Understanding the Law of Zoning and Land Use Controls

CAROLINA ACADEMIC PRESS

Understanding Series

UNDERSTANDING ADMINISTRATIVE LAW
Seventh Edition
Kristin E. Hickman

UNDERSTANDING ALTERNATIVE DISPUTE RESOLUTION,
Second Edition
Kristen M. Blankley and Maureen A. Weston

UNDERSTANDING ANIMAL LAW
Adam Karp

UNDERSTANDING ANTITRUST AND ITS ECONOMIC IMPLICATIONS
Eighth Edition
Christopher R. Leslie, E. Thomas Sullivan, and Jeffrey L. Harrison

UNDERSTANDING BANKRUPTCY
Fifth Edition
Jeffrey Ferriell and Edward J. Janger

UNDERSTANDING CALIFORNIA COMMUNITY PROPERTY LAW
Second Edition
Jo Carrillo

UNDERSTANDING CAPITAL PUNISHMENT LAW
Fifth Edition
Linda E. Carter, Ellen S. Kreitzberg, Scott W. Howe, and Celestine Richards McConville

UNDERSTANDING CIVIL PROCEDURE
Seventh Edition
Gene R. Shreve, Peter Raven-Hansen, and Charles Gardner Geyh

UNDERSTANDING CIVIL PROCEDURE
The California Edition
Walter W. Heiser, Gene R. Shreve, Peter Raven-Hansen, and Charles Gardner Geyh

UNDERSTANDING CIVIL RIGHTS LITIGATION
Third Edition
Howard M. Wasserman

UNDERSTANDING CONFLICT OF LAWS
Fourth Edition
William M. Richman, William L. Reynolds, and Chris A. Whytock

UNDERSTANDING CONSTITUTIONAL LAW
Sixth Edition
William D. Araiza

UNDERSTANDING CONTRACTS
Fifth Edition
Jeffrey Ferriell

UNDERSTANDING COPYRIGHT LAW
Eighth Edition
Marshall A. Leaffer

UNDERSTANDING CORPORATE LAW
Sixth Edition
Arthur R. Pinto and James A. Fanto

UNDERSTANDING CORPORATE TAXATION
Fifth Edition
Leandra Lederman and Emily Cauble

UNDERSTANDING CRIMINAL LAW
Ninth Edition
Joshua Dressler

UNDERSTANDING CRIMINAL PROCEDURE VOL. 1: INVESTIGATION
Eighth Edition
Joshua Dressler, Alan C. Michaels, and Ric Simmons

UNDERSTANDING CRIMINAL PROCEDURE VOL. 2: ADJUDICATION
Fifth Edition
Joshua Dressler, Alan C. Michaels. and Ric Simmons

UNDERSTANDING DISABILITY LAW
Fourth Edition
Mark C. Weber

UNDERSTANDING
ELECTION LAW AND VOTING RIGHTS
Second Edition
Michael R. Dimino, Bradley A. Smith, and Michael E. Solimine

UNDERSTANDING
EMPLOYEE BENEFITS LAW
Second Edition
Kathryn L. Moore

UNDERSTANDING
EMPLOYMENT DISCRIMINATION LAW
Third Edition
Thomas R. Haggard and Bruce N. Cameron

UNDERSTANDING
EMPLOYMENT LAW
Fourth Edition
Richard A. Bales, Jeffrey M. Hirsch, and Paul M. Secunda

UNDERSTANDING
ENVIRONMENTAL LAW
Fourth Edition
Kevin A. Reilly and Philip Weinberg

UNDERSTANDING
ESTATE AND GIFT TAXATION
Third Edition
Brant J. Hellwig and Robert T. Danforth

UNDERSTANDING EVIDENCE
Sixth Edition
Paul C. Giannelli and Jules Epstein

UNDERSTANDING FAMILY LAW
Fourth Edition
John Gregory, Peter N. Swisher, and Robin Wilson

UNDERSTANDING
FEDERAL AND CALIFORNIA EVIDENCE
Paul C. Giannelli

UNDERSTANDING
FEDERAL COURTS AND JURISDICTION
Second Edition
Linda Mullenix, Martin H. Redish, and Georgene Vairo

UNDERSTANDING
FEDERAL INCOME TAXATION
Seventh Edition
J. Martin Burke and Michael K. Friel

UNDERSTANDING
THE FIRST AMENDMENT
Ninth Edition
Russell L. Weaver

UNDERSTANDING
IMMIGRATION LAW
Fourth Edition
Kevin R. Johnson, Raquel Aldana, Bill Ong Hing, Leticia M. Saucedo, and Enid Trucios-Haynes

UNDERSTANDING
INSURANCE LAW
Seventh Edition
Robert H. Jerry, II and Douglas Richmond

UNDERSTANDING
INTELLECTUAL PROPERTY LAW
Fourth Edition
Tyler T. Ochoa, Shubha Ghosh, and Mary LaFrance

UNDERSTANDING
INTERNATIONAL BUSINESS AND FINANCIAL TRANSACTIONS
Fourth Edition
Jerold A. Friedland

UNDERSTANDING
INTERNATIONAL CRIMINAL LAW
Fourth Edition
Ellen S. Podgor, Roger S. Clark, and Lucian E. Dervan

UNDERSTANDING
INTERNATIONAL LAW
Third Edition
Stephen C. McCaffrey

UNDERSTANDING JEWISH LAW
Second Edition
Steven H. Resnicoff

UNDERSTANDING JUVENILE LAW
Fifth Edition
Martin Gardner

UNDERSTANDING LABOR LAW
Sixth Edition
Douglas E. Ray, Robert N. Strassfeld, and Ariana Levinson

UNDERSTANDING
THE LAW OF TERRORISM
Second Edition
Erik Luna and Wayne McCormack

UNDERSTANDING THE LAW OF ZONING AND LAND USE CONTROLS
Fourth Edition
Barlow Burke

UNDERSTANDING LAWYERS' ETHICS
Sixth Edition
Monroe H. Freedman and Abbe Smith

UNDERSTANDING LOCAL GOVERNMENT
Second Edition
Sandra Stevenson

UNDERSTANDING MODERN REAL ESTATE TRANSACTIONS
Fourth Edition
Alex M. Johnson, Jr.

UNDERSTANDING NEGOTIABLE INSTRUMENTS AND PAYMENT SYSTEMS
Second Edition
William H. Lawrence

UNDERSTANDING NONPROFIT AND TAX EXEMPT ORGANIZATIONS
Third Edition
Nicholas P. Cafardi and Jaclyn Fabean Cherry

UNDERSTANDING PARTNERSHIP AND LLC TAXATION
Fifth Edition
Jerold A. Friedland

UNDERSTANDING PATENT LAW
Fourth Edition
Amy L. Landers

UNDERSTANDING PRODUCTS LIABILITY LAW
Second Edition
Bruce L. Ottley, Rogelio A. Lasso, and Terrence F. Kiely

UNDERSTANDING PROPERTY LAW
Fifth Edition
John G. Sprankling

UNDERSTANDING REMEDIES
Fourth Edition
James M. Fischer

UNDERSTANDING SALES AND LEASES OF GOODS
Third Edition
William H. Henning, William H. Lawrence, and Henry Deeb Gabriel

UNDERSTANDING SECURED TRANSACTIONS
Sixth Edition
William H. Henning, R. Wilson Freyermuth, and Brook E. Gotberg

UNDERSTANDING SECURITIES LAW
Eighth Edition
Marc I. Steinberg

UNDERSTANDING SPORTS LAW
Timothy Davis and N. Jeremi Duru

UNDERSTANDING TAXATION OF BUSINESS ENTITIES
Second Edition
Walter D. Schwidetzky and Fred B. Brown

UNDERSTANDING TORTS
Seventh Edition
John L. Diamond, Lawrence C. Levine, and Anita Bernstein

UNDERSTANDING TRADE SECRET LAW
John G. Sprankling and Thomas G. Sprankling

UNDERSTANDING TRADEMARK LAW
Fourth Edition
Mary LaFrance

UNDERSTANDING TRUSTS AND ESTATES
Seventh Edition
Roger W. Andersen and Susan N. Gary

UNDERSTANDING WHITE COLLAR CRIME
Fifth Edition
J. Kelly Strader and Todd Haugh

Understanding the Law of Zoning and Land Use Controls

FOURTH EDITION

Barlow Burke
EMERITUS PROFESSOR OF LAW
JOHN S. MYERS AND ALVINA RECKMAN MYERS SCHOLAR
AMERICAN UNIVERSITY WASHINGTON COLLEGE OF LAW

CAROLINA ACADEMIC PRESS
Durham, North Carolina

LIBRARY OF CONGRESS CATALOGING-IN-PUBLICATION DATA

Names: Burke, D. Barlow, 1941- author
Title: Understanding the law of zoning and
land use controls / by Barlow Burke.
Description: Fourth edition. | Durham, North Carolina :
Carolina Academic Press, LLC, 2025. |
Includes bibliographical references and index.
Identifiers: LCCN 2025032011 | ISBN 9781531029258
paperback | ISBN 9781531029265 ebook
Subjects: LCSH: Zoning law--United States |
Land use--Law and legislation--United States
Classification: LCC KF5698 .B87 2025 |
DDC 346.7304/5--dc23/eng/20250721
LC record available at https://lccn.loc.gov/2025032011

Carolina Academic Press
700 Kent Street
Durham, NC 27701
(919) 489-7486
www.caplaw.com

Printed in the United States of America

Contents

PART THREE
ECONOMIC DISCRIMINATION AND ZONING

PART FOUR

WETLANDS AND BEACHES

PART FIVE
REGULATING THE USER, NOT THE USE

Preface

Zoning, land use, and environmental regulation was one of my first professional interests. My students in any course I taught in the early 1970s, can attest to this. Trained as a city planner, I have long been familiar with the literature and discipline of land use planning. Yet, I came to know that the field is a crowded one. A brief survey of the legal periodicals will confirm that land use and takings law is a tough area in which to write and not be preempted by the annual out-pouring of writing, both from law professors and students. Aside from a law review article published to gain myself a promotion, I went elsewhere to find subjects for my writing, all the while teaching and thinking about this subject. I am happy now to return to it in print.

Not only is the field a crowded one, but it is also jurisdiction-specific. The practice of land use law does not travel well across state lines, and few practices are even state wide in scope. The opinions of state Supreme Courts reflect this. It takes time to learn what does travel and what is worth learning in law school about this subject. I'm glad I waited.

This book is the result of that wait. It is written for two types of readers. First, there is the first-year law student whose professor presents the law of zoning, land use controls, and regulations, in the context of the required course on real property. It is also rich enough in detail to appeal to a more advanced student in an upper-level elective course or seminar on the same subject, although this reader can be selective because she will have less difficulty understanding the constitutional and administrative framework for land use controls. For neither type of reader is this book intended as a treatise. I have always tried to include and discuss leading cases, but otherwise citations are kept to a representative-case minimum.

First, I set out the constitutional framework for land use regulation in a discussion of the takings clause, with a summary of the salient constitutional rules as the discussion proceeds and at the end of this part of the book. The United States Supreme Court opinions on the takings clause present a jurisprudence that will provoke useful and lively discussion in class about the make-up of the Court, and its short and long range purposes in deciding these cases. They provide fascinating material for Court watchers. The land use bar provides experts more sensitive to the nuances of these opinions than your constitutional law professor is likely to be. The discussions of these opinions here are intended to give you a background to participate in further analysis of these cases and a context in which to set the Supreme Court's future land use opinions.

Next appears a discussion of the basic form of land use controls—Euclidian zoning. Once the basic form of a zoning ordinance is summarized and presented, the text discusses more complex forms of land use regulation—so-called non-Euclidian regulations; these require an attorney to exercise increasing amounts of administrative and professional discretion and involve negotiation with municipal officials. Along the way, these chapters present and discuss basic problems, as well as problems based on the United States Supreme Court opinions that relate to these types of land use regulations.

Administrative and legislative relief from land use controls is the bread and butter of a land use practice. This discussion proceeds in that way, and from the straightforward to the discretionary. Distinguishing a client's need for a variance, special exception, rezoning, or other administrative actions, is often the first task of an attorney presented with a land use problem. It is basic and imperative that an attorney understand the uses to which each can be put, separately and in combination, and not waste a client's time and money pursuing the wrong one.

Finally, halting further regulation of a client's property by pursuing vested rights and estoppel is the last task of the attorney discussed in the body of the book.

In writing this book, I owe three debts. First, I owe much to the students and research assistants who have read it over the years. They are Esten Goldsmith, Patricia Hammes, Sean Fleming, Julie Richmond, Stephanie Quaranta, and Erika Gaspar.

Second, as my friend and co-teacher for more than two decades, the late John J. Delaney unstintingly provided me with a wealth of knowledge of, enthusiasm for, and professionalism of the highest caliber in land use practice as he has seen it evolve during the four decades of his own law practice. This book, *donum indignum*, is dedicated to John.

Third, and more recently, Phil J. Tierney has added to it with the insights of a state administrative law judge and hearing examiner with a special interest, enthusiasm, and expertise in land use.

To John, Phil, and now in Phil's place, Stephen Orens, all distinguished attorneys, I, my students, and this book owe much.

BARLOW BURKE
Washington, D.C.
June 2025

PART ONE

Fundamental Concepts

The Police Power, Takings, and Zoning

Chapter 1

The Police Power

The practice of land use attorneys depends on their ability to investigate the regulations applicable to a client's land[1] and on their knowledge of a blend of constitutional, administrative, and local government law, with two basic concepts—the police power and the takings clause—underlying most that they do. Land use attorneys constantly refer to both when either challenging, defending, interpreting, or drafting, any regulation, and so an understanding of both is basic to a grasp of the basics in this field of law. Among the best and the brightest of them, a knowledge of the takings cases is, for example, a precondition for discussing almost any type of land use control—and a knowledge of the facts of these cases is equally important. They usually ask something like the following: "If the Supreme Court said . . . , what's the effect on . . . type of control." This Chapter and the next discuss these basic concepts, and later Chapters will review various effects.

The **police power** is the power of the states and their legislatures to enact regulations over persons and property to prohibit all things inimical to their citizens' health, safety, morals, and general welfare. Its name is in a modern context somewhat misleading: It does not refer to the power of the member of a police force. Instead, it is a reference to the political "polity" of a state or municipality. Its aim is to protect the welfare of the citizenry and has at least three attributes:

(1) It is an **inherent** power of a state legislature, meaning that it is within the legislative function.

(2) It is a **plenary** power—a complete and unqualified legislative power, empowering the legislature to do whatever is necessary to ascertain what it needs to know and to enact legislation to implement what it knows based on that knowledge. Whatever affects the general welfare comes within its scope and may be used to secure its ends. It is broad.[2] The breadth of its power is limited by the ends for which it works, even if those ends need not be articulated when the legislature acts.[3] It is also plenary in a

1. *See Atkin v. Tittle & Tittle*, 730 So. 2d 376, 378 (Fla. App. Ct. 1999) (affirming a legal malpractice award against an attorney not sufficiently investigating land use regulations applicable to a client's land).

2. *See* Lawrence Friedman, Government and Slum Housing 7 (1968).

3. *Id.* Does the due process clause of the 14th Amendment restrict legislative power? Can a piece of legislation be *ultra vires* the police power? If the answer is yes, the due process clause of the 14th Amendment refers not just to the procedural safeguards of the judicial process, but also to

second sense, in that it is a legislative power reserved for use by the legislature itself and so that body need not articulate the standards that will guide or limit the exercise of the power.[4] In this sense, it provides authority to set policy underlying legislative enactments.

(3) It is a **reserved** power under our constitutional system; that is, it is reserved, under the Tenth Amendment to the federal Constitution, to the states[5]—and often delegated by the states to local governments or municipalities. Its reservation thus protects states and municipalities against laws by which Congress seeks to go beyond the constitutional powers delegated to it and encroach on state and municipal exercises of the police power. James Madison said that it embodied the "residual sovereignty of the states."[6] Recent United States Supreme Court cases restricting (say) commerce clause powers of the federal government and Congress to enact laws highlight the fact that, in our system, there is no equivalent plenary federal police power.[7] As Chief Justice John Marshall said, the enumeration of powers granted to Congress in Article 1, § 8, of the federal Constitution, "presupposes something not enumerated."[8]

The police power is not the power of eminent domain.[9] Eminent domain takes private property for governmental use, while the police power only denies some use or uses of private property to its owner. Eminent domain is exercised because property is useful to the public; the police power is exercised because some use of private property is harmful to the public.[10]

---

substantive protections of some individual rights, including the right to property free of regulation burdening more than benefitting its owner—*i.e.*, a right to substantive due process. This issue is hotly debated. *See* Ryan C. Williams, *The One and Only Substantive Due Process Clause*, 120 Yale L.J. 408 (2010 (reviewing the evidence and the issue). Substantive due process as a means of invalidating a statute or ordinance appears more in state judicial opinions but seldom, after the 1930s, in federal opinions. See *Ryan*, op. cit.

4. *See, e.g.*, *Tiber Petroleum v. The Parish of Jefferson*, 391 So. 2d 1178, 1180 (La. 1980) (Dennis, J., dissenting) (involving the location of unsafe oil refineries).

5. The federal Constitution does not formally recognize municipal governments. *See* Paul A Diller, *The Partly Fulfilled Promise of Home Rule in Oregon*, 87 Or. L. Rev. 939, 941–42 (2008).

6. *See The Federalist Papers*, No. 43 (Madison).

7. *See, e.g.*, *Sackett v. EPA*, 598 U.S. 651, 679 (2023) (upholding the states' "primary authority" to regulate land and water use by limiting EPA regulatory jurisdiction over wetlands); *Solid Waste Agency of Northern Cook County v. U.S. Corps of Eng'rs*, 531 U.S. 159, 171 (2001) (holding that the Corps did not have regulatory power over intrastate, non-navigable water bodies when claimed solely because of the presence of migrating birds); *United States v. Lopez*, 514 U.S. 549 (1995) (limiting federal power to regulate the use of guns around schools), *as interpreted in United States v. Wilson*, 133 F.3d 251 (4th Cir. 1997). *Wilson* is noted in James Bryant, United States v. Wilson: *A Change in Wetlands and Clean Water Act Jurisprudence*, 28 Real Est. L.J. 37, 45–50 (1999).

8. *See Gibbons v. Ogden*, 22 U.S. 1 (1824).

9. *See, e.g.*, Ernst Freund, The Police Power § 511, at 546–557 (1904).

10. *See Lemp v. Town Board of Islip*, 394 N.Y.S.2d 517, 521 (N.Y. Sup. Ct. 1977) (involving the prohibition of construction of a house on a sand dune on the beach at Fire Island and invalidating an ordinance prohibiting such construction).

The limits of the power were once more apparent than they are today.[11] Earlier statements of the scope of the power covered only the protection of the health, safety, or morals of a state's citizenry. These statements were in response to the 18th and 19th century demand for urban infrastructure in response to narrow, constricted streets, improper waste disposal, and overcrowding. Often, too, they were in response to epidemics of cholera, yellow fever, and tuberculosis, or to fires that devastated large parts of cities where dangerous land uses abutted residences and tenements. So courts early in our legal history upheld ordinances that prohibited certain uses considered noxious or unsavory from certain areas in cities—laundries,[12] taverns,[13] livery stables,[14] and most commonly, slaughter houses,[15] among them. Quite often such prohibitions were implemented by "frontage consent laws." These laws were an oblique method of regulating these noxious land uses, prohibiting them on a particular block when a stated percentage of owners on the block voted in favor of the prohibition. Eventually the anti-nuisance rationale for these laws wore thin, as municipalities used them for more and more land uses, some not so noxious.

By 1915, however, the United States Supreme Court filled the need frontage consent laws embodied when it upheld a land use regulation prohibiting what the Los Angeles City Council found to be a dangerous brick kiln within the city limits that had come to be surrounded by residences.[16] Affirmatively protecting the general welfare was not then the business of the state. For example, the enactment of laws requiring landlords to provide tenants with hot water were beyond its scope; they were said to be *ultra vires* the police power. The states were able to prevent the citizenry's health or safety from deteriorating, but were not able to promote these things.

Today the police power "is not confined to a narrow category; it extends . . . to all great public needs."[17] For example, after 12% of Chicago's population died in a cholera epidemic in 1885, the city regulated the provision of water to enhance the health, safety, and welfare of its citizens.[18] The police power became "a concept of social cost; it validates legislation designed to limit or alleviate the burden of social costs."[19] Thus, even though authorizing a government to legislate for the health, safety, and morals of the community might not seem limiting, to this triad a fourth category was added by the 1930s, the decade of the New Deal. This was a reference to "the general welfare" of the community. Now the community's health was regarded as being protected

---

11. There is a vast body of law about the police power that is today lost to attorneys. See FREUND, *op. cit.*, one of several treatises written on the police power and widely read by the legal profession in the late 19th and early 20th century.

12. *See In re Hang Kie*, 10 P. 327 (Cal. 1886).

13. *See Shea v. City of Muncie*, 46 N.E. 138 (Ind. 1897).

14. *See City of Chicago v. Stratton*, 44 N.E. 853 (Ill. 1896).

15. *See, e.g., Wilcox v. Henry*, 77 P. 1055 (Wash. 1904); *Reichert v. Geers*, 98 Ind. 73 (1884) (finding a slaughter house a nuisance per se).

16. *See Hadacheck v. Sebastian*, 239 U.S. 394 (1915).

17. *See Day-Brite Lighting Inc. v. Missouri*, 342 U.S. 421, 424 (1952).

18. *See* ANNE SPIRN, THE GRANITE GARDEN 148–49 (1984); *see also* J. R. MCNEILL, SOMETHING NEW UNDER THE SUN 126–27 (2000).

19. *See* FRIEDMAN, *supra* note 2, at 7.

and enhanced when apartment house owners were required by statute or ordinance to provide tenants with hot water and heat.[20] Likewise, tenants' safety is enhanced when buildings are limited to a height reachable safely by then-existing fire apparatus; indeed, the whole neighborhood is protected against fire.[21] Legislation could, in other words, be justified by its limiting of the "neighborhood or external effects" of an owner's behavior.

As Judge Cooley comprehensively said:

> Every man has an abstract right to the exclusive use of his own property for his own enjoyment in such manner as he shall choose; but if he should choose to create a nuisance upon it, or to do anything which would preclude a reasonable enjoyment of adjacent property, the law would interfere to impose restraints. He is said to own his private lot to the center of the earth, but he would not be allowed to excavate it indefinitely, lest his neighbor's lot should disappear in the excavation. The abstract right to make use of his own property in his own way is compelled to yield to the general comfort and protection of community, and to a proper regard to relative rights in others. The situation of his property may even be such that he is compelled to dispose of it, because the law will not suffer his regular business to be carried on upon it. A needful and lawful species of manufacture may so injuriously affect the health and comfort of the vicinity that it cannot be tolerated in a densely settled neighborhood; and therefore the owner of a lot in that neighborhood will not be allowed to engage in that manufacture upon it, even though it be his regular and legitimate business. The butcher, in the vicinity of whose premises a village has grown up, finds himself compelled to remove his business elsewhere, because his right to make use of his lot as a place for the slaughter of cattle has become inconsistent with the superior right of community to the enjoyment of pure air and the accompanying blessings and comforts. The owner of a lot within the fire limits of a city may be compelled to part with the property because he is unable to erect a brick or stone structure upon it, and the local regulations will not permit one of wood.[22]

Consider, as an exercise of the police power, the traffic ticket you get for running a light at midnight with no other traffic in sight? A law which requires riders of motorcycles to wear a helmet or prohibits building on a flood plain or in a wetland or marsh? That regulates the aesthetics of a building, down to the type of material and facade? Down to the door handle? All of these are valid exercises of the police power.

---

20. This broadened conception of the police power came about gradually. *See Early v. Housing Board of Review of the City of Providence*, 174 A.2d 117 (R.I. 1961) (holding that hallway lights could be mandated by the city's housing code, but not the provision of hot water to tenants).

21. *See Welch v. Swasey*, 214 U.S. 91 (1919) (validating height restrictions on buildings in Boston's Back Bay neighborhood).

22. *See People ex rel. Detroit & Howell RR v. Township Bd. of Salem*, 20 Mich. 452, 481–82 (Mich. 1870).

Even the building of large public parks—Central Park in New York City, Fairmont Park in Philadelphia, or the Fens in Boston—have been conceived as public health measures.[23] Today, for example, farmland preservation is viewed as a matter of police power creating "food security," securing environmental benefits, and controlling urban sprawl.[24] And land use regulation enabling statutes are construed to include the adoption by municipalities of flexible and innovative urban design schemes, including the provision of open space land by subdivision developers.[25]

Once enabling statutes for zoning were in place, some state courts upheld the constitutionality of zoning as an exercise of the police power,[26] but others did not. The Maryland Court of Appeals did not, finding that the zoning ordinance under review replaced the forces of the private market with a segregation of land uses.[27] A few municipalities saw the advantages of zoning, but used their eminent domain powers to effectuate it.

In 1926, zoning was held to be a facially[28] valid exercise of the police power.[29] The United States Supreme Court held that there was no violation of due process in a municipality's enactment of a zoning ordinance that was: (1) comprehensive in scope—that is, covered all of the municipality's land area; (2) classified various land uses of property (residential, commercial, etc.), all the land being placed in one classification or another; and (3) created geographic use districts where each land use was permitted. Such an ordinance is facially valid. What the Court did not validate was (say) the placement of the land owner's land in a residential instead of an industrial land use district. So the Court was able to avoid more than passing consideration of the fact that the owner thought that the fair market value of its land was drastically affected, and reduced, by the ordinance. If the Court had decided that case as an "as applied"[30] challenge to the ordinance, it may well have been decided in favor of the owner. When decided, *Euclid* was a close case, and the vote of one particular Justice—Justice George Sutherland[31]—has been thought to be crucial to its result.

---

23. *See* Mel Scott, American City Planning 11 (1971).

24. *See* Mark Cordes, *Takings, Fairness, and Farmland Preservation*, 60 Ohio St. L.J. 1033, 1041–50 (1999).

25. *See River Birch Assocs. v. City of Raleigh*, 388 S.E.2d 539, 544 (N.C. 1990).

26. *See Lincoln Tr. Co. v. Williams Bldg. Corp.*, 128 N.E. 209 (N.Y. 1920).

27. *See Goldman v. Crowther*, 128 A. 50 (Md. 1925) (invalidating a county ordinance).

28. "Facially" is a word often used in land use practice. It means "on its face." Thus, to say that a zoning ordinance is facially valid means that there is nothing in the text of the ordinance to invalidate it upon its enactment, before it is applied to particular facts and circumstances. This is to say that it is not overbroad or written in vague language, and so is valid as enacted. By the same token, to find an ordinance facially valid is not to say that later it might be found invalid "as applied" in particular situations. Land use attorneys thus speak of challenging an ordinance as invalid either "facially" or "as applied."

29. *See Village of Euclid v. Ambler Realty Co.*, 272 U.S. 365 (1926) (noted at 40 Harv. L. Rev. 644 (1927) and 36 Yale L.J. 427 (1927), and discussed *infra*, Chapter 5).

30. See note 28, *supra*, for a definition of this term.

31. George A. Sutherland served as an Associate Justice of the United States Supreme Court from 1922 to 1938, after having served in both houses of Congress representing the state of Utah. In Congress, he supported much President Theodore Roosevelt's legislative program, but opposed that of

Two years later, in another case, the Supreme Court used the police power and the due process clause again, this time to invalidate a zoning ordinance that, although facially valid, was applied to a particular parcel in a way that made the parcel of little value.[32] The land in question was restricted to residential uses; was bisected by the boundary between residential and industrial land use districts; and was adjacent to parcels actually used for industrial purposes. Moreover, the landowner had lost a contract of sale because of the ordinance's regulation. This invalidation too was grounded in the police power. The opinion was written by the same Justice, and seemed to indicate that the Supreme Court would review zoning ordinances with care. Two lessons of *Nectow* were clear: municipalities should place the boundaries of use districts in the middle of their streets, and pay more attention to surrounding uses. However, the Supreme Court's close supervision of the exercise of the police power in zoning matters was not to be. The events of the next decade intervened, producing the Depression, the New Deal, and judicial restraint in many areas of constitutional law, and the Court's next zoning case would be decided in 1974.[33] This hiatus came about despite attempts to appeal zoning decisions to the Court. Between 1949 and 1955, for example, writs of certiorari were denied 21 times.[34]

In the meanwhile, however, the Court did decide some cases that had implications for the use of the police power as a basis for zoning. In *Berman v. Parker*,[35] the Court—Justice Douglas writing the opinion—upheld the use of the power of eminent domain as part of an urban renewal program. The Court upheld a municipal land use decision to condemn a neighborhood it found blighted and riddled with substandard housing, even though the property of the plaintiff was well maintained and not sub-standard. The *Berman* opinion spoke of the legitimate concern of a municipality to become "beautiful as well as healthy," "spacious as well as clean," and "well-balanced as well as carefully patrolled."[36] All these quotations became famous phrases in the history of zoning and land use controls. In another phrase with implications for the police power, the Court said that the "concept of the general welfare is broad and inclusive."[37] An area approach, rather than a structure-by-structure approach to urban renewal, was justified, wrote the Court, adding: "Miserable and disreputable housing conditions may do more than spread disease and crime and immorality. They may also suffocate the spirit . . . [and] may despoil a community as an open sewer may ruin a river."[38] Once the purpose of the legislation was found to be within the police power's general welfare rubric, the use of eminent domain was justified as well. The

---

President Woodrow Wilson, By the time he assumed his seat on the Court, he was a conservative Republican who was influential in striking down important pieces of New Deal legislation.

32. *See Nectow v. City of Cambridge*, 277 U.S. 183 (1928).

33. *See Village of Belle Terre v. Boraas*, 416 U.S. 1 (1974).

34. *See* John Johnson, *Constitutional Law and Community Planning*, 20 L. & Contemp. Prob. 199, 208 (1955).

35. 348 U.S. 26 (1954).

36. *Id.* at 33.

37. *Id.*

38. *Id.*

breadth of the police power licensed the use of eminent domain. All this was good news for attorneys working for municipalities.

In another case in the 1960s, the Court upheld an ordinance that prohibited rock quarrying below the water table and required that the quarry below the water table be filled unless there was a showing that the land lacked other reasonably profitable uses.[39] This case in effect prohibited quarrying in the area. A later case involving another quarry, whose appeal to the Supreme Court was dismissed, was even more drastic.[40] These cases confirm the authority of a municipality to exclude nuisance-like uses. Not only does an owner have no right to zoning that permits the extraction of minerals from a parcel of land, but the total exclusion of mining (an otherwise valid activity) may be upheld as a valid exercise of the police power. Extraction of a piece of land's natural products may be regulated by a municipality in a way no different from other commercial uses of its undisturbed land surface.

The urban renewal and quarry cases confirm the ability of a municipality to impose reasonable regulations on the conduct of a business when delegated the authority to do so and when the regulation is rationally related to some legitimate police power objective. For example, the municipality's total prohibition on curb service street vending by ice cream trucks may be invalid, but an ordinance prohibiting them from conducting their business along heavily traveled streets may be reasonable as a method of regulating the flow of traffic while providing such street vendors with a means of doing business elsewhere. Likewise, prohibiting billboards along residential streets may be valid, while no such prohibition along commercial streets would likely be sustained. Prohibiting so called "adult" entertainment or bookstores from locating near churches and schools may be reasonable, but broader bans on such uses may not. And requiring that residential properties partially rented to students around a university be owner-occupied may be reasonable as a means of controlling rowdy behavior,[41] but a broader ban on renting residential properties or on renting to students may not.[42]

What may be prohibited may also be regulated. Thus, prohibiting door to door solicitation may be too severe, but requiring that such solicitors be licensed is not. Likewise, junkyards and car lots may be required to be surrounded by fences, and businesses such as laundromats or gas stations may be required to have an attendant on the premises when open for business. Thus, police power regulations of street vending, billboards, obscenity, and even a reasonable regulation of a municipality's aesthetics are today all valid exercises of the police power.

---

39. *See Goldblatt v. Town of Hempstead*, 369 U.S. 590 (1962).

40. *See Consolidated Rock Products Co. v. City of Los Angeles*, 370 P.2d 342 (Cal. 1962), *appeal dismissed*, 371 U.S. 36 (1962) (a case in which there was evidence that there was no other profitable use for a quarry zoned residential).

41. *See Anderson v. Provo City Council*, 108 P.3d 701 (Utah 2005).

42. *See Gangemi v. Zoning Bd. of Appeals*, 763 A.2d 1011, 1015 (Conn. 2001).

§ 1.01 Dillon's Rule

Federal and state governments each operate under their own constitutions. Municipal government is constitutionally weak when compared with them. As one Connecticut opinion said, "Under our law, a municipality, as a creation of the state, has no inherent powers of its own."[43] It obtains all of its power and authority from the state.[44] It is the creature of that state government.[45] Therefore, any activity that municipal government undertakes: (1) must be expressly authorized by the state legislature—it must be authorized in express words in a state statute; or (2) it must be reasonably necessary to the achievement of an activity that is expressly authorized—it must be incidental to or implied from an express authorization; or (3) it must be essential to the declared objects and purposes of the municipality.[46] Under the rule, then, municipal authority can be express, implied, or essential.

As of 2023, 39 states subscribe to some version of this rule, and an additional nine states apply it in limited circumstances and to specific types of local government.[47] Three-quarters of those states apply the rule to all municipalities. Some, including California, Illinois, and Tennessee, apply it to only certain municipalities.[48] One state does not apply it to intergovernmental agreements.[49] Some courts require that a municipality meet only one of the three components of the rule,[50] while others give weigh to all three evenly.[51] Thus the rule has been interpreted both liberally to favor a municipality,[52] and narrowly to constrain it.[53] It applies not just to a municipality's direct exercise of its authority, but also to its ability to assert that authority in a lawsuit.[54] In each jurisdiction, local research is required to decide which version of the rule applies.

---

43. *See Capalbo v. Planning & Zoning Bd. of Appeal of the Town of Greenwich*, 547 A.2d 528, 533 (Conn. 1988).

44. *Id.* at 534 (holding that a town could not regulate the color of billboards when the enabling statute permits regulation of their "height, size, and location").

45. *See Trustees of Dartmouth College v. Woodward*, 17 U.S. 250 (1819) (Chief Justice John Marshall's conclusion when distinguishing a private college from a municipal corporation).

46. *See Smith v. City of New Bern*, 70 N.C. 14, 18–19 (1874) (using this canon of construction); *City of Philadelphia v. Fox*, 64 Pa. 169 (1870) (same); David Barron, *The Promise of Cooley's City: Traces of Local Constitutionalism*, 147 U. Pa. L. Rev. 487, 506–09 (1999) (tracing the history of Dillon's Rule).

47. *See* State of Nebraska, Legislative Research Office, *LRO Snapshot* (Feb. 2020).

48. *See* The Brookings Institution, *Is Home Rule the Answer*? (Jan. 1, 2003).

49. *See Brotze v. City of Carlinville*, 183 N.E.3d 251 (Ill. App. Ct. 2021).

50. See Gregory Taylor, *Dillon's Rule: A Check on Sheriffs' Authority to Enter 287(g) Agreements*, 68 Am. U. L. Rev. 1053, 1069, 1070, n. 96 (2019) (citing cases from Maryland, New York, and North Carolina).

51. *See* Taylor, *op. cit.*, 68 Am. U. L. Rev. at 1069.

52. *See State ex rel. Cole v. Keller*, 176 So. 176, 180 (Fla. 1937).

53. *See Dodge City Humane Soc'y v. City of Fremont*, 992 N.W.2d 747, 754 (Neb. 2023) (concurring opinion); *Keller*, 176 So. at 180 (holding that if a reasonable doubt exists as to whether a municipality has been granted express authority, the issue will be resolved against the municipality).

54. *See Endo Health Sols. Inc. v. Second Jud. Dist. Ct.*, 492 P.3d 565 (Nev. 2021).

Dillon's Rule is a rule of delegation of authority as well as a canon of construction for municipalities and their ordinances and resolutions.[55] It has been called a "bed-rock legal principal" of local government law.[56] As such, it is named after a nineteenth century Iowa judge who was one of the first to use this formulation.[57] John F. Dillon was a Justice of the Iowa Supreme Court and also the author of an early, influential treatise on local government law.[58] He wrote in defense of state power. One of his opinions struck down a state statute that authorized municipalities to levy taxes to aid railroads coming to the municipality.[59] Two related things are wrong with such a statute, he wrote: first, it lacked a "public" purpose, and second, it intruded into the realm of the private markets and corporations that worked best if left unregulated.[60] In the area of land use regulation, the analogous debate is between municipalities and private property. Using Dillon's Rule, the municipality is restrained by the very creature that created it—a state's government.[61]

The United States Supreme Court later restated Dillon's Rule. It stated: "Municipal corporations owe their origin to, and derive their powers and rights wholly from, the legislature. It breathes into them the breath of life, without which they cannot exist. As it creates, so may it destroy. If it may destroy, it may abridge and control. . . . [Municipal corporations] are, so to phrase it, the mere tenants at will of the legislature."[62] The Supreme Court reiterated in 2009 that municipalities are the "subordinate governmental instruments" of the states.[63] Nowhere in the federal Constitution are they mentioned or recognized: their powers can be granted or withdrawn without federal Constitutional objection.[64]

The lesson of the Rule is always to check the statutory authority of a municipality to act or enact its ordinances because any reasonable doubt as to the power or authority of a municipality is to be resolved against it. The Rule is a canon of strict construction.[65] As one court said, it "controls our determination of the powers of

---

55. For cases discussing Dillon's Rule, see *City of Montpelier v. Barnett*, 2012 Vt. LEXIS 32 (May 11, 2012), and *Schefer v. City Council of Falls Church*, 691 S.E.2d 778 (Va. 2010).

56. *See Pa. Rest.& Lodging Ass'n v. City of Pittsburgh*, 211 A.3d 810, 816, n.3 (Pa. 2019).

57. *See City of Clinton v. Cedar Rapids & Mo. River R.R.*, 24 Iowa 455, 475 (1868) (Dillon, C.J.).

58. *See* John F. Dillon, The Law of Municipal Corporations, 448–55 (2d rev. ed., 18723). John Forrest Dillon (1831–1914) was a judge on the Iowa Supreme Court from 1862–1868, a judge on the 8th Circuit Court of Appeals from 1869–1879, and thereafter a law professor at Columbia Law School until 1882, when a resumed private practice. He practiced law in N.Y.C. until his death in 1914.

59. *Hanson v. Vernon*, 27 Iowa 28 (1869).

60. *Id.* at 31.

61. *See Ysursa v. Pocatello Educ. Ass'n*, 555 U.S. 353, 364 (2009) (referring the municipalities as "subordinate governmental instrumentalities" from which a state may withdraw "powers and privileges as it sees fit").

62. *See Hunter v. City of Pittsburgh*, 207 U.S. 161, 178 (1907). The term "municipal corporation" is a traditional name for a municipality of any type—city, county, town, township, borough, or village, depending on the jurisdiction and how it organizes municipal governments.

63. *See Ysursa v. Pocatello Education Ass'n*, 555 U.S. 353, 362 (2009) (quoting *Reynolds v. Sims*, 377 U.S. 533, 575 (1964).

64. *Ysursa*, 555 U.S. at 362.

65. *See Home Builders Ass'n of Lincoln v. City of Lincoln*, 711 N.W.2d 873, 877 (Neb. 2006).

local governing bodies. The rule provides that municipal corporations have only those powers that are expressly granted, those necessarily or fairly implied from expressly granted powers, and those that are essential and indispensable."[66] Thus, the Rule is a judicial gloss on the judiciary's relationship with its state legislature,[67] and provides a standard of judicial review for municipal actions. It is also a preference for judicial dispassion over the passions of local politics. When there is a fair and reasonable doubt as to whether a municipality possesses the powers it claims, the existence of the power is resolved by the courts against the municipality and the power is denied.[68]

Dillon's Rule has been used both to invalidate ordinances and well as to uphold them. It has a benefit for municipal governments. Judge Thomas Cooley of the Michigan Supreme Court provided it. As a Justice on the Michigan Supreme Court, he held unconstitutional a state law that permitted a pledge of municipal credit to aid the construction of a private railroad running from Detroit to the municipality.[69] A municipality, he wrote, could not be compelled by the state to issue bonds for the benefit of a private corporation—the deal struck between the railroad and the state legislature was beyond the legislature's authority.[70] This vindicated a municipality's right to be free of the bankruptcies that followed such pledges.[71] Municipalities cannot be forced to use their delegated powers.[72] Once the legislature acts, and absent an express mandate otherwise, municipalities have discretion whether or not to take up the delegation. More generally, Dillon's Rule has been most actively used to strike down municipal ordinances imposing taxes not clearly authorized by the state.[73] The Rule has also been used as an incentive for giving municipalities home rule powers.[74]

The Rule was present at the inception of municipal land use and zoning regulation,[75] and has informed its progress.[76] For example, the Rule's third element, operating without an inquiry into statutory authority common in its first two elements and

---

66. *City of Chesapeake v. Gardner Enterprises, Inc.*, 482 S.E.2d 812, 814 (Va. 1997), *used and quoted in City Council of Alexandria v. The Lindsay Trusts*, 520 S.E.2d 181, 182 (Va. 1999). *See also City of Richmond v. Confrere Club of Richmond*, 387 S.E.2d 471, 473 (Va. 1990).

67. *See Arwine v. Union Cty. Bd. of Education*, 120 SW.3d 804, 807–08 (Tenn. 2003).

68. *Id.* at 808 (quoting John F. Dillon, 1 Law of Municipal Corporations 173 (1st ed. 1872)). Dillon's treatise went through several editions, the fifth being published in 1911.

69. *See People ex rel. Detroit & Howell RR v. Twp. Bd. of Salem*, 20 Mich. 452 (Mich. 1870).

70. *Id.* at 494.

71. *See* Thomas M. Cooley, A Treatise on the Constitutional Limitations Which Rest upon the Legislative Power of the States of the American Union 459 (1874).

72. *See People ex rel. Le Roy v. Hurlbut*, 24 Mich. 44, 107–08 (Mich. 1871) (Cooley, J., concurring).

73. *See Durham Land Owners Ass'n v. City of Durham*, 630 S.E.2d 200 (N.C. App. 2006).

74. *See City of Asbury v. Iowa City Dev. Bd.*, 723 N.W.2d 188, 198 (Iowa 2006) ("Home rule power was intended to renounce the common law Dillon Rule."); *David v. Board of Comm'rs of Norton Cty.*, 89 P.3d 893 (Kan. 2004); *Village of Sugar Grove v. Rich*, 808 N.E.2d 525, 530 (Ill. App. 2004).

75. *See, e.g., State v. Whitlock*, 63 S.E. 123, 124 (N.C. 1908) (finding municipality with power to regulate billboards, but invalidating the instant ordinance doing so).

76. *But see generally*, John R. Nolan, *Death of Dillon's Rule: Local Autonomy to Control Land Use*, 36 J. Land Use & Envtl. L. 7 (2020) (arguing that the Rule has been modified and narrowly interpreted in 40 states).

concerning powers "essential to the objects and purposes" of the municipality, has often been used to justify regulations enacted in the name of safety and health problems.[77]

The breadth of the police power and the limitations in Dillon's Rule combined to bring about an era of conflicting cases regarding the constitutionality of local land use regulation in the first three decades of the twentieth century. There is no inherent municipal power to zone.[78] Neither does such a power spring from the creation of a municipal corporation or local government. Absent home rule powers, some specific state enabling act or statutory authority is required. Such authority in fact exists today in every state. Even a general delegation of police power would probably be insufficient.[79] It would at best only provoke litigation. Municipalities might be delegated functions that might also be performed by state government, but their power and authority is not plenary; in this sense, they may not question the policies underlying the delegation.

§ 1.02 Home Rule

In many states, municipal governments are authorized to exercise the police powers of a state legislature.[80] Known as Home Rule, this authorization grants legislative autonomy and appears either in the state's constitution or in a state statute. More than half of all state constitutions authorize home rule. These constitutional provisions modify the law governing municipal corporations in two ways, (1) granting municipalities the right to legislate for themselves without prior authorization from the state legislature or (2) restricting the right of the state legislature to enact provisions concerning "local or municipal affairs." Often constitutionally-granted, home rule is subject to conditions, limited to certain subjects, to specific types of local government, or to municipalities with a certain threshold population. When such conditions are spelled out in the constitution, the authorization is otherwise regarded as self-executing—that is, no enabling legislation is required to implement it. Twenty states fall into this category. Eleven other constitutions require enabling legislation.

Eight states authorize home rule by statute. These statutes typically identify the types of municipal governments that may use home rule. In several of these states, constitutional provisions state that home rule grants of power are to be "liberally construed," meaning that Dillon's Rule is inapplicable to home rule municipalities.

Home rule is loosely known as self-government for a municipality, county, or another unit of government at a level below that of the state. It is not in our

---

77. *See* Chapter 9, *infra* (a discussion of moratoria).

78. *See Detroit Osteopathic Hosp. v. Southfield*, 139 N.W.2d 728 (Mich. 1966).

79. *See, e.g.*, *Tiber Petroleum v. The Parish of Jefferson*, 391 So. 2d 1178 (La. 1980).

80. The materials in the following paragraph are found in State of Nebraska, Legislative Research Office, *LRO Snapshot* (Feb. 2020).

constitutional system the equivalent of federalism. Why? Because states have a guaranteed status in our country. Home rule jurisdictions have no such thing. They can be changed, amended, or reformed by statute in some states, or by an amendment to the state constitution in other states. A change in the boundaries of a home rule jurisdiction will *pro tanto* change the population given home rule authority.

A precise definition of home rule is difficult because its elements vary from state to state. No state devolves all police powers on home rule municipalities, just as no state reserves all legislative power to itself. Local research is necessary to define home rule for any one state. In general, it is a device for allocating powers and authority over legislation between the state and municipalities within it. Prior to the Magna Carta, "some English cites, boroughs and towns had various customs and liberties, which had been granted by the Crown, or . . . through long use, and among them was the right to elect certain local officers from their own citizens and with some restrictions, to manage their own purely local affairs."[81]

In this country, home rule began as a reform of corrupt state legislatures during the late 19th century and the Progressive Era of the early 20th century.[82] Its theoretical basis was a concurring opinion of Justice Thomas M. Cooley[83] of the Michigan Supreme Court in *State ex rel. Leroy v. Hurlbut*.[84] Judge Cooley's reputation[85] long insured the survival of the "Cooley Doctrine," to the effect that municipalities had an "inherent right" to self-government beyond the control of the state legislature.[86] The eventually prevailing counterweight to the Cooley Doctrine was provided by Judge Dillon,[87] who denied the existence of municipal autonomy out of a concern for corruption, poor management, and self-interest. The legal backbone of this denial was Dillon's Rule. Its underlying doctrine was that the state had plenary power over the structure and organization of municipalities within it. This plenary power doctrine[88] made municipalities into mere creatures of the state. Reaction to Judge Dillon's Rule gave birth to home rule, first in the 1875 Constitution of the state of Missouri,[89] and swiftly thereafter in other state constitutions and statutes. Home rule became

81. *See Metropolitan St. R.R. v. Tax Comm'rs*, 67 N.E. 69, 70–71 (N.Y. 1903).

82. *See* Howard L. McBain, Law and Practice of Home Rule (1916).

83. Thomas M. Cooley (1824–1898) was a professor of property and constitutional law at the University of Michigan Law School while he simultaneously (1864–1885) served as a Justice on the Michigan Supreme Court.

84. 24 Mich. 44, 108 (Mich. 1871) (noting the creation prior in time to state governments, of colonial local governments in New England and Mid-Atlantic states, and stating: "local government is matter of absolute right, and the state cannot take it away").

85. Cooley was also the author of leading treatises on constitutional law.

86. *See* R. Perry Sentell, Jr., *The Georgia Home Rule System*, 50 Mercer L. Rev. 99, 100 (1998) (reviewing the history of home rule in the United States).

87. *See City of Clinton v. Cedar Rapids & Mo. River R.R. Co.*, 24 Iowa 455, 475, 479 (Iowa. 1868) (first announcing the Dillon Rule).

88. *See* Howard L. McBain, *The Doctrine of an Inherent Right of Local Self Government*, 16 Colum. L. Rev. 190 (1916) (forcefully rejecting of the Cooley Doctrine).

89. California, Colorado, Minnesota, and Washington had followed suit by 1906.

the "next best thing" to the Cooley Doctrine.[90] Early on, home rule powers were extended to cities. Most major cities today structure their governments as home rule municipalities. In the 20th century, home rule authority was extended to large urban counties, notably as a way of addressing regional problems and concerns.[91] One-half of the states permit counties to exercise home rule authority.

Once authorized, a municipality usually adopts a Home Rule Charter. This charter must be consistent with the state constitution, the general laws of the state, and the United States Constitution. In states in which home rule is granted by statute, absent a constitutional provision on the subject, the charter is interpreted using Dillon's Rule. In other states, the Rule has precedent on its side, but that precedent is often conflicting.[92]

---

90. *See* Sentell, *op cit.*, 50 Mercer L. Rev. at 168.

91. *See* Daniel R. Mandelker, et al., State and Local Government in a Federal System 129 (2d ed., 1994).

92. *See* Hugh Spitzer, *"Home Rule" vs. "Dillon's Rule" in Washington State*, 38 Seattle U. L. Rev. 809 (2015) (reviewing conflicting opinions in one state).

Chapter 2
The Takings Clause and Its Public Use Requirement

§ 2.01 The Takings Clause

". . . [N]or shall private property be taken for public use, without just compensation." So reads part of the Fifth Amendment to the United States Constitution. It is known as the takings clause.[1] It serves as a limitation on the exercise of the police power. Its antecedents go back as far as the Magna Carta.[2]

The clause may not be read literally: it does not mean that if property is taken for a *private* use, no compensation need be paid. That reading would, if adopted, stand the clause on its head, so ignore such constitutional literalism. The clause assumes the exercise of a governmental function in taking private property is proper, but puts a limitation on that use—to the effect that it can only be exercised after just compensation is paid.

The clause is read backwards. It means that "[w]hen private property is to be used by the public and until just compensation is paid, no such property shall be taken by the government."[3] James Madison initially proposed a draft of this clause that read this way. His version stated: "No person shall be . . . obliged to relinquish his property, where it may be necessary for public use, without a just compensation."[4] Read

1. This clause is also sometimes known as the just compensation clause.

2. *See* Magna Carta, Ch. 39 (1215) ("No free man shall be . . . disseised . . . except by lawful judgment of his peers or by the law of the land."). Similar language was incorporated in Parliament's Petition of Right, signed by King Charles I of England in 1628. *See generally* Richard Pipes, Property and Freedom 120–158 (1999) (and summarizing the Petition at 142).

3. *See* 1 William Blackstone, Commentaries on the Laws of England 139 (1776) (stating that compensation had to accompany any exercise of the government's power to take private property).

4. *See* Speech Proposing the Bill of Rights (June 8, 1789), 1 Annals of Cong. 451–452 (J. Gales, ed., 1834). Madison intended that his draft limit only the acquisition of property and prohibited only direct, physical takings, and even then only by the federal government, not the states. His focus was on a near total diminution of the value of the property taken. In practice, it is difficult to focus on diminished value and on the thing taken without also focusing on the actions of the government doing the taking—hard to focus on just compensation without also focusing on the government's fairness or arbitrariness in the taking. So the use of the takings clause today overlaps with that of the due process clause immediately preceding it in the text of the Fifth Amendment—reading "nor [shall any person]

this way, the clause is not a prohibition on government's taking private property; instead, it requires that what is taken be property[5] and then only imposes a condition on the taking of such property—that is, the government's taking is conditioned by its first paying just compensation for its actions. This reading does not validate the citizenry's right to acquire, hold and sell property. The drafters of the federal Constitution intended that the recognition and protection of such a right be in the states' constitutions then in force; some of them then recognized that there was a "natural right" to property.[6] In general, however, most of the drafters of the federal Constitution recognized the right to hold property as an "adventitious" right—that is, a right created by convention and arising out of the social compact. This was one reason why Thomas Jefferson substituted "life, liberty, and the pursuit of happiness" in place of the more typical triad of 18th century rights to "life, liberty, and property" in our Declaration of Independence.

No one argued against recognizing a right to property during the debates over ratification of either the federal Constitution or its Bill of Rights. In addition, because the drafters of the Bill of Rights recognized the law of eminent domain, it made no sense to word this clause like the First Amendment—i.e., "Congress shall make no law concerning [property]." Eminent domain certainly did affect property and, after all, the enactment of practically any law or legislation affects some form of property. If the clause read this way, the scope of the eminent domain power would arguably be narrower than it is. As it is, this is not the way the clause reads and the power of eminent domain is broadly used. For example, in over thirty states, easements of necessity may be condemned by a land-locked private landowner. In many states, the power is available to and frequently used by public utilities and mining companies, in addition to governmental entities.

All but one of our state constitutions today contain a similar clause. North Carolina's constitution is the sole exception.[7] That the Fifth Amendment's clause protecting property is located in a portion of the Bill of Rights that also restrained the federal government's criminal procedures shows that property and personal liberty were closely associated in the drafters' minds. Because they thought the right to property adventitious, many of them were content to permit institutional and political arrangements to become the chief protector of property rights. Many doubted that property

---

be deprived of... property, without due process of law." *See also* Andrew Gold, *Regulatory Takings and Original Intent: The Direct, Physical Takings Thesis "Goes Too Far,"* 49 Am. U. L. Rev. 181, 184, 186, nn. 27 & 28 (1999) (arguing that Madison's post-ratification writings support a broader view).

5. *See Eastern Enterprises v. Apfel*, 524 U.S. 498, 540 (1998) (Kennedy, J., concurring and providing a fifth vote, finding a statute unconstitutional but not a taking, there being no infringement of a specific property interest).

6. *See* John Ely, *"That due satisfaction may be made:" The Fifth Amendment and the Origins of the Compensation Principle*, 36 Am. J. Leg. Hist. 1 (1992) (arguing that colonial governments pre-1789 often paid compensation).

7. In North Carolina, the courts have read similar protections into that state's constitution by implication.

was a "natural right." Instead, they preferred to think of it as one that would be utilitarian—that is, instrumental in developing the nation's economy.

This clause is not an express grant of authority to use the power of eminent domain. Eminent domain is sometimes referred to as the power to condemn land or property. It is the power to acquire and take possession of property in order to promote the health, safety, and welfare of the citizenry.[8] The takings clause does not grant this power; it is rather a power inherent in sovereignty. The clause only imposes a governmental responsibility when using it. It long predates our Constitution, being recognized by law treatise writers in the 16th and 17th centuries, and as previously mentioned by Blackstone in his famous and widely read commentaries. The clause in our federal Constitution makes the government's duty to pay just compensation express. That was, at the time, a unique requirement when made a precondition to the power's exercise.

Moreover, the takings clause not only makes plain that a "taking" includes a condemnation under the power of eminent domain, but also that it is more: it extends also to state actions that result from police power regulations such as zoning and other types of land use controls. In this respect, the protection of property in our federal and state constitutions is broader than is provided in other countries.[9]

The clause is self-executing: that is, it provides a direct remedy for a taking and its consequential damages without requiring the government to waive its sovereign immunity. There is no sovereign immunity for an action for which the sovereign, in its authorizing document, is responsible.[10] This direct remedy is known as a cause of action for inverse condemnation—a claim that the government committed an action that required the use of eminent domain, but did not use this power, and should be forced to.

The United States Supreme Court reaffirmed Madison's reading of the takings clause and his view that it was a restriction on the federal government, but not on the states.[11] That was the way things stood up to the passage of the Fourteenth Amendment; then, in 1866, John Bingham, a Congressman from Ohio and one of the leading drafters of the Fourteenth Amendment, proposed to include within that Amendment a clause to protect the property of loyal Southern unionists from confiscation by rebels in control of state governments after the Civil War. This clause became the clause that reads "nor shall any State deprive any person of life, liberty, and property, without due process of law"—including the law that had developed around the takings clause of the Fifth Amendment. This latter clause implicitly authorizes the regulation of property, short of its being taken. Soon after the debate and passage of the Fourteenth Amendment, the takings clause was applied to the actions of a state government and the definition of a taking was expanded to include a diminution in the usefulness of

---

8. *See, e.g.*, *Board of Health v. Van Hoesen*, 49 N.W. 894 (Mich. 1891).

9. *See* A.J. van der Walt, Constitutional Property Clauses 423 (1999).

10. *See, e.g.*, *Colman v. Utah State Land Bd.*, 795 P.2d 622, 630–35 (Utah 1990) (discussing self-executing nature of federal and state provisions).

11. *See Barron v. Baltimore*, 32 U.S. 243 (1833).

land, even though the title to the land was not taken from the owner.[12] So, by the end of the 19th century, both the takings and the due process clause of the Fifth Amendment applied to the states.[13]

Once the Fourteenth Amendment made the Bill of Rights (including the takings clause in the Fifth Amendment) applicable to the states, there was a need to consider the extent of the clause's protection of private property. Thus began the development of federal takings jurisprudence that would guide and control state court interpretation of similar clauses in all state constitutions and that today limits the regulation of land under the police power.

§ 2.02 The Public Use Requirement

"... [N]or shall private property be taken **for public use**. ..." The traditional view of this requirement is that it is a threshold test for the proper use of the power of eminent domain.[14] The issue to which the phrase gives rise is whether the purpose or objective of the government in taking private property is a legitimate one. "It is just as important that the proposed use ... be limited to what the court decides is a 'really public' use as it is that the property owner be given just compensation."[15]

An early test read the requirement as a "use by the public."[16] That is, when the state legislature authorized the digging of a canal or the placement of a wharf, the flooding or injury to abutting lands caused by the digging or placement gave rise to no cause of action.[17] The economic development of the country required no less. Inverse condemnation actions were unavailable—no invasion by the public, no cause of action. These canals and wharfs, operated by private parties and companies, were authorized by statutes that were liberally construed, giving benefits to abutting land owners placed near the channels of commerce they created. Early on, condemnation for roads and mill-dams were the uses permitted—in the latter instance, the mills for grinding corn and grain were open to the public, but not operated by the government. Likewise, the widening of an irrigation canal across private land in the West to benefit a neighboring landowner was considered a public use in the opening years of the 20th century.[18]

---

12. *See Pumpelly v. Green Bay Company*, 80 U.S. 166, 181 (1871) (finding a taking in the construction of a dam, authorized by state statute, backing water up on plaintiff's land). *See generally* Kris Kobach, *The Origins of Regulatory Takings: Setting the Record Straight*, 1996 Utah L. Rev. 1211 (1996) (citing pre-*Pumpelly* federal and state cases recognizing non-trespassory, non-destructive, incremental takings all during the 19th century). *See, e.g., Gardner v. Trustees of Newburgh*, 2 Johns Ch. 162 (N.Y. Ch. 1816).

13. *See Chicago, Burlington and Quincy RR Co. v. Chicago*, 166 U.S. 226, 235–41 (1897).

14. *See* Matthew Zinn, Note, *Ultra Vires Takings*, 97 Mich. L. Rev. 245, 260–69 (1998); *see also* Joseph Lazzarotti, *Public Use or Public Abuse*, 68 UMKC L. Rev. 49 (1999).

15. *See Hogue v. Port of Seattle*, 341 P.2d 171, 193 (Wash. 1959).

16. *See Cole v. City of LaGrange*, 113 U.S. 1, 6 (1885).

17. *See Steele v. Western Inland Lock Navigation Co.*, 2 Johns. 283 (N.Y. 1807).

18. *See Clark v. Nash*, 198 U.S. 361 (1905).

However, the general rule (co-existing with these cases) was that condemning the land of one person for the use of another was viewed as impermissibly playing favorites among the citizenry—and prohibited solely on that basis. Historically, it was also on this ground that some state courts struck down state cartway statutes, permitting a landlocked owner to condemn and take a private roadway off the property to obtain access to the nearest public road. Such statutes in part codified the law of easements by necessity,[19] but were essentially for the benefit of a private, landlocked, landowner as a condemnor.

There are also fairly recent examples of this view,[20] and the economic development issues involved remain hot button topics.[21] The use of condemnation powers for the development of a casino was once held to lack a sufficient public use.[22] Similarly, condemning land for parking garages around shopping and retail centers was once found to fail this test. Turning property over after condemnation to private parties was then forbidden; such was not a use by the public.[23] In an urban setting, however, courts in the 1880s and 1890s upheld statutes authorizing the building of elevated railways above public streets, but also allowed an inverse condemnation action against the operators of these railways. These operators were private companies, some newly acquired by the financial speculator Jay Gould, found to have damaged the land parcels of plaintiff abutting owners.[24] The property interest often found taken in these cases was an easement, implied from the facts and circumstances for light, air, and access, or arising from special benefit street assessments, benefitting the plaintiffs' abutting parcels but taken by the coming of the railways passing the abutting owners.

A second test was devised for urban renewal and redevelopment programs. The statutes on which these programs were based were enacted after World War II. Their purpose was to redevelop blighted urban areas, replacing sub-standard structures with new ones. The renewed area typically comprised new housing. In these programs, the land condemned was held only briefly by the public condemnor. The condemnor was usually a special purpose housing or redevelopment authority with the power to issue local revenue bonds to finance its program. Once it acquired the blighted area, it re-subdivided the area and transferred the titles to the parcels in it to previously unidentified private parties.[25] The parties were typically, though not necessarily, low-income persons or households. In cases reviewing these programs, public

---

19. *See* Joseph Kalo & Monica Kalo, *Putting the Cartway Before the House: Statutory Easements by Necessity, or Cartways, in North Carolina*, 75 N.C. L. Rev. 1943, 1946, n.14 (1997) (reviewing state court results).

20. *See Riden v. Philadelphia, B. & W. RR Co.*, 35 A.2d 99, 102 (Md. 1943).

21. *See Kelo City of New London*, 545 U.S. 469 (2005) (discussed in more detail below).

22. *See Mayor of Vicksburg v. Thomas*, 645 So. 2d 940, 941 (Miss. 1994) (so holding and requiring that the public purpose for the condemnation be direct, not indirect or speculative).

23. *See Karesh v. City Council*, 247 S.E.2d 342, 344 (S.C. 1978) (holding that the city could not condemn land for a parking garage and convention center).

24. *See, e.g.*, *Story v. N.Y. Elevated Railroad Co.*, 90 N.Y. 122 (1882), *discussed in* Elizabeth Arens, *The Elevated Railway Cases: Private Property and Mass Transit in Gilded Age New York*, 61 N.Y.U. Ann. Surv. Am. L. 629 (2006).

25. *See, e.g.*, *New York City Hous. Auth. v. Muller*, 1 N.E.2d 153 (N.Y. 1936).

use was held to mean "public benefit." Eminent domain here created a public benefit through better land planning and the elimination of blighted housing, so the "public use" requirement was indirectly met.[26]

Under this second test, it is not essential that a majority of the public benefit from the governmental action or program.[27] Thus, the condemnation of hunting rights in order to establish a migratory bird preserve was found a "public use" in *Swan Lake Hunting Club v. United States*,[28] even though only limited public hunting would be permitted in the future by the government.

In the process of expanding the definition of what was a public use by incorporating public benefit or purpose analysis, the definition of public use became a legislative function. Thus, an action of a state administrative agency requires the authorization by the state legislature in order to further a public use.

[A] The *Berman* Case

In *Berman v. Parker*,[29] an urban redevelopment authority in Washington, D.C., sought to condemn the plaintiff's property. That property was not itself run down or blighted, but it was located within a neighborhood that was. That neighborhood was an extensive one, comprising most of the Southwest quadrant of the District of Columbia. The United States Supreme Court held that the takings clause's public use requirement was satisfied when the urban redevelopment had a "public purpose." In this third reading of the requirement, a legislative finding of a public purpose in the statute authorizing the use of eminent domain was "well-nigh conclusive"[30] that the public use requirement was met. Defining whether a public use was present, the court said, was "essentially the product of legislative determinations addressed to the purposes of government."[31] In this case, Justice Douglas wrote for the court:

> The concept of the public welfare is broad and inclusive. The values it represents are spiritual as well as physical, aesthetic as well as monetary. It is within the power of the legislature to determine that the community should be beautiful as well as healthy, spacious as well as clean, well-balanced as well as carefully patrolled. . . .[32]

26. *See Berman v. Parker*, 348 U.S. 26 (1954) (upholding an urban redevelopment program for the District of Columbia, and discussed in more detail below).

27. *See Rindge Company v. County of Los Angeles*, 262 U.S. 700, 707 (1923) (involving the condemnation of coastal land for a county highway, and stating: "It is not essential that the entire community, nor even any considerable portion, . . . directly enjoy or participate in any improvement in order [that the improvement] constitute a public use. . . . Public uses . . . extend to matters of public health, recreation and enjoyment.").

28. 381 F.2d 238, 245 (1967).

29. 348 U.S. 26, 32 (1954).

30. *Id.*

31. *Id.*

32. *Id.* at 33. *Berman* was noted at 53 Mich L. Rev. 883 and 40 Iowa L. Rev. 659 (1955).

In *Berman*, the public use requirement was measured on an area, rather than a structure by structure, basis. The court rejected the argument that the public use requirement must be satisfied structure by structure. Not every property for which condemnation was sought need be blighted or sub-standard under applicable housing codes.[33] It was enough that its surroundings were blighted in some measurable way. After all, urban planning, not just architecture, was the governmental function involved. Moreover, the reuse of the land for a factory was also valid when the public purpose was to create jobs for the community. That the property is to be passed to a corporation identified at the time of condemnation, does not lessen its public purpose. That purpose need not involve the property directly, but could be tied instead to the effects of the end-use of the property.[34]

Berman's holding was later to extend in state courts beyond urban planning. Economic development legislation was later validated, particularly in "rustbelt" states in which the industrial economy was then sagging.[35]

[B] The *Midkiff* Case

The title to large portions of land on the Hawaiian Islands is held by only a few large holdings. Traditionally used for agriculture, some of these holdings have over the years been split into smaller residential leaseholds. Hawaii's state legislature enacted a statute permitting the holders of these long term leases to buy the underlying fee simple. In *Hawaii Housing Authority v. Midkiff*,[36] the court (Justice O'Connor writing for the majority) held that this state statute, technically authorizing the condemnation of lessors' ground lease reversions that were, it said, held by a "landed oligopoly," was a use of eminent domain for a public use. The system of land tenure at issue here was relatively specialized and not found everywhere, but the court did not focus on the needs of the state in dealing with its tenure system. While not passing on the merits of the condemnation program, the court found that the legislative finding of a widespread problem with land tenures was conclusive.[37] "Where the exercise of the eminent domain power is rationally related to a conceivable public purpose, the [C]ourt has never held a compensated taking to be proscribed by the Public Use Clause. . . . "[38]

---

33. *Berman* was taken as license for many urban renewal projects nationwide. For a discussion of the ensuing problems for low income neighborhoods, see Richard Rothstein, The Color of Law (2017).

34. A *Berman*-like case upholding the condemnation in order to eliminate blight is *City of Los Vegas Downtown Redevelopment Agency v. Pappas*, 76 P.3d 1 (Nev. 2003).

35. *See New Jersey Housing & Mortgage Fin. Agency v. Moses*, 521 A.2d 1307 (N.J. Super. Ct., App. Div., 1987) (condemning land for private shopping center proper, but condemnation action dismissed for failure to bargain with landowners in good faith).

36. 467 U.S. 229, 240 (1984).

37. *Id. See also Kansas ex rel. Tomasic v. The Unified Government of Wyandotte Cty./Kansas City, Kansas*, 962 P.2d 543, 553 (Kan. 1998) (using language similar to *Berman*'s).

38. *Midkiff*, 467 U.S. at 245.

The court made three doctrinal points about its holding. First, the court said that state legislatures are better able to assess the need for condemnation than the courts are. Judicial deference and the resulting breadth of the public use requirement is in turn the result of a prudential concern of the court for the relative competencies and fact-finding abilities of the legislature and the judiciary.[39] Thus, so far as courts are concerned, the public use requirement is more descriptive and proscriptive—not at all intended to be limitation on governmental actions. This deference is also rooted in separation of power concerns, and might further be rooted in a reluctance that courts sometimes exhibit for engaging in discussions of political theory. Second, the court said that only if the definition of a public use is without palpable reasonable foundation, will a legislative determination in this area be invalidated.[40] Third, the court stated that the public use requirement of the takings clause "is thus coterminous with the scope of the sovereign's police power."[41] Thus, a taking is for a public use if it is within the bounds of the police power.

One further point might be made—if only to show how far beyond the plausible one might go in analyzing this holding. The court stated that the public purpose need only be "conceivable." This word might suggest to some that it need not be articulated—meaning that it need not be articulated during the legislative process and prior to being challenged. The writer meant no such thing. "Conceivable" means conceivable in a rational mind and is another way of saying that the public purpose must be conceived by the legislature in such a way that it is supported by substantial evidence—that is, by that amount of evidence that a reasonable mind would require when choosing one of several options—even if it must be "conceived" from the text of the statute itself or from the facts and circumstances surrounding its enactment.[42]

Two more basic points need to be made about the holding as well. First, as to the court's language about the takings clause being "conterminous" with the police power, the important point is that the power of eminent domain is regarded as a corollary or implementing power of government, not a plenary or primary one. If the police power could properly be used, then so could the eminent domain power. The former licenses the latter.[43] This works both ways. Because the eminent domain power is coterminous with the police power, anything permissibly done by condemnation can also be achieved by regulation. Thus Hawaii might have regulated the ground lease reversion out of existence by limiting the landlord's right of reentry or his ability to sue in trespass to enforce the reversion. Second, it converts the public use requirement into a descriptive term, rather than a limitation on government. It requires only that

39. *Id.* at 244.

40. *Id.* at 240–41.

41. *Id.* at 244.

42. *Id.* at 245.

43. This is thinking suitable for government in which economic regulation is far-reaching and in which uncompensated regulation is more far-reaching than the use of eminent domain.

the legislature articulate a "clear and significant" public purpose. This articulation must both precede the condemnation and provide a "rationale basis" for it, and must also relate the purpose of the condemnation and the program used to implement that purpose. (Respectively, these are, in constitutional law terms, the "rational basis" standard for judicial review, and the "reasonable nexus" required of any police power regulation.)

The holding in *Midkiff* is not limited to residential land reform. Consider some applications. If the land reform effort of Hawaii is valid, then the condemnation of scattered residential lots for public housing is valid too. Its public purpose is that it avoids the problems associated with large hi-rise public housing, even if those problems are created by prior governmental programs. In the same vein, the condemnation of scattered site shopping center leases may also be expected to expand low income businesses.[44] Housing is just as important as jobs.[45] Using *Midkiff*, a reviewing court asks, not whether the legislation will in fact achieve its goals, but whether the legislature "rationally could have believed" that the legislation "would promote its objective."[46]

Lawrence Tribe, a Harvard law professor and author of a prominent constitutional law treatise, was the attorney for the State of Hawaii in *Midkiff*. Apparently seeing his work in the broadest terms, he is said to have told a reporter that states had acquired authority to "rearrange property interests" in this opinion.[47] However, the *Midkiff* opinion states that the Housing Authority could begin condemnation proceedings when requested to do so by twenty five or more lessees or lessees of more than fifty percent of the leased lots, whichever is less, in a residential subdivision with an area not less than five contiguous acres. Analogous groups may be hard to find, and this feature of Hawaii's program significantly narrows the holding of the case.

After *Midkiff*, a municipality might condemn a scheme of restrictive, residential only covenants in a subdivision which has been zoned commercial as a means of encouraging the expansion of its downtown.[48] The argument against such a purchase is that downtown building developers could negotiate as easily as the municipality,[49] but another "rational belief" for validating such a condemnation is that it will reduce

---

44. However, some state statutes prohibit the condemnation of an on-going enterprise.

45. *See* David Callies, *Requiem for Public Purpose*, 36 Zoning Dig. 194 (1984) (who suggests these hypos). What about a middle western state's legislature deciding to condemn all farmland held by corporate interests in a program to reestablish family farming? Or, to condemn farmland held by absentee owners, or foreign investors? Such programs seem no less permissible.

46. *Midkiff*, 467 U.S. at 242–43.

47. Note, Hawaii Housing Authority v. Midkiff: *A Wolf in Sheeps' Clothing?*, 12 Cal. West. L. Rev. 325, 341, n. 118 (1984) (reporting Tribe's remarks).

48. *See* Stephen Jones, *Trumping Eminent Domain Law: An Argument for Strict Scrutiny Analysis under the Public Use Requirement of the Fifth Amendment*, 50 Syracuse L. Rev. 285 (2000) (citing several instances reported in newspapers).

49. *In re City of Seattle*, 638 P.2d 549 (Wash. 1981) (suggesting not).

transaction costs that "conceivably" no developer would bear: Residential land has been subdivided in parcels too small for downtown development; condemning the covenants "clearly and significantly" makes redoing this pattern of parcelization easier. *Berman* first requires that the subdivision be blighted and its housing a threat to public health or safety, but that was not true in *Midkiff*. So when the holdings in *Midkiff* and *Berman* are combined, a municipality might condemn a general scheme of private, residential only, restrictive covenants in a subdivision in order to permit its downtown area to expand more easily.

[1] Later Developments

Some state courts refused to go along with the holdings in *Berman*.[50] Urban renewal statutes were invalidated in Florida, Georgia, and South Carolina. Likewise, some state courts rejected *Midkiff*.[51] Some of these cases involved parking lots and facilities adjacent to private commercial uses—when operating such facilities is a matter of competing with private activities of a similar nature. Thus, a municipality could not condemn land for a convention center containing rental commercial space and a parking garage that the public had "no fixed and enforceable right to use" and so the condemnation lacked a public purpose.[52] In some of these cases, the private benefit is too widely regarded as a private activity, and in others, the persons benefitted are too prominent to clothe themselves in the mantle of a public purpose. The condemnation of land adjacent to a privately run riverboat casino has also been found to lack a public purpose.[53] And a tax credit agreement with a private developer that does not guarantee that the public use will be maintained is insufficient justification for a finding of a public purpose for a condemnation.[54] Many of these cases are typically litigated when the municipality proposes to issue municipal bonds whose proceeds will be used to acquire the condemned land, but one recent case held that a statutory right of first refusal given to tenants in a mobile home park to purchase the pad on which their mobile home sat, was an exercise of eminent domain for a private instead of a public purpose.[55]

---

50. *See Karesh v. City Council of Charleston*, 247 S.E.2d 343 (S.C. 1978) (decided before *Midkiff*); *Baycol, Inc. v. Downtown Dev. Authority*, 315 So. 2d 451 (Fla. 1975) (refusing to authorize condemnation of land for a parking facility). *Price v. Philadelphia Housing Authority*, 221 A.2d 138 (Pa. 1966), gave its state statute a close look equivalent to the heightened scrutiny later given in other states. *See infra*, this chapter.

51. *See, e.g., Casino Reinvestment Dev. Authority v. Banin*, 727 A.2d 102 (N.J. Super. Ct., Law Div. 1998) (refusing to authorize condemnation of a house owned by an elderly widow for a parking lot adjacent to the Trump Plaza casino), *noted in*, Jones, *supra*, 50 Syracuse L. Rev. 285.

52. *See Karesh v. City Council of Charleston*, 247 S.E.2d 343 (S.C. 1978).

53. *See Mayor of Vicksburg v. Thomas*, 645 So. 2d 940 (Miss. 1994).

54. *See Casino Reinvestment Dev. Authority v. Banin*, 727 A.2d 102 (N.J. Super. Ct., Law Div. 1998).

55. *See Manufactured Hsg. Communities of Washington v. State of Washington*, 13 P.3d 183 (Wash. 2000) (*en banc*).

[C] The *Poletown* Case

Another important state court opinion on "public use" has been *Poletown Neighborhood Council v. City of Detroit*.[56] There, the city[57] proposed to condemn what amounted to a whole neighborhood for a new General Motors plant, to be located just inside the city's limits: 465 acres, 3,000 residents' homes, and sixteen churches. The condemning authority was the state Industrial Development Corporation. Reviewing this condemnation, the Michigan Supreme Court held that (1) this condemnation had a public purpose with "clear and significant" public benefits, and (2) because of the presence of clear private benefits as well, it was applying "heightened scrutiny" to identify those benefits to make certain that the public benefit was the predominant one.

The Michigan court acknowledged that the case involved the transfer of property from one private party to another. For many state courts, this alone makes the case problematic.[58] It suggests that the takings clause is not a requirement that property taken be for a public use, but only that when the taking is for a public use, just compensation must be paid. This narrower interpretation of the clause leaves open the possibility that takings for what is ultimately a *private* use, are valid.[59]

The Chrysler Corporation got the same treatment as GM in *City of Detroit v. Vavro*,[60] in which the court again upheld the condemnation of land for an auto plant. This time the opinion was written by Michigan's intermediate appellate court, which expressed its reluctance and distaste for the condemnation: "While we agree with defendants that the use of the power of eminent domain . . . is unconscionable,

---

56. 304 N.W.2d 455 (Mich. 1981), *discussed in* Timothy Sandefur, *A Gleeful Obituary for* Poletown Neighborhood Council v. Detroit, 28 Harv. J. L. & Pub. Pol'y 651 (2005).

57. In *Poletown*, the Detroit city council, not the state legislature, articulated the public purpose. A local legislative judgment is "conceivably" entitled to less weight than a state legislature's. Even if the city has plenary, home rule powers, it does not have jurisdiction over a large enough sector of the economy for its council to be representative of its needs. So when legislative authority is not as clear as in *Poletown*, the judicially permissive attitude in this opinion might disappear: the less clear the articulation of the public purpose is, and the less comprehensive and more localized the legislative mandate is, the greater the possibility of heightened scrutiny and a different result.

58. Two "slippery slope" hypotheticals show some of those problems. (1) Suppose, with the plant established, General Motors receives complaints from neighbors about pollution from it. In response, what about condemning pollution easements over neighboring land in order to immunize the plant from nuisance suits? If the initial condemnation has a public purpose, shouldn't this one be valid too? Granted that, anytime it wants, the legislature can restrict condemnation powers by statute, this condemnation still intrudes on the judicial function in nuisance cases and interference with judicial remedies doesn't come close to involving a public use. (2) Suppose further, once the plant is old and out-dated, it is condemned anew when General Motors proposes to move its operations out of town. This condemnation doesn't develop the local economy, it preserves it, but what's wrong with that? The state's being in the auto manufacturing business is one answer. *See infra*, this chapter, for a discussion of the *Oakland Raiders* case.

59. *See* Nathan Sales, *Classical Republicanism and the Fifth Amendment's "Public Use" Requirement*, 49 Duke L.J. 339, 344–49 (1999).

60. 442 N.W.2d 730 (Mich. App. Ct. 1989) (in which Chrysler had not entered into a binding agreement with the city ensuring the public purposes' achievement).

the doctrine of *stare decisis* constrains us to affirm the trial court."[61] The court also called on its Supreme Court to overrule *Poletown*.[62] Later, the heightened scrutiny announced in *Poletown* was used in *City of Center Line v. Chmelko*,[63] and in Delaware to prohibit the condemnation of several small businesses to permit a Japanese auto dealership to expand its operation.[64] Finally, the Michigan Supreme Court decided to retreat from its decisions in *Poletown* and its progeny. *Poletown* was reconsidered in *County of Wayne v. Hathcock*.[65] In its opinion, the Michigan Supreme Court called *Poletown* a radical departure from prior law and stated that condemnations in which land goes to a private party or entity requires "public necessity of an extreme sort otherwise impractical" and are only permitted so long as (a) land assembly is required, (b) "the private entity is accountable to the public in its use," and (c) so long as "the selection of private land is subject to a public concern." In an economic development context, a municipality would most likely find the authority to condemn the interests of holdout-owners for a development project requiring assembly of a large amount of land. The court's majority made the phrase public use into "words of art," having a more "technical meaning within the law" and providing Michigan with a state constitutional litmus test for all condemnations.

[1] Industrial Parks and Mining

The condemnation of land for municipal industrial parks has been a controversial topic in the law of public use.[66] When the statutory authority for such activity was clear, this alone persuaded many courts. For some not persuaded, express statutory authority to issue municipal bonds to finance such projects made plain that the legislature considered luring industry to a jurisdiction to be a public purpose. Similarly controversial are state statutes that today authorize a power of condemnation for mining and natural resource extraction companies—on the theory that the development

61. *Id.* at 731 (subject to a strong dissent, *id.* at 644–45, noting that: "Any business enterprise produces benefits to society at large. Now that we have authorized local legislative bodies to decide that a different commercial use or industrial use of property will produce greater benefits than its present use, no . . . property is immune from condemnation for the benefit of other private interests that put it to a 'higher' use.").

62. *Id.* at 732.

63. 416 N.W.2d 401 (Mich. App. Ct. 1987).

64. *See also Wilmington Parking Auth. v. Land with Improvements, Situated in Wilmington, New Castle County*, 521 A.2d 227, 231 (Del. 1986) (quoting *Poletown* and finding no public use in a city condemnation proceeding for land for a parking garage, part of which would be used to permit an adjoining newspaper plant to expand, because the condemnation would not have occurred without the newspaper's involvement).

65. 684 N.W.2d 765 (Mich. 2004) (a unanimous decision, with concurrences, involving a business and technology park, emphasizing that the standard of review is heightened when specific parties are identified as beneficiaries of a condemnation, and reversing the lower court's upholding of the condemnation), *noted at* 33 Real Est. L.J 478, 484 (2005), 50 Vill. L. Rev. 341 (2005), and in a Symposium at 2004 Mich. St. L. Rev. 837 (2004).

66. *See Hogue v. Port of Seattle*, 341 P.2d 171 (Wash. 1959) (finding no public use).

of such resources is a public benefit.[67] Such statutes have been enacted in ten states in the interior West, and four more states have constitutional provisions conferring the same authority.[68]

[D] The *Oakland Raiders* Case

City of Oakland v. Oakland Raiders[69] held that the Raiders, attempting to move its football franchise to Southern California, was not entitled to summary judgment on the question of a public purpose for the franchise's proposed condemnation by the city. If the city could condemn park-land, own and operate the stadium in which the Raiders played their games, it could condemn the team's franchise as well. The team was first franchised in Oakland and played there for 20 years before moving. Isn't it possible to say that the franchise owes its value to the city and to its fans? Tempting as it is to answer the question affirmatively, the court's substantive holding was limited. There is nothing, it said, in the takings clause that would prevent its application to intangible personal property such as a franchise; the clause does not distinguish between real and personal, or tangible and intangible property—and all of these categories of property are subject to being taken by the exercise of eminent domain.[70]

Although the *Oakland Raiders* opinion held that the operation of a sports franchise might constitute a valid public purpose, the California Court of Appeal later held that the City's condemnation of the franchise by eminent domain violated the commerce clause of the federal constitution.[71] The football league was operating a business in interstate commerce and the City's use of eminent domain was, the court said, "precisely" the type of "meddling with the national economy that the commerce clause was designed to prohibit."[72] This commerce clause finding precluded further consideration of the public use issue. The *Oakland Raiders* decision is sparsely cited, perhaps because when a business decides to relocate to another state, the state of its current location exercising its eminent domain power would likely meet the same fate.

After *Midkiff*, *Poletown*, and *Oakland Raiders*, there were few limitations left on a legislature's reach under the takings clause. Thus, when a municipal government imposes a rent control ordinance on mobile home parks and a provision of the ordinance requires

---

67. *See* Nathan Sales, *Classical Republicanism and the Fifth Amendment's "Public Use" Requirement*, 49 Duke L.J. 339, 376–77 (1999) (reviewing the genesis of such statutes).

68. *See* Alexandra B. Klass, *The Frontier of Eminent Domain*, 79 U. Colo. L. Rev. 651 (2008).

69. 646 P.2d 835, 840 (Cal. App. Ct. 1982).

70. The football team's league's charter prohibited the long-term ownership of a franchise by the city, so the court envisioned that upon retransfer to private owners, the public purpose of the condemnation would have to be suitably protected, probably by a covenant in the franchise prohibiting its relocation out of town.

71. *See City of Oakland v. Oakland Raiders*, 220 Cal. Rptr. 153 (Cal. Ct. App. 1985) (finding that moving the franchise affected the income stream of every other NFL team, all operating at the national level sharing income from the operation of each team).

72. *Id.* at 157.

the owners of such parks to offer tenants assignable leases of unlimited duration, such a provision might have a public purpose even though it is not a taking.[73]

Three limiting lines of attack, however, are still possible: (1) state legislatures might enact legislation limiting the reach of its state constitution's public use clause; or (2) the courts might narrowly interpret that clause or statutes enacted under it; or (3) they might impose a heightened scrutiny (a higher burden of proof than just requiring a rational basis) regarding a public use or benefit.[74]

[E] *Kelo v. City of New London*

[1] The Decision

In this case,[75] the plaintiffs were 15 homeowners in the Fort Trumbull park area of the city. The City, like many other municipalities hoping for an economic rebirth with redevelopment, in 1998 approved a $5.3 million bond issue to condemn the 90 acres of land, including the much-improved, long-held homes of the plaintiffs.[76] A month later, Pfizer Inc. (a Big Pharma company) announced that it intended to build a $300 million research facility adjacent to the condemned acreage. Pfizer arrived before the City started to formulate its plan for the Fort Trumbull area, but the plan built on its private redevelopment. Under the plan, the City's economic development corporation was the condemnor.[77] It was to take the 90 acres and lease it for 99 years to a developer—not yet chosen—at $1/year. That developer would have the sole discretion to select those who would occupy the land. So Pfizer's interests were well represented in the corporation's redevelopment plan for the area—a hotel, upscale housing, and office space were part of the corporation's plan intended to compliment the Pfizer facility. The plaintiffs' land was to be used for office space and some for "park support"—riverfront walkways and a marina. The plaintiffs' land was 1.54 acres of the 90 acre project.

The facts of this case offered courts an opportunity to address the charges that the public use clause had been left without teeth and made to play favorites among the citizenry—"the seizure of the property of innocent persons for reasons that are

73. *See Yee v. City of Escondido*, 503 U.S. 519 (1992).

74. Before this reconsideration, seven state supreme courts in Arkansas, Florida, Kentucky, Maine, New Hampshire, South Carolina, and Washington, had decided that economic development standing alone is not a public use.

75. *See Kelo v. City of New London*, 843 A.2d 500, *aff'd*, 545 U.S. 469 (2005).

76. *See* Daniel Curtin, *The Implications of* Kelo *in Land Use Law*, 46 Santa Clara L. Rev. 787, 792–93 (2006) (reporting that the city was designated by the state a "distressed municipality," having an unemployment rate double that of the state, 54% of its property tax-exempt, and having lost large but unreplaced manufacturing facilities).

77. State money from the state's redevelopment agency was available for planning and land acquisition. *See* Abraham Bell & Gideon Parchomovsky, *The Uselessness of Public Use*, 106 Colum. L. Rev. 1412, 1438–39 (2006) (reporting that if the condemnor condemned the area for being blighted, no state money would follow, whereas a declaration of condemnation for economic development resulted in state money being granted to the condemnor).

distributionally unjust."[78] The charge of an "unjust distribution" is at bottom a charge that property is being taken and given according to the political influence of the recipient—who is thus tempted to lobby instead of engaging in more economically productive activity. Further, when other recipients receive a lesser benefit, they have less incentive to oppose the lobbyist for the recipient obtaining the greater benefit. The results are a skewed politics and captive legislatures.

Although the *Kelo* case set off a fierce debate among the public and in state legislatures,[79] as well as many law review commentaries,[80] the court declined to address such charges. Instead, it opined that it was bound by the precedents in *Berman* and *Midkiff*, and so the case presented no new or elaborate issue, being decided by *stare decisis*. The *Kelo* decision was consistent with precedent. Declining to see *Kelo* as a different sort of case precluded the court from engaging in a wider debate about the purpose of the public use clause.

What did the court hold? Three Justices subscribed to the plurality opinion written by Justice Stevens. He held that the City's economic development plan "satisfied the public use requirement of the Fifth Amendment." Public use, he said, did not require use of the public. He rejected any literalist "public use" test—too difficult to administer, and too impractical given the evolving and regionally based needs of government—for a broader test equating public use with "public purpose." Then, characterizing the issue as whether the City's economic development plan has a public purpose, he reviewed the cases—particularly *Berman* and *Midkiff*—finding it "incongruous to hold that the City's interest in the economic benefits to be derived from the development of the Fort Trumbull area has less of a public character than any of those other interests" (referring to the interests asserted in those prior cases) without imposing "an artificial restriction on the concept of public use." "A strong theme of federalism" underlies this decision and past cases, he said, "emphasizing the 'great respect' that we owe to state legislatures and state courts in discerning local public needs." The *Kelo* decision, he thought, broke no new legal ground.

Justice Stevens went further, however. He also rejected expressly two arguments made by the petitioners. The first was a claim that a "bright-line rule that economic development was not a public use." Such a rule was proposed as a prophylactic one—in effect a presumption that when economic development is concerned, the political process is skewed against existing owners. There was no principled way of adopting such a claim as a rule, he said, considering the court's past decisions, and so no way of holding that the government's pursuit of a public purpose could not benefit private parties. Further, Stevens rejected the argument that the court "should require a

78. *See* Thomas Merrill & Henry Smith, *The Morality of Property*, 48 Wm. & Mary L. Rev. 1849, 1880 (2007).

79. Over 40 states enacted legislation in response to *Kelo*. *See* Donald E. Sanders & Patricia Pattison, *The Aftermath of* Kelo, 34 Real Est. L.J. 157 (2005); Patricia Salkin & Margaret Lavery, *Irresponsible Legislating: Reeling in the Aftermath of* Kelo, 34 Real Est. L.J. 375 (2005).

80. *Kelo* was noted and discussed in, e.g., 119 Harv. L. Rev. 287 (2005), 34 Fordham Urb. L.J. 613, 617–38 (2007), 39 Ind. L. Rev. 449 (2006), 33 Ecol. L.Q. 545 (2006), and 34 Real Est L.J. 206 (2005).

'reasonable certainty' that the expected public benefits will actually accrue." His opinion goes on to reject any heightened scrutiny standard of review, again citing a rule of legislative deference. This discussion leaves the impression that tests of reasonableness and rationale basis were being redefined.

If Justice Stevens left this impression, Justice Kennedy, concurring and providing the fifth crucial vote for the majority, left no doubt. Picking up on the deferential language of the *Midkiff* case, he said that a taking is presumptively valid, he said, if it is "rationally related to a conceivable public purpose."

While Stevens recognized that the City could not transfer A's property to B solely because B would put the property to a more productive use and that such a transfer "would certainly raise a suspicion that a private purpose was afoot," he did not pursue the matter in his opinion. Justice Kennedy did. He noted that the trial court properly inquired into: communications between Pfizer and City officials, the City's awareness of the depressed economy of the area, the substantial commitment of public funds by the state to the project before the private benefits were identified, the review of a variety of development plans and the choice of a private developer in a competitive process rather than picking out the developer beforehand, and the impossibility of knowing other lessee beneficiaries before the project is built. He said: "A court applying rational-basis review under the Public Use Clause should strike down a taking that, by a clear showing, is intended to favor a particular private party, with only incidental or pretextual[81] public benefits. . . . A court confronted with a plausible accusation of impermissible favoritism to private parties should treat the objection as a serious one and review the record to see if it has merit, though with the presumption that the government's actions were reasonable and intended to serve a public purpose."[82] Aside from re-affirming that a rational basis standard controls the case, there is little here of help to trial courts evaluating charges of favoritism.[83]

Thus, the court found that a public-private partnership, mixed use redevelopment satisfied the public use requirement. The requirement authorizes more than blight removal in permitting municipalities to encourage employment and private investment in underutilized commercial areas.[84] Exercising the power of eminent domain

81. "Pretextual" defenses has become well-used by owners facing a condemnation for the purpose of economic development. *See Franco v. District of Columbia*, 39 A.3d 890, 891–92, 894–95 (D.C. App. 2012); *County of Hawaii v. C&J Coupe Family Limited Partnership*, 242 P.3d 1136, 1146–53 (Haw. 2010) (involving the condemnation of a road as a public use); *Middletown Twp. v. Lands of Stone*, 939 A.2d 331, 337 (Pa. 2007) (stating that the public must be the primary and paramount beneficiary of the taking). *See generally* Daniel Kelly, *Pretextual Takings: Of Private Developers, Local Governments, and Impermissible Favoritism*, 17 Sup. Ct. Econ. Rev. 173 (2009).

82. Justice Kennedy suggested that equal protection analysis would provide guidance to the courts on the matter of favoritism.

83. For an article suggesting events raising suspicions of favoritism, see Jennie Nolon, Kelo*'s Wake: In search of a Proportional Benefit*, 24 Pace. Envt'l L. Rev. 241, 287–95 (2007) (suggesting that exactions analysis then provides a heightened standard of review).

84. *See* Marc B. Mihaly, *Living in the Past: The* Kelo *Court and Public-Private Economic Redevelopment*, 34 Ecol. L.Q. 1, text at nn. 23–28 (2007) (arguing that the *Kelo* opinion does not reflect current patterns of redevelopment and that few residential properties are ever condemned for such projects,

transferring property from one private owner, even a long term resident with a great personal and sentimental attachment to their home, to another, did not solely on that account violate the requirement.

The dissenters were Justices O'Connor, Scalia, and Thomas, and the Chief Justice. Justice O'Connor wrote a strongly worded dissent. She thought that the public use requirement had become "hortatory fluff." She relied heavily on distinguishing *Berman*. In *Berman*, the land use was changed—but that is not necessarily the situation under the City's development plan. Moreover, the court's past cases, she said, required the elimination of an "affirmative harm"—"blight" in *Berman* and "land oligopoly" in *Midkiff*—in both cases, the public benefit was immediate, while this was not the case here.

Aside from the difficulties of holding otherwise, what justifies the court's holding is (1) a state or municipal legislature's suitability to judge what is a public use—a legislative judgment compatible with legislative processes and fact finding; (2) a political process will protect widely held property rights and control municipal-corporate conspiracy and abuse; (3) a fear that narrowing the uses of eminent domain will just increase the regulatory burden on landowners and so not be in their interests—after all, the takings clause is the only constitutional provision requiring payment for governmental action; (4) just compensation providing an adequate remedy, even for one's home.

The fourth and last proposition is the most uncertain. It may be that eminent domain is overly expensive, requiring legislatures or condemnors to pay a premium over a fair market value in order to achieve a negotiated settlement that avoids using the procedures required by the eminent domain statutes,[85] but this is a proposition that should be tested before general acceptance. Under it, the exercise of eminent domain is best justified when the proposed condemnee has some type of monopoly power, producing a substantial premium over fair market value if the transfer were left to private negotiations or marketplace. In this regard, *Kelo* teaches that a holdout, even an innocent one, cannot extract this premium and that the exercise of eminent domain may be used against her.

This opinion provides a baseline—states could require a heightened standard of review for use of the eminent domain power in economic development cases. From a federalism point of view, the decision is in keeping with its own traditions, in that it offers the states an opportunity to restrict the public use definition by statute,[86] or

involving as they do too much expense and political controversy; instead, projects are usually aimed at underutilized commercial warehouse districts, parking lots, and other holding uses).

85. *See* Note, *The Supreme Court, 2004 Term: Leading Cases*, 119 Harv. L. Rev. 287, 296–97 (2005).

86. *See* Marcilynn Burke, *Much Ado About Nothing:* Kelo v. City of New London, Babbitt v. Sweet Home, *and Other Tales from the Supreme Court*, 75 U. Cin. L. Rev. 663, 694 (2006) (discussing Alabama, Delaware, Michigan, Ohio, South Dakota, and Texas statutes prohibiting the exercise of eminent domain in circumstances similar to *Kelo*; and reporting that courts in Arizona, Kentucky, Virginia, and Washington have achieved similar results in judicial opinions); Abraham Bell & Gideon Parchomovsky, *The Uselessness of Public Use*, 106 Colum. L. Rev. 1412, 1418, n. 27 (2006).

provide for a standard for just compensation reflecting more than fair market value, thus in effect overruling the court or otherwise "compensating" for its decision. The court refused to analyze the City's development plan in pieces; it only analyzed the plan as a whole; neither did it require necessity or achievability as the standard for the use of eminent domain—it only required that there be a "reasonable certainty that a conceivable public purpose" would be advanced. Disputes over individual property rights, it said, should probably be settled by local legislative calculations of municipal wealth maximization and that, in a dispute between individual property owners and possible future owners, courts should rule in favor of the party capable of bringing about that maximization.

[2] Reaction to Kelo

A week after the decision, the United States House of Representatives passed a non-binding House Resolution 340, on a vote of 365 to 33, expressing "grave disapproval" of the decision. So it went. No federal legislation resulted, but legislative activity in almost all states made it plain that disapproval was widespread,[87] and virtually all states enacted statutes either prohibiting the use of eminent domain for economic development purposes, redefining more narrowly the definition of blight, restricting eminent domain's use to blighted areas or to recognized and traditional public uses, prohibiting use of eminent domain when its beneficiaries were primarily private parties, shifting the burden of proof to the condemnor to demonstrate a public use, requiring negotiations for purchase at an enhanced value with an offer of relocation payments, or else providing enhanced notice and hearing rights to condemnees.[88]

Some state judicial opinions after *Kelo* applied a heightened rational basis scrutiny standard when reviewing exercises of eminent domain. One Ohio opinion also held that the term "deteriorating neighborhood" as a statutory standard for determining whether eminent domain could be used, was void for vagueness.[89] A New Jersey opinion upheld a limitation on the exercise of eminent domain, restricting its use to "blighted areas" as not permitting redevelopment solely because the property is not used in an optimal manner.[90] Thus, the trend of eminent domain law in the states is intentionally at odds with the *Kelo* decision.[91]

87. Some of these forty-odd statutes prohibited condemnation for "economic development" but permitted it for "community development"; some continued to permit it to eliminate "blight." *See* Ilya Somin, *The Limits of Backlash: Assessing the Political Response to Kelo*, 93 Minn. L. Rev. 2100 (2009) (arguing that many state statutes responding to *Kelo* were ineffective and that only six or seven would effectively restrict takings for economic development).

88. *See* Zachary Hudson, *Eminent Domain Due Process*, 119 Yale L.J. 1280 (2010); 13 Powell on Real Property § 79F.03 (2012) (providing a state by state review of statutory changes).

89. *See Norwood v. Horney*, 853 N.E.2d 1115 (Ohio 2006).

90. *See Gallenthin Realty Dev. Inc. v. Borough of Paulsboro*, 924 A.2d 447 (N.J. 2007).

91. *See Rhode Island Econ. Dev. Corp. v. The Parking Co.*, 892 A.2d 87, 102 (R.I. 2006); *Mayor and Council of Baltimore City v. Valsamaki*, 916 A.2d 324 (Md. 2007). *But see Kaur v. N.Y. State Urban Dev. Corp.*, 933 N.E.2d 721(N.Y.2010), noted at 38 Fordham Urb. L. J. 1193 (2011). *See generally* Ilya Somin, *The Judicial Reaction to* Kelo, 4 Alb. Gov't L. Rev. 1 (2011).

What might the City have done differently? Perhaps rezoning the Fort Trumbull area for the types of commercial uses Pfizer represented and then declaring pre-existing uses non-conforming, prohibiting such uses from continuing indefinitely, would have provided an alternative, albeit more long-range, strategy for the city. Perhaps the City could have rezoned the area for office or a residential and commercial mix of land uses. Or perhaps providing Fort Trumbull park residents with a community development agreement[92] would have made the re-development more agreeable to potential plaintiffs. Before the redevelopment plan authorized in *Kelo* could get underway, the real estate recession of 2007–2008 intervened and stymied its implementation. It is hard to say, but an approach less drastic than eminent domain condemnation might have been just as effective.

What sort of litigation over the public use requirement might be expected in the future? Litigation over sport arenas has provided further developments in this area of law when a sports team is the principal and direct beneficiary. Most of the well-known historic stadiums, particularly baseball stadiums, in the country were, after all, built by the teams that play in them, but others, particularly in the South and West, were at least financed by municipalities, principally by the issuance of municipal bonds.

92. A "community development agreement" is a bi-lateral contract between residents impacted by a redevelopment and a developer in which the developer promises amenities (such as the Riverwalk in Fort Trumbull, first hire agreements, low income tenant set asides, or cash) in exchange for public support and a promise not to further litigate against the developer).

Chapter 3

Types of Takings—Physical and Regulatory Takings

§ 3.01 Physical Takings

Over the last five decades, the United States Supreme Court opinions on the Fifth Amendment takings clause have veered between avoidance of set formulas and an embrace of the idea that some regulatory actions will automatically or "categorically" effect a taking. Regulatory takings have no set formula for a taking. Physical takings are categorical takings. This Chapter will treat both types of takings—physical takings first.

A physical taking is an eminent domain, inverse-type of taking. It involves the trespass on, invasion of, or occupation by a governmental entity, or by a third person authorized by such an entity, of an owner's private property. Such a taking is referred to as a *per se* or categorical taking.[1] An initial example occurred in *Loretto v. Teleprompter Manhattan CATV Corp.*[2] There, an apartment house owner in New York City challenged a state statute which permitted a cable television company to place cable television boxes and cables on her property. The statute's purpose was "the rapid development and maximum penetration by a means of communication which has important educational and community aspects." The box on the owner's building was installed before the plaintiff acquired her apartment building. It was located on the exterior of the building, just above and on its roof, but the owner did not notice it until she had owned the building for some time. The box took up one and one half cubic feet. The owner admitted that other apartment building owners thought that the cable connection increased the market value of their buildings and that her tenants might be upset if the connection was removed. Nonetheless, the United States Supreme Court held, 6–3, that any governmentally authorized, permanent, and physical occupation or invasion of private property, no matter the governmental benefit

1. In Chapter 12, *infra*, another type of categorical taking, involving the destruction of all economically beneficial use, will be discussed.

2. 458 U.S. 419 (1982).

and no matter how minor the invasion, requires just compensation—no matter the amount.[3] In this case, no matter how small the amount.

The holding in *Loretto* shows that, with physical takings, the damage done by the invasive action may be close to nil. For example, the building of a road through vacant land is likely to create more value in the remaining land than is destroyed in the land taken. This does not mean that there is no taking—there is; it just means that the resulting just compensation will be nominal if the government is permitted to off-set the benefits that the road confers.

"Physical invasion cases are special," and the "holding today is very narrow," Justice Thurgood Marshall wrote for the majority in *Loretto*.[4] He meant what he said: the Supreme Court left the amount of compensation to state courts to determine. Likewise, the court did not decide whether the nominal damages provided satisfied the compensation requirement: the challenged statute permitted "reasonable compensation" and the regulatory agency in charge of cable-television in New York City had concluded that: (1) compensation would in most cases be nominal, one dollar damages; and (2) the landlord benefitted from being able to offer apartments for rent with access to cable.

Justice Marshall justified the majority's holding in four ways. First, he invoked the "historical rule."[5] Historically, he wrote, "our cases uniformly have found a taking to the extent of the occupation, without regard to whether the action achieves an important public benefit or has only minimal economic impact on the owner."[6] Some fundamental rules can be drawn from this statement: First, (1) the magnitude of, or the necessity for, the public use is not to be balanced against the "extent of the occupation" or taking; (2) that the landowner is also benefitted is irrelevant;[7] (3) that the government acted in good faith is likewise beside the point; and (4) that little or no just compensation is due, cannot justify not finding a physical taking. Second, this historical rule "has more than tradition to commend it": a physical invasion is "the most serious form of a taking."[8] This is so because the government does not merely take one right out of the bundle of rights held by the owner; rather, "it chops through the bundle, taking a slice of every strand." The government denies *pro tanto* the right

3. *Loretto*, 458 U.S. at 441. In this case, the statute was constitutional, but, the taking issue being a separate issue, it effected a taking nonetheless.

4. *Id.*

5. The physical invasion rule traces its jurisprudential roots back to *Pumpelly v. Green Bay Company*, 80 U.S. 166 (1872) (framing the cause of action as trespass on the case), in which the court found a taking by inverse condemnation when the government built a dam which backed the water of a river up further than expected, so flooding the land of the plaintiff.

6. *Loretto*, 458 U.S. at 434–35.

7. *See Vaizburd v. United States*, 67 Fed. Cl. 257 (2005) (holding that the accretion of sand on a sea front parcel was a taking, resulting from an Army Corps of Engineers beach replenishing project and, notwithstanding there was no diminution in fair market value, finding that the cost of removal was the measure of damages).

8. Physical invasions are taken so seriously that, even though Mrs. Loretto stipulated that she did not have a use for the space the cable occupied, this stipulation did not affect her case: Installing the cable along the baseboard on a wall was no bar to Mrs. Loretto's claim of physical invasion.

of possession, the power to use, and decreases the right to sell that portion of the property occupied.[9] Third, the rule avoids "otherwise difficult line-drawing problems." Its alternative lacks crispness and presents proof and evidentiary problems. And, fourth, it is crisp and simple, and "presents relatively few problems of proof." Thus *Loretto*'s rule that "a permanent physical occupation of property is a taking"[10] is justified by (1) the seriousness, permanence, and exclusivity of any physical occupation or invasion, as well as (2) every owner's "historically rooted expectation of compensation," and (3) some notions of judicial economy.

Loretto's three dissenting Justices (Blackmun, writing the dissent, for himself, Brennan and White) thought that the distinction between permanent and temporary occupations will be difficult to draw in practice, and opted instead for a balancing test, weighing the interference with the owner's post-regulation uses against the public benefits flowing from the regulation.[11] Their focus was on the post-regulation, reasonable return available to the owner. The majority's response was that, for physical takings, the resulting benefit available to the owner is irrelevant; the focus of the takings clause is on what is taken, not what remains.

[A] Criticism and Response

The *Loretto* majority's holding has been criticized in the following way: other governmental actions, involving million of dollars,[12] but classified as regulatory takings, go uncompensated, while the actions in *Loretto*, involving much less money, require compensation. A starting point in formulating a response to this criticism and to justifying this seemingly unfair comparison is the idea that the finding of a physical

9. Marshall concluded that all three rights were taken here. This discussion of "rights" is inconsistent with a test used in the Supreme Court's regulatory taking cases—notably in *Penn Central Transportation Company v. City of New York*, 438 U.S. 104 (1978) (upholding historic landmark regulation and so denying an owner the right to lease unbuilt air rights worth $1-3 million a year in rents). But Marshall was building a majority of the court by emphasizing (for those Justices who thought *Loretto* should be a regulatory takings case) part of the *Penn Central* rule that finding a taking requires in part a consideration of the "character of the governmental action." Such emphasis in *Penn Central*, discussed in Chapter 4, *infra*, § 4.01 *et seq.*, was intended to get away from an examination of particular "strands" in the "bundle" of property rights.

10. Definitional questions might be: what is "physical," what is "permanent," and what is an "occupation"? If any one of these is not present, there may be no physical taking. The *Loretto* opinion contrasts a temporary intrusion, then resulting in no taking, and a permanent physical occupation, which results in a taking. A "permanent physical invasion" is, for Marshall, an example of a situation in which the "character of the governmental action" (one of the three parts of the *Penn Central* test) proves dispositive and requires a finding of a taking.

11. *Loretto*, 458 U.S. at 442–56.

12. *See, e.g.*, *Penn Central Transportation Company v. City of New York*, 438 U.S. 104 (1978) (discussed *infra*, Chapter 4, § 4.01); *Keystone Bituminous Coal Association v. DeBenedictis*, 480 U.S. 470 (1987) (upholding a state underground mining regulation controlling surface subsidence and so denying affected miners the right to extract 27 million tons of coal).

taking does not depend on the degree of invasion,[13] or extent of the injury to private property, or to the percentage decrease in the fair market value. The takings clause is self-executing and does not depend on balancing tests because in that way, the property of the citizenry is best protected from governmental intrusion. The majority's holding is prophylactic.[14]

Another way to formulate a response to the *Loretto* holding might be to ask: why is requiring a landlord to install mailboxes in the foyer of an apartment house not a physical taking, while the installation of the cable-TV boxes and cables is a physical taking? The *Loretto* majority's opinion is clear that mailboxes must be provided and other building code requirements met, without having to pay any compensation. This is: (1) because the landlord is there dealing directly with the government, whereas in *Loretto*, the government was authorizing occupation by a third party—the cable company—over whom the government does not exercise everyday supervision; and (2) because the mailboxes and building code requirements are to be met before the apartment house gets its occupancy permits—before, in other words, the right to possession arises.

[B] Citations to Other Cases in *Loretto*

Justice Marshall uses two World War II cases, both finding a taking, but their special wartime situation militates against giving them great weight. Two other cases are more interesting. The *Loretto* opinion distinguished *PruneYard Shopping Center v. Robins*,[15] as involving only a temporary intrusion on an owner's property. There, the intrusion was for the purpose of soliciting signatures for a petition to the government in the owner's shopping center, the right to petition the government being protected by the First Amendment to the U.S. Constitution.[16]

The opinion also relies on *Kaiser Aetna v. United States*.[17] This case involved a Hawaii marina development. The developer asked the Army Corps of Engineers if a navigational servitude[18] would be imposed once a non-navigable lagoon was dredged,

---

13. As we will see *infra*, Chapter 4, § 4.01, *Loretto*'s holding confines Justice Brennan's "whole parcel analysis" in *Penn Central* to regulatory takings, so Justice Marshall does not explain why the whole parcel is the focus of the analysis in *Penn Central*, while here the occupation of merely a portion of the apartment house results in a taking.

14. *Loretto*'s holding is also a decision to confine Justice Holmes' diminution in value test in *Mahon* to regulatory takings.

15. 447 U.S. 74 (1980).

16. *But see Judlo, Inc. v. Vons Companies, Inc.*, 259 Cal. Rptr. 624, 626 (Cal. App. Ct. 1989), *rev. denied*, 1989 Cal. LEXIS 2820 (Sept. 6, 1989) (holding that a shopping center tenant did not create a public forum by permitting news-racks in the front of its grocery store within the center; that the store owner had no constitutional duty to permit the publisher to place racks there; and that the issuance of an injunction requiring it to do so was a taking, citing *Loretto*.)

17. 444 U.S. 164 (1979).

18. This is an easement of passage for the public over navigable waters, even though the bed of the waterway is owned by private persons.

connected to navigable water, and improved with boat slips. The Corps said no. Once the development was completed, the Corps changed its mind and imposed the servitude. The Supreme Court found that the Corps had extracted a right for which compensation should have been paid and its belated assertion of the servitude was a *de facto* taking, taking advantage of the marina owner's improvements to the waterway and defeating his investment-backed expectations.[19] Marshall characterized the servitude as "not being a permanent *occupation* of land," but, even though the public's right was only one of passage, it was permanent from the time it was asserted by the Corps. While Marshall, as previously discussed, recognizes the right to possess, use, and dispose of property, and finds each affected, his discussion in *Kaiser Aetna* reveals that he sees *Loretto* as involving also the right to exclude. He calls this right "one of the most essential sticks on the bundle of rights that are commonly characterized as property" and "one of the most treasured strands in an owner's bundle of property rights."[20] Its deprivation denies an owner control over the property's use, and even though legal title is retained, is likely to "empty" the legal title of value.

[C] Personal Property and the *Loretto* Rule

As is true in state takings law, the categorical or *per se* rule of *Loretto* extends to personal property.[21] Personalty is in some ways more easily subject to a permanent physical seizure than is land, is more easily concealed from its owner after the fact, and so is deserving of protection for these two reasons.[22] Further, seizing items within the improvements on the land, although these items are not technically fixtures and so remain personal property, should also be compensable. However, prior to *Loretto*, another case held that other attributes of personal property, namely the right to alienate or sell personal property, are not equally protected.[23] Thus, the right to protect possession and the right to exclude appear to be *essential* rights of property, with specially high protections. It is an open question whether *Loretto* overrules or weakens the precedential value of *Allard*. It may be enough to say that the statute in *Loretto* involved a governmental monopoly and so placed special responsibilities on the cable operators.

Governmental regulations protecting wildlife roaming from public wildlife refuges onto private lands where they kill domestic animals like sheep and cattle, do not work

---

19. *Loretto*, 458 U.S. at 493.

20. *Id.* at 435.

21. Personal property is subject to condemnation of any type discussed in this book. For example, earlier the text discussed the condemnation of a sports franchise. *See* § 2.02[D], *supra*.

22. *See Nixon v. United States*, 978 F.2d 1269 (D.C. Cir. 1992) (applying the *Loretto* doctrine to a federal statute asserting governmental control over President Nixon's presidential papers).

23. *See Andrus v. Allard*, 444 U.S. 51, 65–66 (1979) (involving a prohibition on the sale of bird artifacts, such as feathers, in order to protect endangered and migrating birds and a trader in such artifacts claiming that the prohibition is a taking; held: there is no taking in this situation because the right to possess, transport, devise, and donate the artifacts is unaffected and there is "no physical property restriction").

a physical taking.[24] While physically invasive actions of government are not limited to its employees and agents, but may also extend to those acting under the authority of its regulations,[25] the wildlife protected while in the refuge are not acting in any such capacity. Similarly, when government-protected wild horses and burros eat the grass on a rancher's pastures, so that a rancher's sheep had little to eat, forcing the rancher to provide forage for them, there would, even then, be no physical invasion.[26]

[D] The Aftermath of *Loretto*

In 1988, rejecting Mrs. Loretto's application for attorneys' fees, a New York court called the finding of a taking "of purely academic interest" because the just compensation requirement of the U.S. Constitution would provide little more than the statutory requirement in place for reasonable compensation. The judge suggested that one dollar would suffice in most cases.[27]

In response to *Loretto*, several state statutes provide for provision of reasonable compensation for cable access to multi-unit apartment houses.[28] Even as cable fades as a means of receiving information, a Maine statute still provides the cable company with access for a nominal sum, but permits the apartment house owner to sue for additional compensation and if successful, to collect costs and attorneys' fees as well.[29] Likewise, Illinois permits a local government to authorize a cable company to exercise the power of eminent domain.[30] In Michigan, the courts have held that a cable company is a public utility and therefore entitled to exercise the eminent domain power on that account.

Also in response to *Loretto*, Congress deleted a mandatory access provision to a federal communications statute and an accompanying compensation requirement—indicating that Congress did not intend to confer condemnation powers on cable companies.[31]

---

24. *See Christy v. Hodel*, 857 F.2d 1324 (9th Cir. 1988).

25. *See State of Ohio ex rel. Jenkins v. Division of Wildlife, Dept. of Natural Resources*, slip opinion (Ohio App., Franklin County, Oct. 10, 1978) (involving an owner that has land adjacent to a state forest, in which the wildlife is protected from trapping and hunting and in which beavers built a dam along a stream, the dam causing the stream's water to back up onto the owner's land, flooding a large portion of it; owner sued the state, claiming a taking of his property). A *Loretto*, permanent physical invasion is not present: the beavers are not the agents of the state.

26. *See Clajon Production Corp. v. Petera*, 854 F. Supp. 843, 852–53 (D. Wyo. 1994); *Mountain States Legal Foundation v. Hodel*, 799 F.2d 1423 (10th Cir. 1986).

27. *Loretto v. Group W. Cable*, 522 N.Y.S.2d 543, 545–46 (N.Y. App. Div. 1987).

28. *See, e.g.*, Nev. Rev. Stat. Ann. § 711.255(3) (2024) (providing for a rebuttable presumption that access is worth $1 a unit, or $1,000, whichever is greater).

29. Me. Rev. Stat. Ann., tit. 14, § 6041(1)(F) (2024).

30. 65 ILCS 5/11-42-11(c) (2024).

31. *See Cable Associates v. Town & Country Management Corporation*, 709 F. Supp. 582, 585–86 (E.D. Pa. 1989).

[E] Easements

When government airplanes use private airspace to approach a government airport, it is required to pay for the airspace invaded—even if the invasion is not continuous, there has been a physical invasion that must be compensated. This result would not change if a county land use height limitation was adopted by ordinance.[32]

If within a residential subdivision or a condominium regime, a developer dedicates a utility easement and subsequently a cable company attempts to route its wires along the easement, courts have divided on the issue of whether *Loretto* compensation is paid to the developer or the utility.[33] On the one hand, the landowner may be seen as previously having given up the right of way, but, on the other hand, the physical occupation of the easement's space is for a purpose unintended at the time of the dedication and arguably a per se physical invasion. If the utility easement uses poles owned by a utility, *Loretto* requires compensation to the owner of the pole for its use, although rent for attaching the cable to the pole can be set by regulation at considerably less than market rates.[34]

§ 3.02 *Yee* Limits on *Loretto's* Categorical Rules

A 1978 California statute restricted the ability of mobile home park owners to terminate the tenancies of "pads" for mobile homes and their ability to disapprove purchasers of the tenancies unless the purchaser was financially unable to pay the rent. The statute also forbade the owners from requiring the removal of a mobile home from the pad upon its sale or transfer. A decade later, in 1988, the City of Escondido rent control ordinance reset rents to 1986 levels and prohibited rent increases, even upon the transfer of the mobile home on the pad, unless approved by the city council. The owners were required to accept their new tenants at controlled rents. Several park owners, including John Yee, sued the city and challenged the statute and the ordinance as a physical taking because they together prevented the owners from setting their own rents and choosing their own tenants. In *Yee v. City of Escondido*,[35] the U.S. Supreme Court decided that there had been no taking. *Yee* indicated that *Loretto*'s holding was not as elastic as some had thought.

---

32. *See McCarran International Airport v. Sistolak*, 137 P.3d 1110 (Nev. 2006).

33. J.G. Howard, *Real Property Issues in CATV Use of Public Rights-of-Way and Easements Dedicated for Compatible Use*, 23 Real Prop. Prob. & Tr. J. 413, 423–27 (1991) (collecting cases).

34. *Federal Communications Commission v. Florida Power Corporation*, 480 U.S. 245, 253–54 (1987).

35. 503 U.S. 519 (1992) (O'Connor, J., writing for the majority).

Yee alleged that the combined effect of this ordinance and statute was to increase the amount for which mobile homes sold (reflecting the lower rent on the pad), thus enabling the tenants to capture the value of living in a rent-controlled park. This premium price showed that the purpose of rent control, to supply affordable housing, was not being accomplished by the ordinance. What was accomplished, Yee said, was a transfer of a benefit from the landlord to the tenant, while the ordinance was not, under *Nollan v. California Coastal Comm'n*,[36] "substantially advancing a legitimate state interest." At the time, between 1987 and 1992, some thought *Nollan* was a physical invasion case,[37] so it is easy to see why Yee alleged that the effect of the regulation amounted to a physical taking of his property. The United States Supreme Court held that the effect was not a physical taking. The park owner voluntarily invited the original mobile home owner onto the pad, so the right to exclude was not affected. No physical, categorical, *Loretto*-like taking was involved.

The court recognized that neither the issue of a regulatory taking, nor the issue of a physical taking, is subsidiary to the other: "they exist side by side, neither encompassing the other."[38] Petitioner had asked whether the state courts below erred in ignoring the applicability of cases, from two federal circuits, involving physical takings and holding that a physical taking was involved in similar settings.[39]

The court's answer was that California's state courts had not erred. The "government effects a physical taking only when it requires the landowner to submit to the physical occupation of his land."[40] Yee and other owners voluntarily opened a mobile home park on their land, and voluntarily stayed in business, and neither the rent-control ordinance and the state statute required that they stay in business, "no government has required any physical invasion of petitioners' property." End of case.[41]

---

36. 483 U.S. 825 (1987), discussed *infra*, Chapter 14, § 14.20.

37. *Nollan v. California Coastal Commission*, 483 U.S. 825 (1987). In the process of garnering a majority of the court, Justice Scalia, in *Lucas v. South Carolina Coastal Council*, 505 U.S. 1003 (1992), had to explain that *Nollan* was not a physical invasion case; instead, it was the deprivation of a well-recognized right, an easement of access, over a beachfront parcel. This uncertainty was prolonged by *Hall v. City of Santa Barbara*, 813 F.2d 198 (9th Cir. 1986), *modified*, 833 F.2d 1270 (9th Cir. 1987) (suggesting that a mobile home ordinance might be a physical occupation), *cert denied*, 485 U.S. 940 (1988). *See also Seawall Associates v. City of New York*, 542 N.E.2d 1059 (N.Y. 1989) (holding that a five-year moratorium on the conversion, alteration, or demolition of single-room occupancy housing and that a statute requiring that the owner restore all such housing to habitable condition and lease it at controlled rents for an indefinite period, resulted in a physical, per se, taking of property and was compensable).

38. *Yee*, 503 U.S. at 537 (language following Justice Scalia's logic in *Lucas*, discussed *infra* Chapter 17).

39. This lesson in Supreme Court pleading leaves the regulatory taking issue open, perhaps as a warning to government attorneys that someday the court might consider benefit-shifting regulations to be a regulatory taking under a *Penn Central* analysis.

40. *Yee*, 503 U.S. at 527.

41. On occasion, a state court decides differently. *See Lee Cty. v. Kiesel*, 705 So. 2d 1013 (Fla. App. Ct. 1998) (recognizing a physical invasion of a riparian right to view a river, the view being blocked by the construction of a state bridge), *noted at* 109 Yale L.J. 849 (2000).

In the final analysis, the court used *Yee* to emphasize the separateness of the type of (physical) taking found in *Loretto*.

If the statute and the ordinance amounted to no more than a land use regulation, the court said, then the property challenge to them was not as a physical taking, but a regulatory one.[42] Unfortunately for John Yee and the park owners, they had not alleged and argued that a regulatory taking took place, so the court in Yee did not consider this issue.[43]

[A] *Loretto* and *Yee* Combined

Conflicts between the results in *Loretto* and *Yee* are often found in the context of the telecommunications industry. In one case, a state public utility commission required that a telephone company install the electronic data transmission equipment—software and data—used by another phone company. Authorized by statute, the commission's joint location requirement is a legislative judgment entitled to judicial deference, is reasonable, and substantially advances the state's interests. However beneficial to consumers it might be, *Loretto* still suggests that there has been a physical taking. However, the holding in *Yee v. City of Escondido* that a regulation giving mobile home park residents a right to transfer their occupancy of the mobile home pad at a controlled rent was not a physical invasion of the park owner's property, refocuses *Loretto*'s core concern with physical occupancy. Even though the invasion here has the same permanence that appeared important in *Loretto*, *Yee* is distinguishable: the mobile home park ordinance in *Yee* was a regulation, not a direct invasion of the property—city officials did not appropriate the mobile home pad.

Still and all, the presence of the electronic data transmission company's equipment on the telephone company's premises looks more like the intrusion of the cable lines

---

42. Here the court cited its own rule of procedure: Rule 14.1(a) states that "only the questions set forth in the opinion [appealed], or fairly included therein, will be considered by the Court." The regulatory taking issue was not in the opinion below and was not, the court held, "fairly included" within it. The theory of notice pleading, as well as the court's reluctance to rule on a matter not fully briefed and litigated below, also counseled against ruling on a regulatory takings issue. "In fact, were we to address the issue here, we would apparently be the first court in the Nation to determine whether an ordinance like this one effects a regulatory taking." No thanks, said the court.

43. The issue of a regulatory taking in the context of a mobile home park was addressed by the Ninth Circuit in *Guggenheim v. City of Goleta*, 582 F.3d 996 (9th Cir. 2009). Goleta had enacted a mobile home park rent control ordinance in order to increase the supply of affordable housing. Park owners argued the ordinance effected a regulatory taking. The Circuit Court panel found that the ordinance singled out park owners to provide affordable housing when that burden should have been borne by all city residents. It also found that the ordinance caused a wealth transfer from the owners to their tenants, forcing rents down to 80% of fair market levels and increasing the value of park tenancies by 90%. Purchasers of the tenancies would enjoy the below market rents and thus pay more for them. The 9th Circuit *en banc* vacated the panel's decision. 638 F.3d 1111 (9th Cir. 2010). It found that because the owners purchased their parks after the ordinance was in effect, they presumably paid a price reflecting the ordinance's effects, so there had been no regulatory taking.

in *Loretto* than a regulatory exaction.[44] Similarly, the company's property might be seen as their operating certificate; once granted by the state, the state commission does not have the right to add to it a condition that destroys the company's right to exclude.

[B] Further Categorical Physical Takings: *Horne v. Department of Agriculture*

The blurry lines between *Loretto* (1982) and *Yee* (1992) remained unexplored for nearly a quarter century. The next physical invasion case decided by the Supreme Court was *Horne v. Department of Agriculture.*[45] The opinion in this case held, as a preliminary matter, that a governmental appropriation of personal property could be a categorical, physical taking. Here a 1937 New Deal federal statute required raisin farmers annually to give up a portion of their crop to a raisin "reserve." The purpose of the reserve was to "stabilize" raisin prices.[46] California farmers Marvin and Laura Horne objected, refused to surrender the required portion of the crop, and argued that placing their raisins in the reserve caused a physical taking. They argued this point all the way to the United States Supreme Court, all courts below rejecting their argument.[47]

The Supreme Court, however, agreed, 8–1, with the Hornes: the statute effected a physical invasion and a taking of his raisins.[48] The court found that nothing in American history suggests that personal property is any less subject to the demands of the takings clause than real property:[49] "The government has a categorical duty to pay just compensation when it takes your car, just as when it takes your home."[50]

Writing for the court, Chief Justice Roberts went on: he said that the just compensation required by the takings clause is the "stabilized" market price of the forfeited raisins, rather than their fair market value of the raisins computed without stabilization. The majority opinion allowed the Hornes to challenge the implementation and enforcement of the reserve regulation before the government actually took a portion of their crop; they did not have to seek just compensation for it after the taking; that

44. *See GTE Northwest, Inc. v. Public Utility Comm'n of Oregon*, 900 P.2d 495 (Or. App. Ct. 1994).

45. 576 U.S. 351 (2015) (hereafter *Horne*), noted at 129 Harv. L. Rev. 261 (2015).

46. There is more here than this brief description of the administrative process reveals. Its details are discussed in Steven J. Engle, *Property Rights after Horne*, 10 N.Y.U. J.L. & Liberty 669, 670–71 (2016).

47. The Hornes' litigation began in 2002 with proceedings against the administrators of the raisin reserve. These proceedings resulted in a nearly $700,000 fine, which the Hornes appealed to federal district court.

48. Don't get caught in the weeds here: the issue isn't how many raisins make a "crop" of them, it is rather that portion of the crop taken, whatever the statute requires.

49. Beware! The Justices are not historians: what they lack in precedent they may find in history—and what they find in history may stand in for what they see as the reasonable expectations of their readers.

50. *Horne*, 576 U.S. at 357.

is, there is a remediable constitutional injury before the administrators of the reserve enforce its order, thus remedies under the takings clause may include a decree invalidating an administrative order.[51]

Nonetheless the only remedy mentioned in the takings clause is just compensation. Dissenting in part, three justices objected to the lack of a remand of the case to determine that compensation, noting that the Hornes retained not only the right to the portion of their crop not reserved, but also the right to the net proceeds of the sale of the reserved raisins.[52] Those proceeds, Justice Breyer wrote, should reduce the amount of just compensation due the Hornes. Just compensation, he thought, should be the fair market value of the raisins taken into the reserve adjusted to account for net proceeds received.[53]

Justice Sotomayor dissented as well, arguing that *Loretto* did not apply because *all* of the Hornes' rights in the crop were not taken, so there could be no physical taking. She wrote that "a claim of a *Loretto* taking is a bold accusation that carries with it a heavy burden."[54] The retention of even one right "defeats a claim" because the governmental action must be so completely destructive to the property owner's rights—all of them—as to "render a regulatory takings claim either a foregone conclusion or unequal to the task."[55]

Toward the end of Justice O'Connor's time on the bench, in 2005, she wrote the opinion in *Lingle v. Chevron U.S.A. Inc.*[56] The opinion attempted to redraw the line between takings and due process claims and in so doing, she summarized the takings cases to date. Justice O'Connor recognized *Loretto* as an example of a regulatory taking, involving a regulation of a cable television company. She assumed that physical and regulatory takings were two variants of the same species. To the contrary, the *Horne* majority assumed that they were mutually exclusive species. As precedent for maintaining that distinction in spite of the fact that the Hornes could still make money from some of their raisin crop, *Horne* has a place in future takings jurisprudence. The appropriation of a percentage of the crop reduces its value, but not to zero. Appropriation here is assumed to be the equivalent of condemning part of the land on which the crop is grown. However, the Hornes were dealing with a fungible commodity, no one trespassed on their farm, no government official "occupied" their raisins, and no one prevented them from selling their non-reserved raisins. In this context, *Horne*, in de-emphasizing the need to find a permanent, physical occupation of the whole crop, expanded the idea of a physical taking.[57]

---

51. *Id.* at 367.
52. *Id.* at 372.
53. *Id.* at 376.
54. *Id.* at 378.
55. *Id.*
56. 544 U.S. 528 (2005).
57. From a policy perspective, the *Horne* holding makes sense: the required raisin reserve was an out-of-date device skewing market forces and presented anti-trust concerns, viewing the reserve as a cartel whose aim was to restrict the supply of raisins and thereby to increase demand for them in the

The *Horne* opinion holds that a government mandate to surrender a specific, identifiable, fungible, portion of an owner's personal property as a condition of engaging in the sale of the rest of the property, is a categorical, *per se*, physical taking. This is not a widely applicable holding. The future of the *Horne* opinion lies in picking it apart. The opinion may become a pastiche of sources for future quotations.

[C] *Cedar Point Nursery v. Hassid*

In 2021, in *Cedar Point Nursey v. Hassid*,[58] the Supreme Court held, 6-3, that whenever the government authorizes by statute an involuntary entry upon real property, no matter how long the duration of the entry, there is a physical, categorical, *per se* taking. Like *Horne, Cedar Point* expanded the doctrine of physical takings: *Loretto* dealt with a permanent physical occupation of land, *Cedar Point* dealt with a temporary one. It dealt with the right of union organizers, after giving notice to employers of migrant farm workers and to the state labor relations board, to enter an employer's farm in order to speak with farm workers not in residence on the farm. The entry was limited in time to one hour before and after work and during the workers' lunch hour. The number of entries was also limited—to up to four in separate 30 day periods annually. This entry was, the court held, a physical invasion no matter its duration, public purpose, or economic impact.

The court dealt with two of its past cases. The employer's farm was not otherwise open to the public, and the court said that this fact distinguished the case of *Pruneyard v. Robbins*:[59] the *Pruneyard* opinion allowed a religious group, on First Amendment grounds, to hand out fliers in a shopping mall. The court also discussed the case of *United States v. Causby*:[60] *Causby* held that the government took property by flying repeatedly over a chicken farmer's coops, thereby causing "substantial damage" and destroying the farm's use as a chicken farm. Here, military aircraft flights were causing the chickens to harm or kill themselves by taking flight into the walls of the chicken coops. Because a categorical physical taking does not consider the economic impact of the entry on the owner, this makes the *Causby* precedent a weak one as precedent for the case of the union organizers' entry. However, neither the slight economic impact in *Robbins* nor the substantial economic impact in *Causby* stood in the way of the court's finding a physical taking in *Cedar Point*.

Why? It is because the court's emphasis here was on the employer's right to exclude, viewed as a stick in the bundle of rights that constitute property. That right was here superior to all other sticks in the bundle. That superiority depended on the workers

---

marketplace. *See* Dean Lueck, *The Curious Case of Horne v. Department of Agriculture: Good Law, Bad Economics?*, 10 N.Y.U. J. L. & Liberty (2016).

58. 594 U.S. 139 (2021). *See generally* Bethany R. Berger, *Eliding Original Understanding in Cedar Point Nursery v. Hassid*, 33 Yale J.L. & Human. 307 (2022).

59. 447 U.S. 74 (1980).

60. 328 U.S. 256 (1946).

not residing where they worked. If the workers lived elsewhere, off-site on a separate parcel and at a location available to the organizers, there would have been no need for the organizers to enter the farm. This distinction emphasizes the narrowness of the court's holding and its applicability to a particular sector of the agricultural migrant workforce not residing where they worked. Like *Horne*, the applicability of the *Cedar Point* holding is narrow, except for its time dimension—its extension of physical takings doctrine to temporary occupations of property.

A further point on the narrow reach of this case. The *Cedar Point* opinion recognized three exceptions to its holding. The first is for "occasional entries" with which the law of trespass deals. This first exception "accounts for," the court said, its opinion in *Arkansas Game and Fish Comm'n v. United States*.[61] In that case, a federal agency, the Army Corps of Engineers, constructed a dam upstream from a state wildlife management area. Periodic water releases from the dam temporarily flooded the management area and destroyed its timber. The court said that a taking might occur, but that the case should be analyzed using a multi-factor, regulatory takings, balancing test. The following factors—how long the flooding lasted, the degree to which the flooding was the intended or foreseeable result of the release, the flooded land's character, and the owner's reasonable investment-backed expectations for the timber—were to be used to determine whether a taking occurred. *Arkansas Game and Fish Comm'n* is made an exception because its opinion is difficult to reconcile with the holding in *Cedar Point*.

The second exception is for "government-authorized" entries consistent with "longstanding background restrictions on property rights," such as the government's right to abate a nuisance and "traditional common law privileges to access private property"[62]—perhaps such as hunters' rights on unposted woodland and open fields. As a defense to an allegation of a taking, this exception was first raised in the 1992 case of *Lucas v. South Carolina Coastal Council*.[63] There Justice Scalia found "common law privileges" in the common law of property and nuisance, but they might also be a matter of tradition, or of an evolving consensus, or be known to the public and applied through doctrines of actual and constructive notice. The one sure thing is that union organizers are not protected by this exception.

The third exception is for a government "requiring owners to cede a right of access as a condition of receiving certain benefits," including "health and safety inspection regimes." The future outlines of this exception are unclear: in one important respect, health and safety inspection regimes might or might not include occupational health and safety for workers—miners, steelworkers, etc.

The second and third exceptions concern, the court said, governmental defenses to a physical taking. These two exceptions are closely akin to governmental defenses to

61. 568 U.S. 23 (2012).

62. *See generally* David R. Dana, *"Background Principles" in the Law of Takings*, 73 Am. U. L. Rev. 1789 (2024) (reviewing the case law and academic treatment (see *id.*, 1790–91, notes 8–12) of these principles and searching for a justification for them other than judicial fiat).

63. 505 U.S. 1003, 1015–17 (1992), discussed further *infra*, Chapter 14, § 14.20.

an owner's allegation of a taking for a total deprivation of a property's economically beneficial uses. They are further discussed with the exactions cases in Chapter 14. The point here is that if these defenses remain undefined, they also remain future litigation-breeders. In state and lower federal courts, the basis for these two defenses has been found in state constitutions, water law, public trust law, wildlife regulations, and judge-made common law—the list is inclusive, but untested in the United States Supreme Court.

§ 3.03 Regulatory Takings

A physical taking occurs when the government takes and occupies property. A regulatory taking is the result of the government regulating a property's use in a way that unreasonably diminishes its value without physically occupying it. Neither type of taking is derivative of the other—each is a separate and distinct type of taking.

[A] Early Nuisance Abatement Cases

In English law, since at least the 12th century, no landowner has had the right to operate or conduct a public nuisance on his or her land and the legislature has had the right to abate such a nuisance. When it did so, American case law on takings in the 19th and early 20th centuries show landowners seeking compensation for the results of governmental abatement actions, losing their cases. In *Mugler v. Kansas*,[64] a brewer contested the validity, under the takings clause, of a statute prohibiting the manufacture of alcoholic beverages to be sold within the State of Kansas. The statute was upheld and the brewer was held not to have suffered a compensable taking of his property, even though his brewery was essentially worthless because of the statutory prohibition.

Again, in *Hadacheck v. Sebastian*,[65] the City of Los Angeles enacted an ordinance prohibiting the manufacture of bricks within its city limits. The court upheld the ordinance because it was within the city's legislative authority; it abated a public nuisance and this purpose was held to render the ordinance valid, even if it at the same time had a severe impact on the fair market value of the owner's property.[66] The severity of that impact did not matter. So long as the legislature stayed within the bounds of the police power, compensation was not due because the diminution in fair market value was the result of a proper regulation.

Both of these two cases have precedential value only when the legislature declares that a particular use of property is a public nuisance, but once this occurs, the judicial

64. 123 U.S. 623 (1887).

65. 239 U.S. 394 (1915).

66. The record had evidence that the fair market value of the property was reduced by 93%.

finding of legislative authority for the regulation immunizes it from being a taking. The legislation was absolutely bullet-proofed against a regulatory taking claim, at least until Justice Holmes reformulated the law of takings in his 1922 majority opinion in *Pennsylvania Coal Co. v. Mahon*.[67] However, it took time, a great deal of time, to recognize the implications of what Holmes had done, so the nuisance abatement line of case survived *Pennsylvania Coal*.[68] By the 1920s, when a legislature was not abating a nuisance, it was instead regulating uses and activities that did not amount to a nuisance. Regulation could nonetheless be heavy-handed and substantially affect property values. In the face of this activism, Justice Holmes thought that a new approach to takings law was necessary.

There are several tests for determining when a regulatory taking has occurred. Two of the most frequently used are (1) the diminution in value test, and (2) the public benefits/private injury test. Both are discussed in the following, 1922 opinion by Justice Holmes.

§ 3.04 *Pennsylvania Coal Co. v. Mahon*

This case held that a state statute requiring a coal mining company to support the surface above its mines is unconstitutional when the company holds a pre-existing waiver of a right to such support from the surface owner; it is a violation of the Fifth Amendment's taking clause.

[A] The Facts

This case is set in Pennsylvania's anthracite coal fields. In 1878, 43 years before the case reached the United States Supreme Court, Mr. and Mrs. Mahon[69] first held a surface estate to land which they long thereafter used for a residence. What they did not purchase was the coal company's subsurface mineral estate. It had earlier been severed from their surface estate; neither did they purchase the right to have their surface supported from below. This right to support was also held by the company. In

67. 260 U.S. 393 (1922).

68. *See Miller v. Schoene*, 276 U.S. 272, 279–80 (1928) (finding no taking when a state regulation required owners to cut down red cedar trees harboring a virus killing local apple trees and noting that the legislative judgment, here preferring ownership of apples over cedars, is one of the "distinguishing characteristics of every exercise of the police power," Holmes, J., voting with the court's majority). *See also Goldblatt v. Hempstead*, 369 U.S. 590 (1962) (holding that a prohibition on further excavation below a quarry's water table valid as a nuisance abatement and so not a taking when other uses remained).

69. Mr. Mahon was an attorney.

Pennsylvania, this right is known as the third estate—the right to the surface, and the right to mine, being the first two. Once notified that the company was about to start mining under their surface, the Mahons sued to enjoin the company from mining their subsurface.[70]

At the time the surface was sold, the risk of the surface caving in or subsiding was low. Coal companies then removed about two-thirds of the subsurface coal and left pillars of coal to support the surface, using the "room and pillar" method of mining. Later however, the original mining companies sold their holdings to scavenger companies. Technology also improved, so a larger percentage of the coal could safely be mined. Meanwhile, the surface population increased in the Mahons' neighborhood when a large portion of the surface verged on collapse.

"Government could hardly go on," Holmes wrote in introducing his two takings tests in this opinion, "if to some extent values incident to property could not be diminished without paying for every such change in the general law."[71] These are famous words.[72] They require both a presumption of validity for land use regulations as well as a first tier rational basis standard of judicial review, applied occasionally (as here) with a rigor sufficient to overturn legislation.

In his *Mahon* opinion, Holmes also wrote: "The general rule . . . is, that while property may be regulated to a certain extent, if the regulation goes too far it will be recognized as a taking."[73] These too are famous words. They required a fact-driven inquiry and often a trial by jury. This "too far" language then, together with the "government could hardly go on . . . " language, encapsulate the issues involved in regulatory takings.

[B] Diminution in Value

"In the field of land use regulation, the emphasis which Justice Holmes placed on the degree of value diminution suffered by the property owner has continued to be the central focus of modern case law on the subject."[74] This "diminution in value" test is measured by the value of the owner's property. It comes out of the previously

70. This made for an unusual takings case. The usual plaintiff in such cases is the owner whose property is harmed by the government. Here the state (Pennsylvania) was attempting to protect the plaintiff's surface rights and it is the defendant company whose property was harmed, allegedly to the point of a taking. Moreover, the company was seeking neither compensation nor any other affirmative relief. It just wanted the regulations to go away.

71. *Mahon*, 260 U.S. at 413.

72. Holmes was past 80 when he wrote them, eager to do the work assigned by the new Chief Justice, William Howard Taft, and at the same time was picking up the threads of a long-term friendship with Justice Brandeis, recently appointed to the Supreme Court and dissenting in the case. *See* SHELTON NOVICK, HONORABLE JUSTICE: THE LIFE OF OLIVER WENDELL HOLMES 343–45 (1989).

73. *Mahon*, 260 U.S. at 415.

74. *Skaw v. United States*, 740 F.2d 932, 939 (Ct. Cl. 1984) (citing *Mahon*).

quoted "too far" language of Holmes' opinion.[75] Cases have long used this test.[76] However, figuring out which unit of property to measure is another question. Recent cases have divided over whether, in the context of mining, it is the value of the surface and the mining rights, or the value of the severed mining rights, standing alone.[77]

[C] Balancing Public Benefits against Private Injuries

In the very next paragraph of his opinion, Holmes presents a second, very different test. This is the public benefit/private injury balance. This is the test which he intends to be dispositive—it has certainly proven to be the most influential over the long term.[78]

It is not always easy to apply. Public benefits are often held very diffusely. In this test, however, they must be weighed against private injury that is often severe and specific. The resulting comparison is like weighing apples and oranges. Moreover, a very great private injury may be outweighed by a greater public benefit, but the test makes no provision for defining a point at which the absolute enormity of the private injury controls.

If *Mahon*'s legal backdrop is *Mugler* or *Hadacheck*, then *Mahon* is a departure from precedent.[79] Holmes' opinion for the majority said that the Kohler Act is not a safety measure: notice to the Mahons to get out in advance of mining would, Holmes said, protect their safety. Nor was the safety of the miners the state's concern: restrictions

---

75. Holmes gives no definite idea of what degree of diminution was necessary; he felt that when "positive law" (his era's term for a statute) upset an owner's expectations as to what he owns too violently, it went "too far" and required compensation. *See Bent v. Emery*, 173 Mass. 495, 496 (Mass. 1899) (Holmes stating that small diminutions are "incident to the free play of the machinery of government" but sooner or later reach limits imposed by the Constitution); *Commonwealth v. Parks*, 30 N.E. 174 (Mass. 1892) (Holmes, J.) (a Holmes opinion structured much like *Mahon*).

76. *See Ruckelshaus v. Monsanto Company*, 467 U.S. 986, 1003–04 (1984) (holding that public disclosure of confidential business data by the EPA constitutes a taking).

77. *Compare Machipongo Land & Coal Co. v. Department of Enviro. Prot.*, 799 A.2d 751 (Pa. 2002) (refusing to measure diminution in value by the mineral rights alone and rejecting "vertical segmentation"), *cert. denied*, 537 U.S. 1002 (2002), *with R.T.G., Inc. v. Ohio*, 780 N.E.2d 998 (Ohio 2002) (deciding to divide the land into surface, mineral and air estates in order to measure the diminution so using "vertical segmentation").

78. Its effects can be seen in the majority opinion in *Penn Central Transportation Co. v. City of New York*, 438 U.S. 104 (1978), and again in the majority opinion in *Keystone Bituminous Coal Ass'n v. DeBenedictis*, 480 U.S. 470 (1987), discussed *infra*.

79. Holmes later wrote a friend: "I have always thought that old Harlan's decision in *Mugler* was pretty fishy." Letter of O.W. Holmes, Jr. to H. Laski, 1 HOLMES-LASKI LETTERS 346 (Mark deW. Howe, ed., 1963). What's "pretty fishy" about *Mugler* is either that it is hard to believe that the brewery in that case is worth nothing after Kansas went dry, or that the legislature thought in terms of Mr. Mugler's brewery being a public nuisance. In any event, Kansas' going dry and moralistic about alcoholic beverages was not a secure enough basis for a constitutional right: one generation's morality might not be the next's—and the Constitution should not depend on swings in public policy or morals.

on mining methods could accomplish that end, he said. The surface itself was not protected: when the surface and the mineral estate were in the same hands, the Act did not apply. The company could destroy, for example, any surface farmlands which it owned. Thus, Holmes found no public purpose or benefit of the type that the state was entitled to seek.

That said, Holmes turned to the specifics of the case: "This is the case of a single private house."[80] This is akin to saying that the Mahons knew what rights and estates they were buying and, more importantly, what they weren't buying. They purchased their home with eyes wide open, but were now receiving an additional right via the Act, thus redoing their original deal. No right that they possessed was interfered with, because they only held the thin crust of the earth's surface. The government was not intruding on that, so the taking was not a physical one from the Mahons' perspective. Instead, the intrusion was on the coal company's rights. It had purchased the right of support and the Act prevented the Coal Company from exercising that right.

Holmes thought that the state was not just choosing to elevate one person's property right over another's. If that were all it was doing, then the "government could hardly go on" language would resolve the case in the Mahons' favor.[81] No, Holmes thought instead that the Act had permitted the Mahons and others to redo their bargain in purchasing the surface, by successfully lobbying the legislature, and he saw no "public benefit" (as previously discussed) in the legislative response to that lobbying. The Coal Company simply was not treated fairly and equally by the Act.

Justice Brandeis' dissenting opinion[82] viewed the Kohler Act as a public safety measure.[83] He said that the purpose of the Act does not cease to be public because some private citizens benefit thereby. If it were otherwise, much legislation would be stymied as a result. In addition, Brandeis said, the coal regulated by the Kohler Act "may be negligible as compared with the value of the whole property." (That is, the private injury may be negligible in comparison with the widespread public benefit achieved, making the diminution in value a relative matter.)

80. *Mahon*, 260 U.S. at 413.

81. Holmes' attitude toward legislatures was often one of judicial restraint. If the dispute in *Mahon* had been between a farmer using the surface profitably and a miner causing sinkholes on otherwise good agricultural land, Holmes may have conceded that the legislature could decide that some of the coal needs to be left in place in order to save the farmland above. If in a Western state the legislature decided to save farmland or pasturage from surface mining, Holmes would probably not have stood in its way. This deference to legislatures stemmed not from a belief that they were wise, or always right, but from his realization that, as a practical matter, every decision they make gives a benefit or an advantage to some portion of society, and by the same token, disadvantages another portion. Hence his "government could hardly go on" language.

82. Because Holmes and Brandeis have been famously paired in their dissents in the contract clause cases early in the twentieth century, you might wonder about their disagreement in *Mahon*. As to Holmes, it might be said that he saw a textual warrant in the Constitution for what he wrote here, but saw nothing similar in the contract clause cases.

83. Brandeis privately attributed Holmes' decision to old age and class bias. *See* Philippa Strumm, Louis D. Brandeis 313 (1984).

Holmes had first resolved the case in a single paragraph. The paragraph for which the statement, "This is the case of a single private house," is the topic sentence, was originally the whole of his analysis in a first draft of his opinion. Holmes circulated his draft to the other justices. Chief Justice Taft read it, liked the draft so far, but wrote Holmes a letter expressing the opinion that the Kohler Act was unconstitutional. The Chief also said that more was needed in view of the interests of the state in the litigation and the *amicus* briefs filed with the court. After receipt of the letter, Holmes added the remainder of the opinion[84] (presumably to gather a majority). He wrote the remainder as it was handed down, continuing in the manner of an "advisory opinion."[85] This portion of the opinion may technically be *dicta*, but it contains the opinion's most quotable material. Three aspects of this second portion of Holmes' opinion are worth high-lighting.

[1] The Property

Holmes first recognizes that the takings clause may be violated, not just by a taking of a person's title to property, but also by a taking of the value in using it, here by mining the coal in it. He is not concerned just with the "thing-ness" of property, but with the value in its use, that it may be "exercised with profit" and in a "commercially practical" manner. Underlying this idea of property is the "bundle of sticks" view of property—the support estate being one of the sticks missing from the Mahons' bundle originally, but impermissibly restored by the legislation under review.

An up-to-date example of a *Mahon* type taking involves information rights. The common law says that the holder of mineral rights has the exclusive power to explore and develop them (known as the exploration right). Suppose that a state's Geological Survey, a state agency, conducts a seismic survey of a region including an owner's mineral properties and releases geologic data showing that there are no minerals within the owner's boundaries. If the third estate is a recognized property right in *Mahon*, then the exploration right should have the same status—Holmes' definition of property can dis-aggregate the property into various sticks in the bundle of property rights, and when a stick is deprived of all its value, then there is a taking. Clearly, the state has an interest in knowing what minerals lie within its jurisdiction, but that only means that the seismic survey was a valid exercise of state power. The interest at issue is an informational one, and information has value when released to the public. Release prevents the owner from capitalizing on the information, even information about the absence of minerals. The state has made exploring for minerals "commercially impractical" in Holmes' words so a taking has arguably occurred.[86]

---

84. *See* J. Dimento, *Mining the Archives of* Pennsylvania Coal: *Heaps of Constitutional Mischief*, 11 J. Leg. Hist. 396, 407 (1990).

85. The phrase is Justice Steven's in *Keystone*, discussed *infra*.

86. For another discussion of this problem, in light of a later Supreme Court opinion, see *infra* Chapter 12, discussing *Lucas v. South Carolina Coastal Council*, 505 U.S. 1003 (1992).

[2] Reciprocity of Advantage

Speaking about a Pennsylvania statute that required mining companies to maintain a pillar of coal between mines to avoid flooding one mine with water from another, Holmes said that the statute "secured an average reciprocity of advantage"[87]—that it was, in other words, good for both the miners and the company employing them. A good way to distinguish Holmes' and Brandeis' approaches to analyzing the case is to look at Holmes' discussion of the idea that a statute regulating the mines might be justified by its "reciprocity of advantage"—that is, by the idea that the mining company whose workplace was regulated by health and safety measures got healthy employees in return. In the context of the Fifth Amendment's takings clause, the idea is that the "reciprocity of advantage" is an owner's implicit compensation, made in kind, for his being burdened by a regulation when his neighbors—that is, other coal mine owners—are subject to the same regulation. Holmes' idea is narrower than that—he sees it as applicable to save a statute from the claim that it works a taking, when there is a benefit back to the owner on the owner's property when his miner employees are healthy and safe. The idea can generally be seen either as a test for a taking (without it, a taking occurs) or as an affirmative defense to a taking (with its presence, no taking can occur).

Holmes dealt with this idea in the second, or advisory portion of his majority opinion. He thought that every statute was to be examined separately to determine whether regulations were reciprocated by conferring some benefit on the employer or owner. On the other hand, Brandeis thought that a regulation might be justified when it provided "the advantage of living and doing business in a civilized community"—by, in other words, a very generalized, society-wide idea of reciprocity.[88] His idea of a proper reciprocity of advantage goes beyond each statute evaluated by the courts.[89] There was no room, thought Brandeis, for considering Holmes' narrow version of reciprocity of advantage, except that of acceptance of the regulation in exchange for "the advantage of living and doing business in a civilized community."[90]

Holmes' next paragraph, starting with "the rights of the public in a street," hypothesized that if the legislature "have been so short sighted as to acquire only the surface rights without the right of support" for the street, the legislature should not thereafter,

---

87. *Mahon*, 260 U.S. at 415. Justice Holmes used this phrase once before, in the case of *Jackman v. Rosenbaum Co.*, 260 U.S. 22, 30 (1922) (concerning the construction of a party wall).

88. *Mahon*, 260 U.S. at 422.

89. Brandeis' general reciprocity is a theme taken up by Justice Stevens 65 years later, writing for the majority of the United States Supreme Court in the *Keystone Bituminous Coal Ass'n v. DeBenedictis*, 480 U.S. 470, 491–92 (1987), discussed in this Chapter: "one of the state's primary ways of preserving the public weal is restricting the uses individuals can make of their property. While each of us is burdened by such restrictions, we, in turn, benefit greatly from the restrictions that are placed on others."

90. This debate between Justices Holmes and Brandeis has continued down to date and can be particularly seen in the opinions in *Penn Central Transportation Co. v. New York City*, 438 U.S. 104 (1978).

once the street is recognized as a public use, be able to acquire the support right by regulation when the takings clause required compensation.[91] This would be a bad faith attempt by the legislature to do on the cheap what it should pay for. Since there is, however, no evidence in the case of legislative bad faith, this paragraph presents a weak argument.

[3] A Regulation that "Goes Too Far"

The closest that Holmes comes to stating a general rule for the *Mahon* case appears (like the discussion of reciprocity of advantage) in the second portion of his opinion in the "too far" language previously discussed. He states: "The general rule is that, while property may be regulated to a certain extent, if regulation goes too far it will be recognized as a taking." Too far beyond what? We are not told: the line between regulation and taking is not defined, nor are criteria for identifying that line given. In another context, a person might say that "citizens are supposed to be good, but when they are not good enough, they are bad—and the worst of the bad people are criminals." Any criminal defense lawyer might object to this as a rule of law. However, Holmes is not proposing the same type of rule for takings cases. What he means is that the Pennsylvania legislature moved too fast or abruptly, unsettling the Coal Company's (and the Mahons') expectations about the deal they had struck when the Mahons took the deed to the surface without either the coal or the support right. You might think of this deal as the Mahons' agreement not to sue the company in either nuisance or trespass for unsettling the surface of the land on which their house stood. Holmes' talk of a taking at the end of this sentence may likewise be taken in the context of the case—that is, a case in which the Fifth Amendment takings clause and its due process clause is made applicable to the states through the due process clause of the Fourteenth Amendment. Thus, there is reason to see *Mahon* as both a takings and a due process case. In the first portion of the opinion, the "this is the case of a single private house" paragraph, Holmes finds a violation of the due process clause, and in the latter portion of the opinion, he finds a violation of the takings clause.

[D] Takings Jurisprudence

The second, advisory portion of Holmes' opinion contains the "too far" language previously quoted. This language is often taken to mean that the two clauses of the Fifth Amendment—the due process and the takings clause—are co-equal and on a continuum. The takings clause immediately follows the due process clause in the text of the Amendment. In context, then, a regulation which goes too far also offends the

91. *Mahon*, 260 U.S. at 415.

takings clause. So the reach and scope of the police power in the due process clause is limited by the clause following.

Another view is that Holmes synthesizes the two clauses in the Fifth Amendment: the due process clause is the place to which the courts look to determine whether a regulation works a taking; if so, then the takings clause is remedial: it provides the remedy of just compensation, as determined by the courts.

The relationship between the two clauses is crucial. If a regulation does provide due process and satisfies the tests for constitutionality under that clause, a litigant after *Mahon* remains free to challenge it again, under the takings clause. Concurrently, evidence of a denial of due process, becomes evidence of a taking.

[E] The Natural State Exception

One of the most interesting ancillary rules to develop from *Mahon*'s discussion of a taking is the holding of *Just v. Marinette County*.[92] There a shorelands zoning ordinance prevented the filling of wetlands without a permit. Because the county ordinance, mandated by and enacted under a state-wide program of shoreline protection, was in furtherance of a pre-existing public right—the state's public trust doctrine—and preserved the property zoned in its natural state, its enactment is not a taking. The ordinance did not create a public benefit (that would require just compensation) where none had existed previously, it preserved a public right and protected the resource held in the public trust. This distinction owes much to a formulation first made at the turn of the 20th century, between a prevention of a harm to the public (no compensation required), as opposed to the extraction of a public benefit (just compensation required).[93]

In *Just*, the preservation of a natural use was held not to be a taking. Like the Mahons, the Justs purchased their land subject to a preexisting right, although here the burden on their fee was not in their deed. For Holmes, that might have made a difference: Holmes' distaste with attempting to redo a private bargain in the legislature may have motivated his opinion in *Mahon* and his disagreement with Justice Brandeis. As to defining the "natural use," the court in *Just* regards forestry as a natural use of land.[94] Today it is best to regard the land protected in *Just* as riparian or littoral forest land, protecting wetlands.[95] Preserving this land in its natural state may be a govern-

---

92. 201 N.W.2d 761 (Wis. 1972), *noted at* 86 Harv. L. Rev. 1582 (1973).

93. *But see Lemp v. Town Bd. of the Town of Islip*, 394 N.Y.S.2d 517, 521 (N.Y. Sup. Ct., Special Term 1977) (rejecting *Just* and invalidating an ordinance prohibiting the construction on a dune on the beach as applied to petitioner's land).

94. For a case with a similar theory, see *Potomac Sand and Gravel Co. v. Maryland*, 293 A.2d 241 (Md. 1972) (finding that the preservation of natural resources is a valid public purpose under the police power).

95. *See, e.g.*, Alan Flenner, *Municipal Riparian Buffer Regulations in Pennsylvania—Confronting the Regulatory Takings Doctrine*, 7 Dick. J. Env. L. Pol. 207 (1998) (discussing the protection of riparian forest land by excluding development thereon).

mental purpose satisfying the public use requirement of the takings clause,[96] but such preservation may still require that compensation be paid in some circumstances.[97]

[F] The Police Power, Nuisances, and *Mahon*

The *Mugler-Hadacheck* line of cases, discussed earlier in this Chapter, continues well past *Mahon*. Its first use after 1922 is found in *Miller v. Schoene*[98] in 1928. The *Miller* opinion said: "When forced to such a choice (choosing between ordering the destruction of cedar trees harboring a pest that also liked to kill apple trees, in a region of the state full of apple orchards), the state does not exceed its constitutional powers by deciding upon the destruction of one class of property in order to save another which, in the judgment of the legislature, is of greater value to the public."[99] This is a statement applying Holmes' "government could hardly go on" language. Holmes joined the majority opinion in *Miller*,[100] so Holmes did not view his opinion in *Mahon* as establishing the exclusive method of analysis for takings cases. For him it remained more obnoxious to run a brickyard in a city (as in *Hadacheck*) than to attempt to undermine that city, as the coal company was about to do in *Mahon*.

A second use was in 1962 in *Goldblatt v. Town of Hempstead*.[101] In this case, the facts established that a sand and gravel pit, into which water was drawn, was amid an otherwise residential community. Here safety concerns seem paramount. The *Goldblatt* opinion assumes that an ordinance must deprive the owner of all reasonable use of a property before a taking will be found. It also holds that the landowner has the burden of proof to establish a taking.

As later chapters will show, this post-1922 line of nuisance cases engendered considerable controversy, and were eventually re-positioned (but not abolished) within the whole of the United States Supreme Court's takings jurisprudence. This re-positioning took place in later cases, particularly *Lucas v. South Carolina Coastal Council*.[102]

---

96. *See* Scott Wilder, *Tree Preservation Methods: Zoning Regulation vs. Conservation Servitude*, 14 J. Nat. Res. & Env. L. 253, 254–59 (1998).

97. *Id.* (suggesting that preservation at the time of subdivision or reforestation using impact fees is constitutional).

98. 276 U.S. 272 (1928) (finding no taking in order of state entomologist to cut down ornamental red cedar trees with cedar rust disease fatal to apple trees cultivated in large quantities nearby).

99. *Id.* at 279.

100. *Id.* at 279–80.

101. 369 U.S. 590 (1962) (ordinance requiring a permit to mine sand and gravel below water table had the purpose of protecting health and safety and was not a taking absent evidence that the prohibition of further mining would reduce the value of the property).

102. 505 U.S. 1003 (1992).

[G] Holmes and the *Euclid* Case

Holmes also signed the majority opinion in *Village of Euclid v. Ambler Realty Co.*[103] There, the court upheld a zoning ordinance when the record showed that the fair market value of the applicant's land was reduced in value between 66% and 75%. In this opinion, the purpose of the zoning ordinance was portrayed as the prevention of development in the village that would locate nuisances side-by-side. The ordinance was held to be a valid exercise of the police power given to the Village by the State of Ohio and as such is not a violation of the due process clause of the Fourteenth Amendment because the ordinance bears a reasonable relationship to the police power—protecting the health, safety, morals, and general welfare of its community. *Euclid*, the court found, was more like *Hadacheck* than *Mahon*. The Village's ordinance was not a regulation going "too far," so no taking.

§ 3.05 *Keystone Bituminous Coal Association v. Debenedictis*[104]

This later United States Supreme Court case extensively discussed and re-considered the majority opinion in *Mahon*. Without overruling Holmes' opinion, it undercut *Mahon* and some of the advisory language in the opinion's second part;[105] respect for Justice Holmes and the number of times his opinion had been cited preclude overruling it.[106] It is hardly necessary to state the facts of this case because they are so similar to those in *Mahon*.[107] The statute in *Keystone* required that 50% of the coal be left in place under certain types of buildings in order to prevent surface subsidence. This Subsidence Act was upheld. The buildings protected included public buildings and dwellings not repaired by the mining company causing subsidence.

Keystone's majority opinion provided a three pronged analysis of the Act derived from Justice Brennan's test for a taking in *Penn Central Transportation Co. v. City of New York*.[108] First, the court considered the nature of the governmental intrusion.

---

103. 272 U.S. 365 (1926).

104. 480 U.S. 470 (1987) (Stevens, J., writing for the majority). *Keystone* was a 5–4 decision. Two members of the majority (and one dissenter) retired within five years of the decision.

105. The majority's purpose was to incorporate new jurisprudence into the facts of *Mahon*, without repudiating Holmes' jurisprudence of the Fifth Amendment, and to embrace the ideas of Brandeis' dissenting opinion in *Mahon*.

106. Carlisle, *The Section 1983 Land Use Case: Justice Stevens and the Hunt for the Taking Quark*, 16 Stetson L. Rev. 565, n. 1 (1987) (reporting that, between 1922 and 1986, *Mahon* was cited nearly 100,000 times).

107. *Mahon* arose in the anthracite fields of Eastern Pennsylvania and *Keystone* in the bituminous coal fields in the Western part of that state.

108. 438 U.S. 104 (1978).

Second, it considered the diminution of value. Third, it considered the degree of interference with the owner's investment-backed expectations.

[A] Distinguishing *Mahon*

The court distinguishes *Mahon* in four ways. First, it emphasizes the *ad hoc* nature of the tests for a taking—in particular, it states that, in the field of regulatory takings, the balancing of private injury with public benefit is dependent on the circumstances of each case.

Second, the court finds that there is a public benefit associated with the Pennsylvania Subsidence Act that distinguishes it from the Kohler Act. The recent statute applied to all the state's land area, not just the anthracite fields, and not just lands where the title to the coal was severed from the title to the surface. Its concern was with conserving the land surface of the state, in its own right, whether in public or private hands, and whether or not the minerals have been previously severed from the surface of the land. The public benefit thus is a general one and involves many factors, not just health and safety, but also the conservation of land and the environmental protection of the state's land surface; it is not merely a re-doing of a private transaction, meant to protect private parties. In this part of the opinion, Justice Stevens assigned a greater value to environmental protection in the 1980s than it was assigned in the 1920s. Then, the economic development of the region depended on the continuation of the coal companies' ability to mine. The region was far less dependent on this one industry in the 1980s. Many of its mines were by then exhausted and abandoned.

Third, Holmes' opinion is called "uncharacteristically advisory": Holmes found that the Act was invalid as applied to a particular transaction and particular parties, but went on to invalidate it generally without having to.

Fourth, the court refers to the *Mugler*, *Hadacheck*, and *Goldblatt* line of authority for precedent in abating "nuisance-like activity." These cases are here understood to represent an instance when the "character of the governmental action" is the predominant consideration in deciding that no taking has occurred.

After defining the public benefit, the court went on to find a minimal impact on private parties—that is, only a minimal adverse effect on "investment-backed expectations" in the profitable mining of coal. Thus, the Act's public benefits outweighed the private injury it inflicted.

[B] Narrowing *Mahon*

Mahon concerned opening of new portions of an existing mine; here the impact surveyed was on to total amount of coal in existing mines (the coal in place) as well as on the coal involved in the support estate (the coal in the pillars of an existing deep mine). In *Mahon*, Holmes focused exclusively on the coal pillar necessary to prevent surface subsidence; here the focus is on the whole coal mine.[109] Justice Stevens said that when a property interest was as a business matter inseparable from other unregulated interests, the regulated interest may not be the sole subject of a takings claim.[110]

Thus, the *Keystone* majority opinion first rejected the definition of property in Holmes' opinion in favor of a review of the profitability of the industry as a whole. Holmes only in passing and in *dicta* assayed the statute in *Mahon* for its effect on the profits of the Pennsylvania Coal Company: there was no showing that the right to mine was made "commercially impractical." Holmes only suggested that it was. Stevens rejected Holmes' suggestion and his narrow analysis of the property taken.[111] Holmes focused on the support estate, Stevens on the profitability of the industry and on the expectation of investment profit.[112] Stevens found that in the western Pennsylvania coal fields, a very small percentage of the coal in the ground would have to stay there because of the regulation—this percentage being between one and nine percent, depending on the mine surveyed. One reason for explaining the difference between Holmes' and Stevens' approach was that in *Keystone*, Stevens treated the issue as a matter of the facial validity of the Pennsylvania Act, and not as an "as applied" case.[113]

Second, the majority opinion used the "reciprocity of advantage" test used by Holmes in *Mahon*, but in a way that Brandeis would agree with, and Holmes would not.[114] Justice Stevens wrote: "While each of us is burdened somewhat by such restrictions, we, in turn, benefit greatly from the restrictions that are placed on others." Note 21, following this statement, states that:

> [t]he takings clause has never been read to require the States or the courts to calculate whether a specific individual has suffered burdens under this generic rule in excess of the benefits received. Not every individual gets a full dollar return in benefits for the taxes he or she pays; yet, no one suggests that an individual has a right to compensation for the difference between taxes paid and the dollar value of benefits received.

Regulation, Stevens said, was the "burden of our common citizenship." His was a broad validation of governmental regulation.

---

109. This again is the "economic impact on the claimant" prong of the *Penn Central* analysis.

110. This accords with *Penn Central*'s view of the matter.

111. The sharpest differences between the majority and the dissent have to do with the definition of the parcel at issue, what is called the third or the support estate.

112. This focus was from *Penn Central*, not *Mahon*.

113. Like Holmes in *Mahon*, the *Keystone* majority indicated that a facial challenge to a regulatory taking was an up-hill battle at best and so difficult as to be not worth bringing when administrative remedies remain. Indeed, later cases, e.g., Justice Scalia's opinions in *Nollan* (1987) and *Lucas* (1992), bear out the idea that the court only wanted to decide "as applied" cases.

114. *Keystone*, 480 U.S. at 492, n. 21.

§ 3.06 Conclusion

Justice Stevens does not embrace Holmes' "too far" language in *Mahon*, noting that it was found in that part of the *Mahon* opinion which he labeled "advisory" or *dicta*.[115] Both that language and the "reciprocity of advantage" language, however, are parts of the *Mahon* majority opinion to survive *Keystone*.[116] Other parts left were Holmes' two tests for a taking. Justice Stevens used both of them in *Keystone*: the diminution in value test was applied in light of the plaintiffs' investment-backed expectations, and, viewing the affected property only in comparison with the industry's unaffected property,[117] the public benefit of the statute was weighed against the private injury it works.[118] The *Keystone* majority thus kept *Mahon* in touch with changing times.

---

115. The dissent, however, made a point of keeping that language alive, reading the due process and the takings clauses together, as Holmes had implied should be done, federalizing the state law used to review the exercise of the police power, and limiting both federal-state comity in our federal system and Brandeis' notion that states should be a place of experimentation in exercising the police power.

116. Stevens rejected both Holmes' definition of the property involved and his discussion of the public benefit of the Act.

117. Stevens' comparative approach to defining the property taken survives today and is known as the "whole parcel" rule. *See Boise Cascade Corp. v. State*, 174 P.3d 587 (Or. Ct. App. 2007) (discussing the history of the rule, involving timber harvest rights and comparing affected timber rights with all the rights owned in fee by the corporation, its unaffected timber rights, over all the corporation's acreage and over time).

118. *See Grasso v. City of New Bedford*, 777 N.E.2d 1264 (Mass. 2002) (adopting *Keystone*'s "whole parcel rule" approach to the definition of property taken); *Machipongo Land and Coal Co. v. Department of Enviro. Prot.*, 799 A.2d 751 (Pa. 2002) (same); *Bernardsville Quarry, Inc. v. Borough of Bernardsville*, 608 A.2d 1377 (N.J. 1992) (same, involving a quarry); *see also Karam v. Deptartment of Envir. Protection*, 705 A.2d 1221, 1226 (N.J. Super. Ct., App. Div. 1998) (same, involving riparian land).

Chapter 4
The Evolution of Regulatory Takings

In 1978, Supreme Court Justice William Brennan wrote an opinion that contains his restatement of the law of takings. His restatement is still influential—although it was modified two years later by Justice Lewis Powell's attempted restatement of the same law, this time in *Agins v. City of Tiburon* (1980), and twenty-seven years later by Justice Sandra Day O'Connor in *Lingle v. Chevron, U.S.A.* (2005). To understand all three opinions, each one giving one Justice's statement of the law of takings, it is first necessary to understand Justice Brennan's opinion in *Penn Central Transportation Company v. City of New York*,[1] to which we will now turn. Understanding all three cases is necessary in order to understand the permissible scope of land use controls.

§ 4.01 The Facts in *Penn Central*

In 1965, New York City adopted a landmarks preservation ordinance designed to protect and preserve historic buildings, including Grand Central Terminal, from decisions to alter and destroy them without public review and permission.[2]

The city agency established in the ordinance to oversee its provisions refused to permit Penn Central to construct a fifty-five story building on the air rights over the terminal. This proposed building was to be cantilevered above the existing facade, resting on the roof of the Terminal, and stripping away some of its facade. The agency justified its decision on aesthetic grounds: it labeled Penn Central's development plans "an aesthetic joke." Penn Central then brought suit in state court, alleging both a due process and a takings claim. The trial court granted Penn Central relief, but the New York Court of Appeals reversed. Amid much publicity, the case reached the Supreme Court, which upheld the ordinance.

1. 438 U.S. 104 (1978).

2. The Landmark Preservation Law enacted by the city was itself a response to the mid-1960s demolition of Pennsylvania Station, a structure equally grand and architecturally significant as Grand Central.

Justice Brennan wrote the Supreme Court's majority opinion. He found: (1) that the ordinance did not interfere with the present use of the building as a terminal; (2) that the ordinance allowed Penn Central to make a reasonable return on its investment; and (3) the transferable development rights (TDRs) helped mitigate the severity of the economic impact of the ordinance.

[A] The *Penn Central* Test

This opinion is often cited for its new, so-called three prong test for a taking. That is, three factors have particular significance in determining whether or not a governmental action is a taking: (1) the **character** of the governmental action; (2) the **economic impact** of the regulation on the owner; and (3) the extent to which the regulation interferes with the owner's **investment-backed expectations**. This test for a taking is still good law and in use today, although its impact is limited by the later establishment of two types of *per se*, categorical taking doctrines for total[3] and physical takings.[4]

The **first factor**, the character of the governmental action, is probably the hardest to classify. First, if this phrase refers to a physical invasion or occupation of property by the government, its focus would then be directed to the intrusiveness of the action. Justice Brennan states that a "taking can more readily be found when the interference with property can be characterized as a physical invasion. . . . "[5] Second, the phrase—particularly the "can more readily be found" language—suggests that something more was meant. So the phrase might refer to the extraction of a public benefit from a private party who is uniquely affected by the regulation. A regulation that affects one or a few landowners substantially more than the general population would be a weighty factor in assessing whether the regulation resulted in a taking. A few should not in fairness be forced to bear a burden or give a benefit that should be paid for by the public. So the sharper the burden and the more diffuse the benefit, the more likely it is that the public should pay and the landowner compensated. Constant and long-continued overflights by government airplanes going over an owner's property that destroys the value of the land surface is an example. Third, the phrase might be applied and the character of the governmental action dispositive when the ordinance or regulation aims at abating a public nuisance, as in *Mugler, Hadacheck*, or *Goldblatt*. All of these meanings are

3. *See Lucas v. South Carolina Coastal Council*, 505 U.S. 1003, 1015 (1992) (finding "categorical treatment appropriate . . . where regulation denies all economically beneficial or productive use of land").

4. *See Loretto v. Teleprompter Manhattan CATV Corp.*, 458 U.S. 419 (1982) (finding a physical taking when a cable wire and box were installed in a N.Y.C. apartment house under statutory authority). Trespass is the essence of a physical taking, so a partial inability to use a right or a partial loss of access due to the construction of a median barrier on a highway is viewed as a regulatory taking, not a physical one. *See, e.g., County of Anoka v. Blaine Bldg. Corp.*, 566 N.W.2d 331 (Minn. 1997).

5. *Penn Central*, 438 U.S. at 124. This seems tentative, but Justice Brennan earlier dissented in the case of *Loretto v. Teleprompter Manhattan CATV Corp.*, 458 U.S. 419 (1982) (holding that, when there is even a slight physical invasion, the "character of the governmental action" overrides the other two factors and requires a finding of a taking), discussed *supra*, Chapter 3, § 3.01.

plausible, so long as the emphasis is on the word "action"—for it is not the government's motives, purposes, or objectives that are in play.

The first meaning seems to have been in Brennan's mind (the next sentence, quoted in the last paragraph, refers to a physical invasion), but all three are possible instances of prohibited governmental action. When a physical invasion is not involved, the focus is on whether the regulation takes a broadly held public benefit. In *Penn Central*, the designation of a property as historic, with or without the consent of its owner, and the restriction of the property to its historic appearance, was found to be for the benefit of the public at large.

The **second factor**, the economic impact, is close to the statements in the case law that state that a regulation must leave an owner with economically viable uses for his property or with a reasonable number of uses.[6] The impact of the governmental action must be great—indeed, it must result in a near complete loss of market value. Thus, its focus is fact-based and is on that portion of the property that is left to an owner after the imposition of a regulation.[7] Here "use" and "value" are used interchangeably. The assumption is that they will be affected together. For constitutional strict constructionists, the focus of takings jurisprudence is on what has been taken, not what's left—so, when considering this factor, they would speak of the number of uses or percentage of the value taken, compared with the uses and value left. In discussing this factor, defining the unit of property to be considered in assessing a takings claim is crucial to its consideration, and is sometimes dispositive of the claim. For example, prohibiting an landowner from drilling a well on his land can deprive him of all his sub-surface water rights, but not decrease the value of the land by much.[8]

The **third factor** opens the way to a holding that, even if the regulation is within the police power, it might still be a taking when it violates an owner's distinct or reasonable, investment backed expectations. Justice Brennan gathered many friends for this notion among the more conservative Justices. He thought that the investment backed expectations of the railroad were met so long as the property remained useful as a terminal—because that was its intended use when it was built. Generally, an investment backed expectation means a reasonable return on the privately contributed ingredient of the terminal's value, and not the ingredient added by the presence of surrounding

6. *See, e.g., Karam v. Department of Envir. Protection*, 705 A.2d 1221, 1226–27 (N.J. Super. Ct., App. Div. 1998).

7. *Id.* (including upland and riparian land in the unit of property considered with regard to a regulatory takings claim).

8. The first two factors resemble, when taken together, the test applied when the facial validity of a police power ordinance is challenged: does the owner have a reasonable return, or economically viable uses, and does the ordinance avoid extracting a public benefit from a landowner (aside from forcing him to abate a public nuisance) or trespassing on private property? If the answers are yes both times, a facial challenge is turned away. *See Keystone Bituminous Coal Association v. DeBenedictus*, discussed in Chapter 3. The *Penn Central* opinion discussed all three factors and treated the situation before it as an "as applied" case, rather than one presenting a facial challenge to the landmark law. Its precedential value in the area of traditional zoning was limited on that account because, although the court asserted that this was a zoning case, it was a very special one.

properties and facilities. The idea of investment backed expectations appealed to a broad spectrum of the Justices—liberals and conservatives alike—then on the court.

[1] Investment-Backed Expectations

The idea of investment-backed expectations (IBEs) has only been part of takings jurisprudence since *Penn Central*. Its meaning is still evolving. Indeed, many courts swiftly exchanged the word "distinct"—the word in Justice Brennan's opinion—IBEs for "reasonable" IBEs. One might have "distinct" and compensable IBEs when investing in raw and unimproved land, but once the investor puts improvements on the land, relying on the regulations in place when the improvements were made, he should have the right to recoup the cost of only reasonable improvements; otherwise the investor could force the government to pay for unwise investments.

These expectations might either be formed when the investment is made or an initial expectation might be subject to change thereafter. Moreover, this aspect of the test might be differently used once the initial investment is recouped along with a reasonable profit. This term suggests that an investor, just by making an investment, has a vested right to pursue his investment, regardless of the later-imposed regulation; this might explain its appeal to some of the Justices, but is arguably overbroad. The expectations of a person who inherits property might be different from a purchaser, but it is also difficult to suggest that an heir can be more strictly regulated than an investor/purchaser. Thus, a legal preference for an investor over other types of owners is difficult to rationalize. A person inheriting property or receiving it as a gift cannot in any principled way be given less constitutional protection than the investor who purchased it yesterday.[9]

The appeal of this term may also lie in its restatement of Holmes' "diminution in value" test stated in *Mahon*; if it had become a dead letter, this term revived it in an updated, modified form. Further, an IBE might vary according to the governmental interest advanced in the regulation, for the expectation of the investor surely lessens in the face of prior regulation, and the purchase of already regulated property would naturally diminish the IBEs of an owner. The same might be said for an owner planning a use of land in a highly regulated industry, such as surface mining. On the other hand, no regulation should be immune from constitutional challenge just because it is long-standing, for the passage of time does not make the economic impact of any governmental action less onerous.

[2] Two Applications of IBEs

First, if we reached back in time and applied the idea of IBEs as presented in *Penn Central* to *Mahon*, the Mahons' investment-backed expectations seem slight. The mineral estate had been severed from the surface in 1878, so that the holders of the Mahons' chain of title had been in possession of the surface since that time. If their

9. *See Palazzolo v. Rhode Island*, 533 U.S. 606 (2001), discussed later in this chapter.

surface interest were regarded as a lease of the surface, then the elapsed time was sufficient to amortize a considerable investment in the site. It is thus arguable that their IBEs had been fulfilled by the time of the Kohler Act. On the other hand, as to the Pennsylvania Coal Company, its investment in the right of support was not recouped yet. Indeed, it had not started to mine under the Mahons' land. Thus, compared with the Mahons, there is still no recoupment of its investment. This is particularly so if the company was a secondary recovery miner—a company that purchased a coal property already mined once by the room and pillar method, and that proceeds to remove the pillars, relying on the waiver of damages provision in the Mahons' deed to the surface. Yet IBEs should be held in good faith: an investment in a secondary recovery of coal that started up in the face of the Kohler Act, can hardly have been conducted in good faith, so what is protected in *Mahon* must have been the primary recovery miner's expectation of the right to sell the pillars.

Second, suppose a developer purchased a site with an old office building on it, paying more for the land than for the building, and thereafter a historic landmark law is enacted, the building is designated a landmark—designated because it is an example of the free-standing masonry building techniques pre-dating the introduction of structural steel. The old building's facade is neither historic nor attractive. The developer alleges that the rental income from a new building would be 10 times greater than the old one, and his building lacks outward aesthetic appeal and historic value. In spite of such allegations, any takings challenge will probably fail.[10] The building's structural components still give it cultural value. There is no reason why paying more for the land under his building should be relevant to the takings issue; were it otherwise, his accountant could create a violation of his IBEs by allocating more of the purchase price to the land. The expectation of higher profits from the new building does not qualify as a "property" interest protected by the takings clause so long as the developer has the ability to make a reasonable return on the whole of what he purchased: the developer must prove an unreasonably low income for the old building, instead of projecting higher income from the new one.

[3] IBEs and Palazzolo v. Rhode Island[11]

The Supreme Court decided that a purchaser or successive title holder, even though on notice of earlier-enacted regulations, is not barred from claiming interference with IBEs and a taking based on the earlier restriction. The purchaser's IBEs may, but need not be, affected by the earlier restriction. Post-enactment purchasers, it said, should be protected in this way because: (1) otherwise unreasonably burdensome enactments would become less so only because of the passage of time; (2) the state would only have to justify unreasonable enactments before either a later transfer of title or the (early) death of the person holding title at the time of enactment;

---

10. This developer's position is stronger than Penn Central's: his investment has not yet been recouped, while Penn Central had 60 years to recoup its investment in the terminal.

11. 533 U.S. 606 (2001).

(3) the enactment would otherwise strip an owner of the right to transfer what he purchased—"a critical alteration in the nature of property"; (4) vendors of property would be in different positions depending on their age and whether they are rich or poor; (5) takings law should be harmonized with eminent domain law, where the owner at the time of the condemnation is always entitled to just compensation, so an inverse condemnation action should have the same rule as a condemnation action for the sake of consistency in the law;[12] and (6) a prior Supreme Court takings case[13] rejected the idea that post-enactment purchasers had no claim. Thus "a regulation that otherwise would be unconstitutional absent compensation is not transformed into [a defense for the regulatory agency] by the mere passage of title."[14] IBEs are not diminished by inaction either.[15]

That post-enactment purchasers have the right to bring a claim, does not mean that they will get a judgment. In *Palazzolo*, on remand to the Rhode Island Superior Court, the court held that the plaintiff's IBEs were "modest" and that he had no *Penn Central*, regulatory takings claim, partly because of his post-enactment acquisition, but mostly because filling a wetland was an abatable public nuisance, the wetland itself being subject to the state's public trust.[16]

§ 4.02 Justice Brennan's *Penn Central* Majority Opinion

[A] The Restatement Section

Justice Brennan began his *Penn Central* discussion of the Supreme Court's takings cases by quoting *Mahon* and the proposition that "government could hardly go on" if some property value decreases were not tolerated as a consequence of governmental regulation. Brennan then discussed the cases most tolerant of that regulation: the so-called "nuisance abatement" line of cases—*Mugler*, *Hadacheck*, and *Goldblatt*. In a footnote in a later section of the opinion, when refuting Penn Central's arguments, he went further and attempted to give these cases the widest possible use, saying that they were best understood not as "noxious" use or nuisance abatement cases, but as instances of governmental action where "the restrictions were reasonably related to the implementation of a policy—not unlike historic preservation—expected to produce a widespread

12. *Id.* at 629–30 (stating the foregoing rationales).

13. *See Nollan v. California Coastal Comm'n*, 483 U.S. 825, 834, n. 2 (1987) (Justice Scalia, responding to Justice Brennan's dissent, *id.* at 860).

14. *Palazzolo*, 533 U.S. at 629-30.

15. *See McQueen v. South Carolina Coastal Council*, 530 S.E.2d 628 (S.C. 2000) (finding that an owner who did not seek development permits "in the face of ever more stringent regulations" demonstrated a "distinct lack" of IBEs) (cert. granted, vacated, and remanded for consideration in light of *Palazzolo*).

16. *See Palazzolo v. Rhode Island*, 2005 R.I. Super. LEXIS 108 (July 5, 2005).

public benefit and applicable to all similarly situated property." Thus were the nuisance exception cases made into cases in which the "character of the governmental action" controlled. Brennan concluded this section with a restatement of *Mahon*'s holding in terms of his own test, one that would have startled Justice Holmes: "a state statute that substantially furthers important public policies may so frustrate distinct investment-backed expectations as to amount to a 'taking.'"[17] Brennan's quotation from *Mahon* and restatement of *Mahon*'s holding, both bracketing the nuisance abatement cases, make those cases an instance of the type of taking (a regulatory one) he thinks involved here. He also here makes *Mahon* squarely into a regulatory takings case.

[B] The Refutation Section

Justice Brennan then set out to refute four arguments made by Penn Central. First, that the ordinance had deprived the company of the gainful use of the air rights. In reply, Brennan stated that simply because the company was denied the ability to exploit the air space above the terminal, space the company previously had expected to exploit, does not convert the city's action into a taking. The terminal property was not, for takings purposes, to be divided into discrete units, for which the denial of development became a taking. Instead, the terminal's parcel as a whole provided the relevant field of inquiry. This is the modern genesis of the so-called "whole parcel" rule.[18]

Second, the company argued that the only means of protecting landmark owners from being singled out to provide a public benefit is to find the preservation of individual landmarks a taking. No merit in this argument, thought Brennan, because the ordinance was the subject of a city-wide comprehensive plan for preservation, and subjected each of over four hundred landmarks designated in the city to the same review procedure—of which the company had not fully availed itself.[19]

Third, the company argued that the ordinance has a disparate, non-uniform impact on each landmark owner, according to the needs of the landmark. Any zoning ordinance impacts more severely on some landowners than it does on others. The ordinance here is no different, states Brennan.

Fourth, Brennan turned aside an argument that the air space had been appropriated for a city enterprise (providing cultural amenities) through the use of a governmental procedure.[20] Not so, said Brennan: neither exploitation of the company's parcel for city purposes nor appropriation occurs here.

---

17. *Penn Central*, 438 U.S. at 127.

18. This rule has been reaffirmed by the Supreme Court in *Keystone Bituminous Coal Ass'n v. DeBenedictis*, 480 U.S. 470 (1987) and *Tahoe-Sierra Preservation Council v. Tahoe Regional Planning Agency*, 535 U.S. 302 (2002), discussed in this Chapter, *infra*, § 4.03.

19. This discussion is the genesis of a "ripeness" rule for takings claims. *See Williamson Cty. Regional Planning Comm'n v. Hamilton Bank*, 473 U.S. 172 (1985).

20. This argument was an attempt to reply to the N.Y. Court of Appeals opinion in this case, an opinion largely ignored by the Supreme Court. *See Penn Central Transportation Co. v. New York*, 366 N.E.2d 1271 (N.Y. 1977).

[C] The "As Applied" Section

In the opinion's next section, Justice Brennan set out to determine whether Penn Central was permitted under the ordinance to make a reasonable return on its investment backed expectations—whether the regulation had interfered with those expectations. This issue, Brennan said, "may be narrowed to the question of the severity of the impact of the law on the appellant's parcel." There was no intent by the city to prohibit the occupation of any of the company's air space, nor was there an intent to prohibit any and all construction within that space. The company could have sought permission to build a smaller, less overwhelming structure—and did not do so. Neither was there any interference, with any of the present uses of the terminal and they, Brennan said, "must be regarded as Penn Central's primary expectation concerning the use of the parcel."

At this point Justice Brennan found it important that the use of *some* of Penn Central's remaining unused airspace had not been denied them. He here measured a taking by what was left the owner, rather than by what was taken from him. The constitutional requirement is for just compensation for what is taken, but he here turned this requirement into an inquiry into whether Penn Central had been denied its right to a reasonable return on the terminal parcel. (What constituted a reasonable return could be either a return on the property in its restricted use, or on its present or future uses.)

In addition, the presence of the transferable development rights (TDRs) meant that Penn Central had not been denied all use of its parcel. TDRs are the rights otherwise available under the city's zoning regulations, not used because of the landmark ordinance, but transferable to other parcels. They (under the city's TDR scheme) could be transferred only to properties that the railroad company already owned. Fortunately for the city, the company already owned eight or so properties further up on Park Avenue, north of the terminal.[21] (It actually owned more than that, but the opinion mentions only eight.) In any event, those properties were available to receive the TDRs unused on the company's terminal site.

The TDRs were relevant, Brennan stated, to the issue of whether or not there was a taking: they may be considered as mitigating the severity of one of his factors for assessing a regulatory taking claim—the economic impact of the regulation. The traditional approach was first to address whether there was a taking, and then, if there was a taking, to confront the compensation issue. Brennan's opinion, in this last section, seemed combine these two issues into a very untraditional whole. Critics have pointed out that the TDRs were certainly relevant to the issue of whether just compensation had been paid, but they were less clearly relevant to the issue of whether a taking had occurred.

---

21. It would have been difficult for the company to add onto its other properties. Imagine 20 more stories added on top of the Waldorf-Astoria Hotel, one of the other nearby properties owned by the company.

[D] TDRs

TDRs separate the right to possess from the right to develop a parcel. Development rights are severed from the sending parcel and transferred to a receiving one. They have been used, not only around New York City's Grand Central Terminal, but around its South Street Seaport as well.[22] Justice Brennan regarded the city's program as less than ideal, but by the time he wrote the opinion, it was clear from state court opinions on the subject that at a minimum, a transferable developments rights program needed a transfer right (1) whose existence was not dependent on further administrative rulings or appeals, (2) whose use was available in pre-determined, clearly mapped, and reasonable large receiving zones,[23] and (3) with the government bearing the risk that the right will prove valueless and be without a market of potential purchasers.[24] The last requirement has sometimes meant the creation by regulators of a "TDR bank" for holding unused and unsold rights—the bank itself "making a market" in the rights, giving their holder immediate money for them. In 1997, the Supreme Court declined to review another TDR scheme.[25] There, in a concurring opinion signed by three Justices, however, Justice Scalia said that their view—not taken in *Penn Central*—was that TDRs were appropriate for determining the amount of compensation due, but not in determining whether or not there had been a taking. Thus TDRs have twice been involved in Supreme Court cases, and each time the court assumed their validity, saying in *Penn Central* that they "undoubtedly mitigated" against finding a regulatory taking there.

§ 4.03 The Holdings

There are five of them. Most narrowly, and first, the Supreme Court majority held that the Company has not met its burden of proof or that it stipulated away its case. Second, using the reciprocity of advantage formula, it held that the benefits to the affected owners of historic landmarks and to the municipality made the injury to the owners non-compensable.[26] Third, it broadly held that aesthetic and historic landmark regulations are justified under the police power, notwithstanding their substantial economic impact on the owner of an affected landmark and, unless the owner's investment backed expectations are taken away, no compensation need be paid for such an impact. Fourth, the majority held that, in assessing whether there was a

22. They have also been used in downtown Chicago and Seattle, as well as for open space protection in New Jersey's Pinelands and for agricultural preservation in Montgomery County, Maryland.

23. *See, e.g., Fred F. French Inv. Co. v. City of New York*, 350 N.E.2d 381 (N.Y. 1976) (invalidating an early scheme for its failure to meet either of the first two requirements).

24. *See* Note, *Past, Present, and Future Constitutional Challenges to Transferable Development Rights*, 74 Wash. L. Rev. 825 (1999).

25. *See Suitum v. Lake Tahoe Regional Planning Agency*, 520 U.S. 725 (1997). *See generally* R.S. Radford, *Takings and Transferable Development Rights in the Supreme Court: The Constitutional Status of TDRs in the Aftermath of* Suitum, 28 Stetson L. Rev. 685 (1999).

26. Only 0.1% of the property in the city was landmarked.

taking, the TDRs were properly considered in assessing the economic impact of the regulation.[27] Thus, *Penn Central* is some evidence that non-monetary compensation is constitutional, since the TDRs provide substitute property instead of cash.[28] The *Penn Central* court considered the value of the TDRs in determining the economic impact of the landmark regulation—that is, a regulation does not "go too far" if it either (1) gives some proportionate benefit back to the landowner or (2) even if it goes too far, it can be pushed back by giving TDRs as just compensation.[29]

[A] The "Whole Parcel" Rule

The definition of the property at issue was the subject of *Penn Central*'s fifth holding, as it had been in other takings cases so far reviewed. This fifth holding has proven the most long-lasting and contentious one. In a regulatory takings claim, a court must compare the value of the property taken with the value that remains after the contested regulation is imposed. This comparison can be expressed as a fraction: the loss in value caused by the regulation (the fraction's numerator) with regard to a particular unit of or interest in property (the denominator). This denominator has turned out to be elusive and difficult to ascertain.

The problem in doing so was first identified by a law professor a decade before *Penn Central* was decided.[30] In the Supreme Court's takings opinions, the problem has sometimes been discussed in the negative, finding what the fractional denominator is not. In *Penn Central*, it was found not to be the right to develop the air rights over Grand Central Station. In another opinion the year after *Penn Central* was decided, the denominator was not the right to alienate or sell property.[31] Nearly a decade after *Penn Central*, the *Keystone* court declined to treat the "support estate" for pillars in the coal mine as the denominator.[32] In the first years of the 21st century, The court declined to treat the right to develop during a planning moratorium as the denominator.[33]

For the Supreme Court, the problem started with *Mahon*. There, Justice Holmes talked about profit and "commercially practical" mining as he was talking about the removal of the coal pillars from a mine. *Penn Central*'s majority talked of the "whole parcel" that Grand Central Terminal occupied, not just the portion then used, and not just the air rights over the terminal. There, Justice Brennan said, both the used portion

---

27. Assessing other landmark programs, the TDRs may be a limiting aspect of the case.

28. If the Constitution means otherwise, its drafters could have used the word "cash" or "money," not just compensation.

29. In eminent domain law, the amount of just compensation due is reduced by the value of the benefit to the non-condemned portion of the parcel that the landowner receives from the condemnation of a part of it. So the use of TDRs in inverse condemnation cases may be consistent with eminent domain law.

30. *See* Frank I. Michelman, *Property, Utility, and Fairness*, 80 Harv. L. Rev. 1165, 1192 (1967).

31. *See Andrus v. Allard*, 444 U.S. 51, 64 (1979).

32. *Keystone, op. cit.*, 480 U.S. at 499, 500–02.

33. *See Tahoe-Sierra Preservation Council v. Tahoe Regional Planning Agency*, 535 U.S. 302, 337 (2002).

and the air rights constituted the "whole parcel." He said: "Taking jurisprudence does not divide a single parcel into discrete segments and attempt to determine whether rights in a particular segment have been entirely abrogated." Later, the *Keystone* court would talk broadly about the holdings of the mining companies in Western Pennsylvania: there, Justice Stevens looked at the mine as a whole, not just at the coal pillars in it. This "whole parcel" rule was then arguably *Penn Central*'s greatest contribution to takings jurisprudence as has been twice reaffirmed by the Court.[34] Still later, in 2002, Justice Steven's majority option in *Tahoe-Sierra Preservation Council v. Tahoe Regional Planning Agency*,[35] dealt with a severance of a parcel based on time: a 32-month moratorium on development that the petitioners argue was a substantial restriction on the right to develop a parcel. Justice Stevens strongly endorsed the application of the "whole parcel" rule. He wrote: "An interest in property is defined by the metes and bounds that describe its geographic dimensions and the term of years that describe the temporal aspect of the owner's interest.... Both dimensions must be considered if the interest is to be viewed in its entirety"[36]

As time passed, the "whole parcel" rule attracted more critics than boosters,[37] and most recently, the Supreme Court has modified the "whole parcel" rule, a/k/a and there known as the rule of "conceptual severance." Justice Kennedy in this opinion started out by stating what the denominator is not: it cannot be, he said, what is taken by the very regulation at issue; likewise, it cannot result from the regulator "improperly ... fortifying" itself against liability for a taking by the use of the state's law of property to consolidate parcels held in common.[38] Rejecting these two poles, he stated in the 2017 opinion in *Murr v. Wisconsin*[39] that its application would depend on the facts of each case and on a variety of factors. Those factors include (1) "the treatment of the land under state and local law," (2) "the physical characteristics of the land," and (3) the "prospective value of the regulated land."[40]

The *Murr* opinion emphasized the third factor in finding no taking had occurred. Application of these three factors should endeavor to "determine whether reasonable

---

34. *See* § 4.02[B], *supra*.

35. *Tahoe-Sierra*, *op. cit.*, 535 U.S. at 337.

36. *Id.*

37. *See, e.g.*, Steven J. Eagle, *The Four Factor Penn Central Regulatory Takings Test*, 118 Penn St. L. Rev. 601 (2014) (arguing that the whole parcel rule is the equal of the traditional three factor test, and a fourth important factor, in *Penn Central*).

38. *See Murr v. Wisconsin*, 582 U.S. 383 (2017), noted at 131 Harv. L. Rev. 253 (2017) and 42 Harv. Envtl. L. Rev. 287 (2018). *Murr* involved two un-developable parcels jointly owned by four siblings and merged into one developable parcel. If the two parcels were considered together, there would be no *Penn Central* regulatory taking, but if considered pre-merger, there would have been a *Lucas*-style, categorical, *per se* regulatory taking of "all economically beneficial use" of one of them. *See infra*, Chapter 17, § 17.04 et seq., for a discussion of *Lucas v. South Carolina Coastal Council*, 505 U.S. 1003, 1018, 1031 (1992) (holding that a state beach conservation statute constituted a taking when it barred the petitioner from developing his two beachfront parcels, leaving them substantially in their natural state).

39. *Murr*, *op. cit.*, 582 U.S. at 393.

40. *Id.* at 397–98.

expectations about property ownership would lead a landowner to anticipate that his holdings would be treated as one parcel, or, instead, as separate parcels. This endeavor is objective, and the reasonable expectations at issue derive from background customs and the whole of our legal tradition."[41] Writing for the 5–3 *Murr* majority,[42] Justice Kennedy also said: "In some, though not all, cases the effect of the challenged regulation must be assessed and understood by the effect on the entire property held by the owner, rather than just some part of the property that, considered just on its own, has been diminished in value."[43] Thus the "whole parcel" rule became an *ad hoc*, facts and circumstances, three factor rule. This modification might be seen either as muddying an otherwise bright-line, clear, if epigrammatic, rule, or as the court's giving up the search for a clear understanding of the rule and falling back into case-by-case analysis and application of it. If the latter proves to be the case, it might be nice to say so, but a common law system of case development sometimes, as here, limits the use of such candor.

The third factor ("the prospective value of the regulated land") has proven more important than the first two.[44] So it was in *Murr.* There, Justice Kennedy stated that courts should pay special attention to the effect of the regulated land on any other holdings of the petitioner; he meant that the regulation might diminish the value of one parcel while increasing the value of other remaining parcels—or vice versa. This special attention is a recognition of Justice Holmes' reciprocity of advantage, taken from his *Mahon* opinion—the idea that a regulation may give a benefit to an owner while at the same time burdening his property.[45] This complimentary relationship between parcels can itself create value when the parcels are combined. As the law professor representing the Wisconsin county in which the Murrs' parcels were located explained to the court at oral argument, a left or right shoe alone is not worth what a pair of shoes is.

As to the other two factors in the *Murr* rule, factor one—the consideration of state and local property and land use law—of *Murr*'s three-factor test encouraged recognition of the effect of municipal regulations in merging the petitioners' two parcels. Factor two—on the physical characteristics of the land—recognized that the two parcels were contiguous, a fact arguing that they should be treated as one, and that they were located in an area regulated by federal and state law—*i.e.*, they abutted a federally recognized wild and scenic river. Finally, Justice Kennedy found that one lot when regulated was worth $40,000 and the other $373,000, but when merged, both together became a parcel worth nearly $700,000—clearly, he thought, an economically complimentary whole, arguing for their treatment as a "whole parcel." Thus, the Murr siblings did not suffer a taking—either a *Penn Central* taking, or a *per se*, *Lucas*-style taking.

---

41. *Id.* at 395.

42. One Justice, Justice Gorsuch, took no part in the case.

43. *Id.*

44. *See, e.g., Goertz v. City of Kirkland*, 641 F. Supp. 3d 990. 999–1000 (W.D. Wash. 2022).

45. *See Mahon v. Pennsylvania Coal Co.*, 260 U.S. 393, 422 (1922), discussed supra, Chapter 3, § 3.04.

§4.04 *Penn Central's* Dissenting Opinion

The dissent, written by Justice Rehnquist, takes as its starting point the "physical invasion" cases. The regulation substantially destroyed the value of the railroad's property, and also destroyed the air rights, viewed as a separate commodity. Further, the use of these rights was neither a nuisance nor prohibited under a comprehensive zoning scheme. For the dissent, this was not a zoning case, for an office building in midtown Manhattan was not out of place and a nuisance on that account. Instead, the dissenters—Justices Rehnquist and Stevens, joined by Chief Justice Berger—thought that the landmark ordinance imposed an affirmative preservation covenant on the company. This servitude imposed on the property was, they thought, the equivalent of a physical invasion of the property. The dissenters' approach is important because of subsequent changes in personnel on the Supreme Court and because later takings opinions by the court reflect their views.

Two things distinguish the majority and dissent. First, they disagree about the proper role of both the physical invasion and nuisance abatement cases. Second, the dissent subdivides and disaggregates the railroad's property interests in order to find a taking, thus using a "vertical segmentation" rule. In contrast, the majority aggregates the use of the terminal with the use of all the railroad's other properties in the area, thus using the "whole parcel" rule.[46]

§4.05 The Aftermath of *Penn Central*

At the time of this litigation, the terminal had a maximum floor area ratio of 18, but was using about 1.5. The railroad owned 23 properties in the area, mostly north of the terminal on Park Avenue. It has leased the air rights on some, and improved some itself. In addition, the railroad owned over forty acres under the Avenue. The terminal site is approximately 130,000 square feet. Under the ordinance, such an area permits a building with about two million square feet. Only about 300,000 were used in the terminal. Thus the TDRs available for transfer represented about 1.7 million square feet. Over a decade later in 1989, none of these TDRs had in fact been transferred.[47]

---

46. A good guide to the dialogue between majority and dissent can be found in M. Davis & R. Glickman, *To the Promised Land: A Century of Wandering and a Final Homeland for the Due Process and Taking Clauses*, 68 Or. L. Rev. 393, 446–53 (1989).

47. *See* S. Kowaloff, *Grand Central Zoning Game*, N.Y.L.J., Sept. 20, 1989, at 33, col. 3 (reporting that the Planning Commission denied the transfer of 800,000 square feet from the terminal site 1,000 feet away to a receiving parcel on Madison Avenue).

§4.06 The *Agins* Test

Penn Central has provided one of two principal tests for a regulatory taking. *Agins v. City of Tiburon*[48] has provided another. *Agins* was a facial challenge to an open space regulation. The landowners purchased five acres of ridgeland property for residential development in the City of Tiburon, California. Their ridgeland overlooked both San Francisco Bay and the Pacific Ocean. It had, in other words, tremendous potential for residential building lots because of its spectacular views. The state of California, some six years after their purchase, required the City to prepare a comprehensive plan governing both land use and the preservation of open space. The plan was implemented by two ordinances that downzoned the land and, when applied, permitted the owners to build between one and five residences on the land. After the rezoning, dwellings were limited to one per acre. The owners had no particular plans for building, and submitted no development proposals to the City, so their later attack on the regulation was a facial one.

The Supreme Court upheld the open space regulation. Its test for doing so initially had two prongs. It asked: (1) whether the regulation advanced a substantial state interest and/or (2) whether the landowner was left with an economically viable use of his land once the regulation was imposed. The two prongs were, in the original opinion, connected by the disjunctive conjunction "or."

> The application of a general zoning law to particular property effects a taking if the ordinance does not substantially advance legitimate state interests . . . or denies an owner economically viable use of his land.[49]

Twenty five years after *Agins*, Justice O'Connor, writing for a unanimous Court, held that the first prong of the *Agins* test was not a takings test at all, but was instead a due process test for a regulation.[50] That is, after *Lingle*, "substantially advancing a legitimate state interest"—and consideration of a state or municipal public purpose or objective substantially advanced by a statute or an ordinance—is generally irrelevant to consideration of a takings claim.[51] A second impact of *Lingle* on *Agins* is that the "character of the governmental action" element of the *Penn Central* test for a regulatory taking will have to be narrowly interpreted, or else eliminated in its entirety. The latter course seems extreme, the former preferred—and that is how this first element of the *Penn Central* test has been presented in the earlier sections of this Chapter. A third impact of *Lingle* on *Agins* is that *Agins'* original second prong can now be taken as encapsulating *Penn Central's* three-pronged test for a taking.

---

48. 447 U.S. 255 (1980).

49. *Agins*, 447 U.S. at 260.

50. *See Lingle v. Chevron U.S.A., Inc.*, 544 U.S. 528 (2005).

51. An emphasis should be put on the word "generally" here, for when considering a *per se* categorical, total taking under the framework of *Lucas v. South Carolina Coastal Council*, 505 U.S. 1003 (1992), a state or municipality might defend a statute or ordinance by invoking one of the common law "background principles" and so make the purpose or objective of a law relevant by way of its affirmative defense.

Applying his test in *Agins* and writing for the majority, Justice Powell cited California statutes mandating the development of open space plans to discourage premature and unnecessary conversion of open space land to urban uses. He thus found the ordinance within the scope of the police power as enumerated in state statutes, finding that there was a substantial state interest in the preservation of open space and avoidance of the harmful effects of premature urbanization, which the regulation (he said) helps to forestall. Justice Powell's opinion did not discuss the ridgeland characteristic of the Agins' parcel, but subsequent state cases have upheld ordinances restricting the height of buildings to protect existing views[52] and one state, North Carolina, has enacted state-wide legislation to protect the view of mountain ridges from lower elevations.[53] Justice Powell also found that the ordinance was of general applicability (in the language of *Euclid* and zoning attorneys, it was found to be comprehensive, although Powell did not use that word). All this is (after *Lingle*) regarded as due process analysis.

Justice Powell also found that, because, the owner had not submitted a development plan or application, it was premature to ask, on the record in front of the court, whether the second surviving prong of *Agins* was involved. He said: "the appellants are free to pursue their reasonable investment expectations by submitting a development plan to local officials." After they did so, the ordinance could be evaluated "as applied." Powell's language on this aspect of the case was later used, in the same way that some of Justice Brennan's refutation of *Penn Central*'s arguments was, to formulate a ripeness rule, requiring first a "meaningful application" to develop a property.[54]

[A] The Uses of *Agins*

The two prongs of the *Agins* test provided influential, but malleable rules for later United States Supreme Court opinions. More specifically, it has been involved in three United States Supreme Court opinions on regulatory takings and exactions. Exactions are development approvals that are granted conditionally and contain within them unconstitutional conditions—that is, conditions that take or exact from a developer more land, and in some jurisdictions, money than is required to contain the

52. *See Ross v. City of Rolling Hills Estates*, 238 Cal. Rptr. 561 (Cal. App. Ct. 1987) (upholding denial of permits for addition to house under ordinance restricting blockage of existing views as a stated objective of ordinance and as needed to protect scenic character of area) (review denied, July 29, 1987); *Landmark Land v. City of Denver*, 728 P.2d 1281 (Colo. 1986) (upholding ordinance restricting height of building in office park to protect Rocky Mountain views); *In re Interim Bylaw, Waitsfield, Vermont*, 742 A.2d 742 (Vt. 1999) (upholding interim ordinance for forest land above 1700 feet elevation in town). *See generally* Lisa Healy, *Trophy Homes and Other Alpine Predators: The Protection of Mountain Views through Ridge Line Zoning*, 25 B.C. Envtl. Aff. L. Rev. 913 (1998).

53. N.C. Gen. Stat. § 113A-205 to -214 (enacted 1983) (ridgelands include all lands up to 100 feet below the crest of the ridge. *Id.* at § 113A-206). *See generally* Robert Kessler, *North Carolina's Ridge Law: No View from the Top*, 63 N.C. L. Rev. 197 (1984).

54. *See, e.g., MacDonald, Sommer & Frates v. Yolo County*, 477 U.S. 340 (1986).

externalities of the development, requiring forced dedications to the public of easements and land.

As to exactions, in 1987, in *Nollan v. California Coastal Commission*,[55] the court used the first prong (while it was still effective) of the *Agins* rule to invalidate a regulation of the commission.[56] Further, in 1992, in *Lucas v. South Carolina Coastal Council*,[57] the court used the second and surviving prong of the *Agins* test to invalidate a council prohibition on building a beach house. The Coastal Council required that no house be built seaward of an historic tide line, leaving Mr. Lucas, the landowner, with no place to build on his lots. Thus he was deprived of all reasonable use of his lots, and suffered a total taking of his property. Finally, in 1994, the *Agins* test was elaborated in *Dolan v. City of Tigard*,[58] in order to invalidate yet another exaction that had conditioned the granting of a development permit. The law of unconstitutional conditions and exactions survives today, even though its underpinning in the first prong of the *Agins* test does not. The *Lingle* opinion in 2005 explicitly reaffirms exactions law as laid down in both *Nollan* and *Dolan*.[59]

Up to 2013 and the case of *Koontz v. St. Johns River Water Management District*,[60] exactions were seen as physically invasive conditions on development. *Koontz* changed that limited vision: It held, 5–4, that *Nollan* and *Dolan* applied to monetary exactions and impact fees as well as physical, land dedications. Writing for the *Koontz* majority, Justice Alito said that both land dedications and impact fees present "the risk that the government may use its substantial power and discretion in land-use permitting to pursue governmental ends that lack an essential nexus and rough proportionality to the effects of the proposed new use of the specific property at issue, thereby diminishing without justification the value of the property."[61]

[B] The Aftermath of *Agins*

Donald and Bonnie Agins had purchased their ridgeland acreage in 1968, for a price of $50,000. Their plans were to build a residence for themselves on one of the five acres, and subdivide the parcel so that they could finance their home from the proceeds of the other (they hoped) four lots. After their case was decided by the United States Supreme Court, they submitted a development proposal and were permitted (about two years after the 1980 opinion) to subdivide their property into three lots, but this approval was a conditional one. A road to the site and a hiking trail would have to be designed to pass through their three parcels. After the decision in *First English Evangelical Lutheran Church of Glendale v. City of Los Angeles*,[62] recognizing

55. 483 U.S. 825 (1987).
56. *Id.* at 834.
57. 505 U.S. 1003 (1992).
58. 512 U.S. 374 (1994).
59. *See Lingle v. Chevron U.S.A., Inc.*, 544 U.S. 528, 546–47 (2005).
60. 570 U.S. 595 (2013).
61. *Id.*
62. 482 U.S. 304 (1987).

a damages remedy for temporary takings of property, their threat of a law suit altered their bargaining power, increasing it considerably. Four lots were approved for development in 1988. Four years later, however, the plans for one of the homes, containing some 14,000 square feet of space, was disapproved. Homes now occupy the ridgelands, but the Agins don't live there. They were divorced in the late 1980s.

[C] Using *Penn Central* and *Agins*

Many commentators have suggested that the more elaborate, three prong test from *Penn Central* is to be used with the "as applied" challenge to a regulation,[63] while *Agins*' no "economically viable use" test is most useful in "facial" challenges to regulations.[64]

§ 4.07 The Just Compensation Requirement

Just compensation requires the equivalent of the computation of damages in a civil suit. This computation is made after there has been a finding that a taking for a public purpose has indeed occurred. The compensation is that which is also available in an eminent domain action. It is to this body of law that the regulatory land use bar looks to when they seek analogies for the types of compensation available in their regulatory takings claims.

The compensation required in eminent domain actions, then, is the fair market value of the property taken, as well as severance damages for the remaining property abutting that taken, but off-set by any benefit accruing to the owner by having the condemned property nearby in the government's hands.[65]

When tangible property is taken, intangible property, such as the goodwill of a business, is also condemnable and compensable when present and diminished by the taking of the tangible property.[66] On the other hand, if a property owner has had the site of his business condemned, but can conduct it elsewhere, intangible property losses are not recoverable.[67]

---

63. The *Penn Central* opinion itself does not completely bear this out, because there the railroad company did not seek all of the administrative relief available to it.

64. *See, e.g., Hodel v. Virginia Surface Mining & Reclamation Ass'n*, 452 U.S. 264, 295–97 (1981); *Hilton Head Automotive, LLC v. South Carolina Dep't of Transportation*, 714 S.E.2d 308 (S.C. 2011); *Blair v. Dep't of Conservation and Recreation*, 932 N.E.2d 267, 271–72 (Mass. 2010).

65. *Cf. United States v. Fuller*, 409 U.S. 488 (1973) (holding that the presence of nearby, leased (from the government) grazing lands not be considered in determining compensation).

66. *See Kimball Laundry Company v. United States*, 338 U.S. 1 (1949) (laundry forced to suspend service, lost goodwill as well).

67. *Cf. West River Bridge Company v. Dix*, 47 U.S. (6 How.) 507 (1848).

[A] Computation Methods

The methods used to compute the compensation do not differ appreciably from those used to appraise real property in other settings. First, a capitalization rate (or cap rate) may be used: this method establishes a fair market value by evaluating the income received from the property (its rental value), assuming that that income represents a percentage of the fair market value (often determined by a comparison of various rates of return offered by alternative investments for a potential purchaser considering buying the property), and computing the ratios involved. That is, if the rental value is 8% of the fair market value, then x is 100%, when x is the fair market value. Second, a fair market value can be established from data collected from the sales of similar properties and adjusted to reflect a sale of the appraised property. A third method is to figure the replacement cost of the property from data collected from construction agreements for similar properties, adjusted for the appraised property, adding a value for the land, established by another method, but subtracting the depreciated value of the property. Often, as the third method indicates, a combination of methods is used. This is so because condemnation trials can be before a jury and it is proper for the jury, or other fact-finder, to consider several methods in reaching a determination of just compensation. Finally, it is well to remember that compensation can be in kind, as well as in money. In *Penn Central*, for example, the majority opinion suggested that the transferable development rights offered by the city might in fact be found to constitute an element of just compensation.[68]

§ 4.08 Summary of the Law of Due Process and Takings

The law of takings discussed thus far has five rules: First, without a public purpose, neither regulation nor condemnation is permitted by the government. Second, even when the government has a public purpose for what it does, only implementing governmental action reasonably related to that purpose is justified and will satisfy the due process clause.[69] Third, no regulation which destroys all use, or an essential right (to exclude, for example), is justified, no matter the purpose. A total taking is a categorical or *per se* taking. Fourth, any permanent physical occupation of property, even if temporary, authorized by the government, is a categorical or *per se* taking, no matter how beneficial to the public and no matter the extent of the occupation.[70] Fifth, a regulation is invalid when it interferes with or takes all reasonable economic use of

68. *See Penn Central Transportation Co. v. City of New York*, 438 U.S. 104, 136–37 (1978).
69. *See Lingle v. Chevron U.S.A., Inc.*, 544 U.S. 528 (2005) (discussed § 4.06, *supra*).
70. *See Loretto v. Teleprompter Manhattan CATV Corp.*, 458 U.S. 419 (1982) (discussed § 3.01, *supra*).

the property.[71] Throughout the United States Supreme Court cases discussed so far, a shifting majority of its Justices have indicated an increasing impatience with *ad hoc* tests for a taking. In order to provide more certainty and black-letter law in this area, the court has created another type of takings: for governmental exactions of land or money imposed as conditions on the granting of various types of development permits. These exactions will be discussed later, in Chapter 14, when the text returns to the constitutional law framework of land use law.

71. *See Lucas v. South Carolina Coastal Council*, 505 U.S. 1003 (1992)), discussed *infra*, Chapter 17, § 17.04.

Chapter 5
Temporary Regulatory Takings

§ 5.01 Background

In addition to *Keystone Bituminous Coal Association*,[1] the United States Supreme Court decided one other significant takings case in 1987. The subject of this case was a temporary regulatory taking, defined as a freeze on (all) uses of real property for the period of time that a regulation going too far is in effect, thus denying development permits for the property. The time involved must be unreasonably long, but otherwise a temporary taking is a type of regulatory taking.

San Diego Gas & Electric Company v. City of San Diego[2] involved the company's claim that the municipality's open space program had deprived it of the "entire beneficial use of the property" when the municipality denied the company a development permit for any uses inconsistent with its open space program. The company asked for a ruling that the program was an inverse condemnation of its property and requested money damages. The court's majority of five Justices found no finding of a taking in the record before the lower courts, and so no final decision on the takings issue; thus the majority felt constrained not to rule on this issue.

In dissent, however, Justice Brennan, along with three colleagues, felt that because a final decision had been rendered below, the court had appellate jurisdiction to rule on the takings issue. Thus freed to address the merits, Brennan reached the question "whether a government entity must pay just compensation when a police power regulation has effected a 'taking' of 'private property' for 'public use' within the meaning of that constitutional provision."[3] Quoting the "too far" language of Holmes in *Mahon*, Justice Brennan saw little distinction between physical invasions (requiring compensation) and land use regulations that go too far (that he saw as requiring compensation, too).[4] He also suggested several factors to consider in measuring whether the regulation goes too far, factors drawn from his majority opinion in *Penn Central*.[5]

1. Discussed *supra*, Chapter 3.
2. 450 U.S. 621, 633 (1981).
3. *Id.* at 646.
4. *Id.* at 649, 652–53.
5. *Id.* at 648.

While recognizing that the traditional remedy for a regulation going too far was merely invalidation of the regulation, Justice Brennan thought that the money damages that the company sought were also an appropriate remedy; even though the government repealed the invalid regulation, the owner was entitled to damages for the time before repeal. "After all," he wrote, "if a policeman must know the Constitution, then why not a planner?"[6] Justice Brennan further explained:

> [T]he threat of financial liability for unconstitutional police power regulations would help to produce a more rational basis of decisionmaking that weighs the costs of restrictions against their benefits. Such liability might also encourage municipalities to err on the constitutional side of police power regulations, and to develop internal rules and operating procedures to minimize overzealous regulatory attempts.[7]

Brennan wrote in dissent, but his views on the merits of the case as well as the damages remedy, were approvingly echoed by Chief Justice Rehnquist in his concurrence with the majority opinion. Thus, a five-member majority of the court thought that a temporary regulatory taking was possible and would give rise to money damages in a case on which a final judgment had been reached below.

While similar cases were granted certiorari during the next six years,[8] it was not until *First English Evan. Lutheran Church of Glendale v. Los Angeles County*[9] that the court was presented with the issue of whether a compensable regulatory taking occurred.

§ 5.02 *First English Evangelical Lutheran Church of Glendale v. Los Angeles County*

[A] The Facts

In *First English Evan. Lutheran Church of Glendale v. Los Angeles County,*[10] a church owned 21 acres in a remote part of Los Angeles County—up a creek, in a canyon. Since 1957, it had continuously used 12 acres of flat land along the creek as a camp for the handicapped, named Lutherglen. A fire destroyed the forest up-stream from the camp in 1977. This reduced the water-retention capacity of the soils, resulting the

6. *Id.* at 661, n. 26.
7. *Id.* (citations omitted).
8. *See, e.g., Williamson County Regional Planning Commission v. Hamilton Bank,* 473 U.S. 172 (1985) (claim not ripe for judicial determination because state administrative remedies were not yet exhausted); *MacDonald, Sommer, & Frates v. Yolo County,* 477 U.S. 340 (1986).
9. 482 U.S. 304 (1987).
10. *Id.*

next year in a flood which destroyed all of the camp's buildings and in which several lives were lost.

Some facts in this case must be seen in their local context. A creek in the context of Los Angeles means, for most of the year, a dry creek-bed. A flood in this context means a combination of flood and mudslide.[11] The "flood" came in 1978. In early 1979, after the flood, the county enacted an interim, emergency ordinance which denied the church the right to rebuild on the flood plain on which the camp's buildings had been located. The ordinance provided in part that "[a] person shall not construct, reconstruct, place or enlarge any building or structure, any portion of which is, or will be, located with the outer boundary lines of the interim flood protection area." The ordinance was effective immediately because the county viewed the situation as a health and safety matter. In quick response, the church sued, but only for damages, alleging a regulatory taking. The interim ordinance was made permanent in 1983. It was enacted in response to a tragedy in which lives were lost. For police power purposes, it was a safety measure, not a general welfare one; so the county thought that the traditional heart of the police power (protecting health, safety, etc.) was involved, strengthening its case. Los Angeles County in effect thought that it was abating a public nuisance, the camp being a nuisance endangering the lives of handicapped campers.

The trial court granted the county's motion to strike the church's allegation that the church was denied all use of the property and so was entitled to damages and so, before the United States Supreme Court granted certiorari in this litigation, no trial on the merits had been held on the takings issue, but the court below had limited the remedy by denying damages.

[B] The Holding

The Supreme Court held that temporary takings, accomplished through regulatory measures rather than a physical occupation, entitle the property owner to damages. When "a burden results from governmental action that amounted to a taking, the Just Compensation Clause of the Fifth Amendment requires that the government pay the landowner for the value of the use of the land during this period."[12] This holding, narrowly read, is that there is a cause of action for a temporary taking as well as a permanent one. "[W]here the government's activities have already worked a taking of all use of property, no subsequent action by the government can relieve it of the duty to provide compensation for the period during which the taking was effective."[13] The holding did not authorize the plaintiff's recovery of damages—that recovery still depends on a trial on the merits and a finding that there was a taking in this case. However, the court further held that "invalidation of the ordinance without payment

---

11. John McPhee, *The Control of Nature*, The New Yorker, Sept. 26, 1988, at 45, 67–72, gives some background on the area.

12. *See First English*, 482 U.S. at 320.

13. *Id.* at 305.

of fair value for the use of the property during the [pendency of the ordinance] would be a constitutionally insufficient remedy."[14]

To reach these holdings, the court proceeded in several steps. First, it found that the issue not presented in *San Diego Gas* and subsequent cases, was "squarely presented here." Second, the opinion noted that the just compensation clause is "self-executing" and that any inverse condemnation action recognizes as much. Third, a regulation that goes too far is a taking and that temporary and permanent takings are different only in degree.[15] Finally, once the government has already taken "all use" of a property, it must pay compensation; the injunctive remedy is inadequate.

A temporary regulatory taking has three elements: it (1) is temporary (lasting only so long as the invalid regulation is enforced or is effective); (2) denies the owner "all use"[16] of the property; and (3) exceeds the police power. The court also said what it is not deciding, i.e., it is not deciding that there is a taking, but rather assuming that the state court below found a taking here. The court's failure to find a taking here opens up the possibility of inconsistent state and federal court results on this issue.[17]

Chief Justice Rehnquist wrote the majority opinion, joined by Justices White, Marshall, Brennan, Powell and Scalia. The three elements of this type of a regulatory taking, recited previously, were not all incorporated into the holding: the third element, the requirement that the regulation be an invalid exercise of the police power, was omitted. Its omission indicates that this element is irrelevant in situations in which damages are given, and that even if the regulation is found to have a public purpose, that finding is irrelevant. This is all consistent with Holmes' "too far" language in *Mahon*. In any event, the majority assumes that an award of damages makes such findings irrelevant.

The temporary taking, once found, is effective when the last required administrative form of relief (such as a variance) is denied by the administrative agency authorized to grant it, and does not include any period of judicial review of the denial. It

---

14. *Id. First English* and its progeny are discussed in Daniel Siegel & Robert Meltz, *Temporary Takings: Settled Principles and Unresolved Questions*, 11 Vt. J. Envtl. L. 479 (2010).

15. *See, e.g., Zeman v. City of Minneapolis*, 552 N.W.2d 548, 553 (Mn. 1996) ("Our takings analysis must begin with the fact that [the plaintiff's municipal rental] license, which was reinstated by the trial court, was thus taken, if at all, only temporarily. However, this will have no impact upon our analysis. The United States Supreme Court has held that temporary takings, even those later invalidated by courts, are not different from permanent takings.").

16. The *First English* opinion repeatedly states that "all use" was denied. This phrase provides a bright line test because the opinion does not use the phrase "all reasonable use." It is intended to be a part of the holding and to make clear the court's assumption about the finality of the decision below. The regulatory taking found here applied from the time of the enactment of the interim ordinance to the time it was made permanent. After being made permanent, if "all use" is still denied, a "total taking" under *Lucas v. South Carolina Coastal Council*, 505 U.S. 1003 (1992) (discussed in Chapter 17 *infra*), occurs.

17. *See Sea Cabins on the Ocean IV Homeowners' Ass'n v. City of North Myrtle Beach*, 523 S.E.2d 193 (S.C. App. 1999) (holding that no taking occurred under *First English* because there was no deprivation of "all economically viable use" when city required an owner to execute a 4-year license agreement for public use of the association's pier), *affirmed in result*, 548 S.E.2d 595 (S.C. 2001) (using *Nollan/Dolan*, physical exaction analysis).

continues until the regulation going "too far" is withdrawn or repealed, and if no express withdrawal or repeal is forthcoming, it continues as a temporary taking until a decision on repeal or withdrawal is reached; it was, in other words, on-going until some decision otherwise is communicated to the complaining landowner.[18]

Citing *Mahon*, the majority emphasizes that policy arguments such as the prediction of "a flood" of litigation coming in the wake of this opinion, the risk of draining the public fisc, as well as the chilling effect of the opinion on land use planners devising regulations, must give way to the taking clause's requirement of just compensation. Thus, *First English* should be seen as a takings clause remedies case, although it might also someday (but not so far) provide a method of analyzing a temporary violation of substantive due process as well. As to the substance of takings law, the majority expected better planning studies and less resort to *ad hoc* exactions and remedies to be the result of *First English*.

[C] The Dissent

Justices Stevens, Blackmun, and O'Connor dissented, urging four points. First, that the case was not ripe for decision. Second, that the ordinance was a health and safety measure (so like *Hadacheck*, in terms of U.S. Supreme Court precedent). Third, that the majority relied on physical invasion cases (like *Loretto*) to find a taking and those cases were inapposite (here the dissent strikes a raw nerve because it is precisely those physical invasion cases that several in the majority would probably at the time have liked to expand). Fourth, that the due process clause, not the takings clause, was involved.[19] Writing the dissent, Justice Stevens stated that the majority opinion would likely have a chilling effect on land use and urban planning, although such effects have proven difficult to measure. After *First English*, some state regulators did indeed explore insurance policies—issued to pay litigation costs and compensation—for the risk of being found to have taken property. States with aggressive urban planning programs found such insurance policies more difficult to acquire; so there was at least one chilling effect on land use planning, just as Justice Stevens' dissent warned.

[D] Effects of *First English* on Other Supreme Court Cases

While *First English* did not overrule public nuisance abatement/character of the governmental action cases, its facts made it look like such a case: the Los Angeles County legislature had visions of handicapped children being sweep away by a flood.

18. *See* Gregory Stein, *Pinpointing the Beginning and Ending of a Temporary Regulatory Taking*, 70 Wash. L. Rev. 953, 961, 979 (1995).

19. Justice O'Connor, agreeing with this dissent, held this opinion to the end of her tenure as a Justice, writing the decision in *Lingle v. Chevron, U.S.A.*, 544 U.S. 528 (2005) (a majority opinion), in her last term on the bench.

(As the dissent points out, lives lost in the flood provoked the ordinance.) The court overlooked this aspect of the case, which indicates that no matter the good intent or objective of a legislative body, the impact on the landowner affected is still the paramount concern of the takings clause, notwithstanding the seriousness of the health and safety problem addressed by an ordinance.

Five years later, in 1992,[20] the Supreme Court made plain that such problems, when serious enough to amount to a nuisance, were also grounds for dismissal of a takings claim. Dismissal was then, however, the result of an affirmative defense by a municipality, to the effect that the background principles of state property law justified the ordinance held to be a taking.

A decade later, in 2002,[21] the Supreme Court made plain that *First English* was a remedies or compensation case, pointing out that the court expressly disavowed any ruling on the "quite different and logically prior" merits of the takings claim. The court also rejected an argument that *First English* established that the interim denial of use by the Los Angeles ordinance was a categorical taking of all use under *Lucas*. Cabined in these three ways, *First English* tells us little or nothing about what a taking is.

[E] The Exception for Normal Administrative Delay

One exception to *First English*'s holding is that there is no compensation for normal administrative delays. The rationale for this exception is that expectations of unregulated use are not reasonable investment backed expectations under *Penn Central* when a regulatory scheme or program is in effect at the time of a developer's purchase. *First English* sanctions normal administrative delays inherent in the regulatory process for the development of property.

Distinguishing normal delay from an excessive delay is difficult. Many state zoning enabling acts contain a provision requiring an administrative decision be made within 90 days of the hearing. Arguably a decision not made until the 91st day is the product of excessive delay, although the excessive delay might be measured either from day one or starting from the 90th day.

Moreover, the good faith of an agency is relevant solely to the question of delay. If a land use agency is given an advisory opinion to the effect that a regulation is constitutional, then great weight should be given to the opinion if the regulation is later held unconstitutional. However, such an opinion does not insulate the agency from the payment of regulatory damages: assuming *arguendo* that the agency acts in good faith reliance on the opinion, there is no judicially-created good faith exception to the holding of *First English*.

20. *See Lucas v. South Carolina Coastal Council*, 505 U.S. 1003 (1992), discussed *infra*, Chapter 12.

21. *See Tahoe-Sierra Preservation Council, Inc. v. Tahoe Regional Planning Agency, Inc.*, 535 U.S. 302 (2002).

Permissible normal delay can also result from litigation. The mere assertion of regulatory jurisdiction is not the start of a temporary taking when the agency is later found to be in error.[22] So the mistaken denial of a permit that an owner must litigate to correct is not a temporary taking so long as the administrative mistake was not unreasonable.[23] The time consumed in a judicial appeal, to either the trial court or the appellate level, is not compensable: there may be harm suffered by an owner as the result of the time consumed, but no matter that the result of the trial and appeal is favorable to an owner, that harm does not rise to the level of a temporary taking.[24] Normal regulatory delays caused by litigation pursued in good faith do not give rise to a temporary taking.

§ 5.03 *First English* and Moratoria

In general, legislative or administrative motives and objectives may be scrutinized in setting damages. For example, when a permit moratorium is enacted and extends for 18 months in order to write and implement an open space preservation plan by the planning board, the moratorium is not a health and safety matter. Therefore, the urgency of the problem should figure in the length of the administrative delay considered reasonable. So there is every reason to continue evaluating moratoria according to the rules in effect preceding *First English*. One example, *Zilber v. Town of Moraga*,[25] indicates that the 18 month moratoria is not an excessive delay—and that the importance of the objective may indeed argue for lengthening the period countenanced as a normal administrative delay. Similar considerations will probably apply to a phased-growth plan, as in *Ramapo*, or to a rate of growth plan, as in *Petaluma*, or to an updating of the comprehensive plan.[26] As the Supreme Court said in *Tahoe-Sierra*, it "may well be that a moratorium that lasts for more than one year should be viewed with special skepticism."[27] There are, however, no hard and fast rules, and *Tahoe Sierra* found a 32-month moratorium reasonable, and the Supreme Court said that defining the allowable length of a moratorium was "a suitable task for state legislatures."

---

22. *See Landgate, Inc. v. California Coastal Comm'n*, 953 P.2d 1188 (Cal.), *cert. denied*, 119 S. Ct. 179 (1998).

23. *Id.* (involving the commission's assertion of jurisdiction over a lot boundary adjustment as involving the "density or intensity" of land use and finding the assertion not unreasonable), *noted at* 7 Hastings W.-N.W. J. Envtl. L. & Policy 55 (2000).

24. *See Sea Cabins on the Ocean IV Homeowners Ass'n, Inc. v. City of North Myrtle Beach*, 548 S.E.2d 595 (S.C. 2001).

25. 692 F. Supp. 1195, 1206 (N.D. Cal. 1988) (holding such moratoria valid).

26. *See Golden v. Planning Board of Ramapo*, 285 N.E.2d 291 (N.Y.), *appeal dismissed sub nom. Rockland County Builders Ass'n v. McAlevey*, 409 U.S. 1003 (1972) (noted in 47 N.Y.U. L. Rev. 723 (1972), 26 Stan. L. Rev. 585 (1974), and 58 Minn. L. Rev. 1009, 1054–58 (1974)), discussed *infra* Chapter 9.

27. *See Tahoe-Sierra Preservation Council, Inc. v. Tahoe Regional Planning Agency, Inc.*, 535 U.S. 302 (2002).

A developer seeking a judgment of a temporary taking must be an owner. A developer with an option to buy land does not qualify, even in a municipality enacting an invalid moratorium on new developments; a developer with an option does not have a claim for compensation for a temporary taking. He only has a contract right to purchase. Although the period of time that the invalid moratorium was in effect might well not be a normal administrative delay, the developer with an option has no title to the land, so the municipality can argue that there is no "property" taken in this instance.[28] An option works no equitable conversion of the title, and so does not give rise to an action for specific performance by the developer. The developer/optionor has no interest in the property compensable under the takings clause.[29] Even if the developer had exercised the option during the moratorium, the takings claim would still fail. The reasonable investment-backed expectations of the developer in exercising the option cannot include the costs of waiting out even an invalid moratorium.

§ 5.04 Determining the Time of the Temporary Taking

The *First English* majority stated that the temporary taking occurred when the regulation takes effect and ends when a court finds the regulation invalid. That will present a question of fact to the courts. A *First English* taking may be effective when the invalid regulation is first enacted or becomes effective by its terms. When the Supreme Court's decisions on the doctrine of ripeness are considered alongside *First English*, however, this conclusion may be applicable to a facial challenge to a regulation, but it becomes tenuous for an as applied challenge. When the challenge is as applied, the time of the taking is when (1) the claim to compensation arises and (2) when the statute of limitations begins to run on it. This is so, first, because property owners cannot discover whether they have a claim until the regulators have denied their application to develop; only a punitive notion of compensation favors awarding it from the date of enactment. And, second, because owners have no vested rights in any jurisdiction until much later in the development process, often at the building permit stage.

A better rule is: after the municipality has considered a reasonable application—along with its attendant applications for administrative relief—for a reasonable amount of time, and finally denied it, a temporary regulatory taking occurs.[30] By then, the identity of the administrative or legislative body in the role of the taker is

28. *See Board of Education, Gadsden Indep. School Dist. No 16 v. James Hamilton Const. Co.*, 891 P.2d 556 (N.M. App. Ct. 1994).

29. *See Pro-Eco v. Board of Comm'nrs of Jay County, Indiana*, 57 F.3d 505 (7th Cir. 1995).

30. *See City of Pompano Beach v. Yardarm Restaurant, Inc.*, 641 So. 2d 1377, 1384-89 (Fla. Dist. App. Ct. 1994) (a two decade dispute over converting a restaurant into a marina and hotel), *rev. denied*, 651 So. 2d 1197, *cert. denied*, 115 S. Ct. 2583 (1995) (adopting a similar rule) (*discussed in* Gregory Stein, *Pinpointing the Beginning and Ending of a Temporary Regulatory Taking*, 70 Wash. L. Rev. 953 (1995)).

apparent and the extent of the taking is clearer. Such a rule melds the law of ripeness[31] with *First English.* First, such a "final decision" rule will encourage owners wishing to develop to work with regulators. Certainly filing an application is not an indication of an owner's final position on what development is economically feasible, and similarly, the regulators' first or preliminary decision may be ill-considered—both sides in the development process should have a reasonable amount of time to consider and re-consider their positions; regulators should not have to pay for their preliminary decisions. Second, this rule recognizes that regulation is a process, requiring a "normal" time to implement. Third, the rule does not reward owners who file development plans prematurely, in an attempt to "vest" a takings claim. Fourth, having a rule such as this avoids an *ad hoc* approach to determining the time of the taking.

In reacting to a finding of a temporary regulatory taking, a municipality is permitted to do one of three things: first, it may repeal the regulation; second, it may move to take the affected property in eminent domain; and, third, it may amend the regulation, eliminating its over-inclusive aspects but achieving as much of its original purposes as are consistent with the takings clause.

A judicial finding of a temporary regulatory taking may sometimes be greeted by municipal regulatory inaction or silence.[32] Such inaction may thereafter be found to be a permanent taking, but such a finding is subject to a high burden of proof. This is so because the exercise of eminent domain is a legislative function and because inaction may just as easily be an abandonment of the municipality's regulatory authority. The path of judicial restraint, then, is to treat municipal inaction as a continuing temporary taking, recognizing that the inaction is most likely the result of indecisiveness, not malice. The need is for minimal intrusion into municipal autonomy while still providing an incentive to repeal, amend, or pay for the regulation.

In *First English*, the time period for which damages can be awarded is the time from the effective date of the ordinance to the time of its invalidation by the courts.

§ 5.05 Measuring Regulatory Damages

The plaintiffs in *First English* wanted millions of dollars in interim damages. They asked for so much because the owner's intent was to force the lifting of the regulation. The church did not really want to force the county to buy their acreage. Indeed, most developers want to develop, not litigate. Filing for damages is the lever with which to lift the regulation. Perhaps a money damages claim against a municipality is only for the developer fed up with the regulators (and who doesn't care if he or she does business in that municipality again).

---

31. Discussed *infra* Chapter 13.

32. *See* Gregory Stein, *Pinpointing the Beginning and Ending of a Temporary Regulatory Taking*, op. cit., 70 Wash. L. Rev. at 1005–09.

When damages are awarded, what is the measure of damages? The majority opinion in *First English* did not discuss this issue. Early in the development process, a developer is likely to spend lots of money on engineering, planning, and market studies of the property proposed for subdivision or development. Such expenses are not recoverable in a temporary takings claim: just compensation for a regulatory taking is measured by the fair market value of the property subject to the taking, not by studies related to the use to which the developer wishes to put it. One proper measure might be a **rate of return available on the difference in fair market value** with and without the invalid regulation. There are better measures. Consider the following four alternatives:

First, damages may be measured by the **value of the public benefits** achieved. In *San Diego Gas*, Justice Brennan first suggested that if the public gained something by the temporary regulation, it should pay for it. However, this measure is flawed by the poor fit between the public benefit and the private injury worked by the regulation. The two will seldom be equal. If the court thought this was the proper measure, it might just as well have adopted Brennan's dissent in *San Diego Gas* verbatim. But it didn't. More generally, in eminent domain cases, measuring damages by the benefit to the government, rather than the loss to the landowner, is unusual. It is used only when other measures are unavailable. Thus using this first measure would not render takings law consistent with the law of eminent domain. The fair market value of what is taken is the normal measure of damages.

Second, the **fair rental value** of the property during the time of the taking could be used. Such rent might either be computed on the basis of the highest and best use of the property, or the use of the property as regulated, but without the confiscatory regulation. However computed, this measure assumes a hypothetical negotiation over rent, but because the government does not have possession during the time of the taking, the rent will be low and speculative: since there is little market for rentals of non-possessory rights, there are few experts to appraise such things and testify in court on them.

Third, the **price of an option to purchase** the real property, effective for the period of the taking, could also be used to measure regulatory taking damages. This would be an amount necessary to keep the land off the market for the period of the regulatory taking. Will most developers want to sell? No. And do most municipalities want to buy? Again, no. So this measure is based on a fiction—untruthful answers to unrealistic questions. Moreover, the lack of a market in options might again make their appraisal speculative—and the results of such an appraisal suspect—and increase the litigation costs involved.

Fourth, a **contractual difference money** measure of damages could be used. This could mean two things. It could mean the difference in the value of the property just before and just after, the invalid regulation is imposed. Or it could mean the difference between the value before the regulation is imposed, and the value after the regulation is removed. The first meaning is usual and workable, but the second meaning seems unfair to the government—unfair to make it pay for fluctuations in value during the period of the taking. That is a risk of ownership.

The latter measure could also include consequential damages, e.g., lost profits. Courts often say that lost profits in a new business are too speculative. This means that, if this measure is used, the effect of strikes, cost overruns, construction delays, and the unavailability of financing will somehow have to be factored into the award. This however may only be an example of a rule stating that an owner should receive his or her actual loss or damage, including but not limited to, any lost profits, carrying costs, any lost option opportunities, or any rent lost—in other words, any measure reasonably susceptible of proof.

In part because all of these measures have some drawbacks, traditionally remedies other than damages have been used for a regulatory taking. One example is affirmative injunctive relief, such as a judicial rezoning and a decree ordering the granting of permits. Anything less faces the prospect that a municipality will rezone the affected property again and again, always to an unreasonable use; permitting the damage claim to proceed is insurance against this prospect. If the court allows the damage action to proceed, but in the end only awards enough damages to make the owner think twice about further appeals, he will just sell to a speculator at a modest profit and quit the field.

§ 5.06 Off-Setting the Takings Award

Another source of law for fleshing out the dimensions of *First English* lies in state eminent domain codes. Once an owner brings a regulatory takings claim and is awarded damages, statutory provisions governing eminent domain actions may permit the condemnor to off-set the condemnation award by an amount equal to the value of having the public improvement for which the condemnation is made, nearby or adjacent to the condemnee's remaining property. So a municipality confronted with paying for a temporary taking might reasonably claim that it is entitled to set-off the award in this way.

§ 5.07 The Effects of *First English* on Zoning Administration

Problems in awarding damages for the enforcement of invalid regulations which go "too far" are likely to arise in one of three situations: (1) a municipality's refusal to rezone; (2) a downzoning; and (3) a situation in which there are damages, incurred in reliance on the existing zoning in which the owner has a vested right.

As to a rezoning into (say) a duplex residential zone, in a district in which apartment houses are the surrounding and prevailing use (so prevalent that duplexes would not be marketable on this parcel), the owner applying for a rezoning of his parcel into a commercial use district could have the application denied and then bring both a temporary takings claim, including a damage claim, to court. However, there is probably no taking, and so no damages are available here. A landowner is not entitled to the highest and best use of his or her property. There is no regulatory taking here because some use is still available. The practical result of this situation is a rule that *First English* damages are limited to situations in which the loss of fair market value is near total.

As to a downzoning, suppose that it is applied to a parcel previously zoned for apartments and occurs after an owner's purchase in which a premium price is paid for the parcel. The downzoning permits only single-family housing. This parcel, in the midst of other apartments and unmarketable for single-family uses, presents a colorable claim. When an up-zoning application to permit the use of the parcel for intensive uses is denied, this would be seen as a case much like *Lucas v. South Carolina Coastal Council.*[33] It is a categorical total taking of all economically viable uses and value of the parcel.

As to the vested rights, suppose an owner with a parcel zoned for apartments secured all necessary permits and commences construction of an apartment house on a parcel. During construction, the property is rezoned for duplexes, to a use district which excludes apartments. In a suit for an injunction against enforcement of the new ordinance and damages, the injunction will issue. Here the rezoning interferes with the owner's development in progress and in almost every jurisdiction, he has acquired a vested right to proceed with his apartments.[34] This claim would arise when the regulators obtain a stop order against the owner's proceeding with further work or deny an occupancy permit; at both of these points, a regulatory taking would be found. Even here, however, the issue arises whether an injunction isn't a more satisfactory remedy. Assuming that it is not, an actual loss measure of damages is appropriate because the owner's situation is closely analogous to a tort claim, and so consequential damages for his loss of opportunities should be awarded as well.

§ 5.08 Ripeness and Regulatory Takings

In earlier cases not resolving the question of interim regulatory damages, the Supreme Court had invoked the doctrine of ripeness—finding those cases not ripe for decision, either because there was no final decision or the plaintiff had not sought a compensation remedy.[35] *First English* is then an exception to the usual standards for ripeness in Supreme Court jurisprudence: California courts had determined that

33. 505 U.S. 1003 (1992) (discussed *infra* Chapter 17).

34. *See infra* Chapter 21.

35. While the United States was looking for the right case to decide the question of regulatory takings, the state courts were busy deciding the same issue in favor of the developer. *See, e.g., Scherr v. Township of Evesham*, 445 A.2d 46 (N.J. Super. Ct., L. Div. 1982). Many of these state cases involved facts in which the state first attempted to condemn the land, but then pulled back and regulated it for the same purpose as would have been served by the condemnation. *See City of Austin v. Teague*,

"all use" was denied, but the administrative process had not yet run its course—the county had not determined with finality the effect of the regulation on the property.

§ 5.09 Section 1983 Actions

As an alternative to a *First English*, a regulatory takings cause of action, brought under 42 U.S.C. § 1983, has some tactical appeal. A § 1983 action is a damages claim against "any person who, under color of any statute, ordinance, regulation, custom, or usage, of any State, subjects or causes to be subjected, any citizen . . . to the deprivation of any rights . . . secured by the Constitution and laws [of the United States]."[36] If a developer wins a due process and takings case, without including a regulatory damages claim, a state court might be quicker to give him or her judgment; a judge who sees the possibility of draining the public treasury will look hard at the case. With the judgment in hand, however, filing a § 1983 claim later provides a forum in which such reluctance will not affect the merits of the prior, regulatory case.

An owner/developer might, however, layer causes of action in federal court after a finding of a taking is made. That is, in addition to the statutory and inverse condemnation claims made in *First English*, he or she might include a § 1983 action as well as a takings claim.[37] Any judgment or monetary award under this federal statute is likely to track a takings claim, but under § 1983, awards may be for actual damages, emotional distress, and punitive damages, although not consequential damages. Also recoverable in a successful § 1983 action are attorneys fees. Recovering the latter is another tactical reason to use this section.

In 1999, the United State Supreme Court decided that there was a right to a jury trial in an inverse condemnation action brought under § 1983, but the court declined "to define with precision the elements of a temporary regulatory takings claim."[38] Such precision might provide a better definition of the nature of the claim. For example, as a tort claim, consequential damages should be available, but in condemnation cases, only actual or direct damages have typically been given.

Another federal statute, 28 U.S.C. § 1331, provides: "The district courts shall have original jurisdiction of all civil actions arising under the Constitution, laws, or treaties of the United States." The law under this section is also likely to track § 1983. But

---

570 S.W.2d 389 (Tex. 1978) (involving the denial of development permits for vacant land); G. Rankin, *The First Bite at the Apple: State Supreme Court Takings Jurisprudence Antedating First English*, 22 Urban Law. 417 (1990) (finding that N.J. and Texas courts found regulatory takings compensable before Justice Brennan's dissent in *San Diego*, Oregon and Rhode Island courts did so afterwards on state constitutional grounds, and Arizona, New Hampshire, North Dakota, and Wisconsin courts did so citing his dissent).

36. 42 U.S.C.A. § 1983 (2007).

37. *See generally Sintra, Inc. v. City of Seattle*, 829 P.2d 765, 770–71 (Wash. 1992) (containing a general discussion of § 1983 actions).

38. *See City of Monterey v. Del Monte Dunes at Monterey, Ltd.*, 526 U.S. 687 (1999).

nothing in the statute requires such tracking, so that an additional plea for consequential damages is appropriate here.

§ 5.10 *First English* on Remand

On remand, the California courts found that "all use" of the plaintiff's property had not been denied in this case and so no damages were payable.[39] The California appeals court also found the ordinance justified as a health and safety measure. It cited *Mugler* and said: "We recognize a brewery is a far cry from a Bible camp. But here the threat to public health and safety emanates not from what is produced on the property but from the presence of any substantial structures on that property."[40] Moreover, the ordinance was not a taking under *Mahon*: "Justice Holmes did not contest the main legal premise of Justice Brandeis' dissent—government has an absolute right to prohibit land uses which constitute a public nuisance."[41] Indeed, the opinion found Holmes' *Mahon* opinion attacking only the minor premise of Brandeis—to the effect that the Kohler Act was not a "private benefit" statute as applied to the facts. The court found that the public safety concerns were more dominant than they were in *Mahon* and *Keystone*:

> It would not be remarkable at all to allow government to deny a private owner "all uses" of his property where there is no use of that property which does not threaten lives and health. So it makes perfect sense to deny compensation for the denial of "all uses" where health and safety are at stake but require compensation for the denial of "all uses" where the land use regulation advances lesser public purposes.[42]

The "lesser" purposes are not enumerated, but they might include moratoria and growth controls. Further, "all use" of the property was not prohibited by the ordinance. Tenting and campfires were still possible: "Meals could be cooked, games played, lessons given, tents pitched."[43] Finally, the later opinion found that, as a moratorium, the ordinance was reasonably drafted to accomplish its purpose.

Shortly after the *First English* case was decided, the United States Supreme Court refused to hear and decide a case that some thought would have expanded its holding, reviewing the constitutionality of a Denver ordinance which was broadly aimed at protecting the view of the Rockies from downtown.[44]

---

39. *See First English Evangelical Lutheran Church of Glendale v. County of Los Angeles*, 258 Cal. Rptr. 893, 894, 899–900, n. 9, 901–02, 906–07 (Cal. App. Ct. 1989).

40. *See First English*, 258 Cal. Rptr. at 899.

41. *Id.* at 900, n. 9.

42. *Id.* at 901.

43. *Id.* at 902.

44. *See Landmark Land Co. v. City and County of Denver*, 728 P.2d 1281 (Colo. 1987), *cert. denied*, 483 U.S. 1001 (1987).

§ 5.11 Governmental Confusion and Bad Faith

As mentioned previously, a line of cases predating and surviving *First English* involves governmental bad faith. An example is *Arastra Limited Partnership v. City of Palo Alto*.[45] There, the locale was the Palo Alto foothills; the city sits in a bowl in their midst and had annexed the foothills in the 1950s in order to gain control over their development.[46]

In *Arastra*, a partnership owned 515 acres in the foothills. In 1967, the city built an overlook on land above the partners'. During the years 1967-1972, the city took steps to acquire the land by eminent domain; it explored financing the acquisition by using federal grants, the proceeds of municipal bonds, and other monies; it searched the title and appraised the land; finally, it enacted a resolution declaring its intent to acquire the land by eminent domain. But it never did; it walked up to the point of acquisition, but never crossed over. Instead, it enacted an "open space regulation," permitting three houses per acre, reducing the fair market value (in the partners' appraiser's opinion) by about two million dollars.

The partners sued in inverse condemnation, claiming that a *de facto* taking had occurred and measuring the damages from the date the open space ordinance was enacted.

Judgment was for the partnership. There was a taking and the just compensation was measured on the date of the ordinance. The city's reversal of policies after so much preparation for eminent domain showed that its true intent was to accomplish by regulation what it could not afford to do by eminent domain. Thus, the regulation was not aimed at preventing over-development of the foothills, but at extracting a public benefit—open space—from the plaintiffs.

The city argued that there was no physical invasion and so no taking. The district court responded that this argument took a lot of nerve, because physical invasion was precisely the thing the city meant to avoid with its ordinance.

Government ineptitude and an inability to decide on a policy, not amounting to bad faith, has also been found to be a taking.[47] The *Benenson* opinion harks back to earlier cases of planning blight, occurring when an urban renewal or redevelopment agency makes plans to condemn an area, which is denied public services in anticipation of the condemnation, with the result that property values fall prior to

45. 401 F. Supp. 962 (N.D. Cal. 1975), *vacated by agreement of the parties*, 417 F. Supp. 1125 (N.D. Cal. 1976).

46. For background on the foothills controversy, see *Eldridge v. City of Palo Alto*, 129 Cal. Rptr. 575 (Cal. App. Ct. 1976).

47. *See Benenson v. United States*, 548 F.2d 939 (Ct. Cl. 1977) (a decade of uncoordinated agency efforts and policy uncertainty, including a reversal of policy on historic preservation of the Willard Hotel on Washington D.C.'s Pennsylvania Avenue, causing the Court of Claims to find a taking as of the date the building had to be preserved).

the date that the condemnation is legally effective. In this situation, the condemnees are compensated for the fair market value of their property before the planning blight occurred.

§ 5.12 State Takings Legislation

Many states have considered and enacted legislation defining (more broadly than does *First English*) situations in which property owners are entitled to compensation when their property is diminished in value by regulation. Twenty five states enacted such legislation between 1991 and 1996. The legislative objective is to provide a bright line to the diminution in value test for a taking cited in the *Mahon* case. The scope of this type of legislation varies from state to state. Some have enacted statutes providing for compensation for owners when a regulation produced a diminution in value amounting to a specific percentage of the pre-regulation fair market value—40% in Mississippi, 20% in Louisiana—but applies it only to timber or agricultural land. Texas uses a 25% decrease, but broadly applies its statute to any regulated real property. Finally, Florida has a statute compensating generally any "inordinate burden" on the use of real property, leaving it to the courts to define such a burden.

Chapter 6
The Structure of Zoning: The *Euclid* Case

§ 6.01 Introduction

All land is held subject to the regulation of its use by government at many levels.[1] As we have seen in previous Chapters, such regulation is authorized by and derived from the police power as well as limited by the due process, equal protection and takings clauses of the federal and state constitutions.[2] Today, along with education and the real property tax, land-use regulation is one of three activities on which municipal officials spend the bulk of their time and effort.[3]

With regard to land use regulation, it was not always so. Until the late 19th century, the law of nuisance, frontage consent laws, and private restrictive covenants were the principal means of controlling land use. Absent those means, the size of a lot or parcel and adjustment of the placement and location of improvements on it were the principal means of avoiding the effects of nearby intrusive or undesirable uses.

The use of zoning became common in the early decades of the 20th century and spread with particular rapidity in the post-World War I era of the 1920s. Zoning is the product of the exercise by state and local governments of the police power. Dillon's Rule[4] applies. Thus, a municipality's planning and zoning activity must be (1) expressly conferred by the state's planning and zoning enabling act or (2) reasonably necessary to achieve a power expressly delegated by the state in that act or (3) essential

1. Any person holding a freehold title to land has "*seisin*" as one component of that title. Seisin is possession that is responsive to governmental authority—what we mean when attorneys say that all titles are "subject to" regulation by the government.

2. Although federal environmental regulations everywhere have an indirect impact on land use, the federal government seldom directly regulates land use and, except for a few states (e.g., Florida, Hawaii, and Vermont), neither do the states. Regional agencies do sometimes regulate land with special environmental problems (e.g., coastal land and wetlands). State regulation may occasionally preempt municipal building height regulations, as the New Jersey legislature did after a storm surge required the elevation of coastal properties. *See Gross v. Iannuzzi*, 210 A.3d 250 (N.J. Super. Ct. 2019).

3. In this and succeeding chapters, "municipal" means either the city, county, town, or township level of government.

4. As discussed *supra*, Chapter 1, § 1.01.

to the existence of the municipality's planning or zoning powers. Only so much of the police power as is necessary to achieve a scheme of land use regulation is conferred. In many states, planning and zoning powers are often delegated in separate statutes.

Every state has enacted a separate, state-wide, zoning enabling act. The purpose of such acts is to delegate authority to municipal governments to formulate and conduct a scheme of land use regulation.[5] The original prototype for these acts is the Standard Zoning Enabling Act ("SZEA"), drafted originally by the United States Department of Commerce and ready for adoption in 1924.[6] It is still, in over 40 states, the model for state enabling acts today. It authorizes the municipal legislative body to enact a zoning scheme (an ordinance[7] containing the text for the regulatory scheme, and a zoning map). It then establishes two administrative bodies to consider matters of zoning administration: first, a **zoning commission** to advise on any changes to the zoning designation of a property ("rezoning") when the municipality's legislative body does not reserve this authority unto itself; and second, a **board of zoning adjustment or appeals**, to hear requests for variances, special exceptions, and appeals from administrators interpreting the ordinance. This two-body administrative structure still prevails in most municipalities today.

The Standard Planning Enabling Act followed in 1928. It establishes a **planning commission** as a quasi-independent agency of local government, presumably to keep it non-political. To this agency was committed the formulation of land use plans. Although many states have since enacted more comprehensive statutes to authorize these activities, many still use the basic provisions and structures of these two early acts.

The subdivision of land is also typically enabled by a separate state statute, and delegations of the police power may be made as well—typically through the enactment of home rule charters for some municipalities. The subdivision review process is often conducted by the municipality's planning commission.

The activities of planning and zoning, undertaken by municipal governments, must be grounded in these enabling acts. So a first question in any controversial action is whether the activity is *ultra vires*—that is, beyond the authority conferred on a municipality by the act.

---

5. All of these delegations of authority are in the first instance to municipal legislative bodies—such as city or town councils, county or township commissioners, or boards of selectmen—who are therein authorized to enact zoning codes and ordinances. Some states delegate the power to enact land use ordinances to two municipal entities at once—say, to counties and towns. *See, e.g., Quinn v. Town of Dodgeville*, 364 N.W.2d 149 (Wis. 1985) (upholding such dual authority). Some states also permit zoning ordinances to be established by voter initiatives and some (but fewer) states permit enacted ordinances to be reviewed in voter referenda.

6. *See* Standard State Zoning Enabling Act, *reprinted in* A.L.I., *Model Land Development Code*, Tent. Draft No. 1, at 210 (1968). The Foreword to the original text was written by Herbert Hoover, the then-Secretary of Commerce.

7. Zoning ordinance refers to legislation enacted by a municipality of some type. In this sense, an ordinance is an enactment made with the consent of the state and authorized by it, valid until the enabling act requires that something else be done. In this sense, an ordinance refers back to its English origins, as an edict of the King valid until Parliament began its next session.

The further, constitutional constraint on the planning and zoning powers of municipalities are found in due process clause of the Fifth Amendment, made applicable to the states through the Fourteenth Amendment, and on comparable constitutional provisions in state constitutions. Due process not only has a procedural meaning—a course of proceedings according to rules and procedures established for the protection of private rights—but it also has a substantive meaning, to the effect that the burden imposed by government, by regulation or otherwise, should be roughly off-set by the benefit engendered by it. This idea of rough equality between the benefits and burdens of a regulation is known as economic, or substantive, due process. A regulation should not be so onerous that there is no benefit back to the regulated person, considered either directly or as a member of the public. In this connection, Holmes' "reciprocity of advantage" phrase in *Mahon* was his attempt to use this type of analysis without identifying it as such—in part because he objected to its use in cases like *Lochner v. People of the State of New York.*[8] Another alternative statement of economic due process is that particular persons not be singled out and forced to bear an unfair burden—that is, a burden disproportionately large when compared to the burden borne by citizens as a whole. A regulation that does not have this reciprocity is labeled "arbitrary, unreasonable, and capricious." This phrase is also commonly used by courts when referring to a standard of judicial review for legislative zoning matters: that is, an ordinance violates substantive due process when it is "arbitrary and unreasonable, having no substantial relation to the public's health, safety, morals or general welfare."[9]

There is traditionally no taking issue raised by economic losses caused by health and safety regulations. The evaluation of such regulations is a matter reviewed under the due process clause or its state constitutional counterpart. There, the judiciary's concern is for the economic burden imposed by a regulation, as well as legislative proceedings that led to its enactment. Thus the clause has both substantive and procedural concerns.

§ 6.02 *Village of Euclid v. Ambler Realty Company*

While zoning became very popular, city and urban planning did not. Even zoning had an uncertain constitutional status until 1926, when the United States Supreme Court handed down its opinion in the case of *Village of Euclid v. Ambler Realty Co.*[10] The petitioner, the Ambler Realty Company, owned a 68 acre tract, shaped roughly like a parallelogram, in the Village of Euclid. Euclid was a suburb of the City of Cleveland. Ambler's tract was bordered on two sides—to the east and west—by residential

8. 198 U.S. 45 (1905).

9. *See, e.g., Gypsum Res., LLC v. Clark County,* 2023 U.S. Dist. LEXIS 11703 (D. Nev., Jan. 23, 2023), *Flint v. City of Kauai*, 521 F. Supp. 3d 978, 955 (D. Haw. 2021), and numerous other cases.

10. 272 U.S. 365 (1926) (hereafter "*Euclid*").

land uses. On its southern boundary, it abutted Euclid Avenue. At the time, the avenue was a major thoroughfare in the Cleveland area. Further in town, it was lined with substantial residences, mostly facing north toward Lake Erie and including the mansion of John D. Rockefeller.

The facts involved in *Euclid* were not in dispute. Indeed, there was no trial in the courts below. There was instead a series of pretrial examinations of witnesses. Thereafter, the trial judge read the record and issued an opinion.

In *Euclid*, the United States Supreme Court upheld, by a vote of 6 to 3, the zoning ordinance of the Village, an Ohio municipality, that divided its land area into use, height, and area districts. The owner was made to look like a land speculator, not a housing developer; it had, at the time of the litigation, no definite plans for the development of the property.

The percentages of fair market value lost by Ambler Realty to regulation were alleged to be severe. Unzoned, the fair market value per acre was allegedly four times what it was zoned. Along Euclid Avenue, the front foot value was supposed to be three times greater unzoned than it was zoned.

Ambler Realty's tract was zoned into three use districts—for two-family dwellings abutting the Avenue, for apartments and hotels in the center of the property, and, on the northerly portion of the property, abutting railroad tracks, for industrial uses.[11] These use districts were "cumulative"—that is, any use permitted in a higher or less dense district were also permitted in lower, more dense districts. Perhaps the most profitable resale of Ambler Realty's property would have been for industrial uses, but while the ordinance permitted industrial uses along the northern edge of the tract, along a railroad, such uses were prohibited in the southern portion of the property which had roadway access along the avenue.[12]

The Village's initial ordinance had placed the Ambler tract into two zones—U-6 and U-2—but Ambler protested and a strip of U-3 district was added along the middle of the tract. Today Ambler Realty would probably have pursued further legislative and administrative remedies before bringing suit to invalidate the ordinance. Indeed, today it would probably be required to do so, unless the further request would be a futile act.

The *Euclid* opinion spent no time disputing Ambler Realty's allegations of loss. Its analysis started by applying a presumption of validity to the legislative acts of the Village and continued with a search for some rational basis for the ordinance—and so did not require a close look. Rather, it looked at the purpose and character of the regulation and the nexus or connection between that purpose and the ordinance's provisions. This involved what was, and is today, called substantive due process analysis.

---

11. *See Euclid*, 272 U.S. at 379–83 (describing the village ordinance).

12. *See* Richard Epstein, *The Conceptual Approach to Zoning: What's Wrong with Euclid*, 5 N.Y.U. Envir. L.J. 277, 286–87 (1996) (suggesting this).

In *Euclid*, the financial impact of the regulation on Ambler Realty's tract, while recognized, seemed to play little role in the Supreme Court's analysis. At the time that the regulations were imposed, there were no industrial uses in the Village. Yet part of Ambler's property was zoned for industrial uses. Other parts were zoned more restrictively, for multi-unit residential structures.

But because Ambler was buying in advance of development, it could not yet show what the fiscal impact of the regulation actually was. It had in fact (though a fact not cited in the opinion) developed some property along Euclid Avenue further in, toward the city, but had imposed covenants which restricted the uses in its development to non-industrial uses.

Justice Sutherland's holding in this case was a broad-brush validation of the Village ordinance, and of zoning ordinances in general, not a look at their details. Its generality is one of its important features. His opinion represents a "facial" analysis instead of an "as applied" analysis of the ordinance. It contains, for example, a discussion of the exclusion of apartments from a single-family residential use district, although this was a matter not raised by the facts of Ambler Realty's ownership. Sutherland's opinion emphasizes the exclusion of potentially conflicting land uses. The ordinance effected the exclusion of a land use that was potentially and prospectively a nuisance. A nuisance, he says, "may be merely a right thing in the wrong place—like a pig in the parlor instead of the barnyard."[13]

It is important that the zoning ordinance laid down a general scheme of land uses rather than permitting the Village officials to permit development of its land area only on a case-by-case basis or by meeting special conditions. At the time, this would have made the Village's case a weaker one, for then it could be said that the legislature had not enacted a general or comprehensive scheme which the jurisdiction's administrators could implement. The *Euclid* opinion was a pre-New Deal one. It was the product of an era when only the narrowest delegations of authority to administrative bodies were likely to survive judicial review. For instance, to secure a zoning permit, a developer had to show that its plans were in accordance with the ordinance and the general welfare of the community and without any adverse impact on adjacent land. Such standards would have to have then been implemented by legislative decisions. Why? Because then the exercise of the police power could not have been delegated to administrators once the state legislature had provided that a particular municipal body should exercise it.

In subsequent years, *Euclid*'s general finding of validity accomplished four things.[14] First, the Supreme Court said that it would use a flexible and case-by-case approach to zoning issues. Second, its lengthy discussion of the background of zoning laws

---

13. *See Euclid*, 272 U.S. at 388 (suggesting that Sutherland had private, not public, nuisance in mind and recalling *Alred's Case*, 77 Eng. Rep. 816 (King's Bench 1611) (involving a pig sty interfering with the use of a house)). A comparable issue today might be the problems posed by livestock feedlots.

14. *See* Michael Allan Wolf, *Euclid at Threescore Years and Ten: Is This the Twilight of Environmental and Land-Use Regulation*, 30 U. Rich. L. Rev. 961, 963–64 (1996).

endorsed the use of urban planning as a useful pre-condition for a zoning ordinance; the court endorsed its use, but did not hold that such planning was a necessary pre-condition to enacting a zoning ordinance. Third, the court found that the validity of an ordinance was measured by the extent to which it sought to prevent a land use pattern or situation that would require nuisance litigation to resolve. In contested and doubtful situations, Justice Sutherland said, "the maxim *sic utere tuo ut alienum non laedas*, which lies at the foundation of the law of nuisances, ordinarily will furnish a fairly helpful clue as to the resolution."[15] The court also said that so long as the owners of the regulated property were still permitted a "reasonable return" on their investments, regulation was valid. Fourth and finally, Justice Sutherland accepted that the Village of Euclid was recognized in Ohio as the primary legal entity authorized to enact a zoning ordinance, provided at the same time that its enactment was in accord with its region's general welfare.[16] This proviso would in future allow regional concerns to override the Village's zoning when and as this broader general welfare might require.

Because of the general nature of the discussion, it is difficult to determine what portions of the Village ordinance are upheld. The ordinance was upheld generally, but the impact of its separate provisions was not assessed, and the applicability of those provisions was not discussed in the context of a specific piece of property like Ambler Realty's. Two years later, the court did, as promised, use a case-by-case approach and invalidated an ordinance "as applied" to a particular parcel straddling the boundary line between two use districts.[17] *Nectow v. City of Cambridge* seemed to presage Supreme Court involvement in the zoning field, but thereafter the court did not consider any zoning cases until the 1970s. So much, then, for the court's promise in *Euclid* of close review of such ordinances in the future. Its next zoning opinion was in 1974, in *Village of Belle Terre v. Boraas*.[18]

Thus the questions raised, but left unanswered by *Euclid* involve the day to day administration of a zoning ordinance. Would the court uphold any or all of the following: a prohibition on motels from a commercial district where hotels are permitted? A prohibition on bed-and-breakfast businesses from a commercial district in which motels are permitted? A prohibition of fast food restaurants from an area permitting sit-down restaurants? A prohibition on residential development on a flood plain? All of these involve close distinctions. All mimic the prohibition of apartment houses from single-family residential use districts upheld in *Euclid*.

All of the forgoing distinctions might plausibly be made today and, using the presumption of validity and the narrow standard of judicial review used in this opinion, upheld by the courts. While they all present interesting questions, there is no answer

15. *See Euclid*, 272 U.S. at 387.

16. In this regard, see Ezra Rosser, *The Euclid Proviso*, 96 Wash. L. Rev. 811 (2021) (arguing for a broader use of the concept of a regional general welfare in zoning matters).

17. *See Nectow v. City of Cambridge*, 277 U.S. 183, 188–89 (1928).

18. 416 U.S. 1 (1974), discussed *infra*, Chapter 18, § 18.01.

for these situations to be found in Sutherland's opinion; rather, he says that the law of nuisance will often "furnish a helpful clew" as to an ordinance's validity. Nuisance law was the one guidepost the law had in his day. However, Justice Sutherland did not say it was the only, or an exclusive guide.[19] He cited it "not for the purpose of controlling, but for the helpful aid of its analogies in the process of ascertaining the scope of"[20] the police power. It also provided him with a way to avoid direct endorsement of zoning as an expansion of the police power. The validity of the zoning ordinance here was a signal to municipalities that in the future they need not rely on nuisance litigation to sort out their land use conflicts; they also need not wait for matters to get so bad that private plaintiffs bring nuisance actions to resolve such conflicts. A zoning ordinance is presumed valid and the presumption remains intact until the ordinance is shown to be arbitrary or capricious. (Of this presumption of validity, more *infra*.)

The *Euclid* opinion dealt specifically with only one such distinction—whether apartment houses[21] could be excluded from a residential district. Justice Sutherland called this the "serious question" of the case.[22] Apartments had long been a subject of controversy.[23] With such a history, it is little wonder that apartment buildings appear in the *Euclid* opinion as a form of urban blight.[24] The apartment house is a "parasite" taking "advantage of open spaces and attractive surroundings created by the residential character of the district,"[25] blocking light and air, bringing noise and traffic, depriving children of a place to play, and finally destroying the character of the neighborhood. Justice Sutherland saw zoning controlling apartments not as a deprivation of property rights, but as a method of conserving residential property values. He also seemed to see overcrowding of uses as one of the problems that zoning might permissibly address, along with safety problems like the danger of fires.[26] Sutherland's emphasis is on the validity of separating and segregating land uses.

---

19. *Euclid*, 272 U.S. at 387–88. The extent to which land use controls must rest on a local legislature's authority to control or abate nuisances is today a matter of renewed debate. *See Lucas v. South Carolina Coastal Council*, 505 U.S. 1003 (1992).

20. *Euclid*, 272 U.S. at 387–88.

21. *See generally*, Maureen E. Brady, *Turning Neighbors into Nuisances*, 134 Harv. L. Rev. 1609 (2021) (discussing the legal history of the apartment house).

22. *Id.* at 390.

23. *See* Kenneth Jackson, Crabgrass Frontier 89–92 (1985); note 25, *infra*.

24. *Id.* Apartments were considered mildly shady until the end of the 1800s: entrances did not front the street and busybodies could not monitor comings and goings; in New York City, until the Stuyvesant Apartments (built in 1870) "overcame the risque image of the French flat," respectable Americans who could afford a private dwelling were not attracted to them. Jackson, *supra*, at 90. Only in the 1880s did multi-unit buildings become good downtown development: the Dakota Apartments were built on Central Park West at 79th St.—so far uptown that they might as well have been in the Dakota Territory, with its liberal divorce laws. *Id.*

25. *Euclid*, 272 U.S. at 390.

26. *Id.*

Because of this emphasis, under *Euclid* the Village could not have zoned its land area into one district, in which only residential uses were permitted. That would have been an admission by the Village that land uses were not a problem, and not in need of separation, one from another. If nuisance was the guideline for permissible zoning, the separation of otherwise incompatible land use was a precondition to the exercise of the police power via zoning.[27]

Today, a court might evaluate a prohibition on apartments in one of two ways. First, the court can look at what other uses, besides apartments, are excluded. Are they uses of similar intensity? If the answer is yes, the ordinance is under-inclusive and invalid. However, if the court finds that there are no other similar uses excluded, then the court can broaden its inquiry: the question then becomes, are there uses of similar intensity, which are included? If the answer is yes, then the ordinance is over-inclusive (except of course, as to the protesting landowner) and invalid.

In the present day, the issue of the need to exclude apartments might be rephrased as an issue of whether apartments cannot be zoned into a residential district, but without the ill side effects Sutherland saw. When Sutherland discussed the impact of apartment houses in single-family residential use districts, he dealt only with the external effects of the apartments.[28] There was no discussion demonstrating that their effects can be dealt within a zoning ordinance. For instance, if automobiles are a problem, apartment house owners can be compelled to provide on-site parking. If they block light and air, set-back regulations can be imposed. And so on. Sutherland did not deal with the fact that real people live in apartment houses. Why not? Because he was concerned primarily with the nuisance-abating provisions of the Village's ordinance. On the other hand, to be fair to Justice Sutherland, it should be said that techniques for including apartment uses in otherwise single-family districts rely on post-1930 views of what it is permissible to delegate to an administrative agency, the later-invented techniques of city planners, and twenty-twenty hindsight. Sutherland was asked to endorse the separation of land uses, rather than validating an attempt to combine or mix them.[29] In particular, the *Euclid* opinion endorsed the separation of homes from more intensive commercial and industrial uses.[30]

---

27. *See Rockhill v. Chesterfield Twp.*, 128 A.2d 473 (N.J. 1956).

28. *See* JACKSON, *supra*, at n. 21.

29. For example, if livestock feedlots need to be abated as nuisances, then ordinances regulating them ought to think in terms of "odor zones" and buffers, holding lagoons for waste, restrictions on size, and impact fees for local roads transporting the animals. Illinois and North Carolina have enacted special regulations for feedlots.

30. *Euclid*, 272 U.S. at 388 (citing court's own cases restricting a brick yard and a stable from a residential area, and permitting height limits on building in Boston's residential Back Bay neighborhood). *See Hadacheck v. Sebastian*, 239 U.S. 394 (1915) (as to the brick yard); *Reiman v. Little Rock*, 237 U.S. 171 (1915) (as to the stable); *Welch v. Swasey*, 214 U.S. 91 (as to the height limits).

§ 6.03 A Post-*Euclid* Presumption of Validity

As in *Euclid*, the usual rule is that a zoning ordinance enjoys a presumption of validity. Yet this presumption does not apply when the exclusion of a particular land use is total, unless this total exclusion is necessary to preserve the overall character of the zoning jurisdiction.[31]

In land use opinions, the presumption is not an evidentiary one, allocating the burden of producing evidence; here the "evidence" (if one can call it that) is a mixture of social science data and legislative judgments. Instead, the presumption of validity typically refers to a standard of judicial review—a statement of the relationship between courts and local legislatures—to the effect that once an ordinance is shown to be fairly debatable, the presumption of validity attaches to it. If there is a plausible rationale for the ordinance, a court will sustain it. (If it truly were an evidentiary presumption, a court would sustain it, a prima facie case having been made out, unless the facts that are developed later overcome it.)

The necessity for an exclusion from a district is judged by one of two ways; first, the need for the use within the use district, and second, the need for the use within the municipality. Incompatibility with the surrounding and permitted uses provides a third way. Similarly, where a use is totally excluded from a zoning jurisdiction, the necessity for the exclusion is judged either by the need for the use within the jurisdiction or within the surrounding metropolitan region.

§ 6.04 Some Background on *Euclid*

The advocates of zoning were, at the time of the *Euclid* litigation, unhappy that this case went to the United States Supreme Court. Alfred Bettman, one of these advocates, and the writer of the most influential of the *Amicus Curiae* briefs before the court, thought the ordinance ill-considered.[32] The Village had done little in the way of studies to support its ordinance and Bettman considered that its industrial zone, along the railroad tracks running through the Village, was too narrow to be of much use to industry. Bettman's brief thus made little of the ordinance as it applied to the

31. *See McNeill v. Township of Plumsted*, 522 A.2d 469, 471 (N.J. Super. Ct., App. Div., 1987) (remanding case to consider conditions requiring ordinance excluding removal of topsoil from the township).

32. *See* Alfred Bettman, Village of Euclid v. Ambler Realty Co. *Brief, Amicus Curiae, in* City and Regional Planning Papers 157, 172 (Arthur Comey, ed. 1946). Ohio attorney Alfred Bettman knew Chief Justice Howard Taft and, when drafting this brief, filtered the views of the most eminent city planning experts of the time, including those responsible for the drafting of the *Euclid* ordinance.

plaintiff's land and defined (or redefined) the issue so that only the general validity of the ordinance was at issue. The Sutherland opinion accepted this premise.[33]

Justice Sutherland was in the process of writing an opinion striking down the Village's ordinance as applied when he changed his mind, had the case reargued, and then wrote the opinion handed down.[34] What had been going to be a loss for zoning advocates was ripped from the jaws of defeat at the last minute; and zoners won the day—gaining general approval for zoning.[35]

The Supreme Court probably knew of the widespread adoption in the states of the Standard Zoning Enabling Act (SZEA)—over one half of the states had adopted it by the end of 1925.[36] Indeed, in a general way, the opinion seemed to take judicial notice of such a fact. Moreover, the SZEA was promulgated by the successive Republican administrations of the 1920s. Finally, Ambler Realty made it easy for the court to uphold the ordinance by bringing what could be characterized as a facial challenge to the ordinance. It had no definite plans for the development of its sixty-eight acres. It probably should have developed a plan before bringing suit. Perhaps it did not because its capital gains would look disproportionate to their initial investment, and so the claim to have suffered any "diminution in value" would have a hollow ring.

§ 6.05 A Presumption + a Rational Basis = Deference

Judicial deference is the dispositive principle of the *Euclid* opinion. It leads to a presumption of legislative validity, which leads in turns to a rule that if the matter before the legislature is fairly debatable, the presumption of validity applies to the ordinance: the legislature need only muster "substantial evidence" or have a "rational basis" for its decision. "Substantial evidence" is "more than a scintilla and less than

33. *Id.*

34. *See* Mel Scott, American City Planning 238–40 (1971) (reviewing the background of the *Euclid* case).

35. Justice Sutherland knew the legislative process, having served in the Utah state senate. He also knew that in the preceding decades, the Supreme Court had heard and upheld many challenges to municipal land use regulations. *See* Joseph G. Hylton, *Prelude to Euclid: The United States Supreme Court and the Constitutionality of Land Use Regulation*, 3 Wash. U. L. & Pol'y J 1 (2000).

36. Early zoning was used differently in different locations. In the central cities of our metropolitan areas, it was used to separate commercial uses. New York City's first zoning ordinance, enacted in 1916, was used to separate department stores from the sewing lofts that produced the goods sold in the stores—particularly women's dresses. (Residential uses were not protected as well because absentee landlords owned much of the residential property.) Cities as large as Chicago were over-zoned for commercial uses, and cities in California, which saw themselves becoming the Chicagos of the future, were overzoning vacant land as well. In the suburbs, in contrast, zoning was used to segregate residential land uses from other uses. In any event, zoning proved a popular device in many locations. By 1926, seventy six cities has enacted ordinances. By 1936, more than 1,300 cities—85% of American cities—had ordinances.

a preponderance" of all evidence adduced to support an ordinance, enough to form a rational basis for it. A "rational basis" is often described tautologically as "what a reasoning mind needs to reasonably come to a conclusion."[37] Often this standard of review is phrased negatively, and means only that the legislature shall not act in an arbitrary or capricious manner. There is no requirement that the legislature pick the best solution to a matter it considers; there is no requirement of legislative efficiency in this sense; on the contrary, the legislature can pick one of several, equally well justified solutions, so long as it is supported by substantial evidence.

§ 6.06 The Remedy

In *Euclid*, as in *Hadacheck v. Sebastion*[38] and *Mahon*, the remedy asked was an injunction against the enforcement of an ordinance. The earlier majority opinion in *Mahon* is not cited or discussed. Would the result in *Euclid* have been different if damages had been sought? The answer is probably not. Arguably then the issue would not have involved the Fifth Amendment's due process clause, but the takings clause of that Amendment. (But without a development plan, Ambler Realty's damages might well have been seen as unproven and speculative.) Citing these different constitutional clauses could have become a wedge driving the *Mahon* and *Euclid* cases apart, into separate lines of authority; the first involving the takings clause, the second involving the due process clause. As it was, in both of these cases, what was sought was an injunction, the traditional remedy in a nuisance suit.

§ 6.07 The District Court Opinion in *Euclid*

The federal district judge in *Euclid* had invalidated the Village's ordinance.[39] The judge said: "The purpose to be accomplished is really to regulate the mode of living of persons who hereafter inhabit" the village. "[T]he result . . . is to classify the population and segregate them according to their income or situation in life."[40]

His authority for this included Holmes' opinion in *Mahon*. That opinion provided a reasonable basis for striking down the ordinance. It was also accompanied in that era by a series of state supreme court decisions which perceived zoning ordinances

37. *See Napleton v. Village of Hinsdale*, 891 N.E.2d 839, 854 (Ill. 2008) (finding a substantial relation to the police power in an ordinance forbidding banks from locating in a commercial use district because the banks did not produce sales tax revenue).

38. 239 U.S. 394 (1915) (upholding zoning out petitioner's brickyard) (discussed *supra* Chapter 3).

39. *Ambler Realty Co. v. Village of Euclid*, 297 F. 307, 309 (N.D. Ohio 1924), *reversed*, 272 U.S. 365 (1926).

40. *Id.* at 316.

as aimed at separating the rich from the poor and from "undesirable" commercial activities.[41]

The Supreme Court's *Euclid* opinion ignored these cases and *Mahon* because the due process and takings clauses for most of the Justices (Holmes excepted) presented distinct inquiries and separate issues.

In the process of invalidating the Village ordinance, the federal district judge also had harsh things to say about the discriminatory effects he expected to flow from the Village's ordinance. He saw the zoning ordinance as a method of economic exclusion and class separation. Single family householders were let in; apartment dwellers were not.

In order to set the scene as the district judge saw it, you need to know that, generally, there are two strains of opinions with regard to the intersection of zoning and civil rights. One is represented by the *Euclid* opinion, in which the rights of persons excluded are not closely examined. Another is represented by the opinion in *Buchanan v. Warley*,[42] in which the United States Supreme Court held invalid an ordinance of the City of Louisville, Kentucky, which prevented blacks or whites from moving into blocks on which resided persons of the other race.[43]

In *Buchanan*, the plaintiff was a white property owner, whose right to alienate his property was impaired by the ordinance, which limited the class of purchasers to whom he could sell. For purposes of the doctrine of standing, he was injured in fact, but the court's substantive holding was premised on a due process concern with an African-American's right to purchase the white person's property. The *Buchanan* opinion reached those in the African-American community (or other protected minority) who could afford to purchase property. Renters could take little comfort from it.

Later cases like *United States v. City of Black Jack, Missouri*,[44] and *United States v. City of Parma*,[45] held zoning ordinances invalid because of their violation of the Fair Housing Act of 1968. Both of these cases were decided on statutory, and not constitutional, grounds.

Later chapters on exclusionary zoning will return to the civil rights implications of the *Euclid* opinion. Justice Sutherland did not, in *Euclid*, deal with the broader context of the impact of the Village's ordinance on the regional population, in the midst of which the Village of Euclid enacted its ordinance. Later cases have done so.

---

41. *See, e.g., Spann v. City of Dallas*, 235 S.W. 513, 516 (Tex. 1921) ("the true reason why some persons live in a mansion and others in a shack . . . is primarily economic").

42. 245 U.S. 60 (1917).

43. *See also Yick Wo v. Hopkins*, 118 U.S. 356, 374 (1886) (invalidating ordinance requiring permit to operate a laundry that, the court found, was motivated by a desire to exclude Chinese laundries).

44. 508 F.2d 1179, 1188 (8th Cir. 1974), *cert. denied*, 422 U.S. 1042 (1974).

45. 661 F.2d 562 (6th Cir. 1982) (a "pattern or practice suit" bought under the Act).

§ 6.08 *Euclid*'s Legacy

When *Euclid* was decided, Ambler Realty's land was located in three zoning districts. One of those districts involved the most intensive, industrial land use. This district and the two others provided Ambler's land with a wider market, meaning that its resale value and use potential was yet to be determined. Most of it was over time rezoned for industrial uses and for the longest time, up to the 1990s, General Motors owned and used it as an automobile parts manufacturing facility. Thereafter most of it was vacant and unused for a time.

In contrast to Euclid's zoning ordinance, *Euclid*'s underlying policy of separating land uses survived, however, and set the pattern for zoning ordinances restricting a land use district to single family residential use. Such districts proliferated after World War II, populated by single-family housing subdivisions. These subdivisions require larger municipal expenditures for infrastructure than do more compact housing. Thus *Euclid* set the land use pattern for the development of a suburbia sprawling across the landscape. Backstopping this pattern of urban sprawl was *Euclid*'s emphasis on (1) the autonomy of municipalities (and the lack of emphasis on the need for consideration of regional interests), (2) the protection of residential neighborhoods (and the lack of emphasis on other neighborhoods within a municipality), (3) its total lack of consideration of the costs of municipal financing on a municipality's transportation and property tax base, and finally (4) its failure to assess the motives of municipalities when enacting zoning ordinances.

These concerns with the *Euclid* opinion might be mitigated by municipalities denying infrastructure to some sprawling subdivisions without some affordable housing, providing urban growth boundaries set on a regional basis and prohibiting rezonings beyond that boundary, setting maximum parcel size restrictions, giving preference to in-filling rezones, parkland, forest, and open space conservation, and regulations relating energy efficiency to the size of a subdivision or development.

Chapter 7

Euclidian Land-Use Controls, Accessory and Non-Conforming Uses

§ 7.01 Zoning and Planning

Zoning is the regulation and restriction of land uses according to a pre-determined plan. Under many state zoning enabling acts, zoning ordinances are required to be "in accordance with a comprehensive plan."[1] This means one of three things: either that (1) some type of urban planning is a precondition to their enactment,[2] or (2) the zoning must initially be enacted on a comprehensive basis, considering whatever planning had been done,[3] or (3) the decisions made in drafting the ordinance must be internally consistent and the ordinance itself implemented and interpreted in a consistent manner. The third and last approach is the majority rule. The first is generally the result of the legislature's making urban planning a mandatory activity of municipalities by statute. California and Oregon are examples of this first approach.

If and when this precondition is met, in any of its three forms, comprehensive land use ordinances are entitled to twin presumptions of constitutionality and validity. They are then upheld when they are fairly debatable and, for purposes of judicial review, have a rational basis, having a substantial relation to or nexus between the statutory authority, the police power, and the ordinance under review.

The presumption of validity is not always accorded. It is not accorded a later piecemeal rezoning of land in several situations: (1) when it is spot zoning[4] (affecting a small parcel in a non-uniform manner), or (2) when there is no showing of either a public need for the rezoning or a substantial change in the neighborhood of the

1. Standard Zoning Enabling Act § 3.

2. *See Town of Jonesville v. Powell Valley Ltd. Partnership*, 487 S.E.2d 207 (Va. 1997) (ordering a building permit issued when the zoning ordinance of the town was not based on a comprehensive plan mandated by statute).

3. *See Udell v. Haas*, 235 N.E.2d 897, 900–01 (N.Y. 1968).

4. Discussed *infra*, Chapter 11, § 11.04.

change requested,[5] or (3) when its application is exclusionary.[6] These exceptions will be discussed in later Chapters.

Enactment of a zoning or land use ordinance is typically subject to procedural requirements: notice,[7] hearings,[8] and comment periods are typical.[9] At legislative hearings, the rules of evidence do not apply and there is no right to cross examine witnesses. There is, however, a requirement that such hearings be conducted with basic fairness.[10] Sometimes an administrative body will first hold a hearing and study the ordinance, and sometimes the ordinance is even prepared by an administrative body, such as the planning commission, and then the ordinance is referred to the municipal legislature for hearings and adoption. Amendments to the ordinance are also likely to be reviewed by the planning commission.[11]

After *Village of Euclid v. Ambler Realty Company*,[12] zoning assumed its current form: that is, as with the process involved in and approved in *Euclid*, local land use control ordinances mapped the municipality, dividing it into different use districts. The "highest" (or one use) district was reserved for residential uses;[13] typically, one residential district was reserved for single-family, detached residences. In another residential district, townhouses, or duplexes might be added to the list of permitted residences.[14] And so on: types of multi-family structures were added, either as uses permitted "as of right"—that is, without further administrative action—or with an application for a special exception.[15] "Highest" in this context does not refer to the most profitable use, or the "highest and best use" of property when it is appraised, but rather to a less dense use. A rezoning from a commercial to a residential zoning use district is sometimes referred to as a "down-zoning" because less density of development is allowed and its market value has been decreased.

All permitted uses assigned to residential zones were also permitted in commercial use districts as well. And all permitted types of commercial uses enumerated as of right in commercial districts are also permitted in manufacturing and industrial districts. This pattern of cumulative permissiveness marked most zoning ordinances until well after World War II.

---

5. Discussed *infra*, Chapter 11, § 11.08.
6. Discussed *infra*, Chapter 15.
7. *See Golden Gate Corp. v. Town of Naragansett*, 359 A.2d 321, 324 (R.I. 1976).
8. *See F.P. Plaza, Inc. v. Waite*, 196 S.E.2d 141, 144 (Ga. 1973).
9. *See Bisson v. Town of Milford*, 249 A.2d 688 (N.H. 1969).
10. *See Alger v. City of Mukilteo*, 730 P.2d 1333, 1336–37 (Wash. 1987); *Smith v. Skaget Cty.*, 453 P.2d 832, 847–48 (Wash. 1969).
11. *See Wilgus v. City of Murfeesboro*, 532 S.W.2d 50 (Tenn. 1975).
12. 272 U.S. 365 (1926), the police power aspects of which are discussed in Chapter 1, *supra*, and discussed generally in Chapter 6, *supra*.
13. *See* Roy Lubove, The Urban Community: Housing and Planning in the Progressive Era 1–22 (1967) (reviewing why this is so and suggesting why the *Euclid* opinion reflects such a hierarchy of uses).
14. *See Pierro v. Baxendale*, 118 A.2d 401 (N.J. 1955) (finding the exclusion of motels from a residential district permitting rooming and boarding houses, to be reasonable).
15. The latter are discussed *infra* Chapter 10.

Use districts, when they are not cumulative, are said to be exclusive:[16] that is, the highest use district is exclusive by definition,[17] but districts "lower" in the hierarchy of uses may be exclusive as well when designated as such by the express provisions of the ordinance. Thus a commercial use district may be designated as exclusively commercial in the ordinance and all residential uses are prohibited unless grandfathered by the ordinance. There is no reason or policy limiting the designation of exclusive use districts to residential uses, and no enabling act has ever been found to preclude expanding these designations to other uses.[18] Exclusive use districts are most often used for manufacturing and industrial uses.[19]

Each use district is defined two ways. First, the zoning map locates the use within the municipality's land area.[20] The totality of a municipality's land area is thus mapped, and the map shows the area divided into territorial districts. With the passage of time, zoning maps have become more detailed, in the sense that the number of districts have increased, even as they (mostly) confirm existing patterns of land use. Second, each district is the subject of part of the text of the ordinance—where the (number of) permitted uses is listed (in an all-inclusive list) as well as any uses that are prohibited. With time, the texts of ordinances have become more restrictive and their definitions have become tighter. Also listed are height and area restrictions. Height is limited to a maximum number of feet. Area restrictions include maximum square footage[21] and coverage restrictions permitted on each parcel, and (in the case of residential uses) minimum dimensions for front, side, and rear yards. Thus the text of an ordinance actually has many different use, height, and area restrictions for each type of district.

Cumulative, map and text, ordinances are at the heart of zoning in most post-*Euclid* zoning schemes. It is no wonder that such zoning was often referred to as *Euclidian* zoning, so called because of both the geometric dimensions of its regulations and its genesis in the *Euclid* case.

Into the 1950s, the hierarchy of land uses continued apace—ordinances would contain several types of cumulative residential use districts—single family detached, duplexes, town houses, and garden apartments, for example—as well as several types of commercial use districts—convenience store retail, light retail, multi-purpose retail, department stores and big box stores, etc. In this decade also, some ordinances first contained not only exclusively residential use districts, but also permitted exclusively commercial use districts as well[22]—that is, permitted districts from which all

16. *See People ex rel. Skokie Town House Builders v. Village of Morton Grove*, 157 N.E.2d 33, 36 (Ill. 1959) (holding an exclusive residential use district valid).

17. *See Brett v. Building Comm'nr*, 145 N.E. 269, 271 (Mass. 1924) (viewing the exclusive residential single family district as justified as a means of preventing the spread of fires and as a health matter).

18. *See* Note, 32 N.Y.U. L. Rev. 1261 (1957).

19. *See Katobimar Realty Co. v. Webster*, 118 A.2d 824 (N.J. 1955) (an opinion laden with the language of Euclidian zoning and upholding an exclusive industrial use district).

20. *See Wheaton Moose Lodge No. 1775 v. Montgomery Cty.*, 397 A.2d 250, 252 (Md. App. Ct. 1979).

21. Sometimes the maximum square footage is expressed as a floor area ratio—that is, a ratio of so many square feet in a building for every square foot of land on the underlying tract.

22. *See Kozesnik v. Township of Montgomery*, 131 A.2d 1, 9 (N.J. 1957).

residential and industrial uses were excluded. Such districts readily found enabling act authority. Often they were used for the light industry emerging during the post-World War II era.

Euclid thus authorized single use zoning districts—particularly single family residential use districts—and land use regulation has used that as its pattern through the 20th century and into the 21st, from the first zoning ordinance in 1916 in New York City. Euclidian ordinances provide that regulations "shall be uniform" within use districts[23]—that is, similarly situated parcels must be similarly treated. This effectively mandates that all parcels conform to the same requirements for a minimum lot size, front and side yard size, and setback distances from neighbors' parcels. Intruding uses for industry and even apartments are zoned out. All in all, these provisions have enabled many municipalities to insulate single family suburbs from their central cities.

Euclid and Euclidian zoning are often blamed for encouraging suburban sprawl, traffic congestion, too expensive housing, social isolation, and racial segregation.[24] Residential, single family uses screened out those who, for reasons of lack of income, could not afford to live in a house. Some have claimed that Euclidian zoning has failed to protect low-income neighborhoods with the same rigor afforded middle and upper income neighborhoods. During the decade of the 1990s, New Urbanism architects and planners strove to create communities with a central commercial district, housing grouped together to create a sense of community, narrower streets to encourage pedestrian use, and parks and public buildings to provide visual focal points.[25]

Euclid's progeny must often flesh out an ordinance's words and phrases describing particular land.[26] In a residential use district, an owner's occasional short term rental may not be permitted when the ordinance permits only a "single residence" there as a matter of right.[27] Likewise, the provision "short term rentals are not allowed as the principal use of a primary dwelling" in a residential use district only limits such rentals when they are not the "principal use" of a "primary dwelling."[28] Further, in an ordinance, "the term 'residential use' depends both upon the function the property serves for its occupant and the duration of time the property is used.... Indeed, the appellate courts of at least nineteen states have decided that even rental stays of less

---

23. *See Schefer v. City Council of the City of Falls Church*, 691 S.E.2d 778, 781 (Va. 2010) ("The crux of the uniformity requirement is to assure that zoning regulations are nondiscriminatory."). This requirement originated in the 1920s Standard State Zoning Enabling Act and has been adopted in nearly every state zoning enabling act. *See Anderson House LLC v. Mayor of Rockville*, 939 A.2d 116, 131 (Md. 2008).

24. *See, e.g.*, James Kunstler, *Home from Nowhere*, The Atlantic Monthly, Sept. 1996, at 43–66.

25. *See, e.g.*, M. Southworth, *Walkable Suburbs? An Evaluation of Nontraditional Communities at the Urban Edge*, 63 J. Am. Inst. Planners 1, 1, 28–44 (No. 1, Winter 1997).

26. *See, e.g.*, *Borough of Demarest v. Heck*, 201 A.2d 75 (N.J. Super. Ct., App. Div., 1964) (whether a riding academy is an agricultural use); *Sioux Falls v. Cleveland*, 70 N.W.2d 62 (S. Dak. 1955) (addressing whether a "dwelling house, double house, or duplex" includes a trailer); *In re Application of LaPorte*, 152 N.Y.S.2d 916 (N.Y. App. Div. 1956) (whether a dorm is a single-family dwelling).

27. *See Styller v. Zoning Board of Appeals of Lynnfield*, 169 N.E.3d 160, 171 (Mass. 2021).

28. *See Ward v. Town of Nantucket*, 2024 Mass. LCR LEXIS 31, 39 (Mar. 14, 2024).

than 30 days—nightly, weekend or weeklong stays—constitute residential uses or purposes."[29] Whether short term residents were using properties for "ordinary living activities" was the crux of many of these cases.[30] Some in contrast assessed whether the short term nature of the rental affected surrounding residential uses.[31] All this is before a court would focus solely on the duration of a rental as a basis for holding that short term rentals lasting overnight or a week did not constitute a "residential use.[32] Summing up its analysis, the court in *Hawai'i Legal Short-Term Rental Alliance* stated: "Whether a use is residential depends much more on *what* is being done at a residence than for *how long*."[33] Unless an ordinance clearly has a temporal or durational component, its reference to a "single family dwelling" as a residential use permits a short term rental.[34] All-in-all, the term "residential use" itself has been by no means self-defining and whether the term is used in the context of interpreting a residential covenant or a zoning ordinance makes little difference.[35]

In further examples using analysis cross referencing other permitted uses, when an ordinance permits "private clubs" in a residential or commercial use district, such a use would exclude a shooting range, a massage parlor, a nudist camp, or a day camp for children.[36] In the same vein, a court might expand on the word "club" to be "a private association not for profit or business."[37] In an agricultural use district permitting "agricultural equipment," a court might not allow keeping a crop dusting airplane on site, in the same way that snakes would not be permitted as "livestock." A structure for recovering alcoholics might be a permitted "boardinghouse" but not a "single family residential" use. An automobile graveyard is still a prohibited "junkyard" even when its owner sells used auto parts.[38] Likewise, scattering cremains on land does not make the land a prohibited "cemetery."[39] When an ordinance for a residential use district defines a" residence" as a non-business use, and further defines a permitted "nursing home" as a "convalescent or rest home for the chronically ill, infirm, or aged, but not including hospitals, clinics, or similar institution devoted to the diagnosis or treatment of injury, disease or mental illness," it has been held to permit an owner, formerly using a parcel as a nursing home, to use it as a home for the mentally disabled.[40]

---

29. *See Hawai'i Legal Short-Term Rental Alliance v. City & County of Honolulu*, 2022 U.S. Dist. LEXIS 187189, **16–17 & n. 16 (D. Haw., Oct. 13, 2022).

30. *Id.* at *17.

31. *Id.*

32. *Id.* (noting that these cases were "outliers").

33. *Id.* at *18.

34. *See Wihbey v. Zoning Board of Appeals of the Pine Orchard Ass'n*, 292 A.3d 21, 37 (Conn. App. Ct. 2023).

35. Another context in which similar analysis is required is the evaluation of a municipal permit regime for short-term landlords. *See Calvey v. Town Board of North Elba*, 2021 U.S. Dist. LEXIS 56686 (N.D.N.Y., Mar. 25, 2021).

36. *See Board of Supervisors v. Gaffney*, 422 S.E.2d 760 (Va. 1992) (as to a nudist camp).

37. *See Montgomery County v Merlands Club, Inc.*, 96 A.2d 261 (Md. 1953).

38. *See Town of China v. Althenn*, 82 A.3d 835 (Me. 2013).

39. *See Shilling v. Baker*, 691 S.E.2d 806 (Va. 2010).

40. *Cf. Kastendike v. Baltimore Association for Retarded Children, Inc.*, 297 A.2d 745 (Md. 1972).

These examples could be multiplied many times over in every jurisdiction with a zoning ordinance. Such definitional decisions are typically made by an administrative or code enforcement official charged with implementing a zoning ordinance.

Several canons of construction control such decisions. First, the particular definition controls the general one;[41] thus the exclusion of businesses from the residential district is not construed as all-inclusive when more particular definitions of these terms are also found in the ordinance. Evidence that most nursing homes were in fact located in residential districts may provide support for the use of this canon. Second, a permissive provision controls an exclusionary one. The closely guarded right to possess and alienate one's property provides a rationale for this canon. Third, a component of a definition may be read permissively. Thus, in the example in the last paragraph, the proposed home for the mentally disabled fits within the "home for chronically ill" language of the nursing home definition. Fourth, absent evidence that a proposed use is more intensive than the past one, an existing definition should be liberally construed. Finally, when an ordinance lists both expressly permitted and prohibited uses, what is expressly permitted will be liberally construed and what is expressly prohibited will be narrowly construed.[42]

When a use is permitted, but defined in only two words, say "gas station," its ordinary and customary meaning must be sought. That a land use appears in one or two words in an ordinance and is not further defined does not render it ambiguous.[43] For example, a gas station owner may wish to open a convenience store in the cashier's area, or, as in one case, a gas station owner wished to sell to a fast food restaurant chain. The regulations for a commercial use district permitted as of right, but without further definition, a "restaurant." A restaurant is a commercial use in which food is prepared only after it is ordered from a menu and served by the restaurant's staff. If this customary definition is used, pre-prepared food served from behind a counter or on a drive thru basis may not fit the definition. Moreover, the hours of operation and the seating capacity might exceed those of any existing restaurant currently located in the district. If, however, the existing use was a business with an even more rapid rate of customer turn-over than a fast food restaurant, this fact provides an argument in favor of a liberal interpretation of the word "restaurant." The suitability of the property for the new use is relevant as well: are curb cuts already in existence? An owner's efforts to contain the external impacts and effects on the fast food business also support a liberal reading: screening for light, automobile fumes, fences, and shrubbery buffers, might be provided.[44] Close cases like this one often produce amendments to municipal regulations, defining fast food restaurants and then specially regulating them.

---

41. *See In re Wright & Rooster Conditional Use Application*, 267 A.3d 659 (Vt. 2021) (definition of boathouse controls accessory use definition).

42. *See Marshall v. East Bradford Twp. Bd. of Supervisors*, 250 A.3d 481 (Pa. Cmwlth. Ct. 2021).

43. *See Working Stiff Partners v. City of Portsmouth*, 232 A.3d 379 (N.H. 2019) (holding "dwelling unit" not an ambiguous phrase).

44. *Taco Bell, Inc. v. City of Mission*, 678 P.2d 133 (Kan. 1984).

"In construing a zoning ordinance, the permissive widest use of land is the rule and not the exception, unless specifically restrained in the valid and reasonable exercise of the police power."[45] As previously discussed, this canon of construction is justified because of the primacy of owners to use their property as they choose.[46] Here, zoning ordinances are regarded as being in derogation of the common law, and narrowly construed as a result. They are not to be extended by implication. Using this canon, a big box retailer was found to be a "retail" commercial use,[47] even though such superstores were not the norm when an ordinance was enacted.[48]

Ordinances are subject to the same canons of construction as statutes are. They are to be given their plain meaning, must be interpreted according to the canon that a reasonable and rational result was intended by the drafters; no clause or provision in it is deemed superfluous, and all its provisions must be construed as harmoniously as possible. When provisions conflict, the one leading to a reasonable result is to be selected over ones leading to bizarre and unreasonable results.[49]

Language in an ordinance that is unambiguous must be given its plain, ordinary, and natural meaning, and the ordinance itself is conclusive. Ambiguities, however, may be resolved by a study of legislative history and intent, or the origins of the ordinance. Resolving ambiguities is generally considered a matter of law to be resolved by the court. When a term is used within a given trade or industry, but unknown outside it, an ambiguity is present, to be resolved by studying its legislative history or origins.[50]

The burden of proof to bring a requested use within the uses expressly permitted in an ordinance is on the applicant.[51] Thus a nudist colony has been found not to be a "recreational facility" permitted in a residential district[52] when the ordinance contained a statement that "uses not specifically permitted are prohibited." The fact that a nudist facility would not seem to support the principal use permitted in a district, is another rationale for the result. To paraphrase Mark Twain, naked people have little or no influence in most use districts. So a lack of inconsistency with the principal use may be insufficient to meet the applicant's burden of proof; the burden is an affirmative one.

Euclidian definitions are applied with reference to the parcel employing the use. Thus the use of a residentially zoned parcel to gain access to a nearby commercially

---

45. *See Amcare 2 Partners v. Zoning Hearing Bd.*, 609 A.2d 887, 891 (Pa. Commwlth. Ct. 1992).

46. *See Jack Lingo Asset Management LLC v. Bd. of Adjustment of the City of Rehoboth Beach*, 282 A.3d 29, 37 (Del. 2022).

47. *See Beale v. Planning Bd. of Rockland*, 671 N.E.2d 1233 (Mass. 1996); *see also Indian Trail Property Owner's Ass'n v. City of Spokane*, 886 P.2d 209 (Wash. App. Ct. 1994).

48. *See Great Atlantic & Pacific Tea Co. v. Town of East Hampton*, 997 F. Supp. 340 (E.D.N.Y. 1998) (reviewing a big box ordinance).

49. *See Graff v. Zoning Bd. of Appeals*, 894 A.2d 285, 291–92 (Conn. 2006).

50. *See Bannum Inc. v. Board of Zoning Adjustment*, 894 A.2d 423, 433 (D.C. 2006) (referring to the words "community correctional facility" as a penal industry one).

51. *See County of Fairfax v. Parker*, 44 S.E.2d 9, 13 (Va. 1947).

52. *Board of Supervisors of Madison Cty. v. Gaffney*, 422 S.E.2d 760 (Va. 1992).

zoned use is itself a commercial use, and may be prohibited in a residential zone.[53] The access is considered to be in the same use as the parcel to which the access leads.[54] Similarly, a pig, pictured at home in his sty in the *Euclid* case only in an agricultural use district, might be considered a "household pet" permitted in a residential use district—in Hawaii,[55] but not in Illinois.[56]

Zoning maps must confirm existing use patterns. When they do not, the ordinance has moved too far in advance of the market and the regulation (say, a restriction to a residential use) has been found to be a taking—the ordinance restriction being as a result invalid and unenforceable.[57] Comprehensive planning for the ordinance may be too far-sighted. The ordinance must be justified by organizing an existing market for (say) undeveloped land, rather than attempting to make a market that has not previously existed. Often this can be accomplished by placing land in a so-called holding zone or a use district that is only slightly more restrictive than persons in the present market would have liked.

§7.02 Accessory Uses

An accessory use is permitted when it is clearly, customarily, and incidentally subordinate to the a principal, permitted use of a parcel.[58] It must aid or contribute to the principal use in some way. For example, millinery work is a permitted "home occupation" because it is an outgrowth of a home-centered activity such as sewing.[59] So might the work of a laundress qualify as a home occupation. Hour by hour evidence might support these results.

No similar support is possible for a stained glass window business operated from a residence in a residential use district that defines a residence as a "non-business, residential use, including customary home occupations." When the owner's business is the principal use of the parcel and not an accessory one, the ordinance is violated. Several types of evidence show such a violation: advertising in the telephone book, the incorporation of the business, its taking federal and state income tax deductions designed for businesses, and signs along the nearby roads directing customers to the parcel. All will provide evidence that the owner is not conducting an accessory use

53. *See City of Providence v. First Nat'l Stores, Inc.*, 210 A.2d 656, 659 (R.I. 1965).

54. *See Beale v. Planning Bd. of Rockland*, 671 N.E.2d 1233, 1236 (Mass. 1996).

55. *See Foster Village Community Ass'n v. Hess*, 667 P.2d 850 (Haw. App. Ct. 1983).

56. *See Village of Glenview v. Ramaker*, 668 N.E.2d 106 (Ill. App. Ct. 1996).

57. *See Averne Bay Const. Co. v. Thatcher*, 15 N.E.2d 587, 590–91 (N.Y. 1938).

58. *See County Comm'rs of Carroll Cty. v. Zent*, 587 A.2d 1205, 1213–16 (Md. App. Ct. 1991) (thoroughly reviewing the law of accessory uses); *In the Matter of N.Y. Botanical Garden v. Board of Stds. and Appeals of the City of New York*, 694 N.E.2d 424 (N.Y. 1998); *Zalarick v. Monroe Cty.*, 467 So. 2d 1088 (Fla. App. 1985).

59. *See People v. Kelly*, 175 N.E. 108 (N.Y. 1931).

or, where permitted, a "home occupation." Because stained glass is not customarily found in homes, its creation on a residential parcel arguably violates the ordinance.[60]

An accessory use is one that is clearly and customarily subsidiary or incidental to a dominant, main, or principal use.[61] Tool-sheds, garages, patios, and small decks might be typical examples of an accessory use in a residential use district. So there, a dog house might be an accessary use, whereas a kennel might not. Further, parking a light truck or sports utility vehicle in a house's garage is permitted, while parking the cab of an eighteen-wheeler is not, even if the householder is a long-distance truck driver; in a residential use district, tractor-trailer transportation is not a customary activity.[62] Likewise, maintaining a greenhouse to grow flowers and houseplants in a residential use district is an accessory use; growing cannabis plants there would not change this result, but expanding the greenhouse to install cannabis-processing facilities would.

When a zoning ordinance does not expressly provide for accessory uses, they may be implied by the courts.[63] Even when carrying criminal sanctions for misuse, accessory uses (defined as customary and incidental to a principal use) have been upheld against a charge of unconstitutional vagueness.[64] Determining what constitutes a use as an accessory one is normally a question of fact and to be determined by the zoning administrator reading the ordinance liberally but reasonably.[65] After all, what's being protected is an owner's right to use and enjoy his or her own property.

The scope of accessory uses is typically expressly defined in terms of smaller, ancillary structures on a parcel,[66] but their definition need not be limited to structures. Events tents at a yacht or golf club might be accessory uses. They must, however, usually be located on the same parcel as the principal use is.[67] Thus, the operation of a marina adjacent to a riparian residential parcel is not an accessory use. An accessory use must be so necessary to the principal permitted use, and thus expected to be present, that it cannot be inferred that the regulation was intended to prevent their

---

60. *See Narbonne v. Town of Rye*, 534 A.2d 388 (N.H. 1987) (finding a stained glass business a violation of regulations for a residential district).

61. *See Whaley v. Dorchester Cty. Zoning Bd. of Appeals*, 524 S.E.2d 404, 410 (Va. 1999) (hereafter "*Whaley*"); *Platts v. Zoning Hearing Bd. of the Borough of Bradford Woods*, 654 A.2d 149, 152–53 (Pa. Commwlth. Ct. 1994).

62. *See County of Twin Falls v. Hettinga*, 254 P.3d 510 (Idaho Ct. App. 2011); *Whaley*, *op. cit.*, 524 S.E.2d at 410 (S.C. 1999).

63. *See Treisman v. Town of Bedford*, 563 A.2d 786 (1989) (so holding).

64. *See DeVoe v.City of Missoula*, 274 P.3d 752 (Mont. 2012); *Arizona v. Trachman*, 947 P.2d 905, 908–909 (Ariz. App. Ct. 1997) (involving the storage of autos for repair and restoration); *Bitts v. Board of Adjustment*, 765 P.2d 1077 (Colo. 1988).

65. *See The UpJohn Co. v. Planning and Zoning Comm'n of the Town of North Haven*, 616 A.2d 786, 789 (Conn. 1992).

66. *See Whaley*, *supra*, 524 S.E.2d at 411 (quoting, in the dissenting opinion, the definition of "a detached building or structure which is detached from and subordinate to a principal building/facility or use on a lot and used for [a] purpose customarily incidental to the principal use, including, but not limited to, garages, greenhouses, guest homes, servants' quarters, custodial or security quarters, swimming pools and tennis courts, cable satellite antenna or other radio transmitting/receiving antenna.").

67. *See Baccouche v. Blankenship*, 2007 Cal. App. LEXIS 1516 (Sept. 11, 2007).

presence.[68] Thus parking a commercial vehicle on the street abutting a residential use is not an accessory use of a parcel.[69] Nor would it become so if the vehicle was parked on the parcel.[70]

The storage of general contracting equipment on a parcel legally used for conducting this business is an accessory use.[71] So might the storage of explosives be an accessory use to a general contracting business.[72] Thus an accessory use must be defined in light of the principal use. An use accessory to a residential use must not be a commercial use. A chicken coop in a residential use district is not an accessory use.[73] But a child care operation might be an accessory to a religious use,[74] and so might an activities parish hall,[75] but a storage shed might not.[76] A sign is an accessory use for an office building.[77] This is particularly so when the sign advertises the use within the building, but is less likely to be found an accessory use if it advertises an off-premises use. Likewise, a gas pump might be accessory to a convenience store,[78] as is a parking area accessory to a travel plaza.[79]

An addition to a residence is not an accessory use or structure, even when one function of a residential use like cooking is transferred to the addition.[80] When the addition replicates the functions of the main structure, it is neither incidental nor customarily regarded as an accessory use.[81] Moreover, when a structure completely replicates the functions of a residence on a parcel, it is likewise not an accessory use: in this situation, both structures are houses, with neither incidental or secondary to the other.[82]

An accessory use definition must be formulated in light of the changing land use pattern of the district. When a parcel is rezoned from agricultural to residential, a riding facility might be grandfathered into the new district, but the owner's rodeo shows

---

68. *See Dawkins & Smith Homes, LLC v. Lowndes Cty.*, 701 S.E.2d 744 (Ga. Ct. App. 2010); *Borough of Northvale v. Blundo*, 203 A.2d 721, 723 (N.J. Super. Ct., App. Div., 1964).

69. *Id.*

70. *See Cty. of Twin Falls v. Hettinga*, 254 P.3d 510 (Idaho Ct. App. 2011).

71. *See Greenfield v. Board of City Planning Comm'rs of the City of Los Angeles*, 45 P.2d 219 (Cal. 1935).

72. *See Clifford v. Zoning Comm'n of the City of Ansonia*, 908 A.2d 1049, 1060–61 (Conn. 2006).

73. *See Chudonov v. Board of Appeals of Bloomfield*, 154 A. 161 (Conn. 1931).

74. *See Shim v. Washington Twp. Planning Bd.*, 689 A.2d 804, 807 (N.J. Super. Ct., App. Div. 1997); *see also City of Richmond Heights v. Richmond Heights Presbyterian Church*, 764 S.W.2d 647 (Mo. 1989).

75. *See Diocese of Altoona-Johnstown v. Zoning Hearing Bd. of the Borough of State College*, 899 A.2d 399 (Pa. Commwlth. Ct. 2006).

76. *See Grandview Baptist Church v. Zoning Bd. of Adjustment of the City of Davenport*, 301 N.W.2d 704 (Iowa 1981).

77. *See Towers Management Co. v. Thatcher*, 2 N.E.2d 273 (N.Y. App. Div. 1936).

78. *See Borough of Fleetwood v. Zoning Hearing Bd. of Borough of Fleetwood*, 649 A.2d 651 (Pa. 1994). *But see Singal v. City of Bangor*, 440 A.2d 1048 (Me. 1982).

79. *See Flying J, Inc. v. City of New Haven Bd. of Zoning Appeals*, 855 N.E.2d 1035 (Ind. Ct. App. 2006).

80. *See Stiff v. Town of Belgrade*, 322 A.3d 1167, 1172 (Me. 2024).

81. *Id.* at 1172–73.

82. *Id.* at n.10.

might nonetheless be considered as requiring a special exception to be applied for and granted before it is permitted to continue.[83] Changing environmental sensibilities may be considered as well.[84] Stabling horses has been much litigated in this regard.[85]

Accessory uses must be both customary and incidental to a principal use. "Customary" has most often been taken to mean common.[86] As such, landing and parking a helicopter in a residential use district might be prohibited as not customarily done.[87] The prohibition might also be justified on the ground that, if every user in the district were allowed to do this, the resulting noise, dust, and disruption would be out of proportion to anything resembling a reasonable use of the parcels in the district.[88] Most people don't customarily commute or travel by helicopter.

A customary accessory use must further be habitual and a long established practice.[89] Thus what is customary need not always be common in the neighborhood, or considered unobjectionable by most, but should instead be evaluated by means of a "community sensitive" but state wide standard.[90] Testimony about whether a use is customary must go beyond whether any two uses are found together on one parcel, but must also indicate that one use is principal, and one accessory.[91] For example, in an agricultural use district, boarding horses is not an established agricultural practice, even though horses might fit the definition of permitted "agricultural livestock"; the noise, dust, and traffic generated by a stable boarding horses owned by others distinguishes this stable from the stabling horses owned by the farmer.[92] Conversely, when a boarding stable is permitted, a riding arena to exercise the horses becomes a customary accessory use.[93]

"Incidental to a principal use" means subordinate to a use, perhaps not the predominant use, but subordinate to another accessory use—much like elephants

---

83. *Murphy v. Town of Chino Valley*, 789 P.2d 1072 (Ariz. App. Ct. 1989). *See also County Comm'nrs of Carroll Cty. v. Zent*, 587 A.2d 1205, 1213–16 (Md. App. Ct. 1991).

84. *See The UpJohn Co. v. Planning and Zoning Comm'n of the Town of North Haven*, 616 A.2d 786 (Conn. 1992) (holding that the storage of waste was not an accessory use).

85. *See LeCompte v. Zoning Bd. of Appeals of the Village of Barrington Hills*, 958 N.E.2d 1065 (Ill. Ct. App. 2011).

86. The word might also mean "customarily incidental." *See Sky's the Limit, Inc. v. Zoning Hearing Bd. of Smithfield Twp.*, 18 A.3d 409, 413 (Pa. Commwlth. Ct. 2011) (describing the combined phrase as bringing objectivity to the test and holding that a campground is not customarily incidental to an airport).

87. *See Redington Ranch Assoc. v. Redman*, 737 P.2d 808 (Ariz. App. Ct. 1987).

88. *Id.* at 809.

89. *See McKinnney v. Kent Cty. Bd. of Adjustment*, 1995 Del. Super. LEXIS 83, *10 (Feb. 13, 1995).

90. *"The Commissioners of Bellefonte" v. Coppola*, 453 A.2d 457, 461 (Del. 1982) (citing Lewis J. Smith, *Zoning: Accessory Uses and the Meaning of the "Customary" Requirement*, 56 B.U. L. Rev. 542, 549).

91. *See Kobyluck v. Zoning Bd. of Appeals, Town of Montville*, 1998 Conn. Super. LEXIS 454, *8 (Feb. 18, 1998).

92. *See LeCompte v. Zoning Bd. of Appeals for the Village of Barrington Hills*, 958 N.E.2d 1065 (Ill. App. Ct. 2011).

93. *See Tennyson v. Zoning Hearing Bd. of West Bradford Twp.*, 952 A.2d 739 (Pa. Cmwlth. Ct. 2008).

marching trunk to tail—a recognition that an accessory use can in itself be attached to an accessory use. Thus, an accessory use might be attached to a home occupation conducted on a residentially zoned parcel.[94] In an agricultural use district, growing a marijuana crop in a greenhouse might be the primary use, and a co-generation facility for the greenhouse might be incidental to growing it there.[95] The word "incidental" here means that the use requested must not be the primary one, but minor in significance or importance in comparison to the primary use.[96] An hour by hour use comparison might be used to show an incidental use.[97] The relative sizes of two structures may be one factor is determining whether one of them is incidental or subordinate to the other.[98] This is particularly true when a newer structure is greater in size than an older one.

Finally, accessory uses may be restricted to side or rear yards in residential districts, or confined to the rear portion of a parcel, or made subject to set-back restrictions.[99] Likewise, even though in an underlying use district where accessory uses are permitted as of right, a structure incidental to a use operating as a special exception or conditional use may not be built as of right.[100] The more specific provisions governing conditional uses control.

§ 7.03 Non-Conforming Uses

A land use which precedes a zoning regulation, but which becomes illegal under the subsequently effective ordinance, is called non-conforming.[101] A lawful nonconforming use is a use that predated the enactment of a prohibitory zoning regulation.[102] Such a use has two elements: (1) it must be a legal use just before the prohibition is enacted and (2) it must be in such a use just before and after the enactment.

"The primary purpose behind zoning is to bring about the orderly physical development of a community by confining particular uses to defined areas. A goal of zoning is to gradually eliminate nonconforming uses because they are inconsistent with the purpose of developing use-consistent areas in communities."[103] The prevailing view is

---

94. *Cf. Dupont Circle Citizens Ass'n v. District of Columbia Bd. of Zoning Adjustment*, 749 A.2d 1258, 1262, n. 11 (D.C. App. 2000) (finding catered events for guest in a bed and breakfast house permitted).

95. *See Valley Green Grow, Inc. v. Town of Charlton*, 173 N.E.3d 395 (Mass. Ct. App. 2021).

96. *See Henry v. Board of Appeals of Dunstable*, 641 N.E.2d 1334 (Mass. 1994).

97. *Id.*

98. *See Risker v. Zoning Hearing Bd.*, 886 A.2d 727, 732 (Pa. Commwlth. Ct. 2005).

99. *See Sundeen v. Rogers*, 141 A. 142 (N.H. 1928).

100. *See Four Seasons Management Services v. Town of Wrightsville Beach*, 695 S.E.2d 456 (N.C. Ct. App. 2010).

101. *See Odegard Outdoor Advertising, LLC v. Board of Zoning Adjustment of Jackson Cty.*, 6 S.W.3d 148, 150, n. 1 (Mo. 1999). *See also Tuzeer v. YIM, LLC*, 29 A.3d 1019, 1029 (Md. Ct. Spec. App. 2011).

102. *See DoMiJo LLC v. McLain*, 41 A.3d 967 (Pa. Cmwlth. Ct. 2012).

103. *See In re Gregoire*, 742 A.2d 1232, 1235 (Vt. 1999) (citations omitted).

that non-conforming uses "should be abolished or reduced to conformity as quickly as the fair interest of the parties will permit."[104] As one opinion more forcefully said: "Nonconforming uses are a thorn in the side of proper zoning and should not be perpetuated any longer than necessary. The policy of zoning is to abolish nonconforming uses as speedily as justice will permit."[105] Each nonconforming use is meanwhile to be strictly construed in light of a strong state policy to eliminate them.[106] Also, no nonconformity is free of nuisance liability, nor is it free of the requirement of a license to operate when other such businesses must be licensed.[107]

Although prohibited expressly in an ordinance, a non-conforming use is permitted because it is grandfathered.[108] They are permitted so that the ordinance will not have a retroactive effect amounting to a taking and in order to damp down litigation over its application. If the uses were to be abolished outright, there would also be a violation of substantive due process: their owners would lose the right to use them as before without receiving any benefit back. They are vested rights entitled to constitutional protection.[109] Their owners have, in property law terms, an interest that runs with the land so long as it is not abandoned or discontinued.[110] That grandfathered interest may be established by a consent decree to end litigation over what use has been grandfathered, although the decree may not bargain away a municipality's enforcement powers when the use is abandoned or discontinued.[111]

Such a use could be condemned through the use of eminent domain procedures, but this is costly, and as early city planners and attorneys advocating zoning thought, unnecessary because such uses would, like the Marxist state, just "wither away." They seldom do. Indeed, sometimes their non-conforming nature makes them more valuable and gives them, as in the instance of a grocery store in a residential district, a monopoly value. They "continue and prosper because of the artificial monopoly accorded them by the law."[112] In this sense, they are valuable rights. They are recognized and permitted to continue, simply because they existed prior to the enactment of the zoning ordinance, but their extension and expansion is limited because of the overall goal of zoning. For example, barns built in a formerly agricultural area become

---

104. *See Hyatt v. Zoning Bd. of Appeals*, 311 A.2d 77 (Conn. 1972). *See also Tuzeer*, *supra*, 29 A.3d at 1029.

105. *See Inhabitants of Windham v. Sprague*, 219 A.2d 548, 552–53 (Me. 1966)

106. *See In re Appeal of Laskins*, 807 A.2d 420, 424 (Vt. 2002).

107. *See Guy v. Town of Temple*, 956 A.2d 272 (N.H. 2008) (licensing is concerned with the operation of the use, not the use itself, and citing cases from Illinois, Iowa, Kentucky, Maryland, Minnesota, New York, and Wisconsin to same effect).

108. *See Pope v. Little Boar's Head District*, 764 A.2d 932 (N.H. 2000) (distinguishing between a variance and a nonconformity: the latter permitted because it is grandfathered without regulatory action, the former permitted by zoning regulators).

109. *See Tuzeer*, *supra*, 29 A.3d at 1029; *Petruzzi v. Zoning Bd. of Appeals*, 408 A.2d 243 (Conn. 1979).

110. *See PAJ Ventures LP v. Zoning Hearing Bd. of Moore Twp.*, 225 A.3d 891, 898 (Pa. Cmwlth. Ct. 2020).

111. *See Pike Industries, Inc. v. City of Westbrook*, 96 A.3d 73, 77 (Me. 2014).

112. *See Bd. of Supervisors of Cerro Gordo County v. Miller*, 170 N.W.2d 358, 362 (Iowa 1969).

non-conforming uses as the farms are given over to residences and are zoned into residential use districts.

Municipal ordinances usually restrict the use's enlargement and prohibit both rebuilding it after destruction and its reuse after abandonment. Typically, sixty to seventy five percent of the value of the improvements must be destroyed before reconstruction can be enjoined.[113] Lapse of time showing an abandonment may also justify a use's discontinuation.[114] Thereafter, subsequent owners of the parcel may be bound by the prior owner's abandonment of the use.

A single parcel may be the source of multiple non-conforming uses. Thus, a hotel can be both a hotel and an entertainment complex.[115] A gas station can be both a gas station and a convenience store.[116] Thus, the present use of a parcel can be non-conforming in more than one sense, just as a parcel can be non-conforming as to later-enacted set-backs, a height restrictions, minimum parcel sizes,[117] or on-site parking regulations.[118] Occasionally a non-conforming use arises due to the erroneously-issued and ambiguous building permit to restore a use which is already non-conforming in some other respect.[119] This last method of establishing non-conformity will usually rely on an authorizing statute,[120] since ordinarily an erroneously issued permit is regarded as a nullity.

The legal doctrines protecting non-conforming uses are a particular instance of the use of estoppel and of the problem of vested rights we will discuss later in this treatise.[121] The earliest situation that might give rise to vested rights occurs when a development project, about to become illegal under a pending ordinance, is not completed before date of the prohibitory ordinance's effective date. Courts addressing this situation use a combination of estoppel and vested rights law from other situations to resolve it. So, when an owner or developer has expended substantial amounts of money[122] and procured all necessary building and construction permits as the development proceeds, vested rights are accorded and he or she acquires non-conforming

113. *See Mayberry v. Town of Old Orchard Beach*, 599 A.2d 1153, 1154–55 (Me. 1991) (non-conforming use for house unoccupied for two years lapses).

114. *See generally* Annot., *Right to resume nonconforming use of premises after voluntary or unexplained break in the continuity of nonconforming use*, 57 A.L.R.3d 279 (1974); Annot., *Right to resume nonconforming use of premises after involuntary break in the continuity of nonconforming use unrelated to governmental activity*, 56 A.L.R.3d 14 (1974).

115. *See Cape Resort Hotels, Inc. v. Alcoholic Licensing Bd. of Falmouth*, 431 N.E.2d 213, 215–16 (Mass. 1982).

116. *See In re Newton Enterprises*, 708 A.2d 914, 915 (Vt. 1998).

117. *See Aydelott v. City of Portland*, 990 A.2d 1024, 1028 (Me. 2010).

118. *See Reich v. Borough of Fort Lee Zoning Bd. of Adjustment*, 999 A.2d 507, 516 (N.J. Super. Ct., App. Div. 2010).

119. *See In re Barry*, 16 A.3d 613, 618–19 (Vt. 2011) (construing the ambiguity in favor of the owner relying on it).

120. *Id.* at 618.

121. *See infra*, Chapter 21, §§ 21.02, 21.03

122. In some jurisdictions, the money must be used for construction, as opposed to (say) attorneys' fees and other activities not directed toward the construction site.

use status.[123] In a minority of states, courts only look at the amount of money expended. However, when a municipality proves that the alleged nonconformity really operates with a variance from local regulations at the time of enactment of a prohibitory ordinance, the burden of proofs shifts back to the owner to show otherwise.[124] If a use previously permitted is rendered nonconforming but does not at the time of the enactment of the prohibitory ordinance meet all of the regulations for conformity with the existing zoning, its owner may be permitted to bring the use into compliance in order to attain nonconforming status.[125]

As previously discussed, an owner claiming nonconformity has the burden of proof.[126] Indeed, to establish a non-conforming use, an owner must prove that the use existed before the ordinance. The components of this burden of proof follow from the definition of nonconformity: the applicant must show that (1) the use existed as a legal use when the ordinance was enacted, and (2) it was maintained thereafter, down to the date of the litigation.[127] The first component essentially means that the applicant must show that his use was once legal, but isn't now, under the ordinance rendering it illegal.[128] (Conversely, preexisting illegal uses cannot become nonconforming uses.) Proving past legality may involve production of prior zoning codes, certificates of occupancy, and municipal building or occupancy permits. It is not up to the municipality to show that no permits were then issued; the burden is on the applicant to produce them.[129] The evidentiary standard imposed on him is typically proof by a preponderance of the evidence.

State zoning statutes may show a protectiveness toward such uses. Their policy is to prevent zoning ordinances from having retroactive application merely because of deterioration and wear and tear. Permitting non-conforming structures to be "reasonably repaired" or rebuilt when "partially destroyed" are typical statutory phrases used to protect them.[130] Without enabling act guidance, however, courts may resist rigid

---

123. *See Western Land Equities, Inc. v. City of Logan*, 617 P.2d 388 (Utah 1980).

124. *See Inhabitants of Windham v. Sprague*, 219 A.2d 548 (Me. 1966).

125. *See Balough v. Fairbanks North Star Borough*, 995 P.2d 245 (Alaska 2000). *See also Snake River Brewing Co. v. Town of Jackson*, 39 P.3d 397 (Wyo. 2002).

126. *See Cosseboom v. Town of Epsom*, 771 A.2d 565 (N.H. 2001) (lot found non-conforming as to acreage requirement of zoning ordinance).

127. *See Griswold v. City of Homer*, 55 P.3d 64 (Alaska 2002) (doing occasional car repairs does not preserve nonconformity for an auto repair shop).

128. *See Galinsky Family Real Estate, LLC v. City of Des Moines Zoning Bd. of Adjustment*, 2011 Iowa App. LEXIS 57, *14–15 (Jan. 20, 2011); *see also McClure v. City of Hurricane*, 711 S.E.2d 552, 559 (W. Va. 2010).

129. *See Town of Front Royal v. Martin Media*, 542 S.E.2d 373 (Va. 2001); *Abbington Ctr., LLC v. Town of Collierville*, 2012 Tenn. App. LEXIS 95, *37 (Feb. 13, 2012).

130. *See Avalon Home & Land Owner's Ass'n v. Avalon*, 543 A.2d 950 (N.J. 1988) (striking down an ordinance permitting non-conforming structure to be rebuilt when the footprint and volume did not exceed the pre-existing structure as *ultra vires* the state enabling act authorizing rebuilding only upon partial destruction). *See also Lamar Advantage GP Co. v. City of Pittsburgh Zoning Bd. of Adjustment*, 244 A.3d 348 (Pa. 2021) (draping a static sign over an electronic one is not a prohibited "enlargement" of a nonconforming sign).

rules about continuing a use.[131] Statutes and ordinances also typically provide that an abandoned non-conforming use is terminated.[132] In this, the common law meaning of an abandonment typically provides the standard for fleshing out the meaning of such a provision.[133] At common law, abandonment is a voluntary, affirmative act, coupled with a clear intent to repudiate the use; non-use is insufficient, even if long continued.[134] However, a frequently encountered approach is an ordinance provision that states that a non-conforming use discontinued for (say) six months is terminated or presumed to be abandoned, without requiring a finding of a common law abandonment.[135] The lapse of time required in this form of statutory "abandonment" varies from as short a time as 30 days to up to two years. It is justified as capable of objective proof, and is less likely than the use of the common law's definition of abandonment to induce perjury as to motive or intent.[136] "A unsubstantiated assertion of intention cannot carry the day for that would substantially impair, if not defeat, advancement of the elimination policy."[137] In this context, abandonment must be "active and actual," focusing not on intent, but on an owner's failure to make an actual use of the property.[138] "An ordinance that by its own terms does not require subjective intent to abandon a nonconforming use is constitutional."[139] Using this form of statutory abandonment, a tenant's discontinuance of a nonconforming use may result in the loss of nonconformity for his landlord.[140]

Consider some land use changes that might occur over time to a Civil War era mansion, first used as a residence, then as a funeral home, and, with the advent of the municipality's first zoning ordinance, remaining a funeral home as a non-conforming use located in a residential district until its owners propose to sell and relocate their business elsewhere. Then consider what would happen if they decided to sell to new owners who propose to use the mansion as a bed and breakfast. Those new owners will need land use counsel to sort this matter out. Why? Because although restoration, resumption, reconstruction, or substantial expansion of a non-conforming use is subject to reasonable regulation, the substitution of one non-conforming use for another

131. *See Ruby v. Carlisle Zoning Hearing Bd.*, 488 A.2d 655 (Pa. Commw. Ct. 1985) (ordinance found invalid when terminating use if 50% of bulk or value was destroyed).

132. *See Washington Arcade Assoc. v. Zoning Board of Review*, 528 A.2d 736 (R.I. 1987).

133. *Id. See also Lewis v. Maine Coast Artists*, 770 A.2d 644, 650 (Me. 2001).

134. *Id.* (involving a renovation permit for a non-conforming art gallery).

135. *See Trip Assocs., Inc. v. Mayor and City Council of Baltimore*, 898 A.2d 449 (Md. 2006) (as to an adult entertainment club); *Toys 'R' Us v. Silva*, 676 N.E.2d 862 (N.Y. 1996), noted in 62 Alb. L. Rev. 323 (1998); *see also Hartley v. City of Colorado Springs*, 764 P.2d 1216 (Colo. 1988).

136. *See Tuzeer v. YIM, LLC*, 29 A.3d 1019, 1037–38 (Md. Ct. Spec. App. 2011).

137. *See S&S v. Zoning Bd. for Strafford*, 862 A.2d 1204, 1211 (N.J. Super. Ct. 2004).

138. *Id.* at 1039.

139. *See Pike Industries, Inc. v. Woodward*, 999 A.2d 257, 261 (N.H. 2010); *McKenzie v. Town of Eaton Zoning Bd. of Adjustment*, 917 A.2d 193, 197 (N.H. 2007) (collecting cases from other jurisdictions). *See generally* Patricia Salkin, *Abandonment, Discontinuance, and Amortization of Nonconforming Uses: Lessons for Drafters of Zoning Ordinances*, 38 Real Est. L.J. 486, 488–500 (2010).

140. *See Gorgone v. District of Columbia Bd. of Zoning Appeals*, 973 A.2d 692 (D.C. 2006) (discontinuance of a nonconforming deli when tenant used property as a restaurant).

raises the issues of (1) whether the substituted use is more or less appropriate than the pre-existing one,[141] and (2) whether there is a substantial similarity between the use as it was at the time it became non-conforming and the changed use. With a more appropriate use or substantial similarity established, the right to the use continues.[142] Because any ordinance should be read so as to uphold its constitutionality, when the substituted use is "determined to be closer to the desired residential use, then it is a move 'up the use chain' and would satisfy the ordinance."[143] When a substituted use is closer to permitted uses than the pre-existing one, the transfer is permitted to protect the alienability of the non-conforming parcel.[144] Thus, a nonconforming use previously used as a sawmill might be converted into a stone crush and grinding operation because of the similarities between both operations.[145] When both the quantity and the quality of the use changes, however, the change will not be permitted.[146] Even if the new use is a more intensive one, that alone is not a sufficient basis to refuse to continue a structure's status as a non-conforming use.[147] For example, a non-conforming deck might be permitted to expand into an existing garage, so that the overall land use is no more intense than it was before the expansion.[148] Non-conforming uses are permitted to continue, even though their survival is not encouraged. Non-conforming uses that do not amount to a nuisance are not to be treated differently from other land uses.[149]

"Courts have consistently recognized that an increase in the scope, the scale, or the extent of a non-conforming use" is an impermissible enlargement.[150] Ordinances typically provide that no non-conforming use may be "enlarged, increased, expanded, or moved." Interpreting these words is a question of law, and courts will not strain them beyond their ordinary meaning; thus increasing the height of a communications tower is not to "move" it.[151] On the other hand, even leasing a tower might signal an expansion under appropriate circumstances.[152] Likewise, replacing hot batch equipment with a continuous flow operation is an impermissible expansion

141. *See Shire Inn, Inc. v. Borough of Avon-By-The-Sea*, 729 A.2d 473 (N.J. Super. Ct., App. Div. 1999) (refusing to permit inn to become a rooming house, even when it would be arguably an affordable housing project).

142. *See Town of Salem v. Wickson*, 770 A.2d 1120, 1123 (N.H. 2001) (involving a pig farm's stockpiling treated manure).

143. *See Kopietz v. Zoning Bd. of Appeals for the City of the Village of Clarkston*, 535 N.W.2d 910, 912 (Mich. Ct. App. 1995) (permitting such a change).

144. *See Adolphson v. Zoning Bd. of Appeals*, 535 A.2d 799 (Conn. 1988).

145. *See Sowich v. Zoning Hearing Bd. of Brown Twp.*, 243 A.3d 1188 (Pa. Cmwlth. Ct. 2021).

146. *See Turbat Creek Preservation, LLC v. Town of Kennebunkport*, 753 A.2d 489, 493 (Me. 2000) (boathouse converted for overnight stays).

147. *See In re Miserocchi*, 749 A.2d 607, 612 (Vt. 2000).

148. *See Sproul v. Town of Boothbay Harbor*, 746 A.2d 368, 371–72 (Vt. 2000) (reviewing legislation for junkyards).

149. *Cf. Husti v. Zuckerman Property Enterprises, Ltd.*, 508 A.2d 735 (Conn. 1986) (prohibiting the use of country club as a concert and theater venue).

150. *See APAC-Atlantic, Inc. v. City of Salisbury*, 709 S.E.2d 390, 394–95 (N.C. Ct. App. 2011).

151. *See Kelsea v. Town of Pembroke*, 771 A.2d 587, 590 (N.H. 2001).

152. *Cf. Zachs v. Zoning Bd. of Appeals*, 589 A.2d 351, 355 (Conn. 1991).

or enlargement of an asphalt plant.[153] Likewise, a marina is an impermissible expansion of a yacht club.[154]

When deciding whether an activity or physical expansion of a nonconforming use renders the use illegal, courts generally examine three factors: (1) the extent to which the expanded use "reflects the nature and purpose of the original use";[155] (2) "any differences in the character, nature, and kind of use involve"; and (3) "any substantial difference on the neighborhood" produced by the expansion.[156] Whether an expansion is impermissible is a question of fact. If the non-conforming use is used to operate a business, most courts agree that an increase in the number of business transactions on the property is not an impermissible expansion. Expansions to protect the economic viability of a business or to take advantage of increases in trade are also protected.[157] Further, the additional of a seating area in a convenience store newly enabled to serve alcoholic beverages by the issuance of a liquor license is likewise permissible.[158] This follows that general rule that municipal licenses and permits active just before the enactment of the prohibitory ordinance accompany the land use achieving non-conforming status.[159] This general rule has been applied even when the on-going permit licensed musical concerts on an adjoining public park.[160]

The continuance of a non-conforming use is at times subjected to a municipal registration requirement, and failure to register initiates a hearing procedure on the use's discontinuance.[161] The expansion of a non-conforming use is, in some municipalities, regulated by requiring the owner to apply for a special exception of some type.[162] Junkyards and auto graveyards are particularly apt subjects for such regulation.[163] The administrative proceeding reviewing such an application is to assess whether the expansion will have a substantially different effect or impact on the surrounding parcels or neighborhood than the non-conforming use had previously.

Operating as a special exception, a non-conforming use can lose its status as such.[164] It must thereafter continue as a special exception, since the non-conforming use is often deemed abandoned when the special exception for it is granted but not acted upon. The granting of the special exception brings the parcel into conformance

---

153. *See APAC-Atlantic, supra*, 709 S.E.2d at 397 (decided under an ordinance providing that a non-conforming use "shall not be expanded, changed, or enlarged").

154. *See Campbell v. Tiverton Zoning Bd.*, 15 A.3d 1015, 1023 (R.I. 2011).

155. *See Donaghy v. Bd. of Adjustment of the City of Green River*, 55 P.3d 707 (Wyo. 2002).

156. *See Zachs v. Zoning Bd. of Appeals*, 589 A.2d 351 (Conn. 1991).

157. *See, e.g., Nettleton v. Zoning Bd. of Adjustment of the City of Pittsburgh*, 828 A.2d 1033, 1037 (Pa. 2003). For an opinion rejecting the doctrine, see *Town of Richmond v. Wawaloam Reservation, Inc.*, 850 A.2d 977 (R.I. 2004).

158. *See Dipal Corp. v. Chartiers Twp. Zoning Hearing Bd.*, 261 A.3d 1099 (Pa. Comm. Ct. 2021).

159. *See Pfister v. Madison Beach Hotel LLC*, 267 A.3d 811 (Conn. 2022).

160. *Id.*

161. *See DoMiJo, LLC v. McLain*, 41 A.3d 967 (Pa. Commw. Ct. 2012).

162. *See Hurley v. Town of Hollis*, 729 A.2d 998, 1000 (N.H. 1999).

163. *See Balough v. Fairbanks North Star Borough*, 995 P.2d 245 (Alaska 2000).

164. *See Purich v. Draper Properties, Inc.*, 912 A.2d 598 (Md. 2006). *See also Lamar Adv. Co. v. Zoning Hearing Bd. of Monroeville*, 939 A.2d 994, 1004 (Pa. Commw. Ct. 2007).

with the zoning and so is inconsistent with the continuance of the non-conforming use. Non-conformity should be narrowly construed, being a thorn in the side of the zoning ordinance: it should be eliminated as speedily as justice permits.

In some jurisdictions, the enlargement or expansion of a non-conforming use requires the owner to apply for an area variance.[165] The standards for such a variance require a showing of practical difficulties in using the property, and that the expansion of an already non-conforming use would be less intrusive on the ordinance's land use pattern than a new use in the same location.[166] Only an area variance is suitable in this situation, it being difficult to imagine that a use variance with its higher standards of proof would ever be granted in this situation.

[A] Amortization

Sometimes ordinances also adopt a more aggressive, municipally initiated policy toward non-conforming uses. This policy is pursued in so-called amortization ordinance provisions. These are permitted in most jurisdictions. They provide for the elimination of nonconforming uses from the zoning map and at the same time permit the continuance of the use for a reasonable but certain time—say, five years—during which time the property is to be brought into compliance, and its termination thereafter.[167] At the time of termination, there need not be a location within the municipality to which the terminated use can relocate;[168] neither need the value of the use then be zero.[169] Moreover, the value of the nonconformity over the amortization period need not amount to what would be just compensation under the takings clause.[170] This last rule is typically reached because amortization ordinances are often enacted under the general police power granted in home rule charters.[171] Likewise, the police power justifies a ban on blinking or flashing signs rendering them nonconforming.[172]

Amortization statutes and ordinances are often challenged by outdoor advertising and billboard companies. Sometimes, these challenges are brought as class actions for a declaratory judgment on issues of constitutionality.[173] However, when the issue

---

165. *See Nuckel v. Borough of Little Ferry Planning Bd.*, 26 A.3d 418 (N.J. 2011).

166. *Id.* at 425–26.

167. *See generally* Patricia E. Salkin, *Abandonment, Discontinuance, and Amortization of Nonconforming Uses: Lessons for Drafters of Zoning Regulations*, 38 Real Est. L.J. 486, 500–06 (2010); M. Ahmad, *Nonconforming Uses: Amortization, Enlargement, and Rebuilding*, 26 Prac. Real Est. L. 37 (2010).

168. *See Hoffman v. Kinealy*, 389 S.W.2d 745 (Mo. 1965) (a leading case), noted at 45 Neb. L Rev. 636 (1965), 44 Tex. L. Rev. 368 (1965), and 11 Vill. L. Rev. 189 (1966).

169. *See Red Roof Inns, Inc. v. City of Ridgeland*, 797 So. 2d 898 (Miss. 2001).

170. *Id.*

171. *See Baddock v. Baltimore County*, 197 A.3d 546 (Md. Ct. Spec. App. 2018) (regulating the hours of operation of hookah lounges not as a zoning but as a police power matter); *Whiteco. Outdoor Adver. v. City of Tucson*, 972 P.2d 647 (Ariz. Ct. App. 1998).

172. *See Fayetteville v. S & H Co.*, 547 S.W.2d 94 (Ark. 1977).

173. *See Klicker v. State*, 197 N.W.2d 434 (Minn. 1972) (involving 2,388 nonconforming signs state-wide).

becomes the reasonableness of the amortization period, courts regard the issue of one of fact and thus summary judgment for the municipality enacting the prohibitory ordinance is inappropriate on that account: an evidentiary hearing is required on issues of due process and when due process is found lacking, takings questions.[174]

Amortization ordinances apply more readily to structures rather than uses. This is because the word amortization itself can refer either to the recoupment of an owner's investment in a structure or to its reasonable depreciation over the time it has been used in a nonconforming manner. Such ordinances are sometimes, but not often, authorized by a state zoning enabling act; they are instead implied from the municipality's exercise of the police power. They are, moreover, most readily implied when the use to be amortized is either a nuisance or substantially abandoned or discontinued.[175] In contrast to other means of eliminating non-conforming uses, amortization brings certainty and swiftness to bear on the task.

A reasonably long period of time must be provided. The amortization period is a reference to the time period necessary for an owner to recoup his investment in the non-conforming structure on the site, but legislatures and courts are not very specific about what exactly is being amortized. Thus, an amortization period of five years, applied to a structure with a remaining economic life of twenty years, is void.[176] An amortization period of seven years applied to on-site signs in which a substantial investment has been made may be unreasonable short—and a taking of property to boot.[177] Besides a structure's life expectancy, an owner's initial investment, the amount of an investment realized up to the date the amortization period starts to run, or leasehold income derived from the use, are all relevant to setting an amortization period.

In general, amortization period provisions must take account of their origins and rationale. A billboard that is found to create a traffic safety problem may be subject to a shorter amortization period on that account. Likewise, a manufacturing plant creating a nuisance or an environmental hazard may be amortized in a shorter time. On the other hand, a non-conforming use that merely disrupts the aesthetic pattern of its neighborhood may take longer to amortize on that account.[178]

Amortization provisions run into trouble when applied to structures tailored to the use because often the period is then too short.[179] Structures are amortized through depreciation, but land does not depreciate. If a non-conforming use exists

---

174. *Id.*

175. This seems to be the rule in Pennsylvania.

176. *See City of La Mesa v. Tweed and Gambrell Planing Mill*, 304 P.2d 803 (Cal. App. Ct. 1956) (so holding).

177. *See Fayetteville v. S & H Co.*, 547 S.W.2d 94 (Ark. 1977) (holding that the owner of billboards might bring an action to compel the use of eminent domain).

178. *See Modjeska Sign Studios v. Berle*, 373 N.E.2d 255 (N.Y. 1977).

179. *See Jones v. City of Los Angeles*, 295 P. 14 (Cal. 1930) (involving a sanatorium, against which a twenty year amortization period was invalidated) (discussed in *City of Los Angeles v. Gage*, 274 P.2d 34 (Cal. App. Ct. 1954), upholding a five year amortization period for a plumbing business, the moving costs of which were 1% of its yearly gross revenue).

in an untailored structure, the amortization period may be short—say three to five years.[180] Long amortization periods present zoning officials with record-keeping problems as well.[181]

Non-conforming uses like junkyards, gasoline stations, and animal facilities like dog kennels, have been subjected to the amortization process. Billboards have been a frequent subject of amortization ordinances.[182] In fact, the majority of courts dealing with such amortization provisions have upheld them, if only facially and generally.[183]

Amortization is rationalized in one of two ways. Prior to the era of zoning, a use could be terminated only by a cause of action in nuisance, so that, first, amortization is upheld as providing for the abatement of a nuisance, probably a public nuisance. Second, it is upheld under a multi-factor rule of reason. The factors weighed are: the character of the structure, its location, its cost, its depreciated value (sometimes using IRS guidelines), its salvage value and remaining useful life, the legal arrangements under which the use is maintained (e.g., a short or long term lease, or absolute ownership), its monopoly value, and the injury to the public in maintaining the use. Under this second test, the validity or invalidity of the provision becomes a matter of degree and non-nuisance uses can be abated.[184] In some jurisdictions, however, express enabling act authority for an amortization scheme has been required.[185]

In *Pennsylvania Northwestern Distributors, Inc. v. Zoning Hearing Bd. of Moon Twp.*,[186] the Pennsylvania Supreme Court joined a minority of state courts holding a ninety day amortization provision invalid as a taking of property under the state constitution. The court found the amortization provision facially invalid and a per se taking of an adult bookstore. In response to an opinion like that of *Pennsylvania Northwestern Distributors*, a municipality might provide for amortization of adult bookstores operating within 100 feet of a school, after one year, and provide further for a transferable development right (TDR), alienable to third parties, for operation of the store elsewhere. Such an amortization procedure is probably valid. TDRs have been broadly upheld as a means of compensating owners for regulation of their uses, otherwise prohibited, and even though the non-conforming use might be the highest and best use of the parcel.[187]

---

180. *Cf. Lone v. Montgomery County*, 584 A.2d 142, 153–54 (Md. App. 1991) (involving a ten year amortization period for converting single family structures with accessory apartments from a multi-family use to single family use and holding that this was not a taking without compensation).

181. *See Lone*, *op. cit.*, 584 A.2d at 153, n. 18 (collecting amortization cases).

182. *See, e.g.*, *Art Neon Co. v. City & Cty. of Denver*, 488 F.2d 118 (10th Cir. 1973). Billboard companies have raised First and Fifth Amendment claims as well. *See, e.g.*, *Naegele Outdoor Adv. Co. v. City of Durham*, 803 F. Supp. 1068 (M.D.N.C. 1992).

183. *See National Adv. Co. v. City of Raleigh*, 947 F.2d 1158, 1164, n. 6 (4th Cir. 1991) (collecting cases); *see also LaChappelle v. Town of Goffstown*, 225 A.2d 624 (N.H. 1967).

184. *See Northend Cinema, Inc. v. City of Seattle*, 585 P.2d 1153 (Wash. 1978) (en banc), *cert. denied*, *Apple Theatre, Inc. v. City of Seattle*, 441 U.S. 946 (1979) (upholding ninety day amortization period for adult theater operating under lease terminable on short notice).

185. *See State v. Bates*, 305 N.W.2d 426 (Iowa 1981).

186. 584 A.2d 1372 (Pa. 1991), noted at 37 Vill. L.Rev. 161, 181–92 (1992).

187. *See Penn Central Transp. Co. v. City of New York*, 438 U.S. 104, 114 (1978).

Other responses to *Pennsylvania Northwestern Distributors* might be a statute providing that a short period of dormancy or non-use terminates a non-conforming use. Such statutes have, in other areas such as mineral interests, been held constitutional against attacks on both due process and takings grounds.[188]

Finally, the distinctiveness of a structure for a non-conforming use may enhance its legal durability: i.e., a hot dog stand located in the middle of a residential area before the neighborhood was zoned residential. If the stand is shaped like a huge hot dog and roll and the municipality enacted a three year amortization period for all non-conforming uses in the district, the architectural uniqueness of the improvement on this site gives its status as a non-conforming use a strength that use non-conformance alone does not possess. Amortization statutes are most effective when other parcels in the jurisdiction are available to receive the use. The uniqueness of this improvement makes that unlikely: compliance with building codes at any new site makes substantial alteration of the improvement the likely consequence of moving it. Portable uses can be amortized much more easily.

Another device for insulating amortization provisions from attack is to devise an administrative process for handling them. Thus, instead of amortizing all gas stations within a certain use district, an ordinance might require that each station undergo an individual appraisal and assessment process reviewing its operation and proscribing an individual amortization period depending on the outcome of that process. In each instance, the burden on the owner of the nonconformity must be weighed against the benefit to the public. Like many another administrative process, the municipality would bear the burden of justifying the outcome with substantial evidence. That outcome can then be embodied in an ordinance for each parcel amortized, and the legislative nature of each ordinance can be immunized from further review as such. (In appropriate cases, even further flexibility might be built into the process by a petition process and an extension of the amortization period.[189]) Why is such a process worth doing? Because it is fairer to the owners of non-conforming uses. One size does not fit all in this area. Thus, a blanket amortization period for gas stations cannot take account of differing fair market values of the parcels affected, the differing rates of investment in the operations of the business, or the differing replacement costs that owners will incur in relocating. An individualized administrative process can consider all such things.

---

188. *See Texaco, Inc. v. Short*, 454 U.S. 516 (1982) (involving a state statute on the lapsing of titles to unused mineral estates). *But see WFS Earth Materials, LLC v. Planning & Zoning Comm'n of the Town of Haddem*, 2010 Conn. Super. LEXIS 2984 (Nov. 22, 2010) (finding invalid a lifetime maximum tonnage that might be excavated by a nonconforming sand and gravel operation).

189. *See AVR, Inc. v. City of St. Louis Park*, 585 N.W.2d 411, 416 (1998) (upholding such a process), *followed and expanded in KOB-TV LLC v. City of Albuquerque*, 111 P.3d 708, 719 (N.M. Ct. App. 2005) (noted in Julie Shank, *A Taking without Just Compensation? The Constitutionality of Amortization Provision for Nonconforming Uses*, 109 W. Va. L. Rev. 225 (2006)).

[B] The Natural Expansion Doctrine

Regulations typically restrict the extension, repair, alteration, or reconstruction (when destroyed or otherwise demolished) of non-conforming structures. However, in some states, particularly those with a heavy industrial base when zoning was in its formative stage, non-conforming uses do not by any means wither away.[190] Instead, these uses are permitted to expand under what is called the "natural expansion" doctrine.[191] There, they are not limited to their size in existence at the time of enactment of the zoning ordinance—not limited, that is, to a plant capacity unused at the effective date of the ordinance, to the machinery in use then if more modern methods are now available, or to the out-put produced as of the ordinance's effective date. Rather, they may be increased in size to the extent required by natural expansion and growth in the use and the trade for which they are used, provided that the expansion has no adverse impact on the general welfare. However, that caveat imposed on the naturally-expanding non-conforming use is usually taken care of by applying the ordinance's usual set-back, height, bulk, density, and other restrictions to the use.

The rationale for this doctrine has been explained as follows: "An ordinance which would allow the housing of a baby elephant cannot evict the animal when it has grown up, since it is generally known that a baby elephant eventually becomes a big elephant."[192] Denying the natural expansion of a non-conforming use is thought to deny its owners the use as effectively as would its out-right prohibition. This doctrine is said to "run with the title," rather than to benefit the owner at the time of the enactment of the ordinance.[193]

While the doctrine permits an owner to develop or expand a business notwithstanding its nonconformity, it is particularly useful to owners of mines or quarries. In the instance of a quarry, it must grow or die. The doctrine would also protect an increase in height of a nonconforming structure[194] or communications cell tower.[195] However, one Pennsylvania opinion refused to apply this doctrine to a billboard whose owner wished to change it to include an LED display, ruling that the doctrine did not apply to a change in the face of a sign.[196] In one instance, this doctrine has

190. *See In re Gilfillan's Permit*, 140 A. 136 (Pa. 1927) (a leading case).

191. *See Hitz v. Zoning Hearing Bd. of South Annville Twp.*, 734 A.2d 60, 67–68 (Pa. Commnw. Ct. 1999) (restating the doctrine and collecting the cases); *see also Lamar Advantage GP Co. v. Zoning Hearing Bd. of the City of Pittsburgh*, 997 A.2d 423 (Pa. Commw. Ct. 2010) (stating that the doctrine is intended to maintain the "economic viability" of the use and "to take advantage of increases in trade").

192. *See Upper Darby Twp. Appeal*, 138 A.2d 99, 102 (Pa. 1958).

193. *See Eitnier v. Kreitz Corporation*, 172 A.2d 320, 323 (Pa. 1961).

194. *See Nettleton*, op. cit., 828 A.2d at 1041 (finding that the footprint of the nonconforming structure remained the same).

195. *See Kelsea v. Town of Pembroke*, 771 A.2d 587, 591 (N.H. 2001) (finding that a height increase did not increase the land coverage of the tower).

196. *See Lamar Adv. Co. v. Zoning Hearing Bd. of Monroeville*, 939 A.2d 994 (Pa. Cmwlth. Ct. 2007).

been heedless of municipal boundaries, expanding onto land in another municipality; in this situation, a court may consider an expansion as it fits into both municipalities in order to maintain nonconforming status at its original site.[197]

In a jurisdiction adopting the natural expansion doctrine, a municipality might impose a 50% limitation on the expansion of non-conforming uses—that is, provide that the footprint of any non-conforming use may increase not more than 50% after the enactment of the ordinance. Such a provision has been upheld.[198] In implementing such a limitation, however, the type of use regulated will have to be considered. A quarry, for example, must expand or die.[199] In addition, the issue of whether a percentage restriction is related to the adverse impact on surrounding uses will have to be considered. For example, the size of a parcel may make the relationship tenuous. Again, imposing such a limitation is problematical in the case of a quarry, for what would be its footprint?

Most jurisdictions do not follow this doctrine.[200] They limit non-conforming uses more strictly than the doctrine does.[201] Neither the use nor the structure may be expanded or enlarged.[202] Municipalities may in general impose reasonable conditions on the expansion of a non-conforming use.[203] Most would also refuse to permit a non-conforming owner to demolish an existing structure in order to replace it with a newer one.[204] Even in a "natural expansion" jurisdiction, the non-conforming use may not be changed to a new use.[205]

A doctrine similar to the natural expansion doctrine is known as the doctrine of diminishing assets.[206] It is useful in the instance of a mine: a mine has a finite useable term. It elements are that: (1) the assets were being mined on the date the prohibitory ordinance was enacted; (2) the area intended for excavation or mining was clearly and objectively measured and reserved for future use; and (3) the impact on the neighborhood will remain unchanged if the doctrine is applied to protect future operations.[207] When applied to mining operations, this doctrine is a more flexible one than the doctrine of natural expansion.

---

197. *See Churchill Realty v. City of Dover Bd. of Zoning Appeals*, 941 A.2d 584 (N.H. 2008).

198. *See Schiller-Pfeiffer v. Upper Southampton Twp.*, 276 A.2d 334 (Pa. Commw. Ct. 1971) (holding, 5-2, that such a restriction is reasonable).

199. *See City of University Place v. McGuire*, 30 P.3d 453, 459 (Wash. 2001) (labeling the problem one of applying the "doctrine of diminishing assets" and citing cases from eight other states using the doctrine for mines and quarries).

200. *But see Hurley v. Town of Hollis*, 729 A.2d 998, 1002 (N.H. 1999) (indicating that New Hampshire follows it). *See also Town of Salem v. Wickson*, 770 A.2d 1120, 1125 (N.H. 2001) (holding that a pig farm's stockpiling treated manure is not a natural expansion).

201. *See State ex rel. Dierberg v. St. Charles Cty. Bd. of Zoning Adjustment*, 869 S.W.2d 865 (Mo. App. Ct. 1994).

202. *Id.*

203. *See Peabody v. Town of Windham*, 703 A.2d 886 (N.H. 1997).

204. *See In re Stowe Club Highlands*, 668 A.2d 1271 (Vt. 1995).

205. *See Pietropaolo v. Zoning Hearing Bd.*, 979 A.2d 969, 977 (Pa. Commw. Ct. 2009).

206. *See, e.g., City of University Place v. McGuire*, 30 P.3d 453, 459–60 (Wash. 2001) (adopting the doctrine and citing cases from Alaska, California, Illinois, Massachusetts, Michigan, New Hampshire, New Jersey, New York, Pennsylvania, Texas, Utah, and Wisconsin).

207. *See Town of West Greenwich v. A. Cardi Realty Assocs.*, 786 A.2d 354, 361 (R.I. 2001).

[C] Changes in Use

A non-conforming use need not stay exactly as it was at the time of enactment of the ordinance. However, a change in the methods or the quantity of production can be so great as to constitute a new use.[208] If a changed use will have a lesser impact on its surroundings, it is permissible; if the impact is greater, then the user runs the risk that it will be found to be a new use and the change will be subject to injunction. A quarry and stone-crushing business cannot build a cement plant. However, a change in the intensity of the present, non-conforming use does not amount to a change or expansion of that use.[209] So a non-conforming night club operating two nights a week might be permitted to add a third night's operation. For this purpose, intensification is not an expansion of the use.[210] However, if the owner of a non-conforming used car lot wishes to change the parcel's use and open a gas station, the likely response of zoning officials will be negative and to the effect that this is a new use and a permit should be denied.[211] Because the methods of operation and the environmental risks and regulation are significantly different when comparing the present and the proposed use, the change is all the more likely to be found illegal. In a further example, suppose that a non-conforming landfill operates in a residential district under a state permit allowing receipt of so many cubic yards of waste per day. When its owner applies for a new permit to take in six times the number of cubic yards, the new permit application is evidence that the use is being illegally expanded.[212] Allowing the storage of "materials" as a non-conforming use is unlikely to permit the storage of motor vehicles, and permitting storage of materials for a chicken farm is not a basis for permitting storage for a cattle feed lot. The change in use is simply too great.

---

208. *See Board of Zoning Appeals of Spotsylvania Cty. v. McCalley*, 300 S.E.2d 790 (Va. 1983).

209. *See Town of Wolfeboro v. Smith*, 556 A.2d 755, 759 (N.H. 1989).

210. *See Guido v. Township of Sandy*, 880 A.2d 1220 (Pa. 2005) (so holding).

211. *See Hanna v. Board of Adjustment*, 183 A.2d 539 (Pa. 1962) (so holding).

212. *See Township of Chartiers v. William H. Martin, Inc.*, 542 A.2d 985, 987–88 (Pa. 1988) (reviewing the Pa. cases on the natural expansion doctrine) (noted in 27 Duq. U. L. Rev. 391 (1989)).

Chapter 8
Aesthetics and Zoning

§ 8.01 The Police Power and Aesthetics

The broadest scope is given the police power when zoning is enacted to protect the aesthetics of the community. This protection is typically needed for the preservation of compatibility amid various architectural styles for housing in a residential use district. Compatibility of uses is a traditional objective for zoning. Sometimes, an ordinance is drafted to foster a diversity of visual or architectural styles. (If compatibility is a valid objective, then so might diversity be, on the ground that compatibility taken too far results in dullness, and spacing distinctive architectural styles might be a proper remedy.) Sometimes too, an ordinance is drafted to create visual beauty—an affirmative and much less traditional objective. The courts have taken three views of aesthetic regulation. Each view represents a stage in the development of a state's zoning law for this area.

The **first stage** is a judicial refusal to validate regulations based on aesthetic considerations. Every state has passed through this stage, thus today it is a historic relic.

In a **second stage**, aesthetics might be considered a legitimate purpose of zoning if it has a substantial relationship to other, more traditional purposes (other than aesthetics), such as the preservation of property values or the local economy. However, the relationship need not be a direct one. For example, aesthetics can protect property values, which affects the tax base, which in turn affects the amount of money in the treasury, which affects the general welfare. This type of analysis looks very much like substantive due process, so often used in zoning opinions.

Most states are currently categorized as passing through this second stage, although some (Massachusetts and Pennsylvania are examples) seem in permanent residence there. Administration of such ordinances is generally left to persons, such as architects, with professional training in the fine arts. Often these ordinances delegate decision-making powers to an administrative board (often called an architectural review board) and contain one of two types of standards. First, architectural details may be provided, down to the type of door-knob or the color of paint which is permitted. (The most detail is provided in historic district ordinances, less detail in the residential subdivision setting.) Merely stating that the style must be "early

American" will not suffice: that phrase justifies adobe, log cabin, Cape Cod styles, or even a tepee. Second, the architectural principles which constitute a particular style may be defined: the relationship of windows to walls, roof lines, voids and solids on the facade, etc. The administrative decision then is whether a proposed development or renovation "looks like" or "does not look like" the prescribed style. The decision is yes or no, and the courts seldom second-guess it.[1]

In order for the ordinance to avoid the charge that it impermissibly delegates the local police power, adequate criteria for decisions are necessary and should be spelled out in the ordinance's provisions.[2] A charge of impermissible delegation usually goes hand-in-hand with an allegation that the ordinance is void for vagueness, although the latter allegation is more often found when the ordinance is deemed facially invalid.[3] The less professional the board, the more detailed the standards must be. Moreover, aesthetics may be a stand-in for other concerns; compatibility with surrounding uses and buildings is one acceptable concern.[4] So architectural review boards are typically authorized to decide that a structure has no adverse impact on surrounding uses, or represents no incompatibility of architectural style.

Deciding what does harm to the existing visual beauty of a neighborhood is easier than deciding, *a priori*, what beauty is.[5] For example, justifying an ordinance requiring screening and land buffers around a junkyard, is a matter of preventing visual blight or harm, rather than conferring a benefit on neighbors of the junkyard by improving their view—thus regulation is appropriate. However, because both the harm and the benefit are visual, some courts may find the traditional police power rubrics translated into this arena hard to accept; that is, preventing the harm and conferring the benefit may seem inseparable,[6] which is why some courts do not accept aesthetics as the sole justification for an ordinance.

Finding itself in this second stage, a municipality might ban all types of billboards from residential use districts and permit them as of right only in manufacturing and industrial districts. Such a regulation is valid. Traffic safety and visual blight would bring this ordinance well within the police power. This can be accomplished without regulating the content of the speech on the billboards. Should First Amendment, free

---

1. *See, e.g., State ex rel Stoyanoff v. Berkeley*, 458 S.W.2d 305, 311–12 (Mo. 1970) (discussed in Peter Salsich, Land Use Regulation 165 (1991); *see also Town of Deering ex rel. Bittenbender v. Tibbetts*, 202 A.2d 232 (N.H. 1964)

2. *See Anderson v. City of Issaquah*, 851 P.2d 744 (Wash. Ct. App. 1993) (standards must give "effective and meaningful guidance to officials and applicants).

3. *See Hanna v. City of Chicago*, 907 N.E.2d 390 (Ill. Ct. App. 2009) (stating: "We believe that the terms 'value,' 'important,' 'significant,' and 'unique' are vague, ambiguous, and overly broad.").

4. *See Rolling Pines Limited Partnership v. City of Little Rock*, 40 S.W.3d 828 (Ark. Ct. App. 2000) (upholding compatibility standards for manufactured housing units involving the pitch of their roofs, the removal of mobile features, permanent foundations, finished exterior walls, as well as off-street parking).

5. *See Burns v. Town of Palm Beach*, 999 F.3d 1317 (11th Cir. 2021) (in which majority and dissent argue over whether illustrations of progressive architecture are admissible in a neighbors' challenge to a permit for a mid-twentieth century house).

6. *See Nollan v. California Coastal Comm'n*, discussed *infra*, Chapter 14, § 14.20[A].

speech based, constitutional challenges arise, the counter argument would be that there are many alternative channels of communication available—newspapers, magazines, circulars, mailings, e-mail and the internet, telemarketing, television, cable TV, and radio. Such arguments are typically persuasive in court.

In this second stage, the disapproval on architectural grounds of a design for an ultra-modern house to be located in a (say) Georgian colonial residential use district has been justified when there is an established pattern of development in the neighborhood. Thus screening out incompatible styles may be seen as akin to preventing a (cultural or aesthetic) nuisance.[7] Similarly, parking vehicles incompatible with a residential district (such as recreational or commercial vehicles) might be regulated on a combination of aesthetic and traffic safety grounds.[8] Compatibility standards are often seen by the courts as a short-hand for promoting aesthetic values.

A **third stage** permits the consideration of aesthetics alone when drafting a regulation.[9] As of 1988, about 21 states were in this third category.[10] In effect, they invite some affirmative definitions of the aesthetic objectives of an ordinance, although such. ordinances may also use architectural details or compatibility standards.

The opinions of the United States Supreme Court can be categorized as being in this third stage. *Penn Central Transportation Company v. City of New York*[11] is an example. In *Penn Central*, the United States Supreme Court sustained the validity of New York City's Landmarks Preservation Law. Justice Brennan, writing for the majority, said: "[T]his Court has recognized, in a number of settings, that States and municipalities may enact land use restrictions or controls to enhance the quality of life by preserving the character and desirable aesthetic features of a city."[12] This sounds broadly permissive as far as municipalities are concerned, but Justice Brennan went on to say, in characterizing what was not in dispute in that case, that Penn Central had not contested either the legitimacy of the city's objective or public purpose, the nexus between that purpose and the regulations at issue, or the fact that the railroad could still earn a reasonable return from the property with the regulations in place. Clearly the attorneys for Penn Central conceded too much in this case, and the result is a broad brush, rather than a closely reasoned approval of aesthetics as a proper police power purpose.

That a substantial number of states (21), though still a minority, endorse this third stage's "aesthetics alone" rule, is explained by the possibility of misuse of aesthetics in

---

7. *See Reid v. Architectural Bd. of Review*, 192 N.E.2d 74 (Ohio Ct. App. 1963). *See also State ex rel. Saveland Park Holding Corp. v. Wieland*, 69 N.W.2d 217 (Wis. 1955), *cert. denied*, 350 U.S. 841 (1955) (both cases upheld architectural design ordinances with compatibility standards).

8. *See Disney v. City of Concord*, 124 Cal. Rptr. 3d 58 (Ct. App. 2011) (regulating recreational vehicle parking as a valid exercise of the police power on traffic control and aesthetic grounds).

9. *See generally* Jeffrey Strouse, *Redefining Trademark Alteration Within the Context of Aesthetic-Based Zoning Laws: A Blockbuster Dilemna*, 53 Vand. L. Rev. 717, 720–25 (2000).

10. *See Asselin v. Town of Conway*, 628 A.2d 247, 249-50 (N.H. 1993) (shifting from second to third stage rule); *see also City of Fayetteville v. McIlroy Bank & Trust*, 647 S.W.2d 439, 441 (Ark. 1983).

11. 438 U.S. 104 (1978).

12. *Id.* at 129.

decision-making. Aesthetics may be a mask for more sinister factors—economic and class prejudice, racial intolerance, etc. What is not tolerated directly should not be tolerated indirectly. However, a dozen or so states regard the matter as an open question. Thus, the majority of states may well soon endorse the "aesthetics alone" rule.

Another reason for judicial reluctance is that beauty, to paraphrase Hume, is in the eye of the beholder and thus aesthetic decisions must either be based on trust in the beholder or else on criteria to guide his sensibilities; most courts still trust criteria and judicial review more than the beholding architectural board member. Is not judicial review really the answer to the criticism that the aesthetics alone rule is an invitation to subjective decisions? If the decision is subjective, it is arbitrary and may be invalidated. Indeed, in the dozen or so jurisdictions remaining hostile to aesthetic regulations, aesthetics and subjectivity are synonymous.

So aesthetic regulation is valid when it has a substantial relationship to a public purpose other than aesthetics and even solely aesthetic regulation is valid when harm to the surroundings is clear and not merely a matter of taste. Thus, for example, a rural mountainous municipality in a scenic region might prohibit the night-time use of "internally lighted signs." In a stage three jurisdiction, the standard of judicial review is a rational relationship or nexus review. "It is reasonable to infer that the scenic vistas sought to be preserved by the town include the splendor of mountains at twilight and the brilliance of stars at night."[13] Thus the restriction on internally lighted signs is reasonably related to the aesthetic goal of "discouraging development that competes with the natural environment."[14]

With the advent of this third stage, the use of aesthetics to justify an ordinance should typically be described in a specific regulatory context. For example, when an ordinance prevents the removal of topsoil without a permit, it has been argued that it can be justified solely on aesthetic grounds. However, the preservation of the natural environment is arguably easier to justify solely on aesthetic grounds if a related public need for an ordinance can be shown.[15] For example, the topsoil ordinance should be justified as preventing the harm of exposing the subsoil of the municipality or by the need to have the topsoil remain to sustain its natural environment. A similar issue might arise in a use district aimed at preserving farmland. Farmland provides aesthetic relief from urbanization, serving as a buffer between urban development and wetlands and riparian lands, as well as serving as a reminder of a region's agricultural heritage.

The use of aesthetics by a municipal architectural review board has provided most of the law detailed thus far; a historic district, landmark preservation, incentive zoning, and the regulation of billboards, provide other contexts for discussing the law in this area.

---

13. *Asselin v. Town of Conway*, 628 A.2d 247 (N.H. 1993).

14. *Id.*

15. *Cf. McNeill v. Township of Plumsted*, 522 A.2d 469, 472–73 (N.J. Super. Ct., App. Div. 1987) (remanding case for consideration of need for ordinance prohibiting topsoil removal).

§ 8.02 Historic Districts

State and federal courts have upheld aesthetic considerations as a proper basis for imposing architectural controls on buildings within a historic use district. Such districts preserve the visual quality of a historic neighborhood.[16] Such districts are typically authorized expressly by state enabling statutes. Many jurisdictions in which aesthetic considerations alone are an insufficient justification for a zoning regulation move from the second to the third stage of aesthetic regulation and permit aesthetics alone to suffice as a police power justification for a historic district ordinance.[17] Even in a municipality denied zoning power in its home rule charter, historic district regulations are permissible as an exercise of the police power delegated under its charter.[18]

In a historic district, more regulation might be justified because of the setting: the neighborhood's character is dependent on maintaining the historic appearance of each property.[19] Most such ordinances focus on a historic property's compatibility and exterior features designed to be exposed to public view. When put in the context of the district, compatibility as a standard will be upheld against void for vagueness and substantive due process challenges.[20] Conversely, a property of little or no historic value can be brought into conformance with the neighborhood's character because of the same inter-dependency. This is the "tout ensemble" doctrine.[21]

Often aesthetics is not a stand-alone justification for the regulations imposing a certain architectural style. Tourism and economic development are also used to justify regulating such districts as the Vieux Carre in New Orleans, Santa Fe in New Mexico, old Charleston in South Carolina, or Nantucket Island in Massachusetts. These areas provided first-generation, multi-purpose historic districts. Every town or city has, in some sense of the term, a historic district: whether it be the home of its first settlers, or merely a somewhat older and quainter areas of town, there is some historic value there. Sometimes a city's economic "glory days" gave birth to a millionaires' row and a historic district.[22] Giving the citizens a sense of what the place was has some value. The issue is whether this is sufficient to justify freeze-framing the district as it is now or forcing it to become what it was. For some advocates of historic preservation, the answer is a definite yes. An example would be the historic district in Miami Beach,

---

16. *See Stevens v. City of Columbus*, 2022 U.S. App. LEXIS 20829, **11–24, 29-30 (11th Cir. July 27, 2022) (upholding regulation governing landscaping in a historic district).

17. *Id.* (upholding a historic district ordinance "for aesthetic reasons" as a valid exercise of police power). *See also Opinion of the Justices*, 128 N.E.2d 557 (Mass. 1955).

18. *See Powell v. City of Houston*, 628 S.W.3d 838 (Tex. 2021).

19. *See Boczar v. Kingen*, 2000 U.S. Dist. LEXIS 11615 (S.D. Ind., Mar. 9, 2000) (collecting cases).

20. *See Mayes v. City of Dallas*, 747 F.2d 323 (5th Cir. 1984).

21. *See Figarsky v. Historic District Comm'n*, 368 A.2d 163, 172 (Conn. 1976) (upholding a regulation for a property located on the edge of the district); *Lafayette Park Baptist Church v. Scott*, 553 S.W.2d 856, 861 (Mo. App. Ct. 1977) (finding that a historic district with architectural controls "is essentially a zoning ordinance"); *see also Burke v. City of Charleston*, 893 F. Supp. 589 (D.S.C. 1995); *Kruse v. Town of Castle Rock*, 192 P.3d 591 (Colo. Ct. App. 2008).

22. *See Norton v. City of Danville*, 602 S.E.2d 126 (Va. 2004).

created to preserve the mid-twentieth century modern style of residential architecture against the pressure for more intensive development.

Another interesting example of a historic district ordinance is found in Houston, Texas. This home rule city has no jurisdiction-wide zoning. Its city charter prohibits this, and its voters have several times rejected a proposal to institute such zoning. The city relies instead on public enforcement of private covenants. However, the city has a historic district ordinance, and the Texas Supreme Court has held that the ordinance authorizing the district is a "comprehensive plan to regulate the alteration, construction, and razing of buildings in historic areas,"[23] even though the state legislation considers historic preservation regulations to be a type of zoning under the state's zoning enabling act. The city ordinance "is not zoning merely because it creates districts"[24] and creates a process of land use regulation resembling zoning.[25]

The justifications for a historic district ordinance prevail even when the market for renovated houses in the historic style is weak. Aesthetics regulation has often been justified as a matter of preserving property values; here, that protection is afforded and indeed expected by the market—herein of *Penn Central*'s "investment-backed expectations." Protecting existing investments, rather than encouraging new investments, is the rationale here; thus the strength of the market is irrelevant.

Even a one-house historic district has been validated. In an Illinois opinion involving the establishment of a four block district planned around one house, the home in Springfield (Illinois) of Abraham Lincoln, such a district was upheld.[26] Several types of uses were permitted in the district, but retail sales were excluded and the plaintiff had sought a permit to operate a restaurant there. The opinion upheld the state legislation creating the district, not only as a matter of applying a presumption of validity for the ordinance, but also with the observation that the plaintiff's property values were enhanced by the proximity of the Lincoln home. This opinion stressed the historical and cultural values justifying the district, not the economic benefits of creating it; the court emphasized the former because the plaintiff's building fronted on a downtown commercial street.

Historic district regulations must, however, have limits. Proximity to a district, standing alone, is an insufficient basis to permit a district's residents to participate in zoning hearings involving property outside the district. In the same vein, district residents lack standing to sue to protect a landmark outside the boundaries of the district. Residents outside the district likewise generally lack standing to challenge decisions

---

23. *See Powell v. City of Houston*, 628 S.W.3d 838, 858 (Tex. 2021) (finding that Houston's historic district ordinance is zoning for purposes of its being in accord with a comprehensive plan and for its uniformity within the district, but not zoning for purposes of the city charter's requirement of referendum approval).

24. *Id.* at 852.

25. *Id.* at 852–54.

26. *See Rebman v. City of Springfield*, 250 N.E.2d 282 (Ill. App. Ct. 1969).

about historic details of properties within the district.[27] A more explicit regulation, involving more than proximity to the district, is required for standing.[28] The general rules for gaining standing in a proceeding apply to a historic district's residents.[29]

§ 8.03 Preservation of Historic Landmarks

Early landmark preservation efforts involved Independence Hall in Philadelphia, Mount Vernon, and the Gettysburg battlefield.[30] Landmarks preservation, when not coupled with a historic district, presents more difficult problems of justifying architectural and aesthetic regulation. There are initially problems of whether the enabling act authorizes a preservation as a category of aesthetic regulation; its purpose is usually to regulate development and so does not clearly bring a preservation regulation within it. This is so because there is no reciprocity of advantage for the owner of an isolated landmark; in economic terms, it could have become a landmark just because it is the single building remaining after similar structures have been demolished or renovated. Its owner gains no benefit from being included in a historic district. Instead, the owner seems singled out and the landmark regulation takes on a the look of "spot zoning."

In Penn Central, the United States Supreme Court gave a tepid endorsement to landmark preservation and regulation. The court found that New York City had a comprehensive plan for the preservation of more than four hundred isolated landmarks. The presence of the plan itself seemed conclusive on the issue of whether there was reciprocity of advantage. However, less than.10% of the property in the city was affected, so that the landmark owners had (in the view of the dissenting opinion by Chief Justice Rehnquist) a good argument that they were being singled out in order to provide a public benefit at their expense.

A landmark may be a complex of buildings, having something in common with a historic district. For instance, a municipality with a rule that any structure more than 50 years old was eligible for designation as a landmark and seeking to designate an amusement park built in 1945 as a landmark, was met with the argument that all of the park's structures had been renovated, modernized, and reconstructed over time,

---

27. *See Gates v. City of Pittsburgh Historic Review Comm'n*, 254 A.3d 803 (Pa. Commwlth. Ct. 2021); *Tenth Street Residential Ass'n v. City of Dallas*, 968 F.3d 492 (5th Cir. 2020) (neighborhood association lacked standing to contest demolition certificate for historic property).

28. *See Monkton Preservation Society v. Gaylord Brooks Realty Corp.*, 669 A.2d 195, 199 (Md. 1995). *See also Bowser v. Dupont E. Civic Action Ass'n*, 2023 D.C. App. LEXIS 239 (D.C. App., Aug. 24, 2023).

29. *See Preservation Soc'y of Charleston v. S.C. Dep't of Health & Envtl. Control*, 845 S.E.2d 481 (S.C. 2020).

30. *See United States v. Gettysburg Electric Railway Co.*, 160 U.S. 668 (1896) (recognizing that historical preservation is within the powers of the federal government).

so that the park was not eligible as a whole.[31] However, if the park gained historic significance over 50 years, it should not lose its significance because it has been renovated, modernized, or reconstructed. The issue was the significance of the park as a whole, not the renovation of the park's units. The "tout ensemble" doctrine applies to the park built all at once, just as it would to a historic district built over time, but not all at once.[32]

The planning for landmark preservation becomes all the more important when the statutory authority for regulation is weak. An owner was held entitled to a demolition permit for a historic building when it was eligible for listing on the National Register of Historic Places, but was not listed there. Without specific authority in the state zoning enabling act for historic zoning, the act nonetheless did permit planning for cultural and aesthetic purposes. So after denying the permit, the municipality then enacted a floating zone for historic buildings and rezoned the building for the use already announced to replace it on its site. This rezoning was found to be *ultra vires* the enabling act, was found not to be comprehensive rezoning, was not entitled to the presumption of validity, and was spot zoning.[33]

Churches and non-profit institutions in a historic district or when subject to a landmark preservation law, rarely make a reasonable return on the property, if that is defined to mean a market rate return.[34] They may not have an investment-backed expectation that they will use the return on their properties to carry out their non-profit purpose, so their taking arguments have been more difficult than those of other landmark owners. Such owners have the burden of showing that the demolition of the protected features of the structure or landmark, such as the facade, is the only way that the owner can realize a reasonable return or is the only solution to the structure's inadequacy for the intended use.[35] That the non-profit user intends to construct a large replacement building is irrelevant to such a showing.

Some municipalities attempt to avoid the legal problems of landmark ordinances by permitting either its legislature or the administrative body designating such landmarks as historic to go as far as the law of takings will permit. They permit demolition of the landmark when not to issue a demolition permit will result in an unreasonable economic hardship for its owner, the ordinance defining such a hardship as a taking.[36] This permits the implementation of landmark regulations to adjust to changes in the law of takings, but such permissiveness leaves landmark ordinances open to charges

31. *See Metropolitan Dade County v. P.J. Birds*, 654 So. 2d 170, 173 (Fla. App. 1995).

32. *Id.*

33. *See Donovan v. City of Deadwood*, 538 N.W.2d 790 (S.D. 1995).

34. *See Society of Jesus in New England v. Boston Landmarks Comm'n*, 564 N.E.2d 571 (Mass. 1990) (interior regulation of church violated First Amendment's religion clauses).

35. *See Society for Ethical Culture v. Spatt*, 415 N.E.2d 922 (N.Y. 1980) (reflecting the decision in *Penn Central*).

36. *See 900 G Street Assocs. v. Department of Housing and Community Dev.*, 430 A.2d 1387, 1389 (D.C. 1981).

of being without sufficiently definite standards.[37] About 1,500–2,000 municipalities around the country have landmark preservation regulations; some apply to the interior as well as the exterior of a landmark.[38]

[A] Landmark Interior Regulation

When interior as well as exterior control of a landmark is involved, the non-uniformity of the treatment is all the more exaggerated. No two interiors are exactly alike and so the impact of the landmark designation is unique. Moreover, any regulation of the landmark owner's interior is non-uniform vis-a-vis surrounding properties.

An ordinance authorizing a municipal landmark commission to designate "those buildings, structures, sites, and objects which the commission determines are significant to the municipality, exemplifies its cultural heritage, or contains elements of innovative design, detail, materials, or craftsmanship,"[39] did not clearly authorize the commission to regulate and preserve the interior of what would otherwise (considering its facade or exterior) be a landmark. The phrases most favorable to interior regulation depend upon the "building or structure" language preceding them.[40] Reviewing this language, the Pennsylvania Commonwealth Court found both that it was adequate authorization for the regulation of historic interiors and that the language was within the police power. An art deco 1928 movie theater was the site of the controversy in this case. However, at the Pennsylvania Supreme Court level, the case became a takings case.

The Pennsylvania Supreme Court issued two opinions.[41] Its first opinion took Pennsylvania out of the mainstream, denying judicial approval of the landmark preservation ordinance, while its second opinion (finding no taking) returned it to the mainstream. The cases were decided under the Pennsylvania Constitution provision[42] analogous to the federal takings clause. The holding of the United States Supreme

---

37. *See Donnelly Assocs. v. District of Columbia Historic Preservation Review Bd.*, 520 A.2d 270, 279–81 (D.C. 1987) (discussing *900 G St.* and temporary, regulatory takings).

38. *See Weinberg v. Barry*, 634 F. Supp. 86 (D.D.C. 1986) (upholding interior regulation); *United Artists Theater Circuit, Inc. v. City of Philadelphia*, 595 A2d 6 (Pa. 1991) (finding interior regulation a taking), *reversed*, 635 A.2d 612 (Pa. 1993) (noted in 22 B. C. Envtl. L. Rev. 593 (1995), reviewing the two opinions in the *United Artists* case).

39. *United Artists Theater Circuit*, 595 A.2d at 10.

40. This is a paraphrase of the language in the Philadelphia preservation ordinance under review in *Sameric Corp. of Chestnut St. v. City of Philadelphia*, 558 A.2d 155 (Pa. Commw. Ct. 1989), *rev'd sub nom., United Artists Theater Circuit, Inc. v. City of Philadelphia*, 595 A.2d 6 (Pa. 1991) (finding a taking).

41. *See United Artists Theater Circuit, Inc. v. City of Philadelphia*, 595 A.2d 6 (Pa. 1991) (holding Philadelphia's landmark preservation ordinance a taking under the state constitution), *on rehearing*, 635 A.2d 612, 622 (Pa. 1993) (finding no taking under the state constitution but holding that the Philadelphia ordinance did not authorize designation of an interior as historic landmark).

42. "Nor shall private property be taken or applied to public use, without authority of law and without just compensation being first paid or secured." Pa. Const., Art. I, § 10, interpreted in *Commonwealth v. Edmunds*, 586 A.2d 887 (Pa. 1991) (presenting the four prong test used in the first opinion in

Court in the *Penn Central* opinion, upholding New York City's landmark preservation law, has quieted any number of challenges to similar laws. It helped in this case. The second *United Artists* opinion used a test much like *Penn Central*'s: (1) an examination of the need for the governmental regulation; (2) the necessity of the means chosen to alleviate the need; and (3) the economic impact of the regulation. After finding no taking, the court moved on to invalidate the regulation as *ultra vires* to the ordinance.

In the first of two significant decisions by the New York Court of Appeals, the interior of a restaurant from the 1950s had also been regulated and preserved.[43] The opinion doing so found that a designation of the Four Seasons Restaurant's interior, to which the public is customarily invited, is subject to regulation, regardless of the purpose for which it was built. Public access to the space justified the regulation. The court found that, even though an interior currently open to the public might be converted to a private space in the future, this should not shield it from regulation. Indeed, the possibility of future closure to the public was the subject of a later, second decision of the New York Court of Appeals, holding that excluding the public from the clock tower in a historic building with a designated interior landmark—the clock—was within the Preservation Commission's discretion.[44] Public access at the time of a landmark's designation was, the court said, merely a jurisdictional predicate to the Commission's later exercise of its discretion.[45] Thus the New York City Preservation Commission may permit the privatization of a landmark's interior spaces that previously were publicly accessible. Unlike the restaurant's landmark status, compelled public access to the clock tower rooms might raise taking issues. To date, the United States Supreme Court has been silent on the takings issues presented by interior landmarks, but a recent decision raises the possibility that these issues might be considered anew.[46]

An ancillary problem involves the law of fixtures. A fixture is anything that is intended to be, and is, permanently annexed or attached to the real property in which it is located. Should the regulation include items not fixtures? The *TIAA* opinion, cited previously, found that the law of fixtures was irrelevant to its decision, and so hanging sculptures, a walnut bar, metal drapes, railings, and ceiling panels created and installed at the architect's direction, were subject to regulation as integral elements of

---

United Artists, examining the text of the state Constitution, its historic evolution, case law including federal cases, and policy considerations).

43. *See Teachers Insur. & Annuity Ass'n v. New York City*, 623 N.E.2d 526 (N.Y. 1993) (hereafter "*TIAA*") (holding, under the N.Y.C. ordinance involved in *Penn Central*, that such a designation was not arbitrary and capricious) (noted in 26 Conn. L. Rev. 1105 (1994)).

44. *See Matter of Save America's Clocks, Inc. v. City of New York*, 124 N.E.3d 189, 196–97 (N.Y. 2019) (also finding that the clock's electrification and LED lighting on its face preserved the clock's landmark status), noted at 133 Harv. L. Rev. 1790 (2020). The background of this case and its lower court opinion in this case is noted in Nicholas Caros, *Interior Landmarks Preservation and the Law*, 116 Colum. L. Rev. 1773 (2016).

45. *Id.* at 196.

46. *Cf. Cedar Point Nursery v. Hassid*, 141 S. Ct. 2963 (2021).

the interior design.[47] This rationale can easily get out of hand: is the glassware integral to the design too?

When a municipality seeks to regulate historic interiors that are private and not accessible to the public, such regulation presents additional problems. The issue is whether there is a public benefit in regulating a space to which the public does not have access. Regulation in this instance is akin to the creation of sound that no one hears. Only with express authority should such a regulation be valid. The lower court *TIAA* opinion expressly states: "this restaurant is not a private club."[48] The New York Court of Appeals, however, did not include such language in its opinion affirming the lower court. So this silence leaves the issue (whether a private club's interior could be regulated and preserved) an open one. Addressing this issue, one might say that interiors can be imagined by people passing by a famous exterior, just as the exterior of Carnegie Hall evokes the sound of orchestral concerts within or Independence Hall evokes a Gilbert Stuart painting of events inside. So too, might the exterior of a venerable private club evoke an image of wood paneling and old leather chairs inside a historic building.

[B] Landmark Designation Procedures

Most landmark designations can be accomplished without the consent of the owner. Many provide for a petition procedure. Neighbors, local preservation groups, and an administrative preservation agency may use it. Filing a petition for landmark designation typically starts a process of expert study and hearings on the structure.[49] In all but a few ordinances, a legislative finding is necessary before a landmark is designated.

Once a structure is designated a landmark, any proposal for repair, renovation, or demolition will require a permit—often called a certificate of appropriateness. In these proceedings, a showing of economic hardship or an insufficient return on investment will result in the issuance of a certificate, although sometimes a hardship showing is the subject of special proceedings for an exemption from the regulation.[50]

Significantly, the New York City landmark ordinance in *Penn Central* guaranteed an owner of a landmark a reasonable return on his or her property. Recall from the discussion of the *Penn Central* opinion that counsel for the company unwisely stipulated that its client could earn a reasonable return on the Terminal. The District of Columbia regulation in *900 G Street* did not contain a similar guarantee: it merely said that if the owner was permitted a reasonable use, as an alternative to the property's historic use, the regulation was not a taking. The *900 G Street* court's acceptance of

---

47. *TIAA*, 623 N.E.2d at 530 (noting that the noted architect Philip Johnson directed installation).

48. 586 N.Y.S.2d 262, 263 (1992).

49. *See Kirwan v. City of Deadwood*, 990 N.W.2d 108 (S.D. 2023). In this regard, the architectural studies of the N.Y.C. Landmarks Preservation Commission, available on the web, are worth reading.

50. *See Second Baptist Church v. Little Rock Historic Dist. Comm'n*, 732 S.W.2d 483, 487 (Ark. 1987) (construing Ark. Stat. Ann. § 19-5001 and upholding denial of permit for church to construct parking lot within district); PETER SALSICH, LAND USE REGULATION 163–64 (1991).

that regulation is a broadening of the holding in *Penn Central* and broadens the legal basis for continuing a property's landmark status.

Some commentators have suggested that a facade easement program, encouraged by provisions of the Internal Revenue Code concerning charitable deductions for the fair market value of such easements, would work as well as regulation for preserving a landmark. The same argument might be made more forcefully with regard to historic interiors. The preservation of interiors prevents owners from modifying the use of the building (otherwise in accord with the zoning regulations) to update and renovate it. At the same time, not being able to renovate the interior may make the preservation of the exterior less economically viable.

§ 8.04 Aesthetics and Incentive Zoning

In the central business districts of many cities, planners have found incentive zoning useful. With the advent of the skyscrapers, many city ordinances abandoned height limits in their downtown core. Instead, the regulations used Floor Area Ratios (FARs). The FAR is a multiplier for the area of the lot used to determine the permitted square footage of the improvement. The sky's the limit, so long as the FAR is not exceeded. Originally intended as a maximum (an "envelope" for development), in some cities bonus FARs are awarded to buildings with features considered aesthetic. In New York City, the first such feature was a street-front plaza. Such plazas appeared on many plans. Then came atriums, gallerias, roof-top gardens, and pedestrian walkways through the building—all justified by lessening the squared-off, block-like appearance of a district and by the better aesthetics achieved.

Added to these bonuses were tax abatements for aesthetic features. The original rationale was: don't penalize good aesthetics with a higher assessment. The controversy in the 1960s over the tax assessments for the Seagram Building in New York City was one focus for this controversy. However, this rationale was later expanded into an affirmative effort to encourage certain architectural features.

§ 8.05 Aesthetics and Billboards

Billboards typically display "commercial speech," defined as an "expression related solely to the economic interests of the speakers and its audience."[51] Until 1976, the United States Supreme Court left commercial speech largely unprotected, along with obscenity and defamatory speech. In that year, however, the court found that the First Amendment protects commercial speech because its auditors have an interest in the

51. *See Virginia State Bd. of Pharmacy v. Virginia Citizens Consumer Council*, 425 U.S. 748, 762 (1976).

free flow of information.[52] Free speech and free enterprise go hand in hand. Regulation of such speech is constitutional when it: (1) is justifiable without reference to its content;[53] (2) advances a significant governmental interest; and (3) provides ample alternative channels of communication for the regulated information. This is the so-called *Virginia Pharmacy* test.

When the first prong of this test is not met—that is, when the content of commercial speech is limited—a different, four prong test is applied. The limitation must (1) confine itself to misleading speech or speech involving unlawful activity; thus, when speech is inaccurate or unlawful, the First Amendment provides no protection; (2) the government must have a substantial interest in the regulation; (3) the regulation must directly advance that interest; and (4) the regulation must be narrowly tailored—no broader than necessary to accomplish its purpose.[54] Together, these four prongs are known as the *Central Hudson* test. A later case discussed the fourth prong, holding that the regulation need not be the least restrictive, but need only be reasonably tailored to accomplish its purpose.[55] For example, when a municipality limits neon, electronic, or digital signs to its commercial use districts as a means of balancing aesthetic and economic development goals, the ordinance is still narrowly tailored, satisfying the fourth prong of *Central Hudson.*[56]

The United States Supreme Court, in *Metromedia, Inc. v. City of San Diego*,[57] invalidated parts of a city ordinance that prohibited outdoor, off-premises advertising from most of the city, along with on-site noncommercial advertisements. The ordinance contained some exceptions, for example in the case of political campaign signs. This exception proved too narrow, leaving as it did many other types of political speech within its ambit and so making the ordinance under-inclusive. The court had no majority opinion and showed itself in disarray over the reason for the invalidation. The result was achieved by a 6-3 vote.

In *Metromedia*, Justice Byron White's plurality opinion said that the first, second, and fourth prong of *Central Hudson* were met. The third prong—whether the San Diego ordinance directly advanced governmental interests—presented the remaining and dispositive issue. Here, there was no evidence that the San Diego's traffic safety and aesthetic purposes were unreasonable and did not represent substantial and important governmental concerns. Likewise, the ordinance's favoring on-site over off-site signs, and so favoring one type of commercial speech over another, was a permissible municipal judgment: municipalities are free to decide that one type of commercial speech is more important to the flow of information and the functioning

52. *Id.* at 763.

53. *See Wag More Dogs v. Cozart*, 680 F.3d 359, 366 (4th Cir. 2012) (defining a content neutral ordinance as (1) not expressing disagreement with the regulated message, (2) supported by a governmental interest unrelated to the message, and (3) regulating only the message's location).

54. *See Central Hudson Gas and Electric Co. v. Public Service Comm'n of New York*, 447 U.S. 557 (1980). This is *Lochnerian*, economic, or substantive due process in a First Amendment context.

55. *Board of Trustees v. Fox*, 492 U.S. 469 (1989).

56. *See Signs for Jesus v. Town of Pembroke*, 977 F.3d 93 (1st Cir. 2020).

57. 453 U.S. 490 (1981).

of business and might reasonably conclude that on-site signs will be better maintained and change subjects less often.[58]

As to the *Virginia Pharmacy* test, Justice White concluded that the ordinance was not neutral because it was not limited to a time/place/manner regulation. It offended the first and third prongs of the *Virginia Pharmacy* test. It could not be justified without reference to the content of the speech and did not provide ample alternative channels of communication.

In a second aspect of its *Central Hudson* analysis, the plurality opinion struck down part of the ordinance. Construing the ordinance as exempting on-site commercial advertisements, Justice White found it failed to exempt non-commercial speech. (Non-commercial speech means political or highly protected speech subject to heightened scrutiny by the courts.) Such speech was regulated unless it fell within some narrow exceptions listed in the ordinance. In essence, the ordinance inverted the hierarchy of types of speech protected by the First Amendment in that it gave greater protection to commercial speech than it did to non-commercial speech, including political speech. Because of this inversion, Justice White found that the ordinance was over-inclusive by limiting non-commercial as well as commercial speech. Thus, the restrictions on off-site commercial advertising were valid, but the restrictions on on-site non-commercial advertisements were invalid. The former restrictions were justified on safety and aesthetic grounds. So, for instance, if a municipality were to ban all commercial billboards, but allow all non-commercial ones, the problem with regard to *Metromedia* would be that municipal officials will run afoul of Justice White's concern that they will be making content-oriented judgments to distinguish commercial from non-commercial speech.

Because six of the Justices focus on *Virginia Pharmacy* and the first and third prongs of its test, content neutrality and the alternative channels of communication have become the focus of later cases. Content neutrality has been the focus of most subsequent cases in this area. For example, the 2015 case of *Reed v. Town of Gilbert*[59] found that only regulations that discriminate based on the topic discussed or the idea or message expressed are content based.[60] Just because the regulator has to read the sign does not make it content based. To be content based, the regulation must (1) target the communicative content of a billboard or sign; targeting its location is a different matter, and (2) even if the regulation is facially content neutral, an improper purpose may be a basis for finding it content based.[61] Establishing that alternate channels of communication are available has not given rise to as much litigation because

---

58. *See Reagan Nat'l Adver. of Austin, Inc. v. City of Austin*, 64 F.4th 287, 293 (5th Cir. 2023) (noting that the U.S. Supreme Court has never questioned on-site/off-site distinctions, part of an "unbroken tradition" since the 1800s), citing *City of Austin v. Reagan Nat'l Advert. of Austin*, 142 S. Ct. 1464, 1475 (2022).

59. 576 U.S. 155 (2015) (using strict scrutiny as the standard of review), noted in 125 Yale L.J. F. 359 (2016).

60. 576 U.S. at 171.

61. *See Reagan Nat'l Adver. of Austin, op. cit.*, 64 F.4th at 293 (discussing *Reed, supra*); *Cent. Radio Co. v. City of Norfolk*, 811 F.3d 625, 632 (4th Cir. 2016).

such channels might include on-site signs, internet advertising, direct mail, radio and TV advertising, and newspapers.[62]

The *Medtromedia* majority of six, although not writing jointly, suggested that billboard restrictions on commercial speech were not a violation of the First Amendment. Indeed, the Justices said enough to indicate that a majority of them thought that aesthetics alone could be sufficient justification for an ordinance. That majority is drawn from those in the plurality and the dissenters. What was wrong with San Diego's ordinance was that it threw a protected class of political speech into a catch-all category of non-commercial speech by not defining the type of restricted speech narrowly enough.

In the wake of *Metromedia*, federal circuit courts have upheld billboard and sign ordinances that prohibited the digitalization of off-site commercial signs, but allowed the digitalization of on-site ones;[63] likewise upheld was an ordinance prohibiting the digitalization of traditional billboards.[64] These cases suggest that, instead of banning off-site signs outright, their gradual elimination through amortization may be the wiser, less economically disruptive course of action for municipalities. They also suggest that ordinances regulating the size and location of signs, distinguishing between on-site and off-site signs, and imposing time restrictions on one-off events, are constitutional as regulation of First Amendment commercial speech.

The standard of review used in most of the cases following *Metromedia* and not involving political speech or religious speech is one of intermediate scrutiny.[65] This is a second level of scrutiny, requiring more scrutiny that a first level, rational basis review, but requiring that an important or substantial governmental interest underlie a regulation, not necessarily a compelling interest (which is required in the third, heightened level of review). Intermediate scrutiny requires the important interest be advanced by means substantially related to the interest asserted.[66]

[A] How Can Cities Like San Diego Respond to *Metromedia* Cases?

Four responses are possible:

(1) Because Justice White concluded that the ordinance valued some types of protected speech over others entitled to greater protection, he found that the city could remedy this defect by banning all commercial billboards while permitting all

62. *See Interstate Outdoor Advertising LP v. Zoning Bd. of the Twp. of Mt. Laurel*, 706 F.3d 527 (3d Cir. 2013).

63. *See Reagan Nat'l Adver. of Austin, Inc., op. cit.*, 64 F.4th at 298.

64. *See Adams Outdoor Adver. Ltd. P'ship v. City of Madison*, 56 F.4th 1111 (7th Cir. 2023).

65. Because of the San Diego ordinance's potential for the regulation of political speech, heightened scrutiny as discussed in this paragraph was brought to bear on the ordinance.

66. *See Adams Outdoor Adver. Ltd. P'ship v. City of Madison*, 56 F.4th 1111, 1119 (7th Cir. 2023). *See also City of Cincinnati v. Fourth Nat'l Realty, LLC*, 214 N.E.3d 1 (Ohio App. Ct. 2023).

non-commercial billboards—in this sense, a total ban is thus better than a partial one. In the alternative, the city might amend its ordinance to permit non-commercial speech wherever and whenever commercial speech was permitted.[67] Further, a billboard ban should be preceded by an amortization period for the prohibited billboards;

(2) A municipality should define commercial speech in greater detail, so that political speech does not inadvertently come within the prohibitions of an ordinance. Defining the commercial speech to be regulated first and providing that non-commercial speech is not regulated, would do the trick;

(3) A municipality should eliminate the ordinance's exceptions that in effect force its officials to interpret messages and to categorize speech; such an effort, the *Metromedia* Court felt, verged on prior restraint of otherwise protected speech; and

(4) A municipality should allow any sign to go up, but require that it be dismantled by the advertiser or the city (at the advertiser's expense) if it falls within the restrictions. This eliminates a claim that the ordinance is a prior restraint on free speech. "In *Metromedia* . . . , a plurality of the court recognized that an ordinance prohibiting off-premise commercial billboard advertising would not have offended the first amendment if it had not preferred commercial over noncommercial advertising."[68] The *Naegele* opinion continues: "Contrary to Naegele's contention, the location of the billboard in commercial and industrial areas does not preclude the city from relying on aesthetics to justify its exercise of police power. The San Diego ordinance banned billboards in similar areas."[69] Apparently "once ugly, always ugly" is *not* the law.

Six years after *Metromedia*, the Supreme Court in *Members of the City Council of the City of Los Angeles v. Taxpayers for Vincent*,[70] upheld an ordinance prohibiting posting of a local political candidate's signs on utility poles.[71] The court, however, went out of its way to endorse the aesthetic purpose of the ordinance, which was to eliminate "visual assault on the citizens of Los Angeles presented by an accumulation of signs posted on public property."[72] The *Vincent* opinion makes plain that a prohibition on signs justified by aesthetics is valid, just as it was clear after *Metromedia* that a prohibition of commercial advertising is valid.

The *Vincent* opinion clarifies several points unclear after *Metromedia*. The opinion is an "aesthetics alone" case.[73] In addition, the poles were found not to be a public forum necessary to the dissemination of political ideas—there was plenty of private property around on which Vincent could have his signs placed. As one state court said later, "the *Vincent* opinion makes it clear that a content-neutral regulation limiting expressive activity on non-forum public property is tailored narrowly enough if it is

---

67. *See Wag More Dogs*, *supra*, 680 F.3d at 362.

68. *See Naegele Outdoor Advertising, Inc. v. City of Durham*, 844 F.2d 172, 173 (4th Cir. 1988).

69. *Id.* at 174.

70. 466 U.S. 789 (1984).

71. *Id.* at 814–15.

72. *Id.* at 827. *See also Act Now to Stop War & End Racism Coalition v. District of Columbia*, 846 F.3d 391 (D.C. Cir. 2017) (upholding the regulation of flyers on public lampposts).

73. *See Mahoney v. Doe*, 642 F.3d 1112 (D.C. Cir. 2011).

not 'substantially broader than necessary' to protect the interest. . . . "[74] In the same vein, the *Vincent* opinion states: "By banning these signs, the City did no more than eliminate the exact source of the evil it sought to remedy."[75] What is required here is not legislative efficiency, but rather only a reasonable nexus between the public purposes sought to be advanced and the regulations in the ordinance.

The distinction between on-site and off-site advertisements is unnecessary in some jurisdictions today. In jurisdictions which have endorsed aesthetics alone as a valid reason for an exercise of the police power, the difference between on-premises and off-premises signs and billboards should logically disappear.[76]

There is a large amount of case law in the area of billboard regulation. This is so because, first, the outdoor advertisers are tenacious litigators and the urge to "beautify" is strong at the local level. In *National Advertising Co. v. City and County of Denver*,[77] the court upheld an ordinance banning all off-site commercial signs within 600 feet of a freeway, but permitting non-commercial and on-site signs in the same proximity to a freeway. In *National Advertising Co. v. Town of Babylon*,[78] the court held that a town's billboard ordinance was unconstitutional for its failure to state the substantial governmental interest advanced by it, or because the town in the alternative failed to offer extrinsic evidence of that interest.[79]

Second, basic definitions for a sign are likely to provoke disputes. One ordinance usefully defined a sign as "any structure, part thereof or device attached thereto, or painted or represented thereon, which displays or includes any messages or representations used as an announcement, advertisement, direction, or designation of any goods or services located on any land or any building in such a manner as to draw attention from beyond the land or building." Likewise, a message was "any number, word, symbol, emblem, insignia, trademark, model, banner more than four inches high."[80] Before regarding this definition as too vague, consider the variety of sizes and shapes for signs that any definition must cover: there are standard roadside billboards, but there are also corporate logos atop buildings, signs painted on the side of a building, and signs declared historic landmarks. Signs can be neon, flashing, or fiber optic—and regulated as traffic safety matters. Signs can be permanent or portable.[81] Inclusivity is not vagueness.

---

74. *State v. Hodgkiss*, 565 A.2d 1059, 1064 (N.H. 1989).

75. *Vincent*, 466 U.S. at 808.

76. *See generally Bell v. Township of Stafford*, 541 A.2d 692, 696–99 (N.J. 1988) (reviewing U.S. Supreme Court cases).

77. 912 F.2d 405 (10th Cir. 1990).

78. 900 F.2d 551, 555 (2d Cir. 1990).

79. *See generally* Peter Salsich, Land Use Regulation 445–49 (1991).

80. *See Blockbuster Video, Inc. v. City of Tempe*, 141 F.3d 1295 (9th Cir. 1998) (noted in Jeffrey Strouse, *Redefining Trademark Alteration Within the Context of Aesthetic-Based Zoning Laws: A Blockbuster Dilemma*, 53 Vand. L. Rev. 717 (2000)).

81. *See Harnish v. Manatee County*, 783 F.2d 1535 (11th Cir. 1986) (upholding a prohibition of portable signs). The ordinance also provided: "No sign shall have more than eight messages, although a premium of one message is permitted if the sign is lower than ten feet in height."

Third, many types of signs have some protected, political content—for example, a garrison flag flown by a car dealership. Some make use of public space either (1) directly—for example, a billboard hung on a elevated light-rail track over a public street—or (2) indirectly—for example, a sign for a local political candidate suspended between a utility pole and a tree. Consider the free speech implications of prohibiting the latter sign, situated between the pole and tree, as before, but while a candidate for public office stands under it on the sidewalk distributing leaflets to passers-by.[82] Thus regulation of signs by physical type easily runs afoul of the free speech clause of the First Amendment. So, many sign definitions are likely to be challenged "as applied."

§ 8.06 Low-Income Neighborhoods and Billboards

Some local problems with billboards will require less than jurisdiction-wide regulation. For instance, nation-wide surveys show that much of the revenue from billboard companies comes from tobacco and liquor companies advertising their products to low-income persons. Local groups have whitewashed the billboards advertising such products; they also have engaged in civil disobedience when billboard owners attempt to have the police stop them. Faced with such a situation, a municipal legislature might permissibly ban such advertising from low-income neighborhoods. A local municipality need not do its own studies on this matter.[83] If national studies show that tobacco and liquor has adverse effects on health, the municipality may regulate this advertising on that account. This will not likely be found to be content neutral regulation, but the adverse health effects of such billboards are arguably included within a regulation of offending billboards' "secondary effects."[84] Those effects bring the matter within the police power. They provide a rational basis for a municipality to enact a neighborhood ban on such billboards, or else to require placing tobacco or liquor advertising alongside public service announcements with an anti-smoking or sobriety theme.

---

82. *See State v. Hodgkiss*, 565 A.2d 1059 (N.H. 1989).

83. *See City of Renton v. Playtime Theatres, Inc.*, 475 U.S. 41 (1986) (finding that no independent localized study is required before regulating adult movie theaters when secondary effects of the regulated use are reasonably considered to be present) (discussed *infra* Chapter 19).

84. *See Young v. American Mini-Theatres, Inc.*, 427 U.S. 50 (1976) (Powell, J., writing a plurality opinion, finding that regulation of adult movie houses might be justified by the secondary effects occurring around them—e.g., incidental criminal conduct).

§ 8.07 A Ban on Billboards

Faced with the complexity of the law in this area, a municipality might be tempted to ban all types of billboards. Courts have said in dicta that a municipality might limit the number of billboards to a certain maximum number or prohibit them altogether.[85] In *Lucas v. South Carolina Coastal Council*,[86] the United States Supreme Court held that "when an owner of real property has been called upon to sacrifice *all* economically beneficial uses in the name of the common good, that is, to leave his property economically idle, he has suffered a taking."[87] Reading this, a municipal attorney might suspect that a total ban raises the possibility that *Metromedia* and *Lucas* may intersect for the benefit of the billboard industry. What *Metromedia* seems to permit—a total prohibition on billboards—may deprive the billboard company of "*all* economically beneficial uses" of its property in the municipality. In this instance, the company's property will be a collection of billboard leases, licenses, and easements, as opposed to the fee simple underlying the billboard or the land improved with a billboard and incapable of another use. Imagining an alternative use for a billboard is difficult. So the "total takings" analysis of *Lucas* might apply, unless the state's background common law of nuisance and property permit the ban. As background law, numerous state cases upholding billboard regulations should suffice to show that they are a visual blight and a nuisance. Therefore, a ban on billboards, when content-neutral and when other means of advertising are available, makes, in the words of *Lucas*, "what was previously permissible no longer so."[88] The widespread judicial approval of aesthetic regulation should trump *Lucas*.

---

85. *See Bell v. Township of Stafford*, 541 A.2d 692 (N.J. 1988) (holding that the township failed to justify a total ban, but admitted the possibility on aesthetic grounds).

86. 505 U.S. 1003 (1992).

87. *Id.* at 1019.

88. *Id.* at 1031.

Chapter 9
Moratoria and Growth Controls

§ 9.01 Moratoria

In order to meet an emergency, municipal legislatures sometimes enact moratoria on building permits, sewer hook-ups, or other permits and approvals. These are stop gap, time buying measures. Often moratoria are enacted in order to prevent the overloading of public facilities such as schools, sewer systems, or water supply facilities. Sometimes they are enacted to prevent a permitting rush in the face of proposed new regulations or to keep the status quo in place while decisions are made on capital budgeting and improvements.

The United States Supreme Court has said that moratoria are not per se unconstitutional.[1] As such, they are important planning tools to ensure that problems and emergencies are not exacerbated while a plan for solving them is formulated.[2] The enactment of a moratorium ordinance is a legislative act, subject to rational basis review and to electoral review by referenda in many jurisdictions, but also entitled to a presumption of validity.

A long-running problem to which the legislature suddenly responds with a moratorium, when unaccompanied by a simultaneous increase in the seriousness of the problem, does not lay the basis for a valid moratorium.[3]

Authority for enacting moratorium is often found as an implied power in a state's zoning enabling act to exercise the police power to protect a municipality's zoning and planning authority, and by liberally construing the act.[4] Such implied authority is in

---

1. *See Tahoe-Sierra Preservation Council, Inc. v. Tahoe Regional Planning Agency*, 535 U.S. 302, 338 (2002).

2. *Id.* at 337-38.

3. *See Westwood Forest Estates Inc. v. Village of South Nyack*, 244 N.E.2d 700 (N.Y. 1969) (involving a rezoning prohibiting multiple dwellings throughout the town); *see also Q.C. Construction Company v. Gallo*, 649 F. Supp. 1331 (D.R.I. 1986) (due process violation found, with injunctive remedy given).

4. *See Brazos Land, Inc. v. Board of Cty. Comm'nrs*, 848 P.2d 1095 (N.M. App. Ct. 1993) (moratoria to protect groundwater from pollution). *But see Board of Supervisors v. Horne*, 215 S.E.2d 453 (Va. 1975) (finding moratoria *ultra vires* a county's express and implied authority).; *See also Biggers v. City of Bainbridge Island*, 169 P.3d 14 (Wash. 2007) (finding on implied authority for a moratorium in a coastal management statute) (noted in 84 Wash. L. Rev. 67 (2009)). *Cf. Naylor v. Twp. of Hellam*, 773 A.2d 770, 777, n.8 (Pa. 2001) (rejecting a rule of incidental authority but citing cases embracing it from numerous other states).

effect taken from the second prong of Dillon's Rule—the moratorium being a municipal action reasonably necessary to achieve a power (the power to zone) expressly delegated to it. When a statute authorizes zoning or planning for a particular purpose, there is implied authority to adopt a moratorium for that same purpose.[5] Likewise, if a municipality has authority to operate sewer and water facilities, implied authority for a moratorium on providing them may be readily implied.

For those who think it illogical that a moratorium suspending zoning decisions is implicitly authorized by a statute enabling zoning decisions, or that the authority to halt development is not incidental to the authority to regulate it, an alternative ground for a moratorium, for home rule municipalities in particular, is the police power itself. A moratorium that does not suspend or prohibit all zoning applications is simply not a zoning matter. Neither is a moratorium ordinance that contains rules on vested rights, even though the zoning ordinance contains other such rules.[6] In both instances, the moratorium is emergency legislation and as such is not final municipal legislative action.[7] Some would see such an action as an interim zoning control, allowing some types of zoning control to continue while pausing others.[8] For example, a moratorium on some land uses, rather than permitting procedures, gives time to study the off-site impacts of those uses: video arcades, fast food outlets, adult entertainment, or billboards are well studied examples. Wind farms and cannabis operations and outlets are newer ones.[9]

If a moratorium is enacted (1) in good faith, (2) on a temporary basis, (3) is nondiscriminatory, (4) is an interim step while a comprehensive plan is worked out to deal with the emergency, and (5) a prompt adoption of the plan follows, then the moratorium is a valid exercise of the police power and by the same token is not a taking.[10] While the moratorium is in force, a municipality must continue to conduct its administrative business as usual while the moratorium on other types of permits is in place. The permits denied must be linked to the problem addressed in the moratorium and may not be denied on an arbitrary or case-by-case basis.[11] However, if valid, a moratorium can reach even vested rights, permitting a municipality to revoke prior approvals.[12]

---

5. *See Samson v. City of Bainbridge Island*, 683 F.3d 1051 (9th Cir. 2012) (moratoria on pier permits valid under the police power to protect fish and wildlife and prevent an expected increase in permit applications while doing coastal planning required by the state, and not a violation of the due process clause).

6. *See Green Dev. LLC v. Town of Exeter*, 297 A.3d 931, 939 (R.I. 2023).

7. *See City of Roswell v. Outdoor Systems, Inc.*, 549 S.E.2d 90 (Ga. App. Ct. 2001).

8. *See infra*, this Chapter, § 9.02.

9. *See Seven Hills LLC v. Chelan Cty.*, 495 P.3d 778 (Wash. 2021) (validating a moratorium on cannabis operations).

10. *See Droste v. Board of Cty. Comm'rs of Cty. of Pitkin*, 159 P.3d 601 (Colo. 2007) (ten month moratorium held valid); *see also WCI Communities, Inc. v. City of Coral Springs*, 885 So. 2d 912 (Fla. Dist. Ct. App. 2004); *Adams Outdoor Advertising v. East Lansing*, 483 N.W.2d 38, 44 (Mich. 1992).

11. *See Pritchett v. Nathan Rogers Const. & Realty Co.*, 379 So. 2d 545 (Ala. 1979).

12. *See Almquist v. Town of Marshan*, 245 N.W.2d 819 (Minn. 1976) (applying moratorium on permits to partially completed development); *Belle Harbor Realty Corporation v. Kerr*, 323 N.E.2d 697 (N.Y. 1974) (problem with the whole sewer system, not just the capacity of a treatment plant involved).

A municipality that is contemplating a moratorium should plan for it. That is, a municipality contemplating a year's moratorium should be able to complete its plan to address the emergency within that time. If the studies to address it are not completed with the year, an extension of the moratorium at year's end will be on weaker ground than originally. Why? Because the rationale for the moratorium cannot be as originally stated. The reasonableness of the moratorium's length is now at issue as well. For those who see the adoption of a moratorium as a failure of the municipal planning process, the moratorium itself must be planned at its adoption, with steps outlined to be taken during its effective period, and with steps to be taken at its end, all consistent with the moratorium's original stated purpose. When the studies of the emergency and the drafting and promulgation of legislation necessary to address it will take two or three years, the municipality had best say so before the start of the moratorium: transparency in this regard will make the moratorium more defensible later. In this regard too, the remedial actions taken at the end of the moratorium must be within the grasp of those affected by it. For instance, a study of soil stability of affected parcels should not conclude by setting conditions on development that are impossible to meet.[13] Setting such conditions would amount to a permanent moratorium, a matter not considered in the *Tahoe-Sierra Preservation Council*[14] case but, as a facial matter, raising takings and due process issues. The issue of the reasonableness of a moratorium's length is fact-dependent and subject to rational basis judicial scrutiny, but when permanent in effect, may still become a *Lucas*-type total taking.[15] Likewise, a moratorium should avoid unintended effects: One on development and occupancy permits for new office buildings should take account of the fact that both landlords and tenants are affected: a moratorium that lasts as long as an existing lease on office space restricts development for the entire remaining term of the lease and becomes a 100% total taking under *Lucas*.

The seriousness of the problem to which the moratorium responds is more easily justified and defensible when the health and safety of the public is at stake (as with water treatment or inadequate sewers).[16] Even more serious and defensible is the problem that amounts to a nuisance.[17] On the other hand, moratoria on the provision of public facilities are harder to justify, in large part because the municipality's problem is then general in nature, and in this situation, forcing particular property owners to bear the consequences of its failure to solve a municipal problem violates the "reciprocity of advantage" required in substantive due process cases. Likewise, the need to protect public facilities, such as a municipal hospital, from competition

---

13. *See Monks v. City of Rancho Palos Verdes*, 84 Cal. Rptr. 3d 75 (Cal. Ct. App. 2008).

14. *Tahoe-Sierra Preservation Council, Inc. v. Tahoe Regional Planning Agency*, 535 U.S. 302, 338 (2002), cited *supra*, this section.

15. *See Lucas v. South Carolina Coastal Council*, 505 U.S. 1003 (1992), discussed in Chapter 17, § 17.04.

16. *See Kaplan v. Clear Lake Water Authority*, 794 F.2d 1059 (5th Cir. 1986).

17. *See Ecogen v. Town of Italy*, 438 F. Supp. 2d 149 (W.D. N.Y. 2006) (involving a wind farm's turbines). In this regard, there might be aesthetic, noise, and public trust nuisances, the latter based on endangering wildlife.

in order to preserve its fiscal position, will not justify a moratorium on building hospitals.[18] Lesser municipal needs, such as the protection of tourism or aesthetics, are even less defensible. A moratorium should defend the heavyweight objectives of the police power—health and safety.

Factors indicating the seriousness of a problem are: (1) inter-governmental disputes over how to solve it (a longer moratorium is justified here); (2) the protection of natural resources (e.g., a river, into which sewage might overflow from an inadequate sewage treatment plant); and (3) the presence of state or regional effects wider than the jurisdictional writ of the moratorium (e.g., state administrative actions producing a ban at the local or regional level—in effect saying, "we did not create this problem, we're under orders").[19] Ambiguities in an ordinance, its need for more definition, and the possibility that the ordinance is void for vagueness, are insufficient grounds for a serious problem and a moratorium. However, the novelty or newness of a problem might rise to the point of emergency, as with the advent of cell phone towers, or wind or water farms in a region.[20] So might the coming of a natural disaster, such as a hurricane.

A defensible moratorium must also be limited in its physical dimensions, affecting as small an area as possible and as few land uses as possible. A moratorium on sewer system connections should be limited to development permits in neighborhoods where sewer hook-ups produce the heaviest burden on the system—or to land uses, such as large apartment buildings, that threaten to overload the system.

When a moratorium may more defensibly target land uses rather than permitting procedures, the land uses targeted should be those already developed to the point where a reasonable, beneficial use remains for their owners during the moratorium. Likewise, the permitting procedures denied them during that time should allow them to fall back on the existing uses of their property.

There is no bright-line rule concerning the length of a valid moratorium. The United States Supreme Court has said that a moratorium lasting more than a year is suspect, but on the other hand it approved a moratorium lasting thirty two months.[21] On the other hand, a moratorium on billboard reconstruction after a hurricane lasting twenty two months has been held subject to a temporary restraining order because of its length.[22] Often moratoria are the herald of the imposition of growth controls—when there is no health and safety problem, but instead there is an on-going

---

18. *See Kentuckiana Med. Ctr. LLC v. Clark Cty.*, 2006 U.S. Dist. LEXIS 3298 (S.D. Ind., Jan 18, 2006).

19. *See Smoke Rise, Inc. v. Washington Suburban Sanitary Commission*, 400 F. Supp. 1369 (D. Md. 1975) (upholding five year sewer hook-up moratorium against due process and taking claims); *see also Unity Ventures v. County of Lake*, 631 F. Supp. 181, 197-199 (N.D. Ill. 1986) (a civil rights case discussing *Smoke Rise*).

20. *See Ecogen, LLC v. Town of Italy*, 438 F. Supp. 2d 149 (W.D. N.Y. 2006) (involving a wind farm, upholding a moratorium against a facial challenge, but requiring that the town develop its plan within ninety days)

21. *See Tahoe-Sierra Preservation Council, Inc., supra*, 535 U.S. at 341–41.

22. *See Bill Salter Advertising, Inc. v. City of Brewster*, 486 F. Supp. 2d 1314 (S.D. Ala. 2007).

planning process, the effectiveness of which the local legislature wishes to preserve. Here, a quick spike in development permits can provide the precipitating emergency.

Similarly, moratoria may be used particularly in rural, agricultural areas containing second home communities for which there are no public sewer lines and treatment facilities;[23] a three-year moratorium on the installation of new septic systems in order to protect the groundwater supplies in the municipality tests the scope of the good faith element for a moratorium. The time period during which criteria for adequate septic systems may be devised is unreasonably long when lasting more than 2 or 3 years; such a lengthy ban is neither "temporary" nor does it provide a solution to be put in place within a reasonable time, so it also violates both the second and the fifth criteria for a valid moratorium. On the other hand, a moratorium lasting as long as the process needed to respond to the emergency is valid and not a taking.[24] A second, similar example involved a moratorium on mobile home sales stores. It was enacted to prevent a municipality from having "an unwanted reputation" as the mobile home sales capital of its region, but was struck down.[25] Its good faith was suspect. On the other hand, a moratorium to study the effects of an excess of cement and asphalt plants in a municipality has been upheld.[26] Here the court would not impute the bad faith motives of two legislators to the municipal legislature as a whole.

On occasion, moratoria have even reached matters that might be regarded as title matters, such as the creation of time shares in apartments in a destination resort municipality.[27] Moratoria may sometimes to limited to certain urbanizing areas of a municipality, particular land uses, or types of very intensive development.

Property owners affected by a moratorium followed by a valid downzoning might wish to consider further steps, one of which might be to appeal their next property tax assessment.[28] If a client's parcel is worth less than before the moratorium, then the assessment, premised on the "full value" of the parcel, should logically be reduced. Such a reduction will not result automatically and must be applied for, but is more easily achieved than would be a judgment in a takings claim brought as a result of the moratorium and downzoning.

---

23. *See Kaplan v. Clear Lake Water Authority*, 794 F.2d 1059 (5th Cir. 1986) (upholding such a moratorium against due process and equal protection challenges).

24. *See Tahoe-Sierra Preservation Council*, *supra*, 535 U.S. at 342 (finding no total taking under the *Lucas v. South Carolina Coastal Council* opinion).

25. *See Herrington v. City of Pearl*, 908 F. Supp. 418 (S.D. Miss. 1995); *see also Begin v. Inhabitants of the Town of Sabbatus*, 409 A.2d 1269 (Me. 1979) (invalidating moratorium applicable only to mobile homes as a violation of the equal protection clause).

26. *See Watson Construction Co. v. City of Gainesville*, 433 F. Supp. 2d 1269 (N.D. Fla. 2006).

27. *See Jackson Court Condominiums, Inc. v. City of New Orleans*, 665 F. Supp. 1235 (E.D. La. 1987) (upholding the interim regulation as preserving the residential integrity of the use district by discouraging transiency and promoting a sense of belonging, and by preserving the aesthetics of the district, citing *Penn Central Transp. Co.*).

28. *See State Department of Assessments and Taxation v. Clark*, 380 A.2d 28 (Md. 1977).

[A] Statutory Prohibitions on Moratoria

Several states—e.g., New Jersey[29] and New Mexico—have enacted statutes prohibiting certain types of moratoria. New Jersey prohibits them when used in order to prepare a comprehensive plan. New Mexico prohibits them when they are used to buy study time to impose impact fees. Arizona, Montana, and Washington also have some type of statutory restrictions on the use of moratoria, requiring specific legislative findings, limiting its duration, or imposing hearing requirements, respectively.

The New Jersey statute provides:

> (a) The prohibition of development in order to prepare a master plan and development regulations is prohibited.
>
> (b) No moratoria on applications for development or interim zoning ordinances shall be permitted except in cases where the municipality demonstrates on the basis of a written opinion by a qualified health professional that a clear imminent danger to the health of the inhabitants of the municipality exists, and in no case shall the moratorium or interim ordinance exceed a six-month term.

Although the language of subsection (a) is stilted—a "prohibition" being there "prohibited"—the prohibition on a development moratorium to develop a plan and regulations is clear enough. Most of the litigation under this statute concerns subsection (b). A moratorium on development *applications* might permit a moratorium on land uses, except that because interim zoning ordinances are also prohibited in subsection (b), and zoning is intended to regulate development, no moratorium that requires a municipality to amend its existing zoning is permitted. However, then follows the exception permitting a moratorium to prevent a "clear imminent danger" to public health when supported in writing by a "qualified health professional." So a professional opinion that a sewage treatment plant is over capacity and threatening nearly watercourses with untreated sewage provides a rationale for a "health and safety" moratorium lasting no more than six months (hardly by itself time to remedy such a problem). Likewise, a "boil water" order issued by a state department of health will validate a moratorium under this exception. Because the opinion must "demonstrate" the health danger, its contents will, when challenged in court, result in questions of fact precluding summary judgment—that is, an opinion not containing substantial evidence of the danger will be insufficient support for a moratorium. Growth controls, timed and phased development controls, growth caps, and urban boundary ordinances (all discussed in later sections of this Chapter) are all within the scope of this statute's subsection (a) prohibition because they all require new "development regulations" mentioned in subsection (a).

---

29. *See* N.J. Stat. Ann. § 40:55D-90 (1997) (used in *New Jersey Shore Builders Ass'n v. Mayor and Twp. of Middletown*, 561 A.2d 319 (N.J. Super. Ct., L. Div. 1989), and *Toll Bros., Inc. v. Mayor and Council of the Twp. of West Windsor*, 712 A.2d 266 (N.J. Super. Ct., App. Div. 1998) (invalidating a timed, sequential growth control and distinguishing *Golden v. Planning Bd.*, discussed *infra*)).

§ 9.02 Interim Zoning Controls

Municipalities sometimes experience a problem with a land use for which its land use regulations are unprepared. Fast food restaurants in commercial use districts, bed and breakfasts in residential land use districts, and adult entertainment uses in commercial districts,[30] provide examples. An interim regulation may restrict the rezoning of sites for such purposes, or the subdivision of such sites, or the issuance of special exceptions for them.[31] A moratorium on applications for building permits, utility connections, or occupancy permits may then provide a bridge between the planning necessary to deal with such uses and the implementation of that planning by preserving the status quo in the affected use districts while the planning takes place.[32] It may even be used in part to provoke public debate about such uses. Reasonably prompt planning and implementation of the plan is all that is required. "Moratorium" and "interim regulation" are interchangeable terms in many jurisdictions.

This use of interim regulations with a moratorium on applications has a public purpose.[33] It prevents a plan's defeat before it is implemented.[34] However, the duration of the moratorium is crucial: its duration should not be so long as to provide the affected property owner with a cause of action for a temporary taking.[35] Two to three years provide the outside limits on the duration of interim ordinances.[36] Some states limit such moratoria by statute, but about ten states authorize some use of interim and restrictive regulations so long as the municipality diligently pursues the enactment of new or amended regulations.[37]

Express statutory authority exists for interim zoning in several states.[38] At least eighteen state courts in different jurisdictions have held that interim zoning is within

---

30. *See CR of Rialto, Inc. v. City of Rialto*, 975 F. Supp. 1254 (C.D. Cal. 1997) (striking down an interim ordinance and enjoining its enforcement on First Amendment grounds).

31. *See Liberty Cove, Inc. v. Missoula Cty.*, 220 P.3d 617 (Mont. 2009) (interim regulations for excavation of minerals not illegal reverse spot zoning).

32. *See State ex rel. SCA Chemical Waste Services, Inc. v. Konigsberg*, 636 S.W.2d 430, 435 (Tenn. 1982).

33. *See Schafer v. City of New Orleans*, 743 F.2d 1086 (5th Cir. 1984) (rejecting a substantive due process claim involving fast food restaurants and upholding an interim ordinance applying to five city blocks and whose duration was 10.5 months long).

34. Robert Frielich, *Interim Development Controls: Essential Tools for Implementing Flexible Planning and Zoning*, 49 J. Urban L. 65, 66–67 (1971).

35. *See First English Evan. Lutheran Church v. City of Los Angeles*, 482 U.S. 304 (1987) (finding that an action for a temporary regulatory taking occurs when the time passing is more than a "normal administrative delay").

36. *See Zilber v. Town of Moraga*, 692 F. Supp. 1195, 1207 (N.D. Cal. 1988) (upholding a 1.5 year development moratorium while open space preservation regulations were developed); *see also Kawaoka v. City of Arroyo Grande*, 796 F. Supp. 1320 (C.D. Cal. 1992).

37. *See, e.g.*, Minn. Stat. Ann. § 394.34 (1998).

38. *See Gateway Opencut Mining Action Group v. Bd. of Cty. Comm'nrs*, 260 P.3d 133 (Mont. 2011) (interpreting a state statute limiting the enforceability of an interim regulation to one year).

the general police power delegation inherent in zoning enabling acts.[39] An electoral initiative or referendum may attempt to take such matters out of hands of the local authorities, but such preemption has been held invalid when the state legislature has enacted an express authority to enact interim land use regulations.[40]

Finally, when expressly authorized by statute, in some states interim regulations may be used for land beyond a municipality's borders that will soon be subject to annexation.

§ 9.03 Growth Controls

In the landmark case of *Village of Euclid v. Ambler Realty Co.*,[41] land use regulation that permits a landowner the reasonable use of his land was authorized; there, reasonable use was measured once, at the moment of the regulation's enactment. Later cases recognized that what is a reasonable use may change with the approach of urbanization. Moreover, it was recognized that such uses needed to be measured differently as urbanization approached—that what was reasonable without urbanization was not the same as what was required when it came. Thus was born the idea of regulating the shift to a more intense use of land over a reasonable length of time—in short, growth controls. Growth controls require land developers to wait a reasonable period of time until public services and facilities catch up with their projects. Municipalities with growth controls have expressly required that a subdivision may only be approved where there are facilities with adequate capacity to provide water, treat wastewater and sewage, handle traffic smoothly on abutting roads, and provide other public facilities like fire protection, libraries and public open spaces. Often such growth controls are known as adequate public facilities (APF) ordinances. They involve planning in and over time in addition to spatial planning.[42]

The need for such controls may be seen, in relief and in the alternative, in the phrase "urban sprawl."[43] It is costly in many ways to society as a whole—for example, in the uneconomical provision of urban facilities and services over long distances, or

---

39. *See Sprint Spectrum L.P. v. Jefferson Cty.*, 968 F. Supp. 1457, 1464–65 (N.D. Ala. 1997) (finding no Alabama statutes or decisions on the matter, but listing, *id.* at n. 9, California, Colorado, Kentucky, Michigan, Minnesota, Montana, New Jersey, Oregon, Washington, and Wisconsin as providing express statutory authority for interim land use regulations; and also listing Arkansas, Connecticut, Florida, Georgia, Hawaii, Illinois, Maryland, Massachusetts, New York, Ohio, Oklahoma, Pennsylvania, South Carolina, Tennessee, Texas, Utah, and Wyoming as having judicial decisions on this matter).

40. *See Bank of the Orient v. Tiburon*, 269 Cal. Rptr. 690 (App. Ct. 1990) (so holding in a situation in which the municipal legislature already enacted a similar interim regulation).

41. 272 U.S. 365 (1926) (discussed *supra* Chapter 6).

42. In this regard, see *Marx v. Zoning Board of Appeal of the Village of Mill Neck*, 529 N.Y.S.2d 330 (N.Y. App. Div. 1988), denying a BZA the right to alter a subdivision approval of the village planning board in an attempt to maintain the distinct jurisdiction of each agency.

43. The effects of sprawl are hotly debated. *Compare* Timothy Dowling, *Reflections on Urban Sprawl, Smart Growth, and the Fifth Amendment*, 148 U. Pa. L. Rev. 873 (2000), *with* Clint Bolick,

in a spreading and low density of population and land use affecting the rate at which land is urbanized and denied to other uses, such as agriculture.[44] It is also seen in the lack of control over the quality of public services and facilities, as when a dependence on the automobile defeats the purposes of public transportation. It is sometimes further described as a lack of balance among various land uses, or in the lack of control over the specifics and eventual development of a municipality. In contrast, the alternative to urban sprawl is seen by urban planners as the use of compact, high-density urban designs of mixed land use—an updated version of a traditional town, with a town center.[45] There is considerable debate in economic circles over the costs of sprawl as opposed to un-sprawled, compact dense development. Some urban costs, e.g., schools, are less related to sprawl than to a concern with quality.[46]

Thus, after a jurisdiction enacts a moratorium on permits, its officials may start a planning process resulting in the enactment of some type of growth controls ordinance, involving the timing and sequence of development. These controls are an overlay on already existing zoning and subdivision regulations and so require a developer to obtain special permits certifying that the development is served by certain public facilities. Only essential and the most costly public facilities are typically involved: waste water sewers, drainage facilities, roads with a capacity to handle subdivision traffic, parks, and fire protection.

Growth controls must not be just a moratorium in disguise. They are aimed at preventing the imposition of moratoria in the future by dealing with the provision of essential services. One case, however, concluded that a mandatory phasing ordinance for a large development otherwise permitted as of right, was an invalid moratorium.[47]

Thus and as previously noted, growth controls impose additional requirements on the platting of subdivisions, requirements that channel subdivisions into areas of the municipality for which public facilities are available. The purpose is to coordinate the subdivision of land with the provision and availability of such facilities. An additional, underlying purpose is to regulate the flow of municipal financing devices such as municipal bonds, making sure that a municipality does not overleverage its ability to incur debt in amounts over what its tax base can support. Sometimes this regulation of municipal debt is mandated by ratios of tax revenue to debt imposed by state government.

In APF ordinances, the availability of public facilities means one of two things. It can mean proximity. This is the simpler definition: the public facilities must be within

---

Subverting the American Dream: Government Dictated "Smart Growth" Is Unwise and Unconstitutional, 148 U. Pa. L. Rev. 858 (2000).

44. *See generally Mayhew v. Town of Sunnyvale*, 964 S.W.2d 922 (Tex. 1998) (finding that the denial of a development application is not a regulatory taking when designed to steady a municipality's rate of growth and remedy the "ill effects of urbanization" with the expansion of the urban areas within the municipality).

45. This is sometimes called "New Urbanism," discussed *supra* Chapter 7.

46. *See generally Points of View: Paying for Sprawl*, http://www.reocities.com/erietown/sprawl.htm.

47. *See Toll Bros., Inc. v. West Windsor Twp.*, 712 A.2d 266 (N.J. Super. Ct., App. Div. 1998).

a certain distance of the proposed subdivision or development. Somewhat more difficult to apply is a definition in which availability means adequacy—with this definition in place, the discretion of the administrators of the system becomes much greater. Adequacy standards are appropriate and most used when the capacity of municipality wide facilities, such as the provision of water and sewer services are in doubt. This type of municipality wide phasing does not forecast where development will occur within the municipality. More typically, adequacy standards are used in phasing development in municipalities with room to grow. Such development, phased by area, allows a municipality to target its investment in public facilities for developing areas within its boundaries and to plan its capital budget for public facilities accordingly.

For proximity standards, a point system is often used in granting growth control permits. If the services required to be available are in fact available, then the subdivision application receives so many points. A minimum number of points must be assembled by the application and its proposed plat before a subdivision permit is issued. This is the system used by the Town of Ramapo, validated by the New York Court of Appeals in *Golden v. Planning Board of Ramapo*.[48] The United States Supreme Court's dismissal of the appeal in *Ramapo* should not be interpreted as its validation of the town's ordinance. Caution is warranted, particularly after the Supreme Court's temporary takings opinion in *First English*.[49]

§ 9.04 The Ramapo Plan

With growth controls imposed on land in residential-use districts in the Town of Ramapo, a landowner, Mrs. Golden, wanted to develop at a density below the level permitted in the zoning ordinance, but without meeting the extra requirements for the town's growth control permits. The planning board would not permit her to do so.

Mrs. Golden had contracted to sell her land for development purposes to a commercial builder. The planning board denied approval on the ground that she had failed to obtain the special permit required by the town's growth controls ordinance. (Such a system had better apply to a wide spectrum of owners, as here, or else equal protection clause concerns are raised.) Golden sued the planning board, seeking to annul its denial of her purchaser's subdivision plan.

Ramapo is one of five towns in Rockland County, a suburban and rural municipality twenty-five miles north of New York City. Between 1960 and 1970, its population more than doubled and its county's population increased 68%. So the town had grown rapidly during the 1960s and had grown nearly 300% in population during the years 1940–1968.

---

48. 285 N.E.2d 291 (N.Y.), *appeal dismissed sub nom. Rockland County Builders Ass'n v. McAlevey*, 409 U.S. 1003 (1972) (noted in 47 N.Y.U. L. Rev. 723 (1972), 26 Stan. L. Rev. 585 (1974), and 58 Minn. L. Rev. 1009, 1054–58 (1974)).

49. Involving temporary takings, discussed *supra*, Chapter 5, § 5.02.

The town adopted its growth control plan in 1969. Behind the Ramapo plan and ordinance lay eight years of planning studies, sewage and drainage studies, adoption of an official map, master planning, and capital budgeting. Moreover, the town's ordinance was not an exclusionary device. Its plan and ordinance also provided for some, though not a lot, of low and moderate income housing. Moreover, its planning board was given the authority under the ordinance to issue permits granting the right to proceed with development in future years, once capital improvements called for in the town's capital budget were constructed.

In Ramapo's ordinance (the ground for denying Mrs. Golden's subdivision plan), the eligibility of each project for a special permit was based on the availability of five essential services:

1. sewers or an approved substitute,
2. drainage facilities,
3. parks or recreational facilities,
4. public roads improved with curbs and sidewalks, and
5. firehouses.

A variable number of points was given, the greater number given for proximity of the proposed subdivision to these five types of facilities. A score of fifteen was the minimum required, and no more than five points could be awarded in any one of the five categories. An applicant had to obtain the fifteen points and with them a special permit before beginning the subdivision process.

Ramapo's controls applied to all residential districts, to single family as well as multi-family development districts. This aspect of the controls is reminiscent of the "reciprocity of advantage" discussed by Justice Holmes in *Mahon*. Underlying the plan was the fiscal assumption that it would lower municipal bond financing costs for the town. Thus the town obtained these lower costs and reciprocated by extending the developer the financed services. However, the town's growth controls plan would have been in a still stronger position—and probably further lowered financing costs too—if commercial and industrial uses had been included as well.

The court found this scheme "an over-all program of orderly growth" and "a sequential development policy commensurate with progressing availability and capacity of public facilities."[50] Moreover, it found authority for the growth controls in the language of the enabling act "to restrict and regulate" land use;[51] that included by implication the authority to direct the growth of population within the confines of the jurisdiction. New York State's enabling statute governing the town's authority was based on the Standard Zoning Enabling Act—enhancing the persuasive value of this opinion for other states.

50. *Ramapo*, 285 N.E.2d at 144.

51. For a contrary view, see *Lanvale Properties, LLC v. Cty. of Cabarrus*, 731 S.E.2d 800 (N.C. 2012).

Finally, it is important to note that any developer whose property was prohibited from development by the controls until some future year might provide the facilities himself and so accumulate enough development points to gain the right to subdivide. Thus, the developer willing to pay the price of his development in municipal facilities was not precluded from going ahead. It is likely, though, that only well-financed developers could do so, choosing the facilities that they could build most cheaply.

Ramapo's sequence of development proceeded in three six-year phases. This phasing was necessary because the enabling statute for capital budgets provided for six-year plans. For those holding some property back from development for eighteen years, the town gave decreased real property tax assessments. Such decreases were reminiscent of contractual consideration and of an agreement between the developer and the town—based again on a reciprocity of advantage.

[A] Summary

Ramapo's growth control plan was approved because it:

1. was supported, before-the-fact, by a comprehensive planning process,
2. involved no permanent land use restrictions (although 12-18 years—the program's life—does stretch the meaning of the word "temporary"),
3. admitted exceptions, variances, and some tax relief for burdened landowners, and
4. found authority in the state's enabling statute.

Ramapo establishes the rule that a comprehensive planning process, resulting in a plan neither designed to exclude population growth nor involving permanent restrictions on land, justifies both (1) a refusal to rezone, and (2) if no rezoning is needed, a denial of an overlay development permit required before subdividing when available public facilities are inadequate and the subdivision is "premature."[52] In contrast, a finding that a municipality's road system is inadequate, and the consequent enactment of a capital improvement program for it, envisioning its completion in fifty years' time, but in the meanwhile imposing a point system delaying development from one to fifteen years, are neither temporary nor reasonable because the completion of the system and the delay in development were not in sync.[53] Likewise, an ordinance finding that schools are overcrowded and so awarding more points to apartment projects with units of two bedrooms or less, is likely to be an impermissible delay on development.

Perhaps municipalities with fewer financial resources are more justified in using growth controls like Ramapo's, but since the case was decided, similar ordinances

---

52. For another discussion of the control of premature subdivision, see *infra* Chapter 14, § 14.10.

53. *See Toll Bros., Inc. v. West Windsor Twp.*, 712 A.2d 266, 271 (N.J. Super. Ct., App. Div. 1998) (distinguishing *Ramapo* because N.J. Stat. Ann. 40:55D-90 limited moratoria to situations certified as a "clear imminent danger" to health by a qualified public health professional and also stating that otherwise no moratoria on development applications or interim zoning shall be permitted).

have not been used in such a limited way. Those already residents of a municipality, rich or poor, are the real winners under such controls.

[B] Open Issues

Several issues are left open by this opinion. Initially, the court noted that the underlying mix of land uses and their exclusionary impact were not before the court. Because of this, the opinion might be viewed as a planning response to early exclusionary zoning opinions, like that of the Pennsylvania Supreme Court in *National Land and Investment Company v. Kohn.*[54] Exclusionary zoning cases present separate and open questions, for this court.

Interesting issues also arose once the town's growth controls ordinance was approved. Whether the town was "committed to the construction and installation of capital improvements" in the sense that a waiting developer could, in the year named in the capital budget, sue for specific performance of the commitment, was an open issue. The court suggested that the town was committed. Later, however, the town might find that when it spent the money committed in its budget, the money bought less facilities than the town had expected. The town's commitment to developers like Mrs. Golden probably does not rise to the level of a development contract when unforeseen events intervene.[55] What looks like contractual consideration—postponed development followed by an decrease in the real property tax assessment—should not be confused with the reciprocity required to sustain the ordinance as a development agreement. The town's failure to meet its capital budget obligations may well be excusable. Today, however, a development agreement between the town and the developer would detail the facilities that each will provide.

Ramapo's holding involved the facial validity of the town's plan—rather than "as applied." Thus, the court left open the issue of the actual effect or impact of the town's plan. There was no discussion of whether a few or many parcels could gain subdivision approval, of the precise need for the controls, or of the exclusionary effects of those controls. They too are all open questions. On the last unaddressed question, critics have noted that 65% of the town was zoned into districts with large lots.

[C] Creating Sounder *Ramapo* Plans

The Ramapo ordinance singles out residential subdivisions, but would be more comprehensive and uniform in its treatment of owners if it encompassed other land uses as well. So, first, municipalities like Ramapo will achieve sounder planning if all types of developments—residential, commercial, and industrial—were included in the future. This comprehensiveness is particularly important when (as here) the town

---

54. 215 A.2d 597 (Pa. 1970) (discussed *infra*, Chapter 15, § 15.02).

55. *See infra*, Chapter 21, § 21.09 (discussing development agreements).

does not control all of the facilities whose availability gave developers points towards its permits.

Second, a further method of testing a municipality's comprehensive plan lies in its conformance to, and consistency with, regional plans; that consistency provides some assurance that no exclusionary requirements were involved. For example, when another municipality used a state projection of population growth, coupled with a questionnaire distributed to municipal residents asking for their opinion of what the ideal municipal growth rate should be, the municipality's land use plan was found not to be a sound statistical basis for a recommended 3% growth rate.[56] As another growth controls opinion stated, growth controls "should be the product of careful study."[57]

Third, a municipality's capital budgets must be more definitive than they were in Ramapo's case, with regard (for example) to the types of municipal bonds to be used. A shorter period than eighteen years would make budgetary planning projections more secure as well.[58] So further changes in budgeting might (1) shorten the eighteen year restrictive period to (say) a decade, or (2) be more specific in tying the capital budget to the capital program and to the official map of the municipality. The Ramapo ordinance envisioned a complete build-out of the town during the eighteen year financial plan underlying the restrictions; this seemed reasonable because Ramapo was a relatively small town. When in contrast the municipality seeking to control growth was larger and would not be built out during such a period, then shortening of the period for using the restrictions is warranted.

A fourth change for the better involves the *Ramapo* criteria. The proximity criteria in the Ramapo ordinance were tied to services which invoke health and safety considerations: water, sewer, and fire services. These provided the safest of criteria. Thus, for instance, an ordinance using the presence of nearby schools instead suggests a concern to exclude people in families with school age children. According to *Ramapo*, "[t]here is something inherently suspect in a scheme that . . . effects a restriction upon the free mobility of people. . . ." The opinion also suggested that it was on watch for "an array of exclusionary devices" in the guise of growth controls. The presence of a police station, or a water treatment plant, or a trunk line sewer, should be used instead of schools. Moreover, a developer's attorney can point out that a school can be made to appear adequate or inadequate to serve more students by changes in school service-area boundaries.

Ramapo's ordinance required that five essential services be "available" as the precondition to subdivision approval. "Adequate" public facilities is a discretionary and perhaps more desirable term than availability. Adequacy can be measured more objectively, in terms of, to mention a few, calls to the fire house, response times for the

56. *See Rancourt v. Town of Barnstead*, 523 A.2d 55 (N.H. 1986).

57. *See Beck v. Town of Raymond*, 394 A.2d 847, 852 (Me. 1978) (also requiring constant reexamination with a view to ending the controls).

58. For an opinion in which a town singled out sewer hook-up permits and allocated its remaining sewer capacity over twenty years in equal numbers annually, see *Bryant v. Town of Essex*, 564 A.2d 1052 (Vt. 1989) (validating the town policy).

fire truck, etc. Availability might mean proximity, but also might have other meanings as well: for example, public facilities might be found unavailable when the market for municipal bonds needed to finance the facilities turns sour, marked by rising interest rates or by a reduction in capital available to purchase such bonds.

The *Ramapo* opinion sought to avoid giving too much fiscal discretion to municipal officials: for example, *Ramapo* suggests that a municipality could not require that a developer show that tax revenue generated by a project would exceed its costs in public services. *Ramapo* also suggests that a developer does not have the right to insist that a municipality engage in deficit financing to provide public services, but this need not mean that when no deficit financing is involved, the municipality must approve a project.

Fifth, the geographic reach of the growth control ordinance should be considered. The Ramapo ordinance was applicable in all of the town's residence districts and the ordinance looked like the product of comprehensive planning and zoning on that account. Thus, a growth control ordinance only applicable to the urbanizing edge of its jurisdiction, but not applicable throughout the jurisdiction, would be viewed with suspicion by the courts—as reverse spot zoning, as exclusionary zoning, and as a regulatory wall at the municipality's boundary. A narrow reach also runs afoul of the language in the *Ramapo* opinion quoting from Pennsylvania exclusionary zoning cases: "[T]hough the issues are framed in terms of the developer's due process rights, those rights cannot, realistically, be viewed separately and apart from the rights of others 'in search of a [more] comfortable place to live.'" The ordinance must be seen as a method of assimilating new residents, not denying them a place to live. It must "restrict and regulate," but not choke off development.

Sixth, and finally, a Ramapo-like ordinance should provide that the decisions of the planning board on growth control permits are reviewable by the municipal legislature. This review feature tends to make the decisions legislative in nature and so entitled, like rezoning decisions, to the presumption of validity and the fairly debatable, not arbitrary and capricious, standard of judicial review.

A town on the cusp of urbanization, that has not yet experienced population growth while nearby towns have, may also seek to respond with a growth control ordinance in advance of urbanization. In this regard, the planning and growth factors that *Ramapo* recited seem like a factual pre-condition to the court's finding the town ordinance valid. So a review of the planning done previously should be conducted to derive the intent and the terms of the ordinance. If studies detailing these factors have not been done, they should be done and a temporary moratorium imposed while they are being done. However, a moratorium will only be upheld under stringent conditions[59]—one of which is the town's undertaking planning to solve the prob-

59. *See supra*, this Chapter, § 9.01; *see also Toll Bros., Inc. v. Mayor and Council of the Twp. of West Windsor*, 712 A.2d 266 (N.J. Super. Ct., App. Div. 1998) (invalidating timed, sequential growth control as a moratorium prohibited by state statute and distinguishing *Ramapo*).

lem to which the moratorium is addressed.[60] Data on the number of applications for rezonings, variances, special exceptions, or subdivisions pending, and being at historic highs, is one set of statistics justifying both the moratorium and the ordinance. Overall, a growth controls ordinance not preceded and justified by dramatic and objective comprehensive planning estimates on population growth is not entitled to the presumption of validity and may be subject to attack as exclusionary, even if its terms mimic those of the Ramapo ordinance.[61]

Finally, consider whether the holding in *Ramapo* is suspect after the United States Supreme Court opinions in *First English* and *Lucas*.[62] If the municipality has done comprehensive planning in advance of the effective date of its growth controls ordinance, then the compensation remedy for the temporary taking discussed in *First English* is inapplicable because the reasonableness of the period during which the growth controls are imposed has already been addressed in the plan. In addition, if the plan considers the magnitude of the growth as a justification for the ordinance, it imposes no more than normal administrative delays justified by the problem of growth. By the same token, if the ordinance permits very low-intensity development of the affected properties as an interim measure, it does not offend the concern of the *Lucas* court with a total deprivation of all economically viable uses, making *Lucas* distinguishable.

[D] Development Options

Developers finding themselves subject to *Ramapo*-like growth controls have three options: (1) to wait for the municipality to provide the improvements necessary for a parcel to amass the required points; (2) to wait for the period scheduled for the necessary facilities' installation to run and then apply for a permit again; or (3) to install the improvements themselves. In Ramapo, during the period 1969-1983, developers owning tracts large enough to enable them to provide off-site drainage and other improvements achieved the required number of points. Meanwhile, the town provided real property tax reductions for owners waiting out the capital budget period and so lessened the financial impact of the permit program. The reductions lasted only until the improvements were provided or the relevant period in the capital budget lapsed without provision of the improvements. This lower tax burden, once extended to some, required that the assessment and taxes on other properties and their owners be increased.

---

60. *See Ecogen, LLC v. Town of Italy*, 439 F. Supp. 2d 149 (W.D.N.Y. 2006).

61. In this regard, see the cases litigating population projections for the State of Washington's growth controls. *see, e.g., King Cty. v. Central Puget Sound Growth Mgmt. Hearings*, 951 P.2d 1151, 1158 (Wash. 1998) (litigation over allocating county population growth estimates among county's municipalities); *Clark Cty. Citizens v. Resource Council*, 972 P.2d 941 (Wash. App. Ct. 1999) (involving population growth allocations between county's urban and rural areas).

62. *See supra*, Chapter 5, § 5.02 (as to *First English*), *infra*, Chapter 17, § 17.04 (as to *Lucas*).

Two unexpected events also played a part in the use of the town's controls. First, a hurricane (named Agnes) hit the town in 1972, changing its fiscal priorities from support of the Ramapo plan to the rebuilding of existing services and facilities. Second, the 1973 oil embargo made commuting by automobile between Ramapo and New York City more expensive. Soon afterwards, the rate of growth in the town slowed. The plan and the permit system ordinance were repealed in March, 1983—14 years into the 18 year plan, on the ground that it was discouraging needed growth. A newly elected, legislative majority enacted the repeal.

§ 9.05 Concurrency

Statutory regulation of growth has come to a few states. These statutes, applicable state-wide, require in some jurisdictions that some infrastructure and public facilities be available concurrently with development.[63] They link development approval with the provision of public facilities. "Public facilities and services needed to support development shall be concurrent with the impacts of such development."[64] The objective of such statutes is to provide for the sequencing of public and private development in a municipality. This type of concurrency requirement is not in itself a growth control. It is more akin to an adequate public facilities ordinance.[65] However, the failure of a state legislature to authorize funds for the facilities that are required to be in place preceding any development is likely to limit growth—and may be seen as a *de facto* moratorium.

Florida has a broad concurrency requirement,[66] while Washington state has provided for concurrency with regard to roads and transportation.[67] The latter statute makes the provision of a minimum level of service ("LOS") for transportation a concurrent requirement of development.[68] LOS is a ratio of (say) a road's use to its capacity, taking account of all demand for the road.

Both states (Florida and Washington) have amended their programs since 2010. Florida has made property rights a new element in its municipalities' comprehensive plans, exempted certain types of development from its concurrency requirement, and

---

63. *See generally* Boggs & Apgar, *Concurrency and Growth Management: A Lawyer's Primer*, 7 J. Land Use & Env. L. 1 (1991).

64. *See* Fla. Stat. Ann. § 163.3177(10)(h) (enacted 1985).

65. *See* Andrew Balasov, *Keeping a Foot in Each Camp: Adequate Public Facilities Ordinances as Both a Concurrency Tool and a Means of Generating Revenue*, 3 U. Balt. J. Land & Dev. 181 (2014).

66. *See* Fla. Stat. Ann. § 163.3202(2)(g) (1998).

67. *See* Wash. Rev. Stat. Ann. § 36.70(6)(e) (1998) (enacted in 1990 as the state's Growth Management Act, with oversight concerning disputes over consistency between plans and regulations given to a Growth Management Hearing Board).

68. *Id. See generally*, Eric Laschever, *An Overview of Washington's Growth Management Act*, 7 Pacific Rim L. & Policy, 657 (1998).

even exempted some projects by name.[69] Washington has added a climate change element to its required comprehensive plans, but allowed some small communities and counties to opt out of the requirement that they have comprehensive plans.[70] In addition, one hearing board overseeing Washington's growth management statute refused to find authority to include homeless shelters to the list of "essential public facilities" addressed in comprehensive plans.[71]

§ 9.06 Large Lots and Growth Controls

A municipality in the path of urban growth may not zone its land area into large lot use districts so as to zone out all but the most expensive residential housing. Nonetheless, a system of growth controls may in some instances still use large lot zoning.[72] In a state in which the zoning enabling act authorizes ordinances that "regulate and control the timing of development," an amendment of the land use regulations to establish a forestry use district with a 50 acre minimum lot size, locating this district in the rural sector of the municipality, is not a growth control ordinance. It has no time-related or phasing growth controls; that it has the effect of steering development to other sectors of the municipality does not make it so. Were it otherwise, most zoning would be considered growth controls. Whether the large minimum size of the lots in the district is rationally related to the legitimate goals of encouraging forestry is another, separate issue: large lots may be necessary to encourage efficient timber harvests and to give the logger access to the forest under production. The objective of the amendment must be assessed in light of the municipality's zoning goals.[73] There may be other methods of preserving forestry, less restrictive in their impact on landowners, but such an inquiry does not figure in a rational basis, due process analysis of the ordinance. Second-guessing the town's legislature is not usually part of a court's function here. The same device might be used in an active agricultural area.[74]

---

69. *See* Timothy S. Chapin & Lindsay E. Stevens, *Growth Management's Fourth Wave, Revisited*, 5 J. Comp. Urb. L & Policy, 327 (922).

70. *See* https://wsac.org/climate-change-and-the-gma/.

71. *See Homeward Bound in Puyallup v. Central Puget Sound Growth Mgmt. Hearings Bd.*, 517 P.3d 1098 (Wash. Ct. App. 2022).

72. *See Zuckerman v. Town of Hadley*, 813 N.E.2d 843, 849 & n. 14 (Mass. 2004).

73. *See Caspersen v. Town of Lyme*, 661 A.2d 759 (N.H. 1995) (upholding such a fifty acre minimum lot size in a forestry district).

74. *See Oregonians in Action v. LCDC*, 854 P.2d 1010, 1014–15 (Or. App. Ct. 1993) (an 80-acre farming district upheld).

§ 9.07 The Petaluma Rate-Of-Growth Plan

A second generation growth control strategy, adopted by a few municipalities,[75] involves setting a multi-year limit on annual development. Here development is limited to the number of special development permits issued annually—an annual cap on these permits means a later annual cap in building permits. No development permit, no building permit. The limit is set as a percentage of a municipality's total stock of housing and expressed in the number of approved dwelling units. When the demand for these permits exceeds the number of permits planned for, developers must vie for development permit approval.

This type of rate of growth regulation was upheld in *Construction Industry Association of Sonoma County v. City of Petaluma*,[76] which validated a five year plan to limit building permits to 500 per year within the city. The quota on permits was enacted to control the imbalance between types of housing being constructed by the market, to curb urban sprawl, and to slow the city's accelerating growth rates. The quota was set at a level well below what had been demanded by the market. The allocation of permits was distributed both geographically around the city, and divided equally between multi-family and single family developments—whereas 88% of pre-control permits were issued for single family developments. A point system was devised and points were assigned to a development on the basis of conformance with the city's comprehensive plan. Other points were assigned for environmental controls, architectural and urban design, and recreation facilities, as well as the voluntary provision of low and moderate income housing.

The overall purpose of the Petaluma Plan was to develop "in-fill land" (near the core of the city and surrounded by already developed land) before expanding the urban area of the city. The federal circuit court of appeals held that this purpose was carried out in the Plan without any substantial impact or effect on the mobility of residents of the San Francisco Bay region. (Whether the appeals court analyzed the Plan by assaying the purpose of the plan or its impacts was unclear: if this case were a civil rights case, this would be important, but here the effect on the constitutional right of persons to interstate travel was being balanced against the right of the municipality to enact this plan.)

The Petaluma Plan had two interesting features not a part of the Ramapo controls. First, a greenbelt or urban boundary was drawn around the center of the existing city. Second, the allocation of the 500 permits was in effect a design competition between developers—and their architects and planners. The point system gave a great degree of credit to developers who presented interesting, innovative architecture,

---

75. *See Boulder Builders Group v. City of Boulder*, 759 P.2d 752 (Colo. Ct. App. 1988).

76. 522 F.2d 897 (9th Cir.), *cert. denied*, 424 U.S. 934 (1975).

landscaping, and urban designs. These two features (the greenbelt boundary and the design competition) incorporated more administrative discretion into Petaluma's plan than Ramapo's plan contained.

The federal district court and the appeals court reviewing the Plan disagreed about nearly everything regarding the case. Their constitutional analyses appear somewhat dated—the right to travel, for example, was touted in the late 1960s and early seventies as a vehicle for gaining federal review of municipal decisions. It never served that purpose. This right proved to be an inflexible analytical tool—what about intra-state travel?[77]

The Petaluma Plan too was backed by extensive planning studies, so the resulting planning documents were comprehensive. It was limited in time (more so than Ramapo's) to five years. And it was more inclusive of low and moderate income housing than the private market had been in pre-control years. Such features made its validation reasonable. Courts measure the validity of similar growth controls by their

—comprehensiveness

—limited duration, and

—inclusiveness.

The court of appeals held this plan valid against both due process and interstate commerce challenges. Its interstate commerce analysis asked first, whether the state agent (the city, in this case) had a legitimate public purpose in enacting the plan (the court decided it did). If a legitimate public purpose was found, it then asked whether the plan reasonably carried out its purpose (again, it did), and if so, whether its impact or effect unreasonably impedes the flow of interstate commerce. To the last issue, the appeals court responded in the negative.

Its due process analysis relied on an analysis of three cases: (1) *Berman v. Parker*,[78] (2) *Boraas v. Village of Belle Terre*,[79] and (3) *Ybarra v. City of Los Altos Hills*.[80] It was Justice Douglas who wrote the opinion in both *Berman* and *Boraas*; he was also, at the time, the Supreme Court Justice overseeing the 9th Circuit. It was also he who stayed the district court opinion invalidating the city's plan. Much of the opinion in *Petaluma* seems written with him in mind.

In both *Ramapo* and *Petaluma*, the population growth rate that spurred the planning behind the growth controls was substantially above that of other jurisdictions in

---

77. The standing requirements of *Warth v. Seldin*, 422 U.S. 490 (1975), had tossed a lot of the industry's arguments out of federal court. (State courts have not been kind to *Warth*'s tough standing requirements, but state courts are used to zoning and subdivision issues!) *Warth* was concerned with a specific housing project—while Petaluma's plan applied city-wide—so shouldn't the standing requirements have been loosened a bit?

78. 348 U.S. 26, 33 (1954) (opinion written by Justice Douglas, involving the validity of an urban renewal program, that established, in 1954, a broad reach for the police power).

79. 416 U.S. 1 (1974) (an opinion, again written by Justice Douglas, that upheld a more restrictive ordinance) (discussed *infra*, Chapter 18, § 18.01).

80. 503 F.2d 250 (9th Cir. 1974) (which upheld a less inclusive one).

the surrounding metropolitan area. The rate in Petaluma was ten times the metro-rate and Ramapo was the fastest growing unincorporated area in New York State at the time controls were imposed.

Nonetheless, since phased growth and timing controls have turned out to have exclusionary effects, the holdings in each opinion should be narrowly construed for the future.[81] Otherwise, the growth control and the exclusionary zoning case law are on a collision course. This is particularly true in the case of the Petaluma Plan, which might be re-characterized by some developer's attorney as a cap on growth, rather than merely as a regulation of it.

In jurisdictions authorizing zoning by citizen initiative,[82] population growth need not be the original driver for a rate of growth regulation. Nonetheless, the resulting rate of growth regulation, once approved by the voters, may find its validity measured against and in the growth goals of the municipality's comprehensive plan.[83] In this regard, a limitation on building permits (to 280 units *per annum*) has been sustained, even though the municipality secured infrastructure bonds based on a higher population growth rate—in one case, a 3.5% rate as against the regulation's 2% rate of growth.[84] "Because the building cap was based on the 2% growth rate, the 280-unit cap was not arbitrary and capricious."[85]

[A] Challenging a Petaluma-Like Ordinance

A developer seeking to challenge a timing of growth control might wish to bring a **facial challenge** to the control. However, unless the challenged control is a *de facto* moratorium on growth, effective indefinitely and with no accompanying attempt to provide the infrastructure necessary to accommodate a reasonable amount of growth, a facial challenge is unlikely to succeed. Most important here is the fact that growth controls do not deny existing land uses and typically do not prohibit less intensive land uses. Because facial takings claims will likely be judged under what remains of the *Agins* test, they are likely to fail.[86] Additionally, because a growth control ordinance generally allows some growth every year, a *Hamilton Bank* ripeness requirement is likely to prevent a facial takings challenge until the applicant has been denied development permission for several cycles of permit allocations.[87]

---

81. *See Bryant v. Town of Essex*, 564 A.2d 1052, 1056 (Vt. 1989) (noting that the exclusionary effects were not pleaded).

82. An initiative is a procedure in which a percentage of the electorate may propose an ordinance and compel a vote to adopt it. *See* infra, Chapter 20, § 20.02[G][1].

83. *See Sustainable Growth Initiative Committee v. Jumpers LLC*, 128 P.3d 452 (Nev. 2006).

84. *Id.* (finding that, for purposes of reversing a summary judgment, the regulation was facially valid).

85. *Id.* at 465.

86. *See Agins v. City of Tiburon*, 447 U.S. 255, 260 (1980) (requiring that a ridgeland, open-space regulation effectively prevent all reasonable land uses before it will be declared a taking).

87. *See Williamson Cty. Regional Planning Comm'n v. Hamilton Bank*, 473 U.S. 172 (1985).

A further, **"as applied" challenge** might be brought in state court under either a substantive due process or a takings theory. Several variables might affect the decision about which theory to use. The due process claim examines the validity of the government's actions, while the takings claim looks primarily at their impact.

The test for a substantive due process claim is the same balancing of burdens imposed and benefits back used in many other zoning matters. Given the presumption of validity that attaches to municipal controls, they will not violate the due process clause unless they are arbitrary and have no substantial relationship to the police power. A plaintiff has the burden of proving their arbitrariness, showing that the goals of the police power are not even "fairly debatably" related to them. *Petaluma* is the leading case on this claim, and shows how difficult it is to win a case based on it. There, when no link between the infrastructure resources of the city and the controls was apparent on the face of the controls, the city's interests were balanced against their restrictive effects. Indeed, in *Petaluma*, the vague "quality of life" purposes of the controls (taken particularly from *Euclid* and *Belle Terre*) sufficed to sustain them.

The test for an "as applied" takings comes from the *Penn Central* opinion: while it is admittedly ad hoc, it has three prongs—the action's economic impact, its interference with the owner's investment-backed expectations, and the character of the governmental action. The first prong might be addressed in several ways: for instance whether the owner is deprived of much of the fair market value of the property during the period development is delayed; whether the before and after regulation values of the property are substantially different; and whether the owner receives reciprocal benefits back in exchange for the regulation. As for the second prong, a developer's investment-backed expectations are unlikely to contribute to a finding that a taking has occurred. Because growth controls are so common, the fact that one owns the land before the controls were imposed is unlikely to carry much weight. She will be expected to know that such controls are a common regulatory device; this knowledge is imputed to her. Finally, so long as the growth controls are widely applicable and do not single out a few owners for this layer of regulation, the third prong is met.

Three other variables will affect counsel's decision making process. First, the **measure of damages** for a due process violation may be broader than it is for a taking; in the latter instance, the claimant is limited to the value of the property taken, while a due process claim encompasses damages falling outside the realm of measures involving decreased property values—encompassing expectational and consequential damages; for example, engineering and planning fees, the cost of marketing studies, and other soft costs of developing the property. (However, this limitation on takings claims may change when the state constitution provides a remedy for property "taken or damaged.") Likewise, the **statute of limitations** for a taking will be that applying to property interests generally, while the statute applicable to a due process claim will be shorter: limited either to the very short period of time permitted for an appeal from an administrative action, or to the period provided for torts when the claim is pled as a § 1983 or negligence cause of action.[88] Third, **ripeness** requirements[89] apply to a takings claim, but not to a due process claim.

The ordinance in *Petaluma* was suspect just after the later United States Supreme Court opinion in *First English* and then *Lucas*, but such suspicions proved groundless[90] so long as the time delays are reasonable in light of the fiscal responsibilities of the town, a developer's ability to foot the bill for required facilities, and the regulators' need to review and discuss a project. So controls related to capital budgets, from which a developer might seek an administrative exception, and handled in an administrative process flexible enough to encompass many types of projects, will bulletproof a municipality from challenges. The rate of growth ordinance first imposing a limit on the number of development permits and then applying criteria for allocating those limited permits, imposes time delays only on those developers not assigned a permit over the period they seek an approval. So it is advisable for a state wishing to permit its municipalities to enact rate of growth ordinances to enact them only for a limited number of years. So long as the time remaining for development is reasonably short, the parcel has not been denied its reasonable use, and may even benefit from the additional planning underlying the growth controls.

[B] A Petaluma-Like Ordinance for a Rural Municipality

A rural community, even before it experiences uncontrolled growth, might survey its soils and develop a carrying capacity for septic systems, permitting development permits for as many units of housing as the underlying soils will safely absorb.[91] The result might be timing-based growth controls on development in order to preserve its rural character. This carrying capacity approach involves health and safety concerns, thus bringing such controls well within the traditional scope of the police power. This approach to growth controls is particularly suited to municipalities that depend on private wells for their potable water, in that it prevents unnecessary pollution of groundwater supplies. In municipalities concerned also about the proliferation of seasonal, second homes, residency requirements might accompany timing-based controls.[92]

---

88. *Cf. Charles v. Diamond*, 360 N.E.2d 1295 (N.Y. 1977) (discussing the availability of damages in instances of governmental bad faith and physical invasion cases).

89. *See infra*, Chapter 13, § 13.03.

90. *See Tahoe Sierra Preservation Council, Inc. v. Lake Tahoe Regional Planning Agency*, 535 U.S. 302 (2002); *see also Williams v. City of Central*, 907 P.2d 701 (Colo. App. 1995); *Woodbury Place Partners v. City of Woodbury*, 492 N.W.2d 258 (Minn. App. 1992) (both cases deciding that a temporary limitation on use does not result in either a temporary, categorical and total, or regulatory taking, cabining both *Lucas* and *First English*).

91. *See Sturges v. Chilmark*, 402 N.E.2d 1346 (Mass. 1980).

92. *Id.*

As with other rate of growth ordinances, it should be for a limited time; extending it for an uncertain or unlimited time would render it unconstitutional as a violation of substantive due process.

Likewise, in an agricultural area of a municipality concerned about the influx of vacationing seasonal residents, a concern for workforce housing might justify a restriction on building permits for large homes affordable only by seasonal residents; this restriction is stronger when it is a regional planning agency imposing it. Before such an agency, authorized to balance cultural and scenic values against housing for vacation homes, an agency finding that the latter would be a detriment to the former may be upheld and a building permit denied, even when municipal officials might draw the opposite conclusion.[93]

However, any type of growth controls may not be of indefinite or unlimited duration. Timing controls are time limited. Were it otherwise, the detriment to affected landowners would far outweigh the benefit to the municipalities. Timing controls are intended to give a municipality the time to study and determine what controls are necessary for the long term; when the municipality does not perform the appropriate studies, or having performed them, does not enact suitable new regulations to respond to the situation justifying the growth controls when first imposed, substantive due process requires that their enforcement end.[94]

§ 9.08 Growth Controls and Utilities

In some jurisdictions, courts have held that municipalities may use their ownership of water and sewer utilities for planning purposes and may therefore deny permits to hook up to the utilities' lines as a means of growth control. There is no public policy that would prevent municipalities from using their utilities in this way.[95] Normally a public utility (of whatever type) receives a certificate of authority with a duty to serve all citizens requesting service in a definite geographic area, in exchange for being granted a monopoly for that service in the same area. For a municipal utility, even when a proposed subdivision abuts an existing line with the capacity to serve it, a hook-up denial is proper when the subdivision is on an out-lying parcel in an area unserviced in other ways.[96]

---

93. *See Meeting House Way LLC v. Martha's Vineyard Comm'n*, 2023 Mass. Super. LEXIS 24 (Dukes Cty. April 20, 2023).

94. *See Zuckerman v. Town of Hadley*, 813 N.E.2d 843 (Mass. 2004).

95. *See generally, Septic Shock: Wastewater Infrastructure, Urban Growth, and Local Exclusion*, 41 Yale L. & Policy Rev. 170 (1922).

96. *See Dateline Builders v. City of Santa Rosa*, 194 Cal. Rptr. 258 (App. Ct. 1983) (involving a joint agreement between a city and county to share subdivision powers under the city's statutory right to prezone county land within a certain number of miles from the city boundary); *see also County of Del Norte v. City of Crescent City*, 84 Cal. Rptr. 2d 179 (Cal. App. Ct. 1999) (following *Dateline*).

Reaching this point has been difficult in some jurisdictions. In *Robinson v. City of Boulder*,[97] the Colorado Supreme Court held that a municipality could only refuse to serve new development outside its municipal boundaries for reasons relating to its ownership of the utility; it could not justify its refusal with reasons related to implementing its planning and land use regulations. This result may rest on a judicial suspicion of an extra-territorial assertion of legislative power: absent statutory authority, extra-territorial exercise of zoning and planning powers is prohibited. Presumably, a refusal within its boundaries would be permissible, since utility services and regulatory powers could be used concurrently. In Vermont, the state Supreme Court broadly held that the allocation of sewer hookups was not a basis for imposing a phased timing condition on the approval of a subdivision.[98]

When a municipal utility "may" provide service outside its boundaries, the power to do so is discretionary and may not be mandated by injunction. This "no duty" rule has an exception when the municipality holds itself out as willing to supply services or where it is the exclusive provider of services.[99] Thus a duty to provide services may be found by implication. Even then, however, future annexation of the parcel provided with service may be made a condition of its provision.[100] Because annexation is a discretionary act and may not be compelled,[101] enacting conditions on it is permissible.[102]

In the same manner, charging higher utility fees to non-residents than are charged to those within the municipal boundary is justified on the ground that residents have been paying the property taxes used to fund the utility, while non-residents do not. The latter have the burden of proof that the higher fee is unreasonable or discriminatory and, considering that attacking the higher fee as unreasonable is just as complex a piece of litigation as a utility rate regulation case, the case is seldom proven.

There is some question whether the imposition of growth controls is justified only in fast growing municipalities.[103] Infrastructure problems and an urban core surrounded by sensitive or scenic land areas might justify the use of both growth controls, either in their *Ramapo* or *Petaluma* versions, and concurrency requirements without preconditioning their use on there first being a fast growing population.[104]

---

97. 547 P.2d 288 (Colo. 1976), *overruled in Board of Cty. Comm'nrs v. Denver Bd. of Water Comm'nrs*, 718 P.2d 235, 244 (Colo. 1986).

98. *See Brennan Woods LP v. Town of Williston*, 782 A.2d 1230 (Vt. 2001). *Cf. Joy Bldrs. Inc. v. Town of Clarkstown*, 87 N.Y. S.3d 60 (N.Y. App. Div. 2018) (conditioning subdivision approval on holding back some lots from development invalid).

99. *See Yakima Cty. (West Valley) Fire Protection District No. 12 v. City of Yakima*, 858 P.2d 245 (Wash. 1993).

100. *Id.*

101. *See Mayor and Council of Rockville v. Brookville Turnpike Const. Co.*, 228 A.2d 263 (Md. 1967); *Wilkerson v. City of Coralville*, 478 F.2d 709 (8th Cir. 1973).

102. *See Mayor and Council of Rockville v. Brookville Turnpike Const. Co.*, 228 A.2d 263 (Md. 1967).

103. *See* Amy Brandt, *Sedona's Sustainable Growth Ordinance: Testing the Parameters of* Dolan v. City of Tigard, 28 Ariz. St. L.J. 1297, 1302–04 (1996) (reviewing both *Ramapo* and *Petaluma*).

104. *Id.* (arguing this).

Extension of a municipal utility's sewer or water line may be a planning decision, and does not imply an extension of its certificated area of service.[105]

§ 9.09 Inter-Governmental Growth Control Cooperation

For reasons of economy, and to take advantage of the expertise of particular municipal staffs, planning and zoning are often conducted on a cooperative basis among municipalities. This is sometimes expressly authorized by statute. Absent such statutory authority, a municipal government cannot generally contract away or delegate its police powers and, in jurisdictions in which the sum of all zoning and piece-meal rezonings constitute the general or comprehensive plan for an area, this non-delegation rule includes its planning powers as well. The argument against any delegation is particularly strong in states in which urban and regional planning is a mandatory activity of municipalities. Sharing administrative powers over a subdivision[106] is one thing, but it is quite different when planning and rezoning powers are shared without express statutory authority.[107] Thus, when a city and its surrounding county both have zoning authority under the state's zoning enabling act, and both share a concern to preserve a large tract of open pasture lands in both the county's unincorporated areas and the city, their memorandum of understanding that before any rezoning of the tract in the county takes effect, the city must consent to it—and vice versa—is an important delegation when the county approves a pasture rezoning suitable for development, but the city disapproves. The city may not become the delegate of the county, because the police power, with mandatory planning duties attached to it, is non-delegable. Concurrent use of zoning and planning authority is permissible, but their delegation is not.

§ 9.10 Growth Caps

Growth caps have had a checkered history when facing judicial review and, as a result, only a few municipalities have attempted to enact absolute limits on their population. In *City of Boca Raton v. Boca Villas Corp.*,[108] the court reviewed a cap on the maximum number of dwelling units permitted in the city. After the city council failed to enact an ordinance to put the question of adopting the cap as a city charter

---

105. *See Town of Rocky Mount v. Wenco, Inc.*, 506 S.E.2d 17 (Va. 1998).

106. *See Dateline Builders, supra.*

107. *See Alameda County Land Use Ass'n v. City of Hayward*, 45 Cal. Rptr. 2d 752 (App. Ct. 1995) (so holding).

108. 371 So. 2d 154 (Fla. Ct. App. 1979), *cert. denied*, 449 U.S. 824.

amendment to a popular vote, a citizens group brought the question to the voters.[109] The group's proposed amendment to the charter passed with 57% of the votes cast. To this charter amendment (now adopted by popular vote) the city council responded first with moratorium, and then with zoning amendments cutting in half the permitted densities in all multi-family use districts.

The city's planners were not consulted beforehand; planning studies about the cap were only done *post hoc* and to implement the charter amendment. As a result, the testimony of the planning director at trial did not confirm the need for the cap. The court found that the planning department of the local government wasn't even consulted before the cap was imposed. The Florida court in this case held that the cap was a direct and absolute limit on population and was invalid.

It is not difficult to distinguish an annual quota on permits—as in *Ramapo* or *Petaluma*—from a cap on growth—as was involved in *Boca Raton*. The difference is between a direct and an indirect limit. Unlike the Petaluma Plan, Boca Raton's growth cap was a permanent one, fixing an upper ceiling on the number of dwelling units in the city, justified only by after-the-fact planning studies, and based on estimates of future growth, rather than a response to historical growth rates. There really is not much good that can be said for what the city did, but by negative implication and in contrast, a temporary, flexible quota of permits, enacted after study, and applying to a comprehensive set of land uses, would survive judicial review.

The *Boca Raton* opinion contained greater scrutiny of the city's actions than would normally be found using due process analysis. For instance, the city made much of its "water crop"—the amount of rainwater falling within the city limits and available for its water supply. The trial court found that such considerations, while possibly relevant on a regional basis, were not a proper concern of the city when there was no creditable evidence that the regional water authorities would fail to carry out their responsibilities in this area. The city must study factors within its own control to justify the cap, because once the court finds the presumption of validity rebutted, the court reassigns the burden of proof to the city to justify the cap. The city might have considered the following three types of caps.

First, consider an ordinance limiting the number of building permits issued annually for new residential subdivision lots to ten percent of the number of similar permits issued over the past decade. Here, the purpose of the ordinance might be seen as leveling out past growth, avoiding swings in the annual number of permits issued, and there is thus a nexus between growth and the number of permits.[110]

---

109. The question to the voters of Boca Raton was: "Shall the charter of the City of Boca Raton be amended by the addition of the following provisions: 'The total number of dwelling units within the existing boundaries of the city is hereby limited to 40,000. No building permit shall be issued for the construction of any dwelling unit within the city which permits the total number of dwelling units with the city to exceed 40,000.'"

110. This type of growth control was upheld in *Sturges v. Town of Chilmark*, 402 N.E.2d 1346 (Mass. 1980). Chilmark is a town on the island of Martha's Vineyard, a town of 400 persons not in the

Second, consider an ordinance limiting the number of new building permits to a number corresponding to a population growth rate of not more than two percent annually. This ordinance has a nexus between growth and permits that the *Boca Raton* growth caps lacked and would probably survive judicial review on that account.[111]

Third, consider a limitation on the number of dwelling units, whether single or multi-family, up to a number increasing the jurisdiction's housing stock by three percent a year, for the next five years, or by five percent a year if federal regional air quality, water quality, and waste disposal standards are met for the jurisdiction. The nexus between the allocation scheme for permits and the region's environmental health is an important connection to draw if the controls are to be found non-exclusionary. Although flexible, the increase in the overall numbers of dwelling units built in the municipality would help sustain the controls. More dwelling units for low and moderate income housing would add strength too. Moreover, the time period involved in these controls permits revisiting the matter within a reasonable time, and so might be seen as "temporary."

§ 9.11 Urban Boundaries

The state of Oregon is the primary example of a jurisdiction that has a statute, enacted in 1973, authorizing the establishment of a boundary providing a separation between urban and urbanizable lands on one side, and rural lands on the other. Outside the boundary, development is discouraged.[112] These boundaries are set based on seven factors measuring the projected need for urban land over the up-coming twenty years for the city or cities within the boundary. Consistency with each factor is necessary for setting the boundary, but even more crucial has been the designation of the county or city agency to make the population projections for the region.[113]

The state of Washington's Growth Management Act requires that a county's comprehensive plan identify urban growth areas outside of which growth can occur if it is "not urban in nature."[114] In such areas, the expansion or extension of "urban governmental services" is inappropriate, except when necessary to protect public health.[115]

---

path of development sought to preserve its rural character, where land is a scarce resource (and this might well make some difference to the outcome of the litigation).

111. *See Boulder Builders Group v. City of Boulder*, 759 P.2d 752 (Colo. App. Ct. 1988) (upholding such a limitation).

112. *See Sensible Transp. Options for People v. Metropolitan Service Dist*, 787 P.2d 498 (Or. App. Ct. 1998); *see also* Or. Rev. Stat. § 197.296(2) (1997).

113. *See* Edward Sullivan, *Remarks to University of Oregon Symposium Marking the Twenty-fifth Anniversary of S.B. 100*, 77 Ore. L. Rev. 813, 834–36 (1998); *see also* James Bross, *Smart Growth in Georgia*, 35 Wake Forest L. Rev. 609. 610–11, 615, 616 (2000) (reviewing the Oregon history and contrasting it with more recent Georgia efforts).

114. *See* Wash. Rev. Stat. Ann. § 36.70A.110.

115. *Id.* (applying to 18 of Washington's 28 counties, making up over 90% of the state's population).

At the same time, counties subject to this requirement are responsible for defining, expanding, and reducing such areas.

Maryland has a more modest program of "smart growth," enacted in 1997, and prohibiting the development of new, state-funded, water, sewer, and transportation projects outside of "priority funding areas."[116] Such areas are either municipal corporations, designated neighborhoods, enterprise zones, or are areas designated around existing interstate highways. The legislature has authorized and reserved to itself the authority to designate such areas, consistent with municipal or county comprehensive plans.

116. *See* http://www.mdp.state.md.us/OurWork/smartgrowth.shtml.

PART TWO

The Zoning Forms of Action

Chapter 10
Administrative Relief from Zoning Ordinances

§ 10.01 Definitions and Introduction

There are four forms of action which a landowner has to deal with unfavorable zoning. Distinguishing between them is necessary, in the same way that recognizing the common law writs was once necessary, to the practice of land use law. They are the variance, the special exception, the administrative appeal, and the rezoning. Typically, the attorney will combine them to achieve a client's objectives, but knowing each one will in turn enable the attorney to blend them into a creative whole for a client's project.

A variance is a waiver of the application of the terms of an ordinance and is authorized in an ordinance for undue hardship (a Standard Zoning Enabling Act phrase[1]), unnecessary hardship, (a phrase from the *Euclid* opinion) or practical difficulty. Criteria for granting a variance are not usually specified in the ordinance. It provides elasticity in applying the literal terms of the regulations.

Second, a special exception (sometimes called a conditional use permit) can be sought. The uses authorized by such permits are not ones permitted as of right by the ordinance. Rather, they are only permitted on condition that certain criteria are met. Such criteria are specified in the text of the ordinance. Group houses of various types, home offices, and accessory commercial uses are often the subject of special exception provisions in ordinances.

Both variances and special exceptions are issued initially by a municipal administrative board, often called the Board of Zoning Adjustment or Appeals (hereafter the BZA or board). The successful applicant for both of these has the burden of proof and must support his or her application with substantial evidence. Hearing applications for both, the board is the sole judge of the credibility of witnesses, the resolution of

1. *See Stop & Shop Supermarket Co. v. Board of Adjustment of Twp. of Springfield*, 744 A.2d 1169, 1175 (N.J. 2000) (stating that N.J.'s first enabling act authorizing variances was based on the Standard Zoning Enabling Act).

conflicting testimony and evidence, and the weight accorded to the evidence presented; assuming the existence of substantial evidence to support its actions, a reviewing court is bound by board findings.[2] The board being the sole judge of such matters does not mean that it needn't explain itself and make a reviewable record of its actions; indeed, when a written decision is required and the board's decision does not weigh the conflicts in the testimony and witness credibility, or explain its reasoning in reaching its decision, its decision will be reversed on appeal.[3] When a reviewing court does not take new evidence in the course of its review, the court is typically limited to determining whether the board abused its discretion or committed an error of law in rendering its decision.[4] The board typically also hears claims that the scope or terms of a variance or special exception have been violated.[5]

These boards typically function without much in the way of staff, so that it typically falls to the winning attorney to write or draft the board's order. In a minority of jurisdictions, these forms of action are heard by the local legislatures—the village board of trustees, the town or city council, the township commissioners, or the county council or board of supervisors. Performing this function, these bodies may act in either a legislative or an administrative capacity.

Third, an attorney might seek clarification or definition of the local ordinance from a zoning enforcement official or administrator. Such definitions may be sought either in the text of the ordinance, or in the definitions already provided for it. Appeals from these decisions typically are taken to the board, which in such matters sits in an appellate capacity.

Fourth, one can seek to rezone the land, either by amending the text of the ordinance, or by amending the zoning map (without a text amendment). Rezonings are done by the municipal legislature or by a Zoning Commission. This and the next several chapters discuss these four forms of action.

§ 10.02 The Variance

A variance is a waiver of the zoning regulations when they work some difficulty or hardship on a particular parcel of real property. It is generally granted only in exceptional circumstances. It takes the form of an application to the Board of Zoning Adjustment or Appeals (hereafter board or BZA). If granted, it results in an order of the board granting a waiver of, or relief from, the literal enforcement of the regulations,[6] specifying which regulations will not be enforced. When a direct attack

2. *See In re Garcia*, 276 A.3d 340, 346 (Pa. Comwlth. Ct. 2022).
3. *See Metal Green, Inc. v. City of Philadelphia*, 266 A.3d 495 (Pa. 2021).
4. *See Garcia, op. cit.*, 276 A.3d. at 347, n. 4.
5. *See Kenlin Properties LLC v. City of Providence*, 155 A.3d 658 (R.I. 2016).
6. *See Simplex Technologies v. Town of Newington*, 766 A.2d 713, 715 (N.H. 2001) (waiver without sacrifice of the spirit and purpose of the ordinance).

upon the ordinance as applied to the parcel would in a court's view succeed, a variance should be granted.[7] The variance is typically granted when the applicant can show that an "undue or unnecessary hardship" or "practical difficulty" is visited upon him as a result of the application of the ordinance to his property.[8] When a municipal ordinance does not prescribe standards for a variance, the common law of the jurisdiction pertaining to variances controls.[9] Once granted by the board, neighbors opposing the grant lack standing to request a preliminary injunction against implementation. They usually have no due process protected property interest in the outcome of the variance decision.[10]

Variances are of two types: area and use variances. The classification of variances into two types is a judicial gloss on enabling acts, which often do not mention the distinction. The standards of review vary depending on which type is at issue. An **area variance** application asks the BZA or board to lift or modify minimum acreage, height, area, set-back, side or back yard, or other dimensional requirements imposed by the ordinance. It does not concern the applicant's use of his parcel. More broadly speaking, area variances ask for either structural or dimensional deviations from the requirements of the zoning ordinance. Thus, they are sometimes called a "deviation."[11] Area variances require proof that the ordinance presents a parcel owner with a "practical difficulty" in applying the ordinance to the owner's parcel. The parcel may be irregularly shaped and cannot meet the dimensional requirements of the ordinance, or may lack the required minimum frontage, set-back, or back yard minimum area. Likewise, the application may ask for a deviation as to a structure—say, asking for a deviation in a building's height, square footage, or the ratio of the size of the building to the size of the parcel on which it sits.

A **use variance** application asks for a change in the use of a parcel, asking for example for a commercial use in a residential use district. A use is an affirmative use—demolition is not a use and is not a proper subject for a use variance.[12] A parcel owner's application seeks permission or authority to use a parcel in way not permitted either as of right or as a special exception in its land use district. Because granting it is a more drastic change in the zoning ordinance, the standard of proof is higher than it is for an area variance and denial of the application is more likely. Proof is required of an "unnecessary hardship." Use variances are applications to permit an otherwise unpermitted land use. They are more difficult to obtain because the list of permitted uses is, in effect, expanded, for this one parcel. Because the effect on the ordinance is

---

7. Thus, a request for a variance is often a replay of takings jurisprudence, this time set in an administrative forum. *Id.*

8. *See OK Properties v. Zoning Board of Review of City of Warwick*, 601 A.2d 953, 954–55 (R.I. 1992) (stating that the Rhode Island equivalent phrase is "special condition").

9. *See Dan's Mt. Wind Force LLC v. Allegany Cty. Bd. of Zoning Appeals*, 182 A.3d 252 (Md. Ct. Spec. App. 2018).

10. *See Brooks v. Butler Cty.*, 2022 U.S. App. LEXIS 18865, 2022 FED App. 0268N, 2022 WL 2526601 (6th Cir. 2022).

11. *See Sciacca v. Caruso*, 769 A.2d 578, 582 (R.I. 2001).

12. *See Mt. Lookout Community Council v. City of Cincinnati*, 215 N.E.3d 599 (Ohio Ct. App. 2023).

more drastic, and the standard of proof is consequently higher, they are sometimes called "true variances."[13] Such a variance is not viewed as a delegation by the municipal legislature to the board of the power to rezone; as such, the delegation would be unconstitutional in many states and a violation of the state's enabling act in all states.

For both types of variances, an applicant's proof is easiest when the need for the variance is created by the zoning or subdivision regulations themselves. When a tract of land is subdivided into lots by the planning commission, using dimensions called for by the zoning and subdivision ordinances, but there is left over a substandard or remnant lot—a too small lot, not conforming to the minimum acreage requirements—a hardship or difficulty has been created by the general provisions of the ordinances, and the left-over, remnant lot qualifies for an area variance. The law created this problem, and the law should solve it.[14] So too, where a parcel is located in two land use districts by an ordinance's zoning map and is a sub-standard parcel in both, a hardship is shown.[15]

This section will discuss use variances first, presenting the elements of proof usually found in zoning ordinances, realizing that they are sometimes a judicial gloss on the phrase "unnecessary hardship" and sometimes are expressly stated in the ordinance.

[A] Use Variances

An "unnecessary hardship" or variance in the use to which a parcel may be put requires proof of three elements. First, the applicant must show that she is uniquely affected by the literal terms or the implementation of the ordinance.[16] Second, the owner must show that he or she cannot realize a reasonable return or is not left a reasonable number of uses by the terms or implementation of the ordinance.[17] Third, the applicant must show that the use authorized by the variance if granted will not adversely affect the surrounding neighborhood.[18] Proof of each element is required

---

13. *See Sciacca v. Caruso*, 769 A.2d 578, 583 & n. 5 (R.I. 2001) (collecting R.I. cases).

14. *See Eagan v. Zoning Bd. of Appeals of Old Lyme*, 568 A.2d 811, 813 (Conn. App. Ct. 1990) (when locating a house of any size on a residential lot is impossible within the required setbacks, applicant has shown an undue hardship).

15. *See Lewis v. New Castle County Bd. of Adjustment*, 601 A.2d 1048, 1050 (Del. Super. Ct. 1989). *Cf. Victor Recchia Residential Const., Inc. v. Zoning Bd. of Adjustment of Cedar Grove*, 768 A.2d 803, 810 (N.J. Super. Ct., App. Div. 2001) (upholding board decision that a split-zoned parcel could be used in complying manner in two districts upheld and affirming a denial of a use variance).

16. *See Otto v. Steinhilber*, 24 N.E.2d 851, 853 (N.Y. 1939) (hereafter "*Otto*"; *see also Victor Recchia Residential Const., Inc. v. Zoning Bd. of Adjustment of Cedar Grove*, 768 A.2d 803, 810 (N.J. Super. Ct., App. Div. 2001).

17. *See Puritan-Greenfield Improvement Ass'n v. Leo*, 153 N.W.2d 162 (Mich. App. Ct. 1967).

18. These tests have often been combined differently, into one long statement of the elements necessary to obtain a variance. Thus, a variance requires a showing that (1) strict application of the ordinance would produce an unnecessary hardship, meaning that it cannot yield a reasonable return, (2) the hardship is not shared generally by the other properties in the use district, but is attributable to the unique character of the applicant's property, and (3) granting the application will not be a substantial detriment to adjacent property and will not change the essential character of the district. *See*

before a variance is granted. A municipality is free to require stricter standards for a variance than those in the jurisdiction's enabling act.[19] Merely because a particular use is not mentioned at all in an ordinance in any land use district is no reason to grant a use variance for it.[20]

An owner's parcel being irregular in shape, on a very steep slope, or rough terrain, may well be "uniquely affected" (as required by the first element). Highly unusual or extraordinary geography is the strongest evidence for a variance, because it tends to show the uniqueness of the owner's situation.[21] However, if other owners have similar conditions, no uniqueness is shown,[22] unless the enabling statute for the BZA expressly makes allowance for this.[23] Uniqueness must be related to the land, not to its owner, but is not just a physical attribute of land. The attribute must be related to the application of the ordinance from which relief is sought. Thus, a minimum width requirement for a parcel makes little sense for a pie shaped lot—likewise for a set back regulation that puts a house into an arroyo or ravine.[24] A BZA decision on the uniqueness of a parcel for variance purposes has been called a quasi-judicial decision regarding findings of fact about specific property.[25]

An applicant's land is not "uniquely affected" when the application is based on a situation common to other parcels in the neighborhood or use district.[26] Thus, a bad odor in the neighborhood is not unique (everyone can smell it); neither is heavy traffic passing the applicant's land (it passes other parcels as well). An applicant must point to a specific application of the ordinance not suffered by other owners in the district—and for some land uses, even that is insufficient. That land is bisected by a use district boundary is also insufficient to show uniqueness—boundaries must a drawn, and many other parcels may straddle or abut such boundaries. Likewise, an owner of a wetland must show that, considering all other owners of wetlands in the municipality, not just neighboring owners of dry land in the same use district, she is

---

Pepperman v. Town of Rangeley, 659 A.2d 280, 283 (Me. 1995); *Prince William County Bd. of Zoning Appeals v. Bond*, 300 S.E.2d 781, 782–83 (Va. 1983).

19. *See City of Lewes v. Nepa*, 212 A.3d 270 (Del. 2019).

20. *See DeAngelo v. N. Strabane Twp. Zoning Hearing Bd.*, 208 A.3d 156 (Pa. Comwlth. Ct. 2019) (as to medical clinics).

21. *See Tidd v. Lower Saucon Twp. Zoning Hearing Bd.*, 118 A.3d 1 (Pa. Comwlth. Ct. 2015).

22. *See Nance v. Town of Indialantic*, 419 So. 2d 1041 (Fla. 1982).

23. *See, e.g.*, Cal. Gov't Code § 65906 (1983) (which makes "size, shape, topography, location or surroundings" a "special circumstance" and authorizes area variances only).

24. *See Fairview Twp. v. Fairview Twp. Zoning Hearing Board*, 233 A.3d 958, (Pa. Comwlth. Ct. 2020).

25. *See City of Cummings v. Flowers*, 797 S.E.2d 846 (Ga. 2017) (holding that appeal from a BZA fact-based variance decision is available solely by a writ of certiorari and that a local zoning ordinance about variances cannot broaden the basis for appeal). *See also Dolezal-Soukup v. Dodge City Bd. of Adjustment*, 952 N.W.2d 674 (Neb. 2020).

26. *See Victor Recchia Residential Const., Inc. v. Zoning Bd. of Adjustment of Cedar Grove*, 768 A.2d 803, 810 (N.J. Super. Ct., App. Div. 2001).

uniquely affected; if all owners of wetlands are affected in the same way, uniqueness is not shown.[27]

On the other hand, that a parcel has remained unimproved or blighted for decades, that it has three street frontages, and that what could be built on the parcel would result in an unusually long and thin structure, goes to show its uniqueness in a single-family use district sufficient to justify the development of duplex condominiums there.[28] Likewise, that a parcel has a swale or dip in it, or that the ground is uneven or has varying subsurface conditions, goes to show its uniqueness.[29] Likewise, a structure that is valueless as zoned, dilapidated, and could only be converted to a permitted use at a prohibitive cost, may be granted a use variance.[30]

Much use variance litigation revolves around the second "no reasonable return" element. Generally, mere economic hardship alone is insufficient to justify the granting of a variance; other elements must be shown as well. The applicant must show that a literal or strict enforcement of the ordinance results in a substantial loss or an unreasonably low return, resulting in the practical loss of all beneficial use of the parcel for which a variance is sought.[31] Any financial impact on the profitability of the parcel alone is insufficient to establish the unnecessary hardship necessary for a use variance. So is the fact that the applicant is operating the current use on the parcel at a loss.[32] Conversely, the applicant must prove that the currently operated and permitted use of the property cannot continue.[33] In this regard, however, a parcel owner is not required to show that the parcel is valueless if the variance is not granted. The fact that the applicant's parcel may be used more profitably if the variance is granted does not provide grounds for granting it.

Often, when an economic hardship is at issue, the board must find that the variance granted is the minimum required to make a reasonable use of the applicant's parcel.[34] In this regard, reasonable return does not mean maximum return. The applicant is often said not to be entitled to the maximum return that the parcel might yield, and the fact that an applicant might increase the yield on the parcel is insufficient to support a showing of no reasonable return.[35] Other jurisdictions use this element to track takings jurisprudence closely, emphasizing that the applicant for a variance must show "interference with a reasonable use."[36] Then the applicant must show that

27. *See Chester Haven Beach Partnership v. Board of App. for Queen Anne's Cty.*, 653 A.2d 532 (Md. App. Ct. 1995) (holding that an owner's offer to build cluster housing on wetland at lower density than permitted by regulation does not satisfy the uniqueness element necessary for a variance).

28. *See In re Garcia*, 276 A.3d 340, 346–47 (Pa. Comwlth. Ct. 2022).

29. *See Fairview Twp. op. cit.*, 233 A.3d at 963.

30. *See Liberties Lofts LLC v. Zoning Bd. of Adjustment*, 182 A.3d 513 (Pa. Comwlth. Ct. 2018).

31. *See Goldstein v. City of South Portland*, 728 A.2d 164, 165 (Me. 1999).

32. *See Otto v. Steinhilber*, 24 N.E.2d 851, 853 (N.Y. 1939).

33. *See Fowler v. City of Bethlehem Zoning Hearing Bd.*, 137 A.3d 287 (Pa. Comwlth. Ct. 2018).

34. *See Corkery v. Municipality of Anchorage*, 426 P.3d 1078 (Alas. 2018).

35. *Id. See also Rowe v. City of South Portland*, 730 A.2d 673 (Me. 1999).

36. *See Simplex Technologies v. Town of Newington*, 766 A.2d 713, 715 (N.H. 2001); *Garrison v. Town of Henniker*, 907 A.2d 948, 951 (N.H. 2006) (recognizing that the standard for a use variance

there is no other reasonable alternative (to granting the variance) in order to enjoy an otherwise legal use.[37]

When variances are denied, the evidence showing that the property as is has economic value establishes the denial was proper.[38] An economic hardship must be an undue restriction on the use of the applicant's land and a deprivation of value "so great as to effectively prevent the owner from making any reasonable use of the land."[39] The hardship proven must be based on an applicant's rightful use.[40] Operating a reasonable use before the application is conclusive proof that no such hardship is present. Likewise, a failure to comply with a subdivision ordinance requirement concerning the width of a parcel is not a hardship required for a variance.[41] Nor does a hardship arise from a structure located on the parcel for which a variance is sought—as when an application is predicated on extra construction costs incurred because of a parcel's terrain. That the construction is more costly is insufficient—it must be prohibitively more costly. The purpose of such a rule is to discourage investment in sub-standard or non-conforming parcels. Finally, when the extra expenditure results in a greater intensity of use than permitted other owners in the district, a use variance should not be granted.

The third element—that there be "no adverse impact" on the surrounding neighborhood—is sometimes restated as a requirement that the variance not alter the essential character of the neighborhood[42] and if granted would not be contrary to the public interest.[43] In jurisdictions in which the municipality must prepare a master or comprehensive plan before enacting a zoning ordinance, this element is often stated as there being no adverse impact on the plan or that granting the variance will not violate the spirit and general intent of the plan. Thus, this element is generally stated in the negative to avoid granting the board too much discretion and authority. Indeed, the board's justifying the granting of a variance on other objectives that it considers worthy will result in a reviewing court reversing the board's decision. Any adverse impact on the neighborhood requires a showing by the neighbors of a particular impact.[44] The impact may concern traffic, pollution, or noise. An oversized structure must "degrade significant value" of surrounding parcels.[45] In this regard, the element is often interpreted to require the board when granting a variance in the use of a

---

was changed from requiring applicant to make a showing of deprivation of reasonable use of the land, to one requiring a showing of interference with a reasonable use).

37. *See Sciacca v. Caruso*, 769 A.2d 578, 583 (R.I. 2001).

38. *See E&F LLC v. Zoning Bd. of Appeals*, 127 A.3d 986 (Conn. 2015).

39. *See Governor's Island Club v. Gilford*, 467 A.2d 246, 248 (N.H. 1983).

40. *See In re Appeal of Chestnut Hill Community Ass'n*, 155 A.3d 658 (Pa. Comwlth. Ct. 2017) (finding that applicant's hardship showing for a carport was based on the mistaken belief that he had a right to park on his property).

41. *See Dunn v. Middletown Twp. Zoning Hearing Bd.*, 143 A.3d 494 (Pa. Comwlth. Ct. 2016).

42. *See Commons v. Westwood Zoning Bd. of Adjustment*, 410 A.2d 1138 (N.J. 1980).

43. *See Gray v. Seidel*, 726 A.2d 1283 (N.H. 1999).

44. *See I-465 LLC v. Metro Bd. of Zoning Appeals*, 36 N.E.3d 1094 (Ind. Ct. App. 2015) (as to noise emanating from a kennel granted a variance).

45. *See Hill v. Town of Wells*, 254 A.3d 1161 (Me. 2021).

parcel to reconcile its decision with continuance of the legislative prohibition on and exclusion of that use from the list of uses permitted as of right.[46] In some jurisdictions, this element is measured, in a looser fashion, by the otherwise applicable terms of the ordinance: that is, the applicant must demonstrate that "no fair and substantial relationship exists between the general purposes of the zoning ordinance and the specific restriction on the property,"[47] thus requiring that he show no adverse impact on the effectiveness of the ordinance as a whole.

Sometimes a fourth element is added, to the effect that the hardship is not the result of action taken by the applicant or a prior owner of the property.[48] A self-created hardship is a bar to the granting of a use variance.

The enlargement of a non-conforming use (one pre-existing a use regulation currently prohibiting the non-conformity) is generally treated as a use variance rather than as an area variance.[49]

[B] Area Variances

Area variances are applications to lift or modify minimum acreage, height, area, set-back, side or back yard, or other dimensional requirements imposed by the ordinance when there is no prohibition on the petitioner's use of his property. Their purpose is to prevent the overbuilding of land parcels and the overcrowding of structures.[50] They are sometimes called "dimensional variances."[51] Applications for this type of variance are more common than those for use variances, for the obvious reason that they interfere less with a municipality's overall zoning scheme or plan.

An area variance may be granted when (1) there is a unique (meaning exceptional within the applicable use district) condition affecting the applicant's parcel, (2) practical difficulties will occur if the ordinance is strictly and literally enforced, thus impacting the owner/applicant, and (3) relief can be granted without substantial injury to the public welfare or (where applicable) without substantially impairing the intent or integrity of the municipality's master or comprehensive plan.[52] These three elements are all part of an applicant's showing in support of granting the variance. They are not balanced, one against another. Sometimes a fourth element is added, although it may often be implicit in the third: that is, the relief is to be the minimum necessary to

46. *See Medici v. BPR Co.*, 526 A.2d 109 (N.J. 1987) (explaining *Commons, op. cit.*).

47. *See Simplex Technologies v. Town of Newington*, 766 A.2d 713, 717 (N.H. 2001) (the court recognizing that it was adopting a less restrictive approach to the granting of variance, an approach justified in order to keep pace with constitutional law and takings jurisprudence).

48. For a fuller discussion of this fourth element, see *infra*, this Chapter, § 10.02[K].

49. *See NYNEX Mobile Communications Co. v. Hazlet Twp. Bd. of Adjustment*, 648 A.2d 724, 729–30 (N.J. Super. Ct., App. Div. 1994).

50. *See Perreault v. Town of New Hampton*, 193 A.3d 266 (N.H. 2018).

51. *See Sciacca v. Caruso*, 769 A.2d 578, 582 (R.I. 2001).

52. *See Roth v. D.C. Board of Zoning Adjustment*, 279 A.3d 840, 845 (D.C. 2022).

overcome the difficulties shown by the applicant.[53] These elements developed because in the early decades of zoning law, legislative guidance was lacking with regard to the standards necessary for granting an area variance. This judicial gloss on early enabling acts became the "practical difficulties" test.[54]

In some jurisdictions, there is no difference between the applicant's showing of unnecessary hardship (for a use variance) and the lesser showing of practical difficulties (for an area variance).[55] One jurisdiction (Iowa) has recently rejected the rule that area variances require a lesser standard of proof than a use variances.[56] In this case, the higher standard of "unnecessary hardship" is applied to both types of variances: in Iowa, the standard in part requires a showing that denial of the variance will mean that the parcel in question cannot yield a reasonable return for its owner.[57] The Iowa court claimed a sixty year long provenance for its rule as well as legislative acquiescence for it over that time, citing an early New York case as its origin.[58]

The required unique condition may arise from a confluence of factors, but it must affect only one parcel. Inclusion of a structure in an historic district does not make it unique.[59] The same could be said of every other structure in the district. That even a small number of parcels is affected by the same condition indicates that a rezoning rather than a variance is the applicant's proper remedy. An irregular, narrow, small, corner, flag-shaped, or pie-shaped parcel, a condition inherent in a building built to suit a particular land use on a parcel, and even prior zoning actions regarding it, may qualify a parcel as uniquely affected by zoning regulations.[60] Relief from a one-structure-per-parcel requirement is similarly regarded as a request for a finding of uniqueness required for a dimensional or area variance, but not necessarily a mandate for granting the variance. Relief from a tree preservation regulation may be regarded as akin to a request for a structural variance.[61] The small size of a parcel does not by itself make it unique enough to justify an area variance.[62]

---

53. *See Pequea Twp. v. Zoning Hearing Bd.*, 180 A.3d 500 (Pa. Comwlth. Ct. 2018).

54. *See Matter of Colin Realty, LLC v. Town of North Hempstead*, 21 N.E.3d 188, 103–04 (N.Y. 2014).

55. For an expression of this minority view, see *Snyder v. Waukesha Cty. Zoning Bd. of Adjustment*, 247 N.W.2d 98, 102–04 (Wis. 1976).

56. *See Early v. Board of Adjustment of Cerro Gordo Cty.*, 955 N.W.2d 812 (Iowa 2021) (reversing a lower court decision requiring different standards when interpreting a state enabling act).

57. *Id.* at 818 (citing in part N. Williams Hines, *Difficulties Standard for Area Variances*, 102 Iowa L. Rev. Online 365, 366 (2018) (while arguing for different standards for each type of variance, the author nonetheless concludes: "Notwithstanding the distinctively different purposes served by these two types of zoning variances, two-thirds of U.S. states . . . apply the same strict requirements for granting them both.").

58. *See Otto v. Steinhilber*, 24 N.E.2d 851, 853 (N.Y. 1939).

59. *See Dupont Circle Citizens Ass'n v. D.C. Board of Zoning Adjustment*, 182 A.3d 138 (D.C. 2018) (as to a church).

60. *See Roth, op. cit.*, 279 A.3d. at 846.

61. *See West Montgomery County Citizens Ass'n v. Montgomery County Planning Board*, 241 A.3d 76, 82 (Md. Ct. Spec. App. 2020).

62. *See Roth, op. cit.*, 279 A.3d. at 846.

Neither does a conflict between the dimensional requirements of an ordinance and the applicant's personal preferences create the type of practical difficulty necessary to justify granting an area variance.[63] A personal preference might arise, for example, when an applicant is forced to choose between adding an addition to his home with a back deck, or satisfying the dimensional requirements of the ordinance. In such a situation, the applicant should explain why choosing between an addition and the deck would create a practical difficulty. If the parcel's smallness is unique in its land use district, evidence should be presented connecting that uniqueness with some practical difficulty. Likewise, an applicant's inconvenience is insufficient to establish a practical difficulty.[64]

An application that is predicated on building a house of a certain design will likely result in a denial of the variance for not showing the requisite practical difficulty.[65] Such design preferences relate to the person, not the parcel—and the justification for a variance of any type must relate to the land parcel or structure on it, not to its owner.[66] Likewise, an applicant's need for a larger living area for her family does not warrant a variance.[67] A variance is not justified by the personal or life-style needs of the user: zoning deals with land uses, not users. A variance granted "for the life of the applicant" is invalid: variances must run with the land.[68] In addition, a need for a satellite dish in the backyard, for a garden shed, a pergola for a residence,[69] or for a digital sign for a church,[70] is unlikely to establish a practical difficulty or unnecessary hardship. Such an inconvenience is insufficient to support a board's granting a variance.

A BZA has discretion to consider a wide range of factors creating a practical difficulty, including the economic use of the parcel or structure and the increased expense or inconvenience to the applicant.[71] When a structure was built to operate as a corner grocery store, the addition of some coffee and bagel facilities might insure the continued economic viability of the store—and denying a variance might hasten its demise or create difficulties in attracting an alternative operator for the store—such considerations show a practical difficulty necessary for granting an area variance.[72] Once the board has accepted such considerations, even substantial evidence to the

63. *See Kneebone v. Zoning Hearing Board of Twp. of Plainfield*, 276 A.3d 705, 713 (Pa. 2022). *See also Verrillo v. Zoning Bd. of Appeals of Branford*, 111 A.3d 473 (Conn. App. 2015).

64. *See State ex rel. Organic Remedies Mo., Inc. v. Bd. of Zoning Adjustment of St. Louis Cty.*, 674 S.W.3d 508 (Mo. Ct. App. 2023).

65. *See Jaser v. Zoning Board of Appeals*, 684 A.2d 735 (Conn. App. Ct. 1996).

66. *See Amendola v. Zoning Bd. of Appeals of City of West Haven*, 128 A.3d 726 (Conn. Ct. App. 2015).

67. *See Larsen v. Zoning Board of Adjustment of the City of Pittsburgh*, 672 A.2d 286 (Pa. 1996) (finding that an applicant's need for a larger play area for a child did not warrant a variance to build a 400 square foot deck).

68. *See Reid v. Zoning Bd. Of Appeals of Town of Lebanon*, 670 A.2d 1271 (Conn. 1996) (variances cannot be "personal" and must be based on objective facts of the land's condition).

69. *See Early v. Bd. of Adjustment*, 955 N.W.2d 812 (Iowa 2021).

70. *See Antioch Community Church v. Bd. of Zoning Adjustment*, 543 S.W.3d 28 (Mo. 2018).

71. *See Roth, op. cit.*, 279 A.3d at 846.

72. *Id.* at 846–47.

contrary will not justify reversing the board's decision: the resolution of any conflicts in the evidence is left to the board.

As to the third element necessary for an area variance—that it may be granted without substantial injury to the neighborhood or zoning ordinance—the board may not substitute its view that granting the variance would be consistent with certain objectives of the ordinance: the required analysis is that granting it is not contrary to and would not injure the intent and purpose of the ordinance.[73] Often this third element is linked to a requirement that the granting of the variance will be the minimum necessary to afford relief from the disproportionate impact that the ordinance has on the applicant.[74]

With an area variance, there is a tendency to balance the applicant's need for the variance (and/or the public purposes and benefits of the varied use) against the impact on the surrounding uses.[75] Thus, the financial burden on the applicant might (as to, say, a set-back or parking requirement) be balanced against the impact on neighboring parcels, particularly when a requirement was devised with another land use in mind. An area variance application might be supported by an existing site plan, showing the placement of mature trees and screening landscaping, or the use of walkways of brick and sand that decrease water run-off onto surrounding parcels.[76] The approval of an area variance to prevent the destruction of such trees might then prevent an adverse impact on neighboring parcels.[77] The applicant might further argue that alternative but permitted development plans will be more onerous than the one proposed utilizing the variance, with regard to their impact on the neighbors.[78]

When the applicant's structure is leased, the profitability of the leasing business is not directly relevant to the application for a variance: the inquiry into practical difficulties is focused on the owner, not the tenant. The difficulty then must focus on the tenant's ability to maintain the lease and pay the rent due under it. An inability to maintain the lease is thus the owner and applicant's difficulty—and relevant to the board's inquiry.[79]

Neither may the board focus its decision on one element of proof and not address others spelt out either in the ordinance or in the elements of a variance established in the jurisdiction's common law. Such a mono-focus will not yield substantial evidence

---

73. *See Surfrider Fdn. v. Zoning Bd. of Appeals*, 358 P.3d 664 (Haw. 2015) (as to a hotel's proposed encroachment on a coastal zone).

74. *See Paganico v. Zoning Hearing Bd. of the Municipality of Penn Hills*, 227 A.3d 949 (Pa. Comwlth. Ct. 2020).

75. *See Roth, op. cit.*, 279 A.3d at 847; *Kali Bari Temple v. Board of Adjustment of Twp. of Readington*, 638 A.2d 839 (N.J. Super. Ct., App. Div. 1994).

76. *See Mastandrea v. North*, 760 A.2d 677, 696 (Md. 2000).

77. *See Holmes v. Zoning Hearing Board of Kennett Twp.*, 396 A.2d 859, 861 (Pa. Comwlth. Ct. 1978).

78. *See Gilmartin v. District of Columbia Bd. of Zoning Adjustment*, 579 A.2d 1164, 1172 (D.C. 1990) (rejecting variance from parking requirements when alternative means were available).

79. *See Roth, op. cit.*, 279 A.3d at 847 (raising but not resolving this matter).

for granting the variance.[80] Likewise, showing only the reasonableness of granting the variance, even when the applicant's small parcel abuts open farmland and there is no adverse impact on a surrounding neighborhood, does not establish the practical difficulty that the parcel presents with regard to an area or dimensional variance.[81] The reasonableness of an applicant's request for rezoning is for the municipality's legislative body, while the application for a variance calls more narrowly for the board to conduct a quasi-judicial proceeding between the applicant and those objecting to the application.

In a geologically unsettled setting, an ordinance may set a maximum percentage of a parcel that may be disturbed along with a requirement that a parcel owner refrain from disturbing the soil within a certain distance from a parcel boundary. While the geological setting may establish the uniqueness of the parcel, these ordinance requirements take such matters off the table; citing them will not establish the unique effect required for granting an area variance.[82]

Likewise, reducing the impact of a non-conforming use or structure on its surroundings does not justify such a variance.[83] However, a non-conforming use destroyed in a hurricane and not rebuilt within the time allotted by ordinance to rebuild, may be granted variances in height and set-back requirements in order to raise the structure above the water level reached in the storm.[84]

[C] Hybrid Variances

Gathering evidence for a variance from a parking requirement will be harder than for a strictly dimensional variance. The applicant might show that the parking for the proposed use is needed at different times of the day or week, so that the applicant might often require less parking than an ordinance requires, but need more at other times, all without adversely impacting his neighbors.[85] It is for this reason that a variance from parking requirements is often seen as a hybrid between the use and area variance, so that the standard of proof is somewhat lower than "unnecessary hardship" and somewhat higher than "practical difficulties." Nonetheless, an application to relax off-street parking regulations is considered an application for an area variance "so long as the underlying use is permitted in the zoning district; use variance rules prevail only if the variance is sought in connection with a use prohibited in the

---

80. Whether substantial evidence supports a board's decision is a matter of law, which a court reviews *de novo*, not deferentially.

81. See *Kneebone*, *op. cit.*, 276 A.3d at 717.

82. *See Polish Hill Civic Ass'n v. City of Pittsburgh Zoning Board of Adjustment*, 285 A.3d 718 (Pa. Comwlth. Ct. 2022).

83. *See Turek v. Zoning Board of Appeals of City of Milford*, 229 A.3d 737, 750 (Conn. App. Ct. 2019).

84. *See Mayer-Wittmann v. Zoning Board of Appeals of City of Stamford*, 218 A.3d 37, 52 (Conn. 2019).

85. *See NYNEX Mobile Communications Co. v. Hazlet Twp. Bd. of Adjustment*, 648 A.2d 724, 729–30 (N.J. Super. Ct., App. Div. 1994).

district."[86] Because such regulations relate to how a property may be developed, they are "akin to minimum lot size or set-back restrictions."[87]

In one case, a restaurateur sought a variance from the ordinance's parking requirements for his type of business. The ordinance required that 25 spaces be provided within 500 feet of the front door of his business, which was otherwise (aside from this parking requirement) permitted in the commercial zone in which the restaurant was located. Instead of classifying this application as either an area or a use variance, the reviewing court called this a hybrid variance and applied an intermediate standard of proof, mid-way between unnecessary hardship (which can often mean that no reasonable use or return is left to the property owner) and practical difficulties (which balances the adverse impact on the neighborhood with the injury suffered by the applicant). Thus, the hybrid variance used both tests and with such a multi-faceted test, the range of evidence available to the applicant expanded to the point at which the variance was much more likely to be granted.[88]

If the application could reasonably be construed either way, then which way should the board go?[89] In *Taylor*, the applicant overreached; he piled requests for bulk, height, and acreage variance on top of each other, until taken together, all the requests looked like a use variance and caught the applicant in its higher standard of proof. In this regard, the board might recall that classifying an application as a request for one or the other type of variance is a matter best resolved by the board and will likely to subject to a deferential standard of judicial review.[90] Further, given the possibility that a "hybrid" area/use variance might subject the applicant to both practical difficulty and undue hardship inquiries, boards should be careful finding situations in which hybrid variances arise. Counsel's piling on requests for area and dimensional variances should be avoided; that is the rationale for a least-intrusive relief requirement in many ordinances.

[D] Variances and Takings Law

The *Puritan-Greenfield* test, used previously to state the elements of a use variance, has the sound of takings law.[91] This is no more than an analogy. Variance applications are handled by an administrative agency—the board—not a court. Thus failing to raise a constitutional objective before the board is not a waiver, nor does it exhaust any

86. *See Matter of Colin Realty, LLC v. Town of North Hempstead*, 21 N.E.3d 188, 198 (N.Y. 2014)

87. *Id.*

88. *See Palmer v. District of Columbia Bd. of Zoning Adjustment*, 287 A.2d 535 (D.C. 1972). *See also Appeal of Campbell*, 250 A.3d 1263 (Pa. Comwlth. Ct. 2021).

89. *See Taylor v. District of Columbia Board of Zoning Adjustment*, 308 A.2d 230 (D.C. 1973) (toward a use variance, with its higher standard of proof, says the court in an opinion rejecting an area variance for 27 townhouses on land zoned for ten single family residences).

90. *See Neighbors for Responsive Gov't, LLC v. D.C. Board of Zoning Adjustment*, 195 A.3d 35, 62–64 (D.C. 2018)

91. *See Puritan-Greenfield Improvement Ass'n v. Leo*, 153 N.W.2d 162 (Mich. App. Ct. 1967).

administrative remedy.[92] Although variance law does track the constitutional analysis of the ordinance itself, this means that the variance is a buffer, saving the ordinance from an attack on its constitutionality when some property owners are severely affected.[93] Courts recognize an inevitable tension between zoning ordinances and property rights and attempt to respect those rights and protect them from unreasonable regulation.

A zoning regulation that entirely deprives a structure of its legally non-conforming use status "might be confiscatory as applied."[94] In this situation, a variance might save the regulation from its confiscatory effect, but if an appeal is taken before a court, the applicant will need to prove that a regulatory taking has occurred.[95]

One municipality enacted an amendment to its zoning ordinance providing that the board may grant use variances "upon the applicant's showing that he or she cannot reasonably use the subject property for any of the uses permitted under this ordinance and that the denial of the application would constitute an unconstitutional taking of property without compensation as defined by the laws of the state and of the United States." This amendment was improper and *ultra vires* the enabling act. An agency like the board may not act like a court finding an unconstitutional taking without usurping the judicial function.[96] Any direct consideration of a constitutional right is beyond the board's statutory scope of authority in every jurisdiction. By the same token, the denial of a variance does not *per se* result in a taking, and the denial is no pre-condition to the applicant's bringing a takings claim in court.

Parcels that are ecologically-sensitive, such as a wetland, may well be so restricted by a regulation that virtually no development is permitted. Such regulation may give rise to a claim that the property has been the subject of a regulatory taking of "all viable economic or beneficial use" and so the landowner should be given just compensation under the Fifth Amendment's takings clause. When there is an allegation of such a total taking (under rules laid down in *Lucas v. South Carolina Coastal Commission*[97]), such an allegation also entitles the owner to a variance. The related showing for a variance is that the property is not capable of yielding a reasonable return or being used reasonably, and that showing can be made by an owner showing a total taking.[98]

---

92. *See Md. Reclamation Assocs. v. Harford Cty.*, 227 A.3d 230 (Md. 2020).

93. *See Simplex Technologies v. Town of Newington*, 766 A.2d 713, 717 (N.H. 2001) (remanding after board denial of a variance and citing the state constitution's guarantee of the right to acquire, possess, and protect property as limiting a delegation of zoning authority to municipalities and so informing the state's variance rules).

94. *See Mayer-Wittmann v. Zoning Bd. of Appeals of Stanford*, 218 A.3d 37 (Conn. 2019). *See also Nowicki v. Zoning Hearing Bd.*, 91 A.3d 287 (Pa. Comwlth. Ct. 2014).

95. *See Caruso v. Zoning Bd. of Appeals*, 130 A.3d 241 (Conn. 2016).

96. *See Zoning Bd. of Appeals v. Planning and Zoning Comm'n of the Town of Wallingford*, 605 A.2d 885, 889 (Conn. App. Ct. 1992) (holding that the BZA is an aggrieved party with standing to appeal the enactment and further invalidating the amendment because the BZA is deprived of its authority to grant variance under statutory criteria).

97. 505 U.S. 1003 (1992), discussed *infra*, Chapter 17, § 17.04.

98. *See Greenberg v. DiBiase*, 637 A.2d 1177, 1179 (Me. 1994) (involving, but without mentioning *Lucas*, a residential-only, lakeshore set back regulation when the set back would preclude the construction of any residence on applicant's parcel).

Likewise, an ordinance requiring that the board not grant variances for outdoor decks unless the applicant "shall respect the privacy of adjacent properties" is a delegation of authority on a constitutional issue—that of a right to privacy. As such, it is again improper; however, it also may be interpreted so as to only amount to a first-in-time rule of (temporal) priority for improvements or it may also permit the board to condition the grant of a variance by the planting of screening and/or landscaping without enumerating the criteria for doing so.[99] When the delegation to the board has been consistently and narrowly interpreted, a reviewing court may sustain the board's action by giving great weight in interpreting an ordinance by an agency's long established meaning of its terms.

[E] The Burden of Proof and Substantial Evidence

In any variance proceeding, the applicant has the burden of proof. The applicant must present substantial evidence in support of the request.[100] Substantial evidence is that quantum of evidence a reasonable mind will accept as adequate to support a finding or conclusion;[101] or that evidence with which "a reasoning mind reasonably could have reached the same conclusion that the agency reached."[102] It requires a reviewing court to draw inferences from the evidence as the agency or board did in order to make its decision, rather than the court's substituting its judgment for the board's.[103] It affords a substantial basis of fact from which an issue or conclusion might be inferred. It is a conclusion not so lacking in fact and based on a foundation not clearly unreasonable.[104] For example, an applicant's *pro forma* analysis of a project does not provide a foundation for a conclusion about undue hardship; the financial viability of a project and the hardship are two different matters.[105] The test is the reasonableness of the applicant's evidence, not its rightness. In the course of judicial review of an administrative proceeding, substantial evidence is also enough evidence to avoid the charge that the board acted in an arbitrary and capricious manner. In a trial, it is enough evidence to avoid a directed verdict.

---

99. *See Briggs v. City of Rolling Hills Estates*, 47 Cal. Rptr. 2d 29 (App. Ct. 1995) (holding such language not unconstitutionally void for vagueness).

100. When a use variance is involved, substantial evidence is also said to be evidence sufficient to make the matter "fairly debatable." *See White v. North*, 736 A.2d 1072, 1079–80 (Md. 1999).

101. *See Mastandrea v. North*, 760 A.2d 677, 691 (Md. 2000).

102. *Id. See also Montgomery Cty. v. Rotwein*, 906 A.2d 959, 965 (Md. Spec. App. Ct. 2006).

103. Several empirical studies have shown that zoning boards tend to issue variances as an accommodation for the applicant, and that appellate courts serve a disciplinary function for boards, forcing them to consider only the criteria relevant for variances. Nonetheless, there is a great volume of appellate litigation and reported opinions involving variances.

104. *See Hamilton Southside Historic Preservation Ass'n v. Zoning Bd. of Adjustment of the City of Hamilton*, 531 P.3d 584 (Mont. 2023).

105. *See Yates Real Estate, Inc. v. Plainfield Zoning Bd. of Adjustment*, 435 F. Supp. 3d 626 (D.N.J. 2020).

While deference is due the board's decision, greater deference will be accorded a decision to deny a variance than is given one to grant it, and greater deference is given to its decision in an area variance case than is given in a use variance case.[106]

[F] Standards of Proof and a BZA'S Subject Matter Authority

Often, zoning ordinances and regulations concerning variances do little more than mimic the undue hardship language of the enabling act authorizing the granting of variances. However, some statutes and ordinances attempt to narrow the grounds for a variance in an attempt to prevent them from being granted too freely. Consider the impact of the following typical statute on variances:

> Where, by reason of exceptional narrowness, shallowness, or shape of a specific piece of property at the time of the original adoption of the regulations or by reason of exceptional topographical conditions or other extraordinary or exceptional situation or condition of a specific piece of property, the strict application of any regulation adopted under [the zoning enabling act] would result in peculiar and exceptional practical difficulties to or exceptional and undue hardship upon the owner of such property, a variance from such strict application so as to relieve such difficulties or hardship, provided such relief can be granted without substantial detriment to the public good and without substantially impairing the intent, purpose, and integrity of the zone plan as embodied in the zoning regulations and map.[107]

In this statute, variances are authorized for either practical difficulties or undue hardships. In interpreting them, a showing of practical difficulties is necessary when the applicant for a variance seeks an **area variance.**[108] An area variance may properly be granted when (1) the regulation unreasonably prevents the owner from using the property for a permitted use or conformity with the regulation is unreasonably burdensome (meaning that it would cost more to comply with the ordinance as written than compliance is worth), (2) granting the variance does substantial justice between the owner and his neighbors (here is a generalized version of a "no adverse impact on the neighbors" element), and (3) the variance observes the spirit if not the letter of the regulation (here is a generalized version of a "promotes the general welfare" element).[109]

---

106. *See Saddle Brook Realty v. Board of Adjustment*, 906 A.2d 454, 459 (N.J. Super. Ct., App. Div. 2006).

107. D.C. Code Ann. § 6-641(g)(3) (2025).

108. *See Fleischman v. District of Columbia Bd. of Zoning Adjustment*, 27 A.3d 554, 557–63 (D.C. 2011).

109. *See North v. St. Mary's Cty.*, 638 A.2d 1175, 1179 (Md. App. Ct. 1994).

These three criteria for an area variance present an applicant with a substantial burden of proof. However, in interpreting the undue hardship language, courts have held that the *Otto* test for a **use variance** is applicable, and the burden becomes even heavier. Thus an undue hardship means that: (1) a complying use will not yield a reasonable return, (2) the owner's difficulty in complying is unique, and (3) the essential character of the locality will be unchanged if the application is granted.[110] About twenty states use these three criteria to define an undue hardship. One court, however, using its zoning enabling act's undue hardship standard, has held that no variance is authorized unless compliance with the ordinance "would interfere with all reasonable beneficial uses of the property."[111]

Often two standards are not set out in an enabling act. When this is the situation, the default rule is that the undue hardship standard is used for both types of variances.[112] However, labeling a variance as one or the other might make a difference.[113] Good pleading is necessary to exploit that difference. For example, where owners have a 1.9 acre parcel zoned for one house and single-family residential use with a minimum lot size of 1 acre but two houses are located on the parcel, the board granted them a variance in order that they might rent the houses to two families—a single family in each house. When their neighbors challenged the granting of the variance in court, the issue turned on identifying the requirement from which a variance was requested: was it the single family residence requirement, or in the alternative, was it the minimum acreage requirement? The former would be a use variance, the latter an area variance.[114] As previously discussed, the latter is much more common and easier to obtain. However, in this situation, the granting of an area variance for a parcel of 0.9 acres would require that the board condition its grant of a variance on the subdivision of the whole parcel. This the board cannot do. Why? Because the board may not condition its granting of the variance on the subdivision of the property into two parcels. Such a condition is a matter for the planning commission or whatever board is responsible for the subdivision of land in the municipality.[115] The existence of this subject-matter authority elsewhere, in another board or agency, is grounds for finding that the board has no authority to impose this restriction. So a referral to the planning commission should precede the board's consideration of an area variance.

---

110. *See Otto*, 24 N.E.2d 851 (N.Y. 1939), cited *supra*, this Chapter, at n. 16.

111. *See Cochran v. Fairfax Cty. Bd. of Zoning Appeals*, 594 S.E.2d 571 (Va. 2004).

112. *Id.*

113. *See Matthew v. Smith*, 707 S.W.2d 411 (Mo. 1986) (noted in 52 Mo. L. Rev. 537 (1987)).

114. In this regard, consider *Bamber v. Zoning Bd. of Review of the Town of Foster*, 591 A.2d 1220, 1223 (R.I. 1991). In Rhode Island, an area variance is "a deviation," a term of long standing in that state. *See Viti v. Zoning Bd. of Review of Providence*, 166 A.2d 211 (R.I. 1960) (term deviation defined).

115. *See Marx v. Zoning Bd. of Appeals*, 529 N.Y.S.2d 330 (N.Y. App. Div. 1988).

[G] Variances as an Administrative Remedy

The granting of one or more variances to nearby landowners is irrelevant to the consideration of a variance. Each variance is granted—or denied—on the basis of facts peculiar to the property of the applicant.[116] In part, this is so because a request for a variance is an administrative, rather than a legislative, procedure.[117] If a general policy lying behind a regulation is not working well, it is the function of the legislature in the municipality to change it—such changes are beyond both the competence and the jurisdiction of the board.

A zoning ordinance that provides "the board may, with appropriate conditions and safeguards, vary the application of this ordinance in accord with its general intent, if not its literal terms," would be upheld by most courts against a charge that it is void for vagueness. A court would either interpret this provision as authority to decide that a variance if granted is "not inconsistent with the general welfare" or have "no adverse impact on adjacent parcels" or else find that a hardship standard would typically be implied from the word "vary"; the rest of the language about "appropriate conditions and safeguards" would then be authority for the board to impose reasonable restrictive covenants when granting an application for a variance.[118] Privately imposed restrictive covenants applicable to a subdivision may arguably require that an owner undertaking a renovation obtain permission of the subdivision owners' architectural review committee or property owners association before seeking any necessary variances to carry out the renovation. Covenants on which such arguments are based must be clear in limiting the right of access to a public forum such as the BZA, else they will be interpreted as permitting an owner to choose whether to apply for permission before or after obtaining a variance.[119]

When an ordinance does not use its enabling act's hardship standard, but instead substitutes other standards, the board is nonetheless authorized either to imply the hardship standard from the standards that are expressly authorized, or else use the hardship standard in any event.[120] Thus, the enabling act standard is incorporated by reference into the ordinance's standards.

---

116. *See Santos v. Zoning Bd. of Appeals of the Town of Stratford*, 918 A.2d 303 (Conn. App. Ct. 2007).

117. *See Victor Recchia Residential Const. Inc. v. Zoning Bd. of Adjustment of Cedar Grove*, 768 A.2d 803, 809 (N.J. Super. Ct., App. Div. 2001) (stating that a board may not usurp the legislative function when granting variances).

118. *See Driesbaugh v. Gagnon*, 522 N.E.2d 1019 (N.Y. 1988) (restrictions imposed shall relate to the use, not the user of the property, and not to other property not subject to the application).

119. *See Little Whale Cove Homeowners Ass'n, Inc. v. Harmon*, 986 P.2d 616, 620 (Or. App. Ct. 1999).

120. *See Green v. Bair*, 549 A.2d 762, 764–65 (Md. App. Ct. 1988) (holding that the board should use a hardship standard when the word appears in the enabling statute but not in the ordinance, involving an enabling statute defining a variance as "a relaxation in the terms of the ordinance, not contrary to the public interest and owing to unique conditions, not self-created, on the land or intended use, but resulting in undue hardship" and an ordinance authorizing the board to grant variances upon finding that: (1) there are unique circumstances applying to the applicant's parcel; (2) the variance is necessary

[H] The Board and Legislative Judgments

In considering an application for a use variance, it is improper and *ultra vires* the board's authority to conclude that "the neighborhood is changing and becoming a center for [whatever use the applicant proposes]," even though several similar non-conforming uses and variances are present in proximity to the proposed use. This rationale would be appropriate when used by the municipality's legislature to justify a rezoning, but it is inappropriate when used by the board. A variance may not be used to confirm an emerging land-use pattern.[121] An owner need not present evidence of attempting (and failing) to sell the parcel for a conforming use in order to show an undue hardship; although such evidence is helpful, it is not dispositive. Likewise, a board may not, after many applications for use variances for (say) two-family occupancy in a single-family district, announce that hereafter all such requests will be granted, that announcement involving again a legislative judgment, and not one for the board.[122]

In the same vein, if an owner seeks a variance for a "wholesale" business in a commercial use district in which the ordinance permits only "retail" businesses, no variance may be issued because the classification of uses into districts is a legislative function, not an administrative matter delegated to the board; granting such a variance would again be akin to a rezoning—here akin to a change in the text of the ordinance (i.e., a text amendment). It is for this reason that some zoning enabling statutes deny boards the authority to grant "use variances."[123]

On the other hand, if in a deteriorating neighborhood, a corner movie theater is losing money, is out of step with the prevailing market for theaters and unsalable for use as a cineplex, its owner could obtain a variance to change the use on the parcel in order to utilize it for other permitted uses under the zoning ordinance. Here, the board is implementing a pre-existing legislative decision.

Standing alone, however, evidence of financial loss is insufficient to grant a use variance.[124] Likewise, the deterioration of the neighborhood puts every owner at the same disadvantage, meaning that every owner is affected the same way and there is no "unique" hardship.

---

for the applicant to enjoy the same rights as his neighbors; and (3) granting of the variance will have no adverse impact on neighbors).

121. In many older residential neighborhoods, owners want to expand the square footage or add a deck, porch, or other modernizing features to keep their residences up to date, but a variance is not the proper remedy for such improvements, a rezoning being the correct one.

122. *See Feiler v. Fort Lee Bd. of Adjustment*, 573 A.2d 175, 178 (N.J. Super. Ct. 1990) (reversing BZA grant of variance for mixed commercial and high rise residential project).

123. *See* Cal. Gov't Code § 65906 (1983).

124. *City of Pittsburgh v. Zoning Bd. of Adjustment of City of Pittsburgh*, 559 A.2d 896, 903 (Pa. 1989) ("Mere economic hardship will not of itself justify a grant of variance."). *See also Rittenhouse Row v. Aspite*, 917 A.2d 880, 885 (Pa. Commwlth. Ct. 2006) (same).

[I] Variances and Social Benefits

Sometimes an owner wishes a variance for a use which might be regarded as socially beneficial, as when wanting an area variance in order to install solar collectors in his front yard, or a use variance for low income housing. Sometimes the enabling act for the ordinance is specific on this point, providing that the social purpose of the project for which a variance is sought may be considered. New Jersey's enabling statute provides an example.[125] If the statute is not specific on this point, then the "no adverse impact" branch of variance law controls, and might also support the variance: that is, the board might offset the impacts of the proposed use against the benefits obtained from it. This finds, in the "no adverse impact" requirement, the authority to balance the impacts from any off-setting benefits.[126] Some courts, however, reject such balancing, as being without statutory authority.

A "flexible" public welfare standard may be applied when, for example, an apartment house is converted to a homeless shelter by a not-for-profit organization.[127] Such a conversion may be treated as an area variance when height and number of stories permitted as of right in an apartment use district are standing in the way of building the shelter. Here the board has the flexibility to turn the no adverse impact on the public inquiry into a "no substantial detriment to the general welfare or the municipality's general plan," making the public need for the use into an important factor in deciding to grant the variance and giving flexibility to all the elements necessary for granting the variance.[128] Likewise, a legislative determination that the applicant's site is suitable may be considered by the board, "not as overriding applicable zoning regulations, but in applying those requirements to the application at hand," even when the legislature found the parcel suitable with knowledge that the variance would be needed.[129] Such prior knowledge may mean that the need for the variance is self-created or self-imposed, but that is "not a bar to an area variance"[130] when the parcel is the only one feasible in the neighborhood to meet the need for homeless services.[131]

---

125. *See Saddle Brook Realty v. Board of Adjustment*, 906 A.2d 454, 460 (N.J. Super. Ct., App. Div. 2006) (listing schools, hospitals, or public housing as uses serving the public good).

126. *See, e.g., Kaufmann v. Planning Bd.*, 542 A.2d 457 (N.J. 1988) (deciding that granting a variance to permit two non-conforming residences on a parcel would promote the general welfare and that the benefits out-weighed the detriment to the neighborhood; decided under a statute presented as an alternative to a hardship variance); *Burbridge v. Governing Body of the Twp. of Mine Hill*, 568 A.2d 527 (N.J. 1990) (holding that aesthetic benefits justified variance to expand a non-conforming auto body shop use).

127. *See Neighbors for Responsive Gov't, LLC v. D.C. Board of Zoning Adjustment*, 195 A.3d 35 (D.C. 2018).

128. *Id.* at 56.

129. *Id.* at 59. *But see Dupont Circle Citizens Ass'n v. D.C. Board of Zoning Adjustment*, 182 A.3d 138 (D.C. 2018) (refusing to apply a flexible standard to a church).

130. In contrast, a use variance would not be granted for a self-created hardship.

131. *See Neighbors for Responsive Gov't, op. cit.*, 195 A.3d at 60.

[J] Variance Conditions and Remedies

When a parcel for which a variance is sought is unimproved, it is often difficult for neighbors to determine if the "no adverse impact" element for a variance will be met without seeing the improvement proposed. In this situation, a variance may be conditioned on the completion of an improvement within a certain time-period.[132] In this regard, traffic conditions around a parcel may justify conditioning a variance tailored to specific parking requirements[133] or restrictions on operating hours.[134] On the other hand, a variance for an unimproved lot may not be granted upon the condition that the applicant show his development plans to neighbors and obtain their consent to an improvement built according to those plans. Such a condition would be an improper delegation of the authority given the board to the neighbors.[135] There is no provision for it in the Standard Zoning Enabling Act or other enabling statutes. Similarly, no condition can be imposed on granting a variance that prohibits all rental of the property; such a condition is an unreasonable restraint on alienation and violates the policy against creating economic waste of property.[136]

Likewise, if an applicant had no specific plans to develop the lot, neither could the variance be granted on the condition that the neighbors purchase the sub-standard lot, there being no express authority for this either. That condition would offend the owner's right of alienation.

A condition forcing the applicant to sell to neighbors would also be invalid as being something the owner did not expect to happen when filing his application. Moreover, the neighbors might be wary of buying. They would not as purchasers have the same right to apply for a variance thereafter, because then the hardship would be found to be a self-created one, so the sale could only be for the limited purpose of expanding a lawn or garden or buying protection from abutting development. This possibility would decrease what they would pay, unless a merger of a non-conforming lot with the purchasers' gave a right to greater development on the purchasers' side of the boundary. With all of these problems, it is probably safe to conclude that no such condition is authorized—or even good policy.

When a tract can be subdivided into conforming, but odd-shaped lots, the subdivider should do so; failing to do so, a developer will not thereafter have grounds for a variance.[137] Thus, when possible, the subdivider must use the subdivision regulations in such a way as to avoid the necessity for a variance; otherwise, the need for the variance would be self-created, and no variance may be granted when the hardship

---

132. *See Int'l Investors v. Town Plan & Zoning Comm'n of Town of Fairfield*, 277 A.3d 750 (Conn. 2022).

133. *See Brown v. Jefferson*, 203 So. 3d 1213 (Ala. Ct. Civ. App. 2014).

134. *See W.J. Menkins Holdings LLC v. Douglass Twp.*, 208 A.3d 190 (Pa. Comwlth. Ct. 2019).

135. See the discussion of contract and conditional zoning, discussed *infra*, Chapter 12, § 12.01–02.

136. *See Gangemi v. Zoning Bd. of Appeals of the Town of Fairfield*, 763 A.2d 1011, 1015–16 (Conn. 2001).

137. *See Gottlieb v. Board of Appeals*, 527 N.Y.S.2d 258 (N.Y. App. Div. 1988) (finding and imposing a statutory standard of "minimum adjustment" when granting a variance).

is self-created.[138] This leads to the question, why isn't the desire to subdivide a self-created hardship to begin with, no matter what number or odd-shaped parcels result from the process?[139] It is because there should be no penalty for using a public regulation available to all.

[K] The Self-Created Hardship

A self-created hardship is on occasion both an element of the proof of a variance, as well as a defense to the granting of an application for it. A variance may not be granted when the hardship, even when proven by the applicant, is self-inflicted. A "self-created" hardship arises typically when an owner purchases property with the knowledge that the use he proposes for it will require a variance from existing regulations. An applicant for a variance whose design of her house made her realize the need for a variance has created the hardship and no variance will issue.[140] It can also arise when the improvements made on the property, for a specific purpose, become outmoded but might be renovated for another use if a variance is granted. It applies to both use and area variances.[141]

In some jurisdictions, the self-created hardship rule is made an element of the proof that the applicant must offer the board.[142] In others, it is an affirmative defense—not necessarily part of the applicant's proof—but need only be negated when raised by others, such as neighbors or the board's attorney on appeal.

A purchaser's knowledge of zoning restrictions from which her development plan requires a variance traditionally creates a self-inflicted hardship barring variance relief. The knowledge can be actual or constructive, because a purchaser is deemed to know the provisions of the zoning regulations and to have figured out how they will affect her property. This traditional rule has in many jurisdictions been modified so that purchase with the knowledge of the need for a variance does not preclude its granting, but is one factor in the consideration of the application for a variance.[143] For example, a purchaser may have purchased the property with the knowledge that the prior owner obtained variances, but that further variances may be necessary. In such a situation, using the traditional rule might seem to some unfair. Other jurisdictions go further and hold that the right to a variance runs with the land and is available to an applicant's successors in title.[144] By the same token, the specific explanations and

---

138. *See City of Pittsburgh v. Zoning Bd. of Adjustment of City of Pittsburgh*, 559 A.2d 896, 903 (Pa. 1989).

139. *See Aitken v. Zoning Bd. of Appeals*, 557 A.2d 1265 (Conn. 1988) (holding that it is).

140. *See Cox v. City of Madison Zoning Bd. of Appeals*, 2022 WI App. 7 (Wisc. Ct. App., July 8, 2021).

141. *See Sciacca v. Caruso*, 769 A.2d 578, 583 (R.I. 2001).

142. *See Otto*, cited *supra*, this Chapter, at n. 16.

143. *See Twigg v. Town of Kennebunk*, 662 A.2d 914, 916 (Me. 1995); *see also Hill v. Town of Chester*, 771 A.2d 559, 560–61 (N.H. 2001).

144. *See Stop & Shop Supermarket Co. v. Board of Adjustment of Twp. of Springfield*, 744 A.2d 1169, 1177 (N.J. 2000) (so stating and collecting the cases).

representations of an applicant should not be taken to bind the successor in title when the application process is incomplete when taken over.[145] In addition, an owner seeking a variance in order to legitimate improvements to the parcel done in violation of the ordinance, will be granted a variance when that owner did not install the violating improvement—but not if he did.[146]

Self-created hardship issues also often arise during an executory period when an applicant for a variance sells a parcel during the application process, and the board, seizing on the sale as an opportunity to enforce the ordinance, denies the variance, arguing that by buying, the purchaser has a self-created hardship. A variance may not properly be denied in this situation, for to deny the variance is to deny the initial applicant the power to alienate the parcel during the application process. If the vendor is entitled to a variance, the purchaser should be too, even if the purchaser takes the title with knowledge of the restriction from which variance relief is sought. The right to a variance in this situation "runs" with the land. Otherwise, the right to alienate is needlessly impaired.

In another scenario that is a builder's nightmare, a structure may be half-built when an owner discovers that the set-back or other area or bulk requirement of the ordinance is not met. The cases are split when addressing this situation, but "after the fact" area variances have been granted. Surveying and construction errors are sometimes a basis for a variance, but implicitly courts granting the variance are engaging in a type of balancing—balancing the costs of correction versus the impact on the neighbors. This type of case is best regarded as an equitable exception to the rules on variance—not a rule in itself, for then the good faith of the applicant would become an element of the variance.[147] Correction of the mistake must have become prohibitively costly for a variance to be granted in this situation.

A self-created hardship is not created when an owner physically alters the land after the enactment of a regulation.[148] This rule typically applies when proving an unnecessary hardship for a use variance.

---

145. *Id.* at 1178. *See also Dexter v. Town Bd. of Gates*, 324 N.E.2d 870, 871 (N.Y. 1975).

146. *See generally City of Pittsburgh v. Zoning Bd. of Adjustment of City of Pittsburgh*, 559 A.2d 896, 903–904 (Pa. 1989) ("Self-inflicted economic hardship is not justification for grant of variance."); *Appeal of Gro*, 269 A.2d 876 (Pa. 1970) (hardship is self-created only where an increment of the purchase price anticipates the granting of the variance).

147. *See Devaney v. Town of Windham*, 564 A.2d 454, 457 (N.H. 1989); *In re Cumberland Farms, Inc.*, 557 A.2d 486, 488–89 (Vt. 1989) (both cases requiring correction of non-complying structures). *But see Almeida v. Zoning Bd. of Review of the Town of Tiverton*, 606 A.2d 1318 (R.I. 1992) (holding that denial of a variance to permit the conversion of a basement to a separate dwelling unit in a single family residence district was not a hardship and ordering owner to comply with an administrative order halting a partly completed conversion under an illegally issued permit).

148. *See City of Detroit v. City of Detroit Bd. of Zoning Appeals*, 926 N.W.2d 311 (Mich. 2018).

[L] Variances from Regulations for Special Exceptions

Finally, an applicant requesting a variance from the requirements for a use controlled by a provision for a special exception in an ordinance is regarded as seeking a variance from a permitted use; in this situation, a variance may be granted. Special exceptions are the subject of the following section.

§ 10.03 Seeking a Special Exception

While a variance is a waiver of the provisions of the zoning regulations, a special exception\special use\conditional use is something very different. It is a use which, upon application to the board, will be permitted in a use district if certain criteria, already set out in the regulations, are met. "The fundamental distinction between [a special exception and a variance] is that [a special exception] is legislatively permitted in a zone subject to controls whereas the latter is legislatively prohibited."[149] A special exception in some jurisdictions may be known as a special permit or conditional use, but all three terms are synonymous and are customarily used interchangeably.[150]

The special exception has its origin in the zoning ordinance itself (while the variance does not). It is expressly set out in the ordinance, but rather than being incorporated into the litany of uses permitted in a district as of right, its uses are permitted only conditionally. There is no requirement that a zoning ordinance contain provisions for special exceptions.[151] However, when conditions are set out, the board reviewing applications for special use exceptions must apply all of them, and may not pick and choose which to emphasize or apply.

Permitting a use conditionally often sets the stage for a semantic battle between applicants and any opposition. The former argue the requested use is permitted by the ordinance, and subsequent arguments seek to minimize the discretion of the board in hearing the application. The opponents stress the conditions and the discretion given the board. Generally, a special exception is considered to be a permitted use,[152] and so is entitled to a presumption that granting it is consistent with the general welfare

149. *See Value Oil Co. v. Town of Irvington*, 377 A.2d 1225 (1977); *see also Citizens Coalition v. District of Columbia Bd. of Zoning Adjustment*, 619 A.2d 940, 948 (D.C. 1993) (stressing that a use is permitted by a special exception when in harmony with its neighborhood, whereas a variance would be prohibited but for the hardship resulting from the prohibition).

150. *See* Patricia E. Salkin, *American Law of Zoning* § 14:1, at p. 14-5 (5th ed. 2011).

151. *See Piscioneri v. Zoning Hearing Bd. of the Borough of Munhall*, 568 A.2d 610, 611 (Pa. 1990) (holding that special exceptions in residential districts are not required).

152. *See, e.g., Light of Life Ministries, Inc. v. Cross Creek Twp.*, 746 A.2d 571, 573 (Pa. 2000).

of the jurisdiction and its comprehensive plan, and is therefore valid on that account. The authority to issue a permit for a special exception must be express.[153]

A hearing on the application for a special exception is, in almost all states, an administrative procedure. The applicant has the burden of proof, and the state's administrative procedure act controls the proceedings. This burden is to present substantial evidence of compliance with the criteria which condition the use. As previously discussed, substantial evidence is that which a reasonable mind might find relevant and adequate to support a conclusion.

Allocating the burden of proof to the applicant is not always fair, particularly when one of the criteria for the special exception is a finding of "no adverse impact." As with a variance, this requires the petitioner to prove a negative—that there is no adverse impact on the adjacent parcels or (worse yet, from petitioner's standpoint) the public interest. In a majority of jurisdictions, courts require that the municipal legislature adopt standards or criteria for granting or denying an application for a special exception.[154] Express criteria protect an application from arbitrary decisions, prevent discrimination, and facilitate judicial review, particularly when the board must make written findings of fact when deciding to grant or deny the application. A provision for a special exception is entitled to a presumption of validity, just as any provision of a zoning ordinance is.

Under a rule followed in a small minority of jurisdictions, the hearing on a special exception is held by the municipal legislature and is classified as legislative in nature; thus, a presumption of validity attaches to the regulation and, so long as the decision is fairly debatable—that is, so long as reasonable minds could read the record and reach opposite conclusions, including the one reached—it will be upheld.[155] This presumption of validity survives an adverse decision on an application for a special exception, and applies during all judicial appeals of the board decision. It survives until the last court upholds the denial.[156] Even in this minority of jurisdictions, the courts require a written record containing findings of fact pertinent to the ordinance's or any statutory criteria used by the board.[157] In another minority rule jurisdiction, where express criteria are not required, the decision is adjudicatory in nature and is not entitled to a presumption of validity, so the burden is on the decision-maker to justify it.[158]

A better term for a special exception is a conditional use.[159] Indeed, in many jurisdictions, a special exception and a "conditional use" are terms that are used

---

153. *See Farmington-Girard, LLC v. Planning and Zoning Comm'n for the City of Hartford*, 260 A.3d 428, 436 (Conn. 2021).

154. *See Ackman v. Board of Adjustment for Black Hawk Cty.*, 596 N.W.2d 96, 104 (Iowa 1999).

155. *See Board of Supervisors of Fairfax County v. Southland Corp.*, 297 S.E.2d 718 (Va. 1982).

156. *See Board of Supervisors of Rockingham County v. Stickly*, 556 S.E.2d 748 (Va. 2002).

157. *See Ames v. Town of Painter*, 389 S.E.2d 702, 704 (Va. 1990).

158. *See Sunderland Family Treatment Services v. City of Pasco*, 903 P.2d 986, 994 (Wash. 1995).

159. Judges sometimes confuse terms which zoning attorneys routinely use, even to the point of calling a variance a special exception. Such confusion can be traced to inattentive drafting in § 7 of the SZEA. The most famous example of such confusion is Chief Justice Burger's doing just this in his

interchangeably. This term has the advantage of indicating that it is intended to deal with predictable problems of land-use compatibility and anticipate (and keep to a minimum) requests for rezonings. In most jurisdictions, it is still the product of an order issued by the administrative board, setting out the pre-conditions for that use.[160] Such written orders or decision set out each condition, present the board's fact-finding supported by its hearing record, and apply the condition to the facts. The last step—applying the condition to the facts—is what makes the matter before the board a mixed question of law and fact. To such a question on judicial review, the rational basis standard of review applies.

A zoning may permit churches, synagogues, and mosques in a residential use district as a special exception. This is a way of balancing First Amendment, free exercise of religion clause concerns with police power concerns—churches may well create spin-off or external effects on neighboring parcels, but there are reasons to tolerate them.

Other uses that are often the subject of special exceptions in residential neighborhoods, such as funeral homes, nursing homes, age-restricted housing, home offices, and half-way houses for drug addicts and parolees, are less popular than religious buildings. Private schools in residential neighborhoods are sometimes the subject of special exception procedures.[161] In commercial use districts, apartment houses,[162] fast food outlets, branch banks, and other businesses with drive-through windows are often the subject of special exceptions. Sometimes land uses designated as special exceptions are also subject to other regulatory regimes: bars and restaurants, for example, need a liquor license issued by a state alcohol control agency. In this instance, conditions imposed on the grant of a special exception remain land use regulations and are not preempted by that other regime.[163] Finally, no matter where located, if an applicant's parcel is located in two land use districts, development of that split-zoned parcel may be treated as a special exception.[164]

Oil and gas wells and related facilities in the eastern states have also been the subject of special exceptions, even when the land use district involved is residential or agricultural.[165] Sand, gravel, and stone quarries have likewise provided a good deal of

---

opinion in *City of Eastlake v. Forest City Enterprises*, 426 U.S. 668 (1976), discussed *infra*, Chapter 20, § 20.02.

160. *See Steen v. County Council of Sussex County*, 576 A.2d 642, 646 (Del. 1989) ("A conditional use [sometimes called a special exception] is not truly an exception to a zoning ordinance, but is a use in compliance with, rather than in variance of, the ordinance and is allowable when the prerequisite facts and conditions specified in the ordinance are found to exist.").

161. *See Youngblood v. D.C. Bd. of Zoning Adjustment*, 262 A.3d 228 (D.C. 2021).

162. *See Avanru Dev. Group, Ltd. v. Town of Swanzey*, 2022 N.H. LEXIS 103 (N.H., Aug. 16, 2022).

163. *See Lime Lounge LLC v. City of Des Moines*, 2024 Iowa Sup. LEXIS 29, **22–24 (Iowa, Mar. 22, 2024).

164. *See Youngblood, op. cit.*, 262 A.3d at 233 (involving a special exception as an extension of the lesser restrictive use).

165. *See Gorsline v. Bd. of Supervisors of Fairfield Twp.*, 186 A.3d 373 (Pa. 2018).

the appellate case law on the subject of special exceptions.[166] They generate noise and dust and the use of heavy trucks, so sometimes they require proximity to the location where the material excavated is to be used.. Thus, the conditions imposed on granting a special exception for them are detailed—that they not "substantially increase" fire hazards, traffic or the character of the neighborhood.[167] Further, extra and tailored conditions are often added to a grant of all these extractive industry permits.[168] More recently, wind farms have also been subjected to special exception procedures.[169]

All these uses require lawyering in the face of local opposition and that is one reason why the criteria are pre-set. The attorney for the applicant can insist that the board follow the criteria provided in the ordinance, even in a hearing room packed with opponents. There is no neighborhood veto in these hearings. For example, a special exception for group housing or mobile homes in a single family residential zone may be included not just because the legislature wanted to include such uses, but because if it excluded them totally, the exclusion would not promote the police power's general welfare.

The procedural effect of classifying a use as a special exception is to shift the burden of proof to the applicant. The applicant's burden is to present substantial evidence that he qualifies for the exception. This shift occurs even in jurisdictions entitling the conditional use to a presumption of validity, for that is a presumption that attaches only to the legislative classification of the use.

Sometimes the legislative definition of a use made a special exception is not clearly defined or not further defined in an ordinance. If a "private school" is named as a special exception, then what about a music school not offering a general educational program and just giving music lessons? A restaurant giving training to new employees is not a school; nor is a conference center offering continuing education to unrelated groups. However, a music school offering beginner, intermediate and advanced training in many musical instruments, staffed by trained professional musicians and accredited by a national music schools association, whose graduates go on to professional careers in music has qualified as a "private school."[170]

---

166. *See Columbus Bituminous Concrete Corp. v. Harrison Twp. Bd. of Zoning Appeals*, 156 N.E.3d 841 (Ohio 2020); *Como Steak House, Inc. v. Bd. of Supervisors*, 200 So. 3d 417 (Miss. 2016); *EQT Production Co. v. Borough of Jefferson Hills*, 209 A.3d 1010 (Pa. 2019); *Ackman v. Board of Adjustment for Black Hawk Cty.*, 596 N.W.2d 96, 103–04 (Iowa 1999); *Quality Sand and Gravel, Inc. v. Planning and Zoning Comm'n of the City of Torrington*, 738 A.2d 1157 (Conn. App. Ct. 1999).

167. *See Como Steak House*, op. cit.

168. *See, e.g., Markwest Liberty Midstream and Resources LLC v. Cecil Twp. Zoning Hearing Bd.*, 184 A.3d 1048 (Pa. Commwlth. Ct. 2018).

169. *See Monaghan Farm, Inc. v. Bd. of County Comm'nrs*, 527 P.3d 1195 (Wyo. 2023); *Ehlebracht v. Deuel Cty. Planning Comm'n*, 972 N.W.2d 464 (S. Dak. 2022).

170. *See Youngblood v. D.C. Bd. of Zoning Adjustment*, 262 A.3d 228, 237 (D.C. 2021) (discussing *Neighbors on Upton St. v. D.C. Bd. of Zoning Adjustment*, 697 A.2d 3, 5–8 (D.C. 1997)). *See also Freepoint Solar LLC v. Richmond Zoning Bd. of Review*, 274 A.3d 1 (R.I. 2022) (involving the definition of a "utility substation").

A special exception's criteria, set out in the regulations, will have as their subject matter minimum standards for set-backs, side-yards, screening, parking, bulk, density of use—all designed to prevent the conditionally permitted use from exerting external effects on neighboring parcels. Such criteria are meant only in a limited sense to insure the compatibility of the special exception with its surroundings. Under the most commonly used standard, once the applicant has carried his burden of proof as to all of the enumerated and specific criteria, an applicant has carried his burden of proof as to the "adverse impacts" of the proposed use when showing that it is no more burdensome on surrounding parcels than uses permitted as of right are. A more specific standard requires the applicant to show that the use, at the proposed location, would not have adverse impacts *above and beyond* those impacts inherently associated with that use in the use district for which it is proposed. For example, with a special exception for a waste disposal site, the board need not consider all adverse impacts of the applicant's use; the municipal legislature has found them tolerable when providing for a special exception. As an administrative body, the board may not re-consider this legislative decision. Neighbors might allege that the proposed waste disposal use will cause run-off into a stream and that trash trucks entering and leaving will create noise on abutting streets. If the owner then introduces evidence that the run-off will be no heavier than that which occurs at other disposal sites and that the trucks will be no noisier at this site than anywhere else, the owner has met his burden. The issue is whether the adverse effects are greater here than they would be elsewhere: is the drainage pattern unique on this site? Do the trucks using the abutting roads shift gears, or stop and start, more than usually? Those are the appropriate types of questions of fact for the board.[171]

Some external effects are inherent in almost all special exceptions and conditional uses. Why else would they be permitted only conditionally? Some external effects are inherent in the use. Thus, a board may not deny a special exception just because the requested use has external effects. If, however, those effects are above and beyond a level that might reasonably be expected of them at the location for which the applicant seeks the special exception, then a denial is warranted.[172]

What uses may be classified as a special exception has also received judicial attention.[173] Certain uses, considered essential to the zoning jurisdiction's welfare when not incompatible with uses permitted as of right in a use district, but not compatible at each and every location within the district, may be treated as a special exception.[174] In an agricultural use district, it is permissible to classify a junkyard or a machine repair

---

171. *See Schultz v. Pritts*, 432 A.2d 1319, 1325 (Md. 1981) (the leading case for this proposition) (discussed in *Clarksville Residents Against Mortuary Def. Fund, Inc. v. Donaldson Props.*, 162 A.3d 929, 943–47 (Md. Ct. Spec. App. 2017)); *Mossburg v. Montgomery County*, 666 A.2d 1253 (Md. App. Ct. 1995) (reviewing Maryland cases to this effect).

172. *See People's Counsel v. Loyola College*, 956 A.2d 166 (Md. 2008).

173. *But see Ackman v. Board of Adjustment for Black Hawk Cty.*, 596 N.W.2d 96, 103–04 (Iowa 1999) (considering whether a quarry is appropriate in an agricultural use district).

174. *See Tullo v. Millburn Twp.*, 149 A.2d 620, 624–25 (N.J. Super. Ct., App. Div. 1959).

shop as a special exception, but not a landfill.[175] The two former uses are frequently found in agricultural districts and are ancillary to an agricultural use, even though they may have adverse impacts on neighboring uses. Likewise, a special exception for water well drilling, but not oil, may be permissible in an agricultural district because irrigation is necessary for agriculture. Like the definition of a "private school" previously discussed, whether a proposed use falls within those allowed by special exception is a question of law.[176] The language is construed reasonably and with regard to the ordinance's general purpose and structure, and in order to avoid illogical or inconsistent results.[177]

Generalized use of the special exception is invalid.[178] When a small jurisdiction's zoning ordinance contains no residential uses permitted as of right, except for single family housing, but instead requires that special exception permits be obtained for any other residential development, the resulting regulatory scheme can be found invalid on at least three grounds. First, the purpose of zoning is both to integrate compatible uses and separate those which need protection from each other, while this scheme carries out only the last purpose. Second, this scheme has by definition no uniformity and no preexisting comprehensive plan here; instead, every issue is left to the discretion of the local administrative board. Third, viewed as a delegation of power, this scheme is too broad; the local legislature cannot delegate its zoning powers to such a degree.[179] Wait-and-see zoning may not be the primary method of a jurisdiction's land use regulation, that is, without stepping outside the bounds of what is permitted in many zoning enabling acts.

[A] Generalized Mop-Up Conditions for Special Exceptions

While objective criteria conditioning the granting of a special exception are the traditional norm, under which there might arise a presumption of its validity as a provision in an ordinance, there is a more recent tendency to use more generally

---

175. *See Bierman v. Township of Taymouth*, 383 N.W.2d 235 (Mich. App. Ct. 1985) (upholding this distinction).

176. *See Wells v. Portland Yacht Club*, 771 A.2d 371, 374 (Me. 2001) (whether a yacht club is a "private club" and permitting a conditional use for a junior sailing program open for a fee to non-club members).

177. *Id.*

178. *See Massey v. City of Charlotte*, 2000 N.C. Bus. Ct. 4 (Apr. 17, 2000) (invalidating a conditional use district as *ultra vires* the enabling act).

179. *Compare Rockhill v. Township of Chesterfield*, 128 A.2d 473 (N.J. 1956) (criteria for duplexes, quads, townhouses, and multiple family structures were enumerated in the ordinance, in terms of: (1) minimum acreages, (2) set-backs, (3) height restrictions, (4) side and back yard restrictions, and (5) the ordinance provided that no special exception shall issue when to do so would have an adverse impact on adjacent parcels or the public interest), *with Klem v. Zoning Hearing Bd.*, 387 A. 2d 667 (Pa. Commw. Ct. 1978) (where only two percent of the township was zoned and ninety percent was left to the special exception procedure, the court held that the zoning was comprehensively planned).

worded conditions, standing alone or as a mop-up condition. One of the oft-used express conditions for a special exception is a "public need" for its use. This, however, has been attacked as too broad a delegation of legislative power to an administrative board: zoning boards have no authority to regulate competition—for example, to decide how many gas stations should be located at an intersection.[180] A "public need" criterion is inherently too vague because it can be related to matters of competition, a concern beyond land-use compatibility and the authority and competence of the board administering applications for special exceptions. In addition, making findings of public need might be seen as non-delegable duties of the municipal legislature.

The best evidence, but not the only evidence permitted, of a "public need" is in the municipality's comprehensive plan. Thus, a generalized condition like "harmony with the general intent and purpose of the municipality's zoning ordinance" or "harmony with the municipality's comprehensive plan" are two oft used generalized conditions.[181] This is particularly so when the plan has been reviewed and adopted by the municipality's legislature as an ordinance. Then the granting of a special exception may also be challenged on the ground that it is not in accord with the comprehensive plan. A special exception is subject to the comprehensive plan, while a variance (being a waiver of zoning regulations) is not.[182] So an application for a special exception is best challenged by a showing of non-conformance with that plan.

General conditions for special exceptions have also been found void for vagueness.[183] A condition requiring the board to preserve the "natural beauty" is likely void on this account.[184] Conditions that wander far from the idea that the special exception be found compatible with surrounding land uses are suspect. The negative of a compatible use is a nuisance, but an ordinance requiring the board to find that no nuisance exists might trespass on the judicial function, and be void on that account.

[1] "No Adverse Impact" Criteria

Another mop-up criterion for a special exception will be to the effect that "there is no adverse impact on neighboring parcels."[185] Although, for many legislatures, a "no adverse impact" criterion is the next best thing to a public need criteria, its focus is clearly land-use compatibility and so it will survive legislative/administrative line-drawing, and is generally found to be a proper consideration for a board conducting an administrative hearing.

---

180. *See Wesco, Inc. v. City of Montpelier*, 739 A.2d 1241 (Vt. 1999).

181. *See Sheridan Kalorama Historical Ass'n v. D.C. Bd. of Zoning Adjustment*, 222 A.3d 1246, 1251 (D.C. 2020); *Columbus Bituminous Concrete Corp. v. Harrison Twp. Bd. of Zoning Appeals*, 156 N.E.3d 841 (Ohio 2020).

182. *See Anderson v. Zoning Bd. of Review*, 219 A.2d 484 (R.I. 1966).

183. *See Kosalka v. Town of Georgetown*, 752 A.2d 183 (Me. 2000).

184. *Id.*

185. *See Attar v. DMS Tollgate LLC*, 152 A.3d 765, 775 (Md. App. 2017) (whether nearby gas stations might go out of business is irrelevant to issue of adverse impact of an applicant's special exception for a gas station).

"No adverse impact" criteria may mean that, as a practical matter, the applicant has to deal with whatever concerns the opposition raises. Viewed in this light, the burden is less onerous and the criteria is a reflection of the fact that an application for a special exception is heard in a quasi-judicial proceeding—one often designed to settle a dispute between the applicant and his neighbors. Due process principles apply to quasi-judicial proceedings. "Although the ZBA is not a court, it is nevertheless a governmental body charged with applying the law to zoning matters arising in its purview, and the principles of due process apply with the same force."[186] Moreover, whenever a due process violation is reviewed by a court, the standard of review is plenary and *de novo*. In this context, the applicant's attorney should encourage the applicant to discuss the application with neighbors and gain their approval for it.[187] But the hearing record and the board's order should not slip from a discussion of potential adverse impact to a consideration of the general welfare; the board must conduct the hearing and rule on an application on the basis of land-use compatibility criteria. The extent of the adverse impacts considered, however, increases with the extent of the special exception proposed; thus for a big-box discount store, the adverse impacts of a municipality's entire "viewshed" might be considered.[188]

[2] Specific and General Criteria

A frequently litigated issue with special exceptions is whether, when all the enumerated, specific criteria for a special exception are met by the applicant, the board must then issue an order granting the application. One view of this matter is that it must.[189] In this view, specific criteria can be taken to encapsulate mop-up or general, no adverse impact criteria following them. The inclusion of the special exception in a district is a legislative finding that this use, with the conditions met, is in harmony with those uses permitted as of right in the district. In this instance, the specific criteria define the parameters of the police power, and unpublished conditions would be *ultra vires*. This result also follows from the local legislature's duty to provide notice to the applicant of the criteria which it is necessary to satisfy before a special exception will be granted. When the administrative record contains evidence of a dispute about the compatibility or adverse impact of the use, however, this view is less easily justified.

---

186. *See Pascal v. City of Pittsburgh Zoning Bd. of Adjustment*, 259 A.3d 375, 385 (Pa. 2021).

187. *See National Cathedral Neighbors Ass'n v. District of Columbia Bd. of Zoning Adjustment*, 753 A.2d 984, 987 (D.C. 2000).

188. *See Wal-Mart Stores, Inc. v. Planning Bd. of the Town of North Elba*, 668 N.Y.S.2d 774, 776–77 (N.Y. App. Div. 1998) (calling the viewshed integral to a town at the "western gateway" to Lake Placid in a tourism-dependent region).

189. *See Value Oil Co. v. Town of Irvington* 377 A.2d 1225, 1232 (N.J. Super. Ct., Law Div. 1977) ("Once an applicant has demonstrated compliance with the provisions of the zoning ordinance, a duty is imposed upon the board to grant the permit."), *affirmed*, 396 A.2d 1149 (N.J. Super. Ct., App. Div. 1978).

Another view of this issue is that, when the applicant meets the enumerated, specific criteria, a rebuttable presumption generally arises in favor of issuance.[190] This is consistent, courts say, with the presumption of validity accorded a special exception in most states. Once the applicant meets the specifically enumerated criteria, some jurisdictions shift the burden of proof to opponents to show that the use is incompatible or has an adverse impact on its surroundings.

Still another view of this issue arises when the regulation for the exception, after setting out the specific criteria for a group home as a special exception, provides that "when all such criteria are met, the board may by order issue the permit." Here, the discretionary verb "may issue" means that the board has the authority to deny the permit, but need not. When it does not, however, the board needs to make a special showing of its findings and conclusions. The municipal legislature may have only intended to shift the burden of proof to the board to justify its denial or its imposition of additional conditions once all specific criteria are met. This third view is sometimes known as the Pennsylvania rule on this issue.

The opposite view of this issue is that "a zoning commission may deny a special permit application on the basis of general standards set forth in the zoning regulations, *even when all technical requirements of the regulations are met*."[191] This view is consistent with the allocation of both the burdens of proof and persuasion on the applicant. It treats a board's authority to approve a special exception as the equal of its authority to deny one. It treats the general standards as the equivalent of more specific ones and interprets the regulations as a whole, rendering each of equal importance. Moreover, upon judicial review of any denial, it puts on the appellant the burden of showing that there is no substantial evidence to support the denial. It also recognizes that in basing a decision on general standards, the board was deciding a question of law subject to plenary review.

[B] Legislative Review of Special Exceptions

Sometimes a municipal legislature will delegate to itself the authority to hear special exception applications. This is a reservation of authority and is generally regarded as within the legislature's power to delegate.[192] Sometimes too, zoning regulations authorize the board to hear special exception cases, but provide for review by the legislature thereafter. This review provides for a reading of the board order (and discussion of it) in the midst of a legislative session. It may further justify the board's decision and provides insulation from judicial attack on the grounds of an impermissible delegation of a legislative function, but the legislature must still have a written decision to review, because during its review it is functioning in an administrative,

190. *See Steen v. County Council of Sussex County*, 576 A.2d 642, 646 (Del. 1989) (citing cases from Maryland and Pennsylvania).

191. *See McLoughlin v. Planning and Zoning Comm'n of the Town of Bethel*, 240 A.3d 709, 720 (Conn. Ct. App. 2020) (emphasis in original).

192. *See Harford Cty. v. Earl Preston, Jr., Inc.*, 588 A.2d 772 (Md. 1991).

rather than a legislative capacity. As such, it is subject to the standard of substantial evidence and the state's administrative procedure act.

[C] Special Exceptions with Variances Attached

Another category of problems with special exceptions arises when both a special exception and a variance are applied for. When an owner is granted a special exception with the proviso that the development proposed must be built within two years from the date of the grant, such a proviso is valid,[193] having been upheld in other contexts, particularly rezonings. Later delays in obtaining financing will find the applicant seeking to stay the effect of the "use it or lose it" provision in the grant by petitioning for a variance from its requirement. Such an application is in effect asking relief from inaction. Inaction is a self-created hardship—grounds for denying the variance.[194] However, if the delay in financing is caused by a lack of capital in financial markets beyond the control of the owner, the petition may be granted.

A variant of this view affirming the validity of a time limitation is that the limitation on a special exception does not violate the rule that variances and special exceptions are not limited to the tenure of the owner applying for them; instead, they "run with the land." Thus, to the extent that a request for an extension of time to complete development is filed with the board, the request is an integral part of the land use status granted by the special exception. Otherwise, what would normally be a permitted conditional use would become an illegal and invalid one. However, even when (say) a special exception order appears in the land records, it may be time-limited not only by its terms, but also by site plan statutes limiting the life of unbuilt site plans.[195] The underlying assumption here is that a special exception may like many estates in land, be subject to a condition subsequent. In any event, a board is authorized to impose a time limitation on an unbuilt special exception.[196] This authority may be express in some municipalities and implied in others.[197] It is intended to prevent a developer from securing approvals and permits several years in advance of actual construction, thus avoiding more up-to-date and perhaps more rigorous sets of regulations; in this regard, municipalities should be able to exercise their police power and respond to conditions prevalent at the time of actual construction. Stale permits vesting years after issuance thwarts the proper exercise of that power.[198]

A more contentious issue arises when a board grants a variance to allow an applicant for a special exception to satisfy the conditions that are necessary for the board to grant the special exception. May the board, where a variance is proper, use it to vitiate

---

193. *See National Waste Managers v. Anne Arundel Cty.*, 763 A.2d 264, 267 (Md. App. Ct. 2000).

194. *See Farrington v. Zoning Bd. of Appeals*, 413 A.2d 817 (Conn. 1979) (holding that inaction is a self-created hardship).

195. *See Int'l Investors v. Town Plan & Zoning Comm'n*, 277 A.3d 750, 758 (Conn. 2022).

196. *See id.* at767.

197. *Id.* at 766.

198. *Id.* at 767.

the legislatively imposed condition? One court answered this question is the affirmative.[199] This court noted that the zoning ordinance at issue excluded some "areas of the code from being subject to variance relief, but does not exclude the relevant special exception from being modified by variances."[200] Area variances, not use variances, were involved here. Moreover, the court stated, "the granting of the variances may not so substantially alter the criteria for the granting of the special exception so that the criteria ... would be swallowed by the variance to the extent that the special exception would not be a use contemplated in the comprehensive zoning scheme. ... " An occasional ordinance will deal with this issue by inserting a condition that, *inter alia*, a special exception may be granted "in unique circumstances warranting the special exception."[201] When the special exception permitting procedure provides for the relief requested in an application for a variance, the former procedure prevails and the application for a variance will be denied; here, asking for a variance from a height regulation permissible under a special exception makes the board's grant of a variance for the same thing improper.[202]

[D] Special Exceptions and Non-Conforming Uses

Sometimes ordinances make provision for non-conforming uses to become permitted by way of special exceptions.[203] This has been found to be a valid use of a special exception.[204] However, a special exception may not be used to expand an adjacent non-conforming use. Suppose a municipality permitted waste disposal sites by special exception and the board granted a special exception to the owner of both a non-conforming sand and gravel pit and an abutting, proposed disposal site. The owner's proposal, calling for trucks bringing construction refuse to the site from a nearby city to return there, loaded with sand and gravel, might easily be seen as promoting efficiency. Nonetheless, this is an improper use of the special exception. Non-conforming uses (because they are also protected by some enabling statutes and the takings clause) may be expanded, but not substantially changed or increased.[205] Permitting an expansion of the scope of a non-conforming business is more that a mere increase in the rate of quarrying the sand and gravel. Expanding its owner's business off-site is an unreasonable expansion, giving neighbors a case for denying the permit; what results is not substantially the same as what was on site when the use became non-conforming.[206]

199. *See Alviani v. Dixon*, 775 A.2d 1234 (Md. 2001).

200. *Id.* at 1242.

201. *See Bermes v. Summit Cnty.*, 536 P.3d 111, 116 (Utah Ct. App. 2023) (involving a ridgeline lot).

202. *See Comstock v. Zoning Bd. of Appeals of Gloucester*, 153 N.E.3d 395 (Mass. Ct. App. 2020).

203. Discussed *supra*, Chapter 7, § 7.03.

204. *See In re Appeal of Jackson*, 830 A.2d 685 (Vt. 2003).

205. *See Ray's Stateline Market, Inc. v. Town of Pelham*, 665 A.2d 1068 (N.H. 1995) (changed signage and plumbing for convenience store are not an improper expansion of a non-conforming use).

206. *Cf. Lazy Mtn. Land Club v. Matanuska-Susitna Borough Board of Adjustment and Appeals*, 904 P.2d 373 (Alaska 1995).

The board's decision would be struck down as *ultra vires* the protection given nonconforming uses in the enabling act.[207] If the municipality amended its ordinance in order to authorize the quarry as a special exception, the two businesses could then be authorized to proceed with the owner's proposal.

[E] Procedural Due Process

Both the variance and the special exception are the product of an administrative hearing. Conducting such a hearing, the board accords rights of procedural due process: the right to notice, the right to cross-examine the witnesses in some way, and a prohibition of *ex parte* communications with board members. The persons involved in the hearing must have "an opportunity to know the facts on which a board is asked to act" and to offer rebuttals and counter-arguments.[208] These processes govern the conduct of the hearing and assure the adequacy of the record for judicial review.

If at the hearing, the applicant for a special exception produces substantial evidence in support of the application, but the opponents of the application also produce substantial evidence of its adverse impacts, it is then for the board to review the conflicting bodies of evidence and to decide. The applicant need not, in response, produce further evidence such that (say) the application is supported by a preponderance of the evidence. Indeed, the board may refuse to hear further evidence once the hearing is adjourned. Why? Because administrative discretion is given to the board—this is particularly so when the criteria for decision are of the "no adverse impact" type. After all, two bodies of substantial evidence need not be in conflict with one another; there is room for both, and each might just address different impacts of the proposed special exception.[209]

[F] Special Exceptions and Site Planning

In some jurisdictions, "it is common practice . . . to review site plans in connection with special permit applications."[210] The details of an application appear in a site plan. A site plan is a graphic document reflecting the location and dimensions of buildings, from which can be determined compliance with zoning and subdivision regulations as well as any wetlands or conservation regulations applicable to a development. Thus, where available, a BZA is likely to refer a special exception application to whatever agency (often the municipal planning commission) performs site plan review in the

207. *See Nickels v. City of Wildwood*, 658 A.2d 291 (N.J. 1995).

208. *See Taylor v. Planning and Zoning Comm'n of the Town of Westport*, 293 A.3d 356, 367 (Conn. App. Ct. 2023).

209. *See Crooked Creek Conservation and Gun Club v. Hamilton Cty. N. Bd. of Zoning Appeals*, 677 N.E.2d 544 (Ind. App. 1997).

210. *See Int'l Investors v. Town Plan & Zoning Comm'n*, 277 A.3d 750, 764 (Conn. 2022).

municipality.[211] Issues raised in site plan review can reflect the externalities that a development might throw off, such as traffic, and even regional impacts.[212]

§ 10.04 Administrative Appeals

The board or BZA also hears one other type of administrative matter—that is, appeals from administrative determinations and interpretations of the zoning ordinance and regulations. In this capacity, it sits as an appellate agency to review the work of land use administrators. When an administrator oversteps his or her authority, the board may disregard the action as non-appealable as not a legal action, and regard it as a nullity.[213] Its opinion is entitled to a presumption of correctness because harmonizing and defining the terms of the ordinance is often a difficult matter. Administrative appeals may be subject to the doctrine of exhaustion of remedies in some jurisdictions.[214] After all, when a dispute may be resolved by clarifying a definition, rather than litigating the effect of a whole ordinance, judicial efficiency dictates that the parties do the former by going first to the zoning administrator for an opinion. Likewise, the exhaustion doctrine dictates often that appeals from the administrator's decision go the BZA.[215] Once in the hands of a reviewing court, however, questions involving the interpretation of an ordinance are matters of law, reviewed narrowly to determine whether the board abused its discretion.[216] Terms are interpreted either to assign them a plain and sensible meaning (when clear), or to give them (if unclear) their usual meaning in the context of the ordinance. So, for example, a street looping around to end on the same street it began, is not a "dead-end" street.[217] Overall, if the administrator can be shown to have interpreted a term consistently over a long period of time, his interpretation will be entitled to great weight before any reviewing court.

In a more broadly applicable example, when a building is to be constructed on a slope and recessed into the ground, it will matter whether the building's height, for purposes of compliance with a zoning regulation, is measured from the grade of the lot or from the base of the building because a building may be in compliance on its

---

211. *See Stergiou v. City of Dover*, 287 A.3d 717 (N.H. 2022).

212. *Cf. Anthony v. Town of Plaistow*, 301 A.3d 1263 (N.H. 2023).

213. *See Farmington-Girard, LLC v. Planning and Zoning Comm'n of the City of Hartford*, 260 A.3d 428 (Conn. 2021).

214. *See Josephson v. City of Annapolis*, 728 A.2d 690 (Md. 1999).

215. *See McNamara v. Hersh*, 945 A.2d 18 (N.H. 2008).

216. *See Marzullo v. Kahl*, 783 A.2d 169 (Md. 2001) (holding that a facility for breeding snakes is not a "farm").

217. *See Springborn v. Town of Falmouth*, 769 A.2d 852, 856 (Me. 2001) (an ordinance limiting dead-end streets to a 1500 foot length); *see also Swoboda v. Wilder*, 920 A.2d 518 (Md. App. 2007) (as to the "front" of a building on a corner parcel); *Alvord Investments v. Zoning Bd. of App. of Stamford*, 920 A.2d 1000 (Conn. 2007) (interpretation of zoning ordinances governed by the same canons of construction as apply to statutes).

up-hill side, but not on its down-hill side. The location of its front door may be determinative if the height is measured only on its front side.[218]

Similarly, when an ordinance permits a two-story building, sinking the building into the earth, with one grade below ground level and two above, creates a non-complying structure. A "story" is generally defined as an interior measurement. It is "the portion of a building from the upper surface of a floor to the upper surface of the floor next above."[219] On the other hand, a "cellar" or basement may be defined as "being no more than four feet above ground level," but such a definition appearing in a residential-use district permitting houses that are no more than three stories tall, will not prevent a developer from building a fourth floor on a new house by excavating and making the "cellar" deep enough to stand in.[220]

An administrator must exercise common sense. When a building's maximum length is prescribed by a regulation and an administrator is presented with a building plan that puts a "jog" or break in the building's facade, such that the length on either side of the break does not exceed the maximum, the plan fails to comply with the regulation when its two segments have common hallways, elevators, and other facilities and together exceed the maximum length.[221] Likewise, when an ordinance provides that "a use may be non-conforming use as to its area and dimensions," an owner whose parcel does not meet its minimum frontage requirement argues that he owns a valid non-conforming use. Why? Because, he says, its frontage is a "dimension." No, the administrator decides, frontage refers to a parcel's location on an abutting street. Is the administrator correct? Has he used common sense? If his conclusion is doubtful, consider that the owner's remedy is to appeal to the BZA and to apply for a variance. Set in this context, the administrator's decision will be entitled to deference and upheld by the board.[222] Upon further judicial review, however, that same decision will typically be a matter of law and review will be plenary.

An administrator's decision is governed by the same canons of construction that apply to statutes and ordinances, must strictly construe the statute or ordinance, achieve a rational result, and be consistent with past decisions. A strict construction is necessary because the statute or ordinance is considered in derogation of the common law of property; its meaning is not to be extended by implication.

An administrator's interpretative authority should be exercised so that the administrative decision is in accord with the opinions of the municipality's attorney.[223] As a

---

218. *See Laforce v. Bucklin*, 273 A.2d 144 (Md. 1971).

219. *See* Bdlg. Officials Conf. of America (BOCA), *Basic Building Code (an excellent source of many definitions for zoning enforcement officers) (quoted in Nether Providence Twp. v. R.L. Fatscher Assoc.*, 674 A.2d 749, 751 (Pa. Commw. Ct. 1996)).

220. *See* Sandra Fleishman, *When is a Floor a Floor? Therein Lies a Story*, Wash. Post, Apr. 29, 2000, at G1, col. 2.

221. *See Board of Comm'rs of Township of O'Hara v. Hakim*, 339 A.2d 905 (Pa. Commw. Ct. 1975).

222. *See Cosseboom v. Town of Epsom*, 771 A.2d 565 (N.H. 2001).

223. *See Houston v. Town of Waitsfield*, 648 A.2d 864, 865 (Vt. 1994) (where the administrator said that the extraction of spring water for bottling required a variance in an agricultural zone, while

general rule, an administrator may not do more than interpret the regulation; decisions on constitutional or vested rights issues, although not expressly denied him, are nonetheless reserved for the courts.[224] Some further examples show the difficulties that administrators face. For example, "residents" of a parcel might be granted a special exception to engage in various "home occupations" such as babysitting, child care, or renting rooms to boarders. Under this rule, in the last instance, an administrator might rule that residents may not be tenants, summer residents, or even nine months a year residents, and that the boarders be no more than short-term licensees.[225]

In a further example, suppose that an owner had a parcel located in an exclusively agricultural use district: that is, only agricultural uses were permitted as of right. In the applicable ordinance, agriculture was defined as "the growing or harvesting of crops and other farm commodities, including the processing or storage of products harvested on the premises." The owner's parcel had a natural spring that the owner proposed to tap and sell its water in bottled form. Applying to the administrative official to certify that her proposed use of the spring was an agricultural use, she argued: that water was raised from the ground, just as was any crop; that it was a renewable resource, just as wheat or corn; and that water is involved in agriculture, even though not traditionally thought of as a crop, though not sold as a farm commodity, nor an agricultural "product" or the subject of a harvest, as the ordinance seemed to require.[226] The plain meaning of the phrase prevailed, and the owner failed to convince the administrator.[227]

In a final example, an owner obtained approval for a shopping center. The applicable ordinance provided that "in all non-residential use districts in which shopping centers are permitted, no primary entrances or exits shall direct traffic into adjacent residential districts."[228] Neighbors in an adjacent residential district appealed the approval, alleging that, while customers of the center would not be directed into their residential district, delivery vehicles would be. The neighbors won, raising issues regarding the meaning of "primary" access as including both customer and service access. They presented affidavits of engineers and planners to the effect that delivery trucks, including large eighteen-wheelers, would be necessary to service the center and that "primary" access must account for both vehicle trips and the type of traffic generated by the use. Separating customer and delivery traffic would render trip and traffic counts inaccurate, and be overly formalistic: the customer's use of the center

---

legal counsel opined that it was an as-of-right use; the BZA rejected both interpretations, denying the application for an extraction permit).

224. *See Holland v. Johnson, Zoning Administrator*, 403 S.E.2d 356 (Va. 1991).

225. *See Richert v. City of South Portland*, 740 A.2d 1000, 1002–03 (Me. 1999).

226. *See* Annot., *Construction and application of terms "agricultural," "farm," "farming," or the like*, 97 A.L.R.2d 702, 706 (1964).

227. *See Houston v. Town of Waitsfield*, 648 A.2d 864 (Vt. 1994) (considering also the effect of the state legislature's recently enacted statutory program for certifying the quality of spring water and run by the state agriculture department).

228. *See Ryan v. City of Bay Minette*, 1995 Ala. LEXIS 260 (June 9, 1995) (reversing a summary judgment for the owner).

during its peak hours might have been just as noisy as one eighteen-wheeler arriving at midnight.[229]

Conclusion. In the following chapter, we turn our attention to the last of the zoning forms of action—a rezoning. It is not an administrative matter. It is presented, not to the BZA, but to a zoning commission or municipal legislature. It requests a use or textual change in the ordinance. As with the initial zoning of land in the municipality, it is a matter that is legislative in nature.

229. *Id.*

Chapter 11
Seeking a Rezoning

§ 11.01 Introduction

There are two types of rezonings. First, an owner asking to have his parcel taken out of one use district and placed in another is seeking to have the zoning map for the jurisdiction redrawn. Redrawing the map is a rezoning often called a **map amendment**. Second, an application may, in addition or solely, request that the text of the ordinance be modified, usually expanding the list of uses permitted as of right in a district. This second type of rezoning is an application for a **text amendment**. Thus, a rezoning application, once granted, results in either (or both) a map or a text amendment to the zoning ordinance.

Both types of rezoning amendments are typically regarded as legislative actions. Such applications are heard by the local legislative body of the jurisdiction—or, in the alternative, heard by a zoning commission or a hearing examiner, whose decision is subject to legislative review, the legislature being the same body that enacted the zoning ordinance originally. In rezoning hearings, the "minimum procedural protections required by the Due Process Protections vary depending on the context."[1] One result of this is that "those affected by legislation are not entitled to any process beyond that provided by the legislative process."[2] The facts found in a legislative hearing are general in nature, typically do not concern the immediate parties, and are used to decide questions of policy.[3] Legislating necessarily entails "political trading, compromise, and ad hoc decision making" and legislators are "partial to legislation all the time," meaning that they may run for office "promising to use legislative power to accomplish specific policy objectives."[4] Partiality is not a due process violation. Applicants for a rezoning are not entitled then to an impartial hearing. Indeed, property owners have no right to a rezoning.[5] They are only entitled to present their views and to be heard. If, however, the rezoning is a piece-meal one, then courts often regard the matter as a quasi-judicial one, and substantial evidence is required.

1. *See Miller v. Zoning Bd. of Appeals of Lyndon Station*, 991 N.W.2d 380, 384 (Wisc. 2023).
2. *See id.* at 385 (internal quotes omitted).
3. *See infra*, § 11.15.
4. *See Miller, op. cit.*
5. *See Riniker v. Dubuque Bd. of Supervisors*, 884 N.W.2d 223 (Iowa Ct. App. 2016).

In enacting any amendment, municipal legislatures must follow the procedures set out in their own enabling statutes.[6] Typically, these procedures require a notice and a hearing, and usually also, several readings of the amendment before it may be enacted and become effective. No formal written record of the debate (other than the requirements of the state's open meetings laws), or the findings underlying the action, is required, again because the action is a legislative one, and it speaks for itself. The amendment action must, however, be codified (that is, incorporated into the zoning code or ordinance) and made available to the public.

§ 11.02 Twin Presumptions

Rezonings can be comprehensive—broad-based in scale, affecting a diverse number of parcels and uses, or they can be piece-meal, affecting fewer parcels of land. A comprehensive zoning scheme is entitled to twin presumptions of constitutionality and validity.[7] After such a scheme is enacted, if the local legislature changes its mind and rezones an owner's property, is its action entitled to the same presumptions? May not what was reasonable at the time of the original zoning become proof of the unreasonableness of the rezoning?

The answer, as a matter of logic, is that, if the original zoning was justified only by its having a rational basis, then it is possible that the rezoning may have the same basis—and that both actions can fit within the range of all reasonable options open to the local legislature. This is what is meant when a court, reviewing the rezoning decision, states that if the action of the local legislature is fairly or reasonably debatable, then a court will not overturn it.[8]

Any rezoning must be based on evidence making it fairly debatable, meaning that it bears a substantial relationship to the general welfare. Two rules intersect here and should be distinguished. "The substantial relationship rule is a substantive law."[9] It governs the decision of a legislative body. However, the fairly debatable rule is a "rule of procedure or application," stated as follows: when in a piece-meal rezoning the application of a zoning regulation is applied to a specific parcel and that application is reasonably subject to disagreement—that is, if it is fairly debatable—the courts should not disturb the legislative decision.[10] This second rule then provides a standard for judicial review. "Fairly debatable" has come to mean subject to contention

---

6. *See Riggs v. Township of Long Beach*, 538 A.2d 808, 812–13 (N.J. 1988).

7. *See Peter Scotti & Assocs. v. Yurdin*, 276 A.3d 915, 927–28 (R.I. 2022).

8. *See Prete v. City of Morgantown*, 456 S.E.2d 498 (W. Va. 1995) (finding that a rezoning is fairly debatable when the totality of the evidence when viewed "both quantitatively and qualitatively, . . . would lead objective and reasonable persons to reach different conclusions").

9. *See City of Alabaster v. Shelby Land Partners, LLC*, 148 So. 3d 697, 704 (Ala. 2014) (internal quotes omitted).

10. *Id.* (quoting from *BP Oil Co. v. Jefferson Cty.*, 571 So. 2d 1026, 1028–29 (Ala. 1990).

or controversy or open to question.[11] It precludes a court from deciding anew what the municipal legislature has already decided—from becoming a super legislature.[12] When the decision taken by the municipal legislature must be shown to be fairly debatable, a rational basis for the action must be present, but it need be only one of several such bases. Although the decision-maker may explain why one was chosen over another, he or she need not because the choice cannot be further challenged. Typically, several rational bases could fit comfortably within the preponderance of the evidence before the legislature, so that the fairly debatable rule provides the lowest standard of review to a court and accords the greatest deference to the legislative judgment.

Merely because the amendment was initially proposed by private parties (say a land developer) is no reason to overturn it. If the rule were otherwise, few amendments would survive judicial review. Moreover, courts do not generally inquire into or consider the legislative motives for a zoning amendment, unless the reasonableness of the amendment is not facially apparent.[13] An amendment's back story is irrelevant. Even though a particular amendment can serve two purposes, one of them illegal or invalid, the remaining other one, being legal or valid, will be sufficient to sustain it.[14]

§ 11.03 Tests for the Validity of a Rezoning

The tests which are used to evaluate a rezoning application can be used either in conjunction with one another, or used standing alone. They are three in number and focus on:

(1) Whether there is a public need for the rezoning amendment, and whether that need is met by the rezoning amendment.[15] This test requires the identification of the public need, and then the establishment of a rational nexus, or substantive due process connection, between the need and the amendment. It may be seen used in the opening portion of Justice Holmes' majority opinion in *Mahon v. Pennsylvania Coal Co.*[16]

(2) A balancing of the public need for the rezoning against the injury worked on neighbors. For example, if an applicant seeks an amendment making airstrips an

11. *See Davis v. Sails*, 318 So. 2d 214 (Fla. Dist. Ct. App. 1975).

12. *See Dockter v. Burleigh Cnty. Bd. of Cty. Comm'nrs*, 865 N.W.2d 836 (N. Dak. 2015).

13. *See Clary v. Borough of Eatontown*, 124 A.2d 54 (N.J. Super. Ct., App. Div. 1956); *infra* note 23.

14. *See Gallo v. Mayor and Twp. Council of Lawrence Twp.*, 744 A.2d 1219, 1225 (N.J. Super. Ct., App. Div. 2000).

15. *See Campbell Woods Homeowners Ass'n, Inc. v. Village of Mt. Pleasant*, 956 N.W.2d 462 (Wis. Ct. App. 2021) (affirming a rezoning when in the public interest, meaning not solely for the benefit of the applicant, and when consistent with long range planning and the surrounding land uses).

16. 260 U.S. 393 (1922).

accessory use in a use district and seeks to install an airstrip on a parcel rezoned in this way, the issue is whether this type of use will impact in a confiscatory way on the applicant's neighbors, not whether it will reduce the value of their property.[17] Some "diminution in value" is to be expected after many rezonings. If this were not the rule, only up-rezones, to a more intensive use, would be valid, while down-zoning, to a less intense use, would always be invalid; such a result would be an impermissible restriction on the legislative function in rezoning matters. Sometimes this test amounts to a uniformity test that tracks either equal protection clause analysis[18] or Holmes' "reciprocity of advantage" test in *Pennsylvania Coal Co. v. Mahon*:[19] may many landowners, or just the applicant, benefit from the change in the zoning? If the former, then the rezone will be upheld. The uniformity requirement is a foundational rule for Euclidian zoning. It allows classifications with a use district so long as they are reasonable. Thus it will invalidate a rezoning that requires a 25 foot setback throughout a land use district but requires a 50 foot setback on one block.[20] On the other hand, it will find a rezoning uniform when maximum lot coverage depends on the steepness of the slope, even though different lots in the same district have different coverages as a result.[21] Tested this way, a comprehensive rezoning must typically involve many owners or a large area.

(3) Whether the rezoning is "in accord with the comprehensive plan." This is a statutory test,[22] based on a phrase taken from the Standard Zoning Enabling Act, § 3. In using this test, the comprehensive plan is taken as a general guide. It is advisory rather than binding, and need not be a separate and discrete document, being regarded instead as a comprehensive approach or scheme. "It is only as a series of statement and precepts, representing community choice and decision as to the space needs of various activities and the interrelationships of land uses, that the ... plan can effectively fulfill its role as a guide to regulatory action."[23] Nonetheless, a well conceived and implemented master plan for a particular neighborhood or use district, when tied into a larger, comprehensive plan for the region, will strongly influence the outcome of a rezoning case.[24] For example, suppose that an amendment directs

---

17. *See Norbeck Village Joint Venture v. Montgomery County Council*, 254 A.2d 700 (Md. 1969) (stating that decreasing neighbors' property values by two-thirds did not invalidate rezoning and was not a taking).

18. *See, e.g., Thomas v. City of West Haven*, 734 A.2d 535 (Conn. 1999) (holding that requiring a site plan of a rezoning applicant when not all such applicants were required to present such a plan, gives rise to a prima facie violation of the equal protection clause, using federal cases as precedent).

19. 260 U.S. 393 (1922).

20. *See N.T. Hegman Co. v. Mayor & Council of Borough of River Edge*, 69 A.2d 767 (N.J. Super. Ct. 1949).

21. *See Rumson Estates, Inc. v. Mayor & Council of Borough of Fair Haven*, 828 A.2d 317 (N.J. 2003).

22. *See Sycamore LLC v. City Council of Iowa City*, 939 N.W.2d 121 (Iowa Ct. App. 2019).

23. *See* Charles Haar, *In Accordance with a Comprehensive Plan*, 68 Harv. L. Rev. 1154, 1174 (1955) (quoted with approval in *Holmgren v. City of Lincoln*, 256 N.W.2d 686, 690 (Neb. 1977)).

24. *See Mendota Golf LLP v. City of Mendota Heights*, 708 N.W.2d 162 (Minn. 2006) (refusing to order comprehensive plan amendment for land designated as golf course on plan's map; finding the plan and zoning were inconsistent; and holding a writ of mandamus to city would issue to resolve conflict).

urban growth away from a sensitive watershed on which the jurisdiction's water supply depends, or that the watershed itself is down-zoned for large lot zoning to protect the water supply. In each instance, the identification in the plan of the public resource to be protected is an indication to any reviewing court that the rezoning was done in good faith and is not directed at benefitting a small group of owners. Thus the plan is a standard "that commands deference and a presumption of applicability," rather than a legislative straitjacket from which no leave may be taken.[25] Indeed, when a written comprehensive plan is a precondition to a zoning ordinance, the presumption of validity for legislative actions "includes the presumption that the zoning amendments were in accordance with the comprehensive plan."[26] The burden of proof is then on the applicant for a rezoning to show otherwise. In a piece-meal rezoning, being in accord or harmony with the plan, not harmony with the former zoning, is required.[27] The most recent plan gives this guidance.[28]

Down-zonings must be comprehensive in nature.[29] A down-zoning is a type of rezoning amendment that results in lower densities or less intense land uses being permitted than were formerly. It is often introduced by the planning staff of the municipality or a legislator. In order to survive judicial scrutiny, they should be: (1) comprehensive in nature; (2) not solely for the benefit of special interests or existing landowners, but rather directed toward a public need; and finally (3) not directed against any particular person or not confiscatory in nature, but rather conforming to the site and to the uses presently surrounding the downzoned area. To the extent that they are substitutes for a municipality's condemnation of property, they are enacted in bad faith and confiscatory. A taking claim by affected landowners will follow!

§ 11.04 Spot Zoning

The converse of an amendment's meeting the three tests for a rezoning is often labeled "spot zoning." That is a rezoning locating a parcel in a district out of character with the neighborhood which surrounds the rezoned parcel. It is "the process of singling out a small parcel of land for a use classification totally different from that of the surrounding area, for the benefit of the owner of such property and to the detriment of other owners"[30] and "an attempt to wrench a single small lot from its environment and give it a new rating which disturbs the tenor of the neighborhood."[31] Conversely

25. *See Sustainable Growth Initiative Comm. v. Jumpers*, 128 P.3d 452 (Nev. 2006).

26. *See Peter Scotti & Assocs. v. Yurdin*, 276 A.3d 915, 927 (R.I. 2022).

27. *See Friends of the Motherhouse v. City of Portland*, 152 A.3d 159, 162–63 (Me. 2016).

28. *Id.*

29. *See Pal DC Storage v. D.C. Zoning Comm'n.*, 229 A.3d 148 (D.C. 2020).

30. *See Hartshorne v. City of Whitefish*, 486 P.3d 693, 699 (Mont. 2021) (quoting *Thomas v. Town of Bedford*, 184 N.E.2d 285, 288 (N.Y. 1962)).

31. *See Magnin v. Zoning Comm'n*, 138 A.2d 522, 523 (Conn. 1958); *Burd v. Brentwood Zoning Hearing Bd.*, 298 A.3d 431, 441–42 (Pa. Commwlth. Ct. 2023).

when the surrounding parcels are zoned to the same level of development intensity as the rezoned parcel, there is no spot zoning. Spot zoning implicates all the foregoing tests—the public need, the uniformity, and the comprehensive planning tests.[32] It need not flunk all three tests to be labeled spot zoning.[33]

Spot zoning has two elements: (1) treatment of a parcel with a small area—a "spot" of land—in a way (2) not in accord with a comprehensive zoning scheme or plan.[34] Sometimes there is a third element, or perhaps an alternative to the second—viz., (3) a treatment of a parcel benefitting private interests.[35] It is "the use of the zoning power to benefit particular private interests rather than the collective interests of the community."[36] It is the antithesis, then, of zoning "in accord with the comprehensive plan," as required by the Standard Zoning Enabling Act (SZEA). As one court put it, spot zoning "refers to the situation where a small area or 'spot' of land is zoned differently than the surrounding area for the benefit of the owner of such property and to the detriment of others."[37] The detriment can either be shown by the rezoning's being a nuisance, by its having adverse effects on neighbors, or by non-conformance with a comprehensive plan for the neighborhood.

As a substantive doctrine, the doctrine of spot zoning is judge-made and a product of the common law, rather than a statute. It purpose is often (not always) to enable judges to invalidate rezoning decisions which treat landowners in a non-uniform way,[38] even to the point sometimes of bestowing political favors. "Modern courts . . . understand uniformity as the state law counterpart of the Equal Protection Clause."[39] The idea that all zoning regulations shall be uniform for each class or kind of building has is origin also in the SZEA, § 2. The criteria for spot zoning can be generally instructive for any rezoning.

Sometimes the term is used to refer to a reverse proposition—namely, a small parcel being restricted more severely than neighboring parcels. This is known as reverse spot zoning.[40] An island of less intense use surrounded by more developed parcels indicates that the island's owner does not have the development benefits accorded to neighboring parcel owners. Sometimes this situation is the result of a "piece-meal

32. *See Green v. County Council of Sussex County*, 508 A.2d 882, 889 (Del. Ch. 1986) (linking the doctrine of spot zoning with a finding that a rezoning fails to meet the equal protection clause requirement of uniform treatment for otherwise similar owners).

33. *See Hartshorne v. City of Whitefish*, 486 P.3d 693, 699 (Mont. 2021).

34. *See Pal DC Storage v. D.C. Zoning Comm'n.*, 229 A.3d 148, 151, n. 5 (D.C. 2020) and *Blaker v. Planning and Zoning Comm'n of the Town of Fairfield*, 562 A.2d 1093, 1099 (Conn. 1989).

35. *See Kuehne v. Town of East Hartford*, 72 A.2d 474 (Conn. 1950).

36. *See Gallo v. Mayor of Lawrence Twp.*, 744 A.2d 1219 (N.J. Super. Ct., App. Div. 2000).

37. *See Gallo, supra*, 744 A.2d at 1225 (rejecting neighbor's allegation of spot zoning, alleging only that the rezoning request was for a higher density). *See also Eden v. Town Planning & Zoning Committee*, 89 A.2d 746 (Conn. 1952).

38. *See Prince George's Cty. v. Concerned Citizens*, 300 A.3d 857, 875 (Md. 2023).

39. *Id.*

40. *See Riya Finnegan LLC v. Township Council of South Brunswick*, 900 A.2d 325 (N.J. Super. Ct., App. Div. 2006); *see also Riggs v. Township of Long Beach*, 514 A.2d 45, 52 (N.J. Super. Ct., App, Div. 1986), *rev'd on other grounds*, 538 A.2d 808 (N.J. 1988) (rezoning to lower density invalid).

down-zoning."[41] It is typically initiated by zoning officials. A golf course in the middle of a commercial or industrial land use district would be an example.[42]

Generally, the geography, location, and characteristics of the rezoned parcel are considered before a rezoning is found to be a spot zoning.[43] When the rezoning is to locate a regional facility, the public or economic need for it will also be considered.

Although spot zoning cases are likely to be site-specific and have limited value as precedent, two alternative rules have emerged in the case law: first, spot zoning is illegal *per se*; or, second, spot zoning is a descriptive, not a legal, term and the real question is the reasonableness of the action. The second rule considers numerous factors, but particularly stresses the size of the parcel; its compatibility when rezoned with surrounding parcels, its neighborhood, and the community as a whole; and the benefits and injuries conferred and worked by the rezoning on owners of surrounding parcels, in the neighborhood, and within the municipality.

The general issue raised in spot zoning cases is whether the doctrine is a substantive rule of law or represents a shift in the presumption of validity usually accorded rezoning when the court identifies facts (smallness of the parcel, etc.) that are not in accord with surrounding uses or preexisting policies or plans. Because rezoning is a legislative act, the latter is most likely, for so long as the legislature rebuts the factors indicating a spot zoning with evidence making the matter a fairly debatable one, the courts will sustain its decision.[44]

§ 11.05 Rezoning or Special Exception?

With rezonings, how the application is styled matters. For example, an applicant might want to sell only a few of many items permitted for sale in a commercial use district. The municipal legislature might more readily approve an application if it sought to permit only the commercial sale of a few items, not all the other commercial items or uses available in the district to which rezoning is sought. Such limited approval may also be more readily supported by local consumers and might reduce the opposition by residential neighbors. So the application might be styled either as a rezoning or treated as an occasion to draft and then establish a special exception (and referred to the BZA). As a rezoning, moreover, it might be challenged as spot zoning, requiring the legislature to provide additional support in the record when granting it.

41. *See Turner v. Bd. of Cty. Supervisors of Prince William Cty.*, 559 S.E.2d 683 (Va. 2002).

42. *See In re Realen Valley Forge Greens Assocs.*, 838 A.2d 718, 731, n.7 (Pa. 2003) (citing Florida cases).

43. *See Knight v. Lynn Twp. Zoning Hearing Bd.*, 568 A.2d 1372, 1375 (Pa. Commwlth. Ct. 1990) (extending a residential zone into an agricultural use district in such a way as to establish an "island or peninsula" of residential land within another use district, is spot zoning).

44. *See Board of Supervisors of Fairfax County v. Snell Const. Corp.*, 202 S.E.2d 889, 893 (Va. 1974).

Moreover, any conditional approval of the rezoning application might be illegal contract rezoning.[45] So drafting a special exception, having it approved, and then applying to the Board might be the preferable tactic.

§ 11.06 General Considerations in Rezoning: A Summary

(1) The variation in the standard of proof and of review evident in rezoning cases reflects the nature of the rezoning action itself. If broad in scope and affecting a large geographic area, the action looks comprehensive and akin to rule-making under the state's Administrative Procedure Act; but when narrower in scope, the action of the legislature has the appearance of a dispute between neighbors—*i.e.*, piece-meal rezoning—to which procedural due process rules often apply.

(2) The extent of the change will also be considered. A rezoning from residential to commercial, or from commercial to industrial, is more likely to be invalidated than a change which permits garden apartments in a residential zone. Likewise, a rezoning which redraws a boundary line between use districts, rather than places a new use in the middle of otherwise harmonious uses, will likely be upheld. Consideration of current conditions and the character of structures in the land use district, the municipality's comprehensive plan, the conservation of property values, and the adequacy of nearby public facilities and infrastructure—all are considered.[46]

(3) Judicial review of a rezoning tests a reviewing court's attitude about the municipality's legislative body; if it is broadly representative of the body politic, its actions will be given more deference than if it represents a narrow slice of society. So a completely residential suburb's municipal council gets less deference than a large city's council.[47] It is also likely to get more due process challenges. Even in large municipalities, *ex parte* contacts with any municipal legislature can become an issue. As can the right to cross-examine witnesses and experts.[48]

---

45. *See infra,* Chapter 12, § 12.01 (discussing contract zoning); *see also Chrismon v. Guilford County*, 370 S.E.2d 579 (N.C. 1988).

46. *See Rouwenhorst v. Gem Cty.*, 485 P.3d 153 (Idaho 2021) (finding that a BZA's inability to find public facilities adequate was a valid reason to deny a rezoning); *City of Madison v. Demaree*, 77 N.E.3d 1219, 1222 (Ind. Ct. App. 2017).

47. Municipal legislative bias, financial and associational conflicts of interest, *ex parte* contacts, and out-right graft need continuous attention. *See, e.g.*, Conn. Gen. Stat. Ann. § 8-11 (1989) (conflict of interest statute for zoning commissions and other local government agencies); Mark Cordes, *Policing Bias and Conflicts of Interest in Zoning Decisionmaking*, 65 N.D. L. Rev. 161 (1989). Perhaps because of a need to distinguish between legitimate interest group election politics and improper conduct, courts tread lightly in this area. *See Woodland Hills Residents Ass'n v. City Council*, 609 P.2d 1029 (Cal. 1980) (political campaign contributions to a majority of local legislature hearing plat application not improper).

48. *See People v. Village of Lisle*, 781 N.E.2d 223 (Ill. 2002).

§ 11.07 Evidence Needed for a Rezoning

Once a rezoning application is appealed and subject to judicial review, counsel for the applicant must ask a basic question: what types of evidence must be produced in support of or to oppose it? Here we are discussing a piece-meal application for a rezoning by a landowner, rather than a comprehensive rezoning initiated by the government. In many cases, the hearing on the application to convert a parcel to a commercial use often becomes a battle of traffic experts: trip generation and traffic counts become the focus of the hearing. More generally, the adverse impacts of granting the application on surrounding parcels will often be determinative. Other land use changes in the vicinity become of secondary interest.

Two other questions often arise. First, must there be changes in actual uses in the neighborhood since the last comprehensive rezoning and replanning of the area? In many states, the answer is, not necessarily. And, second, what is the evidentiary value of comprehensive and master plans applicable to the neighborhood? In many states, the evidentiary value is considerable. These two questions are addressed in the next section.

§ 11.08 The Change/Mistake Rule

In Maryland and some other states,[49] there must first be substantial changes in the neighborhood before the rezoning can be justified on any other ground.[50] A showing of changes made "on the ground" is a threshold requirement of a rezoning. Population increases, standing alone, will not justify a rezone. This is one portion of Maryland's "change-mistake" rule for rezonings.

Maryland requires planning as a precondition to zoning an area, but a piece-meal rezoning thereafter, requires a showing of substantial change in the actual land uses in the neighborhood. It is not enough that a new plan has been formulated, even if that plan has been adopted as legislation by the municipal legislature.[51] Neither is it sufficient that rezonings similar to the applicant's have been approved, if they have not been acted upon—that is, if no construction followed their approval. Similarly, evidence of an increased flow of traffic past the parcel for which rezoning is sought, widening of nearby streets, the improvement of water and sewer facilities serving

49. *See, e.g., Beard v. City of Ridgeland*, 245 So. 3d 380 (Miss. 2018); *Speyerer v. Bd. of Supervisors*, 139 So. 3d 771 (Miss. Ct. App. 2014).

50. *See The Bowman Group v. Moser*, 686 A.2d 643 (Md. App. Ct. 1996) (also holding that a trial court merely finding that the substantial change "amounted to nothing," would be reversed).

51. *See Chapman v. Montgomery County Council*, 271 A.2d 156, 159 (Md. 1971) (finding that a change in density prescribed in master plan, without substantial change, does not justify rezoning).

the parcel, or a gradual increase in the residential density of the neighborhood, will not show a substantial change. Likewise, actual changes outside the "neighborhood" are irrelevant to a showing of substantial change. In a rural area, the neighborhood may be a large one, and in an urban area, small.[52] Once actual substantial change is shown, however, all three of the foregoing tests for a rezoning might be applied, and so the general need for the use and its suitability on the parcel can buttress a decision to rezone.

The second aspect of Maryland's rule concerns legislative mistakes in the initial zoning. "It is well settled that in zoning an original error or mistake may be established by showing that the assumption, upon which a particular use was predicated, proves with the passage of time to have been erroneous."[53]

Applicants for a rezoning will seldom be able to show such a mistake, but they occasionally do, finding a glaring, legislative error. If at the time of a legislative comprehensive rezoning, the legislators failed to take account of existing land use facts, projects, or trends reasonably foreseeable; or if events subsequent to the rezoning have shown that the legislators' policy assumptions turned out to be incorrect, then the presumption of validity accorded a comprehensive rezoning is overcome.[54]

§ 11.09 Planning Studies and Documents as Justifying a Rezoning

In most other states, it is sufficient that such changes be planned—that is, recommended in the applicable master or comprehensive plan. Then the adopted plan becomes a finding of the public's need for the use subject to the rezoning and becomes evidence of the validity of the rezoning decision.[55]

The SZEA requires that zoning be "consistent with the comprehensive plan." This statutory requirement has (as discussed previously) become the basis for one of the three tests of validity for a rezoning; it has sometimes been taken by courts reviewing rezoning decisions to mean that the rezoning decisions of the jurisdiction, taken as a whole, have to have an internal consistency. If it is what the statutory requirement means, then a changed condition—the advent of new demographic groups, with new housing needs—might justify a rezoning. These conditions can be reflected in planning documents.

---

52. *See Buckel v. Board of County Comm'nrs of Frederick County*, 562 A.2d 1297 (Md. App. Ct. 1989) (summarizing the cases).

53. *See Anne Arundel County v. A-PAC, Ltd.*, 506 A.2d 671 (Md. App. Ct. 1986) (down-zoning based on assumption property would be taken in eminent domain for highway, was mistake warranting rezone).

54. *See Howard County v. Dorsey*, 438 A.2d 1339, 1343 (Md. 1982).

55. *See Pierrepont v. Zoning Comm'n of the Town of Ridgefield*, 226 A.2d 659, 662 (Conn. 1967).

Where changes proposed in planning documents are evidence of validity for a rezoning, some states go further and require that the plan be adopted by the local legislature. For the legislature acting on the changed conditions, it is better to have adopted the plan rather than left it in an administrative limbo. Thus, plans devised by planning staffs of a municipality are often thought to be of less evidentiary weight that those adopted by a municipality's legislature.

Sometimes, the raw data that planners used in devising a plan can prove valuable, too. Census data, housing and building surveys, and statistics on building permits issued are examples.

§ 11.10 Individual vs. Cumulative Change

When an owner applies to have a parcel rezoned from residential to commercial use and the municipal legislature grants the application, there will be a finding that there was a substantial change in the neighborhood and a public need for the rezoning. The basis for such finding might be that the up-grading of neighborhood intersections, the extension of sewer and water lines to the property, and nearby rezonings not yet built all show a substantial change in the neighborhood. Neighbors might still argue that each change (the highway up-grading, the new lines, and the rezonings) in and of itself, does not show substantial change. Such an argument will be unavailing because each change would, in most jurisdictions, be considered cumulatively, rather than separately. A legislature may consider changes separately only when the mix of uses in the neighborhood is substantially the same as they were when the last comprehensive zoning took place. In a piece-meal, non-comprehensive rezoning, the issue of whether to consider neighborhood changes separately or cumulatively in a rezoning is a legislative matter. A reviewing court will not substitute its judgment for the legislature's once the latter finds a matter fairly debatable.[56]

§ 11.11 Invalid Reasons for a Rezoning

Much in the same way courts speak of the presence of spot zoning as a reason why the rezoning is invalid, there are several rationales for a rezoning action or decision often black-lettered as invalid. Invalid rationales include, first, the regulation or prevention of competition, or the increase in market demand for a particular use. The purpose of zoning is not to control competition or to control the number of a

56. *See The Bowman Group v. Moser*, 686 A.2d 643 (Md. App. Ct. 1996).

particular type of land use—say, gas stations—available to the public.[57] A second invalid rationale is the denial of prior applications, unless the application is made within an ordinance's period of repose after the prior request has been denied. Each application must stand or fall on its own merits. A third invalid rationale is the applicant's purchase of the property for which application is made with knowledge of the need to rezone; for rezonings, there is no self-created hardship rule, as exists for variances. Fourth, the decision-maker cannot cite the length of time the zoning of surrounding parcels has been in effect. Zoning does not get stale, even presumptively. Fifth, and finally, the decision-maker may not cite the lack of changed conditions surrounding the parcel—unless the application is made in Maryland, as previously discussed—because the zoning may originally have been unreasonable or a contrary decision fairly debatable.

§ 11.12 Drafting a Complaint to Challenge a Rezoning Amendment

A complaint seeking judicial review of a rezoning should first describe the action taken by the municipal legislature, with particularity as to the time, resolution or ordinance number, and enacting body. It should detail the chronology of the application leading up to the action, and the request made in the application, naming both the prior and the requested use of the parcel for which the application was filed; the date and time of any hearing held on the application, as well as who conducted the hearing; any municipal staff reports, recommendations, or actions taken before the hearing and considered at it, and any findings, report, or description of the action taken. The plaintiffs should be named, the statutory basis for the appeal cited, and the plaintiff's standing as aggrieved and injured parties and/or persons who appeared at the hearing established. Finally, in a final series of paragraphs, the basis for the appeal—the invalidity or arbitrariness of the action, and/or the lack of substantial evidence for it—should be pled. For example, the inappropriateness of the proposed use at the requested location, or the lack of a need for a medium density buffer between lower and higher density of uses, might be pled.

Many zoning enabling acts provide only limited guidance for a judicial review of a rezoning action or decision. Often the legislature has consulted with municipal agencies from whom no appeal may expressly be taken.[58] The need for a record, and the extent of that record, is sometimes unclear. Courts often require a record with findings of fact, even when the enabling statute does not.

---

57. *See Aspen Hill Venture v. Montgomery County Council*, 289 A.2d 303 (Md. 1972).

58. *See Montgomery Preservation, Inc. v. Montgomery Cty. Planning Bd. of the Nat'l Capital Park & Planning Comm'n*, 36 A.3d 419 (Md. 2012) (as to the historic preservation commission consulted by the county legislature)

§ 11.13 Rezoning "in Accord with the Comprehensive Plan" and Environmental Law

A rezoning generally may not be denied because of other applications filed or under review, at whatever stage. This is another way of stating that the cumulative effect of the application case load is not a proper subject for consideration; each application is entitled to be considered on its own merits. This rule was formulated well in advance of the environmental movement. In environmental law, the rule is often otherwise. There, one of its lessons has been that governmental actions have impacts and effects that should be considered with regard other actions because the over-all impact may be a cumulative one; thus, no single action may have a significant impact on the environment, but when taken together, several actions may indeed be significant.

During the 1970s, some states enacted Environmental Policy Acts, modeled on the National Environmental Policy Act, or NEPA, the 1970 federal Act of the same name.[59] Like NEPA, their federal counterpart, SEPA's require that an Environmental Impact Statement (EIS) be prepared by a lead agency whenever a government-sponsored project will have a "significant effect" on the environment.[60] Significant effect is typically defined as resulting from "the existence of two or more *related* actions, none of which has significance, but when considered together would have a significant effect on the environment." An EIS is an evaluation of the short and long-term environmental effects of a proposed action, including its associated and cumulative effects, as well as a recitation of the facts relied on in making its evaluation.[61] It has to contain enough analysis of data to allow an informed consideration of its methodology and the issues it raises.[62] A reasoned elaboration of its conclusions is sufficient.[63] An EIS might also consider hypothetical projects and developments.[64]

Viewed in this light, an EIS can be a substitute for a comprehensive plan in states that do not require one before comprehensive rezonings. An EIS is an attempt to think about the adverse consequences of a governmental action—to foresee them, and if appropriate take steps to avoid or mitigate them, much as a plan does. A rezoning decision, like an EIS, also considers the cumulative impact of land use changes, so a municipality containing state-protected, ecologically sensitive lands, that rezoned

59. *See* 42 U.S.C.A. § 4321–4370(a).

60. *See, e.g.*, N.Y. Envir. Conser. L. § 8-0101–0117 (1992).

61. *See* Cal. Pub. Resources Code §§ 21167, 21168 (1995).

62. *See Akpan v. Koch*, 554 N.E.2d 53 (N.Y. 1990). It is normally also subject to the notice, public comment, and hearing requirements. *See, e.g.*, Cal. Pub. Resources Code § 21167(b)–(c).

63. *See Sutton Area Community v. Board of Estimate of City of New York*, 568 N.Y.S.2d 35 (N.Y. App. Div. 1991).

64. *See Neville v. Koch*, 593 N.E.2d 256 (N.Y. 1992). Conversely, a finding that no EIS is required is called a negative declaration. *See Har Enterprises v. Town of Brookhaven*, 548 N.E.2d 1289 (N.Y. 1989). It is issued by the state environmental protection department.

these lands to permit public facilities improvements, may have to write an EIS during the rezoning process, even though no specific land uses are changed until subsequent piece-meal rezoning applications are approved. The fact that the lands have been zoned all at once or comprehensively gives later rezoning decisions a "relatedness" that calls for an EIS.[65] The EIS provides an early-warning consideration of cumulative impacts, complementing what will later take place in the piece-meal rezoning process.

However, governmental activity by itself does not amount to a plan or policy triggering an EIS when a rezoning is sought. Consider a municipality with a very sensitive aquifer underlying it and regulated by federal drinking water standards, state public health laws, a regional planning agency, and municipal ordinances (prohibiting landfills and solid waste disposal there). When an owner applies for a rezoning for land above the aquifer, the application need not be held in abeyance until an EIS is written. Three rationales explain this result. First, there is no comprehensive plan or rezoning effort for the area—merely a host of uncoordinated federal, state, and local efforts, sharing only a common focus on the aquifer.[66] Second, if an EIS were to be written, it is not clear what agency a court should designate to write it. Third, the courts' role is not to piece together various statutes and regulations in order to fill the gap left by the legislature; a judicial call for legislative action is the best course here.[67]

§ 11.14 The *Fasano* Doctrine

Both spot zoning and the change-mistake rule for rezoning are judicial doctrines for heightening the standard of review for some rezonings. Over the history of zoning, there has been a tendency to zone vacant or developable land for uses that do not reflect its development potential. These zones may permit only agricultural uses and become "holding zones" reflecting a "wait and see" attitude by the municipal legislature. It is one way to ensure control over the future development of the municipality, putting the regulatory and development processes in sync, permitting correction of mistakes or omissions in the original zoning, and perhaps allowing the municipality to review development proposals more closely than would otherwise be possible.

Calling a decision legislative in nature implies that a clash of opposing views prevents hasty, ill-considered actions, and that shifting coalitions of legislators can be trusted to air all views and arrive at a consensus decision reflecting the public welfare, knowing that logrolling and vote trading is the stuff of legislative life. Applying this label to a municipal legislative body, however, may result in a fiction: the small

65. *See Save the Pine Bush, Inc. v. City of Albany*, 512 N.E.2d 526 (N.Y. 1987).

66. *See North Fork Environmental Council, Inc. v. Janoski*, 601 N.Y.S.2d 178 (N.Y. App. Div. 1993).

67. *See Long Island Pine Barrens Society, Inc. v. Planning Board of the Town of Brookhaven*, 606 N.E.2d 1373 (N.Y. 1992) (involving the Long Island Pine Barrens and distinguishing the *Save the Pine Bush* opinion) (noted in 3 Buff. Envir. L.J. 37 (1995), noting that, in response to *Pine Barrens Society*, the state legislature enacted the Long Island Pine Barrens Protection Act).

homogenous nature of a municipality may mean that there is no clash of interests, and that there is rather more of special interest than consensus in its decisions.

The leading case of *Fasano v. Board of County Comm'nrs of Washington County*,[68] heightened the standard of review for rezonings. Its holding is that a rezoning action (to a floating zone via a map amendment) by the municipal legislature was not entitled to a presumption of validity and, when neighbors challenge a rezoning, it becomes a quasi-judicial action, to which requirements of notice and a properly conducted hearing, with the right to cross examine witnesses, applies. Here an applicant for a rezoning of a 32-acre parcel requested a map change from a residential, single family, use district to a planned unit development zone, in order to permit the development of the parcel as a mobile home park. He was challenged by neighboring owners.

The *Fasano* court found that, when the land use issues involve an owner or applicant and his neighbors, the action is a request not for legislative action, but instead seeks a hybrid of judicial and administrative action. It is not judicial action, in part because the decision makers lack the security in office characterizing judges and the rules of evidence are not strictly applied. It is not administrative action, in part because the decision makers lack the expertise and technical background often found in administrators and administrative agencies. Finally, a rezoning is neither purely administrative nor purely legislative because the doctrine of separation of powers does not typically apply to municipalities.[69] Rather, for rezoning proceedings, the *Fansano* court stressed the hybrid nature of the decision. The issues before the municipality involve, not the policies of the legislature nor the community as a whole, but the application of those policies to a specific parcel. With regard to a rezoning, the *Fasano* court held that an applicant has the burden of proving four things:

(1) the requested change conforms to the comprehensive plan of the jurisdiction (this opinion was decided in a state making planning a mandatory activity of municipal governments),

(2) there is a public need for the requested use,

(3) his request best meets the need he proves, and

(4) the request conforms to the general welfare (a mop-up standard).

Each of these four elements of the applicant's burden must be shown by substantial evidence.

The Oregon Supreme Court later modified the *Fasano* doctrine in two respects. First, it dropped the third element in *Neuberger v. City of Portland*.[70] Second, it narrowed the reach of the doctrine to apply it only to piece-meal rezonings. It thus

---

68. 507 P.2d 23 (Or. 1973).

69. *See Building Authority v. State*, 321 S.E.2d 97, 102 (Ga. 1984) (so finding).

70. 607 P.2d 722 (Or. 1980) (hereafter "*Neuberger*") (deciding that the rezoning of a 601-acre parcel was quasi-judicial because, notwithstanding its large size, the rezoning affected relatively few owners, required the application of pre-established criteria and a decision choosing among a set number of options).

excluded from the doctrine's reach a comprehensive rezoning—which the *Fasano* opinion characterized as rule making, rather than the application of a rule to specific individuals or properties, the situation which it sought to control in its original opinion. Still, most map amendments are likely to be regarded as piece-meal, and quasi-judicial and adjudicative, in nature. Urban renewal agencies, boards of zoning appeals, fine arts, historic preservation, and architectural review boards also may be subject to the *Fasano* doctrine.[71] Just because a decision concerns infrastructure and the provision of governmental services does not make it legislative in nature; if such were the case, there would be nothing left of *Fasano*.[72]

Taken as a whole, the *Fasano* doctrine's original elements require a showing that there is a nexus between the plan and the request, and between the public's need and the requested use, that the fit between these two is the "best" one, and that the need and the request fit into the general welfare. Viewed this way, these elements amount to a new elaboration of a substantive due process test combined with the public need test for a rezoning. Its use is easiest in a state that requires comprehensive planning.

In its opinion, the *Fasano* court also makes "some brief remarks" on procedural due process for future zoning decisions taken under the aegis of this decision. "Parties at the hearing . . . are entitled to an opportunity to be heard, to an opportunity to present and rebut evidence (but not a right to cross examination?—Ed.), to a tribunal which is impartial in the matter—i.e., having had no pre-hearing or *ex parte* contacts . . . —and to a record made and adequate findings executed."

[A] The *Fasano* Doctrine in Other States

Kansas, Idaho, and Washington have also adopted the *Fasano* standard. Nebraska has by statute authorized judicial appeals for any final quasi-judicial decision of a legislature of a municipality of a certain class.[73] Courts in Arizona, California,[74] Georgia, Michigan, Minnesota, and South Carolina have rejected *Fasano*. "To regard the act of adopting an ordinance rezoning a single tract as anything other than a legislative act would be to sanction an impermissible encroachment upon the presumption of legislative validity." It would also encourage, argues South Carolina's opinion, "countless" challenges to such actions, "debase the local legislature challenged, and increase the burdens on zoning commissions and the courts."[75] Moreover, the doctrine makes rezoning procedures more costly and cumbersome for all persons involved in them. Its judicialization requires the employment of attorneys, and thus lessens the effective participation of lay citizens; it also strains the resources of some municipalities.

---

71. *See Gold v. City of Portland*, 740 P.2d 812 (Or. App. Ct. 1987).

72. *See Neuberger*, *supra*, 607 P.2d at 722.

73. *See* Neb. Rev. Stat. § 15-1201 (2003) (discussed in *Whitehead Oil Co. v. City of Lincoln*, 515 N.W.2d 390 (Neb. 1994), and *Copple v. City of Lincoln*, 315 N.W.2d 628 (Neb. 1982)).

74. *See Arnel Dev. Co. v. City of Costa Mesa*, 620 P.2d 565 (Cal. 1980).

75. *See Hampton v. Richland County*, 357 S.E.2d 463, 467 (S.C. App. Ct. 1987), *cert. dismissed*, 370 S.E.2d 714 (S.C. 1988).

Florida has found a comprehensive rezoning to be legislative and a piece-meal rezoning to be quasi-judicial, and adopted a modified *Fasano* doctrine, requiring that when an applicant shows that the application is consistent with the comprehensive plan, the burden shifts to the government to show that maintaining the existing zoning accomplishes a legitimate public purpose and that the refusal to rezone is not arbitrary.[76] If the municipality carries its burden, the application for rezoning should be denied. Florida has limited this doctrine to neighbors' challenges to a piece-meal rezoning, on the theory that there is a constitutional right to deal with one's land as one wishes. *Snyder* has not been extended to amendments to a municipal comprehensive plan, even when the amendment was sought in conjunction with an application for a rezoning of a 54 acre parcel.[77] Although this leading case suggested an order of presentation for rezoning proceedings, later cases have detailed the procedural due process requirements of the Florida rule: subpoenaes may be issued to witnesses, who may be sworn and cross-examined, although here as elsewhere no prior discovery is generally available.[78]

The Oregon distinction between legislative and quasi-judicial actions has held up well in that state over the years. The *Fasano* opinion is singular because it makes the municipal exercise of the police power depend on following and according procedural due process rights.[79] Participating citizens need a stable and well thought out procedure at any rezoning hearing. *Fasano* wisely provides that stability. In the last analysis, the distinction between what actions are legislative and which quasi-judicial or adjudicative, is for a municipal legislature to make and depends on the decision itself and the findings leading to it, not whether its effects are felt only by one parcel or just by a small group of owners.[80] Thus the imposition of an impact fee is a legislative action because the legislature has reserved little discretion in the matter.[81] However, the imposition of a special assessment may be quasi-judicial or adjudicative because whether to impose it, as well as the method of assessment, is discretionary.[82]

Some legislative decisions need not involve comprehensive city planning for the municipality. For example, suppose a municipality prohibited the erection of any fences in the town because an endangered species of deer needs to roam freely over

76. *See Board of County Comm'rs of Brevard County, Florida v. Snyder*, 627 So. 2d 469 (Fla. 1993) (also finding that judicial review "is subject to strict scrutiny" meaning that a court should require strict compliance with the plan, but defining the plan as only a guide to maximum future development in the jurisdiction and not setting minimal intensity of land uses) (discussed in Joni Coffey, *Practical Aspects of Quasi-Judicial Hearings: Basic Tools and Recent Fine-Tuning*, 30 Stetson L. Rev. 931, 937 (2001)).

77. *See Martin Cty. v. Yusem*, 690 So. 2d 1288 (Fla. 1997).

78. *See* Coffey, *supra*, 30 Stetson L. Rev. at 947–54 (collecting the cases).

79. *See Eastlake v. Forrest City Enterprises*, 426 U.S. 668 (1976) (classifying matters subject to a referendum as "legislative" in nature); *infra* Chapter 20. The word is not used in the same sense there as it is in the *Fasano* opinion, so beware of cross-citation and confusion of the issues involved in each case.

80. *See Bucktail v. Talbot Cty.*, 723 A.2d 440 (Md. 1999).

81. *See Home Builders Ass'n v. City of Beavercreek*, 1996 WL 812607 (Ohio App. Ct., Feb. 12, 1996) (so holding).

82. *See City of Rockville v. Woodmont Country Club*, 705 A.2d 301, 306 (Md. 1998).

its habitat. Even when an owner with a large parcel within this habitat applies for a permit to erect a fence along its boundary line, this ordinance is a legislative act entitled to the usual deference, and should be regarded as a general policy decision, even though the application affects neighborly relations. It is within the police power of a municipality to protect its environment, including the flora and fauna in it; such a regulation will be upheld, unless it bears no substantial relationship to the police power, and a critically low population count for the deer should be sufficient to show such a nexus. That the regulation is consistent with federal and state environmental policy is additional evidence of its rational basis.[83] An owner wanting to fence his garden might have a strong argument that the ordinance is not generally invalid, but invalid as applied—for while the deer have a right to their habitat, even though it encompasses private property, they do not have a right to take the food off the owner's table.

[B] Some Open Issues

While both *Fasano* or its progeny raise the prospect of local legislators being subpoenaed to testify as to the motives and reasons for their actions, it is more likely that the *Fasano* standards are intended (as the procedural due process quotation indicates) more narrowly to make and protect a record for further judicial review.[84] A legislator who campaigns on a platform generally opposed to urban growth and is elected, is surely not disqualified from voting on all zoning matters, whether or not they are major rezonings. "The quasi-judicial decisions of local general-purpose governing bodies resemble, or should resemble, adjudications in important respects that bear on the procedural fairness and substantive correctness of the decision, but in other respects these bodies remain more 'quasi' than 'judicial.'"[85] Once elected, they have many functions, executive, legislative, and quasi-judicial, and exercise them in overlapping and simultaneous ways. "The combination leaves little room to demand that an elected board member who actively pursues a particular view of the community's interest in his policy making role must maintain an appearance of having no such view when the decision is to be made by an adjudicatory procedure."[86] Even restrictions on the business activities of judges should not apply to local unpaid or low-pay officials.[87]

However many the demands on municipal legislators, an undue delay in decision-making sits on the line between violations of substantive and procedural

83. *See Department of Community Affairs v. Moorman*, 664 So. 2d 930 (Fla. 1995).

84. *Cf. New Castle County Council v. BC Dev. Assocs.*, 567 A.2d 1271, 1275–76, n. 4 (Del. 1989) (citing *Fasano* in an opinion that rejects the labels as determinative, but requires the council to make an adequate explanation of its rejection of a rezoning application beyond inconsistency with the comprehensive plan).

85. *See 1000 Friends of Oregon v. Wasco County Court*, 742 P.2d 39, 43 (Or. 1987).

86. *Id.*

87. *Id.*

due process.[88] Time limits on administrative decision-making are well established: a permit is sometimes "deemed approved" when a decision is not made within a specified time. Should undue delay become actionable under either *Fasano* or *Snyder*? Probably not, as the remedy would be difficult to devise, hasty decision-making might be encouraged, and missed deadlines might endanger the effectiveness of a municipality's comprehensive plan.

§ 11.15 Distinguishing Municipal Legislative from Administrative Actions

When an enabling act requires some type of hearing, a reviewing court must decide whether the proceedings involves a legislative action or whether it involves adjudication. A comprehensive zoning or rezoning decision is legislative: that is, it does not concern the immediate parties to it. Rather, such a decision involves fact finding that decides questions of policy and law. It takes into consideration the public needs of the area as a whole. It is not site-specific. In administrative law terms, it is the equivalent of rule making.

A piece-meal rezoning, on the other hand, involves the interests of the immediate parties appearing before the legislature. It involves adjudicative facts—they are akin to the type of facts given to a jury to decide. The proceeding on a piece-meal rezoning is thus quasi-judicial in nature.[89] It involves facts about the parties and their activities, land uses, businesses and properties. Usually but not always, the proceeding is instituted by private landowners, and a single parcel of land is involved. (Not always, though, because a single parcel's rezoning might affect more than just the adjacent property owners usually given standing to appear.) In Maryland and a few other jurisdictions, the change mistake rule applies to a piece-meal rezoning.[90]

To challenge a piece-meal rezoning, property owner standing is generally required and involves the objector satisfying either a statutory or ordinance definition of an adjacent owner.[91]

For a piece-meal rezoning, more rather than less procedural due process is needed. The proceeding resembles a trial. While there is no discovery, a *voir dire* process is used to introduce expert witnesses. The applicant or counsel may introduce the applicant and supporting experts, and once they testify, cross-examination follows. Supporting

88. See *Norco Construction Co. v. King County*, 649 P.2d 103 (Wash. 1982).

89. *See City of Hyattsville v. Prince George's Cty. Council*, 270 A.3d 959, 973 (Md. Ct. App. 2022).

90. *See* § 11.08, this Chapter.

91. *See Floyd v. City of Baltimore*, 205 A.3d 928 (Md. 2019) (distinguishing property owner and taxpayer standing, the former applying to a piece-meal rezoning, the latter applying to a comprehensive rezoning).

documents and studies are introduced and objections made to their introduction. Modified and simplified rules of evidence apply: objections to the admissibility and relevancy of evidence are permitted. Once the applicant's case is presented, those who object to the rezoning (often neighbors) are heard.

This legislative/administrative distinction matters to zoning litigation in several contexts. The application of the ripeness doctrine,[92] whether or not to apply the takings rules governing development exactions,[93] the issue of a municipal official's immunity from § 1983 or damage suits,[94] issues of procedural due process,[95] the application of referendum and initiative procedures[96]—all depend on the distinction. So as one might expect, calling an action legislative in the rezoning context is no guarantee that the label will stick in another context.[97] Moreover, even when a jurisdiction has not adopted the rules in either *Fasano* or *Snyder*, referenda or initiative procedures still may not be available, even though the legislative label remains broadly applicable.[98]

§ 11.16 Remedies for a Denial of Rezoning

Upon a denial of a rezoning, the issue before the reviewing court is whether a continuation of the existing zoning is unreasonable (and amounts to a taking). That would be the narrowest way to put the question. More broadly put, a court might decide whether the proposed use is a reasonable one.

When a court is willing to consider the remedy issue in its broadest sense, the remedial options would include at least three remedies: first, declaring the existing zoning unreasonable and invalid and enjoining the zoning officials from enforcement of the present regulation, as to that land, leaving no zoning in effect. This will encourage the municipality to act promptly to respond to the applicant, and encourage all applicants to challenge unreasonable regulations. It runs the risk, however, that the municipality will overreact in some way.

Second, the court might order the officials to rezone to the applicant's proposed (or another, similar, and reasonable) use. Giving the applicant his proposed, site-specific

---

92. *See infra*, Chapter 13, § 13.03.

93. *See Dolan v. City of Tigard*, 512 U.S. 374, 379 (1994) (distinguishing between legislative and adjudicative actions and applying exactions rules only to the latter) (discussed *infra* Chapter 14).

94. *See Maynard v. Beck*, 741 A.2d 866, 872 (R.I. 1999) (immunizing planning commission members when performing a component of a legislative rezoning).

95. *See Hyson v. Montgomery Cty. Council*, 217 A.2d 578, 584 (Md. 1966) (finding a piece-meal rezoning quasi-judicial in nature and requiring a right of cross-examination in a rezoning proceeding).

96. *See Arnel Dev. Co. v. City of Costa Mesa*, 620 P.2d 565 (Cal. 1980).

97. *See, e.g., Margolis v. District Ct.*, 638 P.2d 297 (Colo. 1981) (rezoning is a legislative action in the context of a referendum, but quasi-judicial when being judicially reviewed).

98. *See Citizen's Awareness v. Marakis*, 873 P.2d 1117 (Utah 1994) (discussing special criteria to be met before subjecting a rezoning to a referendum vote).

relief will encourage objections to invalid zoning decisions.[99] This will require that the court exercise a judgment similar to an urban planner's—something it might be loath to do. It also requires that the court exercise continuing jurisdiction in the case—again, something it may be loath to do.

Third, the court might order the officials to rezone to any reasonable use. Missouri case law, for example, provides good examples of each of these three options.[100]

Faced with the possibility of a judicial order of the types just discussed, an applicant's counsel along with the municipality's counsel, might enter into a consent decree involving a rezoning. In entering into the agreement to the decree, the municipality will not be deemed to have bargained away the exercise of its regulatory powers. No statute like the Standard Zoning Enabling Act or similar statute should be presumed to deny judicial review and all of its remedial consequences.[101]

---

99. *See Bloomsburg Industrial Ventures, LLC v. Town of Bloomsburg*, 242 A.3d 969, 983 (Pa. Commwlth. Ct. 2020).

100. *See Ohmes v. Lanzarini*, 720 S.W.2d 425 (Mo. App. Ct. 1986) (permitting the parcel to remain unzoned); *Despotis v. City of Sunset Hills*, 619 S.W.2d 814 (Mo. App. Ct. 1981) (ordering officials to rezone); *Home Bldg. Co. v. City of Kansas City*, 666 S.W.2d 816 (Mo. App. Ct. 1984) (ordering any reasonable use, leaving the property zoned in the meanwhile).

101. *But see Warner Co. v. Sutton*, 644 A.2d 656, 661–62 (N.J. Super. Ct., App. Div. 1994) (reporting a split in state court decisions and deciding it did not).

Chapter 12
Non-Euclidean Rezoning: Administrative Flexibility in Zoning

Euclidian zoning is defined as the division of a municipality into districts, classified by height limitations, use limitations, and other regulations regulating the bulk, density, and minimum acreage of a parcel. Its use districts are generally cumulative—meaning that uses in less intensive districts are also permitted in all more intensive ones. It seldom includes exclusive use districts—that is, districts devoted to just one use, say commercial or industrial uses.[1] It is also an alliterative allusion to the *Euclid* case, the leading case, approving this type of land use regulation.[2] Non-Euclidian zoning is taken to include everything else—that is, those regulatory patterns varying the traditional pattern of parcel-by-parcel, district-by-district zoning. It comes in several varieties, with and without standards that are expressly pre-set in the applicable zoning ordinance.

§ 12.01 Contract Zoning

An amendment to a zoning ordinance changing either its text or the zoning map to permit a change of use is called a rezoning amendment. A rezoning amendment that is approved so long as a particular use is maintained on a parcel embodies a reciprocity of rights and obligations between a user and the municipal legislature. This is contract zoning and is invalid.[3] It involves a bargaining away or a delegation of the police power to the user or owner by the municipal legislature. A prohibition on such bargaining rests on three premises. First, the exercise of the police power is a non-delegable duty of a municipality's legislature. Why is the exercise non-delegable?

---

1. *See* Standard State Zoning Enabling Act §§ 1, 3 (discussed *supra* Chapter 6 and *reprinted in* Am. L. Inst., *Model Land Development Code*, Tent. Draft No. 1, at 210 (1968)).

2. *See supra*, Chapter 6, § 6.02.

3. *See Hector v. City of Fargo*, 760 N.W.2d 108, 115 (N. D. 2009); *Chung v. Sarasota Cty.*, 686 So. 2d 1358, 1359 (Fla. App. Ct. 1996); *see also Hale v. Osborn Coal Co.*, 729 So. 2d 853 (Ala. Civ. App. 1997).

Because matters arising under the police power require on-going supervision and oversight. The state zoning enabling act does not authorize any body or persons but those constituting that legislature to enact zoning regulations, and this lack of authority supports the further idea that the legislature may not further delegate such enactment to others. It must exercise the authorized powers itself. This exercise of its authority must be independent and free of any obligation to others. Sub-delegations are prohibited. Thus contract zoning is *ultra vires* the enabling act.

Second, one session of a municipal legislature cannot bind future sessions—the general welfare cannot be bargained away; every future session must be free to respond to the problems of its day and time, unhindered by its predecessors' decisions. Moreover, in the context of one legislative session, contract zoning may introduce a bias into the hearing and deliberative process. It is a strong signal that the legislature has been captured by private interests.

Third, there is the possibility of legislative abuse in contract zoning: legislators might be tempted to demand through agreements what they do not have authority to accomplish by regulation. Such agreements cannot be "voluntary" in any realistic way. Keeping legislatures honest is more important than achieving the flexibility in regulation which the agreements might promote. So bilateral contracts or agreements between a developer and the legislature are invalid.

Such invalid contracts must be clearly shown.[4] "In order to sustain the claim of zoning by contract there must be clear cut evidence of an agreement bargaining away the legislative power. . . . "[5] That the rezoning is granted with conditions is insufficient to show a bilateral contract. That a developer lobbies the legislature hard does not show a bilateral contract with it. That representations were made to the legislature by a developer is likewise insufficient. The legislature must bind itself in advance to grant the rezoning; a notice to an applicant that she may apply for a rezoning without an assurance that it will be granted, is not enough to show contract zoning. Neither is a legislative agreement to amend its generally applicable zoning regulations.[6] In many cases, a showing that the legislative hearing on a rezoning considered all the permitted land uses available in the use district, not merely the use requested by the applicant, is sufficient to show that the legislators did not have an illegal contract with the applicant.[7] This is because contract zoning, at its root, involves an attempt by a parcel owner to gain some special favor not applying to other similarly situated owners in a land use district in exchange for the municipality's giving up its zoning enforcement authority. Thus, the objections to contract zoning are similar to those based on the judicial doctrine of spot zoning and the uniformity requirement found

---

4. *See Century Circuit, Inc. v. Ott*, 65 317 N.Y.S.2d 468 (N.Y. Sup. Ct. 1970), *aff'd*, 327 N.Y.S.2d 829 (N.Y. App. Div. 1971)

5. *Id.* at 471.

6. *See Lamar Advertising of S.D., LLC v. City of Rapid City*, 944 N.W.2d 793, 802–04 (S. D. 2020) (containing a general discussion of contract zoning).

7. *See In the Matter of the Application of Tuxedo Land Tr., Inc.*, 950 N.Y.S.2d 611 (N.Y. Sup. Ct. 2012).

in enabling statutes.[8] When a municipality surrenders its power to enforce future regulations applicable to a parcel, contract zoning is present.[9]

Some jurisdictions declare that contract zoning is illegal *per se* and the contract or agreement is void *ab initio*. Some find it disingenuous to say that the contract benefits a private person since all rezonings will likely benefit the owners applying for them.[10] In the latter jurisdictions, a reviewing court examines "whether the municipality bargained away its police power."

§ 12.02 Conditional Zoning

Contract zoning occurs outside of the legislative process and subverts it. Conditional zoning, on the other hand, occurs within that process. Thus, a variation avoiding this prohibition on contract zoning occurs when the rezoning is sought during an executory period for the purchase and sale of the land subject to rezoning. Here the vendor and/or the purchaser (usually a developer) apply for the rezoning either while the land is under an option to purchase or to fulfill a contingency clause in the contract of sale.[11] Bargains with the legislature are still prohibited, but if the applicant appears before the legislature with a contract or an option to purchase, makes representations to the legislators, and then embodies them in the form of covenants, the presence of the covenants should not invalidate the rezoning. In one state, this process is called "concomitant agreement zoning"; in another, the representations are called "proffers."[12] The process permits courts to analyze, on a case-by-case basis, whether the agreement or proffer minimizes the negative externalities caused by the new development for which the rezoning, is sought.[13]

This variation on the rezoning process is commonly known as conditional zoning. Here, the BZA does not abandon its independent zoning authority. It makes no bilateral promise to a developer or owner. As far as the board is concerned, the promises and representations made to it are unilateral in nature. Conditional zoning instead takes the form of an agreement made between a developer and neighbors or between

---

8. *See Meyer v. Zoning Bd. of Appeals*, 2024 Conn. Super. LEXIS 468, *20 (Conn. Super. Ct., Mar. 6, 2024). A few jurisdictions do not recognize the doctrine of contract zoning, regarding these other doctrines sufficient to guard against it. *See, e.g., Statecraft PLLC v. Town of Snowflake*, 2018 Ariz. App. Unpub. LEXIS 1570, * 11 (Ariz. Ct. App., Oct. 30, 2018).

9. *See Lamar Co., LLC v. City of Columbia*, 512 S.W.3d 774, 785 (Mo. Ct. App. 2016).

10. *See Lamar Advertising of S.D., LLC v. City of Rapid City*, 944 N.W.2d 793, 802–03 (S.D. 2020) (collecting cases for each viewpoint).

11. *See Bucholz v. City of Omaha*, 120 N.W.2d 270, 278 (Neb. 1963) (protective covenants executed by vendor seeking rezoning for the holder of an option to purchase his land did not invalidate the rezoning amendment) (discussed in Comment, *Variances and Parcel Rezoning: Relief from Restrictive Zoning in Nebraska*, 60 Neb. L. Rev. 81, 111–12 (1981)).

12. *See Jefferson Green Owners Ass'n v. Guinn*, 551 S.E.2d 339 (Va. 2001) (noted in 35 U. Rich. L. Rev. 777, 792 (2002)).

13. *See State ex rel. Myhre v. City of Spokane*, 422 P.2d 790 (Wash. 1969).

the developer and the municipal planning commission.[14] It is also sometimes a settlement agreement among the parties to previous litigation over a rezoning decision.[15] Needless to say, the parties to the agreement—neighbors, civic associations, etc.—are given leverage over the applicant owner or developer. In this sense, the authority to engage in conditional zoning may encourage municipal legislatures to initially zone parcels for lower densities and levels of development than they otherwise would.

No matter the parties, the agreement is voluntary and executed in advance of the legislative hearing on a rezoning application filed by the developer. Its subject matter is necessary to make the rezoned compatible with its surroundings, but leaves the legislature free to deal with future enforcement of its police powers. Typically, it results in covenants restricting the use of the developer's property. This set of real covenants runs with the land attaching to the developer's title) and is enforceable by neighbors. The agreement and the covenants are then recorded and thus provide notice to subsequent purchasers of the land that the covenants burden or restrict the rezoned parcel. The covenants may last longer than the zoning which gave birth to them.[16] They terminate in the same ways that real covenants do. Courts have, in most jurisdictions, validated this process and the agreements that come with it.[17]

There are at least five reasons why conditional zoning approvals are, by the weight of the case law today, deemed valid. First, the legislature is not a party to the agreement.[18] Instead, the neighbors, a home owners or civic association, or another municipal agency like the planning commission, is a party to it.[19] Second, the promise of the developer is unilateral, executed prior to the legislative action. In this regard, a developer will promise (through the covenants) to take protective measures to eliminate adverse effects of the development on neighboring or adjacent properties; to control the sequence of development; to assure proper maintenance of the development; or to designate the location or nature of the development. Third, conditional zoning avoids the appearance of an impermissible exercise of power and displays the agreement resulting from the bargaining in the sunshine of the legislative chamber.[20]

14. *See Remmel v. City of Portland*, 102 A.3d 1168, 1171 (Me. 2014); *Hathaway v. City of Portland*, 845 A.2d 1168, 1172 (Me. 2004) (where the planning commission was given the power to enforce the conditions put on the rezone).

15. *See Lamar Advertising of S.D., LLC v. City of Rapid City*, 944 N.W.2d 793, 802–04 (S.D. 2020).

16. *See Equitable Trust Company v. Towson Manor Associations, Inc.*, 340 A.2d 759 (Md. App. 1975).

17. *See Dacy v. Village of Ruidoso*, 845 P.2d 793 (N.M. 1992).

18. *See State ex rel. Zupancic v. Schimenz*, 174 N.W.2d 533 (Wis. 1970) ("We hold that when a city itself makes an agreement with a landowner to rezone the contract is invalid; this is contract zoning. However, when the agreement is made by others . . . and the city is not committed to rezone, it is not a contract in the true sense and does not vitiate the zoning if it is otherwise valid.").

19. Occasionally, the agreement is made between the neighbors, the planning commission, and a developer. Tripartite agreements such as this are not with the legislature either, although at this point, the avoidance of a contractual relationship with the legislature begins to look like a dry exercise. *Compare Pressman v. City of Baltimore*, 160 A.2d 379 (Md. 1960), *with City of Greenbelt v. Bresler*, 236 A.2d 1 (Md. 1967). Both the commission and the legislature are, after all, agents of the same municipal government.

20. *See Prock v. Town of Danville*, 655 N.E.2d 553 (Ind. App. Ct. 1995).

Fourth, it avoids reliance on developer representations at a legislative hearing. Fifth, it separates rezoning issues from those concerning neighbors not resolvable in the rezoning process and permits mediation involving neighbors, municipal urban planners, and attorneys for the parties.

Because the agreement is not tied to the continuance of the new zoning and may even outlast it, the future effectiveness of future land-use regulations may be curtailed by it. Sometimes the municipality will have standing to enforce the covenants underlying conditional zoning, even though these agreements were executed by others. The municipal legislature might enforce them, for example, as a third-party beneficiary. For this purpose, the municipality may be required, absent a statute on the subject, to own some land in the neighborhood to which the benefit of the covenant can attach.[21] Thereafter, a purchaser has to check the local zoning records as well as do a title search in order to find these agreements.

[A] Testing Conditional Zoning

In reviewing conditional zoning situations, the courts have not uniformly required that the negotiations for and the formalities of the agreement not involve the legislature, but instead assumed that the rezoning and the agreement are interrelated, being part and parcel of the same process. With this assumption in mind, the courts have devised four tests for the validity of the conditional (re)zoning.[22] One test focuses on the subject matter and scope of the agreement, no matter who the parties to it are. Thus, when it is reasonably related to the land-use regulation under which the municipal legislature or planning commission acts, it is valid. The agreement's subject matter is tested according to the standard tests for the validity of a regulation. The underlying rationale for this test is that, what could be done by regulation, may also be done by agreement.

If the agreement flunks this test, a second alternative test asks whether its subject is any broader than that any regulation that the legislature could have enacted, judged by the scope of the enabling act, rather than the regulation enacted in fact under it.[23] The underlying rationale for this test is that if the legislature could have

21. *See London County Council v. Allen*, L.R. [1914] 3 K.B. 642, Ann. Cas. 1916C 932.

22. A now generally discredited theory for conditional zoning is that the agreement between the developer and the neighbors is "induced voluntary action" on the developer's part. *See Sylvania Electric Products, Inc. v. City of Newton*, 183 N.E.2d 118 (Mass. 1962). Drawing the line between voluntary and involuntary action proved too difficult a task. *See Meredith v. Talbot County*, 560 A.2d 599 (Md. App. 1989) (upholding an agreement, by which developer agreed to set aside a wildlife preserve in exchange for a plat approval and describing the agreement as voluntary and not executed under duress).

23. *See Giger v. City of Omaha*, 442 N.W.2d 182 (Neb. 1989) (approving a conditional rezoning and requiring that conditions imposed in the rezoning ordinance or by development agreement must be reasonably related to the purposes of the zoning enabling statute, although not expressly authorized there) (discussed in J. Patrick Green, *Giger v. City of Omaha: Of Contracts, Comprehensive Plans, and Master Plans in Nebraska Zoning, Questions With and Without Answers*, 23 Creighton L. Rev. 289 (1990)).

incorporated the subject of the agreement into its regulation, the agreement is an exercise of the authority that the legislature had, but did not use. The agreement in this sense embodies a power that the legislature reserved to itself. Refining this "reserved power" test, one court has said the legislature is exercising a power often delegated to an administrative board, like a board of zoning appeals, authorized to hear applications for a special exception, but here it has reserved that power to itself.[24] That is, the legislature could have responded to a rezoning application by (in part) amending the ordinance with a special exception for the requested land use. The underlying rationale of this test is that the agreement accompanying the rezoning eliminates the adverse off-site externalities or impacts of a development just as a special exception might. In *Chrismon v. Guilford County*,[25] the opinion approves conditional zoning with such a rationale.[26]

In a third test, the agreement is be judged more broadly by the scope of the police power: if the neighbors are benefitted in proportion to the restrictions imposed on the developer, the substantive due process clause is satisfied. If a municipal legislature imposes a condition on an applicant's landfill permit requiring that another landfill of the applicant be closed first, the legislature's consideration of the cumulative impact of two landfills on surrounding uses in order to make the applicant's landfill compatible with its surroundings, is an exercise of valid conditional rezoning.[27] Further, suppose the legislature agrees to approve a rezoning on the condition that the developer execute a recorded covenant that the planning commission may disapprove an enlargement or expansion in the approved use "in its sole discretion, without giving any reason therefor"? What if the developer agrees, executes the covenant in advance of the rezoning's approval, and later asks for permission to expand? When permission is refused without comment or explanation by the municipality, the leading case in this area upheld the refusal as valid conditional zoning. The restrictive agreement pertained to the land use for which the developer sought the rezoning, and its effect was to restrict future development of the permitted use, except when the legislature finds that the general welfare requires its expansion.[28]

---

24. *See Collard v. Incorporated Village of Flower Hill*, 421 N.E.2d 818 (N.Y. 1981) (conditional zoning is not spot zoning, nor an illegal delegation of the legislature's police power, and is implicitly enabled by state statute).

25. 370 S.E.2d 579 (N.C. 1988).

26. *Chrismon*, 370 S.E.2d at 585 n. 2, 586–87 (conflating conditional zoning and special exception procedures and involving an agricultural supply storekeeper's application to rezone land in an agricultural use district for some uses permitted in a commercial district) (noted at 68 N.C. L. Rev. 177 (1989)).

27. *See Brandywine Enterprises, Inc. v. Council for Prince George's County*, 700 A.2d 1216 (Md. Ct. Spec. App. 1997).

28. *See Collard v. Incorporated Village of Flower Hill*, 421 N.E.2d 818 (N.Y. 1981). Another view is that the commission's refusal is a denial of a rezoning request that is not subject to judicial review, but this would be a delegation of the rezoning power to the commission, and so contract, not conditional, zoning.

A fourth, and broadest, multi-factor test has been adopted in Mississippi.[29] There, so long as during the legislative process, (1) all parties are given an opportunity to speak, (2) the record contains no indication that the process is a sham or is not conducted in good faith, (3) the legislators reveal a familiarity with the facts and issues relating to the specific rezoning and (4) support it as in the best interests of the municipality, (5) the conditions imposed are those inherent in the type of rezoning sought, (6) the type of rezoning used is useful in addressing neighbors' land use compatibility concerns, and (7) the conditions last only so long as the rezoning does and any further rezoning of the property annuls them.[30] Meeting all seven conditions, the rezoning is valid conditional rezoning.

[B] The U.S. Supreme Court and Conditional Zoning

A Supreme Court opinion, *Nollan v. California Coastal Commission*,[31] held invalid a condition imposed on a development permit for rebuilding a house along the California coast. The condition required that the applicants (the Nollans) dedicate a portion of their property, located on the dry sand area of a beach in front of their house, for the public's use. *Nollan* thus calls the right of a body like a planning commission to contract with applicants like the Nollans into question, as if the Nollans had signed an agreement promising to dedicate the easement over their beach and then breached it by suing the promisee. This is what they in fact did. Conditional zoning, whose subject is an allegedly unconstitutional exaction, singles persons like the Nollans out for unduly burdensome conditions on their permit. If the condition were the subject of a conditional zoning agreement, it would flunk the third test previously discussed.[32] The court protects the reasonable expectations of private landowners; even though the Nollans had actual notice of the development restrictions at the time they purchased their property, it is singling the Nollans out for the exaction that is improper. Any conditional zoning agreement which does that is improper and violates the takings clause.

Negative or restrictive covenants have fared better than affirmative ones as the proper subject for conditional zoning agreements.[33] So landscaping and design restrictions are more easily approved than obligations to provide public service funds

---

29. *See Old Canton Hills Homeowner's Ass'n v. Mayor and City Council of the City of Jackson*, 749 So. 2d 54 (Miss. 1999) (upholding 23 conditions).

30. *Id.* at 58–59.

31. 483 U.S. 825 (1987) (this opinion is part of the law of development exactions, discussed *infra*, Chapter 14, § 14.20).

32. The Commission would have been wise to ask for an in-lieu-of payment of money from every permit applicant.

33. *See Scrutton v. County of Sacramento*, 79 Cal. Rptr. 872 (App. Ct. 1969) (here the developer was being required to pave a street to which her development had no access).

or land. Automatic reversions, effective upon a breach of the agreement and restoring the pre-agreement zoning, have not fared well either.[34] They are viewed as, in effect, a second rezoning, adopted without compliance with procedural and substantive safeguards. However, a "use it or lose it" provision of the rezoning amendment, requiring application for a building permit within one year of the rezoning or else the prior zoning classification is reinstated, has been upheld if limited and reasonable in time.[35] And similarly, when the developer "loses it" by failing to develop within a set time, the homeowners who meanwhile purchase in reliance on the now-void plat, can take rights in open space reserved on it.[36] Conditional zoning has thus proceeded, even more than other areas of zoning law, on a case-by-case basis. Good politics and the need for flexibility in zoning gets the nod, but a corrupt deal does not.[37]

[C] Enabling Act Authority

Some states have express statutory authority for conditional zoning. California, Hawaii, Nevada, and Florida are examples. Often, hearing requirements are imposed before an agreement is executed. Rhode Island[38] has a narrower statute that authorizes rezonings for a limited time, and if the development is not built within that time, the rezoning may be revoked. Arizona has a similar statute. Other states, such as Maryland, continue to view this type of zoning with skepticism, no matter how labeled.[39] However, a Maryland statute[40] permits continuing design review of a development after a rezoning, but that state's courts have refused to use the statute to authorize conditional zoning.[41]

34. *Id.* at 878.

35. *See Colwell v. Howard County*, 354 A.2d 210, 213–14 (Md. App. Ct. 1976).

36. *See Hickory Point Partnership v. Anne Arundel County*, 557 A.2d 626 (Md. 1989).

37. *See* Judith Wegner, *Moving Toward the Bargaining Table: Contract Zoning, Development Agreements, and the Theoretical Foundations of Government Land Use Deals*, 65 N.C. L. Rev. 957, 978–95 (1987) (providing a good summary of the law on conditional zoning).

38. *See Sweetman v. Town of Cumberland*, 364 A.2d 1277 (R.I. 1976) (citing such a statute).

39. *See Rodriguez v. Prince George's County*, 558 A.2d 742 (Md. App. Ct. 1989) (holding that the exclusion of permitted uses from site plan which forms the basis of rezoning review is an illegal conditional rezoning); *People's Counsel for Baltimore County v. Mockard*, 533 A.2d 1344, 1346 (Md. App. Ct. 1987) ("This Court continues to reaffirm the invalidity of conditional zoning.").

40. *See* Md. Code Ann., art. 66B, § 4.01.

41. *See Board of Cty. Comm'rs v. H. Manny Holtz, Inc.*, 501 A.2d 489 (Md. App. 1985).

§ 12.03 Floating Zones

A Euclidian use district is a geographic area specified on the zoning map, with boundaries previously determined by the municipal legislature. A floating zone has no such pre-designated boundaries.[42] Rather, it is a use district whose permitted uses are spelled out in the ordinance, but is of undetermined size, form, and location. As to its undetermined location, it can be said to float above those Euclidian use districts with which its own permitted uses might potentially be compatible and where it is authorized. So it is known as a "floating zone." It rests on a finding that the state enabling act does not mandate the mapping of every land use permitted in an ordinance.[43] Thus, a municipal legislature may determine such a zone's general location, but its precise location on the zoning map awaits some landowner's application for a rezoning to a use permitted only in the floating zone. That application is then a request for a precise mapping of the boundaries of the zone.[44] "Zoning bodies implement floating zones through two steps: (1) they first pass zoning ordinances with specific zoning classifications for specific purposes, which are said to 'float above the jurisdiction': (2) they then apply the floating zone to a particular property through a map amendment, creating a geographic district."[45]

A floating zone is a useful zoning tool when the need for the presence of a particular land use is hard to predict.[46] Thus, such zones are used to locate affordable housing, quarries, or oil wells; or on a more prosaic level, to locate garden apartments or a bed-and-breakfast in a single-family residential zone.[47] When a particular land use is emerging, or responding to a developing market, a floating zone for locating it on the zoning map is useful when the parcel involved is large enough, or is configured in such a way that potentially negative effects on neighbors can be minimized with standards pre-set in the ordinance.

An early type of floating zone is "cluster development." It is a land use device to encourage flexibility in the design and development of residential housing in order

---

42. *See Cremins v. County Comm'nrs of Washington Cty.*, 883 A.2d 966 (Md. App. 2005); *see also Treme v. St. Louis Cty.*, 609 S.W.2d 706, 710 (Mo. App. Ct. 1980) (collecting the cases and holding valid a commercial use district floating zone).

43. Pennsylvania early determined that a floating zone required express enabling authority in the statute. *See Eves v. Zoning Board of Adjustment*, 164 A.2d 7 (Pa. 1960). New York and Maryland decided *contra*. Today, the floating zone is recognized in all states.

44. There is no limit on the number of landowners who may apply; the only precondition is ownership within a use district above which the floating zone hovers.

45. *See Hartshorne v. City of Whitefish*, 486 P.3d 693, 701 (Mont. 2021).

46. *See generally* Kristine C. Karnezis, Annot., *Zoning" Regulations Creating and Placing "Floating Zones,"* 80 A.L.R.3d 95 (2016); Philip Tierney, *Bold Promises by Basic Steps: Maryland's Growth Policy in the Year 2020*, 23 U. Balt. L. Rev. 461 (1994).

47. *See Rodgers v. Village of Tarrytown*, 96 N.E.2d 731 (N.Y. 1951) (the leading case, where the village's planning board conducted a site plan review before the legislature passed on it, and involving the location of garden apartments in various types of residential use districts, subject to mapping of the floating zone).

to preserve open space. It permits a reduction in parcel area, frontage, setback and infrastructure regulations, provided there is no overall increase in density otherwise permitted in the underlying Euclidian land use district.[48] In return for the regulatory flexibility, the resulting open space may be used for recreation or for preservation of historic, scenic or other natural resources. Parcels qualifying for such treatment typically have a minimum acreage of ten or more acres. Recently, floating zones have been utilized for commercial development as well.

Sometimes the reviewer of the application to locate the zone is the municipal legislature.[49] Sometimes the reviewer is an administrative agency, the planning commission or the board of zoning appeals.[50] Where an administrative agency hears the application, the floating zone is likely to be treated like a special exception and justified in the same way. The legislature has determined the potential compatibility of the use in the zone with the other uses permitted as of right, and the agency's task is to apply the standards (set out in the floating zone ordinance) which assure that compatibility.[51]

For a legislative mapping, locating the zone on the ground, the standard of review is more relaxed than it is in an administrative setting. The leading case treats the location amendment to the zoning map as a rezoning and tests it accordingly.[52]

One case, analogizing a special exception "district" to a statutorily-authorized floating zone, upheld the so-called district.[53] The development context for this holding makes the case unique: while a developer was in the midst of gaining approval for a planned unit development (PUD) in a residential use district, the municipality by amendment prohibited mixed use PUDs in primarily residential use districts, after which the zoning administrator suggested that the developer with a parcel that would have qualified for a PUD, apply for a conditional use (a/k/a special exception) permit for the remaining phases of the PUD.[54] It is in this sense that the court thought that a use district that consists of specially excepted land uses would in effect become a floating zone.

Three justifications for floating zones emerge from the case law. First, the courts say, what the legislature is authorized to do by way of a zoning amendment, it may

48. *See Drewnowski v. Planning and Zoning Comm'n of the Town of Suffield*, 299 A.3d 259, 274, 281, n.1 (Conn. Ct. App. 2023) (holding that a regulation limiting the length of dead end streets in the underlying district was not superseded by the floating zone).

49. *See Rodgers, op. cit.*

50. *See Huff v. Board of Zoning Appeals*, 133 A.2d 83 (Md. 1957) (another leading case, where manufacturing facilities were the subject).

51. *See Rodgers, op. cit., followed in Citizens for a Better Flathead v. Bd. of Cty. Comm'rs*, 386 P.3d 567 (Mont. 2016), *Bellemeade v. Priddle*, 503 S.W.2d 734 (Ky. 1974), *and Sheridan v. Planning Bd.*, 266 A.2d 396 (Conn. 1969).

52. *See Rodgers, op. cit.* (rejecting the charge that this is spot zoning).

53. *See Hartshorne v. City of Whitefish*, 486 P.3d 693, 696–97 (Mont. 2021).

54. *Id.* at 698.

also do by way of a floating zone.[55] This is a both a justification and a test of validity. Second, the zone's consistency with the comprehensive plan provides courts with another test of a zone's validity; the floating zone is thus a rezoning in accordance with a pre-conceived plan, not an exercise of unbridled legislative discretion. Third, some courts have treated the floating zone as a large special exception and if the legislature could have provided for the zoned-in uses by way of special exception, the floating zone too is valid and within the enabling act.[56] However justified, once a floating zone is located, the regulations for the use district in which the parcel was formerly located no longer apply.

§ 12.04 Planned Unit Developments

Another non-Euclidian zoning device involving pre-set standards but allowing negotiations with a developer is a planned unit development (PUD). A PUD is a type of floating zone.[57] Like a floating zone, it permits the introduction of flexibility into the rezoning process,[58] particularly when compared to the relatively rigid requirements of Euclidian zoning.[59] A PUD ordinance lifts the lot-by-lot requirements of Euclidian zoning and substitutes instead a site plan review process, under which the overall density of the pre-existing Euclidian zoning often remains in place, but the placement of individual improvements may be clustered.[60] The land parcel in question is developed as a single large unit, rather than on a lot-by-lot basis, allowing better urban design than is possible in cookie-cutter subdivisions, allowing regulators a more detailed review, and giving PUD applicants a reciprocal advantage because of the efficiencies of clustering and the greater profits permitted by mixing land uses. PUDs became a much-used method of land development after World War II: in PUD ordinances, zoning and subdivision approvals are merged; both types of approvals are typically given by the planning commission.[61]

55. In Maryland, for example, the rezoning rule involving "change or mistake" does not apply to a floating zone determination. *See supra* Chapter 11.

56. *See Carron v. Board of Cty. Comm'rs*, 976 P.2d 359 (Colo. Ct. App. 1998).

57. *See MCB Woodberry Developer, LLC v. Council of Owners of the Millrace Condominium*, 265 A.3d 1140, 1145, n.1 (Md. Ct. Spec. App. 2021).

58. *See generally* Daniel Mandelker, *New Perspectives on Planned Unit Developments*, 52 Real Prop., Prob., and Tr. L.J. 229 (2017) (discussing PUD review procedures).

59. *See generally* Jan Krasonowieki, *Planning Unit Development: A Challenge to Established Theory and Practice of Land Use Control*, 114 U. Pa. L. Rev. 47 (1965).

60. *See Peters v. Spearfish ETJ Planning Commission*, 567 N.W.2d 880, 885 (S.D. 1997).

61. *See In re Appeal of 232511 Investments*, 898 A.2d 109 (Vt. 2006). The planning board or commission is probably the agency best prepared for PUD reviews because its traditional workload includes the review of applications to subdivide land. In some states, the Board of Zoning Adjustment or Appeals may perform this site review. The commission, however, is an administrative body, and where rezonings are an exclusively legislative function, a challenge to the PUD procedure is warranted. *See Lutz v. City of Longview*, 520 P.2d 1374 (Wash. 1974). *But see Cheney v. Village 2 at New Hope, Inc.*,

Permitted uses within the PUD are usually both greater in number and more diverse than are found in a Euclidian use district.[62] The PUDs are mixed and multi-use districts. The developments permitted integrate residential and commercial uses. Thus, a commercial PUD ordinance authorizing "multi-use developments" may not be used for a PUD applicant who wants to locate various types of commercial (warehouse and retail) uses within it.[63] "Multi-use" means a mix of use types that are useful to one another. Used for such a project, the land abutting the highway could easily resemble strip commercial uses—the very pattern that many PUD ordinances are intended to avoid. However, a mixed group of business, or of various types of residential development, would have sufficient diversity of uses to warrant the use of a PUD.[64] PUDs have also been used for exclusively commercial and industrial developments as well as for affordable and workforce housing.[65]

A PUD applicant need not apply for a variance from Euclidian zoning regulations, as the PUD review process itself is intended to contain both variance and special exception processes and procedures within it.[66] When developer/regulator negotiations precede the approval of a PUD, those negotiations are not evidence of contract zoning.[67]

The use of a PUD procedure depends on private initiative. A municipal legislature may not, *sua sponte*, rezone property into a PUD district. Only a voluntary application by a landowner precipitates the rezoning into a PUD district.[68] Thus a developer seeking a Euclidian rezoning cannot be forced to purchase additional adjacent land to meet a minimum acreage requirement in a PUD ordinance.[69]

Pre-set standards, set out in the ordinance, define who may apply for PUD review. As with a special exception, the more specific such standards are, the less discretion the municipality will have to deny an applicant for a PUD meeting all of them. It is these standards that save a PUD ordinance from the charge that the municipal legislature has improperly delegated its power to rezone to an administrative body such as the planning commission, when it reviews PUD applications. A PUD application is

---

241 A.2d 81 (Pa. 1968) (the leading case, deciding that the planning commission is best suited for PUD reviews) (discussed *infra*).

62. *See Woodland Manor III Assoc. v. Keeney*, 713 A.2d 806 (R.I. 1998) (describing a multi-use, phased apartment, condominium, elderly housing, and nursing home development).

63. *See City of Little Rock v. Pfeifer*, 887 S.W.2d 296, 298 (Ark. 1994) (affirming the trial court's finding PUD ordinance invalidly used when applied to such a development when the ordinance authorized PUD use "to encourage orderly, clustered, multi-use development," and the planning board approved a PUD for a 15-acre store with a large showroom, a wholesale warehouse, and a retail area, and holding that this use of the ordinance was improper because the project did not cluster a mix of land uses and that a store serving both wholesale and retail markets did not make the project multi-use).

64. *See Frankland v. City of Lake Oswego*, 517 P.2d 1042 (Or. 1973).

65. *See Vasquez v. D.C. Zoning Comm'n*, 311 A.3d 288 (D.C. 2024).

66. *See Chandler v. Kroiss*, 190 N.W.2d 472 (Minn. 1972) (making this point).

67. *See Rutland Envir. Protection Ass'n v. Kane Cty.*, 334 N.E.2d 215 (Ill. App. Ct. 1975).

68. *See Porpoise Point Partnership v. St. John's County*, 532 So. 2d 727 (Fla. App. Ct. 1988) (invalidating a PUD rezoning initiated by a municipality).

69. *Id.*

typically only available to land owners holding a minimum contiguous acreage, say, ten or more acres, located in pre-determined use districts.[70] Thus the development will be large enough that adverse, off-site impacts can be limited (as would be the case with a special exception). The increased density of the developed portion of the PUD is considered a fair trade for the preservation of other portions as undeveloped or as a buffer against adverse impacts on other parcels.[71] The larger the parcel converted into a PUD, the more likely approval will be "in return for the creation of public benefits or amenities."[72] When this is so, then the density can be greater than that permitted under pre-existing zoning, so long as the planning commission has power to insure that the development is self-contained.[73] Uses may also be restricted to a percentage of the land area; that is, a maximum of eighty percent may be devoted to residential uses and twenty to commercial uses, etc. Proposed commercial uses may be limited to types that will serve only PUD residents.[74] A maximum number of dwelling units may be permitted within any one structure, and there may have to be a minimum number of feet between structures. A minimum percentage may have to be devoted to open space. PUD review must available only in certain pre-designated Euclidian use districts[75]—available, but unmapped precisely—requiring that a rezoning application for a map amendment be made.[76] Only one use district need be named.[77] The application maps the PUD, previously a floating zone—planned for, located generally within specific use districts, but unmapped precisely within those districts beforehand. Thus, with the approval of an application, the proposed development will become a permitted use in a way thought out in advance, being thus also "in accord with the

---

70. The characteristics of a typical PUD have changed over time. The minimum acreage requirement is a good example. Today, more than 30 years after *Cheney*, Pennsylvania does not require either a minimum acreage or a minimum number of dwelling units in its enabling act for PUDs, but the act authorizes a locality to set a minimum number of dwelling units. 53 Pa. Cons. Stat. Ann. § 10705(g) (Purdon 1972). Idaho permits a locality to establish a minimum acreage without prescribing one. Idaho Code § 67 6515 (1980). New Jersey requires a 10 acre minimum. N.J. Stat. Ann. § 40:55D-6 (1988). Massachusetts, perhaps looking to PUDs as a good vehicle for urban in-fill, requires 60,000 sq. ft. or five times the underlying district's minimum lot size. Mass. Gen. L. ch. 40A, § 9 (1987).

71. *See Wheatley v. D.C. Zoning Comm'n*, 229 A.3d 754 (D.C. 2020) (where the open space preserved by the PUD "had long been used for recreation by nearby residents"); *Friends of Shawangunks, Inc. v. Knowlton*, 476 N.E.2d 988, 992 (N.Y. 1985).

72. *See Howell v. D.C. Zoning Comm'n*, 97 A.3d 579, 581 (D.C. 2014), *discussed in Elliott v. D.C. Zoning Comm/n*, 246 A.3d 568, 571 (D.C. 2021) (requiring that the PUD "result in a project superior to what would result from the matter-of-right" zoning), *and Beloved Community Alliance v. D.C. Zoning Comm'n*, 284 A.3d 728, 732 (D.C. 2022) (requiring the commission to balance the public benefits, "the degree of development incentives requested," and the adverse impacts of the PUD).

73. *See, e.g.*, N.Y. Town Law § 281(b) (1987 and Supp. 1989).

74. *See, e.g.*, N.J. Stat. Ann. § 40:55-57(a) (1967) (repealed 1976).

75. *See City of Waukesha v. Town Bd.*, 543 N.W.2d 515 (Wis. Ct. App. 1995) (invalidating a PUD ordinance that did not name the use districts in which a PUD might be located).

76. *See Town of North Hempstead v. Village of North Hills*, 342 N.E.2d 566 (N.Y. 1975).

77. *Id.*

comprehensive plan" advanced by the zoning ordinance;[78] this prevents the development from appearing to be a private deal cut for a particular "aspiring developer."[79]

The foregoing standards are those found in the ordinance validated in *Cheney v. Village 2 at New Hope, Inc.*[80] Decided in 1968, *Cheney* is the first state supreme court case to have validated a PUD ordinance in a jurisdiction without express statutory authority for one in the zoning enabling act.[81] In Pennsylvania, post-*Cheney* legislation required that a PUD comply with the elements of a municipality's comprehensive plan.[82]

[A] The Standard of Review for PUD Approvals

The PUD is sometimes likened to a large special exception. It is analogous to a special exception;[83] it is not the same thing.[84] A PUD is also like a floating zone with cluster zoning features. Like the floating zone for garden apartments in *Rodgers*, it is the legislative response to a felt need, offered in accord with pre-set criteria. Like cluster zoning, it permits variations in density from what the underlying Euclidean zoning would allow.

Considering both analogies side by side, analogizing the PUD to a floating zone seems preferable, particularly when there is no express authority for it in the state's enabling act. Why? Because the special exception is a conditional use expressly provided for in the enabling act and in an ordinance, while a floating zone takes advantage of the silences in an enabling act. If the act does not require that a zoning amendment change the text and the map all at once, then a floating zone may be authorized, and it is but a small step from finding that the act implicitly authorizes a floating zone district to finding the same type of authority for a PUD district.[85]

---

78. *See Amcon Corp. v. City of Eagan*, 348 N.W.2d 66 (Minn. 1984) (remanding matter to planning commission that denied a PUD rezoning when the commission's denial was not in accord with the comprehensive plan, citing the plan as "strong evidence" of arbitrary action).

79. This term is from *Cheney, supra*.

80. 241 A.2d 81 (Pa. 1968).

81. *See also Chrinko v. South Brunswick Township Planning Board*, 187 A.2d 221 (N.J. Super. Ct., L. Div. 1963) (also finding authority for a PUD district in an enabling act based on the Standard Zoning Enabling Act).

82. *See* 53 Pa. Cons. Stat. Ann. § 10702 (Purdon Supp. 1989).

83. *See, e.g., Hotel Tabard Inn v. District of Columbia Dept. of Consumer & Regulatory Affairs*, 747 A.2d 1168 (D.C. 2000); *Cathedral Park Condominium Committee v. District of Columbia Zoning Comm'n*, 743 A.2d 1231 (D.C. 2000) (both cases showing how a PUD can be used for in-fill developments in highly urban settings).

84. *See Todd Mart, Inc. v. Town Board of Town of Webster*, 370 N.Y.S.2d 683 (N.Y. App. Div. 1975) (involving a large commercial PUD and stating: "The distinguishing factor between special use permits and planned unit developments is the size and significance of the proposed development. Whereas special use permits usually seek approval for a specified single use on a small parcel, such as service stations or swimming pools, the PUD is by its very nature a multi-use proposal for large scale developments. . . . ").

85. *See Campion v. Board of Aldermen of the City of New Haven*, 899 A.2d 542 (Conn. 2006) (finding such authority in a state enabling act described as similar to the SZEA).

Analogizing a PUD to either a special exception or a floating zone makes the standard of review for a PUD ordinance difficult to determine. The special exception is the product of an administrative act. The floating zone is the product of a legislative action. Thus a standard of review based on either substantial evidence or a fairly debatable standard is appropriate. Assuming *arguendo* that PUDs are the product of a hybrid process, mixing both legislative and administrative actions, the standards used for reviewing a floating zone and a special exception not only provide substantive rationales for these ordinances, but also standards for the judicial review of actions taken under them.

When a heightened evidentiary standard is required for a rezoning, as in Maryland, the analogy of the special exception has meant that a rezoning to a PUD district does not have to comply with the heightened standard—in Maryland's case, the substantial change rule[86]—and only substantial evidence need be shown.

Nonetheless, heightened first-tier judicial scrutiny may not only sometimes be warranted by the hybrid nature of a PUD proceeding, but may also be warranted on other grounds as well. When the Pennsylvania court validated the ordinance in *Cheney*, it overlooked some of its salient features. The ordinance restricted the development to structures with two bedrooms. This restriction seems "exclusionary" in the sense that it only provided for low-density, upper income zoning. The high costs of the site plan review, as well as some of requirements of PUD ordinances, such as a minimum acreage, indicate that only the best capitalized developers will be able to afford the use of this zoning technique and buttress the conclusion that the ordinance is likely not to be available to all developers, and is exclusionary in that sense as well. Thus the better view is that the *Cheney* opinion is a general validation, rather than as an "as applied" review of the PUD. In jurisdictions with exclusionary zoning rules, residential PUD ordinances today typically include a low income or affordable housing component.

The PUD device is a reaction by municipal government against self-executing Euclidian ordinances that leave too many of the details of development in private hands. Rezoning land without seeing the site development plans for it often seems irresponsible to municipal legislators. PUD ordinances provide developers and the municipality's planning staff and commission with an opportunity to sit down together and discuss the elements of a development, in the hope that better planning should result from such discussions. These discussions, however, are screened from public view, and so subject to a charge of being arbitrary in nature. When this is so, further procedural reforms in the rezoning process may be necessary—either that, or heightened standards of judicial review.[87]

---

86. *See Beall v. Montgomery County Council*, 212 A.2d 751 (Md. 1965).

87. *See Kenart & Assoc. v. Skagit Cty.*, 680 P.2d 439 (Wash. App. Ct. 1984) (remanding for findings to guide further review).

[B] The *Fasano* Rule

A judicial concern with review of PUD approvals lacking a public record has resulted in stricter standards of judicial review in some jurisdictions. A good example, discussed in the previous Chapter, is *Fasano v. Board of County Commissioners of Washington County*.[88] There, the court found that the resolution of a rezoning dispute was a quasi-judicial action (as opposed to a legislative one), and required not only substantial evidence but also procedural safeguards. *Fasano* involved a PUD for a mobile home park, but the type of development involved was less important than the opinion's concern for the record and the standard of judicial review for rezonings:

> Parties at the hearing . . . are entitled to an opportunity to be heard, to an opportunity to present and rebut evidence, to a tribunal which is impartial in the matter—i.e., having had no pre-hearing or ex parte contacts concerning the question at issue—and to a record made and adequate findings executed.[89]

[C] Challenges to PUD Ordinances

PUD-enabling acts or ordinances are very occasionally invalidated on constitutional grounds. The usual ground is that the act or ordinance lacks adequately detailed standards for municipalities to enact ordinances or to decide whether to grant or deny applications brought under their aegis.[90] Most ordinances have been upheld when attacked on constitutional grounds. A home rule municipality might in addition argue it needs no enabling statute to enact a PUD ordinance.

Other challenges to PUDs have been made on several statutory or common law grounds. First, that such ordinances violate the uniformity requirement of the SZEA; that is, that the enabling act requires that the use districts enabled by the Act be "uniform" in nature. So long as the PUD technique is available to all landowners, provided the threshold requirements are met, this argument has been rejected by the courts.[91] Second, that the ordinances violate the "in accord with a comprehensive plan" language of the Act. Again, this is not so: they embody a plan, but one with performance standards, rather than more fixed criteria for development. Third, that a PUD might be "spot zoning." However, such a charge takes account only of the fact that it may be mapped at many locations on the zoning map, not of the conditions placed on their mapping. The large acreage requirement also tends to refute this charge. Fourth, that they are tantamount to letting the planning commission rezone property. This charge

88. 507 P.2d 23 (Or. 1973) (discussed *supra*, Chapter 11, § 11.14).

89. *Id.* at 30.

90. *See Tri-State Generation and Transmission Co. v. City of Thornton*, 647 P.2d 670 (Colo. 1982).

91. *See Orrinda Homeowners Committee v. Board of Supervisors*, 90 Cal. Rptr. 88 (App. Ct. 1970).

is harder to dismiss, particularly when the legislature approves a PUD site plan generally, but the commission later substantially changes it.[92]

This fourth charge has lead to reform in the PUD procedures. Typically today, the site planning process requires that the rezoning application be accompanied by a general schematic plan for the site. The municipal legislature initially approves this, but then, getting down to details, the commission amends it, and then finally the whole plan goes back to the legislature for a final re-approval.[93] Thus, many ordinances require a general plan approval, followed by site plan review by the planning commission, followed by review of the commission's actions by the legislature. With this sequence of legislative-administrative-legislative action established, any judicial review proceeds only after the legislature has had the last word. Then the reviewing court proceeds under the "fairly debatable" standard.[94] By the same token, material changes in the site plan either at the administrative level or in the latter stages of legislative review will require that the general plan be re-approved by the municipal legislature.[95] Such procedures address the concern that the process of rezoning needs to be thoroughly considered, and when it is, the results of the process are unlikely to present opportunities for fraud or the exercise of undue influence wielded by developers when dealing with the public officials.

When a PUD ordinance provides that the municipal legislature "shall give its final approval" to the site plan after the map amendment is enacted and the administrative review by the planning commission is complete, the local legislature need not approve the plan when, although all the express requirements of the ordinance are met, it finds that the development is worse than would be achieved by Euclidian zoning or does not conform to public needs or the general welfare.[96] In *Todd Mart*, the legislative-administrative-legislative action sequence requires, the court held, a standard of review for a legislative action: unless the final legislative action is arbitrary and if it is fairly debatable, it will be affirmed on review. Thus, proceedings to rezone after the administrative site plan review are legislative in nature. Unless expressly negated, the local legislature has reserved to itself a general welfare or mop-up review of the development plan, even after its approval by the planning commission.

---

92. *See Lutz v. City of Longview*, 520 P.2d 1374, 1376 (Wash. 1974).

93. *Cf. Bartlett v. Cinemark USA, Inc.*, 908 S.W.2d 229 (Tex. App. Ct. 1995) (finding that municipal legislators who reject a PUD may not have immunity from suit when acting on a final development plan).

94. *See Todd Mart, Inc. v. Town Board of Town of Webster*, 370 N.Y.S.2d 683 (N.Y. App. Div. 1975). *Cf. Millbrae Association for Residential Survival v. City of Millbrae*, 69 Cal. Rptr. 251 (Cal. App. 1968) (invalidating a rezoning when the commission substantially changed the general plan by changing the location of high rise buildings, parking lots, and open space areas in the course of reviewing a developer's site plan).

95. *Makowski v. City of Naperville*, 617 N.E.2d 1251 (Ill. App. Ct. 1993).

96. *See Todd Mart Inc. v. Town Board of Town of Webster*, 370 N.Y.S.2d 683 (N.Y. App. Div. 1975); *see also Mikell v. Cty. of Charleston*, 687 S.E.2d 326, 330 (S.C. 2009) (holding that the underlying zoning maximum density requirements were applicable in a PUD).

The review process for PUD applications often results in the imposition of easements and covenants applicable to the parcels under review. The enforcement of such less-than fee interests is often given to owners' non-profit associations established during the course of development, but which the developer initially controls. To avoid disputes about the scope and applicability of such interests, their terms and documents should be clear and express.[97] Likewise, it should be clear who has the right to participate in the later modification of any PUD plan.[98] Otherwise the planning commission may have to decide which owners are affected by the modification, and so have the right to participate. This is an area of law (the law of real covenants) traditionally reserved to the courts, and so beyond the competence of the commission.

[D] Staged PUDs

Planned unit developments often involve large enough parcels of land that they are approved in stages. From the developer's standpoint, the staging is useful because it permits him to build to a market which he can foresee at the time of construction. If there are (say) two stages for approval, the first stage is likely a review of the application, submitted with a general schematic rendering of the development proposal, and a finding that the proposed development is in accord with the municipality's comprehensive plan and the spirit of the underlying zoning ordinance. The second stage is a more detailed review, somewhat akin to the review of a subdivision site plan review. Efficient disposition of the reviewing process demands that each stage build on the last, not affording opponents an opportunity to reargue previous objections.[99]

Many times, restrictions on the use of the land in the PUD are written on the plat. While they do not create real covenants and easements encumbering the title to the land and are not recordable in the land records as such, the enactment of the plat and plan in the ordinance rezoning the land as a PUD is sufficient to put future purchasers on constructive notice of the restriction.[100] Such plat restrictions are in effect implied easements.

A PUD applicant, staging a development in three parts and obtaining separate approvals, may run into legal mischief when parcel owners in the earlier stage one wish to assert "residential only" use or "open space" restrictions, noted on the stage one plat and referenced in their deeds, on parcels in stage three. When no such restrictions are noted either on the plat or in the deeds for stage three parcels, perhaps the stage one owners might assert that later owners hold their titles restricted by an

97. *See Glenbrook Homeowner's Assoc. v. Glenbrook Co.*, 901 P.2d 132 (Nev. 1995) (a dispute over the amount of land to be conveyed to a PUD homeowners' association).

98. *See 1330 Conn. Ave. v. District of Columbia Zoning Commission*, 669 A.2d 708 (D.C. App. 1995).

99. *See Fournier v. D.C. Zoning Comm'n*, 244 A.3d 686, 689 (D.C. 2021).

100. *See South Creek Associates v. Bixby & Associates, Inc.*, 781 P.2d 1027 (Colo. 1989) (holding a parking agreement with an adjacent school, noted in the PUD plan, was effective against subsequent purchasers of the PUD).

implied reciprocal negative easement. But not all jurisdictions recognize such an easement. Another theory might be that the developer, in restricting stage one, implicitly promised to restrict later stages in the same way and in fact had no power to create an unrestricted plat in the future. Staged approvals for a PUD require the planning commission to coordinate the restrictions imposed in each stage and, when it does not do so expressly, create legal issues that plague the law of real covenants. The best course here is for the developer to have a preliminary plat plan approved for all stages, so that the more lucrative, later, commercial stages may be built as planned.

§ 12.05 Transferable Development Rights

PUD districts generally allow density transfers within the district—that is, the PUD need not be of uniform density throughout.[101] Some zoning ordinances recognize that a parcel's development rights are a severable estate in land—and are alienable as such. Thus all or a part of the development rights (measured by what the zoning ordinance would normally permit) to a parcel are severed from the "sending parcel," much as the mineral or air rights might be, and transferred to the "receiving parcel" where a developer receives the right to use them to create a project of greater density than would otherwise be permitted under the zoning ordinance.

Once the development rights are recognized as severable from a "sending parcel" to which they would otherwise attach, their owners can either be given a right to develop elsewhere at a receiving parcel, or else they can be paid for the right, in which case thereafter the purchaser (a governmental entity) holds their rights to develop until they can be sold to someone with a "receiving parcel" on which they can be used. The later alternative involves holding the rights purchased in a "development bank."[102]

Transferable development rights (TDRs) are most often used in conjunction with a land use scheme that has become, due to market forces, highly restrictive. They are meant to offset the burden of preserving a landmark or a land use, such as farming or forestry. They shift the costs of preservation to the public, making such programs appear fairer to owners denied capital gains from converting lands away from the preserved use. They thus both compensate owners for lost development opportunities and provide funds for reinvestment in the preserved use. Once sold, TDRs may not be bought back for use on the sending parcel.

TDRs have been used since the 1960s—for example, in New York City for the preservation of historic landmarks; in Collier County, Florida, for the preservation of

---

101. *See In re Snyder Group, Inc. PUD Final Plat*, 233 A.3d 1077 (Vt. 2020) (TDR ordinance not unconstitutionally vague on its face).

102. *See Matlock v. Board of Chosen Freeholders*, 466 A.2d 83 (N.J. 1983) (validating county development bank as purchaser of last resort and prices set for TDRs)

wetlands; in Calvert and Montgomery Counties in Maryland, to preserve farmland against urbanization; and in New Jersey to protect the Pinelands.[103] Municipalities in New York, New Jersey, and Pennsylvania have also attempted to preserve farmland this way. When authorized to protect farmland by statute, they may not be used for other purposes.[104]

The United States Supreme Court recognized TDRs as a valid planning device in its *Penn Central* opinion.[105] TDR programs are easily within the police power when they deal with the carrying capacity of a parcel or land area and recognize that the reasonable use of a parcel with development potential should reflect that potential. In addition, because they preserve and protect existing, and admittedly beneficial, uses of property, the character of the governmental action in running even a mandatory TDR program is not one that triggers a finding of a taking. Likewise, because of the pre-existing uses of the property, there is unlikely to be any undue economic impact on the owner or an interference with an owner's investment-backed expectations. Thus, a regulatory takings claim will not succeed.[106] Moreover, once in place, TDR programs are less susceptible than Euclidian zoning is to shifts in the political climate with regard to land development.

However, a less than fully developed TDR program may result in a taking. An owner of a TDR sending parcel, learning that all receiving parcels are currently developed to the extent permitted by the ordinance, may be offered a very low purchase price for the TDR, one discounted because it cannot be presently used on a receiving parcel. Unless compensation is offered at this point in the program (by a development bank or other device), a taking has occurred. This is so because the "whole parcel" definition of the sending parcel, sanctioned by the United States Supreme Court in *Penn Central*, otherwise results in unfairness "as applied"; that is, when the municipality itself segments the parcel into its existing use and TDR value, the municipality should be estopped from using the "whole parcel" doctrine. It should instead recognize the segmented property interest in the TDR that it has created. In this instance, the takings claim should be measured by either the amount of the discount or the fair market value of the TDR. On the other side of town, once the purchaser owns both a parcel in the designated, but fully developed, receiving district and a TDR, that purchaser has a right to a variance—and a variance denied should result in a takings claim as well. His is, after all, a problem created by the literal implementation of a governmental

103. *See Gardner v. New Jersey Pinelands Comm'n*, 593 A.2d 251 (N.J. 1991) (as to the Pinelands program).

104. *See KGF Development, LLC v. City of Ketchum*, 236 P.3d 1284 (Idaho 2010) (holding that a TDR statute authorizing the preservation of open space and rural land may not be used on a receiving parcel to transfer TDRs to a condominium developer seeking to add a floor making his building higher than the maximum height permitted in the use district of the sending parcel).

105. *See Penn Central Transportation Company v. City of New York*, 438 U.S. 104 (1978) (discussed *supra*, Chapter 4, § 4.02[D]; *see also Appeal of Buckingham Developers, Inc.*, 433 A.2d 931 (Pa. Commwlth. Ct. 1981) (noting their use without reaching their merits).

106. *See Gardner v. New Jersey Pinelands Comm'n*, 593 A.2d 251 (N.J. 1991).

program, and so the purchaser would be in a strong position to negotiate with the municipality for a variance.

Payment for the lost development potential in the sending district typically comes from the purchasers in the receiving district buying TDRs. In the receiving district, TDRs are measured in the extra square feet of development allowed once they are applied. Sometimes TDR programs entitle purchasers to build in a receiving district at a greater density than would otherwise be permitted in the receiving district, with or without a variance.[107] The constitutionality of the TDR program depends on there being active and valuable sending and receiving parcels, otherwise the owner has a takings claim.

Thus, the foundation for a TDR program must be laid out in the comprehensive plan for a municipality and in a comprehensive set of land use regulations. This is particularly so when TDRs are transferred over long distances or to non-contiguous parcels, as when they are used to shift development between agricultural and urban areas. A less than comprehensive program will result in (say) fragmented agricultural holdings that cannot sustain farming as a way of life, and the neighbors adjacent to the receiving parcel will see "spot zoning" when the developer applies for his development permissions. A TDR program established in conjunction with a downzoning of either the sending or the receiving parcels will be particularly suspect.

Another foundation stone in a TDR program is the designation of the receiving use districts. They must be designated in advance and contain a number of receiving parcels sufficiently great to accommodate the market for such rights.[108] A TDR program aimed as preserving open space was invalidated because the TDRs could not be used on the sending parcels and yet lacked any receiving parcels.[109]

TDR programs have received state legislative attention. New Jersey's TDR legislation[110] requires municipalities to adopt (1) a TDR program element in its comprehensive plan, (2) a capital improvement program for any receiving district taking into account the utility services needed there, (3) a market analysis examining the relationship between the number of TDRs generated in the sending district and the capacity of the receiving district to absorb them, and (4) approval of the municipality's TDR program by the state planning commission.[111]

---

107. *See In re Adoption of Highlands Regional Master Plan*, 24 A.3d 314 (N.J. Super. Ct. 2011).

108. *See West Montgomery County Citizens Association v. Maryland-National Capital Park & Planning Commission*, 522 A.2d 1328 (Md. 1987) (failing to designate receiving parcels invalidated a TDR program for farmland).

109. *See Fred F. French Investing Company v. City of New York*, 350 N.E.2d 381 (N.Y. 1976), *appeal dismissed* 429 U.S. 990 (1976) ("it is a tolerable abstraction to consider development rights apart from the solid land from which as a matter of zoning law they derive. But severed, the development rights are a double abstraction until they are actually attached to a receiving parcel, yet to be identified, acquired, and subject to the contingent future approvals of administrative agencies. . . . ") (noted in 90 Harv. L. Rev. 637 (1977)).

110. *See* N.J. Stat. Ann. § 40:55D-137 thru -163 (enacted 2004).

111. *See Builders League of South Jersey, Inc. v. Twp. of Franklin*, 928 A.2d 88, 91–92 N.J. Super. Ct. 2007) (reviewing the state legislation).

[A] TDR Documents

A TDR program requires that participants use three basic documents. All should be recorded on the public real property records after they are executed. They are: first, an easement, from the owner of the sending parcel, restricting the development by however many development rights were transferred to the local government or other holder, such as a private land trust; second, a deed transferring the rights to their purchaser—whether that person be a speculator or a developer; and third, a plat map for the development of the receiving parcel, on which map is noted the use of the rights, referring back to the easement and deed. The easements are by their terms perpetual. Thus, a major advantage of a TDR program is that it relies on the development of a private market to set the prices paid and does not require continuing regulatory supervision.

Chapter 13
Judicial Review of Zoning Actions

§ 13.01 Some Procedural Problems

An applicant for any type of zoning change is entitled to procedural due process in an administrative or legislative hearing. A municipal legislator has the right to state publicly his or her views on the matters before the legislative chamber. However, campaigning for the votes of fellow legislators outside the chamber, or organizing and advising opponents of the application, crosses the line and denies the applicant procedural due process.[1] Likewise, when there has been the appearance of prejudice by a member of an administrative agency, disqualification of a member does not require a reversal of the agency's decision unless there is a showing of control or undue influence over other members.[2] Actual prejudice need not be shown and will not generally be implied from the conduct of a public official: a strong probability of prejudice is required. That may be shown by consistent inattention to the applicant and witnesses appearing before the agency. Moreover, non-dispositive but prejudicial votes do not require that the decision be reversed on appeal.

[A] Standing

Generally, standing is a matter of limiting litigation on the merits to issues that are justiciable, conducted by capable parties sufficiently interested in the outcome to give them an incentive to litigate thoroughly and well.[3] Standing is a threshold, jurisdictional issue. It does not depend on or determine the merits of a party's claim. It is examined independently of those merits, or the lack of them,[4] on a person-by-person basis. It is concerned with whether a plaintiff or other person is the proper party to

1. *See Petrovich Development Co., LLC v. City of Sacramento*, 262 Cal. Rptr. 3d 331 (Cal. Ct. App. 2020).

2. *See Gates v. City of Pittsburgh Planning Comm'n*, 229 A.3d 50 (Pa. Commwlth. Ct. 2020).

3. *See Citizens for the Protection of the North Kohala Coastline v. County of Hawaii*, 979 P.2d 1120, 1126 (Haw. 1999); *Richards v. Planning & Zoning Comm'n*, 365 A.2d 1130 (Conn. 1976).

4. *See Alan v. Wright*, 468 U.S. 737, 750–51 (1984).

assert a claim.[5] It is not conferred on groups or neighborhoods.[6] It is a question of law, subject to a *de novo* review, and may be raised *sua sponte* by a reviewing court.[7]

Standing in land use regulation and zoning matters is always given to landowners of the parcel at issue. Only a minor, adverse consequence is typically required to confer standing on owners.[8] All others have standing when they show special injuries or interests, or more loosely, adverse effect or impact;[9] standing is premised on the principle that the persons who should litigate a dispute are those either injured or about to be injured.

In many states, this limitation on standing is the product of public nuisance cases: a person who seeks to abate a nuisance must be specially affected by it, more affected than by just being a member of the public. This limitation is intended to relieve defendants of litigating multiple suits and to preserve for public officials the power to litigate nuisances that affect the whole populace. A citizen's status as a taxpayer in a municipality is generally insufficient to confer standing;[10] although the Standard Zoning Enabling Act conferred standing on "all taxpayers." (Most jurisdictions did not enact this provision of the Act.) Neither can standing be based on a right to be free of competition.

As a restriction on persons entering into litigation, standing further seeks to limit litigated issues to those that are justiciable, i.e., based on the constitutional limits on land use regulations. Typically, standing is not merely a matter of constitutional law, but rather is a combination of statutory law, ordinances, and judicial administration.

Abutting property owners sometimes enjoy a presumption of injury and standing.[11] This presumption is a rebuttable one.[12] Adjacent owners usually have standing to seek judicial review.[13] Adjacency is defined for this purpose as "abutting, confronting, or nearby" or "in the immediate vicinity" of the parcel subject to a zoning action.[14] It[15] is also usually defined by statute or ordinance as holding property within

5. *See Egan v. City of Lancaster*, 952 N.W.2d 664, 669 (Neb. 2020).

6. *See Ray v. City of Baltimore*, 59 A.3d 545 (Md. 2013).

7. *See Upstream Watch v. City of Belfast*, 298 A.3d 25, 31 (Me. 2023).

8. *See Sproul v. Town of Boothbay*, 746 A.2d 368, 371–72 (Vt. 2000).

9. *See Mangum v. Raleigh Bd. of Adjustment*, 669 S.E.2d 279 (N.C. 2008) (citing such effects as parking overflow, erosion, and safety factors as conferring standing).

10. *See Committee for the Responsible Development on 25th Street v. Mayor and City Council of Baltimore*, 767 A.2d 906, 913 (Md. App. Ct. 2001) (finding state law controlling a home rule county ordinance on standing and finding that a taxpayer is not "aggrieved" under state law).

11. *See Marashlian v. Zoning Bd. of Appeals of Newburyport*, 660 N.E.2d 369, 372 (Mass. 1996); *Center Bay Gardens LLC v. City of Tempe*, 153 P.3d 374, 379, n.5 (Ariz. Ct. App. 2007) (collecting cases from many jurisdictions).

12. *See 81 Spooner Rd. LLC v. Zoning Board of Appeals of Brookline*, 964 N.E.2d 318 (Mass. 2012).

13. *See Burks v. City of Maricopa*, 2018 Ariz. App. LEXIS 114 (Ariz. Ct. App. 2018) (holding that "strict adjacency" is not required in Arizona); *Center Bay Gardens, LLC v. City of Tempe*, 153 P.3d 374, 379, n. 5 (Ariz. Ct. App. 2007) (surveying cases from other jurisdictions, but leaving the issue open in Arizona); *Matter of Sun-Brite Car Wash, Inc. v. Bd. of Zoning and Appeals*, 508 N.E.2d 130 (N.Y. 1987).

14. *See Peifer v. Colerain Twp. Zoning Hearing Bd.*, 302 A.3d 811, 817 (Pa. Commwlth. Ct. 2023).

15. Adjacency is defined for this purpose as abutting, confronting, or nearby.

a certain distance of the parcel affected by the application.[16] When an ordinance or statute gives this more precise definition, a review court will generally defer to and use it. Even if a municipal boundary is crossed, an owner may still be found to be adjacent for purposes of conferring standing. Any adjacency requirement is, therefore, a stand-in for the idea that adjacent owners will likely have a property interest injured by the decision on the application. By the same token, even an out-of-state owner who would otherwise have standing may appear or appeal an "adjacent" zoning decision: the presumption against the extraterritorial enforcement of zoning regulations is no bar preventing out-of-state persons from enforcing in-state regulations.[17]

Some courts have developed a multi-factor test for adjacency; thus, the physical proximity of the use, the character of the neighborhood or use district, the type of zoning amendment or change at issue, and the right to notice, determine whether standing will be awarded.[18] Proximity may sometimes be a privileged factor, particularly when an owner seeking standing is a mile or so away.[19] Conversely, a concern with increased traffic may not be given much weight, it being regarded as a generalized concern and part of any urban development.[20]

Adjacency is a term that is often broadly construed. Typically, participation in administrative proceedings raising issues relevant to the issues before the agency is sufficient to give adjacent owners standing for purposes of judicial review, and more typically, not participating is a reason to deny standing to appeal. Sometimes it is said that an adjacent owner has *prima facie* standing if he or she participated in the administrative proceedings giving rise to the review and is adversely affected by the decision therein.[21]

Participation in the hearing can take several forms: filing a letter with the Board, submitting a written petition with the board, even identifying oneself in the record as a party—any action which puts one's name into the record of the proceedings is likely to be sufficient.[22] Generally, the issue of standing must be raised at trial, not on appeal for the first time.[23]

When a state imposes, by statute or judicial decision, an obligation to provide affordable housing on a municipality, only those persons of low or moderate income

---

16. The American Law Institute's Model Land Development Code, § 9-401(2) (1976), suggests that 500 feet from the applicant's parcel is the right measure.

17. *See Abel v. Planning and Zoning Comm'n of the Town of New Canaan*, 998 A.2d 1149 (Conn. 2010).

18. *See Reynolds v. Dittmer*, 312 N.W.2d 75 (Iowa 1981).

19. *See Cable v. Union Cty. Bd. of Cty. Comm'nrs*, 769 N.W.2d 817 (S. D. 2009).

20. *See Sanitary & Imp. Dist. No. 347 v. City of Omaha*, 589 N.W.2d 160 (Neb. Ct. App. 1999).

21. *See Bryniarski v. Montgomery County Bd. of Appeals*, 230 A.2d 289, 292–93 (Md. 1967). *But see Boulden v. Mayor and Comm'rs of the Town of Elkton*, 535 A.2d 477 (Md. 1988) (when an ordinance granted a right of appeal to a "taxpayer," *Bryniarski* is distinguishable). *See generally Dyer v. Zoning Bd. of Appeals of Arlington Heights*, 534 N.E.2d 506 (Ill. App. Ct. 1989) (holding that adjoining landowner who participates in variance proceeding lacked standing when failing to prove special injury).

22. *Cf. Morris v. Howard Research and Development Corp.*, 365 A.2d 34 (Md. 1976) (involving a statute requiring that any party to the administrative proceeding be given notice of a judicial appeal).

23. *See Baker v. Montgomery County Council*, 215 A.2d 831 (Md. 1966).

who would benefit from such housing have standing to contest the methods the jurisdiction uses to meet its obligation.[24] This test amounts to a "zone of interest" test for standing: that is, a litigant must have the same interest as those protected or benefitted by the ordinance. As we shall see, ruling that those who might benefit but are not yet residents of the municipality have standing is more generous a rule than federal courts provide.[25]

[B] "Substantial Interest/Aggrieved Party" Test

Standing is typically a matter controlled by statute or ordinance: a party given a right to appeal a zoning regulation decision must often show that he or she is, apart from his or her taxpayer status,[26] "a person aggrieved or adversely affected[27] by" the decision of the administrator, BZA, or municipal legislature.[28] This ordinance language cannot confer standing alone, just as a legislature cannot confer standing by any statute alone. All plaintiffs must establish whatever constitutional requirements for standing the courts impose. So statutes and ordinances do not automatically confer standing in the absence of constitutionally imposed requirements. A court's exclusive reliance on the "aggrieved person" or party language is misplaced, and the tests using this language must incorporate constitutional standing requirements.

This "aggrieved person" language originated in Section 7 of the Standard State Zoning Enabling Act. "Aggrieved" in this context means that standing is to be conf erred, not because a decision either granted or denies an application, but rather because, more broadly, the enforcement of the ordinance was involved in the decision appealed.[29] The courts have generally found that this statute requires two things: (1) that the party appealing has a legal interest in the affected or adjacent property and (2) that he or she show special damages, as opposed to an injury suffered by the public at large.[30] Sometimes, the two prongs of this test are stated in the alternative.[31]

---

24. *See Alexander's Dept. Stores of New Jersey v. Borough of Paramus*, 578 A.2d 1241, 1245 (N.J. Super. Ct., App. Div. 1990); *see generally* J.D. Ayer, *The Primitive Law of Standing in Land Use Disputes: Some Notes from a Dark Continent*, 55 Iowa L. Rev. 344 (1967).

25. *See infra.*

26. *See Sons of Confederate Veterans v. Henry Cty. Bd. of Comm'nrs*, 880 S.E.2d 168, 181–82 (Ga. 2022) (reviewing taxpayer standing—seldom involved on zoning disputes—in Georgia).

27. *See Griswold v. City of Homer*, 252 P.3d 1020, 1028 (Alas. 2011) (holding that "adversely affected" and "aggrieved" mean the same thing).

28. *See The Stuttering Foundation, Inc. v. Glynn Cty.*, 801 S.E.2d 793, 797 (Ga. 2017).

29. *See Ladzinske v. Allen*, 626 S.E.2d 83, 85 (Ga. 2006).

30. The two prongs of this test are intended to make plain again that the doctrine of standing is not a surrogate for a test of the merits or the legal theory of the plaintiff's or petitioner's case. Even though judges may be tempted to deny standing to a petitioner with a weak case, they are in error when doing so. That case can be tested, in a procedurally distinct manner, as early as a demurrer can be filed. *See Miller v. Fulton County*, 375 S.E.2d 864 (Ga. 1989).

31. *See Walsh v. Town of Wrightville Beach Bd. of Aldermen*, 2007 N.C. App. LEXIS 2299 (Nov. 6, 2007).

The first prong of this requirement requires not just a legal interest, but a substantial interest as well. It involves the right to use, acquire or enjoy the parcel of the person "aggrieved."[32] For example, it requires factual allegations of an immediate, distinctive, non-trivial, pecuniary harm, distinct from the public at large, and not a remote or indirect harm.[33] It makes standing a preliminary issue for a purchaser under an executory contract of sale or the holder of an option to purchase; in these cases, an equitable interest is involved. Similarly, a lessee may have a lesser, non-freehold interest, but a stronger argument for standing because his interest is a legal estate: unless the lease expressly states it is a usufruct.[34] Even a sale-leaseback, taking place while a rezoning is pending will not change this expansive rule. Both the applicant and the purchaser will still have standing: the purchaser as the title holder and/or mortgagor, and the applicant as a lessee (if the lease is more than a tenancy at will). That the lease is on terms making the landlord's termination rights non-automatic, and that the lessee has guaranteed the rents, makes a lessee's standing all the stronger.[35] So, too, a devisee of real property may have his standing contested.

Although the cases may split on specific results, there is a tendency to extend standing to all the classes of persons listed previously. As to the contract purchaser, courts look at the contingencies in the contract; as to the lessee, courts look at the length of the term, the protections which a lessee has against termination, and whether the lease is oral or written; likewise, the courts look for a contract right of the optionee to participate in or appeal the decision. In each case, the security of the holder's interest in the affected property is the subject of the inquiry. As to the devisee, even though his or her interest in the property affected by a decision is inchoate and not vested, nonetheless, its assignability has proven to be the feature that renders it substantial and qualifies its holder for standing.

In general then, a legal interest conferring standing is a right of use, enjoyment, or possession. Being married to a person with such a right does not confer standing. In addition, a contractor renovating or constructing an improvement on a parcel does not have standing to contest the denial of a foundation permit or any other zoning decision concerning the parcel on which he works.

Because so many zoning matters arise when the title or possession to property is changing hands and the new owner or possessor wishes to change the use of the parcel, the rule of standing must be non-preclusive. Otherwise the matter may not be discussed or litigated sufficiently to make a record for review. Although results vary with local practice, typically both the old and the new owners and possessors (i.e., both vendors and purchasers, landlords and tenants, owners and optionees) have standing once their legal relationship gives both a substantial interest in how a parcel is used.

---

32. *See Edison Bd. of Education v. Zoning Bd. of Adjustment*, 235 A.3d 249, 254 (N.J. Super. Ct. 2020).

33. *See Anders Larsen Tr. v. Bd. of Supervisors*, 872 S.E.2d 449. 452 (Va. 2022).

34. *See The Stuttering Foundation, Inc. v. Glynn Cty.*, 801 S.E.2d 793, 797, n. 5 (Ga. 2017).

35. *See Primerica v. Planning and Zoning Comm'n of Town of Greenwich*, 558 A.2d 646, 650 (Conn. 1989).

The other component of this first "legal interest" prong is the "adjacency" of the parcel. Although not every jurisdiction uses the term,[36] it is generally taken to mean that an "adjoining, confronting, or nearby" parcel owner satisfies this second component; he or she is typically deemed to be specially damaged and thereby "aggrieved."[37] Because proximity creates a presumption of standing, it is the most important factor to be considered. Here obviously what is "nearby" invokes a flexible standard requiring specific allegations to pass the threshold test for standing. A protestant's being with 1,000 feet of the subject parcel while offering "plus factors" discussed in the next paragraph has been held to pass the threshold.[38] More generally, adjacency is a stand-in for those persons protesting a zoning action who will mostly likely "bear the brunt of the changed conditions" created by the decision.[39]

The second prong of this requirement is taken to mean that there must be an affirmative showing of damage, not just judicial notice taken of the probability of damage.[40] The showing of special damages is not made with a showing of increased competition for a person's adjacent business. Nor is it made when the complaint is on the basis of considerations addressed in the zoning ordinance itself.[41] Without adjacency, a parcel owner's lay opinion about increased traffic, the character of the neighborhood, the overcrowding of schools and other public facilities, or the decreased value of his parcel is likewise insufficient. It is only with adjacency that such opinions carry weight.[42] However, the presence of noise, odor, and traffic problems, as well as diminished value, have been found to be the basis of a claim of special damages; if these externalities can be reasonably expected, a claim of special damages will be sustained. Here "adjacency plus" may be sufficient.[43] With regard to the matter of diminished value, for example, expert appraisals may provide the needed plus factor. Likewise, a *de minimis* loss of view is not a plus factor,[44] while a total loss of view would be.[45] Traveling by the affected property would not, by the same token, suffice for standing.

When it is undisputed that at least one party on each side of a dispute has standing, a reviewing court generally does not review the issue further.[46] A corollary to this rule

36. *See Milani v. Irwin*, 840 S.E.2d 700, 705 (Ga. Ct. App. 2020).

37. *See A Guy Named Moe, LLC v. Chipotle Mexican Grill of Colorado, LLC*, 135 A.3d 494, 508 (Md. 2016).

38. *See Heard v. Cty. Council of Prince George's Cty.*, 287 A.3d 682, 699 (Md. App. Ct. 2022).

39. *See Milani, op. cit.*

40. *See 222 East Chestnut Street Corporation, supra*, 152 N.E.2d at 467.

41. *See Columbus, Georgia v. Diaz-Verson*, 373 S.E.2d 208, 210 (Ga. 1988) (addressing protection of residents on a flood plain from flooding).

42. *See Ray v. City of Baltimore*, 59 A.3d 545 (Md. 2013) (collecting cases). *But see Fort v. Cty. of Cumberland*, 721 N.C. Ct. App. 2012) (holding parcel owner's lay opinion of diminished value sufficient for standing).

43. *See* Paul Wilson, *"I don't live next door, but I do drive by": Recent Developments in the Law of Standing in Court Cases Challenging Land Use Permits*, 39 Urb. Law. 711 (2007).

44. *See Marhefka v. Zoning Bd. of Appeals*, 947 N.E.2d 1090 (Mass. Ct. App. 2011); *Kenner v. Zoning Bd. of Appeals*, 944 N.E.2d 163 (Mass. 2011) (noted in B. Lidington, *Massachusetts Standing Laws and Zoning Appeals*, 46 Suffolk U. L. Rev. 603 (2013)).

45. *See Shinall v. Bd. of Zoning Appeals*, 212 N.E.3d 675 (Ind. Ct. App. 2023).

46. *See Heard, op. cit.*, 287 A.3d at 701.

is that the requirement that a party must have standing to appeal "does not disappear when another party appeals first."[47] When standing is challenged and reviewed further, the question is one of law, and the standard of review is *de novo* and plenary.[48] However, when a trial court takes no evidence, the standard of review is narrower and limited to a question of whether the BZA or administrative board erred as a matter of law or abused its discretion. Why? Because the board is the fact finder and the weight and credibility of the evidence it uses to reach a decision will not be second-guessed on appeal.

Although the status of an adjacent competitor with the prospective business seeking a rezoning is insufficient to confer standing in a rezoning decision,[49] neither does competitive status *per se* bar standing. The potential competitor might show increased traffic flow, or new demands on public facilities in the area. Such a showing is not of an economic interest, but is well within the ambit of the type of land use conflicts which can properly be presented to a board or legislature.

The remedy a plaintiff seeks may also affect standing and a showing of special damages. Seeking an injunction in order to ensure future compliance with a zoning ordinance will likely result in dismissal of the plaintiff's compliant; before a permit has been issued, there is no decision that can work damage on the plaintiff's parcel, however nearby it might be. (This is not an action to prevent future damages caused by a decision—for that an injunction traditionally lies.) Likewise, a party that gains the relief it seeks before the BZA or other administrative board "lacks standing to appeal a judgment that grants the relief the party sought."[50] The reason is that the successful party is not "aggrieved" by the board's decision. In this situation, that the party would have preferred a decision based on another theory or reasoning will not change this result. Only if the party's use of collateral estoppel might be prejudiced in some future proceeding would this result change.[51]

Because there is no unfettered right to access to the courts or to an appeal, the legislature may set reasonable qualifications on this right. Participation in the disputed matter is a pre-condition to gaining standing. Some courts call this "procedural standing" as opposed to "substantive standing," referring to having the aforementioned legal interest in the outcome of the dispute.[52] An expression of concern about a pending application to a member of the local zoning appeals board is insufficient to confer standing, even when the member of the board in response states that he will relay his concerns to the board. This is so even when the member does in fact relay such concerns, which thus appear as a part of the record. A municipal ordinance typically requires that in order to appeal, the appellant "shall have participated in the

47. *See Tominsky v. Town of Ogunquit*, 294 A.3d 142, 149 (Me. 2023).

48. *See Dowds v. Zoning Bd. of Adjustment*, 242 A.3d 683, 692 (Pa. Commwlth. Ct. 2020).

49. *See Hendel's Investors Co. v. Zoning Bd. of Appeals of the Town of Montville*, 771 A.2d 182, 188–89 (Conn. App. Ct. 2001) (involving competing gas station owners).

50. *See Tominsky*, *op. cit.*, 294 A.3d at 149.

51. *Id.* at n.3.

52. *See In re City of Philadelphia*, 245 A.3d 346, 351 (Pa. Commwlth. Ct. 2021).

proceeding." Attending the hearing is necessary to establish the necessary participation when the board grants the application. The applicant's or the municipality's later objection that the person expressing concern has no standing to appeal is well taken: A person seeking judicial review of an adverse zoning decision "shall have been a participant in the proceeding" before the administrative board.[53] Whatever interest is found sufficient for standing, it must be maintained throughout the hearing and later appeal.[54]

[C] Standing of Neighborhood Citizens' Associations

Neighborhood and civic groups generally have "organizational or associational standing," although the recent cases on the issue are split. They are the municipal equivalent of the Sierra Club or the Audubon Society, given standing in federal court on questions of environmental concern when their members are injured. Nonetheless, pleading prudence dictates that one of the members satisfy the test for adjacency, legal interest, and/or damage or aggrievement and thus be the nominal plaintiff.[55] Granting standing might, however, depend on whether a variance, special exception or rezoning is at issue. The capacity of the association to take an adversary role, the extent that it can represent the whole interest of the neighborhood, and its ability to spread attorneys' fees, are some of the considerations that courts use to weigh their standing. By the same token, all the owners of a parcel affected by an ordinance applying to a limited amount of a municipality's acreage, have been given standing to contest it.[56]

Jurisdictions divide on the issue of whether one or all members of the group must meet the requirements for standing. Some give standing to a group if one or more members qualify.[57] Others require that all members meet the requirement.[58] The latter rule seems less desirable when one of a group's members, suing in an individual capacity, could carry the litigation forward. Moreover, joining a group permits sharing and spreading the costs of litigation, and so allowing the group to participate makes it more likely that the litigation will proceed and a dispute will be fully aired. Furthermore, the difficulty a group is likely to have coming to a consensus about

53. *See Jaeger v. Sheehy*, 551 A.2d 841, 842 (Me. 1988) (holding that, because the citizen did not appear at the hearing in person or through counsel, she lacks standing to prosecute an appeal).

54. *See Primerica v. Planning and Zoning Comm'n of Town of Greenwich*, 558 A.2d 646, 650–51 (Conn. 1989).

55. *See* Annot., *Standing of civic or property owners' association to challenge zoning board decision (as aggrieved party)*, 8 A.L.R.4th 1087 (1981).

56. *See Lewis v. Planning and Zoning Comm'n of the Town of Ridgefield*, 771 A.2d 167, 172–74 (Conn. App. Ct. 2001) (involving an increase in minimum acreage requirements for new subdivision lots and stressing that "a very limited amount of property" in the municipality was affected).

57. *See Center Sq. Ass'n v. City of Albany*, 780 N.Y.S.2d 203 (2004).

58. *See Northeast Concerned Citizens, Inc. v. City of Hickory*, 545 S.E.2d 768, 772 (N.C. Ct. App. 2001).

bringing litigation makes it unlikely that frivolous suits will result. Finally, groups may have an interest in land's carrying capacity or other environmental effects that, while stretching the definition of special damages or aggrievement, will broaden the scope of the proceedings.

Standing has also been given to native peoples through their tribal organizations. Standing here involves the interests of native peoples and is based on their customary and cultural rights to hunt and fish, aggrievement of those rights being shown in the use of the land affected by an application. Participation in the hearing, by itself, typically gives the natives a right to appeal the granting of the application.[59]

Standing rules in state exclusionary zoning cases are more lenient in state, as opposed to federal courts.[60] This leniency has to do with the familiarity of state courts with the problems of establishing standing in such cases and with the fact that, often, the cases themselves are intended to establish residency within a jurisdiction, so it is antithetical to the very nature of the cause of action to enforce standing rules in the traditional way.

[D] A BZA's Standing to Appeal

Once a BZA or other board is reversed by a trial court in an appeal taken by a citizens' association or an individual protestant from its grant of a variance, special exception, or other zoning decision, the board itself may wish to appeal the trial court's decision. When it has been given notice of appeal to the trial court, and has had to certify the record to the reviewing court, perhaps a right to appeal and appear itself can be implied. The cases, however, are split on this issue.[61]

The better view is that the board may represent interests greater than those of the parties to the decision. Sometimes this greater interest is seen as the public interest. Sometimes it is seen as the board's interest in seeing that the statutes and ordinances that govern its functions and decisions are properly interpreted and applied. Further, when municipalities are granted standing to appeal board decisions with which some other branch of its government disagrees, the right of the board to defend itself on appeal may be recognized. On this basis, granting it standing might become the general rule. Likewise, the municipal legislature might obtain standing once concluding that an appeal involves a matter of legislative policy or the board overstepped its

---

59. *See Public Access Shoreline Hawaii v. Hawaii County Planning Comm'n*, 903 P.2d 1246 (Haw. 1995) (considering standing for native Hawaiians in a hearing on an application for a special exception for a hotel).

60. *See infra*, Chapter 13, § 13.01[E] and Chapter 15, § 15.02.

61. *See Simko v. Zoning Bd. of Appeals of the Town of Fairfield*, 538 A.2d 202, 205 (Conn. 1988). *See generally* Annot., *Standing of zoning board of appeals or similar body to appeal reversal of its decision*, 13 A.L.R.4th 1130 (1982) (indicating a split of authority). *See also Valley & Siletz R.R. v. Laudahl*, 681 P.2d 109, 110 (Or. 1984) (reviewing this split).

authority.[62] Since the issue may boil down to a question of whether a municipality has been authorized by state statute to pursue an appeal, an interest in the integrity of the zoning ordinance or the work of the board should prompt courts to grant standing when the enabling legislation is silent or the authority to appeal may be implied.[63]

The opposite rule (denying standing) is that when the BZA or other board exercises an adjudicatory or quasi-judicial function, it is neither a party to the proceedings before it nor a person or party aggrieved by its own decision and so may not appeal it.[64] The legal basis for this result is usually a statute or ordinance providing only that "persons aggrieved" may appeal. Sometimes this result is reinforced by the fact that some other governmental body within the municipality may proceed with an appeal. The underlying assumption of this result is that the board's interest is solely in conducting a fair and impartial hearing of matter before it.

A middle path might be that a board has standing to defend its decision on appeal from a trial court, but out of deference to the judiciary, lacks standing to appeal a reversal of its decision.[65]

[E] Standing in Federal Civil Rights/Zoning Litigation

The issue of standing in federal court depends on whether there is a case or controversy as a constitutional matter. (As can be seen from the previous discussion, there is no such requirement in state courts.) "Article III of the Constitution limits the judicial power of the United States to the resolution of cases and controversies. This limitation is effectuated through the requirement of standing. *** Standing under the Fair Housing Act is co-extensive with the reaches of Article III standing."[66] In the 1970s, civil rights attorneys hoped that federal courts would review the exclusionary effects of municipal zoning on patterns of housing segregation along racial lines. It was not to be.

[1] Round One

In *Warth v. Seldin*,[67] the United States Supreme Court dashed such hopes with standing rules which in practical effect precluded such a review. Not that it slammed the doors to federal court; rather, it refused to widen them. In *Warth*, the plaintiffs

62. Countervailing considerations are that allowing the board standing to appeal casts doubt on the impartiality of the application process, and just as judges do not appeal their own decisions, so in a variance proceeding or quasi-judicial proceedings for a rezoning—often pitting neighbor against neighbor—granting standing may be unseemly.

63. *See Bd. of Supervisors v. Zoning Bd. of Appeals*, 604 S.E.2d 7 (Va. 2004) (collecting cases).

64. *See Speck v. Zoning Bd. of Appeals*, 483 N.E.2d 685 (Ill. 1982).

65. *See Atticks v. Lancaster Twp. Zoning Bd. of Review*, 915 A.2d 713 (Pa. Commwlth. Ct. 2007).

66. *See Human Research and Management Group v. Cty. of Suffolk*, 687 F. Supp. 2d 237, 248, 250 (E.D.N.Y. 2010) (internal quotations and citations omitted).

67. 422 U.S. 490 (1975).

were residents in the Rochester, N.Y., metropolitan area, home builders, and representatives of fair housing organizations. They sued a suburban town (Penfield) in the same area. None of the individual plaintiffs were themselves residents of Penfield, nor did they own any legal or equitable interest in property there. How could they? To show they couldn't afford housing there, or that it was unavailable, was the whole point of the suit. They did attempt to show that the efforts of a third party to build low income housing were nearly futile under the town's current zoning ordinance: 98% of Penfield's land was zoned for single family detached housing.

Not enough, said the United State Supreme Court. The individual plaintiffs' inability to find housing in the town was not caused by the zoning, nor did they show that they could have afforded to live in projects rejected by the town's officials. Neither did the taxpayers of the central city have standing to challenge the Town's zoning. Moreover, the claims of the builders were not couched in terms of the rejection of a specific project. All this meant that if the court were to grant plaintiffs standing, it would be unable to frame appropriate relief.

Thus, in federal court, there must be a claim that the plaintiff would benefit in some specific way from the judicial relief requested. The facts must concern a specific project. *Warth* gives new meaning to the "injury in fact" test for standing. Its requirements for standing in federal court were the equivalent of the federal courts' declining to take up municipal zoning as a law reform project.

While this case may have been intended to have a chilling effect on federal court review of zoning decisions, there are still several categories of plaintiffs who would indeed have standing after *Warth*. Persons who own parcels in town, a housing authority, a potential purchaser prevented from closing, and residents of the town—any of whom are denied development approvals—would still have standing.

[2] Round Two

In *Village of Arlington Heights v. Metropolitan Hous. Dev. Corp.*,[68] the United States Supreme Court again considered the standing question. *Arlington Heights* was a suit brought on both constitutional and statutory grounds. It clarifies *Warth*. The case presented one plaintiff who worked in a village, this time a suburb of Chicago. However, that individual plaintiff lived in Evanston, some twenty miles away, commuting to work in Arlington Heights. Moreover, he testified that he would move into the plaintiff's non-profit, subsidized housing development should it be built.

Arlington Heights was a suburb that had less than one thousand minority residents, out of a population over 70,000. Here, unlike *Warth*, a specific project on a specific site was rejected by the village zoning officials, after the developer had expended several thousand dollars for planning and market studies for its project. The petitioner held a 99 year lease (granted perhaps for purposes of establishing standing) and an agreement to buy a fifteen acre site within the village. The legal title to the site—and

68. 429 U.S. 252 (1977).

that of a larger, surrounding parcel—was held by a religious order, which had given the plaintiff developer a bargain basement price for the fifteen acres so that it could qualify for federal housing subsidies.

The court held that the petitioner's expenditure of planning funds was sufficient to satisfy the injury in fact test for standing in *Warth*. In *Arlington Heights*, the Supreme Court went on to provide a test for evaluating the village's zoning which held that exclusionary effect alone was not the standard against which the ordinance was to be tested; rather that effect was only one factor among six to be used to determine the intent or purpose of the ordinance. The six factors, however, had more to do with a showing of intent than the impact of the ordinance—the latter being only one of the six factors. The other factors were the background of the decision under review, the sequence of events leading to the decision, departures from normal procedures, legislative and administrative history and the record. These last factors mean that circumstantial evidence is admissible to prove a Fair Housing Act claim of discrimination.[69]

As to standing, *Warth* and *Arlington Heights* seem to be marching in different directions. The former seems to shut the door to the federal courthouse, but the latter leaves it ajar for the egregiously injured plaintiff. Taken together, these two cases highlight the importance of bringing actions to challenge the exclusionary effects of municipal zoning under the Fair Housing Act of 1968.[70] The Act allows plaintiffs to bring lawsuits for intentional, explicit racial discrimination and for facially neutral zoning and land use practices that have a discriminatory effect, including the discriminatory impact of a decision on the racial and minority groups protected by the Act.[71]

Federal court standing thus requires, in addition to Article II standing, that (1) a plaintiff show that his claim is premised on an injury to his own legal rights (an injury in fact, as opposed to a third party's), that (2) the claim is not a generalized grievance, and that (3) the claim falls within the zone of interests protected by the statute invoked.[72]

As to the first two prongs, the FHA confers standing on any person "aggrieved" by discriminatory housing practices. The legislative history of the FHA indicates

---

69. *See Inclusive Communities Project, Inc. v. Town of Flower Mound*, 2010 U.S. Dist. LEXIS 64193, *2–3 (E.D. Tex., June 28, 2010) (collecting circuit court and other cases).

70. *See Olson v. Stark Homes, Inc.* 759 F.3d 140 (2d Cir. 2014); *Human Research and Management Group v. Cty. of Suffolk*, 687 F. Supp. 2d 237, 248–50 (E.D.N.Y. 2010) ("It is axiomatic that '[t]here are three Article III standing requirements: (1) the plaintiff must have suffered an injury-in-fact; (2) there must be a causal connection between the injury and the conduct at issue; and (3) the injury must be likely to be redressed by a favorable decision.' *Cooper [v. Postal Service]*, 577 F.3d [479, 489 (2d Cir. 2009)] ....") (internal quotes omitted).

71. *See infra* Chapter 16, § 16.03.

72. *See Bank of America Corp. v. City of Miami, Fla.*, 581 U.S. 189 (2017) (holding that the City of Miami was a "person aggrieved" under *Lexmark Int'l Inc. v. Static Control Components, Inc.*, 572 U.S. 118, 130 (2014)).

that Congress intended to confer standing broadly. Any person with a "distinct and palpable injury" satisfies the "injury in fact" requirement for standing.[73] Here the injury must be not just foreseeable, but "fairly traceable" to the discriminatory practice at issue. Traceability means that the injury be "causally connected" to the alleged discrimination.

The third prong for statutory standing requires a court to determine, using the tools of statutory interpretation, whether a legislatively created cause of action includes a particular plaintiff's claim. Likewise, the "interests" refer to a plaintiff's interest in remedying or avoiding the injury he has or will suffer because of the statutory violations alleged. Are his injuries—or conversely his interests in remedying those injuries—sufficiently related to the statute allegedly violated and likely to be redressed by a favorable decision?[74]

§ 13.02 Exhaustion of Remedies

Plaintiffs may not sue to challenge the validity of an administrative decision until the agency has made a final decision. Nor may they sue to challenge an ordinance or regulation until they have exhausted their administrative remedies, unless (1) the attack is on the general or facial validity of the ordinance, (2) seeking the remedy would be futile, or (3) the remedy is inadequate.[75] Likewise, a failure to appeal a decision is a failure to exhaust.[76]

This doctrine represents deference to the expertise of administrative agencies to gather information pertinent to their decisions as well as to the legislative judgment that the decision is best made by the agency. Even if the decisions required of the agency are traditionally thought of as judicial, the agency can marshal and sift through the evidence before a court hears the case. Conversely, pursuit of an administrative remedy is no waiver of the right to attack an ordinance generally—otherwise the doctrine of exhaustion would be a Catch-22. Without exhausting administrative remedies, there is in a sense no land use decision to appeal.[77] So long as the decision sought is within the municipal zoning administrator or board's jurisdiction, the exhaustion doctrine applies.[78] Likewise, when the relief sought from the decision

---

73. *See Spokeo, Inc. v. Robins*, 578 U.S. 330, 352 (2016) (requiring that an "injury in fact" be concrete and particularized).

74. *See Lujan v. Defenders of Wildlife*, 504 U.S. 555, 560 (1992).

75. *See Poe v. City of Baltimore*, 216 A.2d 707 (Md. 1966); *Holt v. Town of Stonington*, 765 F.3d 127 (2d Cir. 2014) (applying Connecticut law).

76. *See Town of Pittsboro Advisory Plan Comm'n v. Ark Park, LLC*, 26 N.E.3d 110 (Ind. Ct. App. 2015).

77. *See Durland v. San Juan Cty.*, 340 P.3d 191 (Wn. 2014).

78. *See Bragg Hill Corp. v. City of Fredericksburg*, 831 S.E.2d 483 (Va. 2019); *Bellevue-Ochre Point Neighborhood Ass'n v. Preservation Society of Newport Cty.*, 151 A.3d 1223 (R.I. 2017).

is not authorized by either a state statute or municipal ordinance, the doctrine is inapplicable.[79]

As previously noted, three exceptions to the exhaustion doctrine are typically recognized. First, when the constitutional invalidity of a statute or ordinance is put in question by a facial challenge (as opposed to an "as applied" one), some courts have found that there is no need to exhaust administrative remedies beforehand. One rationale for this is that an agency cannot adequately weigh questions about its own authority, particularly when its very jurisdiction is questioned. This is an argument premised on agency bias.

Second, a person will not be forced to use an administrative remedy, when to do so would be futile—when the result is known in advance. Futility might also be shown by repeated and unsuccessful applications.[80] Likewise, when a person or party is not given notice of a zoning decision before the time for an appeal has passed, the exhaustion doctrine does not apply.[81] However, a party may not wait out the time for appeal and then claim futility.[82]

Third and finally, when the remedy that the agency has authority to give is inadequate, the plaintiff need not seek it, but may instead seek a judicial remedy. The inadequacy of the remedy may be shown by the protracted or onerous nature of the remedy, or its expense.

The doctrine in many states is codified as a provision of the Uniform Declaratory Judgment Act. It provides that when a statute dictates a particular form of administrative remedy, that remedy must be pursued before an action under the Act is brought.

The United States Supreme Court turned aside several takings cases in the early 1980s on grounds related to the doctrine. In addition, the imposition of a procedure for issuance of permits to fill or dredge wetlands by the Army Corps of Engineers makes a taking claim premature.[83]

Further holdings of the Supreme Court may also generally affect this doctrine. For example, the *Keystone* holding[84] may mean that the doctrine will be more rigorously enforced against developers. A further example lies in the holding of *First English*.[85] If municipalities risk interim damages when an ordinance is found to be a temporary taking, this increased risk may give municipalities a right either to seek earlier review on the validity of an ordinance, or in states where it is possible, to receive an advisory opinion.

---

79. *See Dembiec v. Town of Holderness*, 105 A.3d 1051 (N.H. 2014) (regarding the doctrine of municipal estoppel).

80. *See Karches v. City of Cincinnati*, 526 N.E.2d 1350, 1355–56 (Ohio 1988).

81. *See Willow Haven on 106th St. LLC v. Nagireddy*, 228 N.E.3d 481 (Ind. Ct. App. 2024).

82. *See Casser v.Twp. of Knowlton*, 118 A.3d 1071 (N.J. Super. 2015).

83. *See United States v. Riverside Bayview Homes, Inc.*, 474 U.S. 121, 127 (1985) ("the very existence of a permit system implies that permission may be granted").

84. *See* Chapter 3, *supra*, § 3.05.

85. *See* Chapter 5, *supra*, § 5.02.

§ 13.03 Ripeness

An issue arising in an administrative agency must be ripe for judicial review. Ripeness is intended to avoid premature adjudication or review of administrative action. Until the agency has made a final decision and its economic impact is felt in a concrete way, courts are presented with abstract or hypothetical issues. They wish to avoid that situation. They do not wish to decide what that impact is until the full extent of the ordinance or regulation has been fixed and the amount of damage caused by it is measurable. Ripeness is thus a doctrine seeking to protect a court from having to decide an issue with less than a fully developed record. For example, when a developer proposes that a municipal legislature adopt and enact an amendment to the municipality's comprehensive plan permitting a project, any judicial challenge by opponents to this amendment, once it is enacted, is subject to a defense on the grounds of ripeness. There has as yet been no application to rezone on the basis of the amendment, and only if the amendment was proposed and adopted in furtherance of a pending application would this challenge be ripe.[86]

A further example of the application of a ripeness defense would be encountered when early purchasers of lots in a subdivision bring a declaratory judgment action ripe for decision just before a developer loses his subdivision permit mid-project by not proceeding within the period of time during which his permit must be used—by a so-called "use it or lose it" provision. That the developer must first resubmit plans for a plat approval does not operate to extinguish the existing homeowners' rights to a declaration of their rights in the open spaces described on the plat on file when they purchased. The point at which a developer acquires a vested right to proceed is the point at which the plaintiffs' declaratory judgment lies.[87] The early lot purchasers would also still have standing before the planning commission to contest the developer's re-subdivision plat plan.

Ripeness is thus generally related to a court's ability to distinguish and define the claim before it, and in that sense, it goes to the court's subject matter jurisdiction. This is an issue that a court may consider *sua sponte*.[88]

[A] United States Supreme Court Opinions on Ripeness

In the early 1980s, the United States Supreme Court granted the writ of certiorari in several cases which, it apparently thought at the time of the vote on the writ, would resolve the issue of whether or not damages were an available remedy for a regulatory taking. In each, up to the time the *First English* opinion was issued in 1987, the court

86. *See Boyds Civic Ass'n v. Montgomery County Council*, 526 A.2d 598, 601 (Md. 1987).
87. *See Hickory Point Partnership v. Anne Arundel County*, 557 A.2d 626, 631 (Md. 1989).
88. *See Villas of Lake Jackson, Ltd. v. Leon County*, 906 F. Supp. 1509 (N.D. Fla. 1995).

found that the case was not ripe for review. Little was learned in these 1981-1987 opinions about the remedy of damages, but much was learned about the issues of ripeness and exhaustion.

First, in *Agins v. City of Tiburon*,[89] Justice Powell held for a unanimous court that because the appellants "have not submitted a plan for development of their property as the ordinances permit, there is as yet no concrete controversy regarding the application of the specific [down]zoning provisions." The court dismissed an as-applied challenge to the provisions and proceeded to uphold the ordinance on the remaining facial challenge. Thus the threshold test of ripeness is the submission of a development plan by the applicant.[90]

In *Williamson County Planning Commission v. Hamilton Bank*,[91] the petitioner had passed the *Agins* threshold. It had submitted a "plan for development." Nonetheless, the Supreme Court held that a taking claim was not ripe for judicial review because there had been no "final decision" on the plan. No such decision is present until the county agencies authorized to administer the development regulations had not only reached a final decision on the plan, but also on any variance available to the applicant. The court also held that a due process violation was also premature because whether the regulation has proceeded "too far" (Holmes' words in *Mahon*) cannot be determined until the impact of the regulations on the plaintiff is known and that impact also cannot be measured until there is a final decision on variances and other available remedies.[92]

In Hamilton Bank, the developer had also not shown that he had sought a remedy available under a state inverse condemnation statute—and the court required that this remedy be sought and refused as well. This second prong, state-litigation requirement of *Hamilton Bank* was overruled by the case of *Knick v. Township of Scott*.[93] It had been criticized since its inception.[94] It had also encouraged many states to enact an inverse condemnation remedy where none existed beforehand. The court said: "We now conclude that the state-litigation requirement imposes an unjustifiable burden on takings plaintiffs, conflicts with the rest of our takings jurisprudence, and must be overruled." It held: "A property owner has an actionable Fifth Amendment takings claim when

89. 447 U.S. 255, 260 (1980).

90. *Christiansen v. Yolo County*, 995 F.2d 161, 164 (9th Cir. 1993) (holding that the development plan element requires "at least one 'meaningful application'" and that the variance element encompasses the applicant's seeking "compensation through the procedures the state has provided for doing so").

91. 473 U.S. 172 (1985).

92. In contrast, in *United States v. Riverside Bayview Homes Inc.*, 474 U.S. 121 (1985), a wetlands case, the Supreme Court said that as to a wetlands fill permit, the availability of a judicial action for inverse condemnation after a denial of a permit is sufficient to deny an injunction (issued on the grounds of a taking) against the wetlands administrator.

93. 588 U.S. 180, 206 (2019) (Chief Justice Roberts writing for the majority) (noted at 133 Harv. L. Rev. 322 (2019)).

94. *Knick, op. cit.*, 588 U.S. at 203. *See also* Ian Fein, *Why Judicial Takings Are Unripe*, 38 Ecology L.Q. 749, 773 (2011).

the government takes his property without paying for it."[95] Thus an owner "may bring his claim in federal court under § 1983 at that time."[96] Although the court stated that the government need not provide compensation in advance of the taking, "[s]o long as the property owner has some way to obtain compensation after the fact,"[97] the government may not enjoin the regulators' activities in the meantime. So injunctions and damages (just compensation here) are different things: the takings clause refers only to a taking and paying "just compensation" as contemporaneous matters. It does not refer to "an available procedure that will result in just compensation" as contemporaneous with a taking. Thus, once a taking occurs, the door to federal court was opened to the plaintiff to bring an action under 42 U.S.C. § 1983.[98]

Knick arose because the Township of Scott enacted an ordinance requiring that all cemeteries, whether public or private, be open and accessible to the general public during daylight hours. The ordinance also authorized the township's code enforcement officer to enter property to determine the existence and location of a cemetery. Rose Mary Knick owned township property on which a small graveyard was located. She sued for declaratory and injunction relief from enforcement of the ordinance. In state court, she did not sue in inverse condemnation, but because after she filed her lawsuit the township stayed any proceedings against her, she could not show the irreparable harm needed for the injunctive remedy. After this, she filed a § 1983 action[99] in federal court, where her takings claim was dismissed without prejudice, the judge instructing her to pursue a state inverse condemnation action as *Williamson County*'s state-litigation requirement then mandated. The Third Circuit affirmed the district Court judge. This set Knick's case up to appeal the requirement's constitutionality to the Supreme Court.

In the wake of *Hamilton Bank* but before *Knick*, many zoning agencies have instituted administrative appeals in order to forestall takings and inverse condemnation claims. Thus, a response to *Hamilton Bank* is for a board to enact procedural regulations stating that "no appeal from any order or decision of the board shall be taken unless the applicant has first made an application for a rehearing." If at the re-hearing, there are new issues considered and new grounds are used for a further decision, then there must a rehearing on the rehearing.[100] And so on. On the other hand, if the board in its rehearing decision were to invoke new law from the state's highest court, no second rehearing would be required; the new case law raises a "vested rights" matter

95. *Knick, op. cit.*, 588 U.S. at 202.

96. *Id.*

97. *Knick* arose in Pennsylvania, and its Constitution provided the plaintiff with an inverse condemnation action. *See* 26 Pa. Cons. Stat. § 502(c).

98. *See infra*, this Chapter, § 13.04. *Knick* does not prevent a plaintiff from bringing a takings claim in state court using federal law; a plaintiff could have done this both before and after *Knick*, but using a state court to litigate a federal claim would raise questions of issue preclusion and estoppel if the plaintiff later brought a takings claim in federal court.

99. In a § 1983 action, the exhaustion of state remedies is not a prerequisite for filing suit.

100. *See Dziama v. City of Portsmouth*, 669 A.2d 217, 219 (N.H. 1995) (requiring a second application for a rehearing on new issues).

with which a court is better equipped to deal than is the board—and the applicant's judicial appeal should proceed.

After *Knick*, the Supreme Court's sidelining of state inverse takings procedures may turn land-use agencies and regulators (unless they can know in advance whether a regulation constitutes a taking) into law breakers before they know it. It is one thing to require finality before a takings claim is ripe; it is another to ignore the completeness of a claim developed in a state proceeding. The text of the Fifth Amendment's takings clause just requires a swift and practical route to just compensation; it does not require that the award of that compensation be precisely contemporaneous with a taking. Contemporaneousness may be conceptually possible, but impossible as a practical matter. The Supreme Court left it to lower courts to resolve practical issues involving the provision of just compensation. Chief Justice Roberts may have been right to say that the takings clause, like many of the other first ten Amendments to the Constitution, should be self-executing, but he did not say how this should be achieved. If *Knick* ends up diverting some of the flow of takings cases into federal courts, there is no telling how those federal decisions will square with those of state courts. Future conflicting state and federal cases may muddy the law of takings further.

Knick did not displace *Hamilton Bank*'s holding that a takings claim becomes ripe only after the relevant decision maker has made a final decision on an owner or developer's land use application.[101] The *Knick* case may force further elaboration of finality in land use law. To a further discussion of this remaining holding this text now turns.

[B] Premature Takings Claims

With regard to a takings claim, the claim remains premature until the impact of the ordinance is known.[102] After *Hamilton Bank*, the Supreme Court requires an owner or developer do three things:

(1) prepare and submit a development plan,

(2) obtain a final decision on the plan, and

(3) seek and be refused any available variances or other remedies mitigating the impact of the alleged taking,

before seeking federal court review.[103]

101. In this regard, *see Pakdel v. City & County of San Francisco*, 594 U.S. 474 (2021) (holding that a refusal to grant an exemption of an ordinance is a final decision); *South Grande View Dev. Co. v. City of Alabaster, Ala.*, 1 F.4th 1299 (11th Cir. 2021).

102. *See Smithfield Concerned Citizens v. Town of Smithfield*, 907 F.2d 239 (1st Cir. 1990).

103. One tactic for owners is to bring a facial challenge to the ordinance, claiming it invalid upon enactment, alleging arbitrary and capricious action in enacting it, challenging its terms before they are applied to any particular development, and invoking the idea that the injury was done to the plaintiff at the time of enactment. The disadvantage here is that the Supreme Court imposes a heavy burden of proof on such challengers. *See Keystone Bituminous Coal Ass'n v. DeBenedictis*, 480 U.S. 470 (1987)

A year later, the Supreme Court again found another applicant's takings claim not ripe.[104] This case further defined a "final decision" as a "final and authoritative determination of the type and intensity of development legally permitted on the subject property." It also noted that "valuable use" might still be made of the land from continuing its prior, agricultural use (the trial court's conclusion) and that "valuable residential development was open" to it (a state appellate court conclusion).[105] Thus revision of the development plan, after the refusal of all variances, seems to be a fourth requirement for a showing of ripeness. However, the court said that the final decision requirement does not force an owner to "pursue a development application through piecemeal litigation or unfair procedures."[106] This raises the question of how many applications and plan revisions are needed to insure the ripeness of the claim. In this regard, *Penn Central* found a takings claim ripe after the submission and rejection of two development applications.[107] Likewise, the rejection of five applications was sufficient predicate for getting a compensation claim to a jury in *City of Monterey v. Del Monte Dunes at Monterey*.[108] So perhaps a reasonable number of applications—between two and five—must be filed before a decision can be considered final for ripeness purposes. In any event, requiring more than one gives a municipality the opportunity to correct its mistakes before a takings claim ripens.

A year later, the court found that one application and rejection might ripen a takings compensation claim. It held that when an owner must deal (as with development of wetlands) with many agencies at the federal, state, and municipal level, and one agency at any level indicates that no development may take place, that decision may be treated as final, ripening the owner's takings claim.[109] In *Palazzolo*, not being able to fill the wetland was regarded as tantamount to being told no to placing houses on it; thus the owner did not have to further ripen his claim by applying for subdivision and building permissions. "Where the state agency charged with enforcing a challenged land use regulation entertains an application from an owner and its denial of the application makes clear the extent of the development permitted, and neither the agency nor a reviewing state court has cited non-compliance with reasonable state law exhaustion and pre-permit processes . . . , federal ripeness rules do not require the submission of further and futile applications with other agencies."[110] The court further held that, for purposes of asserting a takings claim, purchasing owners acquired everything that their predecessors in interest had, including their takings claim.[111]

(discussed in Chapter 3, *supra*). So a facial challenge is unlikely to succeed, given the presumption of validity and the "fairly debatable" standard used to review such claims.

104. *See Macdonald, Sommer & Frates v. Yolo County*, 477 U.S. 340, 348 (1986).

105. *Id.* at 351–52, n.8.

106. *Id.* at 350, n. 7.

107. *See Penn Central Transp. Co. v. City of New York*, 438 U.S. 104, 116 & n. 17 (1978).

108. 526 U.S. 687, 702 (1999).

109. *See Palazzolo v. Rhode Island*, 533 U.S. 606 (2001).

110. *Id.* (also holding, on the merits of the takings claim made, that "post-enactment purchasers" could ripen a takings claim).

111. State courts had been split on this issue. *See* Stephen Abraham, *Windfall or Windmills: The Right of a Property Owner to Challenge Land Use Regulations (A Call to Critically Examine the Meaning of* Lucas*)*, 13 J. Land Use & Envtl. L. 161, 165 (1997) (collecting the cases).

Decisions about the meaning of "futility" become important here. Futility means being forced to pursue piece-meal, procedurally unfair, time-consuming (involving excessive administrative delays, to the point that the parcel loses its value), or pointless (when the agency has no authority to grant the permission) development applications. There is some warrant in the prevailing case law for each of these four meanings.

[C] Open Questions

What is the future of the ripeness doctrine? Consider that if a landowner wants to develop a 10 acre tract and applicable regulations allow him 10 houses on one acre lots, and the municipality downzones his tract, requiring a minimum of two acres per lot, the development value of the tract is decreased by 50%. *Knick* suggests that when the downzoning ordinance is enacted, the enactment is a "final decision" under *Hamilton Bank*. The owner still has a right to develop, but under a traditional *Penn Central* analysis, he has no takings claim. Suppose, however, that finality is what gives rise to a claim: then the diminishment of that right is compensable upon the enactment of the ordinance. Whether this is so, is an open question. The plaintiff in *Knick* did not challenge *Hamilton Bank*'s finality holding. Would the owner have to apply for a rezoning before bringing a takings claim? Again, the answer is unclear, the issue an open one.

Thus, the reach of the holdings in *Knick* and *Hamilton Bank*, as well as *Yolo County*, and *Palazzolo* is unclear in two respects. First, as in the hypothetical in the last paragraph, it is unclear what types of mitigating zoning decisions an owner must seek. For instance, in addition to seeking a variance under *Hamilton Bank*, a developer may have to seek a conditional rezoning, striking a deal to mitigate his takings claim. Before the deal is struck, a municipality might regard the claim as premature.[112] Second, judicial invalidation or municipal withdrawal of a contested regulation might meet *Hamilton Bank*'s final decision requirement; that would convert a temporary takings claim under *First English* into a permanent takings claim, to which an owner could respond with a § 1983 action.

112. *See Electro-Tech, Inc. v. H.F. Campbell, Inc.*, 445 N.W.2d 61 (Mich. 1989), *cert. denied*, 493 U.S. 1021 (1990).

§ 13.04 Section 1983 Federal Due Process Actions

Hamilton Bank and *Knick* recognized that state procedures by which the invalidity of a zoning or subdivision ordinance can be tested involve a declaratory judgment action.[113] This recognition invokes the federal ripeness doctrine.[114] The federal analog to these state procedures is a federal cause of action based on 42 U.S.C. § 1983. A § 1983 action is for persons who have been "deprived of any rights, privileges, or immunities secured by the Constitution and laws" of the United States by a person or entity acting under color of "any statute, ordinance, regulation, or custom."[115] Section 1983 is "not itself a source of substantive rights."[116] It instead provides "a method of vindicating rights elsewhere conferred."[117] It is viewed often as a supplementary remedy.

Municipalities are entities that may be found liable under § 1983.[118] A plaintiff using § 1983 must show that a protected right was violated by the execution of a municipality's policy or custom made by its legislators or officials. The municipality's agents or employees may not be held individually liable under a theory of *respondeat superior*. Instead, a municipality may be liable for a constitutional tort—the deprivation of a constitutional right—when the execution of an ordinance or policy occurred pursuant to a municipal law, custom or policy.[119] Liability may arise for a single decision by a municipal entity.[120]

Section 1983 does not require that a plaintiff exhaust state judicial remedies before pursuing an action under it. It permits review of any state and municipal action, taken under "color of law," that deprived the plaintiff of some federal constitutional right.

That right might be, as we have seen, the denial of just compensation under the takings clause. However, in the land use area, it might also be a due process clause right to be free of arbitrary governmental action or inaction. A due process claim is

---

113. *Hamilton Bank* has been applied to federal administrative actions too. *See Preseault v. I.C.C.*, 494 U.S. 1 (1990) (holding that because the federal tort claims act provides holders of real property interests with a remedy for obtaining just compensation, a taking claim against an I.C.C. order was premature when asserted before the holder exhausts the act's remedy).

114. Before such a claim is brought, the claim is unripe; after it is brought, and lost, then *res judicata* and collateral estoppel will bar further actions; if won, further actions may be pointless, except to the degree that tort claims would provide significantly more than a takings claim. *See also City of Monterey v. Del Monte Dunes at Monterey*, 526 U.S. 687 (1999) (holding that a jury trial is available in § 1983 claim cases). This may make federal claims more desirable because takings and inverse condemnation claims in state courts are generally held to raise matters of law not going to a jury.

115. 42 U.S.C.A. § 1983.

116. *See Albright v. Olivier*, 510 U.S. 266, 271 (internal quotes omitted).

117. *Id.*

118. *See Robinson v. City of Clarksville*, 673 S.W.3d 556, 576 (Tenn. Ct. App. 2023) (citing *Monell v. Dep't of Social Services of N.Y.C.*, 436 U.S. 658 (1978).

119. *See Robinson, op, cit.*

120. *Id.*

ripe when due process is denied. That means that there must have been some procedure that was arbitrary, so ripeness doctrine applies, but not to the point of requiring repeated applications and plans. A due process claim involves a legitimate right or claim of entitlement to a governmental benefit, typically a permit of some type. Litigation under § 1983 involves the claim of arbitrary action taken under authority of municipal regulations, really a misapplication of a regulation, that violated a plaintiff's substantive due process rights, depriving him of a land use to which he was entitled. Thus § 1983 actions are best regarded as "as applied" challenges.

In these federal court actions, as a foundational or threshold issue, some federal circuits focus on the right at issue, while others focus on the governmental action at issue.[121] In the first category, federal courts require a plaintiff to have a "property right to a permit." These courts define that right so that it is present—or "cognizable" under § 1983—only when the discretion of the municipality is so limited that, absent arbitrariness, the issuance of the permit at issue is certain.[122] Ownership of property alone is an insufficient right and no unilateral expectation that a permit will issue suffices either,[123] even if state law seems to indicate issuance is likely: it is federal common law that is used here. More than a unilateral expectation of a favorable decision in a land use case is necessary. The § 1983 plaintiff's pleadings must disclose that the defendant municipality "lacks all discretion to deny the issuance of a permit or to withhold its approval."[124] A land use ordinance giving an owner or developer the right or opportunity to seek a permit or approval is not the same as a legitimate entitlement to a permit.[125]

Some federal circuits not only require that a right to the permit be involved, but also require, and generally focus on, municipal actions that "shock the conscience of the court."[126] Here the action challenged must be truly irrational, irrational to a point beyond which an administrative agency would be restrained. Merely a violation of state or local law does not qualify.

These requirements represent rules of judicial prudence, insuring that federal courts do not become a super zoning board, merely providing an extra layer of review for land use regulatory decisions.

Yet another federal circuit has provided § 1983 review when political motivation or a personal financial motive of a municipal decision-maker had been shown.[127] This

121. *See* Eric Jenkins, *Challenging Land Use Actions under Section 1983: Washington After* Mission Springs, Inc. v. City of Spokane, 74 Wash. L. Rev. 853 (1999) (reviewing contrasting federal cases and Washington state cases on this issue).

122. *See Scratch Golf, LLC v. Beaufort Cty.*, 2024 U.S. App. LEXIS 3361 (4th Cir. 2024); *Yale Auto Parts v. Johnson*, 758 F.2d 54, 59 (2d Cir. 1985).

123. *See Gardner v. Baltimore Mayor & City Council*, 969 F.2d 63 (4th Cir. 1992) (the 4th Circuit joining 2d, 10th, and 11th Circuit cases so holding).

124. *See Scratch Golf, LLC v. Beaufort Cnty.*, 2024 U.S. App. LEXIS 3361, *3–4 (Feb. 13, 2024).

125. *Id.*

126. *See Creative Environments, Inc. v. Estabrook*, 680 F.2d 822, 833 (1st Cir. 1982).

127. *Compare DeBlasio v. Zoning Bd. of Adjustment*, 53 F.3d 592, 601 (3d Cir. 1995), *with Breneric Associates v. City of Del Mar*, 81 Cal. Rptr. 2d 324, 334–35 (Cal. App. Ct. 1998) (criticizing *Blasio*).

focus on the governmental decision downplays the role of the plaintiff's right to the permit, but only one federal circuit has used it.

No matter what prudential requirement is involved, all these approaches are intended to restrict access to federal court in land use cases so that constitutional challenges are not available on an indiscriminate basis to those denied land use permits in state courts. *Knick* did not displace these three prudential requirements, but did indicate that direct access to federal courts was available to takings claim plaintiffs. It also indicated that federal courts could hear the claim using state inverse condemnation law.[128] This more direct access to federal courts will likely make § 1983 cases in involving takings claims much less frequent in the future, leaving § 1983 to police municipal due process claims.

128. *See Sevilliers v. Texas*, 144 S. Ct. 938 (2024).

Chapter 14
Subdivision Regulations, Impact Fees, Linkage Fees, and Exactions

The subdivision of land requires an application for an administrative action having lasting consequences for the land affected. The forum for such an application is usually the municipal planning commission. In such an agency, the impact of the city and regional planning process is greater than it would be in the other municipal forums discussed previously. The objective of the subdivision process is to fit the parcels of land created into a larger urban form. So, first, a word about urban design.

§ 14.01 Urban Forms

The American pattern of urbanization is a unique one. Our townscapes—whether a New England village, a township, a mining town, a company town, or a utopian community—have often been a "product." It consists first of a core, the oldest part of the city or town, often with a street pattern heavily influenced by the topography of the site. The core may have been the confluence of several roads or paths, with a spine street centering the neighborhood. In New England the core was a central square known as the green or common. It may also have been the location where two forms of transportation met, as with a town on the fall line of a river, requiring that cargo be unloaded from ships there for overland shipment. Starting in the early nineteenth century, the urban pattern emerging around this core was often of rectangular, equally-sized blocks, laid out in a grid, with lots in each block further "subdividing" the landscape.

Most of the colonies of European countries in North America started as planned townscapes, but most had lost their overall planned qualities by the middle of the nineteenth century when a street grid was all that municipalities could do to control the pace of urban development. Starting in the 1890s, however, during the City Beautiful movement, boulevards were superimposed on the grid. In the 1920s and 1930s, as off-shoots of this movement, subdivisions began it be laid out in a curvilinear pattern—having winding streets on very large blocks. Such subdivisions signaled the creation of ever larger, often self-contained, developments, with a shopping center attached or nearby. Whole new towns were built in the 1960s and 1970s, and city planners extensively used cul-de-sacs here to minimize drive-by traffic and promote privacy. They also used clustered land uses permitted by municipal zoning so that large tracts would have open spaces amid the development.

It would be difficult to get a cul-de-sac subdivision approved today. Urban forms wax and wane in popularity with developers, and planning commissions have different concerns from one generation to the next. Today, the fire department would object to having their trucks down a dead-end street.

Whether city or suburban, land uses in subdivisions were first governed by private agreements among the lot owners. Usually such agreements were a series of covenants and easements. Only in the late 1920s would public land-use controls, including subdivision regulations, become widely accepted by municipal governments. In the Standard City Planning Enabling Act, the city planning commission was authorized to approve all subdivision plats whenever it had first adopted a "major street plan" (an Official Map or grid).[1] The Act's emphasis was on coordinating the streets of the subdivision with its street plan.[2]

§ 14.02 The Subdivision Process

Subdivision is the process of dividing a tract of land into a number of parcels. When the number of parcels is of a given number (varying from two to five usually), the subdivider must comply with the requirements of the local subdivision control regulations. Their primary purpose is to ensure that parcels are provided with public services like streets, curbs, and water and sewer lines by the time their developer sells the parcels to homeowners. They also establish a record description of the lots by pinpointing them on an official and recorded map—called a "plat"—which once recorded, is maintained as a public record and may be used for the purposes of referencing a parcel in further conveyances of the title to it. Plats also serve as a record of the location and extent of both underground and above-ground utility lines. Engineering and planning firms are often involved in their creation in order to ensure that the improvements provided meet the professional standards required by regulation. The subdivider is often a home builder and developer as well, but sometimes is not; sometimes he is a person specializing in this aspect of the land development process.[3]

Authority for regulating the subdivision process is grounded in the police power[4] and is found in state codes, modeled often on the 1928 Standard City Planning

---

1. *See* Standard City Planning Enabling Act § 13 (U.S. Dep't of Commerce 1928).

2. *Id.* § 14. The origin of this interest can be seen in *Bauman v. Ross*, 167 U.S. 548 (1897) (justifying the validity of subdivision regulations to the maintenance of streets). *See also Trawalter v. Schaefer*, 179 S.W.2d 765 (Tex. 1944) (upholding subdivision regulations because they enabled tax officials to assess newly platted parcels).

3. *See* D. Listokin & C. Walker, The Subdivision and Site Plan Handbook 129–66 (1989).

4. *See Mansfield & Swett, Inc. v. West Orange*, 198 A. 225 (N.J. 1938), cited approvingly in *Brazer v. Mountainside*, 262 A.2d 857 (N.J. 1970) (Hall, J.).

Enabling Act, § 13–14. Statutory authority is often the first issue in assessing the validity of any particular requirement imposed in the course of the process. Typically the planning commission or board is the municipal agency charged with administering the process. As a precondition to exercising this regulatory authority, the commission formulates at least a street plan for the municipality.

Up to the 1950s, subdivision regulations generally dealt with on-site improvements—that is, improvements constructed within the bounds of the plat. Regulations requiring provisions of off-site improvements became more common in the 1960s—that is, provision was made for the addition of parks, schools, libraries, and recreational facilities, the demand for which was generated by the subdivision. The off-site impacts of a subdivision—particularly storm water runoff, flooding, and erosion—were regulated as well. In the 1970s and 1980s, provision was also made for other types of public facilities—e.g., off-site roads, improvements to nearby intersections, firehouses—requiring developers to pay for or build facilities that would otherwise, after the fact, have to be built or installed by the municipality. As the list of developer-financed and built improvements expanded, it was frequently remarked that many items were being added for which the municipality would otherwise have to tax its residents, and that the cost of these items was being hidden in the price of the new housing in the subdivision. For municipalities with no inherent taxing authority, however, this trend was reinforced by their inability to formulate a program of capital improvements and budgets.

Subdivision of land is different from either a boundary line adjustment, a partial foreclosure on land given as security for a loan, or a testamentary disposition of land.[5] Express statutory exemptions from local regulations are often made for these three types of transfers.

Sometimes problems arise that involve the definition of a subdivision. So long as the title to land underlying a development is not affected, there is no "division of a parcel into two or more parcels" (a common definition of a subdivision) and so no subdivision. For example, as noted in the prior paragraph, the adjustment of parcel boundary lines is not a subdivision.[6] By the same token, adding additional acreage to an existing parcel is not a subdivision. The dispositive inquiry is whether there is a "division" of land into the required number of parcels. The underlying land might, in a further example, continue to be owned by an owners' association established as a non-profit corporation. Thus, more generally, in the majority of the cases addressing this issue, and absent a statute on the situation, no zoning or subdivision approval is

5. *See, e.g.*, *In re Estate of Tettemer*, 26 Pa. D. & C. 3d 745 (1981), *aff'd*, 458 A.2d 287 (Pa. Super. Ct. 1983), *but overruled by legislation* 53 Pa. Cons. Stat. Ann. § 10107 (making a petition by heirs or devisees for distribution of land a subdivision); *see also Hyler v. Town of Blue Hill*, 570 A.2d 316 (Me. 1990) (holding that dividing land into seven parcels granted to family members was an evasion of subdivision regulations); *Mills v. Town of Eliot*, 955 A.2d 258, 260, n. 1 (Me. 2008) (discussing a statutory exemption for "family subdivisions"); Va. Code § 15.2-2244 (exempting the creation of one lot "for the purpose of sale or gift to a member of the immediate family . . . of beneficiaries of a trust.").

6. *See 500 North Ave., LLC v. Planning Comm'n of the Town of Strafford*, 235 A.3d 526, 533 (Conn. Ct. App. 2020).

required to establish a condominium regime.[7] Such regimes are established by statute in all states and involve a change of ownership and of the identity of the owner, but not a change of use. Even when the statute defined a subdivision as a "division or conversion of one parcel into two or more parcels," it is still to be taken as an alteration in use, not a change in ownership.[8]

A more functional definition of a subdivision might be "the division of land for the purposes of a sale for building purposes, the creation of land lots, or a re-subdivision." An owner's development of a mobile home park, in which the pads for each home are to be leased to their holders, is a subdivision under this definition. The issue is not whether the pads are sold or leased, but whether there is an overall intent to undertake a development that requires public scrutiny to determine whether it is in harmony with its environs, even if the pad is not clearly a "land lot." It is close enough. A municipality will interpret the regulatory definition liberally in order to carry out its purpose. Thus, a parcel owner's counsel should be cautious enough to investigate obtaining a subdivision permit before undertaking a development.[9] This investigation is prudent because of the penalties associated with developing without first subdividing—the most common of which to render illegal and thereby void the sales or leases of the individual parcels.

Often an owner of a large parcel wishes to subdivide it piece-meal. The fact that the first division of land is for new parcels that are not adjacent or contiguous is no bar to requiring a subdivision permit. Likewise, the first division need not be for the use made of the remaining parcel—as, for example, where a farmer offers to sell one corner of his farm for a gas station and another corner for a convenience store. The fact that the parcels to be created are not being sold as an integrated development or are not contiguous, is no bar to finding that a subdivision is involved. There are planning concerns even in such a scattered development. Thus, there need be no express residential, integration, or contiguity requirement in the definition of a subdivision for a court to find subdivision regulations applicable.

Typically, subdivision regulations are today seldom restricted to horizontal residential subdivisions.[10] Likewise, it is common to define a subdivision as the division of a tract "being developed as part of an overall plan or as a whole" or "into contiguous lots or parcels." Again, seeking an advisory opinion of the code or enforcement official is advisable. Often too, to make these piece-meal parcelization problems easier to resolve, only so many parcels may be created within a given period of time—say, five years—and to meet this situation, the definition of a subdivision may be "the division of a parcel of land into three or more lots within any five year period."

7. *See In re Lowe*, 666 A.2d 1178 (Vt. 1995) (collecting similar cases to this effect from Florida, Illinois, Maryland, Massachusetts, New Hampshire, New Jersey, North Carolina, Ohio, Rhode Island, and South Carolina).

8. *Id.*

9. *See Sandoval County Board of Comm'rs v. Ruiz*, 893 P.2d 482 (N.M. App. Ct. 1995).

10. *See Appeal of Town of Amherst*, 294 A.3d 1122 (N.H. 2023) (involving a condominium subdivision).

When a definition requires a "division of land into three or more parcels," the remaining parcel must be considered: thus, splitting off two parcels, leaving one larger one remaining in an owner's hands, will likely violate the definition and require subdivision review. However, if the allegedly violative conveyance were of land contiguous to the second parcel to adjust the boundary between the two parcels, no subdivision permission would be needed. A conveyance for the purpose of adjusting the boundaries of the prior conveyance does not count and is not a subdivision. The regulations are not intended to regulate matters pertaining to the title to the property. Likewise, if a conveyance was made, not to adjust a boundary, but so that the owner of a parcel already subdivided without violating the regulations has space to build a garage for the house, no subdivision permission would be needed. Most multi-division definitions implicitly require independent conveyances, and are not triggered by less. Building the garage involves instead a conveyance to adjust the development on the parcel previously conveyed and, while it does involve a title matter, it also involves an accessory use for a previous development. So long as the building is an accessory one, and not the establishment of a separate land use, a subdivision has not been created. (The zoning ordinance may contain separate requirements for accessory uses.[11])

Sometimes a less than fee conveyance creates definitional problems. Suppose that the owner of Blackacre splits his land in two, conveying each half to two persons, one of whom mortgages his land and then defaults on the mortgage, so that the mortgage lender takes possession of so much of the land as is needed to satisfy the mortgage debt. If both half owners are improving their land, building permits for both halves may be revoked when that land comes into the possession of the lender. When the subdivision regulation defines a subdivision as:

> the division of a tract or parcel of land into three (3) or more lots within any five (5) year period after the enactment of this ordinance, whether the sub-division is accomplished by sale, lease, development, improvements, buildings, or otherwise; the first division of a tract or parcel creates two lots, and the subsequent division of either creates a third lot, by whomever accomplished.

the issue is (when all these facts occur within a five year period) whether the execution of the mortgage is the third "subdivision" that violates the regulation. It is certainly the creation of an "interest" in the property—that is, a lien that a mortgagee might foreclose—and so is arguably the third division of the title to the original property known as Blackacre.[12] However, the plain meaning of the word "division" should provide a basis for rejecting this argument.

---

11. *See Catania v. Glastonbury Planning & Zoning Commission*, 1995 Conn. Super. LEXIS 3658 (Dec. 19, 1995).

12. *See Town of Orrington v. Pease*, 660 A.2d 919, 920–20 (Me. 1995) (holding that it is); *see also Baldiga v. Board of Appeals*, 482 N.E.2d 809, 812, n. 4 (Mass. App. Ct. 1985) (describing the process of checker-boarding).

Suppose that, instead of mortgaging his half of the land, its owner executes a revocable license to allow a fourth person to place a mobile home there. The revocable nature of the license and its placement does not inoculate the parties from the requirements of the regulation, but the classification of the mobile home may be determinative here. If it is not classified as real property because it is not attached to the realty, then it is personal property and so the license creates no further division in the parcel. The mobile home might be best regarded as a interim or holding action by the owner (similar to placing a FEMA trailer on a Katrina-damaged parcel), not a further development of the parcel.

The underlying lesson here is, check the applicable subdivision-enabling act for its list of exemptions for: a partition judgment given in kind for concurrent interest holders, cemetery lots, mobile home parks, the division of land for agriculture, re-subdivision, and the division of land where all parcels abut an existing street. All of these situations have been the subject of an exemption. Further, some situations, otherwise regulated, are given expedited treatment by the planning commission, typically by authorizing review of only one plat (thus not requiring the filing of a preliminary plat with the commission). On the other end of the scale, a few jurisdictions require a planning commission with subdivision regulations to review and approve all real estate transfers. Minnesota and Oklahoma have such statutes.

§ 14.03 The Substance of Regulation

Subdivision regulations impose a different type of control on a developer than does zoning. Zoning regulations impose restrictions on the use of real property. They are negative in that respect. Subdivision regulations are applied when land is to be divided into parcels and developed. They require the developer to dedicate land and to install the infrastructure on the parcel which will be needed for the provision of public services—curbs and gutters, streets, grading, utilities, and water and sewer lines of a certain quality—and, where necessary, off-site improvements as well.

Their purpose is to insure that the services will be adequate (as where a sewer line of a certain diameter must be installed), of a prescribed quality (using, say, granite, not concrete, curbing), and mesh with existing public facilities (as where the streets of a subdivision must meet the existing street system in a grid or other pattern without dog-legs or abrupt turns).

Thus, such regulations provide for capacity, quality, and uniformity of a municipality's infrastructure. Imagine that it were otherwise: imagine a municipality where sewer lines were four inches in diameter on one block and eight on another; where the pipes broke after ten years on one block, but lasted a century on another; and where pipes could not be linked in a single system. Imagine a street system in which forty foot wide roads suddenly narrowed to thirty, where curbs were installed on some blocks but not others, and all, for no apparent reason. Protection of public health and safety surely underlie such regulations. For this reason, subdivision regulations are mandatory and typically require that subdividers contribute or dedicate these road, water, and sewer facilities to the municipality.

Specific regulations refer to (1) the content, form, and format of subdivision plats as well as the procedure for approving the application seeking their approval in (typically) a multi-stage process; (2) the regulation of the layout, materials, and dimensions of streets within the project and abutting parcels appearing on the plat;[13] (3) the regulation of parcel sizes, although this is also a subject for zoning regulations as well;[14] (4) the regulation of utility lines and facilities for the subdivided parcels; (5) the regulation of the placement of future improvements on the subdivided parcels; (6) the conservation of existing features, natural and man-made, on those parcels; and (7) requirements that land, or a cash payment equivalent, be dedicated to a public use or fund the provision of parks, playgrounds, schools, and jogging, bicycle, and nature trails.

The approval of subdivisions is generally a conditional one. Conditions are imposed reflecting the specific regulations of the ordinance. Thereafter, upon judicial review of the imposed conditions, the issue is generally whether they are authorized by the ordinance *or ultra vires* its authority.[15]

The process of subdivision plan review is divided into several stages: (1) review of the plan, (2) review of the preliminary plat map, and (3) review of the final map. Thus, subdivision approvals proceed in a designated order. An owner or developer does not, may not, move to the next stage until receiving approval at the prior stage.[16] With that approval in hand, the developer proceeds to the next stage, unless the municipal legislature or a court stays the process. The developer or owner (or his or her counsel) must appear at several public hearings of the planning commission that may be involved in the approval of any plat. Inconsistency between the plats and plans presented in prior stages does not bar issuance of later approvals.[17] In some jurisdictions, a final plat must be approved or denied within a time certain or else be deemed approved.[18] That time may run either from the approval of the prior step or from the filing of the initial application.

Suppose an owner applies for subdivision approval for five acres (half of the acreage to be used for one land use and the other half for another use). Both uses are

13. Whether a platted parcel "abuts" a street has been the subject of litigation: may the abutting street be a paper one, or must it be paved? May a parcel at the end of a *cul de sac* be considering abutting the dead-end street? Jurisdictions can differ on the answers to such questions. *See Kerlin v. Planning and Zoning Comm'n of the Town of Greenwich*, 304 A.3d 148, 164 (Conn. Ct. App. 2023).

14. The typical rule is that when the subdivision regulations are not explicit on the subject of parcel size, etc., the regulations of the underlying land use district control.

15. *See, e.g., Symes Dev. & Permitting LLC v. Ferguson*, 2021 Mass. LCR LEXIS (Mass. Land Ct., June 23, 2021) (invalidating conditions requiring unbuilt parcels to be reserved for three years pending purchase by municipality for affordable housing).

16. *See Wolf v. Planning Bd. of Prince George's Cty.*, 306 A.3d 763, 769 (Md. App. Ct. 2023).

17. *Id.* at 771.

18. *See Wesolowski v. City of Broadview Heights Planning Comm'n*, 140 N.E.3d 545, 553 (Ohio 2019) (state statute requiring approval within 30 days upheld).

permitted in the use district in which the subdivision is to be located. The planning commission in reviewing the subdivision plan has regulatory authority "to require reasonable changes in the applicant's proposed subdivision plan." The owner presents a site plan and a traffic study, but the commission suggests that the traffic generated is excessive and rejects the subdivision. What the commission has done may be beyond its authority, on the theory that it has the duty to propose changes in the road width and vehicle access that would address its traffic safety concerns. The statutory duty to make reasonable changes may mean that the commission may only react to the applicant's proposals with conditions that bring the application into compliance, and also that it has an affirmative duty to propose such conditions where compliance is possible. The latter proposition is particularly appropriate when the use proposed is an otherwise permitted one—a land use permitted as of right in the location proposed.[19] More generally, the commission has no authority to use the subdivision regulations to deny a use that is permitted in the underlying zoning use district.[20]

In the same vein, suppose a planning commission denied an owner's subdivision application because building on the land would require too much fill on the land's (say) 12 degree slopes, require too many trees to be cut down, affect the drainage in the neighborhood, and result in heavy traffic, so that approval of the application would not be in the public interest. The commission has steep-slope regulations for the use of fill on slopes over (say) 15 degrees, the preservation of trees, the slope and contours of drains, and traffic engineering standards for traffic control. In this situation, the board is vulnerable upon any appeal of its decision. When it has specific regulations to apply, as with its 15 degree threshold for the regulation of fill, it is an abuse of its authority to ignore those express standards and decide a case before it on public interest or general welfare grounds. Deciding what the general welfare requires is a legislative function and the commission's doing so oversteps the proper bounds of administrative action.[21] When applicable, only those express regulations and standards in the local subdivision ordinance, not general purpose clauses or general standards in the ordinance or its enabling act, may be used by the commission as grounds for its actions.[22]

---

19. *See Sheetz v. Frederick Planning Commission*, 665 A.2d 327 (Md. App. Ct. 1995) (finding such a statute to be proactive, not reactive, because the planning commission does not have the authority to review the use classification).

20. *See Cty. of Chesterfield v. Tetra Assocs. LLC*, 689 S.E.2d 647, 650 (Va. 2010).

21. *See Pizzo Mantin Group v. Township of Randolph*, 645 A.2d 89 (N.J. 1993).

22. Examples of this principle are widespread. *See, e.g., PTL, LLC v. Chisago Cty. Bd. of Comm'rs*, 656 N.W.2d 567 (Minn. Ct. App. 2003); *Hixon v. Walker Cty.*, 468 S.E.2d 744 (Ga. 1996).

§ 14.04 Vesting an Entitlement to Approval

Even when the subdivision process is drawn out and time-consuming, the filing of a plan or preliminary plat is insufficient to vest a right to develop, absent a statute to the contrary.[23] If the preliminary plat is approved, the right to have approval of a final plat may vest in some jurisdictions,[24] particularly when a substantial amount of money has been spent in gaining that approval.[25] In a majority of jurisdictions, however, an amendment to the subdivision regulations is effective against a pending application, unless the amendment is made in bad faith.[26] Thus an amendment to the zoning map that prohibits some uses that the applicant intends for the subdivision effectively eliminates those uses on the plat. A municipality may amend its land use regulations during the pendency of a subdivision application, even when the amendment is prompted by a particular application. Enacting such an amendment is a legislative act, and so long as it is consistent with the enabling act, a municipality is free to amend its regulations. Its motives are irrelevant. Further, the amendment is entitled to the same presumption of validity attaching to the original regulation and map.[27] Moreover, an illegal plat is void, no matter that it received a final approval or was recorded.[28]

In some jurisdictions, statutory immunity from zoning changes is granted to subdivision applicants during the pendency of their proposals.[29] This immunity is typically based on the interpretation of a statute, but state codes trend the other way, providing no such immunity when the zoning change is pending in the municipality's legislature at the time the initial subdivision application is filed.[30]

---

23. *See In re McCormick Management Co.*, 547 A.2d 1319 (Vt. 1988); *Boutet v. Planning Bd.*, 253 A.2d 53 (Me. 1969) (as to a preliminary plat).

24. *See In re Paynter 2-Lot Subdivision*, 996 A.2d 219, 223-24 (Vt. 2010) (noting that this is a minority rule); *see also Youngblood v. Bd. of Supervisors of San Diego Cty.*, 586 P.2d 556 (Cal. 1978).

25. *See AWL Power, Inc. v. City of Rochester*, 813 A.2d 517 (N.H. 2002).

26. *See Bizier v. Town of Turner*, 32 A.3d 1048, 1050, n. 1 (Me. 2011).

27. *See Manalapan Realty v. Township Committee of the Twp. of Manalapan*, 658 A.2d 1230, 1237 (N.J. 1995); *see also Layton v. Howard Cty. Bd. of Appeals*, 922 A.2d 576, 593, n. 25 (Md. 2007) (noting that this follows from the rule for all types of land use proceedings that the law in effect at the time of the judicial appeal controls the case).

28. *See Union Cty. v. CGP, Inc.*, 589 S.E.2d 240 (Ga. 2003).

29. *See Meadows of Hanover, Inc. v. Board of Supervisors of South Hanover Twp.*, 734 A.2d 854, 857 (Pa. 1999). *See also Youngblood*, *supra*, 586 P.2d 556 (decided based on a Cal. Gov't Code provision).

30. *See In re Appeal of Jaindl Land Co.*, 284 A.3d 1314, 1319–20 (Pa. Commwlth. Ct. 2021) (rejecting this immunity a/k/a "pending ordinance doctrine"). *See also Smith Land & Improv. Corp. v. Swatara Twp. Zoning Hearing Bd.*, 2024 Pa. Commw. Unpub. LEXIS 18 (Pa. Commwlth. Ct., Jan 17, 2024).

§ 14.05 The Matter of Third Party Liability

Subdivision applications—plats, plans, and proposals—are matters between the owner or developer and the regulatory officials. The planning commission's *not* proposing reasonable changes in the traffic patterns or the applications will not render the planning commission liable to a nearby homeowners' association whose members are injured, say by having difficulty accessing the highway running in front of the applicant's subdivision, once it is up and operating as proposed and approved. No municipality is generally liable to third parties, whether subdivision residents or neighbors, when not enforcing its subdivision regulations to the fullest possible extent.[31] Subdivision regulations are intended for the benefit of the municipality; there is generally neither a statutory nor a common law duty to others. Thus, absent some contractual or third party beneficiary right in the association, there is no third-party liability. Moreover, subdivision regulations often involve discretionary actions and conditions imposed by the planning commission. The failure to use its discretion does not increase its liability and does not mean that the failure to impose a condition was unreasonable.

More generally, on the federal level, an owner does not have a state based and protected property interest in a subdivision approval sufficient to bring a due process claim in many federal circuits.[32] The authority to deny the permit is sufficient to destroy any possibility that such an interest exists. Some other circuits reason that ownership of the land involved in the approval process provides a sufficient interest.[33]

§ 14.06 The Extent of Regulation

Typically, a state's enabling act for subdivision regulations authorizes local ordinances governing the grading of lots, and the proper arrangement of streets, lots, and open spaces. A subdivision ordinance thus contains a series of criteria and performance standards for the infrastructure improvements required of developers. Criticized when the pattern emerging from their use is a cookie-cutter monotony of small, same-shape parcels, anti-monotony regulations require that residences located next to, across from, and kitty-cornered to each other have different fronts, elevations, and appearances. The police power premise for such regulations is that monotony in residential design lowers property values, affecting the property tax base; creates

31. *See Stillwater Condominium Ass'n v. Town of Salem*, 668 A.2d 38, 40 (N.H. 1995).

32. *See Gagliardi v. Village of Pawling*, 18 F.3d 188, 193 (2d Cir. 1994); *see also* Christopher Bryant, *Zoning Out Due Process Rights:* W.J.F. Realty v. Town of Southhampton, 73 St. John's L. Rev. 565 (1999).

33. *See DeBlasio v. Zoning Board of Adjustment*, 53 F.3d 592, 601 (3d Cir. 1995); *see also Harris v. County of Riverside*, 904 F.2d 497, 503 (9th Cir. 1990); *Tai Tam LLC v. Missoula Cnty.*, 520 P.3d 312, 320 (Mont. 2022).

confusion when police and fire vehicles seek to locate properties, promoting health and safety; and detracts from the aesthetics of the municipality, thus affecting its general welfare. These purposes implement the authority granted to the village to regulate the "arrangement" of lots.

§ 14.07 The Timing of Regulation

The subdivision process sometimes results in what the ordinances call a "finished" parcel—referring to a lot that is surveyed, cleared, and graded, but is otherwise unimproved. In some contexts, the subdivider is not the builder because a parcel, once finished, is sold to a builder that does nothing else but improve previously subdivided land; so structural regulations are enforced at the building permit stage and subdivision approval as to them is granted conditionally, upon compliance with the ordinance's regulations for structures and with a performance or completion bond to be forfeited for non-compliance.[34] The same type of conditional approval would be given when ordinances require that landscaping or tree cover of a certain density be maintained on subdivided parcels.[35] Likewise, regulations requiring non-glare or directional lighting are approved conditionally with the plat, and for all improvements to be installed, the subidivider or developer posts a performance bond to guarantee the timely installation or construction of improvements as approved by the commission. Such a bond is required when the plat is approved and before any construction starts.[36]

§ 14.08 Exactions of Land and Money

The major types of subdivision exactions involve bonds, land dedications, or a requirement that the subdivider install improvements internal to the subdivision itself. To the extent that subdivision improvements are uninstalled by the developer, but promised in the future, bonds payable to the municipality are required in the event the municipality is put to the expense of doing so. Such bonds may be either payment or performance bonds.[37] When the subdivision is subject to annexation by

---

34. *See Clare v. Town of Hudson*, 999 A.2d 348 (N.H. 2010).

35. *See, e.g.*, Vivian Encarnacion, *More Trees Please: Utilizing Natural Resources in the Urban Environmental Management of New York City*, 26 Fordham Urb. L.J. 1571, 1574–78, 1585–94 (1999) (reviewing ordinances requiring subdividers to preserve trees and landscaping).

36. The importance of a bond lies in part in the potential liability of a municipality accepting dedication of facilities to which have attached unsatisfied mechanics liens. *See Estate of Hazelwood v. City of Bremerton*, 210 P.3d 308 (Wash. 2009). A maintenance bond or a letter of credit may also be required to cover the costs of maintaining a facility until dedication.

37. *See Town of Black Mt. v. Lexon Ins. Co.*, 768 S.E.2d 302, 307 (N.C. App. 2014).

another local government, these bonds are assignable to the annexing municipality.[38] If the bonds are unenforceable and the improvements uninstalled, the municipality may (say) pave the dedicated streets and levy special assessed on those subdivision parcels that are benefitted by the installation.[39]

In addition, land may be set aside in an unimproved state for various public purposes—schools, parks, and other open space. Sometimes these regulations also impose fees, exacted in lieu of requiring land dedications. All these exactions, both in kind and in money, are intended to impose development-related capital costs on developers. Such fees are usually deposited in municipal accounts whose purpose is the future purchase of capital improvements such as schools and parks.[40] Such fees were imposed as early as the 1930s in some jurisdictions.[41] They became much more usual by the late 1950s, however.

§ 14.09 Overlapping Jurisdictions

Sometimes the criteria and standards in a subdivision ordinance overlap with the zoning ordinance of the municipality. For example, set-back and minimum acreage requirements for subdivided parcels may be contained in both its subdivision regulations and its zoning ordinance. Typically, the planning commission will refer the subdivision proposal to the zoning officer to see if it complies with the ordinance; the matter of set-backs is then properly considered by both the planning commission and the zoning officials.[42] Suppose the land being subdivided has an historic building on it. When a planning commission is authorized to consider "historical factors" in reviewing a subdivision plan, its authority overlaps with that of a historic district commission. That another public agency has an oversight function involving the same criteria and standards does not preclude a planning commission's use of them as well.[43] However, when a comprehensive plan would be violated by approval of a subdivision authorized by the zoning ordinance, the zoning regulation controls.[44] It is typically the most recent enactment, having been written to accord with the plan, has the most detail, and so is binding on the commission. Often the fact that the plan has not been adopted as an ordinance gives it no more than the status of a guideline.

---

38. *Id.*

39. *See First State Bank v. Town of Omro*, 873 N.W.2d 247, 254 (Wisc. Ct. App. 2015).

40. *See Bayswater Realty & Capital Corp. v. Planning Bd.*, 560 N.E.2d 1300 (N.Y. 1990) (affirming validity of off-site parkland acquisition fee imposed for cluster subdivision approval).

41. *See* John Reps, *Control of Land Subdivision by Municipal Planning Boards*, 40 Cornell L.Q. 258, 266 (1955).

42. *See Smith v. Town of Wolfeboro*, 615 A.2d 1252, 1255 (N.H. 1992).

43. *See Smith v. Zoning Bd. of Appeals of Town of Greenwich*, 629 A.2d 1089, 1101–02 (Conn. 1993).

44. *See Urrutia v. Blaine Cty.*, 2 P.3d 738 (Idaho 2000).

§ 14.10 Premature Subdivision of Land

Subdivision prior to the need for housing or other improvements on a piece of land is a major problem in the United States.[45] There is sometimes express authority in the enabling act for denying a subdivision permit on this basis.[46] Subdivision approval may also be denied when heavy use by subdivision residents of off-site roads would create a safety hazard. In implementing express premature subdivision regulations, a planning commission may consider both current and anticipated hazards and burdens on off-site facilities. Lacking the authority to deny a premature subdivision, a planning commission generally may not withhold "premature" approval. Neither can it ask the developer to pay for the off-site improvements.[47] In some jurisdictions, without express authority to consider a subdivision as premature, planning commissions are also unable to consider off-site factors in granting or denying an application.[48]

§ 14.11 The Plat Map

The product of the subdivision process is a plat map, showing the parcels, the streets, the utility lines, the open spaces, and the amenities provided by the developer. The public spaces are thereafter dedicated to the appropriate level of government by deed of gift and the parcels are in many jurisdictions thereafter conveyed to private parties using the plat descriptions as the legal description of the parcel, either by using the dimensions on the map, incorporating those dimensions by reference to the map in the deed, or by lot number appearing on the map. In some jurisdictions, the filing of a plat map is a precondition to conveying any parcel in the subdivision to private parties.

A plat map will likewise show the location and dimensions of ways, roads, or streets within a subdivision. Sometimes easements are also shown. These streets are thereafter also dedicated to the county or municipality by deed. When the developer of a subdivision records such a deed, "the developer is said to have made an 'incipient

45. *See* Note, *Premature Subdivision*, 1988 Utah L. Rev. 569 (discussing this problem in the Western states); *see also Garipay v. Town of Hanover*, 351 A.2d 64 (N.H. 1976) (upholding the denial of subdivision approval when the off-site roads were inadequate to handle the traffic to be generated by the subdivision).

46. *See Zukis v. Town of Fitzwilliam*, 604 A.2d 956 (N.H. 1992).

47. *See Frisella v. Town of Farmington*, 550 A.2d 102 (N.H. 1988) (invalidating a commission requirement that a developer pay the cost of improvement of a road not adjacent to the subdivision, even though the developer did not object before the commission).

48. *See Buttermilk Farms LLC v. Planning & Zoning Comm'n of the Town of Plymouth*, 973 A.2d 64 (Conn. 2009); *Pansy Rd. LLC v. Town Plan & Zoning Comm'n of the Town of Fairfield*, 926 A.2d 1029, 1032–34 (Conn. 2007) (holding that off-cite congestion may only be considered in order to regulate traffic within the subdivision).

dedication' of the proposed way for public use."[49] The legal interest conveyed in the deed is either an easement or a fee simple, depending on the law and custom of the jurisdiction. This dedication is unaccepted, inchoate, and incipient, meaning that, under the common law, the municipality has a reasonable time to accept it. Meanwhile adverse users might preempt the municipality's right to accept the dedication. Non-use of the right of way will not preempt the municipality's right of acceptance.[50]

Once approved and recorded, the plat is an official public record. That means that it is self-proving in court and becomes part of the land records of the jurisdiction, giving notice of its contents. It is generally printed on linen, plasticized paper, or something equally durable and heavy, and kept on file with the planning commission or municipal engineer or surveyor.

The plat map is not an "official map" of the jurisdiction. The official map is a map showing where, at some future time, public improvements should be placed. The purpose of such a map is to put owners on notice not to improve property in the path of a future street. If they do, it is at their risk: no compensation in a later eminent domain proceeding will pay for any improvement made after the map is adopted as governmental policy.[51]

§ 14.12 The Merger of Parcels

Subdivided parcels, when used for one structure, are merged into one. When the owner of two contiguous parcels constructs a home that covers both, but later applies to demolish the home and build two homes, one on each parcel, the owner must submit a subdivision plan to do so; the original construction automatically merged the parcels into one lot for purposes of the subdivision regulations.[52] Such a merger is the result of the presumed intent of a common owner. The presumption might be rebutted by the maintenance of a common wall or line of trees along the boundary between the contiguous parcels, but having separate tax parcel numbers and accounts is insufficient to prevent a merger.[53] Similarly, when two parcels are created by splitting off an exempted lot, but later the regulation was changed so that the two no longer meet minimum acreage requirements, these two parcels have also been merged into one.[54] This is a merger by operation of law: the merged parcels more closely meet the

---

49. *See Ocean Point Colony Tr., Inc. v. Town of Boothbay*, 739 A.2d 382 (Me. 1999), quoted in *Pilot Point LLC v. Town of Cape Elizabeth*, 237 A.3d 200, 202, n.2 (Me. 2020).

50. *Pilot Point*, *op. cit.*, 237 A.3d at 207–08.

51. For further discussion of official maps, see § 14.18, *infra*.

52. *See Bridge v. Neptune Twp. Zoning Bd. of Adjustment*, 559 A.2d 855 (N.J. Super. Ct., App. Div. 1989).

53. *See In re Appeal of Moyer*, 978 A.2d 406, 410 (Pa. Commwlth. Ct. 2009).

54. *See Hill v. City of Manhattan Beach*, 98 Cal. Rptr. 785 (Cal. 1971), *rev'd by* Cal. Gov't Code § 66424.2; *see also Dollinger Plaza Assocs. v. Chicago Title Ins. Co.*, 131 Cal. Rptr. 3d 596 (Ct. App. 2011) (holding that merger does not create a title problem covered by the insurer's title policy)

present requirements, and any prior non-conforming status is lost.[55] A presumption is at work here as well, but this time it is the municipality's presumed intent to merge parcels. Prior compliance with applicable codes does not immunize lots from merger. For the city planners and planning commission members, compliance with present standards is what matters.

§ 14.13 Tests for Validating Subdivision Regulations

Four tests have been used to assess these regulations. First, the **right/privilege test**. It assumes that a subdivider is exercising a privilege extended by the government. In consideration for the privilege of subdividing property, the government requires compliance with a statute or ordinance.[56] This "privilege theory" is the historical test. The problem with it is that it does not limit the role of government and the number of requirements which a subdivider must meet. It argues too broadly and justifies many more types of requirements than the subdivision engenders. Thus, many jurisdictions could not find its limits and so adopted other tests, eventually being required to do so by later United States Supreme Court and state court rulings.

Second, a **strict nexus test**. It requires that the exaction be "specially and uniquely attributable to the subdivision." This test is easily met in two situations: (1) when the requirements of the subdivision process conform one subdivision to the rest of the jurisdiction, as where the streets are required to be of a uniform width and meet other streets, or (2) when a jurisdiction has a duty to supply a service or maintain an item which is the subject of its requirement.[57]

In deference to the influence of *Pioneer Trust*, this rule is sometimes called the Illinois rule, although it has also been used in Rhode Island and New Hampshire. Under it, an exaction is borne by a subdivider or developer only if the subdivision or development is the sole cause of the need for the additional public facility financed. The exaction is akin to a special assessment fee, long used to finance sewer and water extensions by municipalities. One court in Florida has found that this test destroys the usual presumption of validity and imposes the burden of proof on the municipality to justify the exaction.[58] There is logic in this ruling.

Third, a test which requires that the exaction be levied uniformly and **according to a comprehensive plan** for the municipality. Often the only evidence of its validity

---

55. *See Shelter Harbor Conservation Society, Inc. v. Rogers*, 21 A.3d 337 (R.I. 2011) (interpreting an ordinance to this effect).

56. *See Ridgefield Land Co. v. City of Detroit*, 217 N.W. 58 (Mich. 1928).

57. *See Krughoff v. City of Naperville*, 369 N.E.2d 892, 895 (Ill. 1977); *Pioneer Trust & Savings Bank v. Village of Mount Prospect*, 176 N.E.2d 799 (Ill. 1961) (the leading case).

58. *Wald Corp. v. Metropolitan Dade County*, 338 So. 2d 863 (Fla. App. Ct., 1976), *cert. denied*, 348 So. 2d 955 (1977) (involving rights of way for canals).

is a comprehensive plan. This is particularly true if the geographic area over which the benefits flowing from the requirement is a large one. When the regulation calls for the use of a subdivision fee across town, rather than close to the subdivision, this third test is useful to justify the fee paid by a subdivider in lieu of dedicating land.[59] School and park funds are often augmented in this way. Traditionally, these funds were deposited in dedicated special purpose accounts, rather than general revenue accounts. Some courts found that this third test gives too much discretion to municipalities in imposing exactions and in-lieu fees.[60] It is now no more than an evidentiary rule, finding admissible statements from an adopted comprehensive plan formulating a public need or benefit involved in a subdivision regulation or exaction.

Fourth and finally, a rational or **reasonable nexus test**. It requires that the exaction be "generally attributable to the subdivision." California and Wisconsin courts have pioneered this test, but it has also been followed in opinions in Maryland, New Jersey, Nebraska, Oregon, and Utah.[61] Using this test, the fact that the municipality's comprehensive plan requires that a condition be put on plat approval is one factor tending to weaken the required nexus.

The leading case for this final test is *Ayres v. City Council of Los Angeles*.[62] Here, a municipality's public facility needs are balanced against the benefits to the subdivision from those facilities. The issue is whether the exaction relates to the need recited by the government and whether its benefits are reserved for and are actually conferred on the subdivision.[63] This test—starting out as a needs/benefit balancing test—has been elaborated into a separate examination of both the needs and the benefits, making sure that the one is rationally related to the other.

In cases using the *Ayres* test pre-1987, a court was unlikely to invalidate a regulation simply because a subdivision did not create the need. Rather, the need could have been created by the approval of many subdivisions over time.

Under this test, the exaction can be challenged only by a subdivider's showing that (1) the municipality has an existing and adequate inventory of land for the purpose of the exaction, or (2) "normal" growth elsewhere in the municipality makes land acquisition unnecessary in any event, or (3) the subdivision will shift the population already within the jurisdiction, rather than cause the in-migration of new residents.

---

59. *See Associated Home Builders v. City of Walnut Creek*, 484 P.2d 606, 610 (Cal. 1971).

60. *E.g., Wald Corp. v. Metropolitan Dade County*, 338 So. 2d 863 (Fla. App. Ct. 1976), *cert. denied*, 348 So. 2d 955 (1977) (applying the reasonable nexus test).

61. *See Jordan v. Village of Menomonee Falls*, 137 N.W.2d 442 (Wis. 1965) (holding that in-lieu fees in place of physical exactions of land authorized by statute and constitutional); *Longridge Builders, Inc. v. Planning Bd.*, 245 A.2d 336, 337 (N.J. 1968) ("[T]he subdivider [can] be compelled only to bear that portion of the cost which bears a rational nexus to the needs created by, and benefits conferred upon, the subdivision.").

62. 207 P.2d 1 (Cal. 1949).

63. *See Brazer v. Mountainside*, 262 A.2d 857, 863–64 (N.J. 1970) (municipality may not condition plat approval on the extension of an existing road taking up 20% of the plat's acreage and citing *Ayres*, *op. cit.*).

In California and other jurisdictions, the *Ayres* opinion became suspect after the 1987 United States Supreme Court opinion in *Nollan* was issued,[64] and after the 1994 opinion in *Dolan v. City of Tigard* followed and elaborated on the *Nollan* opinion,[65] this test became more suspect still. With these two United States Supreme Court opinions in place, it is clear, first, that the reasonable nexus test does not go far enough. It may not be a stiff enough test for a Court that requires that a regulation "substantially advance a legitimate state interest." There have been few attempts to codify this test.[66]

First, there must now be a public need, benefit, or purpose that is "substantially advanced" by the regulation, required dedication, or exaction, and then, second, because of *Dolan*, the municipality must make some individualized effort, beyond making merely conclusory statements of impact, to analyze the impacts created by the subdivision at issue, calculating the increase in the traffic (say) that will occur on roads abutting the subdivision such that resurfacing or increased width is made necessary. This impact analysis need not be precise, but must present a "rough proportionality" between the exactions required of the subdivider and the impact generated by the subdivision. What is now clear is that the exaction enjoys no presumption of validity, and that the burden of proof, when challenged, is on the municipality to document the extent of the impact generated on public facilities by the subdivision.

No matter what test for a regulation's validity is used, some subdivisions do not contain sufficient acreage to warrant the imposition of land dedications. For such a subdivision approval, the previously mentioned so-called "in-lieu fee"—in lieu of dedication—is exacted. If the government could require that land be set aside or dedicated for a particular purpose—again, say, for parks or schools—within a larger subdivision, it will argue that it may exact the fee to purchase land for the same purpose elsewhere to meet the needs generated by a small subdivision.[67]

One lesson of all this is that land use counsel should take early, pre-1987 and pre-1994 statements of a test for the validity of a subdivision regulation with a grain of salt. Those statements do not take account of the later United States Supreme Court opinions in *Nollan* (1987) and *Dolan* (1994).[68] Challenges to subdivision regulations

---

64. *See, e.g.*, *Rohn v. City of Visalia*, 263 Cal. Rptr. 319 (Cal. App. Ct. 1989).

65. *See, e.g.*, *Sparks v. Douglas County*, 904 P.2d 738 (Wash. 1995) (discussing *Dolan*, itself discussed *infra*).

66. *See* Am. L. Inst., *Model Land Development Code* § 2-103 (1976) (used as a guide in *City of College Station v. Turtle Rock Corporation*, 680 S.W.2d 802, 807 (Tex. 1984)).

67. *See Jordan v. Village of Menomonee Falls*, *supra.* See generally three comprehensive opinions reviewing these theories: *Batch v. Town of Chapel Hill*, 376 S.E.2d 22 (N.C. App. 1989), *rev'd*, 387 S.E.2d 655 (N.C. 1990), *cert. denied*, 496 U.S. 931 (1990) (*discussed in* Elizabeth Arias, *Batch v. Town of Chapel Hill: Takings Law and Exactions: Where Should North Carolina Stand?*, 21 Camp. L. Rev. 49 (1998)); *Howard County v. JJM, Inc.*, 482 A.2d 908 (Md. 1984) (holding that a subdivider could not be compelled to dedicate a right of way for a highway through the subdivision without a reasonable nexus between the need for the road and the new subdivision—*JJM* being a case similar to *Nollan*, discussed *infra*); and *Collis v. City of Bloomington*, 246 N.W.2d 19 (Minn. 1976).

68. An exception might be *Rohn v. City of Visalia*, *supra.*

should be assessed with those opinions in mind.[69] Both of them are discussed later in this Chapter.

§ 14.14 Enforcement of Subdivision Regulations

There are three principal methods of enforcement of subdivision regulations. First, a failure to comply with the regulations is sometimes made a misdemeanor subject to a fine and/or a term in jail. Second, other enforcement methods are aimed at transfers of non-complying land: for example, the regulators may enjoin the transfer of non-complying parcels, or in the alternative, a purchaser in a non-complying subdivision has the right to rescind the purchase. A third method of enforcement is the denial of permits for the improvement of non-complying land. Building and occupancy permits are common examples, but the certification of utilities is another potent regulatory pressure-point on the subdivider. Any jurisdiction may use some or all of these methods.

No matter the sanction, an additional, commonly used device for insuring compliance is a requirement that the subdivider post a performance or completion bond, issued by a reputable surety, to assure the completion of the required improvements. If the improvements are not installed, or not installed in compliance with the specifications in the regulation, then the bond is invoked and the surety pays for any further necessary work.

§ 14.15 Summary of Subdivision Fee Rationales

In 1994, in the case of *Dolan v. The City of Tigard*,[70] a majority of the United State Supreme Court attempted to summarize the various rationales for subdivision dedications and fees. Its discussion is informative not only for presenting the court's view, but also as a summary of past law. Here is that discussion:

> The question for us is whether these findings [made by the local planning agency] are constitutionally sufficient to justify the conditions imposed by the city. . . . Since state courts have been dealing with this question a good deal longer than we have, we turn to representative decisions made by them.

69. *See B.A.M. Dev., L.L.C., v. Salt Lake Cty.*, 196 P.3d 601 (2008), *further opinion*, 282 P.3d 41 (Utah 2012) (considering these cases at length).

70. 512 U.S. 374 (1994).

In some States, very generalized statements as to the necessary connection between the required dedication and the proposed development seem to suffice. *See, e.g., Jenad, Inc. v. Scarsdale*, 18 N.Y.2d 78, 271 N.Y.S.2d 955, 218 N.E.2d 673 (1966). We think this standard is too lax to adequately protect petitioner's right to just compensation if her property is taken for a public purpose.

Other state courts require a very exacting correspondence, described as the "specific and uniquely attributable" test. The Supreme Court of Illinois first developed this test in *Pioneer Trust & Savings Bank v. Mount Prospect*, 22 Ill. 2d 375, 380, 176 N.E.2d 799, 802 (1961) (footnote recognizing this test as the minority rule, and citing cases from N.H., N.J., Ohio, and R.I. as examples of the test, omitted.). Under this standard, if the local government cannot demonstrate that its exaction is directly proportional to the specifically created need, the exaction becomes "a veiled exercise of the power of eminent domain and a confiscation of private property behind the defense of police regulations." *Id.* at 381, 176 N.E.2d at 802. We do not think the Federal Constitution requires such exacting scrutiny, given the nature of the interests involved.

A number of state courts have taken an intermediate position, requiring the municipality to show a "reasonable relationship" between the required dedication and the impact of the proposed development. Typical is the Supreme Court of Nebraska's opinion in *Simpson v. North Platte*, 206 Neb. 240, 245, 292 N.W.2d 297, 301 (1980), where that court stated:

> "The distinction, therefore, which must be made between an appropriate exercise of the police power and an improper exercise of eminent domain is whether the requirement has some reasonable relationship or nexus to the use to which the property is being made or is merely being used as an excuse for taking property simply because at that particular moment the landowner is asking the city for some license or permit."

Thus, the court held that a city may not require a property owner to dedicate private property for some future public use as a condition of obtaining a building permit when such future use is not "occasioned by the construction sought to be permitted." *Id.* at 248, 292 N.W.2d at 302.

Some form of the reasonable relationship test has been adopted in many other jurisdictions. *See, e.g., Jordan v. Menomonee Falls*, 28 Wis. 2d 608, 137 N.W.2d 442 (1965); *College Station v. Turtle Rock Corp.*, 680 S.W.2d 802, 807 (Tex. 1984); *Call v. West Jordan*, 606 P.2d 217, 220 (Utah 1979). Despite any semantical differences, general agreement exists among the courts "that the dedication should have some reasonable relationship to the needs created by the [development]." *Ibid.*

We think the "reasonable relationship" test adopted by a majority of the state courts is closer to the federal constitutional norm than either of

> those previously discussed. But we do not adopt it as such, partly because the term "reasonable relationship" seems confusingly similar to the term "rational basis" which describes the minimal level of scrutiny under the Equal Protection Clause of the Fourteenth Amendment. We think a term such as "rough proportionality" best encapsulates what we hold to be the requirement of the Fifth Amendment. No precise mathematical calculation is required, but the city must make some sort of individualized determination that the required dedication is related both in nature and extent to the impact of the proposed development.[71]

This discussion invites closer attention to the so-called "nexus" test for the constitutional validity of subdivision dedications and fees. This test grows out of traditional, substantive due process jurisprudence. It makes plain that there are actually two "nexi" to consider, two nexi that the subdivision ordinance must satisfy at the time of its application, and two nexi whose weakness(es) might be the basis of a property owner's challenge to that ordinance. First, there is the requirement of a reasonable relationship between the purpose of the regulatory dedication or fee and the regulation imposing them. Second, there is the nexus between the regulation and its impact on the particular subdivision under consideration. This second nexus requires that the impact be reasonably tailored to that subdivision. Both must survive challenge for the ordinance to be constitutional.[72]

§ 14.16 Impact Fees

Municipalities have also imposed development impact fees on developers. This type of fee is an attempt to allocate to a developer the fraction of the infrastructure costs caused by that developer's particular project. It is intended, then, to be the developer's payment of a proportionate share of infrastructure costs. The definition of an "infrastructure" is a loose one, but the term is often taken to mean road, sewer, drinking water, storm water systems, sanitation equipment, and occasionally fire and police equipment.[73] A system includes both lines and plants. In the Western United States, impact fees for water consumption are often imposed on developers of new construction.

Impact fees are often levied later in the development process than subdivision exactions and dedications. They are levied and paid as a precondition to obtaining a building permit. Thus they tax developments for which no subdivision approval is required, or for which subdivision approval was given previously or prematurely.

---

71. *Id.* at 389–91.

72. *See City of Annapolis v. Waterman*, 745 A.2d 1000, 1005–25 (Md. 2000) (a comprehensive discussion of *Nollan* and *Dolan*, discussed *infra*).

73. *See Home Builders Ass'n of Tulare/Kings Counties, Inc. v. City of Lemoore*, 112 Cal. Rptr. 3d 7 (Ct. App. 2010) (upholding an impact fee for police equipment).

For example, they are levied when plans to construct, expand or improve existing structures require permits. By levying these fees at this later point in the development process, they may be levied on not just residential subdivisions, but also on commercial, industrial, condominium, and institutional developments; in this sense, they are more equitable than subdivision dedications, since they spread the cost of the infrastructure system across all land uses. The amount of the fee is typically calculated by the use of such factors as the gross square footage in the structure for which a permit is sought or the number of bedrooms in a residence.

In order to justify the impact fee, the municipality must determine what the need for the infrastructure was before the development and what the need will be after its construction or improvement. The tests for the validity of impact fees are the same as those used for testing subdivision regulations. The Florida courts have provided a good line of cases in this regard.[74]

In Florida, the reasonable nexus test is used twice, for, in order to justify an impact fee, the municipality must show two things: (1) a reasonable nexus between the need for additional capital facilities and the growth in population generated by a subdivision or development, and (2) a reasonable nexus between the expenditure of funds collected and the benefits accruing to the subdivision or development. A "dual rational nexus test" is thus required.[75]

Thus, the validity of the fee depends on three things: first, a development creating a need for the creation or expansion of the infrastructure; second, the amount of the fee not exceeding the cost to the government when it provides the infrastructure; and third, the designation and restriction of the fee to meeting the need for the infrastructure.

This double nexus test is in effect the result of the federal constitutional case law embodied in two United States Supreme Court majority opinions in *Nollan v. California Coastal Commission*,[76] and *Dolan v. City of Tigard*,[77] the latter quoted extensively previously in this chapter. This test is roughly in line with *Nollan* and *Dolan* requirements, except that the second nexus measures the benefits received rather than the impacts of the development. For another case following the lead of these cases, see *F & W Associates v. County of Somerset*.[78]

---

74. *Compare, e.g., Contractors & Builders Ass'n of Pinellas County v. City of Dunedin*, 329 So. 2d 314 (Fla. App. 1978), *cert. denied*, 370 So. 2d 458, *cert. denied*, 444 U.S. 867 (1979) (upholding impact fees generally, but striking down the particular fee at issue, using a specifically and uniquely attributable, strict nexus test), *with Hollywood, Inc. v. Broward County*, 431 So. 2d 606 (Fla. App. 1983), *cert. denied*, 440 So. 2d 352 (1983) (using a reasonable nexus test).

75. *St. Johns County, Florida v. Northeast Florida Builders Association, Inc.*, 583 So. 2d 635, 637 (Fla. 1991) (recapping the *Dunedin* opinion in the context of a school impact fee) (noted in 16 Nova L. Rev. 391–93 (1991)).

76. 483 U.S. 825 (1987).

77. 512 U.S. 374 (1994).

78. 648 A.2d 482 (N.J. Super. Ct., App. Div. 1994) (upholding a traffic impact fee).

Rapidly growing states have used impact fees extensively. In California, their use may in part be a reaction to restrictive fiscal measures. Local governments in states such as Colorado, Oregon, Texas, and Washington, have also used such fees. For example, San Diego attempted to price all of its infrastructure costs for its remaining, undeveloped raw land and then assigned these prices *pro rata*, to each unit of land shown on the city's comprehensive plan.[79] These fees are again analogous to special assessments, but are imposed on a larger scale and before the services are provided.[80]

Ordinances for imposing impact fees must be carefully drafted. They must include a definition of the public facilities to which the fees will be devoted, using unambiguous terms. They must be backed by careful cost estimates and a formula to determine the developer's proportionate share of the cost of maintaining, expanding, and supporting the capital facility or system for whose benefit they were enacted. Expenditure of the fees should be limited to those purposes, and the funds earmarked/segregated for those purposes; expenditures should be made within a reasonable time of collection, limited to a specific geographic area, or else refunded. If the purpose is too general, the ordinance runs the risk of being found preempted by state law.[81] An opinion giving careful attention the drafting and to the calculation of the fee is *Banberry Dev. Corp. v. South Jordan City*.[82]

It is not enough that impact fees are economically efficient. They must advance a legitimate state interest, but must also be roughly proportionate in that the developer is not assessed more than a proportionate share of the infrastructure costs his development occasions. What if a developer is asked to finance the cost of a bus to and from the local transit stop? The cost is $75,000. If it reduces traffic congestion at least $75,000 worth, it has an essential nexus, but if it costs $75,000 and attracts $25,000 in riders within the subdivision, it has no rough proportionality, even if it attracts riders from the neighborhood and really reduces traffic congestion by an amount more than $75,000. It could be really efficient, but not roughly proportional.[83]

How then should a fee be calculated? Take the existing cost of the capital facilities for (say) water and sewer service for the relevant area (say, $5,000,000), take the number of existing households served, plus one (so, the 1,000 households served + 1 = 1,001). Thus $5m/1001 = $4,995.004995, or an impact fee (rounded) of $4,995.00 per household. Or, for a more nuanced approach, if we assumed that each household has 10 plumbing fixtures, the formula would be $5m/(1000 × 10 + 10 = 10,010 fixtures) = $499.50004995 per fixture.

---

79. *See J.W. Jones Cos. v. City of San Diego*, 203 Cal. Rptr. 580 (App. Ct. 1984).

80. *See Russ Bldg. Partnership v. City and County of San Francisco*, 750 P.2d 324, 329–30 (Cal. 1988) (upholding a public transit impact fee).

81. *See Albany Area Builders Ass'n v. Town of Guilderland*, 546 N.E.2d 920 (N.Y. 1989) (transportation impact fee preempted by state highway law and taxes).

82. 631 P.2d 899 (Utah 1981).

83. *See* David Dana, *Land Use Regulation in an Age of Heightened Scrutiny*, 75 N.C. L. Rev. 1243, 1278–81 (1997) (providing this example).

Some states have enacted enabling legislation for impact fees.[84] Such fees are a source of political controversy, although in states with declining revenues for local governments or with constitutional limitations on the use of the real property tax (as in California with Proposition 13 now in its constitution), the need for alternative sources of revenue is a pressing one.[85]

Thus, a municipal legislature, enacting a development impact fee ordinance, citing the administrative costs of processing development applications, making the fee payable on the issuance of a building permit, and devoting the amounts charged for construction and re-construction of all types of public facilities, has enacted an invalid ordinance. This is so for three reasons. First, the use of administrative costs of development procedures as a rationale shows that the cost of the services made necessary by the development is not the reason for the fee; rather, the fee looks more like a tax than a regulatory fee.[86] In turn, if the impact fee is based on a state statute permitting the imposition of fees, a study of the legislative intent behind the statute might show that it was intended to generate fees and was not meant to tap a broad base of income and was not designed for revenue generation.[87]

Second, levying the fee at the time a building permit is issued, shows that the fee is levied on the public at large and not just on those increasing the demand for city services; that the fee might be paid by a long-time resident already using the services and not increasing the demand for them, makes the same point more sharply. Third, the ordinance does not ear-mark the fee proceeds to infrastructure in the neighborhood of the permitted construction; it shifts the proceeds from the area of development to the public at large. This fee walks like a tax, talks like one, etc.—and so it is valid only when properly authorized as a tax by a state statute.[88] After asking for legislative authorization for an impact fee and being turned down by the legislature, a municipality cannot fall back on its zoning authority to argue that it has authority for the fee.[89]

Such an ordinance should be redrafted by (first and foremost) conducting a study determining how much demand for the services is generated by different types of new construction, then ear-marking the fees collected for the improvement of municipal facilities in the neighborhood of the person paying the fee, setting up a separate account for administering the ear-marked funds, crediting a developer or owner with a reduction in the scheduled fee when the developer's construction has exceeded the

---

84. Georgia, Hawaii, Maine, Rhode Island, Texas, West Virginia, and Washington are examples.

85. *See* Dana, *supra.*

86. *See Drees Co. v. Hamilton Twp.*, 970 N.E.2d 916 (Ohio 2012).

87. *See Durham Cty. Land Owners Ass'n v. County of Durham*, 630 S.E.2d 200 (N.C. 2006) (invalidating a school impact fee as an unauthorized tax).

88. *See Idaho Building Contractors Ass'n v. City of Coeur D'Alene*, 890 P.2d 326, 329–30 (Idaho 1995) (invalidating an impact fee as an unauthorized tax).

89. *See Durham Cty. Land Owners Ass'n*, *supra* (invalidating a school impact fee and finding that the subject was best handled by the legislature).

engineering standards imposed by applicable codes,[90] and limiting collection of the fee to new construction.

§ 14.17 Linkage Fees

This type of fee is used to pay for some governmental facility or service unused by the developer paying it. The amount of the fee is linked to some unit or feature of the property being developed. For example, a fee of one dollar might be imposed for each square foot of office space developed to fund low income housing for workers using the space. Therefore, a linkage fee is a developer's fee for some broader social program and paid in return for local approval of a developer's project. The program might involve affordable housing, job training, child care, or mass transit. *Holmdel Builders Ass'n v. Township of Holmdel* is a leading case.[91] *Holmdel* held that housing linkage fees to carry out a municipality's *Mt. Laurel* obligation to provide realistic opportunities to developers for the construction of affordable housing are valid. *Holmdel* further held that such fees are neither a taking nor an impermissible tax. Boston and San Francisco have enacted ordinances authorizing such fees, the latter including a fee for child care facilities in commercial structures.[92]

Thus, new office space may generate the need for low income employees to service it and a careful study by the municipality might show that so much office space generates an in-flow of employees in need of housing at a certain income level. Thus an impact fee computed by the square footage of the new space, calibrated to the servicing needs generated by that space, would be shown to have a reasonable nexus between the need for the housing and the population growth generated by the addition of the space to the municipality's inventory of office space.[93] A second nexus based on *Dolan v. City of Tigard*[94] will be harder to show, however. It will require that the fee imposed is proportional to the benefit a developer receives by having ready access to potential employees to work in his office building.

New Jersey has authorized linkage fees for transportation districts state-wide.[95]

90. *See Anne Arundel Cty. v. 808 Bestgate Realty, LLC*, 278 A.3d 731, 741 (Md. 2022).

91. 583 A.2d 277 (N.J. 1990) (noted in Susan Denbo, *Development Exactions: A New Way to Fund State and Local Government Infrastructure Improvements and Affordable Housing?*, 23 Real Est. L.J. 7, 30–36 (1994), and John Payne, *From the Courts: Housing Impact Fees*, 20 Real Est. L.J. 75 (1991)).

92. *See* Symp., *Downtown Office Development and Housing Linkage Fees*, 54 J. Am. Inst. Planners, Spring 1988, at 197.

93. *See Commercial Builders of Northern Calif. v. City of Sacramento*, 941 F.2d 872 (9th Cir. 1991), *cert. denied*, 504 U.S. 931 (1992) (evaluating the fee under the *Nollan* nexus, but not the second or *Dolan* nexus).

94. 512 U.S. 374 (1994).

95. *See F & W Associates v. County of Somerset*, 648 A.2d 482 (N.J. Super. Ct., App. Div. 1994).

§ 14.18 Official Maps as an Aid in Subdivision Regulation

An official map[96] shows anticipated streets, open space, and land needed for future public facilities. Municipal, county, and state governments often use official maps as a part of their transportation planning. When they foresee that a new roadway will be needed in the jurisdiction, and can plot its location—or when an existing roadway will need to be widened—the future right of way, along with drainage facilities and other supporting lands, is located on a map maintained by the government as an official record. (Affected landowners are typically given notice of the mapping and a reasonable opportunity to protest it.) The legal effect of mapping the right of way is to reserve it for roadway use, so that henceforth no further development permits will be issued for improvement within the right of way. The purpose of mapping is two-fold: first, to give notice of the future right of way to affected owners, and second, to serve notice that no condemnation award can be based on the value of post-mapping improvements.

Consequently, if a municipality plans to widen a street, and so maps the widened thoroughfare, showing that in five years' time its right of way will be expanded ten feet on each side, an abutting landowner is likely to argue that this is a taking of his property under the Fifth Amendment. However, it is not a taking. The mapping has no more impact on the abutting property than would a set-back line for an abutting front yard. Establishing a set-back line is well within the police power's health and safety rubrics. Further, the abutting owners are very likely to benefit from the widened roadway to a greater extent than owners in the municipality generally will. Finally, when the mapping limits development only as necessary to insure compatibility of abutting land uses with the widened roadway—and for a limited period of time (say five years)—it is further strengthened against the argument that there has been any taking. The mapping serves a proper municipal purpose and reasonably carries out that purpose.[97] The map substantially advances a legitimate state interest in transportation planning and construction.

The argument for a taking might be strengthened by advising a client to have a development plan drawn up before applying for a permit requiring development within the mapped right of way. Such an "as applied" takings challenge allows the individualized, *ad hoc*, factual showing of deprivation necessary to effect a taking. Facial challenges permit none of this. So long as the law of regulatory takings remains *ad hoc*, an as applied challenge is stronger than a facial one.[98]

---

96. Official Maps were first used in N.Y. City in 1807 to establish the street grid north of Wall Street. Today the widespread use of such map derives from the Standard City Planning Enabling Act, promulgated by the U.S. Dep't of Commerce, § 21 (1928), as model legislation for the states.

97. *See Palm Beach County v. Wright*, 641 So. 2d 50 (Fla. 1994).

98. *See Joint Ventures, Inc. v. Department of Transportation*, 563 So. 2d 622 (Fla. 1990).

Typically, the permitting jurisdiction does the mapping; that way the map can be amended and a variance from its provisions given, when a landowner is able to present evidence of a resulting undue hardship.

Sometimes a reservation map is invalidated for procedural irregularities; in this situation, an owner whose land was shown to be needed for a future public facility may be entitled to a *per se* declaration of a temporary taking under *First English Evangelical Lutheran Church v. County of Los Angeles.*[99] The owner has a cause of action in inverse condemnation, but winning such an action requires a showing that development plans were interfered with while the map was effective; if permits were not applied for, then there is no showing that the map had any effect on the owner's property. Otherwise, assuming that this is taking, it is without injury or damage.[100] On the other hand, *First English* is decided on the theory that once a taking has occurred, it cannot be undone; so damages might be presumed. However, the *First English* plaintiff did not challenge the validity of the regulation, and so such presumption is unwarranted in a facial challenge to a map.

A municipality's official map may also note that some parcels along an existing street will have limited access to the right of way within (say) three years. A first issue to explore is whether a notation of future limited access is within the enabling act for the map and/or the local regulation. The municipality's attorney will argue—and probably prevail on the theory—that if mapping is authorized to limit the use of the land, then the notation about access should be well within that authority. A second issue involves a taking claim. A complete loss of access is not a pre-condition to compensation; any substantial diminution in or loss of access will suffice, even though no land has been taken in the process. Whether there is a taking is a matter of evaluating the remaining access to the property. The loss of the most convenient access is not compensable *per se,*[101] nor would a taking occur when governmental improvements in a roadway cause a decrease in the flow of traffic on abutting streets. The measure of damages for a substantial loss of access is the resulting reduction in the fair market value of the property.[102]

§ 14.19 State Subdivision Statutes

In most states, the processing and approval of subdivision applications is in the hands of county or municipal governments. However, three states have enacted subdivision codes that permit state government to process subdivision applications involving either a large amount of acreage or environmentally sensitive lands. In these states, both state and municipal regulations must be complied with. Vermont has the

99. 482 U.S. 304 (discussed *supra,* Chapter 5).
100. *See Department of Transportation v. Digerlando,* 638 So. 2d 514 (Fla. 1994).
101. *See Jordan v. St. Johns Cty.,* 63 So. 3d 835 (Fla. Ct. App. 2011).
102. *See Palm Beach County v. Tessler,* 538 So. 2d 846, 849 (Fla. 1989).

most comprehensive of these statutes. Maine requires that subdivisions of twenty or more acres, parceled into five or more lots over five years, obtain state approval as well as town permits; many nineteen acre subdivisions were the predictable result. Florida has enacted substantially all the provisions of the American Law Institute's *Model Land Development Code* (1974) as its primary state subdivision law, and is the only state to have done so.

§ 14.20 Development Exactions and Takings

A unique type of taking emerged from two United States Supreme Court opinions. When a municipality or governmental agency allows a landowner to develop, but only on the condition that the owner agrees to dedicate part of his land for some public purpose (a road, a park, or a school), such a conditional dedication is known as an exaction. It is viewed as a hybrid, lying somewhere between a regulatory and a physical taking. Exactions are concerned only with conditional approvals of development, not with denials of a permit. The municipality or government may not defend an unconstitutional exaction claim by saying that an outright denial of the permit would not be a taking and so be permissible. Likewise, the fact that the government might deny the permit does not justify what might seem to it as a more permissive, conditional approval. The conditional approval may nonetheless be a taking.

[A] *Nollan v. California Coastal Commission*[103]

[1] The Facts

Mr. and Mrs. Nollan were interested in purchasing a beach-front bungalow and property on the Pacific coast in California. In front of the bungalow was a chest-high wall, separating the house from the dry sand area of the beach. The Nollans had rented the property for several years, under a lease which contained an option to purchase it. It was located between two public beaches—one a quarter mile to the north and another 1800 feet to the south. The bungalow was in disrepair after several years of use by summer vacationers. The Nollan's option required that, as a condition of the purchase, they would have the right to demolish and replace the bungalow. Their plans called for replacing the 504 square foot structure with a three-bedroom house containing triple the space, 1,674 square feet, but consistent in design with the surrounding properties.

These plans were dependent on approval of the California Coastal Commission. This state agency recommended approval of the Nollan's building plans on the

103. 483 U.S. 825 (1987).

condition that they dedicate an eight-foot wide easement of access across the dry sand area of the beach in front of the property in favor of the public walking between the two public beaches on either side of their property. They refused to dedicate the easement and instead sued the commission.

The United States Supreme Court held, 5–4, that the commission's requirement that the easement be dedicated laterally along the beach was an unconstitutional condition on the issuance of the development permit. Justice Scalia wrote the majority opinion.[104] Requiring the easement dedication was the equivalent of a permanent physical invasion of the Nollan's property, the main citation for this point being *Loretto v. Teleprompter Manhattan CATV Corp.*[105] The public access, although sporadic in fact, was a continuous and permanent right, and akin to a physical invasion.

The court's majority also found that there was no nexus between the purpose of the dedication ("visual access" of the public to the beach) and the way in which that purpose was carried out; access by easement across the beach does not provide visual access to the public traveling along the coastal highway abutting the Nollan property. Thus dedicating the easement does not "substantially advance a legitimate state interest" in that there is no "essential nexus" between the asserted interest of the government and the easement. The majority comments that the commission could have restricted the height or the width of the Nollans' proposed bungalow, or prohibited putting a fence around it—all in the name of the police power. However, "if the condition substituted for the [police power] prohibition utterly fails to further the end advanced as the justification for the prohibition," there is no essential nexus because the commission was acting as if it had imposed a proper prohibition, but then said it would waive it if the Nollans dedicated the easement for public access, a condition unrelated to its stated purpose.

The majority even assumes (without deciding) that a regulation "to forbid the construction of the house altogether" might carry out a legitimate police power purpose—promoting the public's view of the beach from the coastal highway—but the exaction goes further and in a way unrelated to that purpose. This assumption is consistent with *Penn Central*'s expansive view of the police power.

---

104. Joining Justice Scalia were four Justices who were dissenters in *Keystone*'s 5-4 decision. Justice Scalia began with a discussion of *Loretto*. Had he has stopped there, it was reported that he would have gotten Justice Marshall's vote too. Marshall wrote the majority opinion in *Loretto*, but was reported not to approve of the regulatory takings discussion following the opening, physical invasion analysis taken from *Loretto*.

105. 458 U.S. 419 (1982) (holding that any governmentally authorized permanent and physical occupation or invasion of private property, no matter how great the governmental benefit and no matter how minor the invasion, is a *per se* taking, requiring just compensation). *See Loretto*, *supra*, Chapter 3.

[2] The Loretto *Citation*

Loretto was a physical invasion case—the easiest type of takings case, to which a *per se* or categorical rule for a taking applies. Justice Scalia implies that the Nollans' case (where part of the fee simple is taken) is just as easy. The rationale underlying this approach to the case is as follows: if the government exacts a condition that would, if imposed alone, require compensation, then the condition is invalid unless compensation is paid. This does not mean that the petitioner will always be paid; the Nollans, for example, only sought an injunction against enforcement of the exaction. The right which the Nollans had was the right to exclude the public from the dry sand area of the beach—"the right to exclude others is one of the most essential sticks in the bundle of rights commonly characterized as 'property.'" Other essential rights might be the right to use, possess, or alienate (sell) one's property.

This rationale makes dispositive the fact that in this case the public is to be given access to the Nollans' property and, if the Nollans had accepted the condition, they could not thereafter have excluded the public.[106]

Nollan is not just a regulatory takings case; it is a takings clause case in which regulation is the back-drop and provides proof of the regulator's real purpose for an exaction. As an exactions case, its holding is inapplicable to most zoning cases.[107]

Therefore, if *Nollan* is not disposed of with its discussion of *Loretto*, but instead involved the exaction of rights crucial to the owner, then the nexus discussion following is not *dicta*—and not like the "advisory" portion of Holmes' *Mahon* opinion. So an exaction is something close to a physical invasion—a governmental condition that works the same result so far as its effect on an owner is concerned.

[3] Locating This Holding Amid Prior Takings Cases

After discussing *Loretto*, the second section of Justice Scalia's opinion is a discussion of regulatory takings cases. The standard of review used by Scalia here requires that the condition alleged to be an exaction be a "substantial advancement" of a legitimate state interest, such that the permit sought might be denied.[108] This language derives originally from *Nectow v. City of Cambridge*.[109] It was also used in Justice

---

106. *C.f. PruneYard Shopping Ctr. v. Robbins*, 447 U.S. 74 (1980) (holding that shopping center owners had no right under the Fifth Amendment to exclude persons collecting signatures for petitions whose subject was protected by the First Amendment).

107. *See Builders Service Corp. v. Planning & Zoning Comm'n*, 545 A.2d 530 (Conn. 1988); *Adolph v. F.E.M.A.*, 854 F.2d 732, 737 (5th Cir. 1988) (stating it "is apparent that *Nollan* did not revolutionize takings law").

108. When a "substantial advancement of a legitimate state interest" is required, many legislative findings may be insufficient to satisfy this standard. Indeed, here and in his majority opinion in *Lucas*, Scalia has sharp words for legislative staffs: legislative purposes are not merely an "ingenious exercise in semantics and pleadings," Justice Scalia notes: were it not so, only an "exceedingly stupid staff" would fail the test.

109. 277 U.S. 183, 188 (1928).

Brennan's dissent in *San Diego Gas & Electric Co. v. City of San Diego*,[110] by Justice White in a wetlands regulatory case,[111] and by Justice Stevens earlier in 1987 in *Keystone*—Justice Scalia may have been working to gain either of these Justices' votes in this section.[112] So the quoted words had a respectable legal pedigree. However, they had not heretofore been used to strike down administrative action; instead, they had been part of findings that regulations had indeed advanced a substantial governmental interest or purpose. This change in function is an indication that the opinion's reach was intended by its author to establish a new category of takings.

This language also reflects the "substantial relation to the health, safety, morals, and general welfare" standard of *Euclid*—the reasonable relationship test.[113] It provides a more detailed standard of review.[114] The "essential nexus" required here is between the condition and the purpose of the regulation (the purpose generally being "the substantial advancement of a legitimate state interest"). The condition involving an exaction and the purpose of the regulation must advance the *same* governmental interest. This is a nexus of convergence. This "essential nexus" requirement downplays the first prong and emphasizes the third prong of the *Penn Central* test that (you will recall) requires the court to examine (1) the economic impact of the regulation, particularly (2) the investment-backed expectations of the owner, along with (3) the character of the regulation, the third prong requiring a characterization of the regulation as either the acquisition of a public benefit (for which compensation is required) or the remedy for a public injury (no compensation being needed). So *Nollan* creates a new category of takings—what came to be called regulatory exactions.

Nollan finds that an owner's right to build is not unfettered and may be "subjected to legitimate permitting requirements."[115] If the commission had required that the

---

110. 450 U.S. 621 (1981) (the first of a series of cases leading to *First English*, discussed *supra* in Chapter 5, § 5.02).

111. *See United States v. Riverside Bayview Homes, Inc.*, 474 U.S. 121 (1986).

112. While reading the opinion, it may help to edit out Scalia's replies to Brennan's dissent; this will reveal the opinion's skeletal structure. Both the majority and the dissenting opinions cross-reference each other. Justice Scalia's looks like an opinion written first as a dissent. This would account for its defensive and refutorial tone. In the alternative, both opinions might have been written for circulation among the Justices while each had less than majority support, in the hope of attracting a majority or at least a swing vote. The "swing vote" was Justice White, now retired, a member of the *Penn Central* majority.

113. The opinion's footnote 3, however, imposes a higher standard of review and scrutiny than does *Euclid*. Here the standard may amount to mid-level, scrutiny, of the type which the court created for the mentally disabled in *Cleburne Living Ctr. v. City of Cleburne*, discussed in Chapter 15, *infra*. So "substantially advancing" may mean a "least onerous" scrutiny or "neither over nor under-inclusive" scrutiny for land use regulations; more generally, it may mean that mere allegations of public benefit are insufficient and that hard evidence of some type is required.

114. *See Commercial Builders of Northern California v. City of Sacramento*, 941 F.2d 872, 874 (9th Cir.), *cert. denied*, 504 U.S. 931 (1991) (stating that no federal appeals court has interpreted *Nollan* "as changing the level of scrutiny to be applied to regulations that do not constitute a physical encroachment on land").

115. *See City of Austin v. Quick*, 7 S.W.3d 109, 119–20 (Tex. 1999) (in a municipality with land overlying an aquifer from which it drew its drinking water, regulations limiting the percentage and

Nollans paint their bungalow sunflower yellow, this requirement, though extreme, is valid unless the Nollans can show that it has an undue economic impact. It may be irrational, but it is not an exaction. Likewise, if the commission had conditioned its permit by requiring the Nollans to relocate a pre-existing easement over their lot for public access to the beach from the coastal highway, moving it from one location to another on the Nollans' lot, Justice Scalia's comments on the types of regulations that properly carry out the commission's interests easily justify this condition. It too is not an exaction: assuming the commission could relocate the easement without a taking, is to assume that the relocated easement is of the same value to its user and burdens the Nollans' property to no greater extent than it did previously.[116]

If the commission had wanted money to put in a fund for buying similar easements, instead of an easement itself, from the Nollans, nothing would change.[117] The commission would still have the burden of showing the essential nexus. Because the easement alone would require compensation, no traditional deference or presumption of validity is accorded the commission's program—it still has the burden of showing that there is a nexus between (1) the asserted interest of the commission and the money wanted in lieu of the easement, and (2) the purposes of the fund and the Nollan's development—the latter being the type of nexus the court later requires in *Dolan v. City of Tigard.*[118]

[4] Nollan's *Impact on Subdivision Regulations*

Nollan clearly applies to a subdivision development exactions case, and older, leading cases like *Ayres v. City Council* are overruled. In the place of cases like *Ayres*, stands the requirement of the essential nexus, henceforth required of subdivision exactions.[119] *Nollan* requires a crisper articulation of the public interest served. One later opinion said that *Nollan*

> ... does not stand for the proposition that an exaction ordinance will be upheld only where it can be shown that the development is directly responsible for the social ill in question. Rather, *Nollan* holds that where there is

amount of impervious surface covering the aquifer is essentially related to recharging the aquifer and the preservation of its water—and thus to the health of the municipality's residents).

116. Determining the status of the easement involved in its relocation is, however, *ultra vires* the statutory powers of a planning commission. *See Kline v. Bernardsville Ass'n, Inc.*, 631 A.2d 1263 (N.J. Super. Ct., App. Div. 1993); *Smith v. Town of Wolfeboro*, 615 A.2d 1252, 1255 (N.H. 1992).

117. *See Benchmark Land Co. v. City of Battle Ground*, 14 P.3d 172 (Wash. App. Ct. 2000), *rev. granted*, 143 Wn. 2d 1018 (2001).

118. 512 U.S. 374 (1974) (discussed *infra*).

119. *See Weingarten v. Town of Lewisboro*, 542 N.Y.S.2d 1012, 1015–17 (N.Y. Sup. Ct., Westchester Cty. 1989) (recognizing that *Nollan* required a higher standard for in-lieu subdivision fees). *But see Sintra, Inc. v. City of Seattle*, 829 P.2d 765 (Wash. 1992) (finding that the payment of housing replacement fee as a condition of receiving a demolition permit was not subject to *Nollan* nexus analysis).

> no evidence of a nexus between the development and the problem . . . , the exaction cannot be upheld.[120]

When disputing a dedication requirement for a subdivision, however, a claim that the developer's procedural due process rights have been violated is an impermissible attempt to recast a takings claim as a due process violation. It "conflates takings and due process law"; when the developer "has a remedy for unconstitutional exactions under the takings clause" he "cannot claim a redundant remedy under the due process clause."[121]

[5] Other Possible Impacts of Nollan

In addition to subdivision exactions, *Nollan* affects impact and linkage fee ordinances, which provide that a developer is required to contribute to a low-income housing fund or to a fund to expand the highway or public transit system. Further, states using Environmental Impact Statements (EISs) to consider the indirect costs or the cumulative effects of granting the permit might be affected. EISs would then have to consider only direct costs. However, *Nollan* along with the case of *Dolan v. City of Tigard*, discussed in this Chapter, are clearly of great concern to developers of various types of commercial enterprises.[122]

[6] Nollan *as Precedent*

An example of a state court's post-1987 use of *Nollan* is *Rohn v. City of Visalia.*[123] The court there invalidated a dedication requirement of 14% of the area of a parcel, imposed as a condition of rezoning an owner's parcel from residential to office use. The dedication, it said, was found to have been required by a street realignment, not increased traffic from the rezoned parcel. Moreover, the dedication was imposed after the planning commission had found that the rezoned parcel would produce less traffic than previously. So the court held that, under *Nollan*, the dedication requirement was invalid. The opinion in *Rohn* also required that the planning studies done to justify the dedication be particular to the neighborhood, and not be community wide. Neighborhood planning, rather than city wide planning, must be in place when a dedication requirement is imposed. To this extent, *Rohn* limits the third and fourth tests for subdivision exactions discussed previously in this Chapter.

Second, suppose that, enacted under a comprehensive state land use plan, zoning regulations permit existing agricultural uses in a region otherwise zoned for forest

---

120. *See Commercial Builders of Northern California v. City of Sacramento*, 941 F.2d 872, 875 (9th Cir. 1991) (upholding the constitutionality of a housing linkage fee on commercial development measured by the number of low-income workers needing housing and working on the development).

121. *See Pietsch v. Ward County*, 991 F.3d 907, 909 (8th Cir. 2021).

122. For a case using *Nollan*, see *State v. Putman*, 552 A.2d 1247 (Del. Super. Ct. 1988) (town ordinance requiring beach front owners to build retaining walls to protect beach and public road from erosion, held unconstitutional).

123. 263 Cal. Rptr. 319 (App. Ct. 1989).

uses. All non-forestry uses are permitted to continue, provided that a negative covenant (restricting the land to its present use) is recorded at the time the permit is issued. An owner applies for a permit to operate his pre-existing farm, but resists the conveyance of the deed restriction. *Nollan* does not prevent the regulators from requiring the covenant: the easement restriction on the Nollans' title allowed the public access to the Nollans' property, while the negative covenant still permits the owner to exclude the public. Retaining the right to exclude makes this requirement less draconian than the exaction requested from the Nollans. *Nollan* does not impose a requirement that regulators proceed in the least burdensome manner.[124]

Third, suppose that a municipality places land surrounding a lake in a summer cottage residential use district, residences in such a district to be occupied for only 30 days during the winter months (November 1 to May 1). Residents wanting to winter over in their cottages argued that the right to use and possession of the property was at stake and being denied—more serious than the restriction in the last paragraph—for five months out of each year. If this is a health or safety matter (a matter of occupants freezing to death, etc.) during the winter in an uninsulated structure, the ordinance may be sustained. However, the right to possession is an essential right, and if *Nollan* was intended to single out some rights as entitled to special protection, then *Nollan*'s heightened standard of review requires the municipality to justify the ordinance as one "substantially advancing a legitimate state interest."[125] Absent this justification, denying an owner possession is no less crucial than denying the right to exclude the public.

In a fourth example, a hundred yards from an owner's littoral property, the state constructed a public boat launch and, to make launching safer and easier, it installed jetties. The jetties alter the currents along the shore and erosion washes away first the owner's beach, and then his lawn and a tree on fast land. The owner's takings claim might be brought either as a *per se*, physical invasion taking or as a *Nollan* claim for an uncompensated exaction. Even though there has been no permanent physical occupation of owner's land by the state, the effect of the state's action is the same: its action has deprived the owner of possession, so a claim for an exaction is a reasonable response. The state's defense will be that its actions are in furtherance of the well-recognized public trust, giving the public the right to boat on navigable waters. Nonetheless, there is no essential nexus as *Nollan* requires: eroding the owner's land does not substantially further an admittedly legitimate state interest.[126]

---

124. *See Gardner v. New Jersey Pinelands Comm'n*, 593 A.2d 251, 262 (N.J. 1991) (affirming validity of commission negative easement regulations).

125. *See, e.g.*, *Seawall Assocs. v. City of New York*, 542 N.E.2d 1059, 1066 (N.Y. 1989) (holding a five year moratorium on conversion of single room occupancy housing to other uses, unconstitutional and discussing the effect of *Nollan*, *id.* at 1068–69).

126. *See Peterman v. State Department of Natural Resources*, 521 N.W.2d 499 (Mich. 1994) (treating a similar situation as a regulatory taking under *Nollan* and awarding compensation). *But see McQueen v. South Carolina Coastal Council*, 530 S.E.2d 628 (S.C. 2000) (finding no taking in a denial of bulkhead permits for coastal property), *cert. granted and vacated*, 533 U.S. 943 (2001), *rev'd*, 580 S.E.2d 116 (S.C.

[7] *Three Later Supreme Court Discussions of* Nollan

First, in *City of Monterey v. Del Monte Dunes at Monterey, Ltd.*,[127] the Supreme Court implicitly limited *Nollan*'s holding by unanimously saying that "we have not extended the rough proportionality test of *Dolan* beyond the special context of exactions—land use decisions conditioning approval[128] of development on the dedication of property to public use." In *Del Monte Dunes*, the Court thus expressly limited the impact of the other later, nexus case, i.e., *Dolan v. City of Tigard*, but there is no reason to limit one without including the other in the limitation.[129] The "essential nexus" of *Nollan*, between (1) the condition on the permit and (2) the regulation and the public policy used to impose it, applies when an exaction is presented. "Much different questions" are presented, the *Del Monte Dunes* Court said, when a case involves an outright denial of a development permit. However, when *Nollan* was decided the definition of an exaction was in itself unclear. In *Del Monte Dunes at Monterey, Ltd.*,[130] the court said:

> Although in a general sense concerns for proportionality animate the Takings Clause . . . , we have not extended the rough-proportionality test of *Dolan* beyond the special context of exactions—land-use decisions conditioning approval of development on the dedication of property to public use. [Citing both *Dolan* and *Nollan*—Ed.] The rule applied in *Dolan* . . . was not designed to address, and is not readily applicable to, the much different questions arising where, as here, the landowner's challenge is based not on excessive exactions but on denial of development.[131]

City of Monterey involved a situation in which the city had multiple times and after the presentation of several plans, whittled down a developer's proposal until finally the land on which the development sat was shown to be the habitat of an endangered butterfly. This case may properly be regarded as in instance of bad faith on the part of the city.

Second, in *Lingle v. Chevron, USA, Inc.*,[132] the Supreme Court unanimously characterized the law pertaining to exactions as arising only in "adjudicative land-use

---

2003), *cert. denied*, 540 U.S. 982 (2003). *See also Miramar Co. v. City of Santa Barbara*, 143 P.2d 1, 4 (Cal. 1943).

127. 526 U.S. 687 (1999).

128. This phrase "decisions conditioning approval" could refer to either legislative or administrative decisions, or both. State courts have divided on this issue involving the reach of *Nollan* and its related case, *Dolan v. City of Tigard*, 512 U.S. 374 (1994) (discussed *infra*). For an expansive use of these cases, see, for example, *Town of Flower Mound v. Stafford Est. LP*, 135 S.W.3d 620 (Tex. 2004).

129. For a case expressly limiting *Nollan* in this way, see *Bonnie Briar Syndicate, Inc. v. Town of Mamaroneck*, 721 N.E.2d 971, 975–76 (N.Y. 1999).

130. 526 U.S. 687 (1999).

131. *Id.* at 702–03. *See New Port Largo, Inc. v. Monroe Cty.*, 95 F.3d 1084 (11th Cir. 1996) (concluding the same), *cert. denied*, 521 U.S. 1121 (1997); *Spenger, Grubb & Assoc. v. City of Hailey*, 903 P.2d 741 (Idaho 1995).

132. 544 U.S. 528 (2006).

decisions."[133] It further characterized the Coastal Commission's demand in *Nollan* as a demand for an easement permitting public access to "a strip of the property between the owner's seawall and the mean high-tide line" and emphasized that a demand for the easement, had it arisen in the context of a condemnation, would have been a *per se* physical taking. An exaction substantially advancing "the same governmental interest that would furnish a valid ground for denial of the permit" is valid. But not otherwise: *Nollan*, the Court said, involved a dedication "of property so onerous that, outside the exactions context, . . . would be deemed" a *per se* physical taking. The issue was whether the exaction substantially advanced "the *same* interests that land-use authorities asserted would allow them to deny the permit altogether." If there is no essential nexus between these same interests, the *Nollan* case becomes an example of the doctrine of unconstitutional conditions—forcing an owner to relinquish a right, here a right guaranteed by the takings clause of the federal Constitution, to compensation in exchange for a discretionary benefit conferred by the government.[134]

Third, because *Nollan* is an extension of the physical invasion cases, it is important to note that the later case of *Yee v. City of Escondido*,[135] once thought to end further discussion of the physical invasion *per se* takings cases, proved to be a blown-through barrier—again leaving *Nollan* as a leading case for an exaction—a new and flexible category of takings case. The next-discussed *Dolan* case proves the point.

[B] *Dolan v. City of Tigard*[136]

[1] The Facts

Mrs. Florence Dolan applied to the City of Tigard (a suburb of Portland, Oregon) for a building permit to expand her business, A-Boy Plumbing, a plumbing and electrical retail store. She owned a 1.67 acre lot with a 9,700 square foot store on it. It is located in the City's central business district. Fanno Creek flows through the lot's southwest and western boundary and renders part of the lot a "floodplain virtually unusable for commercial development." Mrs. Dolan wished to replace the existing building and expand her store's square footage by 80% to 17,600 square feet, pave the store's parking lot for 39 parking spaces, and later construct a second building for complementary businesses with additional parking. Her proposed development conformed to the City's comprehensive plan and was consistent with its zoning ordinance.

The permit was approved, but with two conditions: first, that she dedicate the portions of the lot within the floodplain for a public greenway, and second, that she

133. This phrase "adjudicative land-use decisions" suggests that these decisions might be made by either a legislative or an administrative body, but that its focus should be, not on general policy, but on the application of such a policy to the owner's property.

134. See *infra* for a discussion of unconstitutional conditions.

135. 503 U.S. 519 (1992) (concerning a limitation on a landlord's right to rent a pad for a mobile home in a mobile home park).

136. 512 U.S. 374 (1994).

dedicate a fifteen foot strip for a pedestrian bicycle path. The first condition (for the greenway) was rationalized as flood control for the increased run-off created by the development. The second condition's rationale was that the bicycle path might ameliorate the impact of additional traffic generated by the development.

After the conditional granting of the permit, Mrs. Dolan sought—and was denied—a variance from the two conditions. The municipal zoning board affirmed and the Oregon courts rejected her argument that neither condition was related to the development and upheld both conditions as reasonably related to her development.[137] The United States Supreme Court reversed.[138]

[2] The Dolan *Majority*

Writing for the five Justice majority, Chief Justice Rehnquist first states that had the city simply required that Mrs. Dolan dedicate a strip of land along Fanno Creek for public use, there would be a taking. "Public access would deprive petitioner of the right to exclude others . . . " so there would be taking.[139] So, he says, this, like *Nollan*, is an exactions case.

The Chief Justice then makes plain that his opinion here builds on *Nollan*. The latter opinion involved the "essential nexus" required between a regulation's public purpose (its "legitimate state interest") and the exacted permit condition. The city's interest in managing flooding and traffic "qualify as the type of legitimate public purposes we have upheld." With regard to the first condition on the permit, an essential nexus exists between preventing flooding and limiting development in the flood plain: because expanding the store increases the impervious surface on her parcel and contributes to the run-off into the Creek, limiting development on the flood plain mitigates the danger of future flooding. Because the city could have denied Dolan her permit in order to handle the flooding problem, the same governmental interest is served by the exaction as would be served by the permit's denial. Similarly, there is an essential nexus between reducing traffic congestion and providing alternative means of transportation (via the bike path), so that the dedication of a bike path will mitigate an increase in traffic congestion resulting from the expansion.

If the first prong (the essential nexus) exists, the degree of the exaction demanded must then be examined. "The second part of our analysis," the Chief Justice continued, "requires us to determine whether the degree of the exactions demanded by the

---

137. *See Dolan v. City of Tigard*, 854 P.2d 437 (Or. 1993).

138. On remand, Mrs. Dolan was granted a permit again subject to the same conditions, but on an amplified record. She sued for a temporary taking and settled this suit for $1.5 million. *See* William Quinland, John Kennedy, & James Niewiara, *Defending against the Takings Claim: A Practical Guide for Municipalities*, 29 Stetson L. Rev. 658, 676–67 (2000).

139. A related point is that, for exactions, the parcel-as-a-whole approach of Justice Brennan in *Penn Central* is not to be used.

city permit conditions bear the required relationship to the projected impact of petitioner's proposed development." The opinion next reviewed the various subdivision regulation exactions tests and concluded that the "reasonable relationship" test—not the "specifically and uniquely attributable" test—best served its needs. The opinion takes pains to say:

> We think [this test] ... is closer to the federal constitutional norm than [those previously discussed]. But we do not adopt it as such, partly because the term "reasonable relationship" is confusingly similar to the term "rational basis" .... We think ... "rough proportionality" best encapsulates what we hold to be the requirement of the Fifth Amendment.

No precise mathematical formula is involved, but "the city must make some sort of individualized determination that the required dedication is related both in nature and extent to the impact of the proposed development." The exaction and the impact or harm created by the project must be roughly proportionate. Some exactions may have an essential nexus (as here), but are so disproportionate to the impact of the proposed development, that they violate the Fifth Amendment (as, it turns out, is also the case here). In addition, the obligation to make an individualized determination of proportionate impact will keep the municipality honest and help to prevent its overreaching and abuse of power; municipalities must make quantifiable, individual findings as appropriate when making a demand for property interests from an owner.

The city failed to meet the "rough proportionality" test. As to the first condition, keeping the flood plain free of development is consistent with the state interest shown, but "the city demanded more—it not only wanted the petitioner not to build on the floodplain, but it also wanted petitioner's property along Fanno Creek for its greenway system" without saying why a public way, rather than a private one, was necessary to achieve its interest. A public greenway entails the "loss of the [petitioner's] ability to exclude others." "It is difficult to see why recreational visitors trampling along petitioner's floodplain easement are sufficiently related to the city's legitimate interest in reducing flooding. ... " As the city had not explained this matter further, there is no reasonable and roughly proportionate relationship between the floodplain easement and the petitioner's proposal for a new store.

As to the second condition, the city also failed to explain how the increased traffic generated by the proposal will be diminished by the bike path. Finding that the bike way "could offset some of the traffic and lessen the increase in traffic congestion" is insufficient and not individualized enough an explanation to meet the reasonable relationship required here.

So the city failed the second, "rough proportionality" test. Applying the federal Constitution's takings clause, *Nollan* requires the essential nexus, and *Dolan* requires a further analysis of rough proportionality. This two-step analysis contains the burden of proof and becomes, with this case, an obstacle course for municipalities demanding subdivision exactions.

[3] *Three Implications of* Dolan

First, the court is fleshing out what it regards as a "rational basis" standard of review. It does not adopt or "federalize" the state law it cites. It talks of "rough proportionality," but cites with approval *Simpson v. North Platte*,[140] as representative of the test that the court adopts. *Simpson* is a reasonable relationship case. Both the essential nexus and rough proportionality tests are only two versions of a reasonable relationship test. First tier scrutiny, applied twice.

Second, note 8 in the opinion indicates that the majority was only imposing a showing of an "individualized determination" of rough proportionality on the city. Traditionally, it is the applicant who carries the burden of proof in land use regulation proceedings, but for exactions, things are different. Here it is not the applicant who must show a lack of a reasonable relationship, but the city that must show one is present, quantifying it as rough proportionality between the impact of the development and the exaction.[141] If Fanno Creek were a watering hole amid grazing lands for endangered wildlife, the government's interest or ownership of wildlife providing an essential nexus, a wildlife corridor could be required through subdivisions along the creek. Similarly, if the exaction's purpose were to give the public a right to fish along Fanno Creek, a right protected in some states by the public trust, a fishing easement might follow.

In the majority opinion, note 8 appears just after the court adopts the rough proportionality test and limits its application to adjudicative, rather than legislative decisions.[142] This distinction proved hard to maintain, considering the myriad of practices for handling land use matters by municipalities. A case in which the court later denied certiorari illustrated this distinction: a municipality had an ordinance with parking requirements and also requiring that parcels, after being subdivided, maintain at least 10% of their acreage in landscaping, and have at least one tree for every eight parking spaces. State courts had found the ordinance constitutional as an exercise of the police power by a municipal legislature; they applied the usual presumption of validity and the "fairly debatable" rule and found the ordinance to substantially advance a legitimate governmental interest. With regard to these findings, *Dolan* was held not to require a more detailed and tailored justification: that is, *Dolan* involves an adjudicative municipal action, requiring that a general policy be applied in an individualized manner, but the action here was distinguishable because it involved only a general policy.[143] The test is not so much whether a legislative or an administrative body makes the decision, but instead focuses on the type of decision made.

---

140. 292 N.W.2d 297 (Neb. 1980).

141. No matter who has the burden of proof, the applicant has the burden of litigation, and must have both the stomach and the money for litigation with the government.

142. *See generally* Inna Resnik, *The Distinction Between Legislative and Adjudicative Decisions in* Dolan v. City of Tigard, 75 N.Y.U. L. Rev. 242 (2000).

143. *See Parking Ass'n of Georgia, Inc. v. City of Atlanta*, 450 S.E.2d 200, 203 (Ga. 1994), *cert. denied*, 515 U.S. 1116 (Justices Thomas and O'Connor dissenting, arguing that lower courts should not have to

Third, had the city required the land dedication in isolation, then a taking would have occurred. This is just another case (like *Nollan*) where the facts look like a physical invasion, in the sense that the right to exclude would with the exaction pass out of the land owner's hands. The court is here, as in *Nollan*, giving owners constitutional law weapons to prevent this. *Dolan* suggests that more traditional, restrictive use regulations remain subject to reasonable basis scrutiny by the courts; the opinion has, for example, statements reenforcing its holding in the *Euclid* decision, mentioning the latter by name. Where the exacted dedication is made necessary by a particular development, it may still be imposed. The test of rough proportionality indicates some remaining deference to governmental decision making. *Dolan* is also not an instance of a taking of a severed interest (and does not repudiate the "whole parcel" rule of *Penn Central*). It is instead a case in which the government sought to require an owner to give up a constitutional right in return for a discretionary benefit without an essential nexus and an individualized determination that the property interests sought are imposed in rough proportion to the harm created by the development.[144]

[4] Dolan *and Subdivision Exactions*

Off-site exactions are particularly suspect after this case. Without evidence that a proposed development requires the widening of the street abutting the property to be subdivided, a municipality seeking to require the dedication of property for widening the street as a condition of approval for a development runs afoul of *Dolan*. Neither the presumption of validity, nor of constitutionality, nor the legislative label that might be attached to such a requirement if it is comprehensive in nature, will likely save this requirement from the judicial scrutiny that *Dolan*'s rule of rough proportionality requires.[145] Even if the municipality were to allege that because the property is underutilized, and that its more intensive development will in the future make the widening necessary, this allegation will likely make no difference: the rough proportionality rule cannot be met by speculation about future construction and development; it must be satisfied in the present and be based on the present or proposed state of development.

Another example of a subdivision regulation running afoul of *Dolan* is a requirement that a subdivider pay for a drainage system serving a whole watershed when

---

struggle with the uncertainties of *Dolan*, and the majority taking pains to distinguish a rational basis test, applicable to most zoning regulations, from its test in *Dolan*).

144. See *infra* for a discussion of unconstitutional conditions.

145. *Cf. William J. Jones Ins. Trust v. City of Fort Smith*, 731 F. Supp. 912 (W.D. Ark. 1990) (applying the *Nollan* nexus test in a similar situation) (discussed in J. Holloway & D. Guy, *Land Dedication Conditions and Beyond the Essential Nexus: Determining "Reasonably Related" Impacts of Real Estate Development Under the Takings Clause*, 27 Tex. Tech. L. Rev. 73, 133, n. 344 (1996)).

the subdivision will only cover one sixth of its land area.[146] Similarly, "premature" subdivision exactions are suspect after this case.[147]

In a further example, suppose that a client wishes to expand his business, located on Center Street, one of two downtown commercial streets leading to an arterial highway overloaded with traffic. The other street is High Street and it generates most of the traffic using the overloaded highway. The municipality refuses to approve his expansion plans unless his curb cuts and parking spaces are limited so that the traffic using Center Street does not increase the overload on the highway. The municipality's response is not roughly proportionate to the impact of your client's expansion plans. If the traffic is generated by High Street businesses and uses, then limiting the expansion of a business on Center Street does not address the problem of the arterial highway's traffic overload. The refusal to approve the expansion of the client's business is not roughly proportionate to the impact of the client's business on the highway and will not proportionately lessen that overload.

[5] Planning and Statistics after Dolan

Past statistics have a limited use for municipal land planners after *Dolan*. For example, a municipality provides in its subdivision regulations that a developer dedicate land for park purposes because its population increased fourfold in the last decade, that every resident needs a minimum of 3,000 square feet of parkland, and that in the last five years, 600 new subdivision lots had been created in 40 new plats. Thus, 1,800,000 square feet (3,000 × 600) of parkland should be required of new subdivision developers. This, the municipality says, works out to one acre per 15 lot subdivision on the municipality's remaining open land. This scheme probably does not satisfy the rough proportionality standard of *Dolan*. The municipality used past growth statistics and they do not provide a basis for predicting the number of new residents needing new parks. The requirement is based on the parcels in the subdivision and not on the new residents expected to live there; this does not provide a standard yielding a rough proportionality between the subdivision and its impact on existing parks and does not quantify findings that apply to the particular developer's subdivision application. This is, however, the sort of data and requirement that was approved in *Jordan v. Village of Menomonee Falls*, a heretofore leading case.[148] *Dolan* therefore makes both the reasoning and the holding of *Jordan* suspect.

On the other hand, if the municipality found that past subdivisions consumed 50% of the municipality's land area available for subdivision, then the 50% remaining—subdivided in lots of a certain size—would likely produce a population of X, needing

---

146. *See Christopher Lake Dev. Co. v. St. Louis Cty.*, 35 F.3d 1269, 1270–71 (8th Cir. 1994) (applying *Dolan* to invalidate the regulation as applied, permitting developer to recoup the cost of installation).

147. *See supra*. *But see Batch v. Town of Chapel Hill*, 387 S.E.2d 655 (N.C. 1990) (refusing to recognize listing plaintiff's land on an official map as an exaction, even though a subdivision plat required "accommodation" recognizing the map), *cert. denied*, 496 U.S. 931 (1990).

148. 137 N.W.2d 442 (Wis. 1965).

a park the size of Y acres, that acreage (or its cost) could then be assessed to future subdivision applicants.[149] This is an important point: the "individualized determination" may be made at the time of application; so the subdivider or developer is denied the argument that he or she did not create the problem that the municipality seeks to solve. The mere fact that prior urbanization created a problem, and that the last developer in an neighborhood is asked to contribute to the solution, is no reason to invalidate an exaction.

When a developer is dealing with an impact fee for increased school district services, he might use district-wide estimates concerning anticipated new residential development and its impact on the district's facilities in order to show the required reasonable relationship between his development and increases in the cost of those services.[150]

[6] The Doctrine of Unconstitutional Conditions

As stated in *Dolan*, this doctrine is to the effect that "the government may not require a person to give up a constitutional right—here the right to receive just compensation when property is taken for a public use—in exchange for a discretionary benefit conferred by the government where the property sought has little or no relationship to the benefit."[151] For example, even though there is generally no vested right to subdivide land and it is generally viewed as a discretionary benefit given by a municipality, subdivision still may not be offered in exchange for giving up the right to just compensation. Bargaining away a constitutional right in exchange for a discretionary benefit is in our polity, a bad deal for the citizenry. So the condition must be justified, and its benefits must be roughly proportional to the cost of the conditions imposed: for a residential subdivision developer, this means that the benefits must be capable of being passed along in house prices that reflect the benefit of the municipality's services.[152]

The doctrine is intended to protect individuals in their dealings with government by preventing government from doing indirectly what it lacks authority to do directly. It is aimed at preventing governmental corruption and coercion. It is a product of the era of *Lochner v. New York*.[153] It requires that a plaintiff owner first establish that a constitutional right is implicated and, second, that the right is being impinged measured by standards applicable to a direct violation of the right. If the plaintiff satisfies these two elements, then the burden shifts to the government to establish the propriety of

149. *See also* Richard Faus, *Exactions, Impact Fees, and Dedications—Local Government Responses to Nollan/Dolan Takings Law Issues*, 29 Stetson L. Rev. 675 (2000).

150. *See AMCAL Chico LLC v. Chico Unified School District*, 270 Cal. Rptr. 3d 868 (2020).

151. *See* Part II of the *Dolan* opinion. *See generally* Michael Kersten, *Exactions, Severability and Takings: When Courts Should Sever Unconstitutional Conditions from Development Permits*, 27 Envir. Aff. 279 (2000).

152. *See Welch v. Paicos*, 66 F. Supp. 2d 138, 180 (D. Mass., 1999) (explaining the doctrine).

153. 198 U.S. 45 (1905) (invalidating a state regulation of maximum working hours in bakeries).

a waiver of the right—and here the essential nexus and rough proportionality must be shown.

As a matter of judicial review, the doctrine is thus aimed at turning what would otherwise be a deferential review into a more thorough look at governmental action conditioning a governmental benefit on giving up a constitutional right.[154] As to exactions, it means that a land use regulator may not condition a benefit—say, a development or building permit—on a developer's ceding constitutional rights. In both *Nollan* and *Dolan*, the ceded rights were the rights to just compensation under the taking clause. In both of these cases, the permit conditions were easements, an interest for which the government would be obligated to pay, but were in both cases, acquired for nothing and without paying just compensation.[155]

The doctrine has been used in many areas of constitutional law, in cases involving free speech,[156] religious exercise, congressional spending powers, and here, with regard to the police power and the takings clause.[157] It is applied here, even though the *Dolan* majority states that the municipality could have withheld the development permit altogether.[158] It applies, in other words, even though an owner has no right to a benefit. It applies to the results of any negotiation, and even to the settlement of a lawsuit. An owner need not accept the government's proposal to state a claim under the doctrine.

The doctrine would not apply when a right was infringed, unless a dedicated exaction or money was transferred to the municipality or government. Thus, an ordinance denying owners around a lake the right to build a dock takes away a valuable riparian right, but does not transfer any right to the municipality, so the doctrine is not applicable, even though a regulatory takings claim may remain.[159]

---

154. *See* Kathleen Sullivan, *Unconstitutional Conditions*, 102 Harv. L. Rev. 1415, 1422 (1989).

155. In order to find out whether the regulators have asked a developer to surrender the right to just compensation, courts must first inquire whether a taking would have occurred if the regulator, instead of asking, simply demanded the easement by force, ignoring whether the regulator granted or the developer sought the permit; thus the doctrine applies when, outside the permitting process, the "ask" would be a taking. *See* Brian Hodges, *Koontz v. St. Johns River Water Management District and Its Implications for Takings Law*, 14 Federalist Soc'y Rev. 38, 41 (2013).

156. *See Perry v. Sindermann*, 408 U.S. 593, 595–97 (1972).

157. *See* Donald Guy & James Holloway, *The Direction of Regulatory Takings in the Post-Lochner Era*, 102 Dick. L. Rev. 327, 349–50 (1998) (reviewing the doctrine in the context of a *Nollan/Dolan* discussion).

158. Justice Stevens, dissenting in *Dolan*, would not have invoked the doctrine because the case involved a business regulation and he regarded the exchange of a dedication for a permit as a mutually beneficial transaction. The majority and the dissent disagree on the extent of governmental coercion that must be present in a "transaction" before the doctrine may be used, and Stevens suggests that the holding in *Nollan* and *Dolan* actually disadvantage owners wanting to bargain with a municipality by putting "exacted" bargains in unconstitutional terrain.

159. The doctrine is not always accepted in state constitutional law. *See Gonya v. Commissioner*, 899 A.2d 278, 282 (N.H. 2006).

[7] Impact Fees, Monetary Exactions, Dolan, *and* Koontz

When a municipality imposes an impact fee on the developer's subdivision permit to build houses, imposing the fee in order to (say) mitigate the loss of open spaces and purchase other open space, *Dolan* arguably applies to these money exactions.[160] *Dolan* burden shifting and heightened scrutiny were for a time thought only apply to land exactions, not money exactions. In part, this is because of Supreme Court precedent: *Nollan* gave reasons why land exactions require special constitutional considerations.[161] Thus for some time, the arguments for not applying *Nollan* and *Dolan* to monetary exactions prevailed;[162] first, that money is not property and so a takings claims does not extend to monetary liabilities and, second, that exactions law applies only to something very much like a *per se* physical taking (because that is the only context in which the doctrine of unconstitutional conditions can be readily applied). However, one court held that *Nollan* and *Dolan* do apply to money exactions.[163] For a time, the Supreme Court left the issue in limbo by vacating an opinion in which a municipality had issued a building permit, but conditioned the issuance on the payment of $50,000 by the developer into a fund for the purchase of public three dimensional art (sculpture, etc.) for public places. This exaction for public space art would have otherwise tested the limits of *Dolan*.[164]

However, the basic issue remained: what is the rationale for distinguishing between land exactions and money exactions when both have a severe and similar impact on a land developer or owner. Neither *Nollan* nor *Dolan* said or even implied that different treatment was required, but state courts dealing with the issue quickly split.[165] Some municipalities avoided using the essential nexus and rough proportionality tests by imposing a monetary exaction according to a schedule enacted in an ordinance or authorized by state statute and imposed on precise classifications of property.[166] Still, one might ask, what principle—other than the applicability of the schedule to a broader population of owners—justifies treating a legislatively enacted exaction

---

160. *See* Richard Ansson, Jr., Dolan v. Tigard's *Rough Proportionality Standard: Why This Standard Should Not Be Applied to an Inverse Condemnation Claim Based Upon Regulatory Denial,* 10 Seton Hall Const. L.J. 417, 440–42 (2000) (collecting cases). *But see Ehrlich v. City of Culver City*, 911 P.2d 429, 434–35 (Cal. 1996) (exaction for fund for placing art in public places in lieu of placing art on the regulated parcel).

161. *See Blue Jeans Equities West v. City and County*, 4 Cal. Rptr. 2d 114 (App. Ct.) (interpreting *Nollan* in this way), *cert. denied*, 506 U.S. 866 (1992).

162. *See West Linn Corporate Park, LLC v. City of West Linn*, 428 Fed. Appx. 700 (9th Cir. 2011).

163. *See Ehrlich v. City of Culver City*, 911 P.2d 429 (Cal.), *cert. denied*, 519 U.S. 929 (1996).

164. *See Hensler v. City of Glendale*, 876 P.2d 1043 (Cal. 1994) (reconsidering the validity of such a fee after *Dolan*).

165. *Compare Town of Flower Mound v. Stafford Est. LP*, 135 S.W.3d 620 (Tex. 2004) (applying *Dolan* to a monetary exaction to improve a road), *with Rogers Machinery, Inc. v. Washington Cty.*, 45 P.3d 966, 983 (Or. Ct. App. 2002), *review denied*, 52 P.3d 1057 (Or. 2002), *cert. denied*, 538 U.S. 906 (2003) (noting the split—45 P.3d at 976—and upholding a traffic impact fee).

166. *Rogers Machinery, op. cit.* In the line of cases including *Rogers Machinery* is *Amoco Oil Co. v. Village of Schaumberg*, 661 N.E.2d 380 (Ill. Ct. App. 1995) (holding than *Dolan* does not apply to legislatively imposed exactions).

differently from an administratively adjudicated exaction? In practice, the effects have indistinguishable effects on the developer or owner's bottom line.

One response to *Nollan* and *Dolan* was and is an ordinance that levied a traffic impact fee on all new development, so that a change in the level of service (LOS) required on nearby roads, pedestrian walk-ways, and public transportation routes made necessary by the development, can be partially paid for by the fee, calculated as a *pro rata* amount of the total costs of the development, placed in a special transportation fund, and returned if not used within five years on a site within three blocks of the development.[167] The developer is also required to pay a relocation assistance fee for any low-income persons displaced by the development. Both of these two fees might be conceded to have an essential or substantial nexus under *Nollan*, and the traffic fee has been legislatively tailored to link it to the public's need for transportation of various types in rough proportion.[168] The relocation fee would not even be subject to *Dolan*. Why? Because no link exists between a developer's property and this fee.[169] The fee is triggered by the developer's actions with respect to the use on his property, not an ongoing burden on the developer's interest in his property.[170]

Thus general legislation, as opposed to an *ad hoc* adjudicatory fee, is probably, after *Koontz*,[171] possibly beyond the scope of *Nollan* and *Dolan*. After *Koontz*, the emphasis is on the word *possibly*, since *Koontz* left the issue an open one. In this regard, the California Supreme Court had found that the "*Koontz* decision does not purport to decide whether the *Nollan/Dolan* test is applicable to legislatively prescribed monetary permit comnditions that apply to a broad class of proposed developments,"[172] citing the cases that held that "legislatively prescribed monetary fees that are imposed as a condition of development are not subject to the *Nollan/Dolan* test."[173]

Another likely response is a state legislature enacting a statute authorizing any municipality with zoning authority to impose a development impact *tax* as an excise tax to the same extent than the state could enact such a tax—payable as a condition of issuing a building permit. General monetary obligations imposed without reference to discrete assets or property are not takings.[174] "It is beyond dispute that 'taxes

---

167. *Cf. Alpine Homes, Inc. v. City of West Jordan*, 424 P.3d 95 (Utah 2017) (holding that a developer had no claim for a refund when the money deposited went unspent and that a *Nollan/Dolan* test applies at the time the impact fee was imposed and did not apply to a claim for a refund).

168. *See McClung v. City of Sumner*, 548 F.3d 1219, 1224 (9th Cir. 2008).

169. For an article suggesting ordinance provisions for impact fees, see Charles Mulcahy & Michelle Zimet, *Impact Fees for a Developing Wisconsin*, 79 Marq. L. Rev. 759, 782–95 (1996), discussing *St. Johns Cty. v. Northeast Florida Builders Ass'n*, 583 So. 2d 635 (Fla. 1991).

170. *See Ballinger v. City of Oakland*, 24 F.4th 1287, 1296–97 (9th Cir. 2022).

171. *Koontz* is discussed *infra*, this section.

172. *See California Bldg. Industry Ass'n v. City of San Jose*, 351 P.4th 974, 989, n. 11 (Cal. 2015).

173. *Id.*

174. *See Eastern Enterprises v. Apfel*, 524 U.S. 498 (1998) (declining to apply the takings clause to coal miners' health benefits). *See generally* Eduardo M. Penalver, *Regulatory Takings*, 104 Colum. L. Rev. 2182, 2206–08 (20004) (distinguishing general monetary obligations and obligations tied to discrete assets).

and user fees . . . are not 'takings.'"[175] Likewise, paying a user fee for the extension of a sewer or water line does not amount to a taking, in part because the developer-payor does not retain any property in the money paid to the utility; to the utility, the fee is revenue. Still, many judicial decisions in several states invalidated impact fees as an unauthorized tax. Developers who paid such a tax under protest after *Dolan* sued to recover the amounts paid, but such suits failed.[176] It does not deny development, but only taxes it.[177] As a tax, the development charge is also subject to equal protection analysis, but this will not detain a court long if developers may reasonably be taxed as a group.

However, after *Dolan*, a flat, per parcel, impact fee not earmarked for use for a capital improvement made necessary by the development to which it is charged, violates two benchmarks of rough proportionality: it does not attempt to correlate the impacts of a subdivision with the amount of the fee, and does not specify the expenditures it will make with the money collected from the fee, even if meanwhile held in a reserve account.[178]

Land use regulators provided work-around methods for dealing with *Nollan* and *Dolan*. Monetary exactions in lieu of land dedications became more numerous in the early years of the 21st century. Taking account of its two unanimous decisions in *Del Monte Dunes* and *Lingle*,[179] the Supreme Court court was put to the task of imposing what it called the heightened review standards of essential nexus and rough proportionatity found in both *Nollan* and *Dolan* when the regulatory body denied a development permit rather than issuing one conditioned on what the developer argued was an exaction. After all, when a denial is issued, the developer has had nothing taken from him, neither land dedicated and taken from him or a monetary obligation falling due and imposed on him. The developer is simply back at square one, fuming perhaps but none the poorer.[180]

Writing for a 5-4 majority in *Koontz v. St Johns River Water Management District*,[181] Justice Alito was up to the task. On the issue of whether a monetary obligation was subject to *Nollan* and *Dolan*, he first conceded that in this case there had been no taking, but that the suggestion by the Water Management District of a monetary condition created a "direct link" to the petitioner's property sufficient to implicate the denial

---

175. *See Koontz v. St. Johns River Water Managment District*, 570 U.S. 595, 615 (2013).

176. *See Waters Landing Limited Partnership v. Montgomery County*, 650 A.2d 712, 720, 724 (Md. 1994) ("To the extent that this tax is a regulation on the development of land, it is not a regulation that 'goes too far' so as to be 'recognized as a taking.'").

177. *See also Homebuilders Ass'n of Central Arizona v. City of Scottsdale*, 902 P.2d 1347 (Ariz. Ct. App. 1995) (finding that an impact fee is a regulatory fee and not a tax).

178. *Cf. Henderson Homes, Inc. v. City of Bothell*, 877 P.2d 176 (Wash. 1994) (so holding, but deciding the case under a state statutory scheme for impact fees).

179. Both cases are discussed *supra*, § 14.20[A][7].

180. *See* Michael C. Miller, *The New Per Se Takings Rule: Koontz's Implicit Revolution of the Regulatory State*, 63 Am. U. L. Rev. 919 (2014).

181. 570 U.S. 595 (2013). *See generally* Timothy M. Mulvaney, *The State of Exactions*, 61 Wm. & Mary L. Rev. 169 (2019).

of a constitutional right (to develop the petitioner's property) that should be tested under *Nollan* and *Dolan*.

The facts of *Koontz* were these:[182] in 1972, Coy Koontz bought an undeveloped parcel, partly wetlands, consisting of 14.9 acres east of Orlando. Over the next decade, land developments surrounded the parcel until, in 1984, a state water conservation statute[183] was enacted and provided that developers of wetland must apply for a permit to develop, but also provided that a permit may be denied if the development will adversely affect wildlife conservation unless the developer offset the adverse damage by taking action to preserve other wetlands in the same water management district. In 1994, Koontz applied for a permit to develop 3.7 acres of his parcel, offering to deed a conservation easement on 11 other acres of his parcel. The district rejected this offer and counter-offered: Koontz might either reduce his development to one acre and increase the conservation easement's coverage to the remaining 13.9 acres, or else to develop the 3.7 acres as Koontz originally proposed, agree that the conservation easement would cover the rest of the parcel, and pay about $10,000 for improvements miles away on district-owned wetlands.[184]

Koontz did not respond to these two proposals. Because he failed to respond to the district's counter-offers, the district denied his permit application and Koontz instead sued the district for damages for an unreasonable use of eminent domain by the state.[185] Koontz died in 2000 while this lawsuit was still on-going. Koontz's estate continued the suit, represented by his son, Coy Koontz, Jr. After the Florida Supreme Court held that the *Nollan/Dolan* tests did not apply to the demand for money, the United States Supreme Court granted a writ of certiorari in 2012 and the next year it held that because the district's monetary condition heavily restricted Koontz's parcel, the exaction should be examined under the *Nollan/Dolan* essential nexus and proportionality standards to determine whether a taking occurred.[186]

The court's holding extends the tests of *Nollan* and *Dolan*, resting on the "direct link" between the district's "demand" for money "operating on an identified property interest" such that "the monetary obligation burdened petitioner's ownership of a specific parcel or land."[187] Really? Not exactly! The district made no demand, unless its last offer of two ways to resolve its negotiations with Koontz can be considered one.

182. *Koontz, op. cit.*, 570 U.S. at 600–02.

183. *Id.* at 600. This statute, the Henderson Act, Fla. Stat., § 403.91 *et seq.*, divided the state into several water management districts intended to enhance regional. but not state wide, control over water resources.

184. The improvements involved improving ditches, replacing culverts, and constructing a new road over some 50 acres of district-owned wetlands. *Id.* at 602.

185. *See* Fla. Stat. Ann. § 373.617(3)(b).

186. *Koontz, op. cit.*, 570 U.S. at 614.

187. *Id.* The court also unanimously held that the fact Koontz did not ever accept the district's offers and so did not submit to any taking, did not also mean that he could not bring a due process clain, a regulatory takings claim under *Penn Central*, or a *Nollan/Dolan* claim to challenge an extortionate exaction as unconstitutional. How this latter view squares with the dissenting Justice's view of the case is an open question.

If the $10,000 had been demanded outright and not as a condition on the permit, it would not have been "linked" to Koontz's parcel in a way sufficient to become a taking. Koontz could have paid cash rather than sold other property to meet the district's condition. Thus Koontz did not have to give up property to meet the demand, and no taking existed on which to base an application of the doctrine of unconstitutional conditions.

Justice Alito responded to this critique by stating that the doctrine "requires us to set aside petitioner's permit application, not his ownership of a particular parcel of real property."[188] For him, giving up the permit process is the property burdened by the district.[189] Alito's language in this context is unclear: no "us" is "required" to do anything under the court's takings' precedents.[190]

It was perhaps the 5-4 nature of the *Koontz* decision that caused Justice Alito to leave some aspects of the opinion ambiguous. For example, his opinion speaks at times of the special risks posed by the discretion regulators have to impose monetary conditions as an alternative to an in-lieu-of fee, advising that use of this discretion justifies the application of the *Nollan* and *Dolan* tests.[191] At another point in the opinion, Justice Alito suggests *Nollan* and *Dolan* should apply when the monetary obligation or condition is imposed even when it is not in lieu of a requirement that a developer dedicate some property interest—this latter suggestion being more broadly applicable than the former.[192] This ambiguity points to the fact that exactions bear a resemblance to both physical and regulatory takings.

Neither *Nollan*, *Dolan*, nor *Koontz* imposes limits on the type of public purpose that a municipality may pursue.[193] Thus, a legislatively-imposed impact fee for the purpose of purchasing art works for display in public parks and squares and in front of public buildings may be valid, so long as the purpose of the fee is defined with clarity, funds collected are to be kept in a separate accounts, used only for the named purposes, and if not so used within a few years, returned to the payor of the fee. The municipality must, however, demonstrate that there is a substantial relationship between the fee's use and the type of development project on which it is imposed,

188. *Id.* at 615, n. 2.

189. *Id.* at 616–17. To this, Justice Kagan in dissent said a real property tax, or a water or sewer line extension fee, was no different from the idea of a taking that Justice Alito advanced. *Id.* at 626. All three are "linked" to a specific parcel or unit of property, perhaps more strongly linked than Koontz's monetary obligation to the district would have been. Justice Alito's view of the proposed counter-offers by the district may chill regulators' willingness to negotiate at all with developers lest their offers be viewed as final demands over which developers can sue. *See* John D. Echeverria, *Koontz: The Very Worse Takings Decision Ever?*, 22 B.U. J. Sci. & Tech. Rev. 1, 34–49 (2014) (a detailed description of why this might be so).

190. *See* Michael C. Miller, *The New Per Se Takings Rule: Koontz's Implicit Revolution of The Regulatory State*, 63 Am. U. L. Rev. 919, 940–42 (2014).

191. *Koontz, op. cit.*, 570 U.S. at 614.

192. *Id.* at 612.

193. *See generally Home Builders Ass'n of Dayton and the Miami Valley v. City of Beavercreek*, 1998 Ohio App. LEXIS 4957 (1998) (a thorough discussion of *Nollan* and *Dolan* in the context of impact fees).

and between the amount of the fee and the cost of the public facility attributable to the development on which the fee is imposed. As to whether an impact fee may be levied for the purpose of paying for public art, if developers may be forced to pay fees for parks, why not art? The quality of town life will be improved: because aesthetics is generally a proper purpose and within the police powers of most jurisdictions, it is difficult to see that the purchase of art displayed in public is not a legitimate state interest.[194]

In a more widely applicable instance, neither of these three cases suggests that a legislatively mandated, inclusionary zoning ordinance, requiring all residential developers to set aside a certain percentage—say, 10-15%—of his new dwelling units for low and moderate income housing, would run afoul of these cases.[195]

Nor do the *Nollan/Dolan/Koontz* standards apply when an applicant for a permit is asked to acquire public easements for wildfire control as a condition of permit approval.[196] Acquisition of the easements is not their appropriation. Only an appropriation results in a taking.

§ 14.21 Summary

Nollan and *Dolan* tell us what it means for a municipality substantially to advance a legitimate state interest. In *Nollan*, the court merely found no essential nexus, but in the *Dolan* case it went further and imposed a finding requirement on municipal governments; it queried not only the sufficiency of the government's findings and how they were drafted, but also queried the quality and specificity of those findings. *Dolan* imposes yet another burden of proof on municipalities, signals greater and heightened judicial scrutiny and review in the context of municipal exactions, but also helpfully tells municipalities what to do to satisfy the courts. Thus under *Nollan*, a legitimate state interest must be rationally related to the exaction and that same interest must be sufficient to justify denial of the permit, and under *Dolan*, the exaction must be rationally related and roughly proportionate to the impact of the proposed development for which a permit is sought. Finally, the Supreme Court, in *Lingle v. Chevron USA, Inc.*,[197] said that it is the doctrine of unconstitutional conditions, rather than a concern for substantive due process that underlies both *Nollan* and *Dolan*. *Lingle* also said that this doctrine can be readily applied only to a governmental action akin to a physical taking, but *Koontz* included monetary exactions within the reach of these two cases.

---

194. *See California Bldg. Industry Ass'n v. City of San Jose*, 351 P.3d 974, 989–90, & n. 11 (Cal. 2015).

195. *See California Bldg. Industry Ass'n v. City of San Jose*, 351 P.4th 974, 989, n. 11 (Cal. 2015).

196. *See Village Communities, LLC v. County of San Diego*, 2024 U.S. App. LEXIS 21783, *8 (9th Cir. 2024) (unpublished).

197. 544 U.S. 528 (2005).

Koontz also untied the doctrine of unconditional conditions from the need to find a taking, or indeed from ceding any consitutional right permitting development. *Koontz* applied exactions law to permit denials. Why? Just because the developer refused to accede to a regulatory request, regardless of whether he had a due process or regulatory takings remedy. (When he has such a remedy, it is difficult to see why any physical or monetary exaction is unconstitutional because the developer has not yet ceded his right to just compensation—but the *Koontz* opinion does not go so far in its analysis.) *Koontz* leaves open the possibility that the unconstitutional conditions doctrine applies, even in the absence of a regulatory action that violates the takings clause or the Constitution, by "burdening" Koontz's right to seek just compensation. This burden is the opportunity cost of refusing to accept the exaction. It is not a taking, but exists in its shadow and is created, for the first time, by the doctrine itself.

Nollan/Dolan/Koontz together mark an implicit elaboration and return of substantive due process analysis to the takings cases. This is all the more surprising after *Lingle* attempted to separate due process analysis from these cases. While the essential nexus and rough proportionality standards of the exactions cases deliver benefits to developers, whether those benefits equal the just compensation required by the takings clause, is doubtful.

PART THREE

Economic Discrimination and Zoning

Chapter 15
Exclusionary Zoning

§ 15.01 Introduction

All Euclidian zoning has some exclusionary consequences or effects—zoning a use into a municipality has the effect of zoning out other uses. The *Euclid* opinion is typical in this respect with its discussion about excluding apartment houses from single family, residential use districts, and, as to its economic effects, this exclusionary aspect of zoning is more forcefully shown in the opinion of the district court judge in *Euclid*. At the same time, the United States Supreme Court opinion in this case recognized expressly that the interest of the general public might, at some indefinite future time, outweigh the interests of the Village.

Another effect of the *Euclid* opinion was to de-emphasize the line of cases culminating in *Buchanan v. Warley*,[1] which explored the civil rights implications of early zoning ordinances. *Euclid* was in this respect a judicial signal either (broadly considered) not to inquire into the legislative motivation for enacting an ordinance, or (more narrowly) a signal not to impute an improper motive merely from the enactment of the ordinance.

Municipalities, even with good intentions, enact zoning ordinances with exclusionary effects. In the leading case on planned unit developments,[2] for example, the ordinance contained a provision limiting the number of bedrooms for some dwellings within the PUD, to two. This has an exclusionary effect on larger families and, if statistically, low income families contain more children, a disproportionate impact on these families. The municipality might be seen to have enacted its PUD ordinance to avoid having to use its tax revenue to build new schools or school facilities.

1. 245 U.S. 60 (1917).
2. *See Cheney v. Village 2 at New Hope, Inc., supra, Chapter 12.*

§ 15.02 Exclusionary Zoning Defined

Exclusionary zoning is a pattern of zoning decisions or ordinances that have one of two effects. The first effect is to exclude low and moderate income housing from the jurisdiction and raise the price of housing beyond the means of low and moderate income persons. As a result, the community is not providing its fair share of its region's need for low and moderate income housing.[3] In the 1980s, such housing came to be called affordable housing—meaning housing that is built without excessive regulatory costs built into its price.

The second effect is to avoid the provision of services and urban infrastructure.[4] Quite often, while a municipality seeks to avoid financing and building an urban or suburban infrastructure, it seeks to build up its tax base with light industry and types of housing which require little in the way of municipal services. This makes this type of exclusion all the more profound.

The "first effect" cases have been more influential. One line of these cases involved large lot zoning. They initially involved 1960s developers' challenges to large lot zoning, in suburbs in which the minimum acreage required in some residential use districts was one acre or more—and in some instances, this minimum was four or five acres.[5]

Another line of similar cases involved the total exclusion of some uses—say apartments, mobile homes, billboards, quarries or gas stations—from a municipality.[6] Here one jurisdiction, Pennsylvania, identifies two types of exclusionary ordinances: "*de jure* exclusion" occurs when an ordinance on its face excludes an otherwise legitimate use and "*de facto* exclusion" occurs when an ordinance appears to permit a use but imposes conditions on it that cannot in fact be accommodated.[7] Together, these two lines of authority stand for the doctrine that if a municipality did not use its zoning powers for the benefit of the general population residing in a metropolitan area or did not provide districts for uses fairly representative of all uses within that area, its zoning was exclusionary.

Using this doctrine to challenge exclusionary zoning is meant to promote metropolitan-wide racial, ethic, and economic integration. When an ordinance or

---

3. *See Home Builders League of South Jersey, Inc. v. Township of Berlin*, 405 A.2d 381 (N.J. 1979).

4. For an early case in which the failure to provide sewers was seen as exclusionary, see *Board of Cty. Supervisors of Fairfax Cty. v. Carper*, 107 S.E.2d 390 (Va. 1959).

5. *See, e.g., Bilbar Construction Co. v. Easttown Township Bd. of Adjustment*, 141 A.2d 851 (Pa. 1958) (one acre lots); *National Land and Investment Co. v. Kohn*, 215 A.2d 597 (Pa. 1965) (noted in 114 U. Pa. L. Rev. 1251 (1966)) (four acre lots); *Appeal of Kit-Mar Builders*, 268 A.2d 765 (Pa. 1970).

6. *See Appeal of Girsh*, 263 A.2d 395 (Pa. 1970) (the exclusion of apartments); *Vickers v. Township Committee of Gloucester Twp.*, 181 A.2d 129 (N.J.), *cert. denied and appeal dismissed*, 371 U.S. 233 (1962) (Hall, J. dissenting) (exclusion of mobile homes); *Town of Conover v. Jolly*, 177 S.E.2d 879, 881–82 (N.C. 1970) (same); *Exton Quarries, Inc. v. Zoning Board of Adjustment*, 228 A.2d 169 (Pa. 1967) (stone quarries); *In re Charlestown Outdoor LLC*, 280 A.3d 948 (Pa. 2022) (billboards).

7. *Charlestown Outdoor*, 280 A.3d at 958. *See also id.* at 961 (holding that ordinance was not exclusionary because its exclusion of billboards was required by state regulation of billboards along highways).

decision is found exclusionary, or in violation of fair housing laws and the result of housing discrimination, courts have fashioned remedies that are premised on this goal. Courts ordered the exclusionary municipality to provide its fair share of affordable housing for low or moderate income persons in the region. Courts impose "fair share" duties reluctantly. For example, if a municipality lay outside of the "path of growth" or its population increases were slight, an exclusion of commercial uses, and even apartments, might be justified.[8] Sometimes this reluctance shows itself in the use of the presumption of validity attaching to an ordinance. If the proposed housing was excluded, but similar housing permitted, the presumption of validity attached and the burden of overturning it fell to the challenger; on the other hand, if the proposal was for a "basic form of housing" that was not provided for in the municipality's land use regulations, then the usual presumption of validity was denied an ordinance.[9]

§ 15.03 The Basis for This Doctrine

In some states, the doctrine has a constitutional basis—the general welfare clause of a state constitution. In New Jersey, an express general welfare provision is sometimes used. Similarly, the general welfare clause of the New York state constitution and its zoning enabling statute are used to invalidate the exclusion of multi-family housing.[10]

In other states, the basis is the fourth rubric of the police power—the protection of the health, safety, morals, and (take note) the general welfare. The U.S. District Court opinion in *Euclid*[11] started this line of cases. More recent Pennsylvania cases are also examples of this line.[12] These cases give the general welfare a weight independent of the other three rubrics. They deliver what was promised, but not delivered, in the Supreme Court opinion in *Euclid*: a close look at the metropolitan regional effects of a zoning ordinance.

---

8. *See Fernley v. Board of Supervisors of Schuykill Twp.*, 464 A.2d 587, 588 (Pa. Commwlth. Ct. 1983), *rev'd*, 502 A.2d 585 (Pa. 1985) (pointing out that factors other than population growth might influence the demand for apartments).

9. *See H.&R. Builders, Inc. v. Borough Council of Borough of Norwood*, 555 A.2d 948, 950 (Pa. Commwlth. Ct. 1989) (finding that townhouses are a basic form of housing and ordering site-specific relief for the builder proposing them to a borough excluding them). *But see In re Appeal of M.A. Kravitz Company*, 460 A.2d 1075 (Pa. 1983) (refusing to extend the *Girsh* holding to an ordinance not providing for townhouses); *In re Appeal of Elocin, Inc.*, 461 A.2d 771 (Pa. 1983) (finding that a municipality need not provide for every category of dwellings in its ordinance).

10. *See Berenson v. Town of New Castle*, 341 N.E.2d 236, 241–43 (N.Y. 1975) (citing the goal of zoning to be "a balanced, cohesive community"); *see also Soares v. Town of Atkinson*, 529 A.2d 867 (N.H. 1987). *But see Asian Americans for Equality v. Koch*, 527 N.E.2d 265 (N.Y. 1988) (noted in 102 Harv. L. Rev. 1092 (1989)) (refusing to apply the N.Y. Constitution to a zoning district allegedly displacing Chinese Americans from New York City's Chinatown).

11. *See Ambler Realty Co. v. Village of Euclid*, 297 F. 307, 313-16 (N.D. Ohio 1924).

12. See the cases cited in note 5, *supra*.

§ 15.04 Judicial Remedies

Exclusionary zoning opinions show a judicial dissatisfaction with the remedies usually provided in land-use litigation. The usual remedy is invalidation of the contested ordinance, in whole or part. If this alone is the provided remedy, then the zoning officials are free to revise the zoning ordinance, even though the revised ordinance does not provide the original applicant with the zoning classification he sought. He may have sought rezoning for an apartment project and, in the revised ordinance, apartments may indeed be permitted somewhere, but not on his parcel. Thus the town may end up with no more apartments than would have been developed if the litigation was never brought. In this event, a developer would have little incentive to contest an exclusionary ordinance.

In response to this remedial problem, the courts in exclusionary zoning cases order the zoning officials to rezone the applicant's land for one of several uses, or for the applicant's requested use. The court might even do the rezoning itself. This broadened remedial power is known as the "builder's remedy." It is a reward, giving the builder plaintiff enough of the rezoning it seeks so as to give it incentive to bring the law suit in the first place. It provides a developer with the means to bring about compliance through litigation.[13] As we shall see, some courts accomplish the builder's remedy procedurally, by assigning the municipality the burden of proof to show that the rezoning or other action that the builder seeks is clearly inappropriate for the site because of planning, environmental, health, or safety reasons.

§ 15.05 The *Mount Laurel* Litigation

The Township of Mt. Laurel was a sprawling, largely undeveloped municipality on the urban fringe of the Camden, N.J., metropolitan area. Its zoning ordinance zoned major portions of its land—some 30%—industrial, envisioning clean, hi-tech industry. Little land was zoned for multi-family housing, and mobile homes were excluded. Mt. Laurel had experienced population growth, however, on the order of Ramapo or Petaluma—municipalities that had responded with growth control ordinances that had some inclusionary aspects.[14]

Mt. Laurel's ordinance had three residential use districts. R-1 had a minimum lot size provision of nearly 10,000 square feet, a minimum lot width of seventy five feet, and a minimum dwelling size of between 1,100 and 1,300 square feet. In the R-2 district, the dwellings were somewhat smaller and the lot size somewhat larger, but otherwise the provisions of the ordinance were the same. In the R-3 district, the largest by far in terms of acreage, the lot size was double that in an R-1 district, but

---

13. *See In the Matter of the Application of Bordentown*, 272 A.3d 413 (N.J. Super. Ct., App. Div. 2022).

14. "Inclusionary" is a word we will return to. *See infra*. this Chapter, § 15.07.

a dwelling's square footage was the same. Some cluster zoning was available in an overlay district within the bounds of mapped R-3 districts, but the clustering reduced the lot and dwelling sizes to R-1 proportions, subject to a maximum of 2.25 dwellings per acre. Thus several devices—minimum lot size and square footage requirements—were used; these had come to be associated with exclusionary zoning by the time of the litigation.

[A] Stage One

Mount Laurel I: In this 1975 opinion, the New Jersey Supreme Court held the zoning ordinance of "a developing municipality" (which it found the township to be) invalid to the extent it did not "provide a realistic opportunity" for the construction of the township's "fair share" of "the present and prospective regional needs for low and moderate income housing."[15]

A writ of certiorari to the United States Supreme Court was denied because this holding was based on the general welfare clause of the state constitution. That clause stated: "All persons . . . have certain natural and inalienable rights, among which are those of . . . acquiring, possessing, and protecting property. . . . "[16] As the New Jersey Supreme Court is the final arbiter of this clause and its state's constitution, the United States Supreme Court was and is without authority to tell it, as the state court of last resort, what its constitution means and how to interpret it.

The idea underlying the holding was that each of the state's municipalities had an affirmative duty to meet a basic need of New Jersey citizens for housing. Their delegation from the legislature of the authority to zone was encumbered by their constitutional obligation to provide this housing. In addition, as a matter of New Jersey constitutional law, the court also held that housing was a basic right. This is not the case in federal constitutional law; with this additional holding, the New Jersey court goes beyond the federal courts, rejecting the analysis of *Lindsay v. Normet*.[17] When municipalities affect this basic right beyond the boundaries of their jurisdiction, they effectively deny general welfare rights. Here the excluded citizen would have no non-judicial remedy because he is unrepresented before the municipal legislature.[18]

Moreover, it is economic discrimination, not racial or ethnic prejudice, which is prohibited by the holding in this case. Once again, the range of persons protected by New Jersey's constitution goes beyond the parties protected by federal constitutional law, where economic discrimination does not define a protected class of persons.

---

15. *See Southern Burlington County NAACP v. Township of Mount Laurel*, 336 A.2d 713, 724–25 (N.J.), *appeal dismissed and cert. denied*, 423 U.S. 808 (1975) (discussed in John Payne, *General Welfare and Regional Planning: How the Law of Unattended Consequences and the Mount Laurel Doctrine Gave New Jersey a Modern State Plan*, 73 St. John's L. Rev. 1103, 1104–08 (1999) (reviewing the case)).

16. *See* N.J. Const. (1947), art. I, para. 1.

17. 405 U.S. 56 (1972) (holding access to housing not a fundamental right).

18. This analysis is like the dissenters' in *Warth v. Seldin*, 422 U.S. 490 (1975).

The court found that the township ordinance was exclusionary. An exclusionary ordinance is in this matter tested and measured, not by the intent of its drafters or the zoning officials, but by the effect or impact of the ordinance itself. A "legal effects" test is used. Again, notice the contrast between state and federal constitutional law here. Under state law, the effect of the ordinance provides the test and an intent to exclude need not be shown. In this respect, as we shall see, *Mt. Laurel I* in effect rejects the comparable federal opinion in *Arlington Heights*.[19]

Environmental planning and timed growth controls are not at issue in this litigation. They are still available to the municipality. It is free to attract uses which require little in the way of municipal services, so long as it also includes its share of uses which require relatively more services too.

This is the basis for the idea of a "fair share" of low and moderate income housing. The geographic area for measuring the need was the Camden metropolitan area in the case of Mt. Laurel. Later cases defined this area either as a county or a metropolitan area: the region from which the housing population of the municipality would be drawn were it not for the exclusionary impact of the ordinance under review. In 1978, the New Jersey Supreme Court further held that this fair share did not have to be reduced to a specific number of dwelling units by the courts,[20] although they later recanted on this holding. Defining two other crucial terms—"fair share" and "a developing municipality"—was still and always has been found to be a judicial matter.

[B] Stage Two

Mount Laurel II: In this 1983 opinion, the same court decided to put teeth into the holding of its 1975 opinion.[21] The state constitutional basis is still the same and the right found there is still a basic one.[22] However, the court held that "a developing municipality" would no longer be defined by the courts. A precise definition of such areas had become difficult and (even if well defined) the use of the definition led to an inequity: the municipalities on the urban fringe of the state's metropolitan areas bore the brunt of the fair share obligation. This inequity led to increased pressure on the state's remaining agricultural areas.

Instead, the idea of a "developing municipality" was replaced by the "growth areas" defined by the state planning office in its development plan for the state. This office is an administrative agency of the executive branch of state government. Its plan,

19. *See infra* Chapter 16.

20. *See Oakwood at Madison, Inc. v. Township of Madison*, 371 A.2d 1192 (N.J. 1977) (holding that fair share obligations need not be precise or based on specific formulae to win judicial approval).

21. *See* John Payne, *General Welfare and Regional Planning: How the Law of Unattended Consequences and the Mount Laurel Doctrine Gave New Jersey a Modern State Plan*, 73 St. John's L. Rev. 1103, 1108–10 (1999).

22. *See Southern Burlington County NAACP v. Township of Mt. Laurel*, 456 A.2d 390 (N.J. 1983) (noted in 15 Rutgers L.J. 513, 526–41 (1984)).

moreover, was not adopted by the state legislature.[23] Entitled the "State Development Guide Plan," it was drafted in an attempt to gain federal grants by an agency abolished by the time the court issued its opinion. Clearly the court was casting around for other agencies to involve in the controversy over *Mt. Laurel I.*

The court also decided that numberless definitions of a municipality's fair share are insufficient. A municipality's fair share must be defined in terms of a number of dwelling units. Good faith in attempting to provide a fair share is likewise insufficient without results.

Mount Laurel litigation would henceforth be assigned to judges selected by the Chief Justice.[24] Initially three judges were used, and a rule of one trial, one appeal, would henceforth be applied to *Mount Laurel* litigation. Special masters were to be employed to rewrite a municipality's zoning ordinance to eliminate barriers to the construction of fair share housing. (New Jersey's rule on the availability of such masters thus became more liberal than the similar federal rule: their appointment was controlled by the Chief Justice.)

Rezoning of plaintiffs' parcels to the requested use (known as a "builder's remedy" here) should be granted unless clearly contrary to environmental or other substantial planning concerns. Thus a builder's remedy is the rule, not the exception, although its timing may be adjusted.[25] The routinization of this remedy was thought necessary to provide builders with an even greater incentive to conduct this type of costly, time-consuming litigation.[26]

If low or moderate income housing cannot be provided in the municipality, then least cost housing will be the back-stop and suffice. Least cost housing is more expensive than low or moderate income housing, but less than middle-income housing; it is a half-way measure, acceptable only when land costs and other market-driven housing costs increase the price of housing beyond the low or moderate range.

[1] Stages One and Two Compared

Mt. Laurel I and *II* have different emphases in several aspects of their respective opinions:

a. Environmental concerns are downplayed in the first opinion because the court felt that the township was using them as an excuse not to plan for its future.[27] *Mt. Laurel II* requires a balancing of environmental concerns with fair share housing needs.

---

23. 456 A.2d at 422–23.

24. *Id.* at 452. Special appeals courts were also created by statute in Connecticut in 1989 to handle appeals for permit denials for affordable housing projects. *See West Hartford Interfaith Coalition, Inc. v. Town Council of the Town of West Hartford*, 636 A.2d 1342 (Conn. 1994). *See infra.*

25. An adjustment of the timing—in the form of a phase-in—was also permitted a municipality in meeting its fair share obligation.

26. *See Southern Burlington County NAACP v. Township of Mt. Laurel*, 456 A.2d at 452–53.

27. *Cf. National Land* and the other Pennsylvania cases, cited in note 5 *supra.*

b. Fair share obligations were defined differently in each opinion. In *Mt. Laurel I*, it is defined in response to the township's quest for land uses requiring few services. The more service-free uses are sought, the greater the fair share obligation. In this sense, the first opinion was an easy case: the township had over-zoned for industry and, using the land available for rezoning, the opinion meant to redress this imbalance. In *Mt. Laurel II*, the fair share is spread across a region and then allocated within that region. Here the emphasis is on the elimination of over-zoning for least-impact, service-free housing.

After *Mt. Laurel II*, the court developed two methodologies for defining the fair share region.[28] One involves the geographic dispersal of low-income housing throughout a region, with the underlying goal of racial and economic desegregation. Another developed the idea of a commuter-shed, based on the idea that all skill levels of a workforce should not have to travel an unreasonable distance to get to work.

c. A floating zone for fair share housing might have survived judicial review of a challenged ordinance under *Mt. Laurel I*, but it would not survive *Mt. Laurel II* scrutiny: there, the sites for fair share housing must be mapped, set aside, and financial incentives and packages provided for their development. Mandatory set-asides, density bonuses for providing low and moderate income housing, and inclusionary zoning are strongly encouraged. The state Supreme Court was increasingly suspicious of non-Euclidian zoning devices because of the discretion involved in administering them.

d. The builder's remedy. In response to the *Mt. Laurel* opinions, the legislature enacted a statute to phase it out. In *Mt. Laurel II*, however, the remedy survived intact, although the opinion warned developers not to use it as a threat to get their projects approved. Evidence of such threats, the court said, would constitute grounds for denying it.

The builder's remedy is a far-reaching one, but raises some remedial problems with a regional flavor. First, an affordable housing project in one municipality may have to be met with compatible zoning in another municipality. Conversely, an affordable housing project in another municipality may have to be met with compatible zoning or rezoning across a nearby border. Thus cross-border arguments for a project or a rezoning reacting to a project are made easier and consistent with the builder's remedy. The builder's remedy is a voluntary but potent tool to encourage developers to propose housing projects with higher densities—and thus higher profits—than would be acceptable in municipalities with exclusionary zoning in place. In this context, it gives developers a function akin to a regulator or a court, compelling municipalities to comply with their *Mt. Laurel* fair share obligations.

Second, a municipality approving a development proposal satisfying, in part, its fair share obligation, requests a neighboring municipality to approve water and sewer line hook-ups for the development to lines in the latter municipality. If the neighboring municipality refuses, the developer, as a part of the builder's remedy, may seek an

28. *See Van Dalen v. Washington Twp.*, 500 A.2d 776, 782 (N.J. Super. Ct., Law Div. 1984).

injunction to mandate the hook-up. There is nothing in the *Mount Laurel II* doctrine to prevent such an injunction.[29]

[2] Two Litigation-Related Tactical Considerations

Counsel representing Mt. Laurel Township during this second stage of the litigation, might have been tempted to consider side-stepping the litigation by repealing its zoning ordinance altogether. A tempting, but also ill-advised strategy. It would have left the Township's land unregulated, and it would probably have earned the Township a contempt of court citation, because once under the obligation to take affirmative steps to confront its fair share obligation, its duty is to use the police power toward this end. Having excluded low income residents for several decades, the township could not suddenly take a libertarian stance toward land use.

Moreover, the likely effect of the court's emphasis on the builder's remedy in *Mount Laurel II* may be a shift in the type of likely plaintiffs engaged in exclusionary zoning litigation. If builders are the type of plaintiff with the strongest incentive to sue, what happens to the interests of plaintiffs like the NAACP, the Urban League, and other groups interested in racial as well as economic integration? What can be done to encourage such groups to participate in testing potentially exclusionary ordinances? The provision of attorneys fees to winning plaintiffs is one incentive not tried in most anti-exclusionary zoning provisions.

[3] Some Political Tactics

The shift from *Mount Laurel I*'s emphasis on developing municipalities to plan-designated growth areas spreads what political pain the first opinion induced. In general, making growth a trigger for imposing a *Mount Laurel* obligation places the obligation where it can most easily be accommodated. If the municipality is willing to accept growth, it should also be willing to accept a number-specific fair share of affordable housing. Not to do so is to cream the land uses available in a metropolitan area, depriving other competing jurisdictions of them. Growth and affordable housing should arguably be linked. *Mount Laurel II* broke that linkage in favor of imposing the fair share obligation more broadly.

[C] Stage Three

In a third stage of this litigation, the state Supreme Court validated a legislative solution and gave increasing deference to non-judicial applications of the *Mt. Laurel* doctrine. The legislative solution came so soon after the decision in *Mt. Laurel II* as to suggest that the legislature was reacting to that decision, thinking it judicial overreach.

---

29. *See Samaritan Center, Inc. v. Borough of Englishtown*, 683 A.2d 611 (N.J. Super. Ct. 1996) (so holding and issuing a mandatory injunction under similar circumstances).

Mount Laurel III: In a third, 1986 opinion, the New Jersey Supreme Court held constitutional a 1985 state Fair Housing Act.[30] The Act established an administrative agency and a voluntary administrative program for defining the fair share obligation of a municipality; it also recognized a new role for state government in the implementation of fair share affordable housing programs, a role intended to replace the courts in implementing *Mount Laurel I* and *II*.[31]

This program was administered by a state agency, the Council on Affordable Housing (COAH). The Act defined a municipality's fair share in terms of a host of planning factors, including the pattern of previous development. It delegated the determination of each's fair share to COAH.

Two features of the Act stand out. First, it incentivized a municipality to adopt an affordable housing plan by granting a municipality immunity from causes of action for a builder's remedy if it was in compliance with COAH procedures and obtained a "substantive certification" of compliance from that agency. Second, it created a system by which a municipality could transfer up to 50% of its fair share obligation to another municipality so long as the second municipality was located in the same housing market. It accomplished this transfer by recognizing so-called RCAs, "Regional Contribution Agreements."[32] (This second feature proved temporary: it was repealed in 2008 amid intense criticism.)

The Act also recognized that another state agency, the Housing and Mortgage Finance Agency, must play a role in implementing fair share housing obligations. The Fair Housing Act required that agency to give priority to projects with development proposals designed to meet such obligations.[33]

Deference to the legislature and comity predominated here. The court gave COAH the time and the flexibility to act. The court determined that the Act would, if properly implemented, provide a realistic opportunity for achieving a fair share of lower income housing. *Mt. Laurel III* once more reaffirmed the "fair share" obligation: "the state constitutional obligation has not changed," it said. The court also warned that the opinion represented "no weakening of our resolve to enforce the constitutional rights of New Jersey's lower income citizens." When considering some of the features of the New Jersey Fair Housing Act, however, perhaps the word "obligation" should be in air-quotes.

---

30. *See* N.J. Stat. Ann. § 52:26D-301 *et seq*. *See also Hills Development Co. v. Township of Bernards*, 510 A.2d 621 (N.J. 1986); John Payne, *General Welfare and Regional Planning: How the Law of Unattended Consequences and the Mount Laurel Doctrine Gave New Jersey a Modern State Plan*, 73 St. John's L. Rev. 1103, 1110–14 (1999).

31. *See* Paula A Franzese, *Mt. Laurel III: The New Jersey Supreme Court's Judicious Retreat*, 18 Seton Hall L. Rev. 30, 37 (1988) (arguing that the Legislature's Fair Housing Act was "destined to promote understatement of the true extent of qualifying municipalities' fair share of regional housing needs.").

32. *See* N.J. Stat. Ann. § 52:27D-312 (enacted 1985, repealed 2008).

33. *See* N.J. Stat. Ann. § 52:27D-307.3a(2)(c) (1986).

[1] Some Legislative History

The Act was the result of a long debate during the 1984 and 1985 legislative sessions. The Governor slowed budgeted state planning office funds to pressure the legislature to speed up its deliberations. Early versions of the Act proposed RCA agreements between municipalities, so that one municipality could transfer a development to another municipality. That proposal proved politically palatable to many legislators and was enacted into law. These statutorily authorized RCA agreements permitted affluent suburbs to satisfy their *Mt. Laurel* obligation by paying many millions of dollars for inner-city affordable housing. Moreover, the receiving municipality could then meet its heightened fair share by rehabilitating its existing, substandard housing stock, using subsidies provided by the sending jurisdiction.

Approval of these RCAs was crucial to the 1985 political compromise that led to the Act. Thus, if a suburban community with a fair share obligation paid for the construction or rehabilitation of low and moderate income units in another municipality, it could partially satisfy its obligation without diversifying its housing stock and diminishing its property tax base.[34]

[2] COAH Proceedings

The Act required that pending Mount Laurel litigation be transferred to COAH, except for litigation commenced more than sixty days before the effective date of the Act when transfer would be manifestly unjust to a party to the litigation. In fact, much litigation was not immediately transferred, and the state Supreme Court had to establish stringent guidelines for a court to retain jurisdiction. Moreover, the Supreme Court said that a municipality could not pick and choose the most lenient of terms as between the terms of any judicial decree and COAH's regulations—so a transfer to COAH must be a complete one.

COAH's regulations are reviewed under an "arbitrary and capricious" standard. In *Mt. Laurel I*, the court acted because the legislature would not. Thus, once the legislature finally acts, if a legislative act is typically entitled to a presumption of validity, legislative action taken in response to judicial concerns should enjoy a similar presumption. Further, the Supreme Court said, when there is apparent authority for a regulation, so should that regulation enjoy the presumption. Using this standard of review, most of COAH's regulations have been upheld, including an affordable housing linkage fee. Only a COAH cap on the number of dwelling units assigned to a municipality's fair share[35] and a municipal occupancy preference for local residents for 50% of the units in COAH-mandated, low income housing[36] have been invalidated by the courts.

---

34. *See In re Township of Warren*, 588 A.2d 1227 (N.J. Super. Ct., App. Div. 1991) (so holding).
35. *See Carlton Homes, Inc. v. COAH*, 582 A.2d 1024, 1030 (N.J. Super. Ct., App. Div. 1990).
36. *See In re Township of Warren*, 622 A.2d 1257 (N.J. 1993).

Finally, the 1985 Fair Housing Act imposed a moratorium on the builders' remedy, removing it from COAH's authorized remedies. The legislature sought to have the agency and the courts provide alternatives to this remedy. In *Mt. Laurel III*, the court found that the remedy was not grounded in the state constitution. Rather, it was only one of several means of meeting the constitutional obligation.

Once a municipality is within COAH's program—which happens when its fair share plan is filed, reviewed and certified by COAH—any person challenging that plan must first exhaust his or her remedies before COAH before going to court. And, once in court, the challenger must present clear and convincing evidence that the fair share obligation is unmet by the certified plan. In this way, certification of a municipality's fair share plan in effect immunizes the municipality from the builder's remedy.[37] However, no action by COAH will prevent neighbors from challenging a rezoning.[38]

[3] Administrative Response to the Act

Along with the 1985 enactment of the Act authorizing COAH came the simultaneous enactment of a State Planning Act.[39] In this legislation, the State Development Plan Guide was repealed and replaced by a State Development and Redevelopment Plan.[40] During the period 1986-1992, New Jersey state planners developed a state-wide plan, but it was not binding on the state's municipalities.[41] While comprehensive, state-wide, land-use planning did not become mandatory in New Jersey, because of the *Mt. Laurel* doctrine, planning for affordable or least-cost housing planning has. Perhaps one lasting achievement of the *Mt. Laurel* cases may be that they brought some state-wide land planning to a state that badly needed its benefits.

[D] Stage Four

Interim COAH regulations expired in 1999. In that year, a new set of COAH regulations were due. They were proposed by COAH but not promulgated. COAH attempted this again in 2004, and again in 2008, but reviewing courts found aspects of these regulations violated the *Mt. Laurel* doctrine and remanded them to the Council. Fourteen years ensued without regulations.[42] COAH's last meeting in 2014 to review draft regulations resulted in a 3-3 tie.[43] No regulations were issued that year. Finally,

37. *See Mt. Olive Complex v. Township of Mt. Olive*, 774 A.2d 704 (N.J. Super. Ct. 2001).

38. *See Saratoga v. Borough of West Patterson*, 788 A.2d 841 (N.J. Super. Ct. App. Div. 2002).

39. *See* N.J. Stat. Ann. § 52:18:A-196 (1985) (requiring a state-wide plan).

40. *See Van Dalen v. Washington Twp.*, 576 A.2d 819, 824 (N.J. 1990) (a previous opinion in this litigation, issued in 1984, is cited *supra*).

41. For more information on New Jersey planning, see http://www.nj.gov/state/planning/index.html.

42. *See* J. Marsico, Note: *A Forty Year Failure: Why the New Jersey Supreme Court Should Take Control of Mount Laurel Enforcement*, 41 Seton Hall. Legis. J. 149, 164 (2016).

43. COAH's authorizing statute does not compel successor appointments when the initial terms for its appointees runs out. *See In re Murphy*, 309 A.3d 128, 130 (N.J. 2024) ("[W]e hold that the Governor cannot be compelled by mandamus to fill COAH's vacancies.").

the New Jersey Supreme Court set a deadline of November, 2014: if COAH did not adopt new regulations by that date, the courts would entertain applications for relief on a case-by-case basis which if granted, would give rise to a cause of action for a builder's remedy.[44] The up-shot was *Mt. Laurel IV*.[45]

Mt. Laurel IV suspended and "dissolved" the doctrine of exhaustion of administrative remedies (before COAH) and ordered all pending COAH cases transferred to the courts, the courts to "resume their role as the forum of first resort for evaluating municipal compliance with *Mount Laurel* obligations." Courts "were authorized to hear and decide actions addressing municipal compliance with constitutional *Mount Laurel* obligations by municipalities that have sought the protections of the FHA through COAH."[46] Municipalities currently achieving COAH compliance certificates or participating in such proceedings were entitled (for a short time period) to bring a declaratory judgment action that its housing plan is "presumptively valid"[47] because it fulfills its constitutional obligation to provide for its needs for low and moderate-income housing. "Only after a court has had the opportunity to fully address constitutional compliance and has found constitutional compliance wanting shall it permit exclusionary zoning actions and any builder's remedy. . . . "[48] Thereafter any party could sue the municipality, the action focused on whether the municipality's housing plan meets its constitutional *Mt. Laurel* obligation. All of these causes of action "shall be directed" to *Mt. Laurel* designated judges.[49]

Once a township achieved its fair share obligations without including a developer's proposed parcel, the township's existing zoning governed the parcel and the developer could not force a builder's remedy on the municipality; thereafter, neither fair share nor realistic opportunity analysis applied.[50]

The New Jersey Supreme Court emphasized that the designated *Mt. Laurel* courts were not a "replacement agency" for COAH. "The action taken herein does not prevent either COAH or the Legislature from taking steps to a viable administrative remedy that towns can use in satisfaction of their constitutional obligation."[51]

---

44. *See In the Matter of the Application of the Twp. of Bordentown*, 272 A.3d 413, 420, n.2 (N.J. Super. Ct. 2022) (reviewing the history given in this paragraph).

45. *See In re N.J.A.C. 5;96 & 5:97*, 110 A.3d 31 (N.J. 2015) (*Mt. Laurel IV*).

46. *Id.* at 51, para. 2.

47. *Id.* para. 5.

48. *Id.* para. 8.

49. *Id.* at 51–52.

50. *See Twp. of Bordentown*, *op. cit.*

51. *Mt. Laurel IV*, *op. cit.*, 110 A.3d at 50–51.

[E] How Successful Is the *Mount Laurel* Doctrine?

By 1988, about 15,000 affordable housing units were either completed, under construction, or the subject of a pending application in 54 municipalities since *Mt. Laurel II.* Most were for sale, rather than rent.[52] Between 1985 and the beginning of the twenty-first century, about 20-25% of the affordable housing units requested by COAH and the state legislature were either newly-built or used existing units rehabilitated for affordable housing residents.[53] A similar percentage of units were zoned into municipal zoning ordinances.[54] When these statistics are compared to the total number of housing units for which building permits were issued in a comparable period, the resulting percentage allotted to low and moderate income housing is low indeed—about 4%.[55]

These accomplishments came with a price—abandonment of the goal of metropolitan-wide racial integration. RCAs administered by COAH permit over 53 suburbs to buy their way out of their duty to have affordable housing located within their jurisdiction. Only one RCA agreement involved an inner city municipality transferring its *Mt. Laurel* obligation to a suburb. RCAs permitted the concentration of affordable housing units in the predominantly minority, poorer, central cities. Moreover, studies of the post-1986 affordable housing built in the suburbs indicates little minority occupancy.[56] Thus, at a time when government funds for low income housing were dwindling, the *Mt. Laurel* doctrine has been diverted from its initial purpose of integrating the suburbs and redirected toward the goal of housing the poor where they currently live.

By 1993, over one-third of New Jersey's municipalities had either participated in or settled judicial or COAH proceedings. That left over 300 of the state's municipalities where COAH's impact is uncertain. Only by 2014 had about two-thirds of New Jersey municipalities had adopted a fair share obligation plan. Moreover, empirical studies of the effectiveness of the *Mt. Laurel* doctrine are decades old, hard to reconcile one with another, and use different methodologies—some study low and moderate income housing consumers, others the housing market.

---

52. *See* Martha Lamar et al., Mt. Laurel *at Work: Affordable Housing in New Jersey, 1983-1988*, 41 Rutgers L.J. 1197, 1204–15 (1989).

53. *See* Dennis Keating, The Suburban Racial Dilemma 39–40 (1994) (reporting also that 3,000 of those 25,000 approved units were the subjects of regional contribution agreements).

54. *See* Henry A. Span, *How the Courts Should Fight Exclusionary Zoning*, 32 Seton Hall. L. Rev. 1, 65 (2001).

55. *See* Malina Sullivan, *The Starting Point: Newark's Land Use Laws at the Outset of Redevelopment to Promote Integration Without Displacement*, 53 Colum. J. L. & Social Probs. 43, 55 (2019). For a review of the studies on the effectiveness of the *Mt. Laurel* doctrine, see *id.* at 55–56.

56. *See* Keating, *supra*, at 40.

§ 15.06 Fair Share Housing Doctrines in Other States

New Jersey courts have been the leader in formulating requirements for the creation of realistic opportunities for the construction of low income and affordable housing. **Pennsylvania** courts have similarly required that municipalities provide a reasonable number of housing types in their ordinances: this means that mobile homes, apartments, townhouses, and duplexes—as well as single-family detached housing—must be zoned into their ordinances. Pennsylvania's townships must permit uses reflective of the housing types offered in the surrounding region—and not on the basis of tokenism either, but in reasonable numbers.[57] The Pennsylvania requirement is based on substantive due process considerations.[58]

In **New York** State, the Court of Appeals has a two-part test for analyzing the validity of a zoning ordinance. First, the municipality shall have a "balanced" plan for development, meeting both present and future housing needs, and second, the municipality must consider the regional general welfare in enacting the ordinance. However, in New York, municipalities can show that the regional housing needs of the poor are being met elsewhere—and so they need do nothing.[59] This second type of showing makes the two parts of the test work against one another. In addition, although standing requirements are often more lenient in state exclusionary zoning cases than they would be in federal court, New York has restricted standing in exclusionary zoning cases in some ways similar to the federal courts.[60]

[A] *Britton v. Town of Chester*

Perhaps the shortest, most comprehensive, best written, post-*Mt.Laurel III* judicial opinion comes from **New Hampshire**. It is *Britton v. Town of Chester*.[61] Here, the New Hampshire Supreme Court invalidated a town's ordinance as exclusionary and an improper use of the delegation of power to the town contained in the state's zoning enabling act. Because this case was decided on a statutory ground, constitutional questions were not reached.

---

57. *See BAC, Inc. v. Board of Supervisors of Millcreek Twp.*, 633 A.2d 144, 147–47 (Pa. 1993) (reviewing the state's case law).

58. *See Precision Equities, Inc. v. Franklin Park Borough Zoning Hearing Bd.*, 646 A.2d 756, 759 (Pa. Commwlth. Ct. 1994); *see also Rauso v. Romero*, 820 A.2d 143 (Pa. 2002) (upholding large lot agricultural zoning based on township's need to preserve farms); *In re Appeal of C & M Development*, 49 D. & C. 4th 71 (Pa. Bucks Cty. C.P. 2000).

59. *See Berenson v. Town of New Castle*, 341 N.E.2d 236, 243 (N.Y. 1975) (involving the denial of a building permit for a large condominium development in a town having a zoning ordinance without a multi-family use district).

60. *See Suffolk Housing Services v. Town of Brookhaven*, 511 N.E.2d 67 (N.Y. 1987).

61. 595 A.2d 492 (N.H. 1991).

The plaintiffs in *Britton* were two individual residents of the town eligible for low income housing, and a developer who had been attempting to build 48 multi-family units, 10 of which were low-income. In the early 1980s, none of the town's land was zoned so as to permit multi-family housing. Its exclusion was then total. Later, the town permitted this type of housing in residential PUD districts, but the court found that less than 2% of the town's land was realistically available for this housing, and even then not "as of right," but only as a part of the specially permitted PUD. The effect of such findings was to shift the burden of proof to the town to justify its ordinance.

As to remedy, the court said that the trial court's order was too broad and left the town unzoned. The order was remanded and the court said that its invalidation applied only to those sections of the ordinance "hindering the construction of multi-family housing units. Accordingly, we defer to the legislative body of the town, within a reasonable time period, to bring these sections of its zoning ordinance into line with the zoning enabling legislation and with this opinion." Thus, the existing ordinance remained in effect in the interim, and the court refused to order a rewrite of the town's entire ordinance.

The court also affirmed the use by the trial court of the site-specific relief in a builder's remedy.[62] As in New Jersey, this remedy is discretionary with the court. To obtain it, however, the plaintiff developer must show that the proposal is a reasonable use of the land; thus, unlike New Jersey's remedy, this builder's remedy requires that the plaintiff carry the burden of proof. In New Jersey, on the other hand, it is the defendant municipality that has the burden of showing that the land is unsuitable for the use proposed by the builder. The better view is found in *Britton*. This burden of proof should be assigned to the builder, requiring him to show a reasonable basis for the proposed use. The municipality is used to making this showing in the course of zoning the jurisdiction, but the developer best knows the impact of the proposed use, and so is best able to bear it under these circumstances.

Britton gives New Hampshire's towns the option of (1) rewriting the ordinance with inclusionary zoning provisions,[63] (2) adopting one of several methods of defining the regional housing needs and calculating the town's fair share to meet those needs, or (3) accepting a builder's remedy. While the state's constitutional provision on the separation of powers might limit the court's future role, nonetheless the court finds authority to fashion relief, even though it might later defer to a state-wide

---

62. This remedy is a judicial order that the land be used as the plaintiff developer proposed; so in effect it is a mandatory rezoning of that land parcel. This relief is a reward for contesting the ordinance and also prevents municipal retribution in rezoning land (but not the plaintiff's land) for multi-family housing. *See Cmty. Res. for Justice, Inc. v. City of Manchester*, 949 A.2d 681 (N.H. 2008) (upholding a builder's remedy for a halfway house); *Great Bridge Properties, LLC v. Town of Ossipee*, 2005 N.H. Super. LEXIS 3 (N.H. Super. Ct., Feb. 7, 2005).

63. *See Sun Coast Properties, LLC v. Town of Windham*, 2012 N.H. Super. LEXIS 10, *4–6, & n. 3 (N.H. Super. Ct., Feb. 29, 2012) (noting that as of 2008, N.H. includes workforce housing in its definition of affordable housing).

legislative housing policy. *Britton* avoids both the pitfalls of New Jersey's *Mount Laurel I* stage and a confrontation with the state legislature.

The New Hampshire Supreme Court later held valid a rural town's zoning regulation that authorized a mountain and forest use district with a minimum lot size of 50 acres to protect forestry, timber harvesting, conservation, and wildlife interests. *Casperson v. Town of Lyme*[64] thus indicates a judicial interest in balancing environmental and affordable housing needs in the state. This case arose in a town near the mid-point of the state's rural western border with Vermont, whereas *Britton* arose in the southern New Hampshire region affected by the growth of the Boston region to the south.

§ 15.07 Inclusionary Zoning

An inclusionary zoning ordinance is one that requires that every housing development proposal include some affordable housing units. New Jersey courts, after *Mount Laurel II*, required that an exclusionary township redraft its ordinance, adding provisions that would provide a "realistic opportunity" for low and moderate income housing. Such provisions often took the form of a requirement that developers set aside a certain percentage of the units built in a development for low and moderate income persons—or in lieu of such a set-aside, make mandatory payments into a township account for the provision of such housing. This is what is known as inclusionary zoning.[65] For such ordinances, a waiver procedure and a density bonus provision weaken arguments that such set-asides amount to a taking of property. Waiver or hardship procedures preclude a facial challenge to the ordinance. Large density bonuses compensate for the set-asides. (In the alternative, an ordinance with impact fee features can be defended by a municipality's performing the essential nexus and rough proportionality studies required by *Nollan* and *Dolan*.) In addition, ordinances without in-lieu fees look less like a exactions.

Most of the recent municipal experience with inclusionary zoning is in two states—California and New Jersey.[66] The outline of a set-aside program is typically as

64. 661 A.2d 759, 761 (N.H. 1995).

65. *See Home Builders of Northern California v. City of Napa*, 108 Cal. Rptr. 2d 60 (App. Ct. 2001) (refusing to apply heightened scrutiny to a 10% set-aside ordinance and finding *Nollan/Dolan* tests inapplicable) (noted in 115 Harv. L. Rev. 2058 (2002)). *But see Board of Supervisors of Fairfax Cty. v. DeGroff Enterprizes, Inc.*, 198 S.E.2d 600 (Va. 1973) (holding invalid an ordinance requiring the developer of 50 or more units to set aside 15% of units for low and moderate income housing), reversed later by statute, Va. Code § 15.1-491.8 to .9 (1991) (requiring that 12.5% of the single family dwelling units, and 6.25% of multi-family units, proposed in plans for 50 or more units, shall be affordable housing, for which the developer receives a 10% density bonus).

66. As to New Jersey, *see* Malina Sullivan, *The Starting Point: Newark's Land Use Laws at the Outset of Redevelopment to Promote Integration Without displacement*, 53 Colum. J. L. & Social Probs. 43, 55 (2019).

follows: (1) Many programs are mandatory, but when they are voluntary, they work (a) as a density bonus, as in California, or (b) are used in conjunction with transferable development rights useable for affordable housing, or (c) are used when the municipality has a growth control/adequate public facilities ordinance similar to Ramapo's or Petaluma's, so that the number of points assigned to affordable housing proposals may be increased and proposals that would not otherwise qualify for a development permit will do so. Most of the California municipalities using this device have mandatory set-aside requirements. California is also a state in which urban planning has been made mandatory by statute, and so state agency certification of the housing element in a municipality's land use plan has provided the hook for implementing inclusionary zoning programs.

(2) Most programs involve setting aside about 10-15% of the proposed housing units. California statutes authorize municipalities to provide for a density bonus of between 10 and 20% of the units when part of a housing development proposal consists of low or moderate income housing—and a 50% bonus if senior citizen housing is included.[67] Whatever the percentage, the units are typically scattered within the development, rather than all clustered in one location.

(3) To provide programmatic flexibility, off-site units are permitted, and fewer interior amenities are required—and generally the affordable- and market-rate units must look substantially the same. Rental as well as ownership units are permitted.

(4) Transfer covenants prohibit future ownership transfers of the affordable units at market rates for a set period following their construction or first purchase, and they must be recorded in a manner that notifies lenders of their applicability. These pricing controls prevent the inclusionary program from becoming a first home program—in California, a 30 year restriction is typical—and just a windfall to first purchasers. The time the restriction applies must be sufficiently long to substantially advance the goals of the ordinance. In some California municipalities, the municipality retains an assignable right to repurchase the unit upon sale, with the assignee being a qualified purchaser on a municipal waiting list. Moreover, transfer covenants require municipal monitoring:[68] ownership units might otherwise be rented, an eligible owner might die leaving ineligible heirs, or an owner might fail to maintain the unit: and purchasers might buy other properties (calling in question eligibility for participation in the program), litigate the legality of the covenants, or build equity with improvements made after occupancy (no bad thing in itself, but an accounting nightmare on resale). Given these scenarios, it isn't surprising that private monitoring firms have grown up in California.

---

67. *See* Calif. Gov. Code §65915 (1996). *See generally* Marc Smith et al., *Inclusionary Housing Programs: Issues and Outcomes*, 25 R. Est. L.J. 155, 166–67 (1996).

68. *See US Bank v. Hough*, 42 A.3d 870 (N.J. 2012) (policing lender who issued a loan exceeding 95% of the maximum allowable resale price of an affordable housing unit).

(5) Finally, small scale projects, typically less than 10 units, are exempted from the program. This exemption is presumably granted because the economies of scale for shifting costs to market rate purchasers are not present in smaller development proposals.[69]

In addition, other features of zoning ordinances might be changed to increase the provision of affordable housing. Here are three examples. First, many residential use district ordinances include regulations prohibiting accessory rental units. So long as over-all density requirements are observed, why not permit, and even encourage accessory apartments in such districts? Doing this would encourage economic diversity. Second, exclusively residential districts are the pattern in some municipalities. Why not encourage mixed-use districts, so that apartments and other forms of housing may be located over commercial uses? That was the pattern of many small town main streets until the advent of zoning ordinances. Why not revert to what has worked in the past? Third, why not prohibit minimum square footage regulations in residential districts? The emphasis on inclusionary zoning should not block a review of zoning ordinances to ferret out their exclusionary features.

In summary, to attempt to insure the constitutionality of an inclusionary affordable housing ordinance requiring set-asides, a municipality should (1) establish by studies the relationship between the new development in which the set-asides are required and the decreased availability of affordable housing (the economic impact of the new development on land prices is perhaps the best approach); (2) the set-aside units of housing should be of a type not likely to be provided by the private unsubsidized market; (3) density bonuses or other voluntary incentives should be provided to maintain the over-all profitability of the development; (4) affordability controls should be maintained: the price of the housing set aside as affordable should be maintained by requiring that future sales or rentals should only be to individuals or families then needing affordable housing; and (5) developers should be given flexibility to decide whether the affordable housing units set aside should be provided on site, by contract providers as opposed to the developer itself, or by the combined efforts of several affected developers.

When in-lieu fees are collected, the regulation should contain precautionary provisions to safeguard the constitutionality of the fee: first, the type of housing meeting the definition of affordable should be defined; second, the neighborhood in which the money will be spent should be limited to one in reasonable proximity of the developer's project; third, the money should be held in trust for its stated purposes, and no other; and fourth and finally, reasonable time limits should be placed on the use of the fees and if they are not used within the prescribed time, the fees should be returned. Such limitations increase the defensibility of such fees.

---

69. *See* Nico Calavita & Kenneth Grimes, *Inclusionary Housing in California: The Experience of Two Decades*, 64 J. Am. Plng. Ass'n 150, 164–66 (1998).

§ 15.08 Appeals of Affordable Housing Permit Denials

In order to counter the effects of exclusionary permit denials, a few states have authorized special permits and administrative appeals to a board with state-wide jurisdiction. Often these appeals arise from a municipality's subdivision review procedures. They concern whether subdivision infrastructure or environmental requirements can trump the need for affordable housing. In **Massachusetts**, an applicant can apply for a comprehensive permit from a BZA for a low and moderate income housing project "subsidized by the federal or state government." When such a permit is denied, or is approved with restrictions making the project uneconomic, the developer has a right to appeal to a special state Housing Appeals Committee (HAC).[70]

The HAC then determines if the denial is "consistent with local needs." Consistency is found (and the denial is upheld) when 10% of the town's housing stock is currently devoted to low or moderate income housing; when subsidized housing is occupying more than 1.5% of the town's land area; or when the approval would affect more than 10 acres or consume more than .3% of the town's land area. Otherwise the presumption of validity does not apply during the appeal: the town has the burden of showing that the denial was supported by a consideration overriding the region's needs for qualifying housing. A town's decision to deny a permit based on the "possibility" that nitrogen contamination of nearby wells will occur, may be overturned by the HAC and affirmed on appeal when the HAC deems the developer's experts more creditable than the town's: the HAC concluded that "the much smaller risk [of contamination] did not outweigh the need for affordable housing."[71] Nor will a town's concerns about blasting noise during site preparation override the HAC's finding of a need for local workforce housing declared in a state statute.[72]

A showing of consistency is a question of fact for the HAC. However, an HAC appeal is subject to the exhaustion of administrative remedies at the municipal level. The HAC is authorized to order that the applicant's permit be issued.[73] When an application is granted, it is still consistent with local needs if it overrides a town's zoning to the extent of including incidental commercial uses.[74] Likewise, a town board may grant an application when considering a regional need for affordable housing,

70. *See Board of Appeals of Hanover v. Housing Appeals Committee*, 294 N.E.2d 393 (Mass. 1973) (upholding the 1969 version of Mass. Gen. L., ch. 40B, §§ 20-23 (2007)).

71. *See Town of Hingham Zoning Bd. of Appeals v. Housing Appeals Comm.*, 2024 Mass. LCR LEXIS 55, *18 (Mass. Land Ct., Apr. 12, 2024) (distinguishing *Reynolds v. Zoning Bd. of Appeals of Stow*, 37 N.E.3d 656 (Mass. Ct. App. 2015).

72. *See Zoning Bd. of Appeals of Woburn v. Housing Appeals Comm.*, 2017 Mass. App. Unpub. LEXIS 1023 (Mass. Ct. App., Nov. 21, 2017).

73. *See Boothroyd v. Zoning Bd. of Appeals of Amherst*, 868 N.E.2d 83, 85 n. 3 (Mass. 2007); *see also Pheasant Ridge Assoc. Limited Partnership v. Town of Burlington*, 506 N.E.2d 1152 (Mass. 1987).

74. *See Jepson v. Zoning Board of Appeals of Ipswich*, 876 N.E.2d 820 (Mass. 2007).

even though the town has met its own need for affordable housing.[75] However, a town board may not accept a cash contribution for affordable housing because the governing state statute, as of 2023, "unambiguously required the physical reservation of 10% of the proposed housing as affordable."[76]

The **Connecticut** legislature has enacted a somewhat similar statute.[77] The Connecticut statute applies to denials of both federally subsidized and unsubsidized affordable housing. If the application qualifies, its denial may be appealed regardless of whether or not the original application was designated as for affordable housing. Appeals from permit denials lie when the affordable housing stock in a town is less than 10% of the total stock. They are heard by the judiciary, with specially-assigned judges presiding over the appeal.[78] The evidence heard by the trial court is scrutinized *de novo* by the reviewing court. The municipal board or commission has the burden of proof in this review.[79] This review is plenary and independent.

The standard of review is twofold. First, a reviewing court must determine that the municipality's decision from which the appeal is taken is "supported by sufficient evidence in the record." Sufficient evidence is a lower standard than substantial evidence. Sufficient evidence is "more than a theoretical possibility, but not necessarily a likelihood, of a specific harm to the public interest if the developer's application is granted."[80] Second, the municipal decision must be shown to (1) advance a substantial public interest in the health, safety, or other police power concern, (2) clearly outweighing the need for affordable housing, and (3) involving such an interest that cannot be protected by reasonable changes in the applicant's housing development.[81] Thus the municipality must show more than non-compliance with its ordinances.[82]

---

75. *See Boothroyd*, 868 N.E.2d at 83. *See generally Zoning Bd. of Appeals of Holliston v. Housing Appeals Comm'n*, 953 N.E.2d 721 (Mass. App. Ct. 2011); *Scituate Zoning Bd. of Appeals v. Herring Brook Meadow LLC*, 2012 Mass. LCR LEXIS 85 (Land Ct., July 27, 2012) (both opinions discussing amendments to the HAC statute similar to Rhode Island's single comprehensive permit); *Welch v. Paicos*, 66 F. Supp. 2d 138, 142–45 (D. Mass. 1999) (reviewing the history of the Mass. statute).

76. *See 50-56 Mkt. St. LLC v. Town of Ipswich*, 2023 LCR LEXIS 119, *11 (Mass. Land Ct., Oct. 30, 2023). The Land Court also held that the Subdivision Control Law did not authorize planning boards to reject compliant subdivisions just because they propose to include affordable housing. *See Estate of Isola v. Town of Stoneham*, 2024 Mass. LCR LEXIS 2 (Land Ct., Jan 4, 2024).

77. *See* Conn. Gen. Stat. § 8-30g(a)-(b) (1991, amended in 1999); *see also Kaufman v. Zoning Comm'n of City of Danbury*, 653 A.2d 798 (Conn. 1995) (finding that a developer of affordable housing did not have to submit more detailed plans for this appeal than would any other applicant for rezoning).

78. *See West Hartford Interfaith Coalition v. Town of West Hartford*, 636 A.2d 1342, 1356 (Conn. 1994) (reversing a local permit denial for a proposed affordable housing project).

79. *See Bremor Props., LLC v. Planning & Zoning Comm'n of Lisbon*, 161 A.3d 545 (Conn. 2017), adopting the appellate court's opinion, 136 A.3d 24 (Conn. App. Ct. 2016) (holding no need for strict compliance with street requirements of subdivision ordinance in affordable housing appeals).

80. *See Bremor Props, op. cit.*, 136 A.3d at 31.

81. *Id.*

82. *See Garden Homes Mgmt. Corp. v. Town Plan & Zoning Comm'm of the Town of Fairfield*, 216 A.3d 680, 691–92 (Conn. Ct. App. 2019) (collecting Connecticut cases on the municipality's burden of proof to quantify harm to a watershed, as well as the impact on traffic, water, and sewer systems).

The possibility of harm to public infrastructure, wetlands, or water wells does not suffice.[83]

Where the reason given for the denial is based on a land use plan which fails to include a program for the eventual satisfaction of a municipality's duty to zone for affordable housing, the reason is suspect and will be carefully scrutinized by the court. When land is designated as open space in a plan, but lacks water and sewer service, is steep and rocky, and is located near a watercourse, the denial may be based on reasons substantial enough to outweigh the need for affordable housing there.[84]

A denial may be reversed outright, or with conditions, and be subject to appeal.[85] A denial may also be remanded to the municipality's board or commission with directions to issue the permit previously denied.[86] When for example, a municipality refused to rezone for affordable housing, it must show that the goal it advanced for not doing so will be harmed, although its showing need not be as high as a preponderance of the evidence.[87] "Specifically, the court must determine whether the record establishes that there is more than a mere theoretical possibility, but not necessarily a likelihood, of a specific harm to the public interest if the application is granted."[88] So the denial must have been based on less than a preponderance of the evidence, but more than a "mere possibility." Generalized fears of affordable housing, or vague quality of life concerns, not lending themselves to some objective measure, do not outweigh the strong public interest in the statute. Likewise, if permits must be obtained from other agencies and boards, there is a strong presumption in these appeals that those permits can be obtained. Thus a denial must be based on (1) a substantial public interest clearly outweighing the need for the affordable housing, and (2) a finding that there are no more modifications to the application than would permit it to be granted.

In addition to the sort of exemptions Massachusetts provides for municipalities with (e.g.) 10% of its housing stock already devoted to affordable housing, Connecticut exempts from this appeals process municipalities that voluntarily participate in a state inclusionary housing program and have built a number of affordable units equal to 1% of all residential units built in the municipality within the last year.[89] However,

---

83. *Id. See also Autumn View LLC v. Planning & Zoning Comm'n*, 218 A.3d 1101 (Conn. Ct. App.), *cert. denied*, 218 A.3d 1048 (Conn. 2019).

84. *See Landmark Development Group, LLC v. East Lyme Zoning Comm'n*, 2004 Conn. Super. LEXIS 2566 (Sept. 3, 2004).

85. *See Carr v. Planning & Zoning Comm'n of The Town of Bridgewater*, 872 A.2d 385 (Conn. 2005).

86. *See Bremor Props., LLC v. Planning & Zoning Comm'n of Lisbon*, 161 A.3d 545 (Conn. 2017), adopting the appellate court's opinion, 136 A.3d 24 (Conn. App. Ct. 2016) (holding no need for strict compliance with street requirements of subdivision ordinance in affordable housing appeals).

87. *See Quarry Knoll II Corp. v. Planning and Zoning Commission of Greenwich*, 780 A.2d 1 (2001) (noting that the statute does not shift burden of proof in these appeals but rather further refines it and reviewing the amendments of the 2000 legislature as to the burden of proof). *See generally* Robert Carroll, *Connecticut Retrenches: A Proposal to Save the Affordable Housing Appeals Procedure*, 110 Yale L.J. 1247 (2001).

88. *See Avalon Bay Communities, Inc. v. Zoning and Planning Comm'n of The Town of Stratford*, 931 A.2d 879, 890, n. 14 (Conn. 2007) (also discussing *Kaufman, op. cit.*).

89. *See* Conn. Gen. Stat. § 8-30g(f)-(g).

when less than 10% of a municipality's stock is devoted to affordable housing, the burden of proof is shifted to the municipality to justify the denial.

In **Rhode Island**, a statutorily authorized "single application for a comprehensive permit" for affordable housing projects may be submitted to the zoning board in lieu of several permits to many municipal boards. Thereafter, with notice to the several boards otherwise involved, the zoning board holds a hearing and decides to grant or deny the application within a prescribed time frame. Failure to decide within the time prescribed means that the application is deemed to have been approved.[90] Denial of the application must be based on one of four grounds: the proposal is inconsistent with local needs, is not in conformance with the comprehensive plan of the municipality, is made in a municipality that has 10% of its housing stock already devoted to low and moderate income housing,[91] or raises environmental concerns and does not adequately address the health and safety of current residents.[92] If the application is denied, an appeal may be made to a State Housing Appeals Board (SHAB).[93] A reviewing court uses a deferential standard when reviewing a SHAB decision.[94] It cannot reweigh the credibility of testimony or evidence relating to questions of fact; instead, it is limited to a review of the record to determine whether there is "any legally competent evidence" to support SHAB's decision.[95]

Granting an application with many conditions may amount to an effective denial and also be subject to appeal.[96] The tight time frame for decision at the municipal level does not apply to the state Board. There, the most important reason for denials has so far been "local needs" basis.[97] In this respect, the scale of the project and its effect on its surrounding area may be considered.[98] That the application would have a negative impact on traffic conditions, exhibited fire risks, and was excessively dense, has been found an insufficient local concern to override the need for affordable housing.[99]

---

90. *See Town of Smithfield v. Churchill & Banks Cos.*, 924 A.2d 796 (R.I. 2007) (noted at 13 Roger Williams L. Rev. 854 (2008) (reversing State Housing Appeals Board (SHAB) decision due to incompleteness of the application).

91. *See JCM LLC v. Town of Cumberland Zoning Bd. of Review*, 889 A.2d 169 (R.I. 2005).

92. *See East Bay Community Development Corp. v. Zoning Bd. of Review of the Town of Barrington*, 901 A.2d 1136, 1145-46 (R.I. 2006) (containing a general description of the municipal procedure).

93. *See New Harbor Village v. New Shoreham Zoning Bd. of Review*, 894 A.2d 901, 904, n. 2 (R.I. 2006) (describing the appellate hearing by the board).

94. *See Town of Hopkinton v. Clarks Falls Realty, LLC*, 2021 R.I. Super. LEXIS 64, *18–19 (R.I. Super. Ct., Aug. 20, 2021).

95. *Id.* at *19.

96. *See Gifford v. Rhode Island State Housing Bd. of Appeals*, 2007 R.I. Super. LEXIS 108 (Aug. 7, 2007).

97. *See New Harbor Village*, *op. cit.*, 894 A.2d at 908, n. 8.

98. *See Housing Opportunities Corp. v. Zoning Bd. of Review of the Town of Johnston*, 890 A.2d 445, 452 (R.I. 2006).

99. *See East Bay Community Development Corp. v. Zoning Bd. of Review of the Town of Barrington*, 901 A.2d 1136 (R.I. 2006) (indicating that the fire risks could be handled at the building permit stage).

In addition, several states have required that municipalities adopt comprehensive land use plans that include an affordable housing element.[100] Such an element requires that the municipality analyze its existing and projected needs for affordable housing. California, Florida, Oregon, and Washington have such statutes in their planning enabling acts. In Oregon, for example, a state agency periodically reviews and certifies these elements as in compliance with the statute; if they are not, administrative orders are authorized to bring them into compliance and local grant funds for planning can be withheld until there is compliance. Oregon designates urban growth boundaries to encourage higher densities and growth rates within these boundaries; municipalities within such boundaries are under an obligation to zone sufficient land to meet its share of the regional need for affordable housing.[101]

§ 15.09 Conclusion

Whether a jurisdiction should enact the Massachusetts or the New Jersey approach to exclusionary zoning and fair share obligations involves a choice made according to the view taken of the courts' and administrative agencies' relative capabilities to oversee housing programs. The Massachusetts administrative approach has achieved more, more quickly, and with less fanfare. What began with a law suit in New Jersey to address the effects of racial segregation in suburban housing, has lost its race-based identity and become instead an attempt at economic, rather than racial integration in housing. New state constitutional law has been made there, but the political cost has been high and the original goal blurred over time; meanwhile, the state's revised administrative process for state-wide land use planning has become the lasting, if unintended, consequence of that long ago law suit in Mount Laurel.

---

100. *See, e.g.*, Cal. Gov't Code § 65584 (1993).

101. *See* Note, *State-Sponsored Growth Management as a Remedy for Exclusionary Zoning*, 108 Harv. L. Rev. 1127, 1133–36 (1995).

Chapter 16
Civil Rights and Exclusionary Zoning

§ 16.01 Introduction

Sometimes an applicant for a variance, special exception, or rezoning, or other land use permit alleges that the denial of a permit is motivated by discrimination of a type prohibited by the federal civil rights statutes. In most cases, the prohibition is contained in Title VIII of the Civil Rights Act of 1968 (the Fair Housing Act or FHA),[1] providing in part that it is unlawful "to make unavailable or deny . . . a dwelling to any person because of race, color, religion, sex, handicap, or national origin." This statute is concerned with the actions of vendors, landlords, real estate brokers, and lending institutions; it does not explicitly mention land use regulators. Nevertheless, discrimination by regulators has been held to "make unavailable" housing of many types. Discrimination is never defined in the civil rights acts; rather, its definition is left to the courts.

As we have seen in discussing the question of standing,[2] the doors of the federal courthouse are not particularly wide for plaintiffs claiming discrimination in land use cases. Once the merits of a discrimination claim are reached, moreover, the plaintiff's path is not an easy one, particularly when the discrimination is urged to be a constitutional matter.

§ 16.02 Constitutional Claims

Village of Arlington Heights v. Metropolitan Housing Development Corporation[3] holds that, when asserting a constitutional claim of discrimination under the Fourteenth Amendment's equal protection clause, a claimant must show more than that the decision has a disparate impact on minority groups (of which plaintiff must be member) protected by the Constitution. Rather, the disparate impact of the decision

1. As amended, 42 U.S.C. § 3604(a) (2024).
2. *See supra* Chapter 13, § 13.01[A].
3. 429 U.S. 252 (1977).

is only one of several other factors reviewed in determining whether the decision was motivated by a discriminatory purpose. The discriminatory purpose need not be the predominant purpose of the decision. It must be a motivating factor: that is, but for the discriminatory purpose, the decision would have been otherwise, the permit would have been granted, etc. Its impact—e.g., whether the decision bears more heavily on one race than another—is not determinative.

The other factors that a court must consider are:

(1) the historical background for the decision,
(2) the specific sequence of events leading up to the decision,
(3) the departures in the contested case from the normal procedural sequence,
(4) any substantive departures from normal law and policy,
(5) the administrative and legislative history of the case, as well as
(6) the impact of the decision.

All must be considered in determining whether discrimination was the motivating purpose of the decision.

The first five factors, all those other than impact, are all process-oriented. No substantive law, intrusive on the state law relating to exclusionary or any other type of zoning, is being made here. This brings this opinion in line with the state law rule that generally legislative motive is generally irrelevant in zoning cases. What the Supreme Court is doing is attempting to inquire into motive without permitting direct evidence of motive. Moreover, the factors are extremely flexible: for example, the planning policies justifying a decision are malleable indeed, so that whether or not there is a departure from them is a matter of first defining them—a matter involving a large amount of discretion.

The land use pattern in the Village of Arlington Heights was much like the town involved in *Warth v. Seldin*:[4] its predominant land use was single family detached housing. While the town in *Warth* was 98% single family detached, however, Arlington Heights did have some apartments. However, they were not low or moderate income housing. The Metropolitan Housing Development Corporation (MHDC) was a not-for-profit corporation proposing to place 190 clustered townhouse buildings on 15 acres, with 100 of the dwelling units having one bedroom.

The racial pattern of the Village was overwhelmingly white: only 27 of the village's approximately 64,000 inhabitants were black. Even so, so long as its rezoning appeared in line with its usual and customary practice and procedures, there was slim-to-none chance of its running afoul of the Court's five factors. The Village *might* have run afoul of the Court's five factors if it had first rezoned the MHDC's land for

4. *See supra* Chapter 13, § 13.01[E][1] (discussing *Warth v. Seldin*, 422 U.S. 490 (1975) (denying numerous parties standing in an exclusionary zoning case under Article III's case or controversy rules)).

multi-family housing, but then down-zoned the land when faced with an affordable or low income housing developer's rezoning proposal.

Under *Arlington Heights*, a housing decision with a disparate racial impact is not *per se* a violation of the Fourteenth Amendment: no equal protection clause violation can be shown without proof of a predominant discriminatory intent. (Both federal courts below had held that there was no showing of such an intent.) Further, even when discrimination is a motivating factor, the effect of this showing is procedural—the burden of proof needed to justify the decision shifts to the municipal decision-maker; there is no liability yet. The latter gets a further opportunity to justify what it did: the defense may show that it acted for mixed motives, some of which are permissible. Given the multiplicity of factors involved here, even if a motivating discriminatory intent is proven, there would still be a defense for the Village—i.e., that its motives in the rezoning were mixed, with the result that the Village would have reached the same decision without its discriminatory motive.[5] So when the Village's discriminatory motive was one of many factors in its decision, it caused the developer no harm that it would not otherwise have suffered: thus a motivating factor that was not a predominant factor can be buried within the five factors presented in the *Arlington Heights* opinion. The result is that a zoning ordinance may be found to be an equal protection violation, as an impermissible racial classification, only when it is proven that both the intent and the impact of the ordinance exclude a racial group.

Arlington Heights is a constitutional case. Its analysis is a search for the meaning of impermissible intent to discriminate on the basis of race. Economic discrimination is not impermissible as a constitutional matter, even if it produces a disparate racial impact. If the decision were brought under Fair Housing Act's Title VIII, the disparate impact (known as the "legal effects" test) would be sufficient to make out a prima facie violation of § 3604(a) of the Act.[6] However, the litigation in *Arlington Heights* was, after the remand, settled by consent.

§ 16.03 Federal Fair Housing Act Claims

In a Fair Housing Act (FHA) case, whose central provision was quoted previously, the courts usually consider four factors when interpreting the statutory provision and considering whether or not the plaintiff has made out a *prima facie* case:

(1) The strength of the plaintiff's evidence of discriminatory effect or impact. Typically this evidence will be statistical and will involve local

---

5. *See Mt. Healthy City School District Bd. of Educ. v. Doyle*, 429 U.S. 274 (1977) (a companion case to *Arlington Heights*).

6. *See Huntington Branch, NAACP v. Town of Huntington*, 844 F.2d 926 (2d Cir. 1988) (where the town restricted multi-unit housing to an urban renewal area whose population was 52% black).

statistics, although statistics are usually accompanied by an identification of the suspect practices linked with the adverse impact they demonstrate; this evidence is presented along with:

(2) evidence of discriminatory intent: who said what, when, and in what context the statement(s) were made.

(3) The defendant's interest in making the decision. Is a bona fide governmental purpose otherwise advanced?

(4) The remedy sought to reverse the effect of the discrimination. Is the plaintiff seeking to build housing for those persons discriminated against, or merely to remove some obstacle to the construction of such housing? The more benefit the remedy provides, the lesser the evidence of discrimination need be.[7]

These four factors were set out in the Circuit Court opinion on remand in the *Arlington Heights* litigation—often called *Arlington Heights II*—holding that in at least some circumstances, a FHA violation may be "established by a showing of discriminatory effect without a showing of discriminatory intent."[8] This was so because the four factors were balanced, each against the others. In the remanded case, the court found no discriminatory intent, a strong state interest, and a willingness on the plaintiff's part to build the affordable housing. Balancing these, it found the "no intent" factor outweighed by the other factors; hence it held for the plaintiff. Thus, a failure to rezone having an adverse impact or effect on racial minorities as "the natural and foreseeable consequence" of that failure, makes a municipality liable under the Act.

This four-prong test, although developed to adjudicate racial discrimination claims, is equally applicable to claims of religion, handicap and familial status discrimination.[9] However, the Sixth and Seventh Circuits have refused to adopt the second prong of this test. In these circuits, then, the other three prongs are used and a plaintiff need not present any evidence of discriminatory intent on the defendant's part.[10]

7. This is the four-prong test of the Seventh Circuit, on remand in *Arlington Heights*, 558 F.2d 1283, 1288 (7th Cir. 1977), *cert. denied*, 434 U.S. 1025 (1978). *See also Smith v. Town of Clarkton, N.C.*, 682 F.2d 1055 (4th Cir. 1982) (adopting the four-prong test of *Arlington Heights* for a claim against a governmental entity).

8. 558 F.2d 1283, 1288 (7th Cir. 1977).

9. *See United States v. Southern Management Corp.*, 955 F.2d 914 (4th Cir. 1992).

10. *See Groach Assocs. # 33, LP v. Louisville/Jefferson Cty., Metro Human Relations Comm'n*, 508 F.3d 366, 372 (majority opinion), 383 (dissenting opinion) (6th Cir. 2007) (refusing to adopt the prong involving discriminatory intent and finding it the "least important" of the four); *see also Arthur v. City of Toledo*, 782 F.2d 565 (6th Cir. 1986).

[A] Two Applications of the *Arlington Heights II* Four-Factor Test

Religion can also be a basis for alleging illegal discrimination. In one case an Orthodox[11] Jewish rabbi was held to have been discriminated against when denied a certificate for the conduct of a home occupation when such certificates were issued only to members of "learned professions." The court considered the application of the four elements. With regard to the first two factors explained previously and in proving a *prima facie* case, a discriminatory and disparate **impact** will be shown when doctors' and attorneys' offices and other religious groups were given certificates. Where necessary, **intent** to discriminate against the applicant's religion might be *prima facie* shown by the change in a prior interpretation of a home occupation for conducting services. As to the third factor, the noise, traffic, and impacts caused by in-home services to which congregants walk, are minimal and do not justify the **municipality's interest** in denying the certificate. In contrast, a municipal regulation requiring that churches, synagogues, and other places of worship be located on parcels at least two acres might require that the rabbi apply for a variance and have it denied before showing that the regulation is a barrier to the exercise of his religion. As to the fourth factor, the exercise of religion provides a clear benefit of giving the applicant the **remedy** sought.[12] With two of the four factors—the interest and remedy prongs—showing discrimination, an order to issue the certificate should result.

"Familial status" is also protected against discrimination,[13] and Title VIII is applicable to private parties. For example, when a trailer park could not accommodate modern, double-wide mobile homes on its pads and so had a density of 10 mobile homes per acre, 5 more than newer parks, the park owner permitted no more than 3 persons to occupy a mobile home when nationally half of all families with minor children had more than 4 members. A woman applied to occupy a pad with her 3 minor children. The park owner refused to rent to her, citing the 3 person maximum. When charged with discrimination, the park owner's defense will be that the woman cannot show at least three of the four factors relevant to finding a violation of Title VIII. As to a showing of discriminatory **intent**, she would have to allege that households of the same size, but without minor children, were offered trailer rentals in the park. As to a showing of the disparate **impact** factor, national statistics are so far removed from the market in which the discrimination is alleged to have occurred that they will have little probative weight. The leading case uses local, not national, statistics as its basis

11. As here relevant, Orthodox Judaism requires that worshipers walk to Sabbath services and conduct daily prayer services in small groups.

12. *See Leblanc-Sternberg v. Village of Airmont*, 67 F.3d 412 (2d Cir. 1995) (involving an alleged defensive incorporation of the Village).

13. *See Hooker v. Weathers*, 990 F.2d 913 (6th Cir. 1993).

for finding a FHA violation.[14] As to the defendant's **interest** factor, the owner has a legitimate, bona fide reason for its occupancy limits: they rest on a concern for the quality of life in its park and for limiting the use of old infrastructure like sewer and water lines for its pads—an interest sufficient to overcome the plaintiff's *prima facie* case. As to the **remedial** factor, no housing for single-parent families with children will be built as a result of granting the plaintiff an injunction. Thus the owner prevails on three of the four factors in *Arlington Heights*.[15]

[B] *Huntington Branch, NAACP v. Town of Huntington*[16]

This case concerned allegations that the 95% white Town had restricted the private construction of subsidized, low income, multi-family housing to a 52% minority, urban renewal area and refused to rezone a parcel outside this area where the plaintiffs sought to build such housing. The Second Circuit found that it is too onerous a burden for plaintiffs to have to show all four *Arlington Heights II* factors to make out a *prima facie* case; i.e., *Arlington Heights II* was too deferential to municipalities. Thus only a showing of disparate impact or effect is initially necessary there: the challenged practice or ordinance must actually or predictably have a discriminatory effect. The four factors need only be considered together and balanced when finally determining the merits of the case. This is a so-called burden-shifting, rather than a balancing approach to discrimination claims.

Huntington Branch modified the *Arlington Heights* test in two other ways. First, it required that in presenting statistics under the first prong, the plaintiff must compare the racial composition of the group which received—or predictably would receive—the benefits of the ordinance or action with the racial composition of the group from which beneficiaries would otherwise have come. It rejected the town's defense that more white renters than black would be injured by its denial of the developer's application for the multi-unit housing project. Second, in order to reply to any third-prong interest asserted by the defendant, the *Huntington Branch* opinion permitted evidence that better land-use planning would resolve the dispute. Some regard this evidence as an additional factor, inserting it between the last two.

These additions make *Huntington Branch* like many civil rights cases in which the parties play a type of legal ping-pong: (first) the discriminatory impact is shown to establish a *prima facie* case for the plaintiff, then (second) the defendant establishes that it has a legitimate interest in the decision, as it came out, thus (third) shifting the

---

14. *See Huntington Branch, NAACP v. Town of Huntington*, 844 F.2d 926 (2d Cir. 1988) (discussed *infra*, this Chapter, § 16.03[B]).

15. *See Mountain Side Mobile Estate Partnership v. Secretary of Housing and Urban Development*, 56 F.3d 1243 (10th Cir. 1995) (adopting three of the four *Arlington Heights* factors for that Circuit); *see also Reinhart v. Lincoln Cty.*, 482 F.3d 1225, 1229 (10th Cir. 2007).

16. 844 F.2d 926 (2d Cir. 1988).

burden back to the plaintiff to show that a less onerous method—or land-use planning solution—could have been used to protect the defendant's legitimate interest without causing the allegedly discriminatory effect. In *Huntington Branch* and some other federal circuits, the second and third showings are taken as one—that is, the municipality must show that its zoning decision is both "a legitimate, bona fide governmental interest" and that no less onerous zoning—"the absence of a less discriminatory alternative"—could have been used.[17]

When a plaintiff establishes the first of these three showings, making out a *prima facie* case, the result is to overthrow the usual presumption of validity that attaches to local land use ordinances and decisions. Thus under *Huntington Branch*, the Fair Housing Act may have a dramatic impact on land use litigation. After the plaintiff establishes a *prima facie* case, the burden of proof shifts to the defendant municipality to prove that "its actions furthered, in theory and in practice, a legitimate, bona fide governmental interest."[18] Having dropped any showing of intent as a part of a *prima facie* case, once a disparate impact is shown, *Huntington Branch* would weight "the adverse impact of the defendant's [municipality's] justification." Here the municipality must show that its failure to rezone advanced a legitimate, bona fide governmental interest and that no alternative action would serve the same interest with less discriminatory effect. Thus, once the burden of proof shifts to the municipality, it stays there.

The approaches of other Circuits has been described as follows:

> The First, Third, and Eighth Circuits evaluate FHA disparate-impact claims against government entities according to burden-shifting frameworks and do not employ any final balancing test derived from the *Arlington Heights II* factors to evaluate the merits of the defendant's justification. The burden-shifting standards employed by these circuits are similar, with the only significant variation being that the Eighth Circuit requires plaintiffs to prove the existence of a less discriminatory alternative, while the Third Circuit requires defendants to prove the absence of such an alternative. . . .[19]

Huntington Branch added that two other factors may affect the finding of a violation: first, whether there is any evidence of discriminatory intent, and second, whether the plaintiff is suing to force a municipal defendant to build housing or whether it is suing only to require such a defendant to remove a land use regulatory obstacle to housing that the plaintiff proposes to build. The less onerous a plaintiff's remedy is, the stronger the interest asserted by the defendant must be. Changing a regulation should be easier than forcing an affirmative duty on a municipality.

In other federal circuits like the Sixth Circuit, when the defendant municipality is successful in establishing a legitimate governmental interest, then the burden shifts

---

17. *See Dews v. Town of Sunnyvale*, 109 F. Supp. 2d 526, 531–32, 565 (N.D. Tex. 2000) (in the 5th Circuit).

18. *See Huntington Branch*, 844 F.2d at 936, *citing Resident Advisory Bd. v. Rizzo*, 564 F.2d 126, 148–49 (3d Cir. 1977).

19. *See Groach Assocs. # 33, LP, supra*, 508 F.3d at 384 (dissenting opinion).

again, to the plaintiff, who is then given an opportunity to show some alternative that would further that interest just as much, but with less discriminatory effect.[20]

In summary, *Huntington Branch* modified *Arlington Heights II* in important ways: first, it rejected any balancing of intent and impact or effect; second, it used a "comparable group" standard for compiling statistics alleging a discriminatory impact; and third, it employed once-for-all burden shifting after that impact was *prima facie* proven.

[1] Applying Huntington Branch

To assess the reach of *Huntington Branch*, suppose that Huntington restricted to a small area the land zoned for use by a battered women's shelter. The rationale used by the court to protect against racial discrimination, can be adapted a claim based on sex. The issue in *Huntington Branch* was whether a greater proportion of blacks are affected by the zoning ordinance restriction than the proportion of whites affected by the ordinance, both groups being considered as a class. So, first, ask whether the harm caused to women is greater than the harm caused to men by the ordinance. Battered women have to get away from their batterers, so there is justification for giving them greater housing opportunities. Second, ask whether women are denied what men have—that is, the right to be safe in their homes. If women are more often the battered, then they are denied what men have and so the ordinance may reasonably be held to have a disparate legal effect on women. This finding would, under *Huntington Branch*, shift the burden to the municipality to show that, by weighing the municipality's refusal to rezone against its bona fide, governmental interests, the municipality was advancing those interests and that no lesser alternative would do.

[C] Rezoning Remedies

In *Huntington Branch*, the court, finding a substantial adverse impact on minorities,[21] ordered that the plaintiff's land be rezoned for the use it sought. This site-specific remedy may seem extreme, but another federal Circuit, finding extreme, self-evident, and blatantly discrimination by municipal officials, went further and ordered not only a rezoning of the plaintiff's parcel, but also devised mandatory, inclusionary, multi-family housing districts to be included in the text of the defendant's zoning ordinance, locating these districts on its zoning map as well.[22]

The Fair Housing Act's Title VII has, however, the potential to go farther. If 42 U.S.C. § 3604(a) makes it unlawful "to make unavailable or deny . . . a dwelling to any person because of race, color, religion, sex, handicap, or national origin," may it not be

---

20. *Id.* at 374. *See also Huntington Branch, op. cit.*, 844 F.2d at 936.

21. In Huntington, 7% of the town's population needed the applicant's subsidized housing; 24% of black residents needed it. Similarly, 60% of those eligible to participate in applicant's housing subsidy program, and 61% of those on its waiting list, were black.

22. *See United States v. City of Black Jack*, 508 F.2d 1179 (8th Cir. 1974).

found to contain anti-exclusionary and fair share housing obligations for municipalities? The answer is that, yes, someday it may. Such a finding must realistically be seen as remote today when the civil rights law is viewed through the prism of case precedents like *Huntington Branch*, where the impact was so distinct. But there is nothing in the statute precluding its broader use.

[D] *Texas Department of Housing & Community Affairs v. Inclusive Communities Project, Inc.*

This is not a land use case, so the facts do not matter. Inclusive Communities argued that federal and state tax credit subsidies for low income housing were allocated by the Department on a discriminatory basis between inner cities and suburbs. The Supreme Court held that the Fair Housing Act's Title VIII incorporates disparate impact theory as a means of exposing discriminatory intent.[23] The court gave four reasons for this holding: (1) Title VIII refers to the effects of state and private action, not to the actions themselves; (2) Title VIII is intended to deal with systematic racism, not just racial classifications: (3) nine Federal Circuits use disparate impact analysis in Title VIII cases; and (4) the federal Department of Housing & Urban Development approves this analysis.

The court also held that state actions not classifying individuals by race do not violate the equal protection clause when motivated by racially integrative policies. It further held that disparate impact theory does not yield to equal protection analysis unless the policy involved classifies individuals by race. Finally, it discussed the traditional stages for litigating a claim of discrimination: it held that, in formulating a *prima facie* case, a contested policy must cause the disparate impact; that the rationales presented in defending the policy must be race neutral and valid, and that discrimination is not shown when the policy is intended to be a benefit to a class otherwise protected by Title VIII.

After *Inclusive Communities*, proof of a disparate impact alone is insufficient to prevail on a Title VIII claim. There must also be proof that the contested policy *caused* the disparate impact. This "robust causation" requirement functions much like proximate cause does in tort law, serving to limit the number of actions brought to court. Different views of this robust causation requirement have been adopted in different federal circuits.[24] One circuit requires that an "artificial, arbitrary, and unnecessary" policy caused the disparity.[25] In another, a "sufficiently substantial" statistical disparity is

23. *See Texas Dep't of Housing and Community Affairs v. Inclusive Communities Project, Inc.*, 576 U.S. 519 (2015) (noted at 44 Real Est. L.J. 387 (2015)).

24. *See Inclusive Comtys. Project, Inc. v. Heartland Cmty. Ass'n*, 399 F. Supp. 3d 657, 669 & n.3 (N.D. Tex. 2019) (reviewing the following views of this matter in the 4th, 8th, and 11th Circuits).

25. *See Ellis v. City of Minneapolis*, 860 F.3d 1106, 1114 (8th Cir. 2017).

sufficient to raise the necessary inference of causation.[26] A third view is that the causation requirement must not be based on statistics showing "disparities that preexisted the policy, as preexisting disparities cannot logically be characterized as the consequence of a policy."[27] Still another view is that racial imbalance alone cannot establish a disparate impact:[28] the policies surrounding the disparities must cause them, as it is those policies that will lead a court to accept disparities as proof of discrimination. All this is to say that Circuit Courts have not reached consensus on what limitations a "robust causation" requirement itself requires of Title VIII claims.

Another federal Circuit opinion refused to adopt any of the foregoing alternatives defining a "robust causation" of a disparate impact.[29] In the *Lincoln Property* case, a landlord refused to accept tenants presenting "Section 8 vouchers" in lieu of rent. The court found that the city-wide and census tract statistics presented by the plaintiff did not support a reasonable inference of discrimination—i.e., that the refusal to participate did not cause any protected group—blacks—to become the dominant holders of vouchers in the metropolitan area or that the defendants caused the geographic distribution of protected groups in the area prior to the implementation of the no vouchers policy, or that the policy changed any of these things after it was in effect. The court dismissed the disparate impact claim, finding that the landlord's decision to opt out of the voucher program was voluntary and as such cannot be arbitrary.[30]

A defendant's second stage rationales defending a policy must remove "artificial, arbitrary, and unnecessary" discriminatory barriers to racially integrated housing, and housing authorities and developers may meanwhile maintain a policy proven necessary to achieve a "valid interest"—one weighty enough to overcome an interest in racial integration. One such interest might be supported by health and safety concerns. Thus a municipality's aggressive policy of housing code enforcement is valid, even though the result is the loss of occupancy permits for low income housing that would otherwise be available to tenants, a disproportionate number of whom are members of a Title VIII protected group.[31] On the other hand, statistics showing only that protected minorities are geographically isolated in a region are not weighty enough unless the contested policy would have a *significant* integrative impact.[32] The Supreme Court did not define what a "valid interest" is, so future litigation will have to determine that. (Meanwhile, fewer low income housing units might be built.) However, it is clear from the *Inclusive Communities* opinion that policies are not constitutionally suspect because they are intended to further racial integration.

---

26. *See Reyes v. Waples Mobile Home Park Ltd. P'ship*, 903 F.3d 415, 428–29 (4th Cir. 2018).

27. *Id.* at 434–35 (dissenting opinion).

28. *See Oviedo Town Ctr. II LLP v. City of Oviedo, Florida*, 759 Fed. Appx. 828 (11th Cir. 2018).

29. *See Inclusive Communities Project, Inc. v. Lincoln Property Co.*, 930 F.3d 890 (5th Cir. 2019) (noted in 133 Harv. L. Rev. 1476 (2020)).

30. *Id.* at 906–07.

31. *See Ellis, op. cit.*, 860 F.3d at 1112–13.

32. *See* Note, 133 Harv. L. Rev. 1476 (2016); Samuel R. Bagenstos, *Disparate Impact and the Role of Classification and Motivation in Equal Protection Law After Inclusive Communities*, 101 Corn. L. Rev. 1115, 1141 (2016).

§ 16.04 Discrimination Against the Handicapped

In the 1988 amendments to the FHA, the handicapped were added to the list of persons protected by the statute. These amendments prohibit discrimination against the handicapped in ways that are more distinctive than with other types of discrimination. For example, both mental and physical handicaps are protected by these amendments,[33] and it is discrimination not to make a reasonable accommodation for the handicapped in renting an apartment to them.[34] The land use analog of reasonable accommodation arises when a municipality refuses to rezone land for the use of a group home for the handicapped, or to grant a variance to accommodate their occupancy.

In *City of Edmonds v. Oxford House, Inc.*,[35] a municipality issued criminal citations to Oxford House[36] for leasing and operating a group home for recovering drug addicts and alcoholics. The home was run for 10 to 12 persons. Its operation was, the municipality said, in violation of a regulation permitting only "family" occupancy in its single-family, residential use district. A "family" was an "individual or two or more persons related by genetics, adoption, or marriage, or a group of five unrelated persons." Thus the ordinance banned more than five unrelated persons from living together in a single-family dwelling. Oxford House alleged that it needed more occupants to make its operation financially and therapeutically practical, but the municipality refused its application for a variance, so Oxford sued, alleging a FHA violation and arguing that the city had violated the FHA.

An exemption to the FHA's anti-discrimination provisions allows enforcement of "any reasonable local . . . restriction regarding the number of occupants permitted to occupy a dwelling."[37] The trial judge found that Edmunds' definition of family was a regulation exempt from the FHA and dismissed the suit.[38] The Supreme Court disagreed.

The court held that the exemption for local regulation was not an absolute one. It held that thc municipality's definition of a family was not a maximum occupancy restriction exempt from the FHA's requirements under § 3607(b)(1) and so the exemption was not applicable. For the court, it was crucial in interpreting the exemption

33. 42 U.S.C. § 3602(h).

34. *Id.* at § 3604(f)(3)(b).

35. 514 U.S. 725 (1995) (a 6-3 decision).

36. Oxford House operates in 36 states. M. Briggs, *Ruling May Boost Group Home Suit Against Palatine*, Chicago Sun Times, May 16, 1995, at 59. It does not apply for variances or special exceptions for its homes; it moves the group in, reasoning that eviction is harder than denying permits for a municipality.

37. 42 U.S.C. § 3607(b)(1) (exempting "any reasonable local, State, or Federal restriction regarding the number of occupants permitted to occupy a dwelling").

38. *See Elliott v. Athens*, 960 F.2d 975 (11th Cir. 1992) (upholding a local definition of family against an FHA challenge).

to recognize a distinction between land use restrictions and maximum occupancy restrictions: families in Oxford House's use district could contain as many persons as need be, but unrelated handicapped persons were limited to five. This amounted to disparate treatment of the handicapped. Moreover, the biological and legal relationships defining a family had nothing to do with health or safety factors the municipality might properly consider in formulating its definition.

Holding that the municipality, with regard to its definition of family, was not immune from a charge of discrimination and could not invoke the maximum occupancy exemption, the court did not hold that the municipality violated the FHA or that the municipality actually discriminated against the plaintiffs. Nor did it decide whether the municipality made a reasonable accommodation by amending its regulations to permit group homes in multi-family and commercial use districts. It held only that the city might not claim immunity from suit on such grounds on the basis of the exemption. It gave tacit approval to reasonable restrictions on single-family dwellings and maximum occupancy restrictions.[39]

Thus a maximum occupancy restriction applicable to all persons in all types of dwellings, would have an absolute exemption. The *Edmonds* opinion stated that regulations that "cap the total number of occupants in order to prevent overcrowding fall within § 3607(b)(1)'s absolute exemption. . . . " Such restrictions are typically figured on the basis of square footage or floor area. So if a municipality had a definition of family requiring that every person subject to the definition occupy a minimum of 200 square feet for the first 2 persons in a dwelling, and (say) 100 square feet for each additional person, this requirement would be exempt. This type of minimum square footage requirement is related to public health concerns and qualifies for the exemption.

Moreover, under the FHA, definitions of "family" are exempt only when reasonable. What if a municipal definition of family provided in part that no more than five persons, related or not, could occupy any single-family dwelling? There is no discrimination on the face of the regulation because related and unrelated persons are not treated differently. This municipality, however, might still have to make some showing that overcrowding would result if its regulation were not enforced: "reasonable" here means reasonable in its impact. Further, there still might be a disparate impact if Oxford House can show that therapeutic relationships among the handicapped can only be established when they are in larger groups.

Similarly, a municipality's ordinance might permit a related family, or no more than five unrelated individuals, or no more than eight unrelated individuals living together in a group home for purposes including those of Oxford House. This ordinance has a facial acceptance of handicapped or disabled persons, but Oxford House might

39. *See* H.R. Rep. No. 711, 100th Cong., 2d Sess. 24 (1988), *reprinted in* 1988 U.S. Code Cong. & Adm. News 2173, 2185 (indicating that, in the 1988 FHA amendments, Congress intended in the exemption to codify the holding of *City of Cleburne v. Cleburne Living Center*, 473 U.S. 432 (1985), where restrictions were imposed on persons with handicaps, but were not imposed on similarly situated persons). The *Edmonds* ordinance did not discriminate between persons with and without handicaps, but between those who are related and unrelated.

then argue that the maximum of eight persons leaves it in the position of operating unprofitable facilities. *Edmonds* did not pass on this argument. Many ordinances have negative financial impacts on owners, but that does not *per se* render them invalid. A larger group of occupants would make the facility more profitable, but no owner is entitled to a property's "highest and best" or most profitable use. Unprofitability does not make the maximum number unreasonable because the municipality may have other overriding factors, other than profitability, in mind. Moreover, under the FHA, the municipality must only make reasonable accommodations for the persons protected by the Act. That is not to say that it requires that facilities be profitable; reasonable accommodation need not mean profitable accommodation. In addition, unless the plaintiff applies for a variance, the "no reasonable accommodation" argument is a difficult one.[40]

Edmunds' distinction between land-use and maximum-occupancy restrictions is not without precedent. The United States Supreme Court recognized it in *Moore v. City of East Cleveland*.[41] Once the exemption is characterized in this binary manner, the city's ordinance clearly fell outside the exempt category of ordinances.[42]

§ 16.05 Conclusions

Three lessons emerge from *Edmonds*: first, that the courts may use the FHA to scrutinize land use regulations; second, that municipalities must offer reasonable accommodation through their zoning procedures to persons with disabilities; and third, that municipalities may impose reasonable occupancy restrictions applicable to all persons alike. The mentally disabled, the elderly, recovering drug addicts, and alcoholics—when living in a group home—are likewise protected.

§ 16.06 The Fair Housing Act and Private Covenants

The FHA can help municipal land use regulations and non-profit groups trump private restrictive covenants. For example, when a non-profit agency seeks to establish a group home for medically disabled patients in a residential subdivision in which all of the homes are controlled by a restrictive covenant permitting only single-family residential uses, the contention that enforcement of the covenants violates the Fair

40. *See Oxford House-C v. City of St. Louis*, 77 F.3d 249 (8th Cir. 1996).

41. 431 U.S. 494 (1977) (striking down a definition of family overly dependent on the nuclear family).

42. In response to *Edmonds*, a state enabling statute might require municipalities to treat group and single family homes in a uniform manner.

Housing Act's prohibition on discrimination against the handicapped is sound.[43] Assuming that the medical disability is recognized by the Act and its regulations, even though nothing in the covenant expressly prevents a patient from owning or renting in the subdivision, a facially neutral restriction, applicable to both handicapped and non-handicapped persons, may still implicate the Act. First, the covenant's attempt to limit group homes by its single family restriction denies housing to the handicapped. Second, any interest served by decreasing noise and traffic with regard to the covenant is likely to weigh less than the interest served by enforcement of the Act. Third, enforcing the covenant denies housing to a class of persons protected by the Act. In this situation, evidence of a discriminatory intent is not likely to be necessary. There is a *prima facie* violation of the Act.[44]

Some commentators have suggested that covenanted subdivisions can be filled with so many amenities that purchasing a home in them can be financially prohibitive for some groups of persons protected by the FHA. That is, a subdivision can have a golf course attached with protected persons unlikely to play golf, swimming pools when such persons do not swim, etc. Has the provision of unwanted amenities denied or made housing "unavailable"? The answer lies in the future.

§ 16.07 FHA Violations Must Be Development Based

An allegation under the FHA cannot stray too far from an actual transaction or real estate development. When a local official is accused of embezzling funds earmarked in a municipal budget for housing for the handicapped, the embezzlement is not a FHA violation. It is not, even although it does indirectly make housing "otherwise unavailable" and denies use of the funds for the benefit of a protected class. The Act is intended to reach a municipality's policies and practices, as well as its housing decisions that are intentionally discriminatory, but only to control a discriminatory impact or effect. Criminal intent is not discriminatory. Other statutes are available to handle this matter; one statute does not reach all governmental decisions affecting the classes of persons protected by the Act, without doing violence to the legislature's prerogative to enact statutes dealing particularly with the misuse of public funds.[45]

43. *See Baxter v. City of Belleville*, 720 F. Supp. 720, 729 (S.D. Ill. 1989).
44. *See Hill v. Community of Damien of Molokai*, 911 P.2d 861 (N. Mex. 1996).
45. *Cf. United States v. Incorporated Village of Island Park*, 888 F. Supp. 419 (E.D.N.Y. 1995).

§ 16.08 Civil Rights and Environmental Justice

Environmental justice seeks to end any policy or practice that has differential effects or disadvantages, whether intentionally or not, on individuals, groups, or communities, based on race, ethnicity, or color. This includes the disproportionate location of hazardous waste facilities, sold waste disposal sites, contaminating industrial sites, and other undesirable land uses, in minority communities. Title VI of the 1964 Civil Rights Act[46] provides a cause of action for persons able to show that they have been discriminated against in programs receiving federal funds. A showing of discriminatory intent has been held to be an element of a Title VI cause of action.[47] However, taken as a whole, two statutes[48] in Title VI leave open the possibility that merely showing a discriminatory impact may be sufficient when federal agency regulations require the non-discriminatory administration of an agency's programs without requiring a showing of intent.[49] Thus the right of a private community group to sue, seeking to show a discriminatory impact in the administration of Environmental Protection Agency programs, has been upheld under Title VI.[50] Such a cause of action might cause a re-allocation of funds for federal and state programs for "brownfields." Brownfields are abandoned, unused, or under-used industrial and commercial sites whose development is stymied by toxic contamination, often located in minority communities. Brownfield programs clean such sites up and then provide immunity from federal or state lawsuits based on the site's continuing toxicity.

Claims of environmental justice highlight the fact that some 40 years after the enactment of the FHA, housing availability and land use regulations can still pose effective barriers to a fully integrated municipality. So while the FHA provides a good start, critics say, more is needed, and that more may be governmental funds and programs.

---

46. 42 U.S.C. § 2000d *et seq.* (Title VI, §§ 601, 602) (1999).

47. *See Alexander v. Choate*, 469 U.S. 287, 292–94 (1985) (interpreting Title VI, § 601).

48. 42 U.S.C. §§ 601, 602 [the latter authorizing federal agencies to implement § 601 by regulations barring discrimination—EPA did so with a regulation—40 C.F.R. § 7.35(b) (1998) (using a disparate impact test)].

49. *But see Rollerson v. Brazos River Harbor Navigation Dist.*, 6 F.4th 633 (5th Cir. 2021) (requiring a § 601 claimant to cite a specific recent act of discrimination, not just a history of racial segregation) (noted at 135 Harv. L. Rev. 1955 (2022)).

50. *See Chester Residents Concerned for Living Quality v. Seif*, 132 F.3d 925 (3d Cir. 1997) (finding a private cause of action for discriminatory administration of EPA program funds for a showing of disproportionate effect).

PART FOUR

Wetlands and Beaches

Chapter 17
Protection of Sensitive Lands

§ 17.01 Wetlands

Land use controls are often justified as environmental protection. Thus, when the lands protected are especially sensitive for some reason, special regulation may be justified. Such regulation is often here justified as a means of protecting (1) unstable lands, such as riparian lands or the thinly soiled Santa Catalina mountains around Los Angeles, or flood plains, steep hillsides, and tidal wetlands; (2) lands that involve a public resource—like navigable water, groundwater aquifers, or wetlands; or (3) lands which serve some crucial biological or ecological function in their region—again, such as wetlands. Little wonder, then, that wetlands have spawned litigation as well as fish.[1]

Most of the coastal states, and some interior states as well, have enacted statutory schemes for restricting the development of wetlands (fresh and saltwater marshes, bogs, and swamps) and shorelands.[2] Many of these statutes are not wetlands protection schemes *per se;* they focus on the dredging and filling that changes the use of a wetland, converting it into something else, and on minimizing the many changes in drainage, soil run-off, and the destruction of plant life that can destroy a wetland. Some of these statutes authorize land use regulations for wetlands, but minimize land uses there. State courts have upheld many state regulatory schemes for wetlands themselves.

Federal regulation exists as well. In *United States v. Riverside Bayview Homes, Inc.*,[3] the Supreme Court reviewed and upheld U.S. Army Corps of Engineers' regulations defining "navigable waters" as including the tributaries of such waters, as well as

1. Wetlands filter and store water. Preserving them provides a cost-effective way to deal with some soluble pollutants and to manage storm water and run-off to prevent floods—all the while providing habitat for plants and wildlife. The loss of wetlands by dredging, filling, and compacting them for development has been (by some estimates) more than one half of our wetlands over the last two centuries, rising to a loss of about 300,000 wetland acres in the early 1980s. The Back Bay in Boston, New Orleans, and the canalized subdivisions in Florida, are examples of such losses, made vivid by Hurricane Katrina in 2006.

2. *See* William Want, Wetlands Regulation Ch. 13 (1989) (reviewing 26 state statutes).

3. 474 U.S. 121, 134–35 (1985) (involving the Clean Water Act's § 404 wetlands dredge and fill permitting program).

non-navigable intrastate waters with an impact on interstate waters, and all freshwater wetlands, defined as an area periodically inundated or saturated at a frequency to support the prevalence of vegetation adapted for life in saturated soil. In *Riverside Bayview Homes*, a unanimous opinion of the court recited the Corps' extensive, technical findings on the environmental importance of wetlands and upheld the Corps' expansive regulatory jurisdiction over them, based on the Corps' definition of a wetland "adjacent" to "navigable waters of the United States." "Navigable waters" is the term defining the Corp's jurisdiction under the Clean Water Act (CWA) of 1972.[4] In recent years, however, more isolated wetlands have presented the Supreme Court with issues of "adjacency" and so with jurisdictional issues for the Corps.[5] This is so because the term "waters of the United States" is not further defined in the CWA.[6]

SWANCC required a "significant nexus" between a wetland and navigable water. In *Rapanos*, there was no majority opinion. A plurality of the court again required a "significant nexus" requiring "a relatively permanent body of water connected to traditional interstate navigable waters" having "a continuous surface connection with that water." Streams, rivers, and lakes have the required permanency; storm tile drains, culverts, and dry arroyos do not. A fifth Justice (Kennedy) concurred, requiring the same nexus, but required that the wetland "significantly affect the chemical, physical, and biological integrity of other covered waters more readily understood as 'navigable.'"

In *Sackett v. Env'l Prot. Agency*,[7] the Supreme Court attempted to clarify the jurisdictional reach of the Corps navigable waters and the definition of protected wetlands. The court first held that "waters of the United States" included only those waters that were "relatively permanent, standing, or continuously flowing" geographic water bodies such as "streams, oceans, rivers and lakes."[8] Second, it held that while some wetlands qualify as "waters of the United States," those wetlands must have a "continuous surface connection" so as to be "indistinguishable" from one of the geographic bodies previously mentioned.[9] The second holding meant that wetlands must qualify as "waters of the United States" in their own right; in so holding, the court declined to defer to and adopt the significant nexus test the EPA previously adopted, finding that

---

4. 33 U.S.C. § 1251 *et seq.* (2024) (CWA).

5. *See Rapanos v. United States*, 547 U.S. 715 (2006) (denying the Corps jurisdiction when the wetland was adjacent to a ditch connected to a navigable water body); *Solid Waste Agency of Northern Cook Cty. v. U.S. Army Corps of Engineers*, 531 U.S. 159 (2001) (hereafter "*SWANCC*") (same as to non-navigable, intrastate, seasonal and isolated wetlands) (both noted in 32 Colum. J. Envtl. L. 141 (2007) and 31 Vt. L. Rev. 355 (2007)).

6. *See* 33 U.S.C. § 1362(12).

7. 598 U.S. 651 (2023) (noted at 137 Harv. L. Rev. 390 (2023)).

8. *Id.* at 671 (citing and paraphrasing the plurality opinion in *Rapanos* rather than Justice Kennedy's concurrence).

9. *Id.* at 678. *See also* 33 C.F.R. § 120 (2023) (a joint memo of the Corps and EPA in response to *Sackett*).

the EPA's test was not supported by the CWA itself and by clear evidence of Congressional intent in enacting it.[10]

In *Sackett*, the Supreme Court chose geography over geology and hydrology as the measure of the jurisdictional reach of the Corps' authority. Another of its opinions, this time in *Cty. of Maui v. Hawaii Wildlife Fund*,[11] held that the discharge of pollutants into waters not "the waters of the United States" were still covered by the CWA when the discharge made its way into a body of water covered by the CWA.[12] This discharge was, in the language of the Act, "the functional equivalent of a direct discharge . . . into navigable waters."[13] The discharged water running through groundwater or other intermittent source to reach CWA-covered bodies of water may take time, but that creates no exception to the Corps' CWA authority or permitting procedures.[14] *Hawaii Wildlife Fund* gives seven factors to determine what constitutes the functional equivalent of a direct discharge: (1) transit time; (2) distance traveled; (3) the nature of the material through which the pollutant travels; (4) the extent to which the pollutant is chemically changed or diluted during its transit time; (5) the pollutant amount entering navigable water relative to the amount leaving the source; (6) the manner or area of the entry; and (7) the degree to which the pollutant has maintained its identity at entry.[15]

[A] Defining Wetlands

Most of the definitions of wetlands establish the scope of state regulatory programs and take the presence of vegetation either needing or surviving periodic inundation, together with soil types capable of saturation for some portion of the year, as the most important indicators of a wetland.[16] It is not necessary that the saturation be visible at the surface. Subsurface saturation by groundwater on a periodic basis is sufficient. By the same token, the periodic collection of rainwater on the ground does not indicate the presence of a wetland. Water saturating the soil drives oxygen out of the soil, and plants indicating the presence of a wetland must have adapted to this lack of oxygenation. Under some definitions, the inundated soil and the saturated vegetation must

---

10. In this regard, the court's interpretation of the Act and of Congressional intent is much disputed. *See. e.g.*, Dave Owen, *Sackett v. Environmental Protection Agency and the Rules of Statutory Misinterpretation*, 48 Harv. Envtl. L. Rev. 333 (2024).

11. 590 U.S. 165 (2020) (involving partially treated wastewater pumped into underground wells that made its way into the Pacific Ocean).

12. *Id.* at 186.

13. *Id.*

14. *Id.* at 181.

15. *See Stone v. High Mt. Mining Co., LLC*, 89 F.4th 1246, 1254 (10th Cir. 2024) (stating these elements of the *Hawaii Wildlife Fund* test).

16. *Compare* N.Y. Envtl. Conser. Law § 24-0701 (2024), implemented by N.Y. Comp. Codes R. & Regs., tit. 6, § 662.1(k) (a detailed regulatory definition specifying types of vegetation required), *with* 33 C.F.R. § 328.3(b) (1990) (the pre-*Sackett* federal definition with both a soil and vegetation component).

co-exist: if the soil qualifies, but is below the root line of the vegetation, the area is not a wetland; likewise, if the land is not vegetated at all, but has qualifying soil at the surface, it is not a wetland either. With the U.S. Supreme Court cases like *Sackett* limiting the U.S. Army Corps of Engineers' permit programs for dredging and filling wetlands under § 404 of the CWA, broad state definitions become all the more important a regulatory tool.[17]

At the state level, the thread connecting these regulatory efforts is often found in the majority opinion in *Euclid*. There, the law of nuisance was recognized as the basis for police power regulation. This law has great flexibility and relies on much judicial discretion. The result is a welter of conflicting cases. To quote *Euclid*, "whether a particular thing is a nuisance, is to be determined . . . by considering it in connection with the circumstances and locality. A nuisance may be merely a right thing in the wrong place, like a pig in a parlor instead of the barnyard." The implication of this quotation is that stronger regulation is required for more fragile land, such as a wetland. Regulation of wetlands is consistent with established nuisance doctrines. A second basis for wetland regulation is the public trust. Under the trust, the state "holds shorelands in trust for the use of the public."[18]

[B] State Regulation

The scope of regulation of wetlands varies from state to state. Some regulations are scattered throughout a state's code, while other states assemble their regulations into code form.[19] Regulation can extend not only to tidal, but also to freshwater wetlands.[20] The objective in enacting such regulation is often tied to aesthetic, conservation, and flood control purposes.[21] Another objective is sometimes public use of shorelands for recreational purposes.[22] Wetland and shoreland regulations have been upheld against a variety of takings claims as well.[23]

17. *See In re Freshwater Wetlands Protection Act Rules*, 852 A.2d 1083 (N.J. 2004) (reviewing wetland rules requiring a buffer around them).

18. *See Boston Waterfront Dev. Corp. v. Commonwealth*, 393 N.E.2d 356 (Mass. 1979) (the trust traditionally provides the public rights to sue waters for fishing, hunting, and navigation); *see also Phillips Petroleum v. Mississippi*, 484 U.S. 469, 476 (1988); *Illinois Central R.R. v. Illinois*, 146 U.S. 387, 435 (1892). The trust is discussed *infra*.

19. *See Secretary, Vermont Agency of Natural Resources v. Irish*, 738 A.2d 571, 575–78 (Vt. 1999) (reviewing Vermont Wetland Rules).

20. N.Y. Envir. Conserv. L. § 24-0301 (2024) (providing mapping and regulation for freshwater wetlands). *See also In re Freshwater Wetlands Protection Act Rules*, *supra*.

21. *See Zealy v. City of Waukesha*, 548 N.W.2d 528, 529 (Wis. 1996) (noted in 8 Fordham Envtl. L.J. 691, 708–09 (1997)).

22. *See Raleigh Ave. Beach Ass'n v. Atlantis Beach Club, Inc.*, 879 A.2d 112 (N.J. 2005).

23. *See Karam v. State of New Jersey, Dept. of Envir. Protection*, 705 A.2d 1221 (N.J. Super. Ct., App. Div. 1998) (finding no regulatory taking in a state shoreland development permit system).

A municipality's designation of property as a wetland is not itself a compensable taking.[24] That is, a regulatory requirement that plaintiff apply for a permit to dredge or fill a wetland is not a taking.[25] In this as in other areas of takings law, just the enactment of a regulation works no *prima facie* or facial taking.

Likewise, "as applied" challenges to wetlands regulation have been rejected.[26] Most of the judicial decisions upholding such statutes at this stage use a balancing test—balancing the private harm or injury against the public benefit involved.[27] By using this test, courts generally have evaluated wetlands regulations as a regulatory taking.[28] With regard to an analogous federal claim, Justice Scalia stated, in *Lucas v. South Carolina Coastal Council*, that "the owner of a lake bed . . . would not be entitled to compensation when he is denied the requisite permit to engage in a landfilling operation that would have the effect of flooding others' land."[29] Justice Scalia's example is, he says, an instance in which the law of nuisance would traditionally prevent an owner from visiting injury on a neighbor; a land use regulation to the same effect would, he concludes, be constitutional and not a taking of property. Given a wetlands context, every wetland serving as a flood control and pollution filtering device, such language is likely to have wide application.

After defining a wetland, the statutes often further define the uses permitted in a wetland: e.g., the Virginia Code permits such uses as harvesting shellfish, recreational uses, boating, trapping, and horticulture—usually permitted only with the proviso that the natural contours and functions of the wetland not be disturbed.[30] Other uses require a permit, issued by a wetlands board. The criteria employed by the board in issuing such permits involve no adverse impact, no feasible alternative, and replacement standards. There is also typically a provision for judicial review of permit denials.[31] Often "special exceptions" for other than the permitted uses are allowed when they are "in the public interest."

More recent state regulations sometimes recognize a right to develop a wetland when the developers replace the lost wetland with comparable acreage. This is called

---

24. *See Zerbetz v. Municipality of Anchorage*, 856 P.2d 777 (Alaska 1993); *Carabell v. Department of Natural Resources*, 478 N.W.2d 675 (Mich. App. Ct. 1991).

25. *See Wedinger v. Goldberger*, 522 N.E.2d 25 (N.Y.), *cert. denied*, 488 U.S. 850 (1988) (involving Staten Island wetlands).

26. *See Claridge v. New Hampshire Wetlands Bd.*, 485 A.2d 287 (N.H. 1984) (upholding the application of state permit regulations as not amounting to a regulatory taking under *Mahon*). Cases like *Claridge* may have been undercut by the U.S. Supreme Court opinions in *Nollan* and *Lucas*, although some courts have distinguished these cases. *See Mock v. Department of Envtl. Resources*, 623 A.2d 940, 946 (Pa. Commw. Ct. 1993); *Plantation Landing Resort, Inc. v. United States*, 30 Fed. Cl. 63, 69 (1993) (both cases distinguishing *Lucas*).

27. *See Just v. Marinette Cty.*, 201 N.W.2d 761 (Wis. 1972) (a seminal case because before it, the leading case was contra); *State v. Johnson*, 265 A.2d 711 (Me. 1970).

28. *See Brace v. United States*, 72 Fed. Cl. 337, 356–58 (Fed. Ct. Ct. 2006), 250 Fed. Appx. 359 (Fed. Cir. 2007), *cert. denied*, 552 U.S. 1258 (2008).

29. *See Lucas v. South Carolina Coastal Council*, 505 U.S. 1003, 1029 (1992).

30. Va. Code Ann. § 28.2-1302(3) (2024).

31. Fla. Stat. Ann. § 373.421 (2024).

the "no net loss" policy.[32] Transferable wetlands development rights and mitigation banking for wetlands are available in several states.

Municipal government is generally given some role in wetlands regulation. Sometimes the municipality is authorized to enact special regulations for wetlands. On the municipal level, a planning commission has been held to have authority to consider the effect of a subdivision's water wells on groundwater and adjacent wetlands.[33] In *Busse*, the proffered evidence concerned the need to reduce bird and animal habitat disruption. The Court concluded "that it is not arbitrary, unreasonable, or discriminatory to accept opinions that a plat would probably adversely affect groundwater which feeds an important wetland."[34]

[C] Federal Regulation

In 1972, the federal Clean Water Act (CWA) was amended so that water-borne "pollutants" were defined so as to include "fill material."[35] With this amendment, federal control over wetland development became pervasive.[36] The discharge of dredged or fill materials into the "navigable waters of the United States" is forbidden unless the developer obtains a permit from the Army Corps of Engineers.[37] Both civil and criminal penalties follow an illegal dredging or filling.[38]

The jurisdiction of the Corps has federal commerce clause origins, but its permit program is authorized by the CWA.[39] The 1972 CWA Amendments never used the word "wetlands."[40] It is the Corps' definition of wetlands that controls the scope of the Corps' authority over them.[41] So, for example, a land developer who proposes to drain a wetland covered by that definition, arguing that because draining is not filling, will

---

32. *See* Richard McNeer, *Nontidal Wetland Protection in Maryland and Virginia*, 51 Md. L. Rev. 105, 133–35 (1992).

33. *See Busse v. City of Madison*, 503 N.W.2d 340, 343 (Wis. App. Ct. 1993).

34. *Id.*

35. 33 U.S.C. § 1362(6) (1996).

36. *See generally* THEDA BRADDOCK (WITH REED HUPPMAN), WETLANDS: AN INTRODUCTION TO ECOLOGY, LAW, AND PERMITTING 61–84 (1995). Prior federal regulation of industrial pollution was based on the Rivers and Harbors Act of 1899. *See Zabel v. Tabb*, 430 F.2d 199 (5th Cir. 1970).

37. *See United States v. Mills*, 817 F. Supp. 1546, *aff'd*, 36 F.3d 1052 (11th Cir. 1994); *Slagle v. United States*, 809 F. Supp. 704, 708 (D. Minn. 1992) (wetlands are "waters of the United States" subject to the Clean Water Act).

38. *See United States v. Rapanos*, 115 F.3d 367 (6th Cir. 1997) (upholding state environmental officials, search of defendant's property for a CWA violation, and involving a criminal penalty—this opinion began further litigation to narrow Corps jurisdiction).

39. *See* 33 U.S.C. § 1344 (known as the "§ 404 permit program," a reference to its section number in the 1972 legislation).

40. *See Natural Resources Defense Council v. Callaway*, 392 F. Supp. 685 (D.D.C. 1975) (a citizen suit forcing expansion of Corps prior definition of "waters of the United States" to wetlands).

41. *See, e.g.*, 33 C.F.R. § 328.3 (2008).

still need a § 404 permit from the Corps.[42] Corps jurisdiction is not confined to waters traditionally considered to be navigable.

Permit decisions of the Corps are appealed to the federal Environmental Protection Agency (EPA) and the Agency's decision,[43] if in conflict with the Corps', controls.[44] Any mistake by the Corps in requiring an owner to submit a permit application and go through the process might give rise to a due process claim, but not a takings claim.[45] In practice and to date, it has proven difficult to overturn a decision of the Corps that land constitutes a wetland. This may change with the opinion in *Sackett*[46] because the reach, some would say the narrowing, of Corps' jurisdiction over wetlands is debatable after the decision.

In addition, the EPA can designate a state's government to run the federal permit program.[47] After this designation, the Corps and the EPA suspend their issuance of permits when a permit may be issued under the state program: applicants need not file for a federal permit provided that they apply for the state one. EPA meanwhile retains the right to object to the issuance of any particular permit.[48] Similarly a state has the right to issue a "state only" permit. The EPA may also suspend its approval of a state's permit program, and in Michigan, it did so in 1994 after the litigation in *Friends of the Crystal River v. EPA*,[49] reinstating the program that same year.

The Corps and the EPA have also been, since 1995, engaged in a program of establishing mitigation banks for wetlands,[50] creating or restoring wetlands after development of various types has injured or destroyed existing wetlands, and banking the activity against unavoidable future impacts.

Coastal wetlands are additionally regulated by the Coastal Zone Management Act. The Act requires each coastal and Great Lakes state to file a management plan for its coastal zone and territorial sea.[51] The state plans are approved (or not) by the

---

42. *See* N.Y. Envtl. Conser. Law § 24-0701(1) (prohibiting "any form of draining, dredging, excavation, removal of soil, mud, sand, shells, gravel or other aggregate" as well as "any form of dumping, filling, or depositing of same," without a permit).

43. *See* Memorandum of Agreement Between the Department of the Army and the Environmental Protection Agency (Jan. 19, 1989), *available at* http://www.usace.army.mil/Portals/2/docs/civilworks/mous/enfmoa.pdf.

44. *See Bersani v. EPA*, 850 F.2d 36 (2d Cir. 1988), *cert. denied*, 489 U.S. 1089 (1989) (involving one of the few instances of EPA's veto of the issuance of a state permit for wetlands).

45. *See Tabb Lakes, Inc. v. United States*, 26 Cl. Ct. 1334 (1992), *aff'd*, 10 F.3d 796, 802–03 (Fed. Cir. 1993).

46. 598 U.S. 561 (2023), previously discussed in this Chapter.

47. *See Friends of the Crystal River v. EPA*, 35 F.3d 1073 (6th Cir. 1994) (reviewing standards for the Michigan program designated by EPA to be as least as stringent as EPA standards, but acting arguably under state statutes and regulations).

48. *See Friends of the Crystal River v. EPA*, 794 F. Supp. 674 (W.D. Mich. 1992) (treating federal authority as having been transferred to the state), later opinion, 35 F.3d 1073 (6th Cir. 1994).

49. 35 F.3d 1073 (6th Cir. 1994).

50. *See* Lawrence Liebesman & David Plott, *The Emergence of Private Wetlands Mitigation Banking*, Nat. Resources & Envir. J., Summer 1998, at 341–42, 370 (describing the federal program).

51. *See* 16 U.S.C. §§ 1451–1466.

Office of Coastal Resource Management in the National Oceanic and Atmospheric Administration after reviewing the state plan's consistency with the federal act.[52] State plans typically include coastal lands not wetlands. For example, California's Coastal Commission has encouraged the development of vineyards on coastal properties as a means of protecting open space for agriculture.[53]

State plans define the land uses permitted within a state's coastal zone, identify areas of particular fragility, establish a priority of uses, and plan for the shoreline's erosion, the siting of energy facilities, and access to beaches. Coastal plan implementation is typically delegated to municipal government, but some states, particularly on the Pacific coast, have established state coastal regulatory agencies; California and South Carolina's state agencies provided the legal background for the *Lucas* and *Nollan* takings cases.[54]

In addition, the Coastal Barrier Protection Act[55] delineates the low-lying barrier lands (often islands paralleling the mainland), requires their mapping, and monitors their development. It applies to both coastal and Great Lake states and limits federal expenditures and financial assistance to development on these barrier islands.

[1] Corps Jurisdiction and State Programs

When a state wetland protection program has a "no net loss" policy or when that policy informs the Corps' jurisdiction, the answer is that artificially-created wetlands may be just as subject to its program as natural wetlands. Many states and the Corps find a "no net loss" policy a politically appealing one. If the Corps created the wetland conditions, the Corps has jurisdiction over the wetland it creates.[56] The Fourth Circuit held (in advance of later Supreme Court rulings) that the Corps has no jurisdiction over isolated wetlands and that a regulation asserting such jurisdiction exceeded federal authority under the Commerce Clause.[57] The United States Supreme Court later

52. *Id.* § 1454(h).

53. *See Mountainlands Conservancy LLC v. California Coastal Comm'n*, 260 Cal. Rptr. 3d 683 (Cal. Ct. App. 2020) (upholding the Commission's authority also to declare some lands within Los Angeles County as unsuitable for vineyards because its authority to support "feasible" agriculture gave it the authority to find some land "unsuitable" for vineyards on "economic, environmental, social and technological grounds").

54. Discussed *infra* and *supra*, Chapter 14.

55. 16 U.S.C. §§ 3501–3510.

56. *See United States v. Southern Investment Co.*, 876 F.2d 606 (8th Cir. 1989) (holding that wetlands created by a dam remain under Corps jurisdiction). *But see United States v. City of Fort Pierre*, 747 F.2d 464 (8th Cir. 1984) (holding that a dry slough exhibiting wetland characteristics because of Corps river dredging, was not subject to the § 404 permit program).

57. *See United States v. Wilson*, 133 F.3d 251, 257 (4th Cir. 1997) (interpreting *United States v. Lopez*, 514 U.S. 549 (1995)) (noted in James Bryant, United States v. Wilson: *A Change in Wetlands and Clean Water Act Jurisprudence?*, 28 Real Est. L.J. 37, 38 (1999)).

agreed.[58] Noting that the jurisdiction of the Corps is limited to the "navigable" waters of the United States, the court in *SWANCC* said that Congress intended that word to be a limiting one, and continued: "it is one thing to give the word limited effect, and quite another to give it no effect whatsoever." Moreover, the court said, to recognize the Corps' jurisdiction over such isolated wetlands would impinge on the traditional rights of the states to regulate land and water uses. Therefore, the court invalidated the Corps' regulatory authority over isolated, non-navigable, intrastate waters in wetlands whose only connection to interstate commerce was the presence of migratory birds.[59] However, if the pond is an intrastate body of water, without a navigable tributary or outlet, but used as fishery whose products entered interstate commerce, the Corps would arguably still have jurisdiction.[60]

After mapping all state wetlands, one state wetlands commission imposed a two mile buffer requirement between wetlands and private waste management company landfills. Against the argument of a waste management company claiming that there is no evidence that the proximity of a landfill is a reliable indicator of landfill pollution, this buffer regulation is reasonable, and even when it is only fairly debatable, it nonetheless may be sustained as having a rational basis and supported by substantial evidence.[61]

§ 17.02 The Public Trust

The doctrine of the public trust was received in the United States as part of the English common law.[62] It is the right of the people to use freely the lands within the trust—including coastal lands for certain purposes, originally navigation, commerce, and fishing, but today in some states, encompassing recreation as well. Originally it applied only to the 13 colonies, but eventually, under the equal footing doctrine for the admission of other states to the Union, the trust was incorporated into every state's sovereign powers.[63] In keeping with its colonial origins, only tidal wetlands were originally subject to the trust; on a beach, this meant that trust lands lay between the high and low tide marks—that is, to the wet sand area of a beach, but not its dry sand

58. *See Rapanos v. United States*, 547 U.S. 715 (2006) (denying the Corps jurisdiction when the wetland was adjacent to a ditch connected to a navigable water body); *Solid Waste Agency of Northern Cook Cty. v. U.S. Army Corps of Engineers*, 531 U.S. 159 (2001) (both discussed *supra*).

59. *Id.* (also limiting the reach of the holding in *Riverside Bayview Homes*, *supra*, 474 U.S. 121, by emphasizing the latter's focus on the reasonableness of the hydrologic connection between a body of water and its wetlands).

60. *See Utah v. Marsh*, 740 F.2d 799 (10th Cir. 1984).

61. *See Johnson v. Sunray Services, Inc.*, 816 S.W.2d 582 (Ark. 1991).

62. *See* Erin Ryan, *Short History of the Public Trust Doctrine and Its Intersection with Private Water Law*, 38 Va. Envtl. L. Rev. 135, 135–81 (2020); Alexandra Klass, *Modern Public Trust Principles: Recognizing Rights and Integrating Standards*, 82 Notre Dame L. Rev. 699 (2006).

63. *See Pollard v. Hagan*, 44 U.S. 212 (1845).

area. The trust then was gradually expanded to apply to all navigable waters—lakes, ponds, rivers and streams.[64] Thus it is that the state has title to both tidal and fresh navigable waters, and their underlying beds, in trust for the free use of them by the public.[65] The trust has been expanded in some states to cover wetlands adjacent to navigable waters,[66] groundwater used for drinking,[67] the dry sand area of beaches, wildlife, and wildlife habitat. It also authorizes regulation by permits and otherwise prohibits removal of the beds of navigable bodies of water.[68] It protects both the public nature of trust lands and assigns the duty of protecting them to the state government as trustee.[69] The trustee can neither alienate trust lands nor allow their destruction. In reality, however, there is no one public trust doctrine, each state has its own.[70] In a few states, state constitutional provisions supplement the protection of the environment given by the public trust.[71] In many other states, citizen suit provisions of environmental statutes and environmental rights statutes provide additional support for enforcing statutes and the trust.

§ 17.03 Beaches

The ecological functions of a barrier beach are several. First, the beach is a unique habitat for plants and wildlife. Second, its sand has a capacity to absorb great amounts of water. The dunes absorb the force of waves, as do the back-of-the-dunes area of a beach, coastal ponds, and wetlands. Thus the beach is the coast's first line of defense against heavy seas, such as are created by hurricanes. When hurricanes come, the escape routes from beaches on barrier islands, such as were the backdrop for *Lucas v. South Carolina Coastal Commission*,[72] are limited.

---

64. *See Glass v. Goeckel*, 703 N.W.2d 188 (Mich. 2005); *Vermont v. Vermont Central Ry.*, 571 A.2d 1128, 1132 (Vt. 1989). *See generally* J. Archer & T. Stone, *The Interaction of the Public Trust and the Takings Doctrine: Protecting Wetlands and Critical Coastal Areas*, 20 Vt. L. Rev. 81 (1995).

65. *See Shrively v. Bowlby*, 152 U.S. 1 (1894); *The Daniel Ball*, 77 U.S. 557, 564 (1871) (holding also that the test for navigability is "navigability in fact").

66. *See Just v. Marinette Cty.*, 201 N.W.2d 761, 769 (Wis. 1972).

67. *See Mayor v. Passaic Valley Water Comm'n*, 539 A.2d 760, 765 (N.J. Super. Ct., Law Div. 1987).

68. *See Reuter v. Department of Natural Resources*, 168 N.W.2d 860 (Wis. 1969).

69. *See Ill. Cent. R.R. v. Illinois*, 146 U.S. 387 (1892), discussed in J.D. Kearney & T.W. Merrill, *The Origins of the American Public Trust Doctrine: What Really Happened in Illinois Central*, 71 U. Chi. L. Rev. 799 (2004).

70. *See* Robin Kundis Craig, *A Comparative Guide to the Eastern States Public Trust Doctrines*, 16 Penn. St. Envtl. L. Rev. 1 (2007).

71. *See* Alaska Const. art. VII, §§ 3, 4 & 14; Haw. Const. art XI, § 1; La. Const. art. IX, § 4; Mont. Const. art. II, § 3, art. IX, § 1; R.I. Const. Amend. 9; Pa. Const. art. I, § 8.

72. 505 U.S. 1003 (Blackmon, J., dissenting, text at n. 1).

§ 17.04 Total Takings

Lucas v. South Carolina Coastal Council[73] created a new category of takings cases involving the so-called "total taking." The court held that an owner losing all economically beneficial uses under a regulation has suffered a taking—that is, a development denial resulting in a total or 100% diminution in value is a taking—except when the owner's proposed development violates the background principles of nuisance and property law.

[A] The Facts

David Lucas purchased two unimproved beachfront lots in 1986. Both lots were then zoned in a single-family use district. He paid $975,000. The lots didn't abut each other and Lucas intended to construct separate residences on both—one residence for himself and his family and the other on speculation. Neighboring lots on each side of Lucas' had been developed previously: on each were homes.

Two years later, in 1988, the state enacted a Beachfront Management Act—an Act made necessary by the federal Coastal Zone Management Act previously discussed. The Act prohibited any substantial development of the lots, including the construction of residences: only wooden decks or narrow raised boardwalks were permitted. The beach in front of Lucas' lots was unstable; parts of it had been underwater within the past 40 years. More recently, however, the beach had not been subject to erosion; in fact, over the last several decades it had been built up by the accretion of sand. Nonetheless, the Coastal Council administering the Act drew a line connecting the landward most points of erosion during the past 40 years—a line to the rear of Lucas' landward lot boundaries. This had the effect of making Lucas ineligible for a building permit and abruptly ended his construction plans.

Lucas did not apply for a building permit. (The Act's administrator testified at trial that applying would have been futile.) Instead, Lucas sued, conceding that the Act was within the well-recognized police power of the legislature, but alleging that it was, notwithstanding, a violation of his constitutional right not to be deprived of his property without first being paid just compensation for it.

While the suit was pending in 1990 and 4 years after Lucas' purchase, the state legislature amended the Act to permit administrative relief in the form of variances from the Act's provisions. Lucas did not apply for this relief either.[74] The trial court found a regulatory taking, awarding Lucas over $1.2 million in compensation.

---

73. 505 U.S. 1003 (1992) (noted at 71 N.C. L. Rev. 928 (1993)). For a state court opinion following *Lucas*, see *Maryland Reclamation Assocs, Inc. v. Harford County*, 227 A.3d 220, 261 (Md. 2020).

74. After the 1990 amendments, the issue arose whether Lucas' takings claim was ripe for judicial review: when further administrative review that might lead to the granting of a variance, the developer should seek such review or else risk a determination that the regulators have not yet reached a final decision about the Act's application. *Lucas* is unclear as to whether ameliorative amendments enacted

[B] The State Supreme Court Opinion

The Supreme Court of South Carolina reversed and, over a strong dissenting opinion, found no taking under the 1987 United States Supreme Court opinion in *Keystone.*[75] The state supreme court concluded that once Lucas had conceded that the Act was intended to protect the coast from erosion, its primary purpose became harm prevention, rather than the creation of a public right or benefit. This concession led the court (like most state courts reviewing similar statutes) to use the private harm/public benefit test (found in Justice Holmes' opinion in *Pennsylvania Coal Co. v. Mahon*[76]) for a taking and to uphold the Act. Thus it found that there was no taking, notwithstanding the severe economic impact on Lucas.[77]

[C] The United States Supreme Court—The Majority Opinion

The United States Supreme Court reversed the state court. Justice Scalia wrote the majority opinion. He first conceded that the takings clause as originally proposed by James Madison, applied only to "physical deprivations,"[78] but he further argued that as ratified, it "can be read to apply to regulatory as well as physical deprivations."[79] Then reaching the merits of Lucas' takings claim, Scalia's opinion described two types of regulatory takings claims: first, those involving a physical invasion of a plaintiff's land and second, those involving a regulation denying "all economically beneficial or productive use" of property. This case, he states, is of the second type.[80]

---

after an owner purchases can affect both his investment-backed expectations and the ripeness of his takings claim. At least three Justices found Lucas' claim not ripe. So this issue was revisited after *Lucas.* (In any event, developers should document their investment-backed expectations at the time that they purchase a property.) *See Palazzolo v. Rhode Island,* 533 U.S. 606 (2001) (holding that a post-enactment purchaser, once procuring a final regulatory decision denying a permit, making clear the extent of the development that would be allowed, and citing no non-compliance with state exhaustion rules or pre-permit processes, would have ripened a takings claim).

75. Discussed *supra,* Chapter 3, § 3.05.

76. Discussed *supra,* Chapter 3, § 3.04.

77. In contrast, the dissent focused on the impact—and on *Agins v. City of Tiburon,* 447 U.S. 255, 260 (1980), discussed *supra,* Chapter 4, stating that a taking occurs when "the ordinance . . . denies an owner economically viable use of his land." The dissent found that the Act's primary purpose was to confer a benefit on the public by preserving the coast as a tourist attraction and habitat for wildlife, plants, and natural processes.

78. *See* John Hart, *Land Use Law in the Early Republic and the Original Meaning of the Takings Clause,* 94 Nw. U. L. Rev. 1099, 1156 (2000) (arguing that early land use regulation was broad and inclusive and so Madison's and others' view of the takings clause was narrow, not encompassing regulatory takings as Justice Holmes found in *Pennsylvania Coal Co. v. Mahon*).

79. The majority and dissenting opinions disagreed about the Act's primary purpose, affecting their views of the Act's constitutionality. The dissent contended that the takings clause applies only to physical takings.

80. This second type of taking has three sources: (1) Justice Holmes' diminution in value test in *Mahon,* in connection with which Holmes states that, when the diminution "reached a certain

These two types of takings, the court said, are "two discrete categories of regulatory action ... compensable without case-specific inquiry into the public interest advanced in support of the restraint" on the plaintiff's property rights. (Thus he made the state court's disagreement about the Act's purpose irrelevant to the taking here.) To mold a rule for the second type of taking involved in this case, the court states: "[W]hen an owner of real property has been called upon to sacrifice *all* economically beneficial uses in the name of the common good, that is, to leave his property economically idle, he has suffered a taking."

The first, and most important, thing done in this opinion is that its majority recognizes this second type of categorical taking—for a deprivation of "all economically beneficial uses," compensable even when supported by the strongest of police power justifications. Here is a clear, bright-line right for the property owner. The second thing done is the holding that this new type of categorical taking is inapplicable when the state justifies the otherwise offending regulation as a public nuisance or as justified under another equally well established principle of real property law.[81]

[1] Lucas *and* Penn Central

The majority opinion states that *Lucas* deals with a "relatively rare" situation, a 100% taking: when, as is the more typical situation, the reduction in value is less than 100%, the substantiality of the legitimate state interest is analyzed as well. This involves balancing the state's interest ("the character of the governmental action") against the degree of restraint on private property ("the impact of the regulation and ... the extent to which the regulation has interfered with distinct investment backed expectations").[82] While *Penn Central* provides the default rule for evaluating a non-*Lucas* regulatory takings claim, such balancing is unlikely to yield crisp results easily put into statements of black letter law.

[2] The Nuisance Cases

The South Carolina Supreme Court, Justice Scalia said, was too quick to conclude that "harmful or noxious uses of property, amounting to a public nuisance, may be abated by regulations without the payment of compensation." Here he intends to clarify[83] the status of the so-called noxious use cases in which some land use has

---

magnitude" it is a taking—so a 100% magnitude is a sure threshold for invoking Holmes' language; (2) Justice Brennan's dicta in *Penn Central*, stating that the case would be different if the terminal were useless (see *Penn Central Transportation Company v. New York City*, 438 U.S. 104, 138, n. 36 (1978)); and (3) the "economic viability" prong of the *Agins* test.

81. The *Lucas* opinion, taken as a whole, is an elaboration of the private harm/public benefit test for a taking found in *Mahon*, discussed *supra*, Chapter 3.

82. *See Penn Central Transportation Company v. New York City*, 438 U.S. 104 (1978) (discussed *supra*, Chapter 4).

83. Scalia's restatement of the law here employs the same analysis as Justice Rehnquist's dissent in *Keystone Bituminous Coal Ass'n v. DeBenedictis*, 480 U.S. 470, 513 (1987), discussed *supra*, Chapter 3.

been halted by legislation: e.g., *Mugler, Hadacheck, Miller v. Schoene*, and *Goldblatt*.[84] Justice Scalia, quoting from a majority opinion of Justice Brennan, thought that these cases are best understood "as resting not on any supposed 'noxious' quality of the prohibited uses but rather on the ground that the restrictions were reasonably related to the implementation of a policy—not unlike historic preservation—expected to produce a widespread public benefit and applicable to all similarly situated property."[85] These cases, Scalia adds, used analysis that is "simply the progenitor of our more contemporary statements" like the statement in Justice Scalia's 1987 opinion, that "land-use regulation does not effect a [regulatory] taking if it 'substantially advance[s] legitimate state interests.'"[86] Thus the noxious use cases cannot be singled out for a special status in takings law.[87]

The distinction—crucial to the state court opinion below—between preventing a harmful use (no compensation required) as opposed to extracting a public benefit from an owner (compensation required), is difficult to make and, for Justice Scalia, is in "the eye of the beholder." At root, his concern with this harm-benefit distinction is a distrust of legislative findings and a refusal to accept them at face value. Were it otherwise, "[s]ince such a justification can be formulated in practically every case, this amounts to a test of whether the legislature has a stupid staff."[88] He thus refuses to accept conclusory legislative declarations of purpose.

[3] Total Taking Analysis

In preparation for the first of Justice Scalia's two important statements in this opinion, he identified two types of discrete categories of regulatory action compensable without case-specific inquiry. That there were <u>two</u> categories is in itself noteworthy because before this opinion, it was clear that there was one, exemplified by *Loretto*. The second "total taking" category involved in this case did not exist beforehand. What had been clear was that there was a group of cases involving physical invasions that always required compensation, and another group involving abating a public nuisance, that did not.

---

84. In three of these four cases (*Miller* excepted), all discussed *supra*, Chapter 3, the regulation was alleged to have completely shut down a business.

85. *See Lucas v. South Carolina Coastal Council*, 505 U.S. 1003, 1023 (1992), *quoting from Penn Central Transportation Company v. New York City*, 438 U.S. 104, 133–34 (1977) (Brennan, J.).

86. Here Justice Scalia is quoting from his own prior opinion in *Nollan v. California Coastal Commission*, 483 U.S. 825, 834 (1987), discussed *supra*, Chapter 14.

87. After *Penn Central*, where these cases were crucial to Justice Brennan's restatement of the law of takings, Supreme Court opinions on takings had discussed these cases either as an exception to a majority rule in takings jurisprudence, or as a distinct line of cases within that jurisprudence. Then Justice Rehnquist, however, treated the cases as an exception in his dissent in *Penn Central*. His dissent in *Keystone* made plain that the nuisance cases provided no safe harbor from taking claims: "Our cases [he said] have never applied the nuisance exception to allow complete extinction of the value of the parcel of property." *Keystone*, 480 U.S. at 513.

88. *See Lucas*, 505 U.S. at 1025, n. 12.

The prior lack of clarity in takings case law existed because of the too general rules in the court's opinions in the 1980s—starting with *Agins*. Many Court watchers spent that decade debating whether Justice Scalia's second category existed at all. That second category was identified as the *Agins* test concerning the denial of all "economically viable use."

While making clear that the noxious use or nuisance abatement cases are not a separate line of authority, Justice Scalia assigns this second, total taking, category stand-alone status.

The opinion offers three justifications for this status: first, that the total taking is the functional equivalent of a physical invasion;[89]; second, that government's continuing ability to operate is not threatened by it; and third, that there is here "a heightened risk that private property is being pressed into some form of public service."

Justice Scalia proposed that a plaintiff like David Lucas prove that, under state law, (1) the use he proposes is one that he might traditionally expect to engage in, (2) one not prohibited by nuisance law, (3) one other owners indulge in, and (4) that has been an expected part of the bundle of sticks for the real property he acquired, but (5) has been destroyed.[90] Most important in this regard is that Lucas' coastal lots were surrounded by others that were already built upon.

Once a landowner proves a deprivation of all economic use, the state or regulator has the burden of proof to show that the "proscribed use interests were not part of his title to begin with" and that there are "background principles of nuisance and property law that prohibit the uses" the owner intends. Such a showing is necessary to sustain the regulation. Without it, the state's proscribing "a productive use that was previously permissible" under relevant property and nuisance principles, means that the state's regulation has "gone too far" and requires compensation.[91]

Justice Scalia elaborates on "this logically antecedent inquiry" with a list of considerations from nuisance law: the degree of harm to public or private lands posed by the proposed use, the social value of the use, its suitability to the land in question, and the ease of avoiding the harm by the user or the government.[92] As Dean Prosser once noted, the law of nuisance is an "impenetrable jungle"—a welter of conflicting decisions, hard to harmonize and emphasizing one factor in one decision only to ignore it elsewhere. Scalia, however, was trolling for votes from his fellow Justices (particularly Justices O'Connor and Kennedy), and so he sets nuisance law up as a means of

---

89. Justice Alito would use this functional equivalency analysis in later takings cases. *See, e.g.*, *Koontz v. St. Johs River Water Management Dist.*, 570 U.S. 595, 619 (2013) (holding that money exacted from a developer was the functional equivalent of land taken from him); *Sackett v. EPA*, 598 U.S. 651, 684 (2023) (holding that for Clean Water Act purposes, the discharge of a pollutant into groundwater not covered by the Act was the "functional equivalent of a direct discharge" into a water course covered by the Act).

90. *See Lucas*, 505 U.S. at 1031.

91. This is Scalia's attempt to reconcile *Mugler* and *Mahon*.

92. *See Lucas*, 505 U.S. at 1030–31 (citing Restatement of Torts §§ 826, 827, 828(a)–(c), 830, 831).

justifying a regulation, however much he elsewhere deplored the type of analysis he was importing into takings jurisprudence.

Returning to private nuisance law as the touchstone for the regulators' arguments in support of a regulation, will present regulators with many problems of proof. Since the advent of environmental laws and statutes, nuisance law has been relatively, but not completely, static. Justice Scalia assumes that nuisance law might immunize state regulation against the state's having to pay compensation, but nuisance law also contains some precedent suggesting that nuisance cases have resulted in the abatement of a use, but only if the plaintiff is willing to pay for the abatement.[93] This is not what Scalia seems to have in mind (although he might not object).

Moreover, defining the type of "background" property law that the state may use to defend against a total takings claim has some further definitional difficulties. For example, many states recognize the public's customary right to use the dry sand area of a beach as part of its public trust, so when a coastal landowner in Oregon wished to construct an improvement and protect it with a seawall over the dry sand area of the beach, the issue arose whether a municipality may deny a building permit for the wall, citing the public's customary use right as preventing the owner from expecting to be able to build the wall. The owner claimed that in this situation a taking has occurred, but the United States Supreme Court refused to hear his case.[94] Justice Scalia criticized the state court opinion rejecting this claim here, calling it "a land grab running the entire length of the Oregon coast," finding that the state's doctrine of custom had been limited in Oregon opinions and so did not justify the denial of the building permit at issue.[95]

In another case involving a building permit to construct a shoreline resort complex, the beaches involved encompassed tidal pools which contain mollusks, shrimp, and vegetation. Native (Hawaiian) Americans had gathered these as food since time immemorial. When the state granted the application for the permit, customary and continuous native access was a permit condition not subject to a later takings claim challenge.[96]

Other sources of "background" principles might be other customary rights, a navigational servitude, natural rights such as the right of lateral and subjacent support, reasonable use rules in riparian water rights law, the beneficial use doctrine in water appropriation law, Native American treaty rights, state constitutional provisions protecting the environment, or the public trust. The extent of each of these sources will vary from state to state, but all might provide regulators with justifications for a contested regulation. The *Lucas* opinion does not limit the possible sources

---

93. *See, e.g., Spur Industries, Inc. v. Del E. Webb Dev. Co.*, 494 P.2d 700 (Ariz. 1972).

94. *See Stevens v. City of Cannon Beach*, 854 P.2d 449 (Or. 1993) (upholding the permit denial under *Lucas*), *cert. denied*, 510 U.S. 1207 (1994) (Scalia, J., dissenting, *id.* at 1334).

95. *See State ex rel. Thornton v. Hay*, 462 P.2d 671 (Or. 1969).

96. *See Public Access Shoreline Hawaii v. Hawaii County Planning Comm'n*, 900 P.2d 1313 (Haw. Ct. App. 1993), *aff'd*, 903 P.2d 1246 (Haw. 1995).

of background principles to nuisance law, so long as the source is well established in the "real property law" of a state.

The public trust has proven to be particularly useful to regulators in defending total takings cases. The public trust doctrine applies to "all water resources" in many states.[97] Where there is no private property interest in water there is no takings claim. An owner or developer of waterfront property may be required to provide public access and a pathway along the waterfront;[98] the public trust denies owners a right to exclude in such situations because the public trust is superior to the developer's riparian rights and, in the view of one court, is an encumbrance on those rights.[99] Even when land was submerged after a developer took title, the newly submerged land is subject to the trust and subjecting them to the trust was a defense to a takings claim.[100] So too when a developer proposes to build on an elevated platform over public trust wetlands.[101] The high water mark as a boundary for public trust lands is not so much a "mark" where water ceases to impact soil and vegetation as it is the result of the course of the tides.

As a background principal of state law, the public trust has also trumped takings claims when used as a defense to a developer's assertion of a regulatory takings claim with regard to a developer's "reasonable investment backed expectations." That is, the developer cannot have any expectation to develop coastal wetlands subject to the state's public trust below the high tide line.[102]

[4] Euclid *and* Lucas

In 1926 in *Euclid*, Justice Sutherland's majority opinion stated that nuisance law will "furnish a helpful clew" as to the validity of a particular zoning regulation. His admonition was disregarded until *Lucas*, particularly so since the New Deal expanded the scope of permissible government activities. *Euclid*'s validation of zoning is cited earlier in the *Lucas* opinion, though not prominently and not in such a way as to give it a continuing, sweeping effect. *Euclid* recognized that the development value of land—up to as much as two thirds to three quarters of its unregulated, fair market value—may be reduced without compensation. So *Euclid* is thus not a "total taking"

---

97. *See, e.g., Kauai Springs, Inc. v. Planning Comm'n of the Cty. of Kauai*, 324 P.3d 851, 982 (Haw. 2014).

98. *See Nat'l Ass'n of Homebuilders v. N.J. Dep't of Envtl. Prot.*, 64 F. Supp. 2d 354 (D.N.J. 1999).

99. *See R.W. Docks & Slips v. State*, 628 N.W.2d 781 (Wis. 2001). *But see Severance v. Patterson*, 370 S.W.3d 723 (Tex. 2012) (rejecting a public trust easement arising after an avulsive change in a water boundary).

100. *See McQueen v. S.C. Coastal Comm'n*, 580 S.E.2d 116 (S.C. 2003). *But see Estate of Teney v. S.C. Dep't of Health & Envtl Control*, 712 S.E.2d 395 (S.C. 2011) (holding that islands within wetland not subject to the public trust); *Matter of New Cr. Bluebelt, Phase 4*, 168 N.Y.S.3d 505 (N.Y. Sup. Ct., App. Div., 2022) (recognizing a taking claim for wetlands subjected to the trust after claimant took title).

101. *See Esplanade Properties LLC v. City of Seattle*, 307 F.3d 978 (9th Cir. 2002).

102. *See Palazzolo v. State*, 2005 R.I. Super. LEXIS 108 (R.I. Super. Ct., July 5, 2005) (on remand from the U.S. Supreme Court whose decision in this takings case in discussed *supra*, Chapter 4, §4.01[A][3].

case: a third to a quarter of the fair market value remained with the owner. In an earlier footnote, Scalia opined that, while some owners who retain only 10% of their land's value would receive compensation under the multi-factor test laid down in earlier opinions,[103] others would not, and Scalia adds that "takings law is full of these 'all or nothing' situations." The Supreme Court continued in *Lucas* to avoid cases dealing with the most frequently-used land use regulations, such as zoning, while citing the more unusual cases as support.

Nuisance law plays a singular role in Justice Scalia's analysis. It really plays two roles: the first in the rejected noxious use cases, where its centrality was rejected; and the second, in which it reappears, as relevant to a defense to a categorical total taking. Justice Scalia reduced the impact of the noxious use cases, only to reintroduce them later as a justification for a regulation. Nuisance law becomes, not a primary justification for a regulation, but when a total taking is present, it becomes an affirmative defense for regulators. The noxious use cases had inoculated from takings challenges a diminution in value—no matter how great, and even if only a fraction less than 100%. Thus, a total taking is compensable, except when the harmful aspects of the use would permit its abatement as a public or private nuisance or under state real property law. This changes the function of nuisance law in total takings cases: what was once an initial showing inoculating a regulation from a taking claim has become an affirmative defense to an initial proof of a total taking.

Whether nuisance law is at the beginning or the end of a rule does not matter much when local zoning and subdivision ordinances are concerned. This is so for two reasons: (1) the presence of non-Euclidian design review procedures, variances, and special exceptions, when combined with ripeness requirements, protect municipalities against a finding of a total taking; (2) Justice Brennan's position in *Penn Central*, treating the railroad's parcel as a whole, and used again by Justice Stevens' treatment of the coal mine as a whole in *Keystone*, also protect municipalities in the same way; that is, this parcel-as-a-whole approach, although the subject of debate, protects municipalities from a finding of a total taking. So if Lucas owned two lots as before, but one was on the landward side, and another on the seaward side of the building line, the parcel as-a-whole-approach would save the state the money otherwise required for compensation.[104]

Since *Euclid*, federal and state environmental laws have largely taken the place of public nuisance actions. Public nuisance law in particular has languished in the decades after *Euclid* upheld zoning in the 1920s. So it is unlikely that state regulators will be forced to look only to nuisance law and ignore a state's zoning and environmental law precedents. Both will likely be used to establish the traditional background principles relevant to defending total takings cases.

---

103. *See Lucas*, 505 U.S. at 1019, n. 8 (citing *Penn Central*, 438 U.S. 104, 124 (1977)).

104. *See Murr v. Wisconsin*, 582 U.S. 383 (2017) (using a multi-factor test to determine whether the state may treat two continuous parcels bought at different times as a merged parcel-as-a-whole) (noted at 131 Harv. L. Rev. 253 (2017)).

The proof of this lies in Justice Kennedy's concurring opinion in *Lucas*. It would permit the state to look broadly as its environmental laws as well as its nuisance case law. Kennedy saw nuisance law as too limiting a model for determining the validity of land use and environmental regulations. The unique environmental concerns involving coastal land made this limitation of special concern to him. He would have used a balancing test, weighing the public interest involved against the owner's investment backed expectations (thus giving these greater prominence than they had in *Penn Central*). His dispute with Justice Scalia is well joined, because balancing is what Scalia hopes to avoid by expanding the role of categorical takings. Probably Justice Kennedy's approach will protect many land use regulations and environmental laws from being impacted by *Lucas*.[105]

[5] Legislatively Created "Background" Law in State Courts

In responding to Justice Scalia's prompting that a regulation be justified if at all by an inquiry into the "background principles of state property and nuisance law," some state courts have included state statutes and regulations,[106] while others have not, using only common law principles in their inquiry.[107] The common law/statutory distinction has the advantage of a bright line, but does not do justice to Scalia's language.

For example, subdivision enabling acts and ordinances conditionally permit developers to subdivide land into building lots. If the developer is forced to leave more than one buildable lot in its natural state, 100% of his right to sell that lot has been denied by the regulation, but a "total taking" inquiry is inappropriate.

Most subdivision ordinances require that the developer set aside portions of the subdivision for streets, parks, schools, and other public purposes. A long tradition of subdivision regulation diminishes a developer's expectations to the point that these very detailed regulations are no surprise. Likewise, an inclusive view of background principles works no unfairness on such developers and a non-inclusive view gives them a windfall. The majority opinions in *Penn Central*, *Keystone*, and *Murr* counsel consideration of the subdivision operation as a whole, rather than on a lot-by-lot

105. Writing for the majority in *Palazzolo v. Rhode Island*, 533 U.S. 606 (2001), Kennedy showed the same flexible approach to finding what is a background principle of property or nuisance law, "those common, shared understandings of permissible limitations derived from a State's legal tradition," unaffected by the time the owner acquires title of the regulated property or the date of the enactment of a regulation.

106. For two cases using statutes as justifying a regulation, see *Soon Duck Kim v. City of New York*, 681 N.E.2d 312, 315–316 (N.Y. 1997) (involving regrading of land to meet a regraded street), and *Hunziker v. State*, 519 N.W.2d 367, 371 (Iowa 1994) (denying developers a building permit because the state's archaeologist found a Native American burial ground on the developer's parcel).

107. *See City of Miami v. Keshbro, Inc.*, 717 So. 2d 601, 604–05 (Fla. App. Ct. 1998) (involving a nuisance abatement order of the city); *Stevens v. City of Cannon Beach*, 854 P.2d 449, 456 (Or. 1993).

basis, and for inclusion of these regulations as within the ambit of relevant background principles.[108]

Similarly, a pre-existing federal environmental statute might provide a background principle for state law. For example, a federal mining statute might provide a principle upon which to deny a state mining permit.

Moreover, background principles may include notions of fairness and the prevention of windfalls, as well as recognition that common law duties may be based on statutes, the encouragement of purchasers to conduct a wide-ranging legal analysis of their purchases, and the long tradition of allowing statutes to affect property rights retroactively.[109]

[6] *What* Lucas *Does Not Decide*

First, the court did not find that a taking had occurred. Instead, it remanded the case to South Carolina courts for a consideration of this issue and also for a consideration of whether Lucas suffered a temporary regulatory taking under *First English*. Second, the court does not say whether the search for background principles will provide a defense not only in a "total taking" case, but also in any regulatory takings case.

[a] Footnote 7

How do we tell when there has been a "total taking"? The value of what's left after the regulation—the value of the economically viable uses remaining once the regulation is in effect—is the numerator of a fraction, the denominator of which is its value before the regulation is imposed. The "composition of the denominator" in the court's "deprivation fraction" is in Scalia's view problematical.[110] This fraction is:

$$\frac{100 - [\text{value after regulation}] \times 100 = \%\text{ of value lost to regulation}}{[\text{value before regulation}]}$$

Justice Scalia says that it is unclear whether a real estate developer forced to leave 90% of land that he proposed for subdivision in its natural state, would have his deprivation measured by the total acreage—in which case there would be 10% remaining and the "total taking" inquiry would not apply—or whether the 90% of the acreage

---

108. *See, e.g., Loveladies Harbor, Inc. v. United States*, 21 Cl. Ct. 153 (1990), *motion to vacate and dismiss denied*, 27 F.3d 1545 (Fed. Cir. 1994) (noted and discussed in Eric Freyfogle, *The Owning and Taking of Sensitive Lands*, 43 U.C.L.A. L. Rev. 77 (1995)). *See generally* Richard Ausness, *Regulatory Takings and Wetland Protection in the Post-*Lucas *Era*, 30 Land and Water L. Rev. 349, 379–87 (1995) (collecting these cases).

109. *See* Kerri Millikan, *The* Lucas *Exception: Inclusion, Exclusion, and a Statute of Limitation*, 68 Geo. Wash. L. Rev. 134, 140–47 (1999); *see also* John Hart, *Land Use Law in the Early Republic and the Original Meaning of the Takings Clause*, 94 Nw. U. L. Rev. 1099, 1107–16 (2000) (arguing that early land use regulation, when regarded as background law, was broad and inclusive).

110. *See Lucas*, 505 U.S. at 1016, n. 7.

should be considered separately, giving the developer a case involving a 100% deprivation of 90% of the acreage.[111]

As an example of this confusion, Scalia cites what he sees as the conflicting results in *Mahon* and *Keystone*. *Pennsylvania Coal Co. v. Mahon*[112] involved the elimination of a right to avoid surface subsidence liability that was recognized as a distinct property right in Pennsylvania law. A regulatory statute "restricting subsurface extraction of coal" was "held to effect a taking." *Keystone Bituminous Coal Ass'n v. DeBenedictis*[113] involved a "nearly identical law held not to effect a taking." What Scalia does not say is that the recognition of many statutes generally codifying environmental law standards for the coal mining industry brought a new understanding of the permissible scope of regulatory activities and their permissible impact on mining properties. Justice Scalia's failure to accept this point of view showed his skepticism of *Keystone*'s majority opinion.[114] However, a later case sustained *Keystone*'s majority viewpoint.[115] In a general sense, however, Justice Scalia is correct: any trial court must define the property taken before it can determine that a total taking as occurred, and air rights were not considered separately in *Penn Central*, but the third estate was in *Mahon*.[116]

[b] Discrete Rights

Some other state-created rights are easily separated from others and considered separately, just as the third estate right of support was in *Mahon v. Pennsylvania Coal Co.*[117] For example, the common law right to explore for minerals has been the basis for an owner's right to bring a trespass action when someone else does. If the state conducts a geological survey of a region including an owner's mineral properties and releases data showing that there are no minerals on the owner's land, there is a taking of the owner's exploration right. An assertion of a total taking of the exploration right is akin to the taking of a segmented right in property similar to the third estate found to be a taking in *Mahon*. Once a right is recognized as distinct, it is subject to a *Lucas* total takings inquiry. That the state has a substantial interest in knowing where minerals are located within its borders, in (say) steering urbanization elsewhere, and in planning for the regulated extraction of the minerals, justifies the regulation but

111. *See Palazzolo v. Rhode Island*, 533 U.S. 606 (2001) (the majority rejecting a total taking claim and refusing to settle the "denominator issue" when plaintiff framed his case as the taking of a whole parcel, not merely its regulated wetland portion).

112. 260 U.S. 393 (1922).

113. 480 U.S. 470 (1987).

114. *Lucas* represents a change in the standard of judicial review and a new heightened scrutiny for regulations. *See Cleburne Living Ctr. v. City of Cleburne*, 473 U.S. 432 (1985) (discussed *infra*, Chapter 18). *Cleburne Living* also exemplifies this trend, as does *Nollan v. California Coastal Commission*, 483 U.S. 825 (1987) (discussed *supra*, Chapter 14).

115. *See Palazzolo v. Rhode Island*, 533 U.S. 606 (2001) (Kennedy, for the majority, and O'Connor, J., concurring).

116. *See* John Delaney, *Advancing Private Property Rights: The Lessons of* Lucas, 22 Stetson L. Rev. 395 (1993); Robert Washburn, *Land Use Control, The Individual, and Society:* Lucas v. South Carolina Coastal Council, 52 Md. L. Rev. 162 (1993).

117. 260 U.S. 393 (1922) (discussed *supra* Chapter 3).

does not avoid the finding of a total taking. In the alternative, the state might argue that, regardless of its interest in geologic information, there is no exploration right outside of a trespass action; so the exploration right is not a property right at all, but only a tort cause of action.

Thus, before filing the takings claim, an attorney should consider whether, when a right is recognized in state law, it cannot adequately be defended by a trespass action. Suppose that the trespass was a seismic one—the invasion of electronic impulses measuring the density and shape of geologic formations. If it can be defended in trespass, there may be no need for recognizing a takings claim. Thus an inquiry into the adequacy of other remedies is part of an antecedent inquiry into a state's background principles in its common law of property.

In another example, the right to drill a well to recover groundwater is a widely recognized, traditional right inherent in the ownership of land. Suppose that an owner with land zoned only for agricultural uses, but overlying groundwater of great purity, wants to drill a well and sell bottled water, but drilling requires a permit from municipal officials when the water is not to be used for irrigating an agricultural crop. If the permit is denied, a total takings claim is worth filing because the right to drill is a discrete ownership right and traditionally a landowner also has the right to capture or make reasonable use (depending on the state) of groundwater.[118]

[c] Worthless or Unsuitable?

Lucas leaves open the issue of whether a total taking requires that (1) the permitted uses of the land are worth nothing or that (2) it becomes unsuitable for any economic development that produces a reasonable return. The return on renting the land to beachgoers looks small in comparison to the return on the sale of neighboring properties, but still may be a reasonable return.[119] So there may be total deprivation in terms of fair market value, but not in terms of a reasonable return. If the Coastal Council had permitted David Lucas to build a very small, seaside bungalow, on pilings and with dry toilets, Lucas' case would have been considered under *Penn Central* and *Keystone* rules, as Justice Scalia had earlier indicated in *Nollan*. Similarly, when a building is required by the fire code to be retrofitted with sprinklers, necessitating the removal of hazardous material (like asbestos) and resulting in a cost to the owner

---

118. *Cf. Houston v. Town of Waitsfield*, 648 A.2d 864, 866 (Vt. 1994) (where the regulator decided that water is not an agricultural product and denying a permit to drill, recognizing that the owner can still drill for water and apply it to an agricultural crop or water livestock with it, and so not reaching the *Lucas* claim).

119. If David Lucas had permitted the public, for an access fee, to use his lots as a beach, and had realized, over ten years, 1% of the income he would have obtained building and selling houses, but 15% of the rental income he would have received from the lots with the houses on them, then only a sale of the houses had been denied. This right to alienate or sell the lots is an important right, well recognized and protected in every states' property law—and it is not 100% taken away. If the state could show that Lucas can sell the lots for 10% of his purchase price to someone who wanted to operate a beach business, with the expectation that someday houses would be permitted on them, then based on what Justice Scalia has said, Lucas would have had difficulty showing a total taking.

of more than the present fair market value of the building, there may be no *Lucas* or total taking claim if an occupancy permit will at the end of the day be issued to the owner; the value of the building is affected, but its use is not. In a similar situation, the required restoration of expensive architectural features might cost more than fair market value, but also not result in a total taking claim.

§ 17.05 Takings Claims—*Per Se* and Balancing Cases

Both *Loretto v. Manhattan Teleprompter CATV Corporation*[120] (finding a taking in a state statute permitting a cable TV company to attach a wire to the plaintiff's apartment building—a physical takings case in which there is little or no economic impact on the owner) and *Lucas* (involving the most substantial, 100% impact) represent two types of categorical or *per se* takings in which there is to be no inquiry into the statute's advancement of a legitimate state interest.

By contrast, in the broader, middle range of regulatory taking cases, exemplified by *Penn Central* and *Keystone*, when no categorical taking is present, the substantiality of the state's interest will still be balanced against the economic impact on the owner, particularly the impact on his or her investment-backed expectations. This balancing, emphasized by the dissenting opinions in *Lucas*, there had two aspects. First, it would take account of the gravity of the harm that a regulation sought to prevent. Erosion and storm protection weigh into this balance. Second, general regulations aimed at protecting and state's entire coastline do not target individual property owners, but seek to protect a whole population of coastal dwellers, and so do not give rise to a takings claim that otherwise seeks to redress individuals being singled out to bear public costs. Considering the need for coastal protection after recent severe hurricanes, such balancing may figure more urgently in future beach front takings cases, making more of them subject to *Penn Central* or *Keystone* regulatory taking as opposed to a *Lucas* total taking analysis.

120. 458 U.S. 419 (1982) (discussed *supra* Chapter 3).

§ 17.06 Federalism and Categorical Takings

Justice Marshall in *Loretto*,[121] resorting to such words as an "occupation" and "invasion" to describe a physical taking, did not specify what interest in property is being taken; nor did he use the usual classifications offered by New York state's law of real property. He was likely using such strange terms as "occupation" in part to avoid the use of more traditional descriptions of state real property interests, such as easements or licenses for the cable operator.

Similarly, when Justice Scalia in *Lucas* refers to the background principles of nuisance or real property law, Justice Scalia is referring to state law used for federal purposes. The issue for both is whether or to what extent the federal constitutional law of takings rests on state law, or whether there is a federal property law. After *Erie Railroad v. Tompkins*[122] ended the era of federal common law begun with *Swift v. Tyson*,[123] it is unlikely that Scalia was bringing back the era of *Swift*.[124] He wrote in *Lucas* that he was not. Yet he is walking a fine line: giving constitutional deference to state law, and writing as if South Carolina had a unified, coherent body of background principles in its nuisance and property law, he writes: "it seems unlikely that common-law principles would have prevented the erection of any habitable or productive improvements" on David Lucas' land.[125] This conclusion is one better left to South Carolina courts. Later, in *Lingle v. Chevron U.S.A., Inc.*,[126] the Supreme Court's de-emphasis on the purposes and objectives of a regulation in favor of looking in a takings claim solely at the impact of a regulation[127] does not mean that those things are irrelevant to a state court's inquiry into background principles as a defense to a *Lucas* total takings claim.

---

121. *Id.*

122. 304 U.S. 64, 78 (1938).

123. 41 U.S. 1 (1842).

124. Critics of *Lucas* point out the danger of federalizing the concept of property much the way the "freedom of contract" was federalized during the *Lochner* era. *See Lochner v. New York*, 198 U.S. 45 (1904); *see also United States v. Carolene Products Co.*, 304 U.S. 144, n. 4 (1938) (treating "liberty" similarly).

125. See *Lucas*, 505 U.S. at 1031.

126. 544 U.S. 528 (2005).

127. For a state court opinion following this change of emphasis, see *Diversified Holdings LLP v. City of Suwanee*, 807 S.E.2d 876 (Ga. 2017) (the dissenting opinion at p. 891) (questioning whether state takings law should follow federal precedents in light of the difference between the federal Constitution's takings clause and Georgia's constitutional equivalent).

PART FIVE

Regulating the User, Not the Use

Chapter 18
"Family" and Group Homes

§ 18.01 Defining a "Family" in a Zoning Ordinance

Most zoning ordinances establish single family, detached housing, use districts. Such districts were the "highest" and least intensive use districts established in Euclidian zoning ordinances enacted during the 1920s and 1930s. Indeed, establishing such districts was a major reason for the spread of Euclidian zoning during those decades. One aspect of any such district is the definition of a family.

This definition was not the subject of much litigation until the 1960s. A family was usually defined as a number of persons keeping house together. The housekeeping unit as a definition was probably not meant to encompass fraternity or religious group living, and certainly did not foresee the various types of communal living arrangements popular from the 1960s onward. New life styles, particularly amongst the young of that and later decades, and more particularly in communities surrounding college campuses, made some communities redefine a family by including a blood, marital or adoption tie.

Today one of the most common problems in interpreting a zoning ordinance involves the definition of a family. It is a common problem not only because of the wide-spread use of single family, exclusive use, residential districts in ordinances, but also because, in suburban and low-density communities, the presence of this type of use district is indeed the principal reason for having an ordinance in the first place. In addition, in 1974, the United States Supreme Court gave its blessing to a definition restrictive enough to exclude a group of college students renting a house near their university.[1] This case—*Village of Belle Terre v. Boraas*—was the first United States Supreme Court opinion since the *Nectow* opinion in the late 1920s to review a zoning ordinance. The Village's definition of the family was essentially a group of persons related by blood, marriage, or adoption, but not more than six persons, so related or not. This definition was upheld in *Boraas*. It was held to prohibit college students living together in a house in a single family use district.

1. *See Belle Terre v. Boraas*, 416 U.S. 1 (1974).

With Justice William O. Douglas writing for the majority in one of his last opinions as a Justice, the court viewed the ordinance's definition as the economic regulation of the landlord, thus involving no fundamental right or right of privacy. Its opinion went on, in words typical of Justice Douglas, to extol the virtues of the ordinance:

> A quiet place where yards are wide, people few, and motor vehicles restricted are legitimate guidelines in a land use project addressed to family needs.... The Police Power is not confined to elimination of filth, stench, and unhealthy places. It is ample to lay out a zone where family values, youth values, and the blessings of quiet seclusion and clean air make the area a sanctuary for people.[2]

Several years later, the United States Supreme Court again dealt with the family definition issue, but this time with more sensitivity to its impacts. Here the City of East Cleveland's zoning ordinance defined single family as "a group of persons consisting of parents and their unmarried children, but not more than six persons"—in other words, the nuclear family. Such a definition would by its terms prohibit grandparents and grandchildren from living together, and so it was, the court said, too restrictive.[3] The East Cleveland ordinance also contained an exception, to the effect that a family might also include a head of household, a spouse, plus one dependent child and that child's child—this would include three generations of a family, but in the case that went to the Supreme Court, *Moore v. City of East Cleveland*, a second grandson (the child of another son) moved in. The grandmother was then made the subject of criminal charges; convicted of violating the ordinance, she was fined and also sentenced to five days in jail. On appeal, the United States Supreme Court, 5-4, found *Boraas* inapplicable and reversed.[4]

Writing for the plurality of the court, Justice Lewis Powell found that the family values upheld in *Boraas* effected only unrelated individuals, but East Cleveland's ordinance "slic[ed] deeply into the family itself" by expressly selecting categories of related individuals who may live together. It made a crime of a grandmother's choice to live with her grandson. Thus, a plurality of the court invalidated the ordinance on substantive due process grounds. Some of the plurality also found the ordinance to be in violation of the Equal Protection Clause. Justice Stevens cast the deciding vote: he

---

2. *Id.* The dissenting Justices in *Boraas* viewed the case very differently. For them, the ordinance unduly burdened the student's First Amendment rights of association and privacy, resulting in discrimination on the basis of personal lifestyles. The dissenting Justices saw no constitutional prohibitions on density restrictions in a zoning ordinance so long as related and unrelated persons were regulated alike. For example, an ordinance might provide that no more than 10 persons, related in any way, or not, may occupy a house or dwelling for health reasons, and survive scrutiny by both the majority and the dissent in *Boraas*. Similarly, an ordinance might establish a minimum floor area per person.

3. *See Moore v. City of East Cleveland*, 431 U.S. 494 (1977).

4. *See* Robert Ellickson & Vicki Been, Land Use Controls 853, n. 1 (1999) (suggesting that the impetus for the definition in *Moore* was to prevent school children from taking up residence in the municipality).

wrote separately and, in a brief opinion, found that the ordinance was a both taking of property and was arbitrary under the test of *Euclid*.[5]

The *Moore* opinion might be seen as a limitation on the opinion in *Belle Terre*, but if it is, then when viewed from the perspective of a non-traditional family or other grouping, it is not much of a limitation. Both opinions reenforce the idea that zoning for the benefit of the family tied by blood or marriage is a proper focus of concern for municipal legislatures.

While both *Boraas* and *Moore* were decided in the same spirit, that of protecting the family, there is a difference between deciding that a municipal legislature, exercising the police power in a zoning ordinance, may protect family values—or rather, more precisely, that family values may provide a reasonable basis for the exercise of the police power (this is *Boraas*)—and deciding that the same type of legislature shall not prohibit grandparents from living with grandchildren who are cousins, but not brothers or sisters, under a restrictive definition of a "family" (as in *Moore*).[6]

Justices Douglas and Thurgood Marshall, writing for *Boraas'* majority and in dissent respectively, not only have a very different view of the issues before them, they also have different views of the plaintiffs: for Douglas, this is a case of a municipal legislature restricting the rent roll of a landlord; for Marshall, the tenants, the students at Stony Brook, are the plaintiffs, and he thus sees the issue as the students' rights to associate and to privacy. These views inform the analysis of each Justice. For Douglas, family values license the use of the police power. For Marshall, the use of the police power conflicts with the tenants' rights and must yield when the reach of the police power is "overinclusive." *Moore* stands for more than *Boraas* because it establishes a constitutional right to "family privacy"—heretofore an individual right—and more particularly, a right to choose to live in either a nuclear or an extended family. But Justice Powell's opinion was written for a plurality of 3 Justices. Viewed as a major extension of the right to privacy, the trouble which Powell had mustering a Supreme Court majority, is more easily understood.

Definitions of a "family" such as the one in *Boraas* are written the way they are, in part, because the family is seen as a self-limiting group—if by no other means than by biology and the period of gestation. However, many state courts in the immediate wake of *Boraas*, did not follow it.[7] Even if seven first cousins and an extended family could live together under the *Boraas* definition, the same number of unrelated persons, no matter how quiet, could not. The first cousins might fight, but quieter groups, say, an equal number of clerics, would be excluded. The clerics might have more of

5. Three dissenting Justices found no substantive due process violation, thinking the plurality opinion intruded on municipalities' authority without providing clear standards. Burger, C.J., dissenting, thought that Mrs. Moore should have applied for a variance and so did not exhaust her administrative remedies.

6. Taking the Supreme Court's lead, the Ohio Supreme Court held that a family unit that rears children, regardless of its composition, is constitutionally protected. *See Saunders v. Clark Cty. Zoning Dep't*, 421 N.E.2d 152 (Ohio 1981).

7. *See, e.g., Borough of Glassboro v. Vallorosi*, 535 A.2d 544 (N.J. Super. Ct. 1987) (collecting cases).

a common life-style than the first-cousins would. Again, the definition appears too restrictive.

The Brady Bunch might also be excluded under the *Boraas* definition. Brady and the spouse were married, the children were their family, but step-children, one's children not adopted by the other spouse, should be provided for in any modern definition—there are lots of Brady Bunches around these days.[8] As family compositions change, the problems of defining a family are unlikely to diminish.[9] As a matter of social policy, for example, a definition should take account of step children and for that matter, foster children as well.

Communal groups have fared somewhat better in state courts than they have in federal court.[10] As to college students, young singles, foster children, and the mentally-disabled, they could still be excluded in the two federal opinions considered so far. Some ordinances considered in state court attempt to remedy this with definitions of family that include both related and some unrelated persons, up to a specific maximum number. The maximum is presumably justified by some density studies indicating that a person needs a certain amount of square footage for comfort and mental health.[11]

Most state courts did, however, eventually follow *Boraas'* lead. In one case involving college students in Ann Arbor, Michigan, the court upheld an ordinance definition, stating a "ragtag collection of college roommates" were characterized as a family only "by the most cynical."[12] In *Dinan v. Board of Appeals of the Town of Strafford*,[13] the court upheld a definition under which no unrelated persons could live together. Its opinion discussed the differences between unrelated persons and related family members. Consider (the court said) a group of tenants (say) living together occupying premises on the basis of individual tenancies. Although they might share facilities, their ties were not likely to survive their separate tenancies, and viewed as transients, they were not as prone to form friendships with neighbors and care about

8. *See, e.g., City of Ladue v. Horn*, 720 S.W.2d 745 (Mo. 1986) (involving a Brady Bunch group in which the parents were not married but living together and upholding the ordinance, using a rational basis standard of review and finding no fundamental rights involved in the "economic and social legislation" under review and quoting from *Boraas*: "The essence of zoning is selection, and, if it is not invidious or discriminatory against those not selected, it is proper," said the court).

9. *See* Katia Brener, *Belle Terre and Single Family Home Ordinances: Judicial Perceptions of Local Government and the Presumption of Validity*, 74 N.Y. U. L. Rev. 447 (1999).

10. *See Charter Twp. of Delta v. Dinolfo*, 351 N.W.2d 831 (Mich. 1984); *City of Santa Barbara v. Adamson*, 164 Cal. Rptr. 539 (Cal. App. Ct. 1980) (both cases invalidating definitions of a family that are found too restrictive).

11. *See Baer v. Town of Brookhaven*, 537 N.E.2d 619 (N.Y. 1989) (involving an ordinance that excluded five unrelated elderly women from a single family district in which a family was defined to include no more than four unrelated persons, as well as others related by blood or marriage).

12. *See, e.g., Stegeman v. City of Ann Arbor*, 540 N.W.2d 724, 727 (Mich. Ct. App. 1995). *See also Dvorak v. City of Bloomington*, 796 N.E.2d 236 (Ind. 2003); *City of Brookings v. Winker*, 554 N.W.2d 827 (S.D. 1996).

13. 595 A.2d 864 (Conn. 1991).

the long-term interests of the community.[14] Another Nebraska opinion concluded that a restrictive definition of a family was entitled to a presumption of validity, and although the municipality did not justify the ordinance with studies, the burden of proof was on the party opposing it—and that burden went unmet.[15] A 1999 survey reported that fifteen states have followed *Boraas*, while four have not.[16]

§ 18.02 A Better Definition

In order to take account of these problems, a revised definition of family might now provide: "One or more persons occupying a dwelling unit as a single non-profit housekeeping unit, who are living together as a stable and permanent living unit, being a traditional family unit or the functional equivalent thereof." This definition has no upper limits on the number of unrelated persons authorized to live as "a family." Moreover, unrelated persons living together is not the subject of a separate provision in this ordinance. In short, the ordinance contains neither of the two provisions which would render it subject to litigation.

A further issue is whether the numerous students are functioning as "a family unit": students are not transients, but they are not necessarily members of a stable, permanent living unit. They will need evidence that they are functioning as the equivalent of such a unit—and evidence of taking meals together, joint purchases, or joint bill-paying, would bolster an argument that they are living in the equivalent of a "living unit." This type of evidence, as long as their communal living is non-profit, makes their use residential in nature. That one of them is a head tenant making a profit is arguably irrelevant. Use at the occupant level, rather than the leasehold level, is the measure of the "residential use" required in an ordinance. Student tenants need not violate the suggested definition.[17]

When an ordinance includes a functional "family unit" within its definition, it might also provide criteria by which to judge the functionality of a group: stability akin to a family, similar lengths of stay, the presence of children, the presence of someone acting as the head of the household, shared living expenses, and common ownership of personal property are some of the criteria that might be used.[18]

---

14. *Id.* at 870–71.

15. *State v. Champoux*, 566 N.W.2d 763 (Neb. 1997).

16. *See* Brener, *supra* note 9, at 454 n. 39 (reporting that 29 states have no decisions on this issue), 457–59 (and reporting that Cal., N.J., and N.Y. have not followed *Boraas*). *See also McMaster v. Columbia Bd. of Zoning Appeals*, 719 S.E.2d 660, 664-65 (S.C. 2011) (following *Boraas*).

17. *See Vallorosi, supra*, 535 A.2d 544 (involving a college town in which the annual "spring fling" at the college spilled over one night into the town, with drunkenness, loud and abusive language, public urination, and many arrests; responding to this situation, the town's ordinance was amended to adopt the foregoing definition).

18. *See In the Matter of Bayram v. City of Binghamton*, 899 N.Y. S.2d 566, 568–69 (N.Y. Sup. Ct. 2010) (upholding these criteria); *see also* Ames (Iowa) Mun. Code §§ 29.201(71), 29.1503(4)(d).

Sometimes home occupations and definitions of "family" conflict. For example, suppose a municipality's ordinance permits home occupations in a residential district, but restricts the right to conduct such an occupation to "the immediate family residing in the dwelling." An ordinance restriction on home occupations is presumptively valid. The fact that the municipality could have chosen another means to regulate home occupations is irrelevant so long as the means it did choose were reasonably related to the end it sought. The court might also turn away an equal protection challenge by a non-family occupant on the ground that the occupant has not shown that she was treated any differently from others similarly situated.[19]

Sometimes a changing housing market runs afoul of the definition of a "family." A builder, constructing homes in a neighborhood in which land prices are extremely high, may respond to the high land costs by reconfiguring the floor plans of his structures so that a common living/dining room and kitchen, is shared by two living units, one off to the right, the other to the left of the living room, each with its own baths and bedrooms. Calling this floor plan "homes for couplets or mingles is a way," he says, "to permit families to buy housing in this area who otherwise couldn't afford it." In *McMinn v. Town of Oyster Bay*,[20] the New York Court of Appeals struck down an ordinance defining the family as any number of persons related by blood, marriage or adoption or 2 persons over 62 years of age not so related, when owners leased to 4 unrelated persons in their twenties, all of whom sought to live in the town where they grew up, but not with their parents and not at home: they wanted to be near their families, but not reside with them. *McMinn* held that the ordinance is facially unconstitutional under the state constitution's due process clause.

Finally, consider the following, more comprehensive definition, one that takes account of the foregoing problems:

> A family consists of:
>
> (a) a householder plus one or more persons related by blood, marriage, adoption, or custodial agreement and limited to the spouse, parents, grandparents, children, foster children, grandchildren, brothers or sisters of the householder or of the householder's spouse, residing together as a single, non-profit, housekeeping unit sharing a kitchen; or
>
> (b) a group of persons headed by a householder caring for a reasonable number of children in a family-like residential arrangement which to all outward appearances is the functional and factual equivalent of a family of related persons; or
>
> (c) a maximum of two persons not sharing a relationship described in paragraphs (a) or (b).

---

19. *See City of Manassas v. Rosson*, 294 S.E.2d 799, 804–05 (Va. 1982) (involving an applicant—a widow, without immediate family—for a permit for a home occupation running a telephone answering service employing two part-time workers to assist her and holding the ordinance valid as applied to her).

20. 488 N.E.2d 1240 (N.Y. 1985).

[A] Short Term Rentals

The advent of on-line rental platforms has given rise to a short term rental (STR) market for persons traveling to locations not their primary residence and there renting housing for a period less than would be the case for a residential lease. Neighbors often protest the disruption to the neighborhood that STRs cause.[21] However, it is an occupant's use of the property, not the owner's, that traditionally dictates how it is used for purposes of a zoning ordinance. This is in line with the idea that zoning regulates the use, not the user. So the duration for which such a property is used does not affect whether the property is used for "residential" purposes as stated in an ordinance.[22] However, when an ordinance's definition of a family is a functional one, requiring that persons subject to the ordinance are "living as a family," the further issue may be whether the family connotes a degree of stability and permanency not present in a STR.[23] In a similar vein, the term "residential dwelling" unit may indicate a legislative intent to refer not just to a residential use, but to a primary residence as well, thus zoning out a STR. Such arguments narrowing the definition of a residential use are particularly persuasive where the STR is the exclusive use of a property—that is, where the owner is seldom or never in residence.[24] A transient use is then incompatible with the definition of a "family" and of a "house-keeping dwelling" unit.

§ 18.03 Group Homes and Other "Families"

Many municipalities continue to maintain definitions of a "family" tied into "residential" use definitions because of a desire to restrict or exclude group homes from single-family residential districts. For example, a foster children's group house located in a single family, residential use district, may function like a family and so qualify under the all inclusive definition just presented. The group is likely to have a common head, a house mother and/or father; on that ground, all of its unrelated persons are responsible to a common head and become a single housekeeping unit.[25] Such a functional approach recognizes that an ordinance is designed primarily to regulate land uses, not users, and this being so, the spirit of the ordinance is satisfied even if its letter

---

21. *See Ward v. Town of Nantucket*, 2024 Mass. LCR LEXIS 31, *27 (Mass. Land Ct., Mar. 14, 2024) (involving noise and light from a STR). *See also Currituck County v. Letendre*, 102 F.4th 252 (4th Cir. 2024) (involving a coastal structure with 24 bedrooms and 25 bathrooms with two wings and finding it to be one dwelling).

22. *See Wihbey v. Zoning Bd. of Appeals of the Pine Orchard Ass'n*, 323 A.3d 324 (Conn. 2024); *Town of Conway v. Kudrick*, 2023 N.H. LEXIS 65 (N.H., May 2, 2023).

23. *Town of Conway*, *supra*, 2023 N.H. LEXIS 65 (Bassett, J., dissenting) (collecting similar cases, *e.g.*, *Slice of Life, LLC v. Hamilton Twp. Zoning Hearing Bd.*, 207 A.3d 886 (Pa. 2019)).

24. *Slice of Life*, *supra*, 207 A.3d at 899.

25. *See City of White Plains v. Ferraioli*, 313 N.E.2d 756 (N.Y. 1974).

is not. When an ordinance does not further define "family," the general conclusion is that the word is not ambiguous and that it includes "functional families"—meaning persons living together in a "relatively stable and bona fide single-housekeeping unit."[26] In addition to stability, courts are likely to consider whether the unit possesses a family-like authority structure, functions as an integrated economic unit, and does not negatively impact the family character of the neighboring residential area.[27]

Such a home may, however, still be excluded from a municipality for non-compliance with the letter of a *Boraas*-authorized definition of a family, using one of two reasons. First, the group might contain too many unrelated persons under the same roof, or second, none of the required affinities would exist;[28] so the group's sponsor will likely seek a variance. In some ordinances, group homes are subject to a requirement that the home be located at a minimum distance from other group homes.[29]

When the foster home is intended for juvenile delinquents, the idea that a house with a common head of household is a single unit is harder to maintain. Faced with this situation, sponsors may seek a permit as a charity or educational institution, or bulldoze their way into the neighborhood as a state agency immune from local zoning. Local law must be researched on all of these legal routes; they are by no means everywhere available. For example, it will be difficult to argue that a home for incorrigible youth is an "educational institution," even if that use is available in a single family district.

Similar problems exist for groups of parolees in half-way houses, justice-involved youth,[30] persons recovering from addictions,[31] the homeless[32]—and the mentally disabled. For some of these groups, the question of violations of the Fair Housing Act arises as well.[33] Sometimes an ordinance's definition of a family will not apply to those disabled or handicapped protected by the Act.[34] Moreover, for the handicapped, the revision of an ordinance's definition of a family may be found to be a reasonable accommodation for their status.[35] When this is the case, an ordinance specially

---

26. *See Maricopa County v. Rana*, 461 P.3d 439, 444 (Ariz. Ct. App. 2020).

27. *Id.*

28. *See Estvanko v. City of Perry*, 2011 U.S. Dist. LEXIS 48632 (M.D. Ga., May 6, 2011) (finding that the legal custodian of foster children is the state and their in-home caretakers are its employees); *Macon Ass'n for Retarded Citizens v. Macon-Bibb Cty. Planning and Zoning Comm'n*, 314 S.E.2d 218 (Ga.), *dismissed for lack of a federal question*, 469 U.S. 802 (1984) (distinguished in *Cleburne*, majority opinion, at n. 8).

29. *See Sailboat Bend Sober Living, LLC v. City of Fort Lauderdale*, 46 F.4th 1268, 1274 (11th Cir. 2022) (involving a group home requiring a location 1,000 feet from other group homes).

30. *See In re Vermont Permanency Initiative, Inc. Denial*, 312 A.3d 491 (Vt. 2023).

31. *See Sailboat Bend Sober Living, supra*, 46 F.4th at 1274 (involving a group home for alcoholics).

32. *See Westhab, Inc. v. City of New Rochelle*, 2004 U.S. Dist. LEXIS 9926 (S.D.N.Y., May 3, 2004).

33. *See Smith & Lee Assocs. v. City of Taylor*, 102 F.3d 781 (6th Cir. 1996). *See also supra*, Chapter 16.

34. *See City of Clairton v. Zoning Hearing Bd. of Clairton*, 246 A.3d 890 (Pa. Commwlth. Ct. 2021).

35. *See Carunchio v. Swarthmore Borough Council*, 237 A.3d 1183 (Pa. Commwlth. Ct. 2020).

tailored to the needs of the group may be the best course for a municipality;[36] this approach avoids the allegation, often used to attack an ordinance, that a definition of family is being used for surrogate, exclusionary purposes. When persons protected by the Fair Housing Act are involved,[37] moreover, the burden of proof (that the ordinance furthers a substantial government purpose) may be assigned the municipality, just as a defendant in a fair housing case involving the disabled must show a reasonable accommodation to the needs of the protected class.[38] Then (again) a specially tailored ordinance may aid a municipality in meeting its burden.

§ 18.04 Groups Homes for the Mentally Disabled and the Equal Protection Clause

In *City of Cleburne v. Cleburne Living Ctr.*,[39] the City denied a special exception application to an organization setting up a group home for the mentally disabled. The home had four bedrooms and two and a half bathrooms. It was to provide housing for 13 mentally disabled individuals, under constant staff supervision. It complied with all applicable state and local housing regulations.

The City's zoning regulations placed the home in an R-3 use district, in which apartment houses, boarding houses, fraternity and sorority houses, and hospitals, sanatoriums, and nursing homes for the aged (other than for the "insane or feeble-minded") were permitted as of right. City officials found that the Living Center was a "hospital for the feeble-minded" and so required an annually renewable special exception permit, which both the city planning commission and the city council denied.

In response to this denial, the Living Center sued in federal court, alleging a violation of the Equal Protection Clause. When the case reached the United States Supreme Court, the court held: first, the denial of the application was to be reviewed, as a violation of the Equal Protection Clause of the Fourteenth Amendment,[40] under a "rational basis" standard of review,[41] unless the ordinance was aimed at a suspect

36. *See Erdman v. City of Fort Atkinson*, 84 F.3d 960 (7th Cir. 1996) (raising this issue without resolving it).

37. *See Courage to Change Ranches Holding Co. v. El Paso Cty.*, 73 F.4th 1175 (10th Cir. 2023).

38. *See Hovsons, Inc. v. Township of Brick*, 89 F.3d 1096 (3d Cir. 1996) (assigning burden of proof to municipality).

39. 473 U.S. 432 (1985).

40. This first holding was unanimous, although only a plurality of four Justices fully joined the majority opinion and agreed fully with its method of analysis.

41. This minimal standard is used when an ordinance or legislation is neither drawn along suspect lines nor is injurious to fundamental rights; it entitles the ordinance to a presumption of constitutionality, requiring only that it be rationally related to a legitimate governmental purpose, even though the ordinance is either under-inclusive or over-inclusive.

class of persons (in which case a higher standard would apply, as it does for gender or race based classifications).

Second, the court held (6 to 3) that the mentally disabled as a group were not a suspect class—that is, not a class entitled to any type of heightened scrutiny upon judicial review.[42] Thus the application procedure, as applied to the Center, only need have a rational basis. The standard of review was rational basis scrutiny, here strictly applied.

[A] Determining the Level of Review

As to the first issue, the court found that the mentally disabled were so different from each other in their abilities, that they could not be regarded as a class; that state and federal lawmakers had sufficiently responded to their needs so as to "belie a continuing antipathy or prejudice and a corresponding need for more intrusive oversight by the judiciary"; that this legislative response "negates any claim that the mentally [disabled] are politically powerless"; and that it is difficult to distinguish them as a group, from other groups—the aged, the disabled, the mentally ill, and the infirm.

[B] Reviewing the Ordinance

On the second issue in *Cleburne*, the court held that the negative fears of adjoining property owners were not a permissible basis for treating the mentally disabled specially in the ordinance. It held more particularly that (1) the fear that students from a nearby junior high school might harass the occupants was (again) just that, a fear, not a basis for legislation—indeed, about 30 mentally disabled students were already enrolled in the school; that (2) the home's location on a flood plain was not a basis for treating the mentally disabled differently from a nursing home, home for the aged, sanitarium, or hospital. Similarly, (3) the court found no more basis for worrying about who would be legally responsible for the actions of the mentally disabled than would be justified in the case of a fraternity or boarding house. Finally, (4) the court states that worrying about the size of the home and the number of occupants was not justified when state and federal guidelines for such facilities were met. In fact, all square-footage-per-patient regulations of state and federal programs for the mentally disabled were met on this site by the Living Center. Thus there was no basis for imposing different density standards on the mentally disabled than are imposed on (say) boarding house residents, and the city had not justified the view than the mentally

42. Three Justices dissented from this second holding, arguing that the mentally disabled were entitled to suspect class status. The group had argued for finding middle level, heightened scrutiny as the appropriate standard: the mentally disabled were a quasi-suspect class, because of (1) the past, gross mistreatment of the mentally disabled, reflecting (2) a deep seated prejudice against (3) an immutable condition in (4) persons lacking political power to remedy their mistreatment themselves or legislatively. Using that standard, the circuit court had invalidated the ordinance both on its face and as applied to the plaintiff.

disabled require more living space than do others. All this adds up to a conclusion that there is no rational basis for the permit denial.

These four grounds for invalidating this ordinance seem to treat the mentally disabled as a class. The opinion looks like one protecting a class of persons, rather than one preventing an injury to them—and in that sense, this is protection of a class common in equal protection opinions. What the mentally disabled are not for purposes of imposing a standard of review, they become for the purpose of examining the ordinance.

This inconsistency is indeed some proof that the opinion is an example of "exacting or heightened rational basis" review. Indeed, one federal circuit court opinion said that *Cleburne*'s exacting rational basis review was limited to "politically unpopular groups."[43] So a shelter for battered women or a home for juvenile delinquents might be treated the same way. Community treatment centers for federal offenders have received a mixed welcome in the courts, some using *Cleburne*'s standard of review, others refusing to do so.[44] This split occurs because of the mixed reception statistics on recidivism and a municipality's reaction to them get in court. Making such statistics applicable to municipal decision-making is difficult. In *Cleburne*, the Supreme Court was conducting a rational basis review, but it took a hard look at the city's rationale for its decision. Not all courts have accepted the prevailing view that *Cleburne* does something new or different.[45] Rational basis review is too well settled, this traditional view maintains, and besides, this approach has the advantage of taking the Supreme Court at its word.

The *Cleburne* opinion is one in which the Equal Protection Clause works for a litigant protesting a zoning regulation. It usually does not because, by their very nature, zoning regulations seeks to differentiate between different users of property.[46] So when neighbors give into their "fears" and the decision-makers have accepted them as a reason for denying an application, thus depriving their decision of a rational basis and substantial evidence, the sponsors of group homes are likely to win.[47]

---

43. *See Jacobs, Visconsi & Jacobs Co. v. City of Lawrence*, 927 F.2d 1111, 1119, n. 6 (10th Cir. 1991) (refusing to apply it for the benefit of a shopping center developer).

44. *See Bannum, Inc. v. City of St. Charles*, 2 F.3d 267 (8th Cir. 1993) (refusing to apply *Cleburne* and collecting cases).

45. *See DeSisto College v. Town of Howey-in-the-Hills*, 706 F. Supp. 1479, 1503 (M.D. Fla.), *aff'd*, 888 F.2d 766 (11th Cir. 1989).

46. *See* James Ellis, *On the Usefulness of Suspect Classifications*, 3 Const. Comm. 375 (1986). Site visits confirm that Cleburne was a poorly zoned city, with mixed and non-conforming uses in abundance. One visitor stood in the middle of the street on which the Living Center was to be located for 45 minutes without having to move for a car. *See also* Note, 99 Harv. L. Rev. 161 (1985).

47. *See Gladden v. District of Columbia Bd. of Zoning Adjustment*, 659 A.2d 249 (D.C. 1995) (when dispersal spacing regulations are satisfied, court is not called on to assess whether a neighborhood has a disproportionate number of group homes); *see also Wilson Cty. Youth Emergency Shelter, Inc. v. Wilson Cty.*, 13 S.W.3d 338 (Tenn. Ct. App. 2000).

[C] The Line Between *Boraas* and *Cleburne*

Between *Village of Belle Terre v. Boraas*[48] and *Cleburne*, there is a conflict, unless we pigeonhole each of these cases by the constitutional provision at issue. May a town limit, with conditions on a special exception, the number of persons living in a group home, using the values protected in the *Boraas* opinion? *Doe v. City of Butler, Pa.*[49] provides an affirmative answer, finding that just because the city could not constitutionally limit the number of family members living together, "the absence of an occupancy limitation on the members of a family who can live together cannot be bootstrapped into an argument that therefore there can be no occupancy limitations for unrelated persons living together. . . . " Once having accepted that related and unrelated occupants may be rationally placed in different classifications, *Doe* holds that an occupancy limitation of six unrelated persons is valid, thus limiting the number of abused and battered women living a group home under a special exception.

In contrast, *Kirsch v. Prince George's County*[50] shows that once a special purpose ordinance is enacted dealing with a particular sub-group of occupants, the provisions of the ordinance also require a substantial basis. *Kirsch* held that, under a rational basis standard, the equal protection clause is violated by a "mini-dorm" ordinance limiting the number of students in rental housing in a college community. It found also that no fundamental right—to housing—or suspect class—of students—is involved. The invalidated ordinance required that when 3–5 students rented housing, bedrooms had to have at least 70 square feet *per* resident, with all parking on-site, and with only one driveway entrance from the street—and all the while, the appearance of the property should remain residential.

Cleburne has not signaled any new judicial activism in reviewing single-family zoning or group home requirements on equal protection grounds. It also did not settle the question of whether an equal protection violation could be claimed that was not group-based. The case has often been limited to litigation involving the mentally disabled.

[D] *Village of Willowbrook v. Olech*

However, in *Village of Willowbrook v. Olech*,[51] the United States Supreme Court permitted a plaintiff suing a municipality for its failure to issue a permit to extend its water lines to her property under the equal protection clause, to assert that she, Grace Olech, was a class of one for purposes of the clause. Her complaint involved no racial or other invidious classification. It simply alleged that the refusal to extend the line was out of spite and in retaliation for Olech's prior success in an unrelated lawsuit against the Village. The Village had agreed to extend its waterline on the condition

48. 416 U.S. 1 (1974), discussed *supra*.
49. 892 F.2d 315 (3d Cir. 1989).
50. 626 A.2d 372 (Md. 1993).
51. 528 U.S. 562 (2000) (a short opinion of about 500 words).

that the Olech grant a 33-foot-wide easement to it, while other landowners had been required to grant only 15-foot-wide easements. The Supreme Court agreed that the condition imposed on Olech was arbitrary and irrational and that Olech has alleged adequate grounds for an equal protection claim against the Village. One concurring Justice stated that the decision was not to be taken to "transform run-of-the-mill zoning cases to cases of constitutional right."[52]

Olech recognized that a person treated in a discriminatory manner, even though a class of one, has an equal protection claim—and, as the court recognized, similarly-based claims can be that the municipality acted in an arbitrary or irrational manner. If this proves so, then equal protection may take its place alongside the takings and due process clauses as a basis for challenging municipal actions. More likely, *Olech* will be used sparingly: a flurry of class-of-one, equal protection claims followed the release of the *Olech* opinion; most were dismissed by the courts.[53] In particular, a plaintiff has three burdens: (1) of showing that his or her treatment was intentional and perhaps malicious, (2) of finding those similarly situated but treated differently while engaged in the same activity with the same governmental agency without distinguishing or mitigating circumstances making the comparison not worth making, and (3) of proving that there is no rational basis for the difference in treatment, negating any and every reasonable, conceivable state of facts that could provide a rational basis for the difference in treatment.[54]

The third element may turn on the cost of providing municipal services to a plaintiff like Grace Olech: cost will typically provide a rational basis for denying a permit. If not, other aspects of a development—commercial benefits, land use planning objectives, community needs, a developer's pro forma or financial statement and ability to complete the development—may provide a basis for a permit denial.

As if the third element is not difficult enough,[55] the second burden will require "particular rigor" because land-use agencies "will often, perhaps almost always, treat one landowner differently from another."[56] Further, ripeness and exhaustion doctrines may bar many such claims or confine many of them to state courts,[57] takings exaction cases may absorb some others,[58] and due process claims still others.[59]

Federal circuits have split as to whether to recognize similar, class-of-one challenges by developers, as well as the evidentiary standard required to support such a

---

52. *Id.* at 566 (Breyer, J., concurring).

53. *See, e.g., Freeman v. Town of Hudson*, 714 F.3d 29, 38 (1st Cir. 2013). *See also, Two Parks LLC v. Kershaw County, S.C.*, 2021 U.S. Dist. LEXIS 25525 (D.S.C., Feb. 10, 2021) (upholding a denial of a rezoning in a class-of-one claim).

54. *See Andrews v. City of Mentor*, 11 F.4th 462 (6th Cir. 2021) (failure to plead the precise location of the property at issue not fatal to a class-of-one claim).

55. *See Miller v. City of Monona*, 784 F.3d 1113, 1121 (7th Cir. 2015).

56. *Olech, op. cit.*, 528 U.S. at 565 (Breyer, J., concurring).

57. *See supra* Chapter 13, § 13.03 (regarding access to federal courts to assert takings claims).

58. *See supra* Chapter 14, § 14.20 (regarding subdivision exactions).

59. *See Bello v. Walker*, 840 F.2d 1124 (3d Cir.), *cert. denied*, 488 U.S. 851 (1988) (recognizing a due process claim for spiteful governmental action, a claim *Olech* did not address).

claim. An intentional and deliberate denial of equal protection has been required in most federal circuits, the first being the Seventh, the Circuit in which the *Olech* case originated.[60] That is the correct standard, unless the denial can be explicitly traced to a completely illegitimate purpose—such as a refusal to contribute to a regulator's political campaign.

60. *See Greenwald Family L.P. v. Village of Mukwonago*, 100 F.4th 814, 822 (7th Cir. 2024).

Chapter 19
The First Amendment and Zoning

§ 19.01 Introduction

When speech is restricted and the First Amendment implicated, the first inquiry is whether speech is involved[1] and the second is what type of speech it is. Political speech deserves the fullest protection. Other types are not given the same level of protection. These other types include advocacy of unlawful action, false statements of fact, fighting words, obscenity, child pornography—all have no protection—and commercial speech—which has some protection.[2]

So classifying the types of speech is a way of assigning the level of protection that the courts extend. An example of commercial speech is found on outdoor billboards, and they are entitled to some protection under the First Amendment. Obscene speech is not entitled to such protection; however, it must be distinguished from "adult" speech, which is.

When some level of First Amendment protection is accorded commercial speech, then, the content of the speech cannot be regulated without provoking a heightened level of judicial scrutiny; on the other hand, regulation of the time, place and manner of the speech can be regulated without provoking such scrutiny.

Entitlement to First Amendment protection means that the usual presumption of constitutionality given to zoning ordinances and regulations is withdrawn and the ordinance alleged to interfere with First Amendment speech must be justified as embodying a substantial governmental interest, directly advanced by the ordinance, no more extensive in scope than is necessary to accomplish its ends, and leaving

1. *See Adam v. Eve Jonesboro, LLC v. Perrin*, 933 F.3d 951 (8th Cir. 2019) (holding that the sale of sex toys is not speech).

2. For an indication of Supreme Court interest in the commercial speech/zoning line, see *Lorillard Tobacco Co. v. Reilly*, 533 U.S. 525 (2001) (holding that state restrictions on tobacco advertising on billboards were pre-empted by a similar federal statute, based on the First Amendment ground that the restrictions were "more extensive than necessary," but recognizing that a tailored regulation of the location and size of advertisements is not pre-empted; Stevens, J., dissenting, called the regulation merely a zoning matter).

alternative methods of communication available to the speaker. No matter the type of speech involved, a threshold issue is whether it is the type of speech alleged.[3]

§ 19.02 Sex Businesses

Two United States Supreme Court opinions dominate this area. The first is *Young v. American Mini-Theatres, Inc.*[4] There a plurality of the court upheld a Detroit ordinance requiring the de-concentration of sex businesses. The ordinance accomplished this with two requirements: first, by requiring that such businesses be located a minimum distance of 1,000 feet from any two other similarly regulated uses, and second, by requiring that each such business be at least 500 feet from a residential zone. The de-concentration ordinance was upheld by a majority of the court.[5]

A plurality opinion found that it was content-neutral (not content-based), regulated a type of speech not accorded as much protection as political speech, and served a substantial purpose (the preservation of "the quality of urban life," which must be accorded high respect, said Justice Stevens for the plurality). Justice Stevens, in a footnote, also said that the ordinance, like all zoning, sought to limit the secondary effects of a particular land use (here of crime), "not the dissemination of 'offensive' speech."[6] Joining the plurality to make it a majority of the court was Justice Powell, who said that he thought the speech involved in adult sexual expression was to be accorded as much First Amendment protection as political speech, but that for him the regulation of its secondary effects[7] provided a sufficient rationale for validating Detroit's ordinance. Its control of those secondary effects was, he said, sufficient to render the ordinance constitutional, noting also that the court had upheld innovative zoning techniques in the past. When an ordinance was aimed at secondary effects, and not speech itself, it was proper, Justice Powell thought, to treat it as a case in which the issue was the reasonableness of the regulation with regard to its time, place, and manner. The time/place/manner regulation issue is one that has been used when a regulation advances a substantial governmental interest while not having, as its primary purpose, the regulation of speech protected by the First Amendment.

There are alternatives: instead of de-concentrating sex businesses, a city council may decide that a better approach would be to concentrate them into a small area adjacent to its downtown. There is little doubt that it may do so. The choice of

3. *See City of Lewiston v. Verrinder*, 275 A.3d 327, 334, n.7 (Me. 2022) (trash randomly thrown into a front yard is neither art nor political speech).

4. 427 U.S. 50 (1976).

5. *Id. See also Stringfellow's of New York, Ltd. v. City of New York*, 694 N.E.2d 407, 413 (N.Y. 1998) (upholding similar "anti-clustering ordinance" based on a local study of the increase in such business from 9 in 1965 to 177 in 1993, and concluding that, if unregulated, they tend to concentrate).

6. *See Young v. American Mini Theatres, Inc.*, 427 U.S. 50, 71, n. 34 (1976).

7. Such effects are increased crime rates, depreciated property values, and deteriorating property values in the vicinity of such uses. *See Stringfellow's of New York*, *supra*, 694 N.E.2d at 410.

de-concentration or concentration is a legislative decision and as such is valid when fairly debatable. Concentration may make police services easier to provide and may make other types of regulation more efficient. Even the businesses may gain from concentrating their customer base. These considerations provide a rational basis for concentration.

[A] *Renton v. Playtime Theatres*

The permissibility of controlling secondary effects was stressed in the second case, *Renton v. Playtime Theatres, Inc.*[8] Writing for a majority of the court, Justice Rehnquist delivered the opinion of the court in sweeping terms, as if this were a routine First Amendment case. As in *Young*, the facts of the case involved a challenge to the location of an adult movie theater. An ordinance regulating the location of sex businesses was again involved. Unlike Detroit (the city involved in *Young*), Renton was a suburban jurisdiction. Its population was approximately 32,000 persons. Its area is 15.3 square miles. It is located within a few miles of Seattle, Washington. It contained 1,450 businesses, 18 parks, and 62 churches. Its businesses provided employment to 81,000 persons.

Renton's ordinance was more restrictive than Detroit's. Under it, adult movie theaters could not be located within 1000 feet of any residential zone, apartment house, church, park or school. The word "adult" was not further defined; it may have been taken to mean non-obscene in the context of this case, for further definition might have opened the city up to the charge of focusing on the content of the speech involved. This ordinance is not, on its face, a de-concentration ordinance, but its impact (the dissent notes) is to restrict regulated sex businesses to about 520 acres of the city's land area.

The majority found that the ordinance was content-neutral, not content based, and because it is neutral, it is valid so long as it meets two tests: (1) it serves a substantial governmental interest and (2) provides reasonable alternative avenues of communication of the regulated speech. This is a less exacting test than was thought to be applicable before this opinion was handed down.[9] The majority claimed that its decision was based on *Young*—a difficult claim to make or scrutinize because of *Young*'s lack of a majority opinion.

---

8. 475 U.S. 41 (1986) (noted in 100 Harv. L. Rev. 190 (1986). An early discussion of *Renton* is found in *Husti v. Zuckerman Property Enterprises, Ltd.*, 508 A.2d 735, 738–39 (Conn. 1986).

9. *Central Hudson Gas & Elec. Corp. v. Public Serv. Comm'n*, 447 U.S. 557 (1980) (using a more expansive, four prong test for commercial speech, asking whether the ordinance asserted a "substantial," "governmental" interest that is "directly advanced" by its terms, in a manner "not more extensive than is necessary" to achieve it.). The fourth prong was the one re-emphasized in *Lorillard Tobacco Co. v. Reilly*, 533 U.S. 525 (2001). Because the *Renton* opinion did not repudiate *Central Hudson*, it may be assumed to summarize it in a new way for adult, but non-obscene, speech used in a commercial context.

Unlike the City of Detroit in *Young*, the City of Renton had not conducted its own studies to support the ordinance it enacted. No matter, said the court, expanding on *Young*. A municipality can rely on the studies of other jurisdictions and adapt them to its purposes; it need not reach the same conclusions or adopt the same type of ordinance as did the jurisdiction that did the study.[10]

This opinion's six holdings were as follows: (1) First, the ordinance was not an outright ban on sexually oriented businesses, but was instead a content-neutral, time/place/manner regulation, designed to combat the undesirable secondary effects of the adult speech involved, rather than an ordinance aimed at the content of that speech. The permissible secondary effects are the increase in crime rates, decreases in property values, and the quality of life in the surrounding neighborhood. In reality, the Renton ordinance only seemed to regulate the place, but not the time or manner of the speech. As to the content-neutrality of the ordinance, commentators have often said that it is difficult to find it content neutral, since a regulated theater is one given over to displaying visually specified sexual activities and anatomical areas of the body. The court must mean that the time/place/manner regulation is more important to defining the primary purpose of the ordinance than its content regulation is.

(2) The ordinance furthered a substantial governmental interest—the regulation of adult speech. Where does adult speech fit into the hierarchy of types of speech for First Amendment purposes? It is not political speech (which is the most protected of all types); it is not commercial speech, as in *Metromedia* (discussed in § 19.03), which receives considerable but limited protection too. However, it is not obscene speech, which receives even less protection and shelter under the Amendment. So the speech involved in *Renton* must be classified as falling somewhere between commercial and obscene speech—a fourth type, which in the face of a substantial governmental interest in regulation, receives special, but not particularly close, scrutiny under the First Amendment. Effectively the speech here received a heightened, but still a first tier, standard of review.

(3) The municipality (the City of Renton) was entitled to rely on the studies conducted by other municipalities in enacting its ordinance, and need not conduct its own studies.[11] Its own studies would have been hard to do, because there were

---

10. This has meant that Renton-type ordinances have been copied around the country. *See, e.g., DiRaimo v. City of Providence*, 714 A.2d 554, 563–66 (R.I. 1998) (finding ordinance a time, place, manner restriction on speech, serving a substantial governmental interest, not over-inclusive, and not foreclosing alternative means of communication); *Centaur, Inc. v. Richland Cty.*, 392 S.E.2d 165 (S.C. 1990) (upholding ordinance). However, other jurisdictions have built upon and expanded the type of ordinance involved in *Renton* too. *See, e.g., 7250 Corporation v. Board of County Commissioners of Adams Cty.*, 799 P.2d 917 (Colo. 1990) (upholding a live nude-entertainment control ordinance).

11. After *Young*, such studies discuss the regulated use's harmful secondary effects. For an extension of this holding, see *Phillips v. Borough of Keyport*, 107 F.3d 164 (3d Cir. 1997) (upholding such a regulation when the enacting municipal legislature did not have before it, at the time of adoption, evidence of such effects). *See also The Pack Shack, Inc. v. Howard Cty.*, 770 A.2d 1028, 1037–38 (Md. App. Ct. 2001) (18 studies of secondary effects in other municipalities relieved trial court of making further findings in upholding ordinance); *Buzzetti v. City of New York*, 140 F.3d 134 (2d Cir. 1998), *cert. denied*, 525 U.S. 816 (1998).

no adult movie theaters in the city when the ordinance was enacted, so there was nothing to study. The importance of this third holding is that the city need not wait until it has a problem, but may act prospectively and before the problem arises. The authority to act in advance of actually having a "problem" may be the most important holding in the case because the enactment of the ordinance may regulate an industry in advance of its locating within the jurisdiction, perhaps even dissuading some adult movie theater owners from locating in the enacting municipality.[12] In such a posture, the jurisdiction cannot be accused of enacting a reactive ordinance, making what it does enact seem like good planning in advance of developments. Moreover, independent studies may well be an unreasonable burden for municipalities like Renton, with limited staffs, expertise, and budgets for such studies, undertaken with little hope that their conclusions would differ markedly from those conducted in (say) Seattle, whose studies were discussed in the *Renton* opinion.[13] This holding also suggests that studies might be conducted, and model legislation drafted for municipalities, at the state level.

(4) An ordinance that regulates this type of use is entitled to disperse them: dispersal is a reasonable regulatory means of dealing with the regulated uses, even if the dispersal results, as here, in concentration of the uses. "Cities may regulate adult theaters by dispersing them, as in Detroit, or by effectively concentrating them, as in Renton." This language has the effect of permitting what was, in *Young*, a big city method of regulation, in smaller suburban jurisdictions like Renton. In any event, commentators wondered of this opinion, wouldn't it be better to concentrate "adult" land uses, the better to deal with their secondary effects by providing more supervision and police in the area of concentration? Concentration and dispersal are arguably both equally reasonable as land use regulatory methods.

(5) The ordinance is neither over- nor under-inclusive. Arguing that an ordinance is either over- or under-inclusive is like challenging it under the equal protection clause, alleging that the classification of adult theaters is unreasonable. That argument loses here. Absent a showing that it will not, Renton may be presumed, in the future, to be ready to amend its ordinance to deal with other types of sex-oriented, adult businesses as they appear, so the ordinance is not under-inclusive. Dealing with such uses as they appear means that the ordinance is "narrowly tailored" and so is not over-inclusive. Its scope is, in other words, just right.[14]

(6) Ample acreage is available and accessible to businesses like the movie theater owners, so that the city has provided reasonable alternatives to conducting its business on the site proposed. In fact, 520 acres were available in the city—more than 5%

---

12. *Cf. Township of Saddle Brook v. A.B. Family Ctr., Inc.*, 722 A.2d 530 (N.J. 1999) (holding that the constitutionality of a state statute restricting the location of adult businesses within 1000 feet of other protected uses, need not be evaluated solely by reference to the boundaries of a township invoking the statute).

13. Seattle chose a concentration rather than a de-concentration strategy.

14. This is the same analysis Goldilocks gave the porridge in the three bears' den: the regulation is not too hot and not too cold, but just right.

of the city's total area. (As to the sixth holding, one might respond, "only 5%—that's not much!")[15]

These six holdings became a framework for reviewing zoning ordinances regulating sexually oriented businesses using an intermediate standard of review. First, if the ordinance is not an outright ban on such businesses, but merely regulates their location, the ordinance is considered a time, place, manner regulation. Second, a court must decide whether the ordinance is content based or content neutral; to do this, the ordinance's purpose and motivating concern is examined indirectly by examining the municipality's justification for it: if the municipality justifies it by an examination of the businesses' secondary effects on their surroundings and not by reference to the content of the regulated speech, then the ordinance is reviewed as a content neutral ordinance subject to intermediate scrutiny. Third, if a court finds the ordinance content neutral in step two, the court applies intermediate scrutiny and considers whether the ordinance advances a substantial governmental interest and the otherwise regulated speech is accessible through reasonable alternative avenues of communication.

[1] Time, Place, Manner Ordinances

A time, place, manner ordinance is one that does not impose an all-out exclusion of sexually oriented businesses; it prohibits them from operating in certain locations but permits them elsewhere. It regulates where sexually oriented speech may be spoken or delivered within the municipality without providing that it may not be delivered at all. This step is easily met by examining the face of an ordinance and is often stipulated as met by litigating parties.

[2] Content Neutral Ordinances

[a] The Governmental Interest and Content Neutrality

The Renton ordinance was found to be content neutral, even though it singled out a particular type of speech for regulation. It is content neutral because the ordinance aims at the secondary effects of the speech, not at the speech itself. (This idea is taken from Justice Powell's concurrence in *Young*.) Content-neutrality appears to relax here either for one type of speech (adult speech, involving sexual expression) or for all speech with secondary effects. The opinion does not indicate the reach of its holding in this regard, so it is proper to ask how the courts will determine when to relax content neutrality standards. Justice Stevens in *Young* said that few would march their sons and daughters off to war to defend this type of speech, but he probably did not mean to say that only speech approved of by the majority receives full First Amendment protection.[16]

---

15. As to this holding on accessibility, more *infra*.

16. A court that would approve of the *Young* and *Renton* ordinances may be backing out of this field altogether: land use controls and First Amendment values are often intertwined. There is some evidence from later opinions that where First Amendment values are involved, courts will read the

Content neutrality, as used in *Renton*, means that the governmental interest in regulating the speech is unrelated to the content of the speech itself. This "unrelatedness" feature of the interest is what is meant by side or "secondary" effects. The regulated secondary effects are not regulated because they involve speech. Under this rationale, it might be difficult to regulate as an adult business a DVD rental store with adult DVDs that may not be viewed on-site, but even such a store might be regulated because of the costs due to the viewers it attracts, not because of the "views" in the rented DVDs. This is one of three rationales for content neutrality. The second is that the regulation was not enacted because of any disagreement with the content of the speech. This is an intent-based rationale. Adult business ordinances of course identify the affected speech by its content, but only as a means of identifying the secondary effects surrounding it. Even finding speech offensive is not to disagree with it, but a municipal official who expresses disgust with an adult business should recuse himself from further regulatory activity applicable to it. Finally, a third rationale is that regulating the places where (and the time and manner when) speech may occur does not limit its content at those places (and at those times and in that manner). Thus it is permissible to regulate the square footage or building coverage of the marquee of an adult theater, or to subject it to design review. This third rationale is the most common one used to find an ordinance content-neutral, but all three achieve the same end.

Here an ordinance must be targeted, not at an activity or speech, but at its secondary effects. The traditional method of showing these secondary effects is an offer of proof involving the conclusions of legislative hearings adopting reports or studies associating the regulated businesses with increased criminal activity, reduced real estate values, decreases in the quality of urban life, public disturbances, or a heightened police presence that would leave the speech involved substantially undisturbed and available. Qualifying studies may be taken from studies conducted in other municipalities, need not examine each regulated business individually, and need not be conducted concurrently with the enactment of the ordinance under review. They need not find a link between the regulated businesses and their secondary effects. It is sufficient that the studies correlate the businesses with the secondary effects, sufficient to infer that the secondary effects might be rationally addressed through a restrictive zoning ordinance. Preserving the quality of urban life sufficed for the first test (taken from Stevens' plurality opinion in *Young*) when data on the secondary effect can reasonably be relied upon.

Constitutional implications may be multi-faceted. When a municipal regulation prohibits adult businesses within 1,000 feet of a church and when such a business applies to locate within 1,000 feet of the municipal correction center, one zoning administrator denied a certificate of occupancy. The grounds for doing so were that the

---

ordinances narrowly to protect those values. *See Richardson v. Wile*, 535 A.2d 1346 (Del. 1988) (video rental store found not to be an "adult entertainment establishment" regulated by ordinance). There is also some evidence that Renton-like ordinances are the norm. *See, e.g.*, *DiRaimo v. City of Providence*, 714 A.2d 554, 563–66 (R.I. 1998); *Landover Books, Inc. v. Prince George's Cty.*, 566 A.2d 792, 801–03 (Md. App. Ct. 1989).

center is the site of religious services, held on a regular basis for the center's inmates. When the business appeals this decision, the applicant will argue that the regulation is aimed at separating an actual church building from sexually oriented businesses. The center is not such a building; indeed, unless it contains a chapel, services may be held in shifting locations within it. Moreover, the existence of the business nearby will not directly influence inmates' behavior—so not even the purpose of the regulation is advanced by denying the certificate.[17]

The result of a finding of content neutrality is that the municipality is granted the right to regulate the "time, place, and manner of the speech" so long as the regulation serves a substantial governmental interest and allows for reasonable, not ample, alternative avenues of communication.

[b] Another Approach: Finding Content Neutrality Before Assessing the Governmental Interest

In *Reed v. Town of Gilbert*,[18] the court's opinion in which all the Justices concurred in the judgment but not the rationale, was written by Justice Thomas. He wrote that a sign ordinance (not aimed as particular types of businesses like sexually oriented businesses, but at all signs in the municipality) "justified without reference to the content of the regulated speech" (as with the secondary effects cited in *Renton*) "skips the crucial first step in the content-neutrality analysis: determining whether the law is content-neutral on its face."[19] Who knew? This is largely constitutional First Amendment law written out of whole cloth. "In other words, an innocuous justification cannot transform a facially content-based law into one that is content-neutral."[20]

Justice Thomas' opinion did not cite or discuss *Renton*,[21] and subsequent courts, reviewing and discussing cases reviewing ordinances that restricted but did not entirely ban sexually oriented businesses and applying intermediate scrutiny review, have assumed that "*Reed* did not overrule these cases."[22] But who knows? For some Supreme Court Justices, the issue may be an open one.

Commentators have debated the reach of *Reed*'s putting the issue of content neutrality before a municipality could present its secondary effects justifications for an ordinance.[23] The seeds of future law and First Amendment analysis may lie in Justice

17. *Hooters, Inc. v. City of Texarkana*, 897 F. Supp. 946 (E.D. Tex. 1995).

18. 576 U.S. 155 (2015).

19. *Id.* at 165.

20. *Id.* at 166.

21. Nor did the majority cite or discuss *City of Los Angeles v. Alameda Books, Inc.*, 535 U.S. 425 (2002), discussed *infra* this Chapter, § 19.02[B].

22. *See, e.g., Valadez v. Paxton*, 2023 U.S. Dist. LEXIS 184099, *9 (W.D. Tex., July 26, 2023). *See also Greater Philadelphia Chamber of Commerce v. City of Phila.* 949 F.3d 116, 149 (3d Cir. 2020) (discussing *Alameda Books* without regard to *Reed*); *689 Eatery Corp. v. City of New York*, 2024 U.S. Dist. LEXIS 23372, *99–105 (S.D.N.Y., Feb. 9, 2024) (rejecting arguments that *Reed* changed *Young, Renton*, or *Alameda Books* analysis.)

23. *See* Note: *Free Speech Doctrine After* Reed v. Town of Gilbert, 129 Harv. L. Rev. 1981 (2016).

Thomas' *Reed* opinion, but they are so far dormant.[24] So far, the opinion's reach seems limited to the regulation of noncommercial speech.[25] Indeed, because Justice Thomas' opinion was joined by only two other Justices, and six Justices concurred only in the judgment, his opinion garnered the support of only a minority of Justices. For the present, content discrimination might help courts to identify an unconstitutional suppression of speech, but does not always trigger strict scrutiny; *Renton* remains a case in which the court might have reviewed a content based ordinance but to which the Court applied an intermediate standard of review.[26] An antidote to *Reed* is found in a billboard regulation case, discussed later in this Chapter, that rejected the idea that a regulator's just reading a billboard does not make it content-based.[27]

[3] A Substantial Governmental Interest and Accessibility

A municipality's interest is preserving the quality of urban living is traditionally accorded high respect. So said the *Renton* opinion. Any evidence reasonably believed relevant, connecting the speech regulated with the secondary effects adduced, and fairly supporting the ordinance, will demonstrate a substantial governmental interest and will shift the burden of proof back to the parties challenging the ordinance to dispute the facts that the municipal legislature found to support it. Individual businesses need not be shown to generate secondary effects before an ordinance is enforced. For example, when a municipality finds that some businesses generate secondary effects, it need not find that particular types of or all sexually oriented businesses do the same. Likewise, the ordinance need not be necessary to address secondary effects so long as the ordinance is reasonably tailored to address them.

Further, when a municipality amends its ordinance, it need not show that the secondary effects were abated the first time around. Once the municipality has validly enacted an ordinance, it may enforce it against all regulated businesses without showing that a particular business produces secondary effects. Once enacting an ordinance, the municipality need not further justify its enactment so long as it provides and preserves adequate alternative accessible avenues of communication for the regulated speech or activity. No periodic review of the municipality's findings as to secondary effects is constitutionally required.

As to the accessibility issue, the *Renton* court held that allowing 520 acres on the ordinance's map for a non-exclusive district permitting adult movie theaters, provides a reasonable avenue of communication. These 520 acres amounted to only 5% of the land area and was occupied by a sewage disposal plant, race track, industrial park,

---

24. *See Flanigan's Enters., Inc. v. City of Sandy Springs*, 703 F. Appx. 929, 935 (11th Cir. 2017), *cert. denied*, 584 U.S. 1032 (2018).

25. *Cf. Norton v. City of Springfield*, 806 F.3d 411, 412 (7th Cir. 2015) (subjecting a panhandling ordinance to *Reed* analysis because the topic discussed applies to particular speech).

26. See *Reed, op. cit.*, 576 U.S. at 183–84 (Kagan, J., concurring, joined by Ginburg and Breyer, JJ.), 576 U.S. at 176 (Breyer, J., concurring). *See also* 576 U.S. at 174 (Alito, J., joined by Kennedy and Sotomayor, JJ.) (giving nine examples of permissible sign regulations that might be content based).

27. *See infra*, Chapter 19, § 19.03.

and several heavy industries. The opinion states that the First Amendment does not guarantee that land will be available at bargain prices.[28] Following *Renton*, in *Town of Islip v. Caviglia*,[29] the New York Court of Appeals held that the town could limit an adult bookstore to an industrial use district. Likewise, a Maryland court held that a county with two existing regulated adult entertainment businesses and 23 alternative parcels available for such businesses was sufficient, even though such parcels might not be commercially desirable.[30] The *Renton* opinion gives great deference to municipal decisions on these de-concentration decisions and accords broad discretion to municipal decision-makers.

In *Young*, alternative access was not a problem. Detroit is a large, diverse central city. However, in *Schad v. Borough of Mt. Ephraim*,[31] the court invalidated a total ban on live nude dancing in a suburban community. The ordinance was, as a facial matter, overbroad and unjustified by the borough. The *Schad* opinion also said that the businesses regulated did not present any more land use or police problems than did some of the businesses permitted in the borough. This invalidation is difficult to square with *Village of Belle Terre v. Boraas*,[32] except that the court's concern in *Schad* was that if every community in the metropolitan area did that, nude dancers would have no place to perform. Renton's ordinance too had the effect of zoning out adult theaters, but unlike the situation in *Schad*, Renton had no such theaters within its boundaries.[33]

Courts evaluating whether there are reasonable alternative locations for sexually oriented businesses in a municipality have exhibited flexibility. They have assumed that the Supreme Court's use of acreage and the percentage of land area available to such business did not foreclose other methods of evaluation. Justice Souter, sitting as a judge in the First Circuit, examined "multiple factors."[34] Justice Souter used the percentage of sites available with the land use district compared with the acreage

---

28. *But see Lorillard Tobacco Co. v. Reilly*, 533 U.S. 525 (2001) (where 90% of jurisdiction being off-limits for tobacco billboards was found "more extensive than necessary" under the fourth prong of the *Central Hudson* test, discussed *supra*, note 6).

29. 540 N.E.2d 215 (N.Y. 1989). *See also Stringfellow's of New York v. City of New York*, 694 N.E.2d 407 (N.Y. 1998) (deciding that the ordinance was content neutral, not over-inclusive, and left open reasonable alternative means of communication) (noted in Martin Schwartz, *New York City Zones Out Free Expression*, 43 N.Y. L. Sch. L. Rev. 301 (1999); Herald Fahringer, *Zoning Out Free Expression: An Analysis of New York City's Adult Zoning Resolution*, 46 Buff. L. Rev. 403 (1998)).

30. *The Pack Shack, Inc. v. Howard Cty.*, 770 A.2d 1028, 1040–41 (Md. App. Ct. 2001). In a related issue, reasonable restrictions on the location of gun shops have been found to not violate the Second Amendment. *See In re Appeal of the Gun Range, LLC*, 311 A.3d 1242 (Pa. Commwlth Ct. 2024).

31. 452 U.S. 61 (1981) (the majority composed of five separate opinions). *But see City of Erie v. Pap's A.M. TDBA "Kandyland"*, 529 U.S. 277 (2000) (upholding municipal ban on nude erotic dancing and noting in passing that *Schad* dealt with conduct "only within the outer ambit of the First Amendment's protection.").

32. 416 U.S. 1 (1974) (discussed *supra*, Chapter 18).

33. *See Basiardanes v. City of Galveston*, 682 F.2d 1203 (5th Cir. 1982) (use of 10–15% of the city available to adult movie theaters in industrial zones insufficient).

34. *See Lund v. City of Fall River*, 714 F.3d 65, 72 (1st Cir. 2013).

available to other commercial enterprises.[35] Other measures have been the number of sites available compared to the municipality's population,[36] the number of available sites compared to the number of regulated businesses that will have to relocate,[37] and the number of available sites compared to the number of regulated businesses (finding a 1 to 1 ratio reasonable).[38] These courts agree that neither the Constitution nor the Supreme Court mandate any minimum percentage of a municipality's land that must be available for sexually oriented businesses.

Finally, basic to the *Renton* opinion is the notion that the land use controls are not a prior restraint on protected speech. Arguably the *Schad* ordinance was, because it contained a total exclusion from the municipality. In *FW/PBS v. City of Dallas*,[39] the Supreme Court struck down a licensing scheme for sexually-oriented businesses, a plurality opinion finding that the city had inadequate procedures for assuring prompt inspections of premises before the issuance of licenses, and hence had enacted an ordinance whose effect was censorship. Acting as a censor, the court said, the city had the duty to suppress speech (1) for only a brief period, while (2) according prompt judicial review of its decisions and (3) carrying the burden in court of justifying the prior restraint. Because more than a brief period was involved and because of the delays in issuing the licenses, prompt review could not be accorded; the ordinance was unconstitutional. However, the court said that here, unlike some prior restraint cases, it was not necessary for the city to go to court before denying a license. The court, moreover, did uphold the inclusion by the city of motel operators renting rooms for periods of less than ten hours in its definition of a sexually oriented business.[40]

Now for some specialized problems with the *Renton* opinion:

a. In squaring *Young-Renton* with *Arlington Heights* on the question of legislative motive, *Arlington Heights* is meant to probe legislative motive indirectly without the courts violating the principal of separation of powers. In *Renton*, little concern is expressed about legislative motive: the motive of a municipal legislature abridging First Amendment rights by dealing with the secondary effects of speech is not as important as abridging an equal protection right when the potential of racial discrimination is present. Once the municipal legislature has decided in what districts

35. *Id.*

36. *See Young v. City of Simi Valley*, 216 F.3d 807, 822 (9th Cir. 2000), *cert. denied*, 531 U.S. 1104 (2001).

37. *See Alino Enterprises, Inc. v. Baltimore Cty.*, 10 Fed. Appx. 197, 201 (4th Cir. 2001).

38. *See Fly Fish Inc. v. City of Cocoa Beach*, 337 F.3d 1301, 1310 (11th Cir. 2003).

39. 493 U.S. 215, 225–26 (1990).

40. *See also Township of Pennsauken v. Schad*, 733 A.2d 1159, 1171–72 (N.J. 1999) (reviewing a similar licensing scheme under analogous state constitutional provisions, upholding it, and discussing *FW/PBS*); *Baltimore v. Dembo*, 719 A.2d 1007 (Md. App. Ct. 1998) (status of land use as nonconforming does not exempt owner from licensing ordinance, and characterizing licensing as directed at an activity no matter where carried out in the jurisdiction, rather than regulating them based on location as zoning does); *State of New Jersey v. Russo*, 745 A.2d 540 (N.J. Super. Ct., App. Div. 2000) (finding unfettered police discretion and a First Amendment violation in adult business licensing statute).

an adult business may locate, "neither [a reviewing court] nor a municipal licensing board may second-guess this legislative determination."[41]

b. In *City of Cleburne v. Cleburne Living Ctr.*,[42] the United States Supreme Court invalidated a denial of a special exception for a group home for the mentally disabled as lacking a rational basis. The court held, in part, that the secondary effect there—i.e., an undifferentiated or diffuse fear of the mentally disabled—was an insufficient basis for the denial. A good argument might be made that the fear of sexually oriented adult businesses is no less undifferentiated. However, in *Renton*, the control of secondary effects drives the decision, although there does not seem to be much difference between the neighbors' fear of the mentally disabled and the secondary effects of the sexually oriented business regulated.

c. If the dispersal of the adult businesses is without constitutional significance for the court, but the exclusionary zoning effects of zoning have significance in state courts, then how, and where, one challenges zoning is important. A municipality drafting restrictions similar to Renton's should not permit uses otherwise restricted when the consent of the nearby church, school or residential user(s) is obtained.[43] The police power once delegated to a municipality, may not be again delegated to a user's neighbors. Similarly, a municipality should not permit uses otherwise regulated by similar proximity restrictions when a special exception permit is obtained. Obtaining a special exception permit requires a showing that the land parcel at issue is suitable for the use intended and that there is no adverse impact (or secondary effect) on surrounding parcels. Here the special exception procedure might qualify as a prior restraint on protected First Amendment speech.[44] However, you might advise a city like Renton when enacting its ordinance to also enact an "amortization clause" for regulated businesses in existence on the effective date of the ordinance, permitting them (say) a six month grace period before they have to close down in their present location.[45] (An amortization clause permits the regulated use to stay in place as a non-conforming use, but only for a definite and limited period of time.) There is no reason to advise against having an amortization period, but its length as proposed should be reasonable.[46]

---

41. *See Cadillac Lounge v. City of Providence*, 763 A.2d 993, 996 (R.I. 2001).

42. 473 U.S. 432 (1985) (discussed *supra* Chapter 18).

43. *See Larkin v. Grendel's Den*, 459 U.S. 116 (1982) (religious users could not veto the grant of a liquor license to a business within 500 feet of their premises) (noted in 97 Harv. L. Rev. 70 (1983)).

44. *Id.*

45. *See Landover Books, Inc. v. Prince George's Cty.*, 566 A.2d 792, 804 (Md. App. Ct. 1989) (finding also that the special exception procedures were severable from the ordinance as a whole). *See also FW/PBS, Inc. v. Dallas*, 493 U.S. 215 (1990) (invalidating as a prior restraint licensing for sex businesses when the procedures for obtaining a license did not provide for a time certain for issuance or denial and swift judicial review).

46. *See Town of Islip v. Caviglia*, 540 N.E.2d 215 (N.Y. 1989) (upholding a one to five year amortization period); *Pennsylvania Northwestern Distributors, Inc. v. Zoning Hearing Bd. of Twp. of Moon*, 555 A.2d 1368 (Pa. Cmwlth. Ct. 1989) (upholding a 90 day amortization period).

[B] *City of Los Angeles v. Alameda Books*

Los Angeles' adult business ordinance required that adult businesses be 1,000 feet apart and not within 500 feet of a park, school, or religious institution. Realizing that several adult businesses were located in one building, the City amended its dispersal ordinance to prohibit more than one regulated business in the same building, even if the businesses operating under one roof were owned by one individual or entity. The Supreme Court upheld the amendment.[47] In this sense, *Alameda Books* is an extension of *Renton*. However, the court's opinion was signed by three Justices, accompanied by two concurring opinions, altogether making for a five Justice majority. Four Justices dissented. The case indicates that the majorities of *Young* and *Renton* calls the analysis of those two cases into question.

Justice O'Connor, writing for the plurality, suggested that step three in the *Renton* analysis needed clarification. She wrote that in showing a substantial governmental interest, it is sufficient to show that the municipality's evidence "fairly supports its rationale" for it.[48] The municipality, she wrote, may rely on any evidence that is reasonably believed relevant for "demonstrating a connection between speech and a substantial independent governmental interest."[49]

Justice Anthony Kennedy, concurring, attempted to clarify both steps two and three in the *Renton* analysis. He agreed with the plurality that the central holding of *Renton* remained "sound," but he also agreed with the dissent[50] that sexually oriented business ordinances were content based, but that despite that fact, were entitled to review under an intermediate standard when "designed to decrease secondary effects and not speech."[51] In step two of a *Renton* analysis, the court must verify that the "predominant concern" motivating the municipality is with the secondary effects of speech and not with the speech itself. A municipality, he wrote, "cannot regulate secondary effects of speech by suppressing the speech itself."[52] He wrote that an ordinance is "consistent with the First Amendment if it is likely to cause a significant decrease in secondary effects and a trivial decrease in the quantity of speech."[53]

Enacting the amendment at issue, the City did not do new studies, but relied instead on the studies on which it based its original ordinance. For Justice Kennedy, this fact raised two questions: "First, what proposition does a city need to advance in order to sustain a secondary effects ordinance? Second, how much evidence is required to support the proposition?" On the first issue, Justice Kennedy found that the "necessary rationale" is the promise that the ordinance "may reduce the costs of secondary effects without reducing speech."[54] The rationale for an ordinance had to

---

47. *See City of Los Angeles v. Almeda Books, Inc.*, 535 U.S. 425 (2002).
48. *Id.* at 435 (criticizing as too high a standard the one applied by the 9th Circuit below).
49. *Id.* at 438.
50. *Id.* at 455 (Souter, J., writing for four dissenting Justices).
51. *Id.* at 448–49.
52. *Id.* at 450.
53. *Id.*
54. *Id.*

be not merely to reduce secondary effects; rather, it had to do so without substantially reducing speech. On the second issue, Kennedy thought that the evidence for the ordinance "may appeal to common sense, rather than to empirical data." It must relate to "how speech *will* fare,"[55] not how it has fared. It must provide a sufficient basis to support the belief that the ordinance will reduce secondary effects and that it will not substantially reduce the quantity of protected speech.

Reducing secondary effects by reducing the speech associated with them is impermissible. Likewise, reducing the patronage of adult businesses is not a permissible method of reducing these effects. So prohibiting two adult businesses from operating in the same building cannot have the effect of closing one of them, even though "cutting the speech in half would probably reduce secondary effects proportionately." (Justice Kennedy's phrasing.) Thus dispersal of the businesses allows community control of the secondary effects. In *Alameda*, the city assumed that proximity to a concentration of these businesses is proximity to crime. The crime statistics report justifying the original ordinance included data showing that neighborhoods with a concentration of adult businesses had more robberies and prostitution than did the city as a whole.[56] Since the original ordinance had dispersal guidelines, dispersal of businesses located within one building was justified by the same studies that justified the original ordinance. Thus the amendment required no new studies. In answer to Justice Kennedy's second question, then, no new studies are needed: "The city may . . . infer," he said, "that two adult businesses under the same roof are no better than two next door." If businesses operating next door to each other can be dispersed, so can businesses operating in the same building.

Alameda Books makes clear that adult businesses cannot rely on the synergy between them, or on one-stop shopping for adult products. Even if both lose some profits when dispersed, profitability is not the measure of the ordinance. Likewise, the plurality opinion makes plain that the court will not set a high bar for the evidence needed to support these ordinances, so long as that the studies behind them "fairly support the municipality's rationale."[57] The business owner then has the burden of proof to show that the evidence does not support the rationale or the facts behind the studies are cast in dispute. In that instance, the plurality states, "the burden shifts back to the municipality to supplement the record with evidence renewing support for a theory that justifies its ordinance."[58]

---

55. *Id.*

56. In contrast, see *New Albany DVD v. City of New Albany*, 581 F.3d 556 (7th Cir. 2009) (Easterbrook, J., rejecting as an insufficient rationale for an ordinance that an adult bookstore subjected patrons to thievery), and *Annex Books v. City of Indianapolis*, 581 F.3d 460 (7th Cir. 2009) (Easterbrook, J., rejecting a law review article as an sufficient rationale for an ordinance).

57. For a case using this phrase from the plurality opinion, see *Richland Bookmart, Inc. v. Knox Cty.*, 555 F.3d 512, 526 (6th Cir. 2009).

58. The quotation is from the plurality opinion, but together with Kennedy's concurrence, it has served up as rich case law discussing the evidentiary issues. *See Doctor John's v. Wahlen*, 542 F.3d 787 (10th Cir. 2008); *84 Video/Newsstand, Inc. v. Sartini*, 455 Fed. App. 541 (6th Cir. 2011). *Alameda Books* has also spawned the increased use of expert witnesses in similar cases. *See* David Hudson, *The*

Alameda Books does four things. It clarifies *Renton*'s step two and three analysis for determining when an ordinance serves a "substantial, independent, government interest." It makes clear that while a majority of the Justices considered sexually oriented business ordinances content based, not content neutral, they nevertheless review such ordinances using an intermediate standard of review. It also proceduralizes the rules about studies underlying these ordinances, but does not narrow the type of evidence that, in the words of the plurality, the municipality "reasonably believes to be relevant" to show its governmental interest in the regulation. It further makes clear that regulating secondary effects may not substantially reduce the quantity of protected speech and may not depend on a municipality's emotional reaction to an adult business; this is akin to the Supreme Court's holding in *City of Cleburne v. Cleburne Living Center* that the neighbors' reaction to the mentally disabled is no basis for an ordinance regulating the location of group homes for them.

§ 19.03 Billboard Regulation

In *Metromedia, Inc. v. City of San Diego*,[59] the city enacted an ordinance that banned all off-site advertising billboards. Existing billboards were to be removed after an amortization period. The plaintiff was an outdoor advertising company and sued to enjoin enforcement of the ordinance. The ordinance was found unconstitutional below, but the California Supreme Court reversed, upholding it. "We hold that the achievement of the purposes recited in the ordinance—eliminating traffic hazards and improving the appearance of the city—represent proper objectives [protecting the health, safety, morals, and general welfare of the people—Ed.] for the exercise of the city's police power, and the ordinance bears a reasonable relationship to those objectives." Ordinances eliminating billboards visible from the streets and highways reasonably relate to safety (they divert a driver's attention) and are entitled to a presumption of validity and constitutionality. (In older cases, billboards were additionally seen as places behind which criminals might lurk and criminal activity might take place—but such secondary effects are not invoked here.) In the alternative, the California court found that the ordinance was valid as a second or third stage[60] exercise of the police power for aesthetic purposes, to improve the appearance of the municipality. California scenery, the court says, attracts tourists and commerce, so the aesthetic regulation of billboards is necessary because it is an indirect form of economic regulation.

There was originally no exception to the ordinance's prohibition on political signs, but an amendment permitted temporary political signs, maintained for no longer

---

Secondary Effects Doctrine: Stripping Away First Amendment Freedoms, 23 Stan. L. & Pol'y Rev. 19, 26–27 (2012).

59. 610 P.2d 407 (Cal. 1980), *reversed on other grounds*, 453 U.S. 490 (1981).

60. See Chapter 8, § 8.01, *supra*, for a discussion of these stages.

than 90 days and removed within 10 days after the election to which their content pertains. No matter. This amendment was held too narrowly drawn for the United States Supreme Court.[61] There were five opinions written in this case. A plurality[62] of the court held that the ordinance did not unreasonably restrict commercial speech[63] and directly advanced a substantial governmental interest. However, the plurality opinion in the United States Supreme Court found that the restrictions on non-commercial speech were too narrowly drawn, that the exemptions were too narrow, and so held the potential to become an onerous, content-based regulation of political speech. The ordinance's exemptions were numerous, but lacked an overall rationale: it might be that a generous interpretation of the exempted signs would protect the types of speech commonly regarded as protected by the First Amendment, but because the ordinance was challenged *prima facie*, such a situation was not before the court. After *Metromedia*, content-based sign restrictions raise severe constitutional issues.

The court's plurality accepted the basic distinction between off-premises and on-premises signs. The ordinance only prohibited the former. On-premises signs were not as heavily regulated because the owner had an interest in the on-premises sign that would make self-policing possible on private property. Off-premises signs were more heavily regulated because the owner was not there and in a position to police the sign. This rationale for the distinction is more significant for state police power purposes than it is as a federal constitutional, First Amendment matter. Indeed, in the latter arena, the distinction may make no difference.[64]

This on/off-premises distinction paved the way for *Members of City Council v. Taxpayers for Vincent*.[65] The disarray among the opinions in *Metromedia* required an occasion to clarify the latter, where seven Justices had, in the plurality opinion, or in dissent in whole or part, expressly concluded that the city's interest in avoiding visual clutter was sufficient to justify the prohibition on billboards. The *Vincent* opinion said: "We affirm the conclusion of the majority in *Metromedia*. The problem addressed by the ordinance [in *Vincent*]—the visual assault on the citizens of Los Angeles presented by an accumulation of signs posted on public property—constitutes a significant evil within the City's power to prohibit." The need for regulation "is created by the medium of expression itself. The ordinance curtails no more speech than is necessary to accomplish its purpose." As to not extending the ordinance to private property, the "private property interest in controlling the use of his own property justifies the

---

61. *Metromedia, Inc.*, 453 U.S. 490 (1981).

62. The plurality opinion was in effect a majority opinion because concurring opinions also supported it while dissenting in other respects.

63. *See* Note, *The Supreme Court—Leading Cases*, 110 Harv. L. Rev. 206, 216–26 (1996) (discussing *44 Liquormart, Inc. v. Rhode Island*, 517 U.S. 484 (1996)).

64. *See, e.g.*, *L.D. Mgmt. Co. v. Thomas*, 456 F. Supp. 3d 873 (W.D. Ky. 2020) (invalidating a Kentucky state statute regulating highway signs and finding that the on/off premises distinction fails both intermediate and heightened scrutiny standards of review when the off premises signs' impact on traffic is not proven worse than on premises signs' impact on traffic). This case is an outlier, and its citation sparse.

65. 466 U.S. 789 (1984).

disparate treatment. Moreover, by not extending the ban to all locations, a significant opportunity to communicate by means of temporary signs is preserved. . . . " That is, there are reasonable alternative means of communication available to political candidates on private property, where the "owner's esthetic concerns will keep the posting of signs within reasonable bounds." The ordinance here is content-neutral because the ban on posting signs on public property is a total ban. Thus the Los Angeles ordinance is content-neutral, has a substantial governmental purpose, advances it directly, is not over or under-inclusive, and leaves reasonable alternative means to communicate.[66] It is thus entitled to a presumption of constitutionality that parallels the presumption of validity accorded the police power ordinance reviewed in *Metromedia.*

Vincent in its turn paves the way for *City of Ladue v. Gilleo.*[67] There, the Supreme Court unanimously invalidated an ordinance enacted to ban all residential signs, as applied to a sign 24 by 36 inches on private property, the front lawn of a residence, that did not fall within one of 10 exempted signs. The sign said, "Say no to War in the Persian Gulf, Call Congress now." Here the Supreme Court acknowledged that residential signs pose numerous problems that "legitimately call for regulation." Even though the ordinance is a total ban and might be, on that account, classified as content neutral, it was held to prohibit too large an amount of protected, political speech to be upheld. As a result, the aesthetic considerations supporting the ban are balanced against the broad suppression of speech worked by the ban. In this instance, the ordinance denied an entire medium for speech (yard signs), was over-inclusive, and lacked a reasonable alternative that was as easy and inexpensive to use as are yard signs. Although the Court accorded special respect for individual liberty and expression exercised from and in the home, the balance tipped in favor of invalidating the ordinance.

Restrictions on signs displaying a political message, signs directing people to events nearby, and signs advertising activities off-premises were rendered suspect and so subject to strict scrutiny[68] by reviewing courts in *Reed v. Town of Gilbert.*[69] *Reed* held that a sign is content-based, no matter its purpose, when its text draws distinctions "based on the message the speaker conveys."[70] This test is riotously over-broad and threatened many directional and off-premises signage restrictions.[71]

---

66. This test is taken from *Central Hudson Gas & Elec. Corp. v. Pub Util. Comm'n*, 447 U.S. 557 (1980) (holding that the First Amendment protects commercial speech only when it concerns a lawful activity that it not misleading, seeks to advance a substantial government interest, directly advances that interest, and reaches no further than necessary to advance the interest (*id.* at 566) and used in *Metromedia* (453 U.S. at 507)).

67. 512 U.S. 43 (1994).

68. This level of constitutional review "takes no prisoners." Such review is premised on the idea that strict scrutiny of content-based regulation is necessary when the regulation is motivated by an illicit purpose—here, to suppress otherwise protected First Amendment interests and speech. Few ordinances survive such a review.

69. 576 U.S. 155 (2015).

70. *Id.* at 164.

71. A concurring opinion by Alito, J., listed some sign provisions making distinctions that are not content-based—i.e., regulations making distinctions based on the size, location, lighted or/unlighted,

With regard to off-premises signs, the opinion in *City of Austin v. Reagan Nat'l Advertising of Austin, LLP*,[72] provides a limiting antidote to *Reed*'s breadth. *City of Austin* clarifies *Reed*, holding that billboards regulated with ordinances using on/off-premises distinctions were time-place-manner speech restrictions subject only to intermediate scrutiny review. The City restricted the use of off-premises signs and to mitigate visual blight and promote traffic safety, prohibited new off-premises signs and the digitization of existing off-premises ones. *City of Austin* held that this prohibitory sign ordinance provision is not content-based just because "it requires reading the sign at issue"[73] to decide how it will be regulated and restricted. The court said that holding otherwise would "upend settled understanding of the law" and reach a "bizarre result." An ordinance provision is content-based on its face only if it "applies to particular speech because of the topic discussed or the idea or the message expressed" and so "singles out specific subject matter for differential treatment."[74] Speech restrictions drawing broad, non-specific subject matter distinctions are not content-based when they apply even-handedly to all wishing to advertise off-site matters. However, the weight given to a "settled understanding" of the law in this area remains unclear. *City of Austin* is certainly good news, but the breadth and bounds of *Reed* are still a blur.

§ 19.04 Zoning and Religion

Are religious uses immune from zoning regulations? Until recently, the answer has been yes, when "religious use" is defined as religious worship or education. In New York, for example, until *Cornell University v. Barnard*,[75] religious institutions enjoyed "special treatment" and a "favored status" with respect to residential zoning ordinances.[76] This special treatment was accorded because of the "presumed beneficial effect on the community." This presumption was not a conclusive one, however, and "the controlling consideration" in reviewing a church's request to expand into a residential use district "must always be the over-all impact on the community." In this regard, a special exception may be required so that a municipality may weigh the over-all impact of an institution's request.[77] Thus expanding a church auditorium to serve the needs of a growing congregation would be permitted as well, in deference to the free

---

fixed message or changing message, public or private property location, residential or commercial property, number of signs allowed per mile, and on/off-premises provisions. *Id.*, 576 U.S. at 174–75.

72. 596 U.S. 61 (2022) (noted at 136 Harv. L. Rev. 320 (2022)).

73. This read-the-sign rule was the basis for the Circuit Court's holding reversed here, the Supreme Court remanding for consideration of whether, though the ordinance is facially content-neutral, there is evidence an illicit purpose underlies such facial neutrality, such that strict scrutiny would apply.

74. *Id.* at 74 (followed in *Adams Outdoor Adver/Ltd. P-ship v. City of Madison*, 56 F.4th 1111 (7th Cir. 2023)).

75. 503 N.E.2d 509 (N.Y. 1986).

76. *Id.* (quoted in *Congregational Rabbinical College of Tartikov v. Villiage of Pomona, NY*, 945 F.3d 83, 92–93 (2d Cir. 2019)).

77. *Id.* at 93.

exercise clause of the First Amendment and recognizing that the social activities of the congregation are necessary to their communal life together.

As a result, the exclusion of religious uses from residential use districts has generally been regarded as improper under the free exercise clause, unless there is a substantial showing of a need to exclude.[78] In other words, there has been a preference for the First Amendment values of the free exercise clause over the Fifth Amendment rights of neighbors.[79] However, a completely hands-off policy on the part of courts runs afoul of the establishment clause of the First Amendment or a similar state constitutional provision.

Moreover, many courts have exhibited a tendency to confine the reach of such issues to interpretive problems within an ordinance. Not reaching a constitutional issue unless it is absolutely necessary is a well-established doctrine observed in this field as well as others.[80] On the other hand, all this does not exclude the possibility that all churches can be excluded from residential neighborhoods without offending the free exercise clause, because the proper test is the impact of the church on its neighborhood.[81] The free exercise of religious beliefs need not extend to the location and siting of churches.[82]

In 1990, the United States Supreme Court decided *Employment Div., Dept. of Human Resources of Oregon v. Smith*,[83] and in 1997, it decided *City of Boerne v. Flores*.[84] *City of Boerne* invalidated a federal statute imposing a strict scrutiny standard of review for land use regulations excluding religious institutions from residential use districts. This invalidation re-imposed the rule of *Smith* and made disparate treatment of religious institutions possible if the regulation applied is facially neutral and

78. *See Jehovah's Witnesses Assembly Hall of Southern New Jersey v. Woolrich Twp.*, 532 A.2d 276, 277–78 (N.J. Super. Ct. 1987) (citing cases from nineteen states for this version of the rule, emphasizing inclusion), *rev'd*, 537 A.2d 1336 (1987).

79. *See, e.g.*, *Westchester Reform Church v. Griffin*, 287 N.Y.S.2d 499 (1968) (invalidating set back regulation as abridgment of free exercise of religion).

80. *See Church of the Savior v. Zoning Hearing Board of Tredyfrin Twp.*, 568 A.2d 1336 (Pa. Commw. Ct. 1989) (holding counseling not a church use was an abuse of discretion by the board).

81. *See Lakewood, Ohio Congregation of Jehovah's Witnesses, Inc. v. City of Lakewood*, 699 F.2d 303 (6th Cir. 1983), *cert. denied*, 464 U.S. 815 (1983) (noted in 45 Ohio St. L.J. 1017 (1984)); *Lakewood Residents Association v. Congregation Exocrine Schneur*, 570 A.2d 1032 (N.J. Super. 1989) (upholding bulk standards for houses of worship in residential district). *See also Messiah Baptist Church v. County of Jefferson, Colorado*, 859 F.2d 820 (10th Cir. 1988) (upholding the exclusion of a church from an agricultural district).

82. *See Bethlehem Evangelical Lutheran Church v. City of Lakewood*, 626 P.2d 668 (Colo. 1981) (upholding the requirement of a land dedication from church).

83. 494 U.S. 872, 882 (1990) (holding that neutral, generally applicable state laws need not be justified by a compelling state interest and so are not entitled to any special judicial scrutiny, notwithstanding their impact on religious institutions and free exercise and so long as they are not specifically aimed at or hostile to religion).

84. 521 U.S. 507 (1997) (holding that the statute seeking to overturn the result in *Smith* and impose a higher standard of review exceeded Congressional authority under the Fourteenth Amendment, § 5).

general in nature.[85] To this Congressional-court back and forth, Congress responded in 2000 with the Religious Land Use and Institutionalized Persons Act (RLUIPA).[86] It provides: "No government shall impose or implement a land use regulation in a manner that imposes a substantial burden on religious exercise of a person . . . unless the government demonstrates that imposition of that burden on that person (A) is in furtherance of a compelling governmental interest; and (B) is the least restrictive means of furthering that compelling governmental interest. . . . "[87] This statute requires a court to apply a strict scrutiny standard of review to a land use regulation that burdens a plaintiff's exercise of religion. "Exercise of religion" need not be compelled by a system of religious belief. This means that an exercise of religion includes the operation of religious schools and ministering to addicted persons, the homeless, and the poor. Only "substantial burdens" on that exercise will be subject to strict scrutiny. If a burden resulting from the limitations on a special exception fall on religious landowners and all other landowners alike, no substantial burden results;[88] likewise, when there are no alternate sites or practical alternatives, a substantial burden may result. The burden need not be insuperable, just one that is directly and primarily responsible for making religious exercise effectively impractical.[89] This latter high threshold test predominates among federal Circuit Courts.[90]

In such a legal environment, religious institutions have used several land use litigation strategies. First, they have sought variances[91] and special exceptions for their uses. Second, they have coupled their free exercise claims with other constitutional claims, such as free speech and the symbolic expression of religious beliefs in architecture, or religious activities as religious expression, or parents' rights to educate their children. Liturgics may influence the outcome here: for example, if a Christian congregation wishes to build a religious building in a cruciform shape, recognizing in that shape a symbol that forms a fundamental tenet of its belief, but inescapably violating the set back requirements of the applicable regulation, a liturgical basis for church architecture qualifies for free exercise clause protection.[92] Third, using a compelling governmental interest analysis, they have argued that their institution is being

85. *See* Von Keetch & Matthew Richards, *The Need for Legislation to Enshrine Free Exercise in the Land Use Context*, 32 U.C. Davis. L. Rev. 725 (1999) (reporting a study of the case law finding a "huge disparity" of treatment between majority and minority religious institutions).

86. 42 U.S.C. § 2000ccc, § 2(a)(1).

87. *Id.*

88. *See Guru Nanak Sikh Soc. v. Cty. of Sutter*, 465 F.3d 978, 989 (9th Cir. 2006).

89. *See Civil Liberties for Urban Believers v. City of Chicago*, 342 F.3d 752, 761 (7th Cir. 2003).

90. *See generally* Adam J. MacLeod, *Resurrecting the Bogeyman: The Curious Forms of the Substantial Burden Testin RLUIPA*, 40 Real Est. L.J. 115 (2011).

91. Variances are less flexible than special exceptions and so less useful here because granting "blanket variances" for religious institutions may violate the establishment clause of the First Amendment. *Cf. Citizens United to Protect Our Neighborhoods v. Village of Chestnut Ridge*, 98 F.4th 386, 391 (2d Cir. 2024) (denying standing to a citizens group making this argument).

92. *See First United Methodist Church of Seattle v. Hearing Examiner for Seattle Landmarks Preservation Bd.*, 916 P.2d 374 (Wash. 1996) (applying a strict scrutiny standard of review to a landmarks ordinance with regard to a church).

treated differently than other religious institutions are.[93] Fourth, they have litigated using state constitutional provisions guaranteeing free exercise.[94]

From this welter of cases and competing values, it seems that a municipality may deny a religious institution the right to operate outright, require special exception permits instead, limit such institutions to specific land use districts, exclude them from other districts, restrict the size of their buildings, mitigate the external effects of their operation, and prohibit their demolition when they are a historic landmark.[95]

[A] Churches and Landmarks

Landmark designation for architecturally distinguished churches is a fertile subject for litigation under the free exercise clauses of federal and state constitutions. Comparisons between *First Covenant Church v. City of Seattle*[96] with *Saint Bartholomew's Church v. City of New York*[97] are instructive. Although the sale of church property might permit the church to raise revenue for its ministerial programs, the *Penn Central* test of economic impact, coupled with the rule that the takings clause countenances a denial of the parcel's most profitable or beneficial use, has prevented landmark churches from relocating when the present use of the property is a reasonable one and is consistent with the church's investment backed expectations.

If the landmark regulation interferes with the functioning of the religious group practices on its existing site, a free exercise challenge will be successful. Thus a small church, serving a growing congregation, can physically expand, notwithstanding a landmark designation for the site. However, when the regulation merely diminishes the income flow which the group might otherwise devote to religious activities, the challenge will fail. A regulation imposing a financial burden does not, *per se*, constitute a free exercise violation. A congregation has no right to tear down a landmark church and build a more profitable office building, but a dwindling congregation might be able to tear down a landmark when most of its resources are devoted to property maintenance, as opposed to good works. As with other land owners, a religious group is not entitled to the highest and best use of its property. So long as the regulation is facially neutral, no facial challenge to it will likely succeed.

---

93. *See, e.g.*, *Church of the Lukumi Babalu Aye, Inc. v. City of Hialeah*, 508 U.S. 520 (1993); *Islamic Ctr. of Mississippi, Inc. v. City of Starkville*, 840 F.2d 293, 299 (5th Cir. 1988).

94. *See, e.g.*, *Omar Islamic Ctr. v. City of Meriden*, 633 F. Supp. 3d 600 (D. Conn. 2022) (utilizing a Connecticut statute patterned on RLUIPA).

95. These examples are taken from Shelby D. Green, *Zoning in and out Churches*, 37 Real Est. L.J. 163, 175 (2006).

96. 787 P.2d 1352 (Wash. 1990), *vacated*, 499 U.S. 901 (1991) (using strict scrutiny and invalidating an ordinance preserving the church exterior under the free exercise clause).

97. 914 F.2d 348 (2d Cir. 1990) (upholding a landmark ordinance against both First Amendment and takings claims), *cert. denied*, 499 U.S. 905 (1991) (denying cert. the same day the United States Supreme Court vacated the *First Covenant* opinion). *See* Note, *Free Exercise, Free Expression and Landmarks Preservation*, 91 Colum. L. Rev. 1814 (1991) (comparing the two cases just cited).

Chapter 20

Democracy and Zoning: The Place of the Referendum

§ 20.01 Introduction

Not long after the *Euclid* opinion, a California opinion held that the voters in a municipality could not adopt a zoning ordinance in an election on a voter-introduced initiative ballot. An initiative permits the voters of a jurisdiction, usually by petition, to propose and enact legislation by ballot. It is most useful when the legislature is "wired" against a proposal for legislation, but is limited in its usefulness at the municipal level when it seeks to amend an ordinance enacted under the authority of a state enabling act. "The initiative law and the zoning [enabling] law are hopelessly inconsistent," one opinion said.[1] Thus begins the tale of democracy and zoning, a tale that continues to this day.

At the other end of the legislative process from an initiative, a referendum is an election in which legislation already enacted by the legislature is put to a vote.[2] It is thus the citizenry's veto over legislation previously adopted by a state or municipal legislature. The citizenry's failure to reject the enactment is deemed its approval. This is one of the citizenry's means of protecting itself against the actions of a corrupt, biased, or unrepresentative legislature. It originated in the age of populism in the early 20th century.[3] The referendum process applies only to legislative, and not to administrative or judicial, actions and decisions. It rests on the assumption that if the enactment of an ordinance is a legislative action, that repealing it must also be legislative in nature. It further assumes that the delegation of authority by a state's zoning enabling act to a municipality is not exclusive, but rather that the electorate traditionally retains and reserves the power to overturn legislative actions: thus, referendum provisions in

1. *See Hurst v. City of Burlingame*, 277 P. 308 (Cal. 1929). Most cases today would agree: enacting a zoning ordinance by initiative would by-pass state statutes requiring municipalities to give notice, hold hearings, and provide several readings of legislation before enacting it.

2. *See Grant Cty. Concerned Citizens v. Grant Cty. Bd. of Comm'nrs*, 794 N.W.2d 462, 466 (S.D. 2011) (distinguishing a referendum from an initiative); *Committee of the Petitioners for Referendum v. City of Norfolk*, 645 S.E.2d 464 (Va. 2007).

3. *See Carter v. Lehi City*, 269 P.3d 141 (Utah 2012) (reviewing the history of state constitutional provisions on referenda in Massachusetts, Ohio and Utah).

state or municipal law do not involve an improper delegation of legislative power to a municipality's electorate.

The referendum is not inconsistent with state planning statutes and enabling acts. Why? Because it does not prevent the procedures required by these acts from taking place. By the same token, it does not conflict with a state zoning enabling act or ordinance enacted under its authority. A referendum cannot validate an ordinance enacted *ultra vires* that authority. Its function is rather to challenge a land use decision and resulting ordinance already enacted and to invalidate an ordinance when the voters believe that it is ill-conceived or overly favors development interests.

Ohio has a typical procedure for a referendum.[4] For a defined period of time (say 30 days) after the date of enactment of a zoning ordinance or any amendment thereto, the ordinance or amendment is effective unless, within that period of time, a petition for a referendum is filed. The petition must contain the signatures of a prescribed number of voters in the municipality. The signatures must be solicited by residents of the municipality. The number of signatures required is typically a percentage of either the municipality's total population or the total number of votes cast in a previous election. A short summary of the action proposed and the contested ordinance must accompany the petition or be included within it. Surplus information in the summary will not invalidate the petition if it is otherwise in compliance with applicable statutes and ordinances. If the summary is misleading, the petition will be denied. If the petition seeks a referendum on an amendment to the zoning ordinance, a map of the area affected by the amendment must be attached. The petition is then reviewed for compliance with state law by the municipality's board of elections. If the board finds that the petition is in compliance, the referendum is placed on the ballot in the next election occurring a set number of days (say 90 days) after its filing.[5] If in the election, the proposal in the referendum is defeated, it may not be the subject of a renewed petition for a set number of years. The decision of the board is subject to judicial review. Any court, reviewing the decision of the board, requires strict compliance with the statute. Emergency legislation is not subject to a referendum.

Petitioners for a referendum may not seek to amend an ordinance piece-meal: the petition must typically call for an up-or-down vote on it.[6]

Whether a zoning regulation is enacted by initiative, or upheld or struck down by referendum, the resulting ballot box zoning raises issues of due process.

4. *See* Ohio Rev. Stat. § 519.12 (2024).

5. *See State ex rel. Valentine v. Schoen*, 2024 Ohio LEXIS 1959, *2–3 (Ohio, Sept. 6, 2024). *See also Smith v. Zook*, 487 P.3d 88, 89–90 (Utah 2020).

6. *See Town of Bel Air v. Bodt*, 318 A.3d 570, 582 (Md. 2024).

§ 20.02 *Eastlake v. Forrest City Enterprises*

A landowner held title to eight acres in Eastlake, Ohio. The parcel was zoned for light industrial uses. The owner applied for a rezoning, to have its classification changed to multi-family residential, in order that he might construct an apartment house on it. The planning commission and the municipal legislature both approved the rezoning, but subsequently the voters changed the City of Eastlake's charter to require that 55% of the city's voters approve city council rezonings in a referendum. In a later action, the city planning commission turned down a request for approval of parking and yard facilities because the rezoning had not been approved by referendum.

The Ohio Supreme Court invalidated the city charter's referendum requirement as a delegation of the police power without standards to guide its exercise. It did so, however, as a matter of federal constitutional law—not as an interpretation of its own state constitution. This meant that it did not have the final say in the matter and made the case appealable to the United States Supreme Court. That court reversed, holding that there is no denial of substantive due process involved in the charter's referendum requirement.[7]

The issue before the court was the validity of the referendum requirement *per se*; the court refused to invalidate it *per se*. The referendum, it said, was "an exercise by the voters of their traditional right through direct legislation to override the view of their elected representatives as to what serves the public interest."[8] At the same time, the court left open the possibility that a compatible land-use might be zoned out of the city and that, in such an instance, the application of the referendum requirement might be invalid, judged by its results. Thus the court said that the democratic process is not unfair to the landowner on its face, but may be applied unfairly.

The Eastlake referendum was mandatory and applied to all land uses there. These are limiting facts for this opinion: the mandatory nature of the referendum is not at all typical of most state referenda procedures; most states require that a referendum is held only after a petition for it is filed. The *Eastlake* opinion comes close to saying that the voters may elect the most biased of persons to their legislature,[9] but once elected, those legislators may not enact laws and ordinances on sexist, racial, or other prohibited grounds. The court means to say that the impact of any bias must be separately shown. It assumes that ample remedies for discriminatory action are available—e.g., the federal Fair Housing Act (Title VIII of the Civil Rights Acts of 1968[10]). Its further assumption may be that even if the voters are permitted to vote out of any motive they

---

7. *See City of Eastlake v. Forest City Enterprises*, 426 U.S. 668 (1976) (Burger, C.J., for the majority).

8. *Id.* at 678 (quoted in *Committee of the Petitioners for Referendum v. City of Norfolk*, 645 S.E.2d 464, 466 (Va. 2007)).

9. In this regard, the power of a state legislature over elections is "plenary," meaning that it is subject to only a rational basis standard of judicial review. *See Bush v. Gore*, 531 U.S. 98, 104 (2000).

10. Discussed *supra*, Chapter 16, § 16.03.

choose, once the local legislators are installed in office, they are then subject to the civil rights laws. If this is so, then the court will not be likely to provide an effective review of legislative actions and enactments without looking at legislative motive—a subject that, out of judicial deference, courts are loath to approach.

In many instances, the record which a court has for review, under whatever standard it might use, will include the support for the ordinance before the local legislature. If the applicant has made a credible record there, and the referendum reverses the result, the applicant should be entitled to due process relief. However, *Eastlake* tells us that what the voters do is not by definition arbitrary. A rezoning decision only need be fairly debatable. Voters can be unpredictable, yet not irrational, because what they do must be characterized after the fact as fairly debatable too. Election results in this regard are entitled to the same presumption of constitutionality and validity that the legislature enjoys.

Referendum procedures are available only when a legislative action is involved.[11] Municipal legislation typically focuses on three areas of the law—matters involving schools and education, property taxes,[12] and land use regulation and zoning. Thus, Euclidian rezoning decisions are subject to referenda. Other types of rezonings *may* be subject to referenda—for example, a rezoning to an unmapped planned unit development use district. However, once mapped, a second ordinance imposing a PUD development plan on the site arguably is a quasi-judicial action; it is no more subject to referendum than a court judgment would be, unless the two PUD rezoning actions were taken together—in which instance the rezoning is a legislative matter and subject to referendum.[13] Ordinarily, however, ordinances adopting final PUD development plans and plats are administrative in nature, even though final approval is given by the municipal "legislature" (regarded here as a legislative body acting in an administrative capacity, exercising a power it could have delegated to administrators but chose to reserve unto itself).[14]

Likewise, when a municipality's comprehensive plan is mandated by state statute, its adoption by the municipality's legislature is a legislative matter and subject to referenda. However, if the plan must be both adopted by the local legislature and approved by the state department of planning, the approval requirement shows that it is an administrative document for coordinating municipal land use with state concerns. The plan's adoption could provide a legislative review of an administrative document—an action not in itself legislative in nature and arguably beyond the holding of

11. *See Friends of Maple Mt., Inc. v. Mapleton City*, 228 P.3d 1238 (Utah 2010) (holding that adoption of new zoning classification is per se legislative action).

12. Referenda to lower property tax rates, or to limit future rate increases, are a popular subject for referenda. Their passage diminishes the ability of municipalities to provide public and affordable housing, with the result that municipal legislatures focus on reforming their zoning ordinances to increase the density of housing in existing land use districts—particularly single family districts.

13. *See The Greens at Fort Missoula, LLC v. City of Missoula*, 897 P.2d 1078, 1081 (Mont. 1995) (upholding the use of the referendum in this instance).

14. *See State ex rel. Committee v. Norris*, 792 N.E.2d 186 (Ohio 2003).

Eastlake.[15] Thus the land use element of the plan may not be subject to a referendum: if it were to be, the everywhere-required consistency between planning and zoning will be affected adversely, and the oversight function of state government might be destroyed by subjecting the plan to the voters. It is better, as a practical matter, to hold that the plan is administrative in nature and not subject to referenda.

[A] Reconciling *Eastlake* with Equal Protection Cases

After *Arlington Heights*,[16] some type of showing of improper motive is required before a violation of the equal protection clause will be found. A local decision will only be upset when there is a showing of improper procedures and motive or purpose. Thus an inquiry into legislative motive is proper, however unlikely it is to result in overturning a municipal decision. Further, what if a group home for the mentally disabled—as in *City of Cleburne v. Cleburne Living Center*[17]—is given its permit by the municipal legislature, but this legislative action is rejected by a referendum electorate, as in *Eastlake*? The mentally disabled are not entitled to any type of heightened scrutiny under *Cleburne*; they are only entitled to rational basis review and under *Eastlake* the electoral process is not unfair on its face. This leaves mentally disabled persons without a remedy and out of court. If the courts place the voters on a par with the legislators, the same standard of review attaches: the voters need only have a rational basis for what they do, and their actions are entitled to the same presumption of validity.

[B] Legislative vs. Judicial Decisions

The referendum procedure, to be valid, "must be one within the scope of the legislative power." This is a crucial distinction. In contrast, judicial decisions may not be made by referendum. For example, a piece-meal rezoning is not a legislative action. It is not a matter of general policy, applicable to the whole municipality, but is instead a resolution of a conflict between a developer and his or her neighbors. That makes it quasi-judicial in nature, best seen as a hybrid, involving both legislative and judicial action. This view is the so-called *Fasano* doctrine.[18] As the number of landowners affected by the rezoning becomes fewer, the degree of protection that they receive by way of substantive and procedural due process review rises. Those protections are

15. *But see Devita v. County of Napa*, 889 P. 2d 1019, 1032 (Cal. 1995) (finding the plan to be subject to an initiative because the state legislature in the mandatory planning statute did not expressly pre-empt its initiative statute).

16. 429 U.S. 252 (1977) (discussed *supra*, Chapter 13, § 13.01[E][2] and Chapter 16, § 16.02).

17. 473 U.S. 432 (1975) (discussed *supra*, Chapter 18, § 18.04).

18. *See Fasano v. Board of Cty. Comm'nrs of Washington Cty.*, 507 P.2d 23 (Or. 1973) (discussed *supra* Chapter 11).

weighed against the costs of providing them and as the difficulty of determining who is affected by the decision rises, the rights of the referendum voter should be protected as well, the referendum being regarded as the protector of diffusely-held interests. *Fasano* and *Eastlake* often collide.

For municipal governments, there is no doctrine of separation of powers.[19] The actions of the legislature, cast in the form of an ordinance amending a zoning regulation, can be treated as either legislative or judicial. The outcome of a rezoning hearing by a municipal legislature can be seen as legislative, but the procedure used to reach that outcome can be regarded as quasi-judicial.[20] Such hybrid decisions are not subject to referenda because the hearing procedures cannot be replicated in an election.

[C] Legislative vs. Administrative Decisions

Equally crucial is the distinction between legislative and administrative decisions: referenda may not be used to decide administrative questions.[21] Thus, a referenda on the granting of a variance, a special exception or conditional use, or a decision in an appeal from a zoning enforcement official, would not be valid: these actions are administrative and beyond the reach of referendum.[22] Any action of a Board of Zoning Appeals or Adjustment would thus be seen as administrative. Its decisions are made according to criteria delegated to it by the municipal legislature, and remedies against its actions lie in judicial review to determine whether it followed its mandate or grant of delegated authority.

Eastlake referenda are available only for actions that are legislative in nature. By definition, legislation refers to a specific act or resolution, not general principles.[23] Thus enactment of a zoning ordinance, any amendment thereto, or a rezoning by a city or county council, are the actions of a municipal legislature, are legislative in nature and subject to a referendum.[24] A rezoning ordinance is not merely the implementation of the original ordinance: it is rather a change in a land use classification, entitled to the same status that the original ordinance was accorded. As such, a rezoning is a legislative action subject to referenda.[25] In the same way, an annexation ordi-

---

19. *See Dreyer v. Illinois*, 187 U.S. 71 (1902).

20. *See Hyson v. Montgomery Cty. Council*, 217 A.2d 578 (Md. 1966) (holding this and granting a right to cross examine in the course of a rezoning).

21. *See Save Beaver Cty. v. Beaver Cty.*, 203 P.3d 937, 938 (Utah 2009); *see also* Alaska Stat. § 29.26.110(a) (2010) (when a matter "relates to legislative rather than to an administrative matter," has one subject, and is enforceable as a matter of law, it is subject to referenda and initiatives).

22. *See Redelsperger v. City of Avondale*, 87 P.3d 843 (Ariz. Ct. App. 2004) (holding a conditional use an administrative action).

23. *See Fritz v. City of Kingman*, 957 P.2d 337, 339 (Ariz. 1998).

24. *Id.* at 340.

25. In the past, Utah law was to the contrary. *See Wilson v. Manning*, 657 P.2d 251, 254 (Utah 1982) (adopting a minority view that a rezoning was not subject to a referendum and distinguishing an original comprehensive zoning ordinance as a legislative act but characterizing a piece-meal rezoning as administrative in nature), overruled in *Krejci v. City of Saratoga Springs*, 322 P.3d 662, 667

nance is also subject to a referendum: if the setting of the boundaries by the original municipal charter was legislative, so too is the decision to change those boundaries. Likewise, the adoption of a development agreement with a specific developer for a specific parcel is subject to a referendum.[26]

The adoption of a comprehensive plan by a municipal legislature, when required by state statute or ordinance, is legislative in nature.[27] Even the adoption of a general plan by resolution may be a legislative act.

[D] The Soundness of *Eastlake*

Politics is a thing to be kept out of rezoning decisions, not encouraged as it is here, because rezoning matters are too easily politicized. Three policy arguments can be made against the holding in *Eastlake*. First, referendum elections may easily be captured by special interests and the result will not truly be the will of the democratic majority in the municipality. Second, even where the electoral process is not subject to manipulation, the electorate may not represent all the interests that need to be considered: outsiders are by definition not included, and racial and ethnic minorities may be more heavily affected than other groups. Third and finally, even if the electorate is perfectly reflective of the society as a whole, they may lack the information to make an informed decision on the matter.[28] Thus, considerations involving the manipulation of the election, the unrepresentativeness of the electorate, and a lack of information, suggest that *Eastlake* is unsound.

On a more detailed level, the majority opinion suggests that a variance may be available if the results of the referendum work a hardship on the applicant for a rezoning. This is wrong. The court was displaying its ignorance of zoning procedures.[29] Generally however, the availability of a due process claim might provide a method for providing relief for a landowner aggrieved by the referendum decision. Perhaps the court was confusing substantive and procedural due process concerns. What's wrong with ballot box zoning is its lack of substantive due process protection; this lack might be cured by the ready availability of procedural due process protection, but such protection is not today readily available.

(Utah 2013). The analysis in *Wilson* may hold some appeal for comprehensive and master plans not mandated by a state statute.

26. *See Workers for Responsible Development v. City of Tempe*, 524 P.3d 1161, 1170 (Ariz. Ct. App. 2023).

27. *See Carruth v. Henderson*, 606 S.W.3d 917 (Tex. Ct. App. 2020).

28. *See Griswold v. City of Homer*, 186 P.3d 558 (Alaska 2008) (initiative bypassing the advisory input of the planning commission is invalid).

29. See the majority opinion in *Eastlake, supra*, 426 U.S. at 679 (text at n. 13).

[E] State Court Responses to *Eastlake*

State courts have followed *Eastlake.* Several state supreme courts, however, hold that the use of the referendum is a due process violation when injected into the rezoning process.[30] For example, West Virginia, Oregon, and Nevada permit zoning referenda only in comprehensive rezoning decisions. New Jersey and Utah have state statutes exempting zoning and land use decisions from their more general statutes with regard to referenda. However, courts in Colorado, California, Minnesota, and Oklahoma have followed the lead of the United States Supreme Court.

State courts use several lines of argument. The first involves the characterization of the action under review: thus typically only "legislative" actions are proper subjects for initiatives and referenda. For example, as previously discussed, judicial decisions are not subject to elective scrutiny; neither are administrative ones.[31] In some states, a heightened standard of review for rezoning decisions has led courts to find a rezoning decision to be quasi-judicial in nature.[32] In Colorado, a rezoning is legislative in that it may be reviewed by the voters in a referendum, but is also quasi-judicial for purposes of judicial review.[33] This situational analysis seems appropriate when dealing with municipal actions. Such distinctions might mean, for example, that a comprehensive remapping and amendment of the zoning regulations might be legislative and subject to referenda review, but a piece-meal, one small parcel rezoning is not because it is classified as quasi-judicial. Labels matter: the labeling of an action as judicial or legislative is easily seen as outcome-determinative. Such classifications afford one line of argument for state courts distinguishing *Eastlake.*

A second line of argument involves the procedural requirements for zoning actions. The electoral process affords the voters no method for meeting the notice, hearing, and other decision-making restrictions imposed on planning commissions, zoning boards, and municipal legislatures. This shows the incompatible nature of zoning and electoral decisions and has justified state courts in refusing to apply initiative or referendum requirements to zoning matters. In a state in which (1) city planning is a mandatory matter, (2) consistency requirements are imposed by state statute on municipal comprehensive plans, (3) municipal plans must be coordinated under a state growth management statute, or (4) procedural requirements apply to the formulation of comprehensive plans, the results of that planning process are arguably immune from

---

30. *See I'On LLC v. Town of Mt. Pleasant*, 526 S.E.2d 716 (S.C. 2000); *Leonard v. City of Bothell*, 557 P.2d 1306 (Wash. 1976); *West v. City of Portage*, 221 N.W.2d 303, 306–10 (Mich. 1974); *see also Township of Sparta v. Spillane*, 312 A.2d 154 (N.J. Super. Ct. 1973) (where the right to referendum was a statutory, not a constitutional, matter).

31. *See Buckeye Community Hope Found. v. City of Cuyahoga Falls*, 697 N.E.2d 181 (Ohio 1998) (site plan approval an administrative action), related opinion at 538 U.S. 188 (2003); *Citizens Awareness Now v. Marakis*, 873 P.2d 1117, 1124–25 (Utah 1994).

32. *See Fasano v. Board of Cty. Comm'nrs of Washington Cty.*, 507 P.2d 23 (Or. 1973).

33. *See Margolis v. District Ct.*, 638 P.2d 297 (Colo. 1981).

electoral review as well.[34] In general, the mechanisms detailed in the enabling act for adopting or amending a zoning ordinance should be considered because, the more substantive and procedural details an ordinance contains, the more likely that a court will limit the scope of the referendum and initiative.

A third line of argument is that the nature of the decision cannot be spelled out with sufficient clarity on the ballot.[35] In a state rejecting the *Eastlake* holding, and holding a rezoning decision to be quasi-judicial and not subject to referendum, a municipality may still hold a non-binding referendum on a rezoning application. A referendum is legislation by the voters. Even if state law precludes the adoption of a rezoning ordinance by referendum, it does not prohibit the use of a non-binding referendum during the adoption process.[36] The plain meaning of the word referendum is the power in the people to review, reject, or confirm legislative action—and a non-binding referendum does not do that.

Perhaps the most articulate, but complex test for elaborating whether a zoning decision is subject to referenda is Utah's.[37] If the issue falls within the general purpose or policy of the zoning ordinance, it is immune from referenda. If not, the court should then decide whether the decision for which a referendum is sought, is a material change in the ordinance; if it is, then the court must decide whether the change is "a policy-making decision amenable to voter control."[38] The complexity of the issues, the time and attention they take, and the operational effect on municipal government, must all be considered as a part of this last decision.

[F] *City of Cuyhoga Falls v. Buckeye Community Hope Foundation*[39]

In this case, the United States Supreme Court revisited the subject of referenda. Justice O'Connor wrote the opinion for a unanimous court. It held that a nonprofit housing corporation, having its site plan approval subjected to a referendum that resulted in the disapproval of its plan, failed to state either a due process or an equal protection claim against the city allowing the referendum to proceed. The Ohio Supreme Court later declared the referendum invalid and unconstitutional, so that the necessary permits and approvals were given to the corporation. However, the corporation then

34. *See 1000 Friends of Washington v. McFarland*, 149 P.3d 616, 625 (Wash. 2007); *Sustainable Growth Initiative Committee v. Jumpers, LLC*, 128 P.3d 452 (Nev. 2006).

35. *See Committee of the Petitioners for Referendum v. City of Norfolk*, 645 S.E.2d 464 (Va. 2007) (petition not invalid because it asks for referendum election on four ordinances because nothing in petition precludes a separate vote on each).

36. *See Great Atlantic and Pacific Tea Co., Inc. v. Borough of Point Pleasant*, 644 A.2d 598 (N.J. 1994) (holding that a statute prohibiting rezoning by referendum, but not defining the word "referendum" further, does not prohibit a non-binding referendum).

37. *See Citizens Awareness Now v. Marakis*, 873 P.2d 1117 (Utah 1994).

38. *Id.* at 1123–25.

39. 538 U.S. 188 (2003).

sued in federal court, maintaining that the city violated the Fourteenth Amendment in stalling the issuance of those permits and approvals.

The Supreme Court disagreed. None of the official acts complained of in the petitioning process reflected the intent required to support an equal protection claim. The municipality acted in accord with its charter. That charter set out a facially neutral procedure. The municipality followed the procedure. End of the claim—no equal protection liability. As to the substantive due process claim, the court's opinion did not address the issue of whether the permits were the corporation's property because, in any event, the municipal official's refusal to issue permits did not constitute an arbitrary action necessary to undergird a due process claim. The official acted on advice of counsel (the city attorney interpreting the city charter). Neither was the municipal action *per se* arbitrary. Refusing to make a distinction between administrative and legislative actions (indeed, finding the distinction irrelevant for federal constitutional purposes, even though the action at issue was clearly an administrative one under Ohio law), the court repeated its endorsement in *Eastlake* of the referendum procedure. Just letting the referendum process take its course was not *per se* arbitrary conduct and so no due process clause violation.[40] Refusing to issue a permit while the referendum is pending is not a due process violation. Thus the Supreme Court continues to be well disposed to referenda—and perhaps from a federalism point of view, this hands off of state policy, whatever the state law view of referenda is, is not a bad thing.

[G] Other Issues in *Eastlake*

[1] Referendum vs. Initiative

When a state statute expressly allows a referendum to "repeal" a zoning ordinance, the word cannot reasonably be interpreted to mean rezone the property. Unlike a referendum that changes the zoning applicable to a parcel, its repeal results in a return to the *status quo ante*. Thus a statute only allowing the repeal of an ordinance by the referendum process does not imply authority to rezone it by the same process.[41] There is disagreement on this matter among state supreme courts.[42] The better view is that when the referendum process is restricted to repealing an ordinance, the danger of unsystematic, unplanned, or partial zoning changes may thus be avoided and so

40. The corporation did not challenge the referendum's outcome; it just challenged the referendum procedures themselves.

41. *See Comm. of the Petitioners ex rel. Taylor v. City of Norfolk*, 2015 Va. Cir. LEXIS 11, *14–15 (Va. Cir. Ct., Feb. 6, 2015) (collecting cases).

42. *Id.* at *13, n.2. (collecting cases from Colorado, Florida, Michigan, Minnesota, Ohio, and Virginia allowing "the use of referendum to rezone property"). *Cf. Egan Slough Cmty. v. Flathead Cty. Bd. of County Comm'rs*, 506 P.3d 996, 1010 (Mont. 2022) (holding that an initiative may both repeal an ordinance and propose a substitute). *See generally* Annot., *Adoption of Zoning Ordinance or Amendment Thereto as Subject of Referendum*, 72 A.L.R.3d 1030 (2015).

rezoning by referenda is best limited to ordinances already in effect and otherwise left to an expressly authorized initiative process.

Thus the general issue is whether, if referenda are a valid part of the rezoning process, an initiative is to be similarly treated. Using it, voters might initiate a rezoning when current zoning regulations permit a use of which they do not approve. The cases are split on whether its use in this regard is a due process violation.[43]

An initiative arguably raises more due process concerns than does a referendum. First, a referendum is held after the usual procedural formalities, e.g., notice and hearing, have been observed, but a rezoning by initiative does not.[44] Second, if a parcel is rezoned by initiative, the comprehensive planning requirement of the enabling act is not met, while a rezoning rejected by a later referendum reinstates the preexisting zoning regulation which (presumably) is "in accordance with the comprehensive plan."[45] *Kaiser Hawaii* suggests that there should be a statutory mechanism for review of the constitutionality and the planning implications of initiative proposals before they are circulated for the signatures needed to put them on the ballot.[46]

In a state in which the right to an initiative is reserved to the electorate and provided for in the state's constitution, a court may regard that right as a fundamental one.[47] This means that judicial review of a dispute over the exercise of the right is subject to a strict scrutiny standard of review. Thus an otherwise valid petition exercising the right can only be denied when the objectors assert a compelling governmental interest. While the legislature may prescribe how the right of initiative is to be exercised, it may not limit or place onerous conditions on its exercise.[48] For example, placing conditions on who may vote for a proposed initiative may be considered onerous and thus unconstitutional as a matter of state law.[49]

A comprehensive plan, however, as a pre-condition to zoning—and rezoning—might more easily be adopted by initiative.[50] In part, this result is the view of a general plan as a set of guiding principles for the development of a municipality rather than the implementation of those principles.

[2] Voting on Exclusionary Zoning

What if either electoral device is used in an exclusionary manner, to slow the growth of the jurisdiction? In *Arnel Development Company v. City of Costa Mesa*,[51] a court set aside the results of an initiative which prohibited multi-family housing in

---

43. *See Wilson v. Manning*, 657 P.2d 251 (Utah 1982) (distinguishing between them), overruled in *Wilson v. Manning*, 657 P.2d 251 (Utah 1982); *Margolis, supra*, 638 P.2d 297 (not distinguishing).

44. *See Transamerica Title Ins. Co. v. City of Tucson*, 757 P.2d 1055 (Ariz. 1988).

45. *See Kaiser Hawaii v. City and Cty. of Honolulu*, 777 P.2d 244 (Haw. 1989).

46. *Id.*

47. *See, e.g., Reclaim Idaho v. Denny*, 169 Idaho 406 (Idaho 2021).

48. *Id.* at 430.

49. *Id.* at 431–32.

50. *See Allison v. Washington Cty.*, 548 P.2d 188 (Or. App. Ct. 1976).

51. 178 Cal. Rptr. 723 (App. Ct. 1981).

the city. Eastlake, Ohio, was one of 15 Cleveland suburbs that had enacted mandatory referenda requirements. Most of the votes taken on rezonings rejected the legislative action. Courts should take account of this pattern of rejections and the resulting exclusionary impact of the referenda. California jurisdictions have been presented with quite a few growth control programs by initiatives and most passed.[52]

[3] Eastlake's *Use in Other Municipalities*

In almost any New England town, particular zoning regulations might be put to a vote of the annual town meeting. The *Eastlake* opinion speaks glowingly about the town meeting as a reservation of rights by the electorate, but the facts of the case do not involve a small New England town, where the town meeting is still in use. Even if the opinion is right for a small suburban Ohio municipality, it might work badly in a large city. There the voters may well have trouble understanding the issues in a rezoning referendum involving land across town and special interests might well use the existing political machine to carry the election. Further, when the referendum is isolated in the context of a political party's primary election, the electorate may well be too small to be an adequate sampling of voter opinion. Not much imagination is necessary to see that this holding is inappropriate in a large, diverse city where the volume of applications and the diversity of the issues would make ballot questions difficult to frame, campaign on, and decide. Moreover, local politicians may not like running in elections in which they have to take a stand on such questions.

The *Eastlake* holding should be limited to electorates small enough to interact, on decisions with very visible consequences for the jurisdiction, and on issues of interest widespread enough to induce a good voter turnout at the polls, so that all affected parties can be informed about and participate in the electoral process.

[4] The Timing of Judicial Review

Judicial review of the decision of the board of elections or other agency reviewing a petition is available through two common law or codified writs. When the board declines to certify a petition for inclusion on the ballot, a writ of mandamus is typically available to petitioners. Here petitioners ask the court for an affirmative action and must show a clear and convincing legal right to have the petition certified and a clear legal duty on the board's part to certify it.[53] A writ of mandamus thus asks for the board to perform a so-called ministerial act. In addition, when a petition is certified but objectors appeal, a writ of prohibition may be used. This writ is typically brought only after the board has held a quasi-judicial hearing on the objections.[54] To obtain either writ, petitioners must show fraud, corruption, or an abuse of discretion

52. *See* Daniel Curtin & Michael Jacobson, *Growth Management by the Initiative in California: Legal and Practical Issues*, 21 Urban Law. 491 (1989).

53. *See State ex rel. Pinkston v. Del. Cnty. Bd. of Elections*, 226 N.E.3d 894, 900 (Ohio 2023).

54. *See State ex rel. Thomas v. Wood Cnty. Bd. of Elections*, 233 N.E.3d 608, 616–17 (Ohio 2024).

on the part of the board. In the last instance, the appellants must show that the board acted in an unauthorized manner or acted in disregard of applicable law.[55] Both of these writs are typically described by courts as equitable in nature and extraordinary. Extraordinary circumstances justifying their issuance is often shown by the closeness-in-time of the upcoming election in which the referendum or initiative will appear on the ballot.

Referenda and initiative questions should arguably be reviewed in the courts only after the election.[56] When the petitioners win at the ballot box, for example, a petitioning landowner has nothing about which to complain. Thus the reviewing court may arguably use a stricter standard of review before the vote, looking only for strict compliance with the applicable statute. Not all courts have agreed. Pre-election judicial review may save a municipality the costs of running the election.[57] Judicial review before the vote may also save the developer precious up-front capital that would otherwise go into building the project. Thus judicial review should be available, early and late.

A developer who knows that there is going to be a vote can continue to spend money on the development that the voters may reject, but only at his own peril. The developer has no vested rights in the development subject to a vote. As we shall see in the next Chapter, spending money before a referendum calls into question the developer's good faith and reasonable reliance as an element of establishing an estoppel and vested rights.

[5] Neighborhood Democracy and Zoning

The Eastlake decision distinguishes the opinion in *Eubank v. City of Richmond*.[58] In *Eubank*, the plaintiff obtained a building permit, but using an ordinance, his neighbors petitioned the city for the establishment of a set-back which would be violated by the plaintiff's otherwise permitted bay window. The city had no discretion to review the petition, and the set-back became law. The Supreme Court invalidated the ordinance as (1) a delegation of the police power to one set of neighbors to control the rights of others as well as (2) a failure to exercise discretion in accepting the decision of the neighbors embodied in their petition; thus the ordinance was both an invalid delegation and an arbitrary and capricious action.

Eastlake also distinguishes *Washington ex rel. Seattle Title Trust Company v. Roberge*,[59] Here the court invalidated an ordinance which required a two-thirds majority of the owners in a residential use district to approve before a home for the aged

55. *Id.* at 617.

56. *See Elevation Enters., LLC v. City of Springfield*, 646 S.W.3d 716 (Mo. Ct. App. 2022).

57. *See DeBottari v. Norco City Council*, 217 Cal. Rptr. 790 (Cal. App. Ct. 1985) (stating that the expenditure of public money to run an election on a matter that would eventually be invalidated, should not be encouraged).

58. 226 U.S. 137 (1912).

59. 278 U.S. 116 (1928).

could be located there.[60] Thus, giving the neighbors the right to waive a prohibition is valid so long as there is some review of the neighbors' actions by the municipal legislature; what neighbors may not do is impose a restriction (*Eubank*) or block the entry of a use into a district when the legislature has not prohibited that entry (*Roberge*). Waiving a restriction is within the province of neighbors, but establishing one is not.

The *Eastlake* court refuses to equate the referendum procedure with the consent provisions of ordinances considered in these older opinions. Consideration by all the citizens of a jurisdiction of a zoning question is not the same as the consideration of the same question given by neighbors. This is so because self-interest might cloud the neighbors' judgment or because the referendum is a check on the possible corruption of the legislature. For this purpose, consideration by a larger electorate is better than consideration by neighbors, but this "larger is better" idea has limits, fading at some point into an electorate's lack of concern.

[6] Veto and Consent

Two situations that look alike, then, are likely to be treated very differently. For example, suppose first that an ordinance provides that a school can file objections to the location of an establishment requesting a liquor license, which location will be denied if within 1000 feet of the school. This ordinance is invalid: filing an objection looks like a veto power.[61] However, suppose second that an ordinance requires that an applicant for a rezoning obtain the consent to the rezoning from a majority of adjoining land owners. The cases are split on the validity of such a regulation.[62] The argument for its validity is that obtaining the consent is merely advisory to the decision-maker and serves to alert the agency to the source of any potential problems with granting the application.

The difference between waiting for objections which will amount to a veto and obtaining consent is a slight one in practice. The applicant's burden is greater in the latter situation, but no matter, the consent provision is also likely to be found invalid unless the legislature reviews and addresses the reasonableness of the neighbors' judgments. In one state, Illinois, the consent provisions invalidated "as applied" have involved uses with some aspects of a nuisance.[63] One neighbor may neither judge another's right to sue in nuisance, nor present the law of nuisance to the decision-maker for consideration.

---

60. *But see Cusack v. City of Chicago*, 242 U.S. 526 (1917) (upholding an ordinance which prohibited the erection of a billboard unless the billboard owner obtained the consent of a majority of the owners on the blocks abutting both sides of the street).

61. *See Arno v. Alcoholic Beverages Control Comm.*, 384 N.E.2d 1223 (Mass. 1979).

62. *Compare Robwood Advertising Assoc., Inc. v. City of Nashua*, 153 A.2d 787 (N.H. 1959) (yes), *with Janas v. Town Bd. & Zoning Bd. of Appeals*, 382 N.Y.S.2d 394 (N.Y. App. Div. 1976) (no).

63. *See Drovers Trust & Savings Bank v. City of Chicago*, 165 N.E.2d 314 (Ill. 1960).

[7] Structural Reform of the Referendum Process

When the referendum process is statutory, not constitutional in nature, it is possible to amend the process so that it accommodates some of the concerns raised previously. An election code might be amended to require that the election be preceded by a hearing at which the issues involved could be aired, giving the electorate at least an opportunity to inform themselves about the issues.[64] Another possible reform is to require those presenting the petition also to present findings of facts and conclusions that could be reviewed for sufficiency under substantive due process standards.

§ 20.03 Public Participation

Citizen participation in land-use matters is generally regarded as a positive thing. Cities such as Atlanta and Washington, D.C., have built such participation into their planning and zoning procedures—but participation at the planning or hearing stage is very different from participation later. Ordinances with such provisions must be drafted to reflect the difference between advisory participation and decisional control. Similarly, requiring that decision makers give weight to citizen views is only to say that citizen concerns should be addressed, not that they should carry the day.

---

64. *See Rzepka v. City of Solon*, 904 N.E. 2d 870 (Ohio 2009) (reviewing ordinance requiring referendum majority in both the city and the affected ward).

PART SIX

Halting an Owner's Further Regulation

Chapter 21
Vested Rights and Governmental Estoppel

§ 21.01 Enforcement of Land Use Regulations

Land use regulations are only as good as they are clear, producing predictable results for both owners and regulators, and are enforceable and are enforced.[1] The drafting of any regulations should be undertaken with an eye to effective enforcement—not necessarily draconian enforcement, but enforcement by a staff skilled in the terms of the regulation as well as sensitive to the rights of the owners against whom enforcement will be sought. "It is better that the law should be certain, than that every judge should speculate upon improvements in it."[2]

Typically both civil and criminal penalties and remedies are available for violations of land use regulations.[3] The municipality's burden of proof is heavier in a criminal case than in a civil one and includes the burden of showing a criminal intent to violate the regulation. For this reason, and also because normally the primary concern of the regulators is abatement of the violation, civil equitable remedies, particularly an injunction against the violation, are usually sought.

Enforcement officers lack broad powers to enter private property to enforce regulations; in order to enter over the written or verbal objections of owner, a valid search warrant is necessary, obtainable upon a showing of probable violation of the regulation.[4] Typically, the issuance of any building or construction permit is conditioned upon compliance with zoning and land use regulations. To enforce the condition,

---

1. "Certainty is the mother of repose, and therefore the law aimed at certainty." *See Walton v. Tryon*, 21 Eng. Rep. 262, 262 (Ch. 1753).

2. *See Sheddon v. Goodrich*, 32 Eng. Rep. 441, 447 (Ch. 1803).

3. Recall that Mr. Hadacheck, in the case of *Hadacheck v. Sebastian*, 239 U.S. 394 (1915), discussed *supra*, Chapter 3, § 3.03[A], was attempting to avoid criminal penalties.

4. *See People v. Northrop*, 410 N.Y.S.2d 32 (N.Y. City Ct., Nassau Cty. 1978), *rev'd mem.*, 420 N.Y.S.2d 486 (App. Div. 1979); *see also* 1976–77 A.G. Opin. (Va.) 338–39 (Oct. 6, 1976).

officers are on site at crucial times during the construction process—for example, when the foundation is poured—to assure themselves that the owner is in compliance—and that the construction is not proceeding in a way that will threaten the owner's future compliance.

When the municipality seeks enforcement long after the violation occurs, an owner may interpose a defense based on the statute of limitations, the doctrine of laches, or estoppel.[5] Rarely are these defenses successful. Absent an appeal, an enforcement officer's decision is final and so may not be collaterally attacked, even when the attack is on the merits of the decision.[6] If the violation is continuing, a defense based on the statute of limitations is denied by finding that the statute is not tolled: no limitation period runs out when the violation is a continuing one.[7] In some states, statutes of limitations may not apply in equity when the government seeks to enjoin the violation.[8]

Laches is an equitable defense.[9] It applies independently of any defense based on a statute of limitations because it involves an allegation of (1) unreasonable delay in enforcement (2) causing prejudice to the plaintiff, regardless of the period permitted by the statute.[10] Each element must be found as a fact by the trial court. Thus delay in enforcement alone is insufficient to make out this defense; some prejudice to the owner must be proven as well.[11] The regulator must be shown to have slept on its enforcement rights, to the owner's prejudice. Even when the owner's intervening financial investment is substantial, laches may still be no defense to delayed enforcement. One commentator has said that the weight of authority is that laches may not bar enforcement by a municipality of its regulations.[12]

Estoppel looks not at the delay in enforcement, and consequent prejudice to the owner, but rather at the actions of the government. Used as a defense, it is not often successful because it is typically difficult for an owner to show that the government meant to issue a permit in violation of its own ordinance or regulation.[13] Thus it is rare that either of these three defenses—statute of limitations, laches, or estoppel—is successful.

---

5. *See Town of Pawlet v. Banyai*, 274 A.3d 23 (Vt. 2021).

6. *Id.* at 30–31 (imposing a $46,000 fine on a firearms training facility operating without permits).

7. See *IT Corp. v. Solano County Bd. of Supervisors*, 820 P.2d 1023 (Cal. 1991).

8. *See West Hartford v. Rechel*, 1459 A.2d 1015, 1019 (Conn. 1983).

9. *See Town of Seabrook v. Vachon Management Inc.*, 745 A.2d 1155, 1161 (N.H. 2000) (a de novo application of the doctrine in the land use context).

10. *See DeFazio v. Washington Public Power Supply System*, 679 P.2d 1316 (Or. 1984) (containing an extensive discussion of laches).

11. *See Fabini v. Kammerer Realty Co.*, 175 N.Y.S.2d 964 (1958) (involving a delay of 33 years).

12. *See* Robert Anderson, Am. L. of Zoning § 29.15, at 733–34 (4th ed. 1997).

13. *See Hurt v. Caldwell*, 279 S.E.2d 138 (Va. 1981).

§ 21.02 Vested Rights and Governmental Estoppel

Whenever a legislature, whether at the congressional, state, or local level, enacts a statute, the issue arises whether the statute should be made retroactive, or if retroactive expressly, so interferes with existing rights and interests as to be unconstitutional.[14] Vested rights and governmental estoppel are doctrines that are applicable to all retroactive civil legislation[15] but apply particularly to the area of land use controls.[16] Both doctrines are informed generally by the due process clause of the Fourteenth Amendment to the United States Constitution and its state analogues.[17]

[A] Distinguishing Them

A vested right is a right to develop one's property in accord with regulations in effect when the right is acquired—or "vests." It involves the right to have an application, development plan, or building permit processed or used in accord with the regulations in effect at the time. "From the developer's perspective, time stops when rights vest."[18] It concerns the actions of an owner or developer to use his or her property in a new way; it is thus is not the same as the continuation of a use right, as is the case of a non-conforming use.[19] Doctrines involving non-conforming uses and vested rights "go hand in hand," but a non-conforming user has "only the right not to have the use immediately terminated in the face of an ordinance which prohibits" it.[20] In contrast, a vested right is an immunity from further regulation.

Governmental approval for the development of real property is often a multi-phase process. There is no vested right in existing zoning. There is also a presumption that enactment of a zoning ordinance does not create contractual rights for land owners and their neighbors.[21] The mere purchase of land for development creates no right to develop the land in accordance with current zoning.[22] A "general knowledge" that other similar developments have received permits does not give rise to a vested

14. *See* Charles Hochman, *The Supreme Court and the Constitutionality of Retroactive Civil Legislation*, 73 Harv. L. Rev. 692 (1960) (arguing broadly for retroactivity as the default rule).

15. *See* Jill Fisch, *Retroactivity and Legal Change: An Equilibrium Approach*, 110 Harv. L. Rev. 1055 (1997).

16. *See* Jan Laitos, *Legislative Retroactivity*, 52 Wash. U. J. Urb. & Contemp. L. 81 (1997).

17. *See Valley View Industrial Park v. City of Redmond*, 733 P.2d 182 (Wash. 1987) (*en banc*) (recognizing the need for "fundamental fairness" and "fixed rules").

18. *See Charles A. Pratt Construction Co. v. Cal. Coastal Comm'n*, 76 Cal. Rptr. 3d 466, 469 (App. Ct. 2008).

19. *See Seven Hills LLC v. Chelan County*, 495 P.3d 778 (Wash. 2021).

20. *Id.* at 791.

21. *See McKee Family, LLC v. City of Fitchburg*, 893 N.W.2d 12, 21 (Wis. 2017).

22. *See Town of Vienna Council v. Kohler*, 244 S.E.2d 542, 547 (Va. 1978).

right.[23] Neither does any "contemplated use" of the property by a developer at the time of purchase create a vested right in that use.[24] Likewise, in many states, the filing of a petition for municipal approval of a subdivision map does not give a right to have the petition reviewed under the *existing* subdivision regulations.[25] However, preliminary plat approval may vest a right to a final approval, although some state statutes require a final plat to be submitted within a certain time after approval of a preliminary one, or not at all.[26] Florida courts have held that substantial expenditures made in reliance on a preliminary plat approval, vests a right to final approval.[27] None of this guarantees in many states the issuance of a building permit for structures within the subdivision, absent special statutory protection.[28]

Thus a municipal legislature often retains the power to enact new regulations applicable to petitions in the regulatory pipeline at the time of enactment. Indeed, for a large development, at the time of the filing of the petition, the process is just commencing: subdivision approval, board (of Zoning Adjustment) permissions, planning commission permissions, environmental permits, and finally building permits—all lie in the future. Thus here an intent to use or improve a parcel, without actual use, vests no rights.[29]

Government has an inherent power to revise its regulations and enact legislation. Legislation is generally applicable to pending applications for a permit retroactively. In particular, a public need in the form of a health or safety problem justifying a moratorium, trumps all pending permits.[30] At the same time, the parcel owner/developer has an interest in being protected from changes that destroy sunk investment costs. These are the themes developed in opinions dealing with vested rights and governmental estoppel.[31]

The vested rights doctrine has a constitutional basis: the issue is the retroactive impact of the regulation on the owner and due process.[32] Stated another way, vested rights arise to prevent the retroactive application of the law that offends the due

23. *See Ocean Bay Mart., Inc. v. City of Rehobeth Beach*, 285 A.3d 125, 140 (Del. 2022).

24. See *Grays Hill Baptist Church v. Beaufort Cty.*, 850 S.E.2d 29, 34 & n. 10 (S.C. 2020).

25. *See Sherman-Colonial Realty Corporation v. Goldsmith*, 230 A.2d 568 (Conn. 1967) (filing subdivision plan, without any expenditure of money, does not vest a right to approval).

26. *See, e.g.*, N.J. Stat. Ann. § 40:55D-49 (1988) (three years).

27. *See Florida Companies v. Orange County*, 411 So. 2d 1008, 1011 (Fla. App. Ct. 1982) (mortgagee acquiring vested right by loan of money on basis of preliminary plat approval).

28. As discussed *infra*, there are a few states in which final subdivision approval, plus substantial reliance in the form of expenditure of money, will vest a right in the existing land use regulations for a reasonable period of time.

29. *See Green Dev. LLC v. Town of Exeter*, 297 A.3d 931, 936–37 (R.I. 2023) (participation in a pre-application meeting vests no rights).

30. *See Ford v. Bellingham County*, 558 P.2d 821, 826–27 (Wash. App. Ct. 1977); *Metropolitan Dade County v. Roseli Construction*, 297 So. 2d 46, 48 (Fla. Dist. Ct. App. 1974) (calling this the "new peril doctrine").

31. *See Tremarco Corp. v. Garzio*, 161 A.2d 241, 245 (N.J. 1960) (containing a good statement of the need for these doctrines).

32. *See Valley View Industrial Park v. City of Redmond*, 733 P.2d 182 (Wash. 1987) (*en banc*).

process clause. As one state supreme court explained: "Constitutional protection of vested rights properly resides in Maine's due process clause."[33] More recently, takings clause requirements of protection for investment backed expectations have also been cited as a basis.[34]

Estoppel has an equitable basis: it examines the actions of the government. There is ample reason to distinguish between these theories because of their different initial focus; in fact the distinction between them is blurred by the cases. The reason is that, for estoppel to work, there must be reasonable reliance on the estopping actions of government. In the final analysis, both doctrines call for an examination of the impact of the change in the regulation on the owner.

[B] Restatement of the Doctrines

As to a **vested right**, a property owner establishes such a right when he or she (1) obtains or is assigned a permit to construct improvements in compliance with then applicable land use regulations, and (2) reasonably relies in good faith on the permit and (3) substantially changes his or her position or incurs expenses in further reliance on the permit. Once obtained, a vested right is non-transferrable and applied only to the development described in the permit.[35]

This is the rule in the majority of states, referred to as the "building permit rule."[36] It requires that, when owners obtain the permit, they must have no knowledge of any impending change in the law affecting its legality.[37] Receiving subdivision approval does not satisfy its requirements: if approval is granted for a 100 residential lot subdivision, an owner might wish to install an efficient sewage treatment plant for all 100 lots. Under the building permit rule, a permit is required for each lot in order to acquire a vested right to develop it. So under this rule an owner can safely install infrastructure for only as many lots as he can vest rights for because, without an improvement on each lot, the second element of that rule is not satisfied.[38] Vested rights are acquired lot by lot, not for the subdivision as a whole. Thus in this example

---

33. *See NECEC Transmission LLC v. Bureau of Parks & Lands*, 281 A.3d 618, 633 (Me. 2022). *See also Browning-Ferris Indus. v. Guifor Cty. Bd. of Adjustment*, 484 S.E.2d 411, 414 (N.C. 1997).

34. *See H.R.D.E., Inc. v. Zoning Officer*, 430 S.E.2d 341 (W. Va. 1993).

35. *See Seven Hills LLC v. Chelan County*, 495 P.3d 778 (Wash. 2021).

36. *See Golden Sands Dairy LLC v. Town of* Saratoga, 913 N.W.2d 118, 129 (Wis. 2018); *McKee Family, LLC v. City of Fitchburg*, 893 N.W.2d 12, 20–22 (Wis. 2017). *See also Seven Hills LLC v. Chelan County*, 495 P.3d 778 (Wash. 2021); *Western Land Equities v. City of Logan*, 617 P.2d 388 (Utah 1980). *See generally* Gregory Overstreet & Diana M. Kirchheim, *The Quest for the Best Test to Vest: Washington's Vested Rights Doctrine Beats the Rest*, 23 Seattle U. L. Rev. 1042 (2000).

37. The requirement is in a majority of states referred to as the "pending ordinance rule." *See Ocean Bay Mart., Inc. v. City of Rehobeth Beach*, 285 A.3d 125, 141 (Del. 2022); *1350 Lakeshore Assocs. v. Healey*, 861 N.E.2d 944 (Ill. 2006). *See also Cribbin v. City of Chicago*, 893 N.E.2d 1016, 1026 (Ill. Ct. App. 2008).

38. *See Gosselin v. City of Nashua*, 321 A.2d 593 (N.H. 1974) (requiring actual improvements, lot by lot); *Yeh v. County of Cass*, 696 N.W.2d 115, 131–32 (Minn. App. Ct. 2005) (same).

the rule may encourage the use of (inefficient) septic systems for each lot, the owner arguing that each system is the improvement satisfying the rule's second element.[39] The rationale for the rule is that the unimproved parcels may require adaption and improvement in compliance with future municipal requirements. An owner installing 100 septic systems instead of a centralized sewage treatment plant strengthens his vested rights, but at the cost of some inefficiency.

In states mandating comprehensive planning, the majority rule has a corollary: an owner acquires a vested right only when obtaining the last discretionary permit for a development. As previously discussed, this permit is usually a building permit, but it may not be when a multi-level governmental approval system is applicable to the development. Under this so-called "last discretionary act" rule, an owner with subdivision approval, petitioning later for an amendment to a new state-mandated comprehensive plan, will find that he has not acquired vested rights. This is because after plan approval typically come applications for a rezoning, further subdivision permits and plats, impact and linkage fee payments, site plan review, and building permits. Each of these reviews provides ample opportunity for the exercise of municipal discretion.[40] When this rule applies, an owner/developer must also prove reasonable and detrimental reliance on any and all permits granted.

A well-known use of the "last discretionary act rule" occurred in Hawaii, when that state's supreme court held that (1) a referendum on a rezoning was the last discretionary approval and (2) a resort community developer did not acquire vested rights, even after expending about a quarter of a million dollars and when holding building permits issued before the election.[41] The developer's knowledge of the voter drive for the referendum, ending in a certification of the referendum question, before the developer filed an application for the permits, was sufficient knowledge to prevent the permits from vesting.[42]

Similarly, the enactment of a growth control ordinance, limiting the number of building permits issued annually, does not change the impact of the building permit rule. An owner/developer has no vested right to control the timing of the issuance of permits—just what this type of growth-control ordinance is intended to do. Thus a developer otherwise qualifying for a building permit is not denied a vested right when the issuance of the permit is delayed by the ordinance's annual quota.

---

39. *Cf. Quirk v. Town of New Boston*, 663 A.2d 1328, 1333–34 (N.H. 1995) (involving a buffer zone regulation around a campground).

40. *See American West Dev., Inc. v. City of Henderson*, 898 P.2d 110 (Nev. 1995) (recognizing the last discretionary act rule for Nevada).

41. *See County of Kauai v. Pacific Std. Life Ins. Co.*, 653 P.2d 766, 775 (Haw. 1982), *appeal dismissed*, 460 U.S. 1077 (1982) (finding that even though the developer had spent over $158,000 after the permit issued, the referendum was the final discretionary act, before which the developer acquires no vested rights).

42. California cases to the contrary state in *dicta* the view that reliance may be reasonable up to the time of the vote. *See Santa Monica Pines, Ltd. v. Rent Control Bd.*, 201 Cal. Rptr. 593, 599 (1984) (involving a vested right to convert rental apartments to condominiums free of the requirements of an intervening rent control ordinance).

Once acquired, vested rights are not violated by the declaration of the moratorium on the issuance of building or other permits by a municipality. Thus, unless the moratorium is subject to another type of legal challenge, it trumps an owner's vested rights.[43] It does not end an owner's vested right, but it suspends that right for the period of the moratorium.

Once a building permit has been secured, if the permittee is forced to litigate its validity and, while doing so, an amendment to the law making the permit illegal is enacted, the original ordinance controls and trumps the amended one, if substantial improvements have been made.[44] This is an exception to the so-called "time of the decision" rule—the idea that the law in effect at the time of a judicial decision controls its reach and consequences. That rule does not apply to vested rights.[45]

Some states provide a limited form of vested rights by statute.[46] Most of the eighteen states enacting such provisions codify a date-certain approach, conferring vested rights on either the date that an application is filed, or the date on which it is approved.[47] Such provisions often state that a municipal government may not modify a prior approval of (say) a subdivision for a certain period of time after approval.[48] The time period is typically set to give the applicant or developer a reasonable time to construct improvements stated in the application.[49] Once the state legislature has enacted such a statute, its action preempts the field and a municipality may not enact its own vesting-period rules.[50] Preemption, however, does not always follow. For example, Arizona has a statute permitting, but not requiring, that a municipality to adopt its own rules for vesting. It is also necessary to check the statutes and the cases decided under it to determine to what type of permits the statute applies. Statutes in California, New York, and Rhode Island, for example, apply only to subdivision applications, conferring a vested right when the application is approved, but only as to municipal ordinances, not state law.

43. *See Matson v. Clark Cty. Bd. of Comm'nrs*, 904 P.2d 317, 320 (Wash. App. Ct. 1995).

44. *See Ackman v. Board of Adjustment for Black Hawk Cty.*, 596 N.W.2d 96, 101 (Iowa 1999) (recognizing also a savings clause in the amendment).

45. *Id.*

46. *See, e.g.*, Va. Code Ann. § 15.2-2307 (2024) (enumerating six situations warranting vested rights arising by reliance on existing law) (early history is discussed in E.A. Prichard & Gregory Riegle, *Searching for Certainty: Virginia's Evolutionary Approach to Vested Rights*, 7 Geo. Mason L. Rev. 983, 998–1009 (1999)); *see also Town of Leesburg v. Long Lane Assocs. Ltd. P'ship*, 726 S.E.2d 27, 31 (Va. 2012) (a landowner cannot acquire a vested right in a proffer); *Bd. of Supervisors of Stafford Cty. v. Crucible, Inc.*, 677 S.E.2d 283 (Va. 2009) (holding that the issuance an administrator's zoning verification letter vested no rights because it was not a "significant governmental act" under the Virginia statute).

47. *See* Brian Steinwascher, *Statutory Development Rights: Why Implemeting Vested Rights Through Statute Serves the Interest of the Developer and Government Alike*, 32 Cardozo. L. Rev. 265, 302 (2010) (listing and characterizing these statutory provisions).

48. *See, e.g.*, Rev. Code Wash. § 19.27.095 (1) (2024) (enacted in 1987, applying to building permits, and codifying a "date of filing the application" rule) (discussed in *Abbey Road Group LLC v. City of Bonney Lake*, 167 P.3d 1213 (Wash. App. Ct. 2007), affirmed, 218 P.3d 180 (Wash. 2009) (requiring the filing of a *completed* application)); *see also Lauer v. Pierce Cty.*, 267 P.3d 988 (Wash. 2011); *In re Sisters and Brothers Investment Group, LLP*, 978 A.2d 448, 451 (Vt. 2009) (requiring a *proper* application).

49. *See Shipyard Assocs., LP v. City of Hoboken*, 230 A.3d 278, 289 (N.J. 2020).

50. *See West Main Associates v. City of Bellevue*, 720 P.2d 782 (Wash. 1986).

Once having acquired and then been denied a vested right recognized by state law, a developer might file a complaint against a municipal official in federal court based on 42 U.S.C. § 1983,[51] for a violation of either the federal due process or takings clauses. The rescission of a vested permit raises two issues with regard to whether a § 1983 claim arises. The first issue is whether the defendant municipal official is acting under the color of state law. That he does was decided by *Monell v. New York City Dept. of Social Services*.[52] The second issue is whether the rescission deprives the owner of a right secured by the federal Constitution.[53] No owner with a rescinded vested right has, *ipso facto*, a § 1983 claim. A federally-protected property right must be first found.[54] The law of vested rights was created to protect an owner's reasonable expectations to develop, and giving compensation, though not originally part of the law's design, is one method of protecting the right; in this sense, "vested" means protected either by a right to specific performance to compel the permit's issuance, or by the right to damages or compensation.[55] It is easier to find a claim for a denial of due process than for a taking; federal courts may, but need not, follow the state-based rules on this point.[56] Some federal courts have said that a property right protected under § 1983 is more than an abstract or unilateral expectation of an entitlement; it must instead arise from an independent source, such as state law, and amount to an actual, realistic claim of entitlement.[57] Other courts have said that the right must involve a substantive restriction on the governmental agency involved and involve arbitrary municipal action.[58]

Comity and abstention doctrines have also been used to avoid federalizing land use disputes. In *C-Y Dev. Co. v. City of Redlands*,[59] one federal judge says:

> Federal courts are not boards of zoning appeals. This message, oft-repeated, has not penetrated the consciousness of property owners who believe that federal judges are more hospitable to their claims.... Why they should believe this we haven't a clue.... Is it that they have omitted the steps necessary to

51. Authorizing a civil suit against any person depriving another of a federal constitutional right, when acting under the color of state law.

52. 436 U.S. 658 (1978) (holding that municipalities are not immune from § 1983 actions).

53. *See Yale Auto Parts, Inc. v. Johnson*, 758 F.2d 54, 59-60 (1st Cir. 1982) (holding that a denial of a variance application does not involve denial of a federally protected property right).

54. *See Stubblefield Construction Co. v. City of San Bernardino*, 38 Cal. Rptr. 2d 413 (App. Ct. 1995).

55. *See* John Delaney & Emily Vaias, *Recognizing Vested Development Rights as Protected Property in Fifth Amendment Due Process and Taking Claims*, 49 Wash. U. J. Urb. & Contemp. L. 27 (1996) (reviewing the state cases).

56. *Cf. Restigouche, Inc. v. Town of Jupiter*, 59 F.3d 1208, 1211 (11th Cir. 1995).

57. *See Spencer v. Pleasant View City*, 80 P.3d 546, 550–51 (Utah App. Ct. 2003); *Hull v. Hunt*, 331 P.2d 856 (Wash. 1958); *Marshall v. Board of County Comm'nrs for Johnson Cty., Wyo.*, 912 F. Supp. 1456 (D. Wyo. 1996).

58. *See Littlefield v. City of Afton*, 785 F.2d 596, 602 (8th Cir. 1985) (reviewing both vested rights under § 1983 and finding a property interest in a building permit subjected to an illegal exaction involving a conveyance to private parties).

59. 703 F.2d 375 (9th Cir. 1983). *See also River Park, Inc. v. City of Highland Park*, 23 F.3d 164, 165 (7th Cir. 1994).

> obtain relief in state courts . . . ? Well, we are not cooperating. Litigants who neglect or disdain their state remedies are out of court, period.

Although the trend in the § 1983 cases has been to turn these cases out of federal courthouses, substantive due process denials have nonetheless on occasion been found to be a basis for § 1983 claims.[60] Increasingly, however, the actions of a municipality must be egregious or in bad faith to survive the pleading stage.

[C] A Blended Rule

In some states, the building permit rule is a bright-line rule. In others it is modified, some would say muddied, by further explanation.[61] A Georgia Supreme Court opinion stated that the court has recognized "four different scenarios wherein a landowner could acquire a vested right."[62] "Those instances are when the landowner relies upon (1) issued building and other permits, (2) the law in existence at the time a landowner properly files an application for a permit, (3) formally and informally approved development plans, or (4) official assurances that a building permit will probably issue."[63] This statement conflates the building permit rule (instances 1 and 2) with examples of equitable estoppel (instances 3 and 4). It is to an elaboration of the last two instances that this treatise now turns.

§ 21.03 The Doctrine of Estoppel

As to **estoppel** of the government, a government is estopped when an owner (1) relies in good faith on some governmental act or omission,[64] and (2) substantially changes position or incurs substantial expenses in further reliance on the permit, such that it would be unfair and inequitable to deny the owner's right to proceed.[65] Estoppel is an equitable doctrine, based on considerations of fair dealing and justice.

60. *See Littlefield v. City of Afton*, 785 F.2d 596, 603 (8th Cir. 1985) (recognizing and joining decisions from the 3rd, 4th, 6th, 9th, and 11th Circuits, to the effect that a § 1983, substantive due process claim may be based on the denial of a land use permit).

61. *See Brown v. Carson*, 872 S.E.2d 695, 697 (Ga. 2022).

62. *Id.*

63. *Id.* at n. 4 (citing a Georgia case "summarily announcing" this rule based on *Cos Corp. v. City of Evanston*, 190 N.E.2d 364, 367–68 (Ill. 1963)). *See also Cribbin v. City of Chicago*, 893 N.E.2d 1016, 1026 (Ill. Ct. App. 2008).

64. *See City of Hutchins v. Prasifka*, 450 S.W.2d 829, 836 (Tex. 1970) (showing that Texas courts for this element require that, first, the act be shown by the owner to be within the governmental employee's scope of employment and, second, not within the performance of a governmental function immune from estoppel).

65. *See Even v. City of Parker*, 597 N.W.2d 670, 674–75 (S.D. 1999) (using estoppel against a municipality); *Town of Largo v. Imperial Homes Corp.*, 309 So. 2d 571, 572–73 (Fla. App. Ct. 1975) (same); *see also Wesco v. City of Montpelier*, 739 A.2d 1241 (Vt. 1999) (finding no reliance or estoppel). *See*

Courts do not generally favor its use against municipalities.[66] The burden of proof on the party asserting the doctrine is a heavy one, involving clear evidence, and the standard of review for the appellate court is deferential to the trial court; seldom is the review de novo, as it might be if the question were one of law.[67] Thus issuance of a zoning certificate for a limited time does not estop a municipality from refusing to renew it.[68]

The necessary "good faith" reliance (the first element of an estoppel) is measured often by the amount of notice of a pending change necessary to destroy it. Knowledge that a permit would likely be required, much less a decision to forego the permitting process, negates this element.[69] The comments of or conversations with a governmental staff member about changing the applicable regulation, are insufficient.[70] Staff studies of the need for a regulatory change, by those persons authorized to propose the change may be sufficient, but a stronger case is presented when the studies are conducted with legislative or administrative authority, or are authorized by legislative or board resolution. Thus, when a change is pending before the governmental body, the question is open to considerable dispute. (As we will see, when an application is pending for purposes of the vested rights doctrine is also subject to dispute.[71])

Another aspect of this element of an estoppel—the governmental act or omission—can be satisfied when the owner procures a rezoning, a special exception, a variance, or a foundation permit.[72] The emphasis here is usually on the affirmative action of the municipality, not on any omission or failure to act.[73] The action must be an "official assurance" by the agent or agency of the municipality, and not solely based on existing ordinances or laws.[74] It must be clear, definite, and affirmative in nature.[75] A letter to the owner from a municipal official might suffice, but if the letter came from the zoning administrator and legislative action was required for a final decision, then even a probability that the decision would be favorable is often insufficient.[76] Firm rules and bright lines are difficult to come by because the doctrine is an equitable one.

---

generally Maryland Reclamation Assocs. v. Harford Cty., 994 A.2d 842, 883–88 (Md. 2010) (Harrell, J., in dissent, extensively reviewing the doctrine).

66. *See Town of Seabrook v. Vachon Management Inc.*, 745 A.2d 1155, 1160 (N.H. 2000).

67. *See City of North Oaks v. Sarpal*, 797 N.W.2d 18, 24–25, n. 5 (Minn. 2011).

68. *Id.* (as to an adult, sex-oriented business).

69. *See Miller v. Walsh Cty. Water Resources District*, 819 N.W.2d 526, 534 (N.D. 2012).

70. *See Brown v. Carson*, 872 S.E.2d 695, 697 (Ga. 2022) (requiring an assurance with a "probability" of a "likely issuance" of a permit).

71. *See Smith v. City of Clearwater*, 383 So. 2d 681 (Fla. App. Ct. 1980), *review dismissed*, 403 So. 2d 407 (Fla. 1981).

72. *See United Parcel Service, Inc. v. People's Counsel for Baltimore County*, 611 A.2d 993 (Md. App. Ct. 1992) (summarizing Maryland case law).

73. *See Even v. City of Parker*, 597 N.W.2d 670, 674 (S.D. 1999) (stating the doctrine so as to require an affirmative action).

74. *See Brescia v. North Shore Ohana*, 168 P.3d 929, 951–51 (Haw. 2007).

75. *See Fox. v. Park City*, 200 P.3d 182 (Utah 2008) (issuance of a building permit is such an act).

76. Except in Illinois, where "reliance upon the probability of issuance" suffices. *See Cribbin v. City of Chicago*, 893 N.E.2d 1016, 1026 (Ill. Ct. App. 2008).

The second element, of substantial change in position, is typically shown by the expenditure of planning and development funds—what a developer calls soft costs. For purposes of this showing, however, a threshold amount is difficult to determine and varies from jurisdiction to jurisdiction. The purchase of non-returnable building materials, of a type an inspector should have investigated prior to the issuance of a permit, provides grounds for estoppel.[77]

With these statements in hand, it is easy to understand that the facts giving rise to a claim of vested right, will also give rise to one for estoppel. In both instances, the *prima facie* case will involve the two elements of reasonable, good faith reliance and a substantial change or expense. This commonality is evident in the so-called "pending ordinance" rule. It is applied in both majority rule vested rights and estoppel cases. It provides that, if during the time that an ordinance imposing a requirement is being legislatively re-considered, an owner applies for a permit based on the existing requirement, the near universal rule is that, when an ordinance is pending when the application is filed, reliance on the old ordinance is unreasonable and no estoppel of the municipality occurs. A race to the planning commission or zoning board would otherwise ensue. Courts applying both the doctrine of estoppel and rules on vested rights give no incentive for a developer to speculate in permits. At the same time, a developer's knowledge that an official or segments of the community dislike his project gives no notice that an ordinance is "pending" against it; the dislike must take the legally significant form of enrolled legislation.[78] An owner may avail himself of compliance with an ordinance only so long as it is on the books.[79]

Differences, however, remain. Vested rights is a permit-specific doctrine; governmental estoppel involves a governmental act, perhaps amounting to a right to a permit not yet in hand. Estoppel lies in equity, whereas vested rights is a remedy at law and which is based on due process considerations. Being equitable in nature, it is perhaps best to think of estoppel as supplementing a state's vested rights rule. After all, if the law on vested rights is clear that a particular permit, usually a building permit, must be obtained, then how can reliance be reasonable for estoppel purposes if the permit is not in the developer's hands?

77. *See Even, supra*, 597 N.W.2d at 674–75.

78. *See Harding Academy v. Metropolitan Gov't of Nashville*, 222 S.W.3d 359, 365 (Tenn. 2007) (collecting the cases, noting that a majority require a legislatively enrolled proposal subject to an open meeting or legislative session); *see also Bucks Cty. Housing Dev. Corp. v. Twp. of Plumstead*, 361 A.2d 447, 448 (Pa. 1976).

79. *See Recycle and Recover, Inc. v. Georgia Board of Natural Resources*, 466 S.E.2d 197 (Ga. 1996).

§21.04 Pre-Construction Improvements and Vested Rights

What about pre-construction improvements made in contemplation of securing a building permit, but before one is actually obtained? If directed toward an improvement, legal at the time, but subsequently rendered an illegal use by rezoning, the courts then look to see whether there is substantial reliance by the owner on the existing regulation. Drilling a well adequate to service the new improvement, heavying up the utilities, and widening abutting roads—these might be reliance costs, admissible to show a vested right. However, these might also be costs directed at the installation of many types of improvements, not just the one proposed by the developer. To the extent a cost supports other improvements, the argument for a vested right in advance of the building permit is weakened.[80]

A few states recognize a right to develop in accordance with existing land use regulations once final subdivision approval is obtained and a substantial expenditure of money has been made in reliance on the existing regulations.[81] Expenditures may be in advance of the issuance of the permit. No building permit is required.

In a majority of states, however, the issuance of a building permit remains a precondition to obtaining a vested right to develop. The date of issuance is the earliest time at which a right to develop can vest.[82] Some states phrase this rule in the negative, with a rule that pre-construction costs give rise to no vested rights. Such costs include planning, engineering, architectural, and legal costs. With a building permit in hand, however, a developer may show substantial expenditures made both before and after the permit is issued; the expenditures thus have an all-or-nothing relevance to the showing of a vested right. In some jurisdictions, the expenditures reach all the way back to the purchase price of the land. However, jurisdictions split on whether to include the purchase price when calculating the substantial expenses element of a vested right.[83] Sometimes this majority rule is modified when consistency with the local comprehensive plan is the issue.[84]

---

80. *But see Mattson v. City of Chicago*, 411 N.E.2d 1002 (Ill. App. Ct. 1980) (approval of apartment plan and of demolition permit sufficient when owner in fact demolished her house).

81. *See Board of Supervisors of Fairfax County v. Cities Service Oil Co.*, 193 S.E.2d 1 (Va. 1972). *See* Grayson Hanes & Randall Minchew, *On Vested Rights to Land Use and Development*, 46 Wash. & Lee L. Rev. 373 (1989) (reviewing Virginia law).

82. *See Town of Paradise v. Gulf Leisure Corporation*, 557 P.2d 532 (Ariz. App. Ct. 1976); *State ex rel. Humble Oil & Refining Company v. Wahner*, 130 N.W.2d 304 (Wis. 1964). *See generally* Michael Shultz, *Vested Property Rights in Colorado: The Legislature Rushes in Where...*, 66 U. Denv. L. Rev. 1, 31–39 (1988).

83. *Compare Hawkinson v. Itaska Cty.*, 231 N.W..2d 279 (Minn. 1975) (purchase price excluded), *with Am. Nat'l Bank & Tr. Co. v. City of Chicago*, 311 N.E.2d 325, 329 (Ill. Ct. App. 1974) (purchase price included).

84. *See Youngblood v. Board of Supervisors of San Diego Cty.*, 586 P.2d 556 (Cal. 1978) (permitting plan consistency to be measured at the review of a tentative development plan and subdivision map).

[A] The Minority Rule for Vested Rights

A minority of states vest a development right at the time of the application for the permit, rather than the date of its issuance.[85] Compared to the majority rule, this rule permits an early vesting of an owner's rights. Early vesting is said to provide a crisp rule, one most easily administered, and free of the uncertainties of phrases like "reasonable reliance" and a "substantial change in position." Moreover, it is said to avoid the problem of developer's speculating in permits. A "date of application" rule does, however, require that a "complete application" be filed, and defining this phrase reduces the crispness of this rule. Accepting an application for a building permit is a non-discretionary, ministerial act, the administrator only checking to see that it complies with applicable existing law,[86] but thereafter, problems of interpreting that law may arise and then the minority rule may result in reducing the discretion that a municipality has in exercising the police power.

In *Western Land Equities v. City of Logan*,[87] the Utah Supreme Court required that a development plan, in substantial conformance with the existing regulations and ordinances, be filed prior to a change in the law; so the date of the application's filing is the date on which the right to develop vests. Thus, if a change in the law is not pending when the development plan is filed and is not necessary to protect the public health or safety, a right to develop vests without substantial expenditure of money or construction. The Utah version of the minority rule also requires that, once the permit is secured, the developer pursue the development with due diligence, and permits the regulators to withdraw it with a showing of a compelling governmental interest. Thus the pending ordinance doctrine,[88] the developer's due diligence, and an exception for a compelling governmental interest, constrain the minority rule.

Idaho, Indiana, Ohio, and Vermont,[89] also adhere to some version of the minority rule: when an application for a building permit is filed, the developer's right to build vests.[90] In addition, six states have codified it: Connecticut, Kansas, Massachusetts, Oregon, Pennsylvania, and Washington.

The minority rule is intended to permit developers to "fix" or "freeze frame" the rules governing their development at the time of the application is filed. This is to insure fairness in subsequent proceedings. "A developer has the vested right to have his application processed under the regulations in effect at the time the complete

---

85. For a good statement of the law and adoption of the minority rule, see *Western Land Equities, Inc. v. City of Logan*, 617 P.2d 388 (Utah 1980), reaffirmed in *Holladay Towne Ctr., LLC, v. Holladay City*, 192 P.3d 302, 304-05 (Utah App. Ct. 2008).

86. *See Fulton Cty. v. Action Outdoor Advertising*, 711 S.E.2d 682, 686 (Ga. 2011) ("Georgia law does make clear that when an applicant submits an application for a permit in accordance with applicable ordinances, the applicant is entitled to issuance of the permit.")

87. *See Western Land Equities*, *supra*, 617 P.2d 388.

88. *See Harding Academy v. Metropolitan Gov't of Nashville*, 222 S.W.3d 359, 364 (Tenn. 2007) (restating the doctrine).

89. *See In re Appeal of Jolley Assocs.*, 915 A.2d 282 (Vt. 2006).

90. *See, e.g.*, *Hull v. Hunt*, 331 P.2d 856, 859 (Wash. 1958).

permit application is filed, regardless of changes in the law."[91] Under such a rule, what vests is the applicant's right to have the preliminary plat or application considered under the ordinances and regulations in effect when the application is acted upon: approval of the application is by no means guaranteed. This means the minority rule is best used when the procedure for approval is an administrative, rather than a legislative matter, because its rationale depends on making decisions based on previously adopted standards.[92]

The minority "date of the application" rule perhaps represents the trend in recent cases, in part because of legislative action codifying a state's vested rights rules. Such statutes are enacted at the behest of the real estate development community and so are more likely to adopt the minority rule than any later vesting rule. The Washington and Virginia statutes cited earlier in this Chapter are examples. They represent the polar opposites among all vested rights statutes: Washington's statute uses a date certain, time of filing, approach, while Virginia's spells out the factors that will be used to determine developer reliance on existing law. Such statutes need, however, to be read carefully to determine their scope and reach.

When a regulation was effective, but its applicability lifted because of a moratorium, an owner is no less on notice of it.[93] A municipality is not, by enacting the moratorium, reserving any right to change the regulation applicable during the course of the owner's later application hearings. Unless the municipality sought to circumvent its minority vesting rule with the moratorium, the pre-existing regulation applies at the owner's hearing held once the moratoria is over. The minority "date of the application" vesting rule does not seek to protect against all uncertainty for developers.

Illinois and Arizona also have cases in which a building permit is not required as a precondition to establishing a vested right.[94] In Illinois, the probability that a permit will issue is a sufficient precondition to a vested right, and thereafter a rule of fundamental fairness balances the financial hardship on the developer against both the benefits to the public and the diminution in surrounding parcel values, in assessing whether a development right has vested.[95] In this balance, the existing uses, the suitability of the proposed use, and the length of time the parcel has been vacant are also considered. The fact that a legislator expresses an intent to introduce a down-zoning ordinance at some future time does not preclude a vested right, as the ordinance is not yet pending.[96]

Maine is another jurisdiction with a developer-oriented rule for vested rights: there, a development plan vests when the government acts on it. More than filing

---

91. *See Thurston Cty. Rental Owners Ass'n v. Thurston Cty.*, 931 P.2d 208, 214 (Wash. 1977).

92. *See Samson v. City of Bainbridge Is.*, 683 F. Supp. 2d 1164, 1168 (W.D. Wash. 2010).

93. *See R.C. Hedreen Co. v. City of Seattle*, 1996 U.S. App. LEXIS 1794 (9th Cir., Jan. 8, 1996) (applying Washington law), *decision affirmed without published opinion*, 74 F.3d 1246 (9th Cir. 1996).

94. *See Town of Paradise Valley v. Gulf Leisure Corp.*, 557 P.2d 532 (Ariz. App. Ct. 1976); *American Nat'l Bank & Tr. Co. v. City of Chicago*, 311 N.E.2d 325 (Ill. App. Ct. 1974).

95. *See Smith v. City of Macomb*, 352 N.E.2d 697 (Ill. App. Ct. 1976).

96. *See 150 Lake Shore Assocs. v. Healey*, 861 N.E.2d 944, 953 (Ill. App. Ct. 2006) (discussing *American Nat'l Bank & Tr. Co.*).

the plan is required, but how much more is unclear.[97] The period during which an application for plan approval is pending should also be a time when the application is diligently pursued through the administrative process. However, here an application is not pending until (1) a hearing on it is commenced, or (2) the hearing is completed and the application is referred to the municipal legislature for a decision on the record. Whether an application is before a legislature or an administrative body, "... when a municipality takes the threshold step of acting on a proposal, the application process has commenced and an application is pending."[98] A substantive review of an application must have commenced for the application to be "pending."

§ 21.05 Substantial Reliance

Substantial reliance on a building permit is an element of a vested right. Reasonable reliance is an element of estoppel. Although they have similar concerns, these terms mean different things—that is, the former is an objective, and the latter a subjective, test. Nonetheless, they are often interpreted to mean just one thing: that construction must be undertaken in some form. This means actual construction, not preparation for it. The reason for this last distinction is that (again) preparatory activities are often consistent with many types of improvements, both legal and illegal under applicable codes. Clearing the land is insufficient because that is consistent with many types of improvements. Likewise, a widening of a nearby roadway or the demolition of an existing building is insufficient.

If in good faith a landowner expends substantial funds or incurs a substantial obligation, or otherwise undergoes a substantial change of position, in reliance on the existing zoning and on obtaining a building permit, then he or she may acquire a vested right. This is not an iron-clad rule. Oregon is an example of a jurisdiction adopting such a requirement.[99] *Holmes* requires that the substantial expenses must be incurred before the zoning change and must be exclusively related to the proposed project.[100]

Substantial reliance is, however, an idea whose importance extends beyond Oregon cases. In majority-rule states, there must be substantial reliance on the permit.[101] How then are pre-construction costs, incurred after the issuance of a permit, to be evaluated? There are three approaches. First, they might be evaluated quantitatively, in terms of an absolute dollar amount. That amount must be spent or exceeded before vested rights in existing regulations arise. When the project is a large one, however,

---

97. *See Littlefield v. Inhabitants of Lyman*, 447 A.2d 1231, 1235 (Me. 1982) (interpreting a state statute preventing the application of intervening regulations to "pending" plans).

98. *See id.* at 1235; *see also Smith v. Town of Pittston*, 820 A.2d 1200, 1209 (Me. 2003).

99. *See Clackamas County v. Holmes*, 508 P.2d 190 (Or. 1973).

100. *See* Comment, *Oregon's Vested Rights Rule: A Statutory Solution for a Troublesome Problem*, 68 Ore. L. Rev. 975, 984–91 (1989) (reviewing the Oregon cases and arguing that the uncertainty of this intermediate rule requires a development agreement statute, as discussed *infra*).

101. *See Geisler v. City Council of Cedar Falls*, 769 N.W.2d 162 (Iowa 2009).

this method is typically used: here the absolute number of dollars spent, without considering the total expenditures required, is the focus of the inquiry.

A second approach is the so-called proportionate ratio test.[102] It takes the expenses incurred and computes them as a percentage of the total cost of the project.[103] Total cost is sometimes defined as comprising both hard and soft costs, but in some cases, soft costs are excluded. Another version of this method is to take the construction undertaken to date as a percentage of the construction required to complete the project. In sum, both versions form a fraction, the numerator of which is the costs incurred and the denominator of which is the total cost of the improvement, however defined. Neither method provides much guidance or predictability about litigation results. Courts move from the first to the second version when they suspect "window dressing," a bad faith expenditure of funds.

In a third approach, the costs incurred so far might be balanced against the costs of redoing the project to conform to the new regulation. This third approach is tailored to the situation in which the cost of compliance with the new regulation is slight compared with the public benefit achieved.[104] This third approach is reminiscent of a test for a taking. A broader version of this third approach takes the form of a balancing test—weighing the owner's right to use the land and the expenses incurred thus far, against the public interest in holding the owner to a new, updated regulation.

In sum, after a building permit is issued, that is not the end of the owner's worries about fickle municipal legislatures because there must be substantial reliance on the permit as well as use of it within a reasonable period of time.

The timing of the expenditure is often a factor in reliance. Construction performed without a permit when one is required, is not performed in good faith. Neither will the costs of such illegally-performed work be considered in establishing substantial reliance. Neither will hastily completed work, performed in anticipation of a change in a law or regulation, be in good faith. Similarly, work performed under the authority of a permit, must be performed in compliance with any conditions specified in the permit. Conditional approval of a development plan or the issuance of a permit gives a vested right that may be forfeited if the development or permitted construction does not proceed according to the conditions.[105]

A permit must be used for the project applied for. Later changes in the project annul any vested right to the project as built, even when the modified project is smaller or in a different location. Any vested right extends only to construction that complies

---

102. *See Town of Hempstead v. Lynne*, 222 N.Y.S.2d 526, 531 (N.Y. Sup. Ct. 1961).

103. *Compare Brennan v. Board of Zoning Adjustment of City of New Orleans*, 371 So. 2d 324 (La. App. Ct. 1979) (95% complete), *with Aries Development Company v. California Coastal Zone Comm'n*, 122 Cal. Rptr. 315 (App. Ct. 1975) (1–2% complete).

104. *See 1350 Lake Shore Assocs. v. Healey*, 861 N.E.2d 944 (Ill. 2006) (adopting a multi-factor test and rejecting a proportionate ratio test).

105. *Browning-Ferris Industries of South Atlantic, Inc. v. Wake County*, 905 F. Supp. 312 (E.D.N.C. 1995) (restating the law of vested rights for North Carolina).

with the terms of the permit and so construction of an altered project is not in good faith.[106] The smallness of the changed project is irrelevant under these circumstances.

Substantial or reasonable reliance on the right to develop depends on the investments made by an owner or developer. The act of investing in an improvement brings the right into being, and the right thus becomes the property of that owner. Its origins in the actions of the owner—not the actions of government—has implications for its transferability. If it is earned or created by the owner's substantial reliance, then the right is personal to the owner—and held one court, non-transferable and personal to its creator.[107]

A final caveat. An owner/developer should not, just after being issued a building permit, move immediately to make substantial expenditures or undertake construction. Moving immediately will mean that these expenditures and construction will be made before the time for appealing the issuance of the permit has expired. An owner may not rely upon any level of expenditure and construction, no matter how substantial, that usurps an aggrieved party's right of appeal.[108] An owner's expenditure of funds prior to an appeal that results in a judgment adverse to the owner cannot be made in good faith and so may not be counted toward meeting the substantial reliance requirement. Respect for the courts and the judicial process requires this rule.

§ 21.06 Applying the Rules: The PUD

It is particularly burdensome to apply the "date of approval" or "building permit rule" when the project is a large one and requires many types of permits. A planned unit development, for example. In one PUD case, a developer planned to construct a 74 acre project amid his nearly 8,000 contiguous acres. Some 5,000 of its 8,000 acres had been rezoned for a PUD containing more than 18,000 dwelling units. As to the 74 acres, the developer had obtained a subdivision map approval and a rough grading permit, and was installing permitted storm drains, streets, and utilities—all at a cost of over two million dollars. The subdivision plat approved divided the 74 acres into 27 parcels, with multi-family housing structures on most of them. (The grading permit did not permit finished grading for building sites.) The developer had in addition sold 11 beach-front acres to the surrounding county at a price below market value.

106. *See Rosenberry Life Insurance Company v. Zoning Hearing Bd. of the City of McKeesport*, 664 A.2d 688 (Pa. Cmmw. Ct. 1995) (involving a permit for a business sign to be used on a building at another location on the same building, the location of signs being a significant factor in their regulation).

107. *See BCC Land and Development, Inc. v. Butts Cty.*, 640 S.E.2d 33, 35 (Ga. 2007).

108. *See State ex rel. Brookside Poultry Farms, Inc. v. Jefferson Cty. Bd. of Adjustment*, 388 N.W.2d 593, 595–96 (Wis. 1986).

At this point, the California legislature enacted the Coastal Commission Act. At the time of enactment, the developer had not been issued building permits for any structures on its 74 acres. However, the developer estimated that it had incurred three-quarters of a million dollars in liabilities, in addition to monies actually spent, and was losing $7,000 a day in rental income.

When the county approved the planned unit development, it saw a general site plan for the whole project. Nonetheless, the California Supreme Court held that the developer was required to obtain a Commission permit or exemption. It had been denied the latter and did not have the former, so it had acquired no vested right to proceed.[109]

Thus, in California and many states, a permit is necessary, but not sufficient to establish a vested right; and no governmental estoppel arises, absent a permit. The *Avco* court stated that something less than a building permit might suffice, but only if the governmental approval relied on has the same specificity and detail that the building permit required. General site plans, forming the basis for a PUD rezoning, will not suffice. Only after the government has given its "final discretionary approval" can a vested right in a specific improvement arise. The risk that the final permit will be denied (the court said) should be borne by the developer when making pre-permit expenditures. The smallness of the 74 acre project in dispute, when compared to the vastness of the PUD as a whole, contributes to the result here.[110]

California's legislature enacted a statute in response to *Avco*.[111] It permits a developer to file a "vesting tentative map" for a subdivision of a multi-permit development and complete the development that is substantially in compliance with such a map.[112] Texas has also enacted a statute that provides that when a series of permits are necessary for a project, the regulations in effect at the time of the application for the first of them controls and "shall be the sole basis for consideration of all subsequent permits required for completion of the project."[113]

---

109. *See Avco Community Developers, Inc. v. South Coast Regional Comm'n*, 553 P.2d 546, 550 (Cal. 1976) (holding that a developer who expended nearly $3,000,000 in planning and site improvements did not acquire vested rights for a 74 acre parcel designed for multi-family use), *appeal dismissed, cert. denied*, 429 U.S. 1083 (1977); *see also CK Dev. LLC v. Town of Nolensville*, 2012 Tenn. App. LEXIS 10 (Jan. 6, 2012) (another example of a developer's *Avco* problem).

110. *See* Paul Nadel, *This Land is Your Land... Or Is It? Making Sense of Vested Rights in California*, 22 Loyola (L.A.) L. Rev. 791, 797–805 (1989) (discussing *Avco* and subsequent California cases).

111. *See* Cal. Gov. Code § 66474.1.–.2, § 66498.1–.7 (Deering 2024) (discussed in *Kaufman & Broad Central Valley, Inc. v. City of Modesto*, 30 Cal. Rptr. 2d 904 (App. Ct. 1994).

112. *Id.* One common law basis for this type of statute is collateral estoppel. *See Becker v. Falls Rd. Community Ass'n*, 281 A.3d 729, 742 (Md. 2022).

113. *See* Tex. Local Gov't Code § 245 (2024) (effective 1999).

§ 21.07 Justifying the Majority Rule on Vested Rights

One advantage of a late vesting rule, such as the "building permit" or "last discretionary act" rule, is that it deters developers trying to beat the clock when a change in the law is in the offing; thus it is particularly appealing in jurisdictions with activist land use regulatory systems. Another is that the right which has vested, is all the more valuable; perhaps it generates fewer, but more substantial, development projects. A third advantage is its clarity. Finally, earlier vesting rules encourage non-conforming uses; late vesting discourages them.

The advantage of the early vesting, date certain, "date of the application" rule is that it is easy to administer. It also recognizes that the changes in the application occurring thereafter have more to do with the developer's negotiation with the regulators than with independent efforts of the developer—the developer's marker is the application. Third, in its rawest form, it involves no weighing of facts necessary to show substantial reliance—and none of the uncertainties that arise from the use of precedent involving such fact finding. Finally, it takes account of the cumulative and increasing amount of regulation: the building permit rule arose in an era of one permit developments and its fairness in a multi-permit era is open to question.

As a consequence of this unfairness, some jurisdictions diverge from the rules in cases like *Avco* at the point at which the developer dedicates land or improvements relating to the entire multi-permit project to government ownership. If the beach dedications in *Avco* had related not just to the 74 acre project, but had instead related to most of the 8,000 acres, the developer would there have acquired a vested right to complete the project in conformance with the regulations in existence at the time of the first permit's issuance.[114] Once making the dedications, the developer is entitled to the permits as consideration for the benefits conferred on the regulator by the dedications. Otherwise, a *Nollan/Dolan* exactions takings claim might arise.

The difference between the minority and the majority rules is one of emphasis. Their respective dates are the fulcrums around which the factors weighed in the rule revolve. Those dates then provide a time for shifting the burden of proof from the developer to prove an entitlement to a vested right to the regulatory body to prove there should be no such right. The same factors weigh into each of the rules, but they are given differing weights as time passes. Both seek a balancing between certainty and predictability on the one hand, and responsiveness to changed conditions on the other, in the law of land use controls.

Once a developer has a building permit in hand, and relied in good faith by a substantial change in position or expenses, equitable estoppel may be used to compel the issuance of related permits. In addition, the issuance of a building permit creates a vested right to compel issuance of dependent permits requiring the same degree of

---

114. *See Preseault v. Wheel*, 315 A.2d 244 (Vt. 1974).

detail as did the initial permit, unless the permit was erroneously issued. There can be no reliance upon an invalid or erroneously issued permit.

§ 21.08 The Illegal Permit Problem

In majority rule states, what if the permit is issued illegally? As one federal opinion applying Maryland law states: "It is embedded in Maryland law that a property interest fails to accrue if the City grants a permit on the basis of ... a violation of the law."[115] The foundation of a common law vested rights doctrine "rests on this principle."[116] The illegal permit is *void ab initio*. Even if the developer has no actual knowledge of the illegality, he or she cannot rely on it and use it as the basis for a vested right.[117] The illegality may appear on the face of the permit, or not. It makes no difference. On the other hand, where the zoning administrator in good faith and acting within his authority interprets the zoning ordinance in a developer's favor, then the developer may rely on the interpretation and vest rights in it.[118]

An illegal permit will not be resuscitated in a court of equity, no matter how great the expenditures made in reliance on it, or no matter how far land preparation has proceeded. In this respect, equity follows the law. No owner has a reasonable expectation that the building permit stage of regulatory review may be avoided.[119] "Vested rights do not arise from an erroneously issued permit."[120] "Generally, a permit issued under a mistake of fact confers no vested right or privilege and may be revoked at any time."[121] It makes no difference that the permit is issued by the legislative body of a municipality with the authority to change the law: "a permit issued by a governing body in violation of an ordinance... is void."[122] The formal or technical nature of the mistake is irrelevant. For example, with regard to a building permit for a business sign, even though the only error in issuing the permit was a failure by the business to present a zoning certificate (certifying compliance with sign regulations) to the official in

115. *See Rockville Cars LLC v. City of Rockville*, 891 F.3d 141, 146 (4th Cir. 2018).

116. *Id.* at 147. *See also St. Martin Parish Gov't v. Champagne*, 304 So. 3d 931 (La. Ct. App. 2020) (commercial use permits issued erroneously after multiples interactions and site visits with zoning officials for a bait shop and grocery operating over many years, created a vested right to continue operating).

117. *See Halla Nursery, Inc. v. City of Chanhassen*, 781 N.W.2d 880, 886 (Minn. 2010); *Levinson v. Montgomery County*, 620 A.2d 961, 974–75 (Md. App. Ct. 1993); *City of Lamoni v. Livingston*, 392 N.W.2d 506, 510 (Iowa 1986) (holding that when the zoning administrator lacked authority to issue a building permit, such a permit was no basis for vested rights: "[W]hen a permit is granted wholly without legal authority, the holder does not gain vested rights in it.").

118. *See Crow v. Board of Adjustment*, 288 N.W. 145, 147 (Iowa 1939) (holding that a veterinarian may rely on an official's finding that a "hospital" as a permitted use includes a veterinary hospital).

119. *See Lake Bluff Hsg. Partners v. City of South Milwaukee*, 540 N.W.2d 189 (Wis. 1995).

120. *See Halla Nursery*, *supra*.

121. *Ebzery v. City of Sheridan*, 982 P.2d 1251, 1257 (Wyo. 1999) (involving a fence built at illegal height); *Bruno v. Zoning Bd. of Adjustment*, 664 A.2d 1077, 1080 (Pa. 1995).

122. *See*, *Union Cty. v. CGP, Inc.*, 589 S.E.2d 240, 242 (Ga. 2003).

charge of issuing the permit, it is still illegal: there is no vested right to proceed under it. Whether the permit violates the substantive regulations of the municipality or the procedural regulations for the issuance of the permit makes no difference; in either event, there are no grounds on which to estop the municipality.[123]

§ 21.09 Development Agreements

The law of vested rights may be limited by either legislation limiting the power of municipalities to apply new ordinances to on-going projects or by statutes or judicial authority for development agreements.[124] The execution of a developer's agreement with a municipality may confer vested contractual rights upon the developer.[125]

A development agreement is a contract that establishes the rights and duties of a developer to build a project.[126] Its precedent in state law often lies in opinions on conditional zoning. It is executed with the municipality: more specifically, it should be executed by representatives of the municipality's legislative body in order to avoid the charge that the legislature has bargained away its police powers.[127]

The most important provision in any such agreement, sometimes made an implied term by statute,[128] is that the project can proceed in accordance with the regulation in place at the time of its execution, subject to any exception or "carve out" spelled out in the agreement itself. Thus, absent a provision to the contrary, the regulations in effect at the time of the development agreement's execution control.[129] In return, the developer agrees to the conditions on development provided in the agreement.[130]

The California statute just cited was a response to the opinion in *Avco*.[131] It was the first state statute authorizing development agreements. Hawaii followed suit.

---

123. *See Marzullo v. Kahl*, 783 A.2d 169, 193 (Md. 2001).

124. *See* Va. Code Ann. § 15.2-2303.2 (2024) (regulating cash given to localities for infrastructure improvements); *Giger v. City of Omaha*, 442 N.W.2d 182 (Neb. 1989) (upholding such an agreement against a charge of contract zoning).

125. *Id.*

126. *See generally* Patricia Hammes, *Development Agreements: The Intersection of Real Estate Finance and Land Use Controls*, 23 U. Balt. L. Rev. 119 (1993); John Armentano, *How Development Agreements Can Protect Developers and Make Certain That Municipalities Receive Benefits Promised*, 28 Real Est. L.J. 259 (2000).

127. *See River Walk Apts. LLC v. Twigg*, 914 A.2d 770 (Md. 2007) (finding that two mayors' signatures were insufficient to bind the municipality).

128. *See* Cal. Gov't Code § 65865.2 (Deering 2024) (reviewed in Armentano, *supra*, 28 Real Est. L.J. at 266–69).

129. *See City of Hollywood v. Beverly Towers, Inc.*, 805 P.2d 329, 334 (Cal. 1991).

130. *See City of Casa Grande v. Tucker*, 817 P.2d 947 (Ariz. App. Ct. 1991).

131. *See supra* § 21.06.

Arizona, Colorado, Florida,[132] Idaho, Indiana, Louisiana,[133] Maryland,[134] Mississippi, North Carolina, Nevada, New Jersey, New Mexico, North Carlina, Oregon, South Carolina, Pennsylvania, Utah, Virginia, and Washington also have such statutes.[135] So far 20 states have enacted them. Most were enacted from the late 1970s to the early 1990s. In addition, Texas has had, and has repealed, such a statute.[136] Generalizations are difficult concerning these statutes. Agreements authorized in them are contracts protected by the federal Constitution's contracts clause or its state analog. Most of them were drafted to supplement, rather than to supplant, the common law doctrines discussed in this Chapter. They also immunize the authorized agreements against charges of spot and contract zoning. Strict compliance with these statutes is required. Non-compliance means that the agreement will suffer the same fate as an illegally issued permit: it vests no rights.[137] Authorized agreements are recordable and run with the land.

These statutes typically describe the subjects that may be addressed in development agreements—that is, "the permitted uses of the land, the density or intensity of its use, the maximum height and size of buildings on it, and the dedication of any land for public use." Some statutes add at this point, "and any subject not inconsistent with [the zoning enabling act] or prohibited by law." Some further require that the dedication or provision of public facilities proceed concurrently with development.

By requiring concurrency, such agreements are one response to the heightened nexus required of subdivision and other exactions after the *Nollan* and *Dolan* opinions. They memorialize the required nexus. At the same time, however, they raise basic issues of whether a later exercise of the police power, contrary to the agreement, may be contracted away. In federal courts, another way of framing this issue is to present it as a tension between the contract and the reserved powers clause of the federal constitution. On this issue, the courts weighing the matter have divided.[138]

The scope of a development agreement must be clear. When a municipality and a developer execute a development agreement, a reference should be made to the zoning ordinance provisions intended to permit the developer's project, with specific

---

132. *See Hollywood, Inc. v. Broward County*, 431 So. 2d 606 (Fla. App. 1983) (involving a development agreement in effect before the county downzoned a developer's land after the developer had spent over two million dollars in site preparation). The Florida statute was a response to this case.

133. *See Azalea Lakes Partnership v. Parish of St. Tamminy*, 859 So. 2d 57, 62–63 (La. App. Ct. 2003) (upholding such a statute as not unconstitutionally delegating legislative power).

134. *See Blentlinger LLC v. Cleanwater Linganore*, 173 A.3d 549, 551–52 (Md. 2017) (reviewing the Maryland statute).

135. See Thompson on Real Property (Thomas ed.), § 111.07, n. 356 (2024) (listing the states and giving statutory citations).

136. *See Save Our Springs Alliance v. City of Austin*, 149 S.W.3d 674 (Tex. App. Ct. 2004) (upholding this statute).

137. *See Summit Media LLC v. City of Los Angeles*, 150 Cal. Rptr. 3d 574 (Ct. App. 2012).

138. *Compare PMC Realty Trust v. Town of Derry*, 480 A. 2d 51, 53 (N. H. 1984) (consent agreement settling a case reversing denial of a variance vests no rights), *with City of Baltimore v. Crane*, 352 A. 2d 786, 790–91 (Md. 1976) (invoking the concept of contractual estoppel for the benefit of a developer).

references to the statutes, regulations, and ordinances that the agreement is intended to effect. An agreement providing that "the development of the subject property shall be in substantial compliance with the municipality's Zoning Ordinance and Comprehensive Plan and sufficient to serve the project's inhabitants" will not prevent the municipality down-zoning that developer's land to a less intense use, or amending its comprehensive plan accordingly. The language quoted is not the equivalent of a regulatory freeze for the land as it was zoned when the agreement was executed. Without an explicit provision for a regulatory freeze, a court is unlikely to imply one because that would involve a delegation of the police power in many jurisdictions.[139]

More generally, the agreement should not be void merely because its executory elements extend beyond the legislative term during which it is executed. Further, so long as the property is developed in accordance with a municipality's comprehensive plan, it is not an abnegation of legislative power—rather it is itself an exercise of that power.[140] When the development agreement is drafted so as to reserve municipal control over its enforcement, it is not an abnegation of the police power but rather a present extension of it, enhancing the municipality's regulatory authority and power.

[A] The Basic Scope of the Development Agreement

The agreement should at a minimum describe the project, the required permits affected, any and every phase of the project to which the agreement applies, public facilities that will serve the project, the remedies available to enforce the agreement, a description of events leading to the termination of the agreement, and compliance with notice, hearing, and other legislative functions necessary to make the agreement binding on the government (this will provide authority for the signatories representing the government). Often the resulting agreement will be adopted by the municipality's legislature either as a resolution or a legislative act. If adopted as legislation, the agreement will be subject to reversal in a referendum, because typically legislative actions are subject to referenda. Sometimes in authorizing statutes, the chief executive of the municipality is designated to negotiate with a developer.

---

139. *See Sprenger, Grubb & Associates, Inc. v. City of Hailey*, 903 P.2d 741 (Idaho 1995) (reviewing also the plan attached to the agreement).

140. *See Santa Margarita Area Residents Together v. Board of Supervisors*, 100 Cal. Rptr. 2d 740 (App. Ct. 2000) (so holding). *Cf. Buckner v. Douglas Cty.*, 615 S.E.2d 850 (Ga. 2005) (litigation settlement agreement unenforceable because it amounts to a zoning decision improperly enacted).

[B] Drafting and Further Considerations for a Development Agreement

An agreement's prologue should contain at least three recitals: (1) its statutory authority if any, (2) its purpose to free the developer from compliance with new regulations replacing existing ones that are specifically referred to by code volume and section number, and (3) its execution being voluntarily and without duress. The third recital is important when the developer executes the agreement in the face of an impending adverse municipal action.[141]

The most important provision of such agreements is a limited term, during which the agreement is enforceable. If limited to a reasonable time, such agreements are more likely to meet with judicial approval.[142] A reasonably short term for such agreements precludes the argument that a development agreement is in effect an exercise of the police power by one legislative session, in an attempt to bind future sessions. Second, agreements should provide that plans for the development are both in conformance with existing comprehensive plans, and are required to conform to any future plans and ordinances not in direct conflict with it. Third, some development agreements permit the developer to construct some improvements, but provide also that the municipality will construct others, financed by bonds backed by a special assessment. The amount of control a developer retains over the municipality's work should be defined in the agreement.[143] Fourth, as to the developer's obligations to provide improvements, this duty should be expressly conditioned on the developer's proceeding with the project diligently and as contemplated in the agreement.[144] Conversely, any of the developer's successors entitled to the benefits, and responsible for implementing the agreement, should be defined.[145] Fifth, the developer's duty to implement the agreement should be conditioned on its finality: when it is subject to a referendum or to judicial review, its effectiveness should be stayed or subject to a termination at a date certain.[146]

Finally, because the agreement is intended to settle disputes that might otherwise involve resort to the courts, an arbitration clause is advisable, particularly when both public and private financing is to be used. For instance, the developer's agreement

---

141. *See Meredith v. Talbot County*, 560 A.2d 599 (Md. App. Ct. 1989).

142. *See Geralnes B.V. v. City of Greenwood Village, Colorado*, 583 F. Supp. 830, 841 (D. Colo. 1984) (agreement not to rezone for twenty-five years is a valid exercise of the police power). *Geralnes* resulted in a development agreement statute.

143. *See Chard Realty, Inc. v. City of Shakopee*, 392 N.W.2d 716 (Minn. App. Ct. 1986) (holding that a developer has no third-party beneficiary rights in a construction contract between the municipality and its contractor for improvements paid for by developer and called for in a development agreement).

144. *See River Vale Plng. Bd. v. E&R Office Interiors, Inc.*, 575 A.2d 55 (N.J. Super. Ct., App. Div. 1990) (holding that an agreement is subject to the implied condition that developer proceed with project).

145. *See Larkin v. City of Burlington*, 772 A.2d 553, 557 (Vt. 2001) (holding that a purchaser at a foreclosure is not a successor to the developer executing an agreement).

146. *See Midway Orchards v. County of Butte*, 269 Cal. Rptr. 796 (Ct. App. 1990).

should last as long as the underwriters of the public instruments (bonds, etc.) advise. Any municipal reimbursement of a developer should be made waiving competitive bidding statutes and other disbursement procedures.[147]

147. *See Achen-Gardner, Inc. v. Superior Court*, 839 P.2d 1093, 1099 (Ariz. 1992) (holding that a development agreement violated a competitive bidding statute).

Table of Cases

Index